Thomas Boghardt
U.S. Army Intelligence in Germany, 1944–1949

De Gruyter Studies in Military History

Edited by
Jörg Echternkamp and Adam Seipp

Volume 5

Thomas Boghardt
U.S. Army Intelligence in Germany, 1944–1949

—

DE GRUYTER
OLDENBOURG

First published: Thomas Boghardt, Covert Legions. U.S. Army Intelligence in Germany, 1944–1949, Washington D.C. 2022, U.S. Army Center of Military History (CMH Pub 45-5).

ISBN 978-3-11-221485-5
e-ISBN (PDF) 978-3-11-098855-0
e-ISBN (EPUB) 978-3-11-098876-5
ISSN 2701-5629

Library of Congress Control Number: 2023940506

Bibliographic information published by the Deutsche Nationalbibliothek
The Deutsche Nationalbibliothek lists this publication in the Deutsche Nationalbibliografie; detailed bibliographic data are available on the internet at http://dnb.dnb.de.

© 2025 Walter de Gruyter GmbH, Berlin/Boston
This volume is text- and page-identical with the hardback published in 2024.
Cover image: Sgt. Marvin E. Sanchez of the 7773d Signal Service Company operates a radio on a U.S. interzonal train, October 1951, National Archives, College Park, Maryland (NACP).
Typesetting: Integra Software Services Pvt. Ltd.
Printing and binding: CPI books GmbH, Leck

www.degruyter.com

To Those Who Served

Foreword by Katrin Paehler

Official histories are a curious genre, sometimes tilting just so toward an organization's favorable perception of itself. It is a testament to Thomas Boghardt and the U.S. Army Center for Military History that this official history—a comprehensive study of Army Intelligence in Germany between 1944 and 1949—is first and foremost an excellent and engaging piece of scholarship. It also fills a major lacuna.

On the surface, there seems to be no shortage of studies, many of them excellent, on U.S. intelligence efforts in Germany in the postwar period. On closer inspection, though, these works have their shortcomings, for they tend to focus on covert operations, or marquee controversial episodes such as Project Paperclip or Operation Rusty, or on the OSS/CIA, which was but a small part of the U.S. intelligence network in Germany (and a subordinate one at that). On the other hand, Army Intelligence stood at the center of U.S. intelligence efforts in postwar Germany. Much of the organization's work was, for lack of a better word, more ordinary intelligence work. But this reality finds little reflection in the historiography.

With *Covert Legions* squarely focused on Army Intelligence, Boghardt provides a needed and comprehensive study. It explores both the organization and its operations; it is nuanced and detail-oriented; and covers an extended timeframe. Out of this approach, which discusses events as disparate as the role of Army Intelligence in the occupation of Aachen in late 1944 to covert actions during the Berlin Blockade, emerges a more fully realized image of Army Intelligence's many roles in Germany during these critical years. Boghardt, finely attuned to the changing situations and contexts on the ground, traces the monumental efforts to denazify and stabilize occupied Germany and to create a new republic out of the ashes of the Third Reich, in cooperation with West Germany's nascent political elite of all democratic stripes, from Konrad Adenauer to Willy Brandt. At the same time, Army Intelligence kept Washington informed about the Soviet Union's military capabilities and designs—two very different things—and managed to establish a long-lasting presence in Germany and Central Europe.

Crucially, Boghardt does not rail against the early decision to shift U.S. intelligence's attention from the recently defeated enemy to the erstwhile ally, the Soviet Union, and Communism writ-large in postwar Germany. Rather, he uses the changing relationship between the United States and the Soviet Union as the "primary prism" of his investigation. Thus, he assesses Army Intelligence not by plans, ideas, and visions of 1942, 1943 or 1944, or even 1945, but by its perception of realities in Germany and Central Europe from 1946 onward. In that sense, the book is both an ode to and a clear-eyed assessment of Army Intelligence. It does tilt the perception "just so" but also rightly so.

This book is also a fantastic read and Boghardt a gifted storyteller. He has a keen eye for telling details and descriptions or pithy quotes, many of them pointed and often quite droll, which he uses to great effect. Rare is the author who can write a solid one hundred pages on "Intelligence Organization in Occupied Europe" and hold the reader's attention. But Boghardt's talents as a writer of elegance and wit are most vividly on display when he discusses intelligence activities, the colorful cast of characters involved in them, and the environment in which these men—and very few women—moved. Writing to a large extent out of the sources, augmented by memoirs and contemporaneous reporting, he conjures defeated Germany and its inhabitants, with a special focus on Berlin, at a level of density and detail all too rare for scholarly monographs. In that sense, *Covert Legions* is also a general history of the occupation period, the early West German postwar, and many of its leading characters, albeit from the unusual perspective of Army Intelligence. It offers insights galore—and a fabulous read.

Normal, IL
13 September 2023

Katrin Paehler
Illinois State University

Foreword by Jon T. Hoffman

The American military occupation of Germany lasted five years. During this time, Germany made great strides along the road from fascism to democracy, Europe became the fulcrum of the Cold War, and the United States emerged as a global superpower. At the center of this turbulent era stood the U.S. Army, the force that helped win the war against Nazi Germany and guaranteed the peaceful integration of postwar Germany's western regions into the transatlantic alliance. The Army, in turn, relied heavily on its intelligence services to guide and implement American policies in the defeated country. This volume details the activities of Army Intelligence in Germany from the Allies' arrival in late 1944 to the end of the military government in 1949.

U.S. military intelligence personnel entered Germany along with Allied combat troops in September 1944. Within days, America's covert warriors apprehended scores of war criminals, removed Nazi officials from public office, and captured scientific and technological hardware and personnel. Over the next five years, Army Intelligence broadened its mission to include the democratization of German society, the surveillance of the communist party, and the containment of the Soviet Union in central Europe. By the end of the military occupation in September 1949, Army Intelligence had established a discreet yet powerful presence in central Europe, which has lasted until the present day.

Covert Legions corrects numerous misunderstandings and fills many gaps in our knowledge about the occupation. The book challenges the prevailing narrative of American softness on former Nazis. It also brings to light the contribution of Army Intelligence to a peaceful resolution of the Soviet blockade of the Western sectors of Berlin in 1948–1949. And it reveals the many links forged between U.S. intelligence and members of the emerging West German elite, including Theodor Heuss, the first president of the Federal Republic; Ernst Reuter, the first mayor of West Berlin; and Willy Brandt, a future West Berlin mayor and West German chancellor.

Army Intelligence was not merely a supporting actor in the occupation. It shaped the American presence in Germany. By suppressing Nazi subversion and monitoring the German Communist Party, intelligence provided breathing space for the fledgling German democracy. By creating a pro-American West German intelligence service, the Army's covert operatives established a lasting security link between victor and vanquished. And by setting up listening posts along the intra-German border, the Army's signals intelligence organization opened a window on the Soviet bloc that would serve the Western alliance for decades. Without Army Intelligence, postwar Germany and the history of the Cold War would have looked very different.

Over the past seventy years, the U.S. intelligence community has burgeoned. Today, the Army constitutes but one of its members. Yet when the Americans came to Germany, the Army stood virtually alone in shouldering the burden of intelligence and counterintelligence operations. Germany was ground zero of the early Cold War, and a generation of American intelligence personnel honed their tradecraft in a constant, heated contest with their communist counterparts. *Covert Legions* affirms the Army's central role in the creation of the U.S. intelligence community and in the struggle to rebuild Europe from the ruins of World War II.

Washington, D.C.
21 September 2021

Jon T. Hoffman
Chief Historian

Preface

"Writing is hard work," asserts the novelist Judith Guest.[1] Most historians will agree. Those of us chronicling the past must not only navigate the shoals of the English language, we also have to locate, read, and process scores of records and secondary sources. All historians need help in this effort, and I received support from many individuals over the past decade. I apologize for my inability to name all of them, but I take great pleasure in thanking many of them here.

The idea for this book was born in the summer of 2011. In June of that year, Joel D. Meyerson, then chief of the Histories Division at the U.S. Army Center of Military History (CMH), asked me if I would be interested in writing an official Army history. My answer was an emphatic yes, and over the ensuing weeks, we discussed possible subjects of the volume-to-be. Eventually, we decided that my project should explore the expansive but little-known operations of Army Intelligence in postwar Germany. The resulting book, we hoped, would make a meaningful contribution to the history of the U.S. Army, of American intelligence, of U.S.-German relations, and of the early Cold War.

Over the following years, I worked under the guidance of knowledgeable, competent, and supportive supervisors. Andrew J. Birtle helped me sharpen the project's focus and ensured its adherence to the requirements of official Army history. W. Shane Story, a veteran of the Iraq War, broadened my perspective by alerting me to similarities and differences between the American occupations of Germany and in the Middle East. James C. McNaughton, who succeeded Dr. Meyerson as division chief in 2013, took a strong interest in my work and offered many helpful suggestions. I am particularly grateful to David W. Hogan Jr., who supervised the project for several years through its conclusion. His patient guidance and his profound knowledge of Army history, World War II, and the Cold War have been invaluable to me.

The CMH leadership steadfastly supported my work. Richard W. Stewart, the Center's chief historian in 2011, championed the volume from its inception. Jon T. Hoffman, who succeeded Dr. Stewart in August 2016, helped me rethink certain aspects of the project to keep it manageable and focused. I greatly appreciated his informed comments, constructive criticism, and words of encouragement over the years. The Center's executive director, Charles R. Bowery, Jr., ensured I had the institutional support I needed, and removed the bureaucratic obstacles that inevitably materialize in a large organization such as the U.S. Army.

---

1 Judith Guest, foreword, in Natalie Goldberg, *Writing Down the Bones: Feeling the Writer Within* (Boston, London: Shambhala, 1986), xii.

The congenial atmosphere at the Center of Military History and the approachability of my colleagues provided a much-needed counterweight against the solitude every writer faces. For many inspiring conversations related to Army Intelligence and beyond, I thank my fellow historians Mark L. Bradley, J. Travis Moger, Kathleen J. Nawyn, Brian F. Neumann, Julie I. Prieto, and Nicholas J. Schlosser. Michael W. DeYoung, Francis Lee Reynolds, and Virginia K. "Ginger" Shaw of the Center's Command Group helped me overcome numerous administrative challenges. Special thanks is due to Donald A. Carter, one of the leading authorities on the Cold War U.S. Army. His expertise and generosity in sharing his knowledge were of inestimable value to me.

The Center's Field Programs Directorate, which includes our library and our archive, provided vital support. I am grateful to Kathleen M. Fargey for locating specific intelligence units in postwar Germany; to Siobhan E. Shaw and Frank R. Shirer for helping me navigate the Center's classified collections; and to Moira E. Zelechoski for assisting me with numerous library requests. Special thanks is due to librarian James A. Tobias, who procured numerous arcane books, articles, and other research material from across the United States for my project. It was with great sadness that I learned of James's passing last year. He will be missed.

The writer Patricia Cornwell emphasizes the importance of "passionate" and "dogged" research, and *Covert Legions* is no exception to this rule.[2] The National Archives at College Park houses the lion's share of the mined documents, and I am indebted to archivists Paul B. Brown, David Castillo, William H. Cunliffe, Martin A. Gedra, Eric Van Slander, and Suzanne M. Zoumbaris for guiding me through the vast collections of their organization. A special thank you is due to the archives' director of declassification, David Fort, who provided me with copies of several thousand classified documents. At Suitland, Maryland, the staff of the Washington National Records Center helped me review several court-martial records pertaining to espionage in postwar Germany.

In my quest for archival records and other research material, I had the support of three indefatigable assistants. From 2017 to 2019, Molly R. Ricks conducted wide-ranging research across the Washington region. Diligent, resourceful, and always upbeat, Molly unearthed a wealth of pertinent material. From 2019 to 2020, Hayley L. Fenton helped me fill several research gaps. In 2021, Kendall E. Cosley compiled the bibliography and collected numerous illustrations during the production phase of the book.

---

2 Patricia Cornwell, "The Passionate Researcher," in *The Writing Life: Writers on How They Think and Work*, ed. Maria Arana (New York: Public Affairs, 2003), 155.

In the course of my research, I consulted two archives outside the greater Washington region. The records of the East German intelligence service at the Stasi archives (BStU) in Berlin allowed me to take a look at intelligence from the other side of the Iron Curtain. I am indebted to BStU archivist Annette Müller for identifying numerous records pertaining to Soviet-bloc intelligence and counter-intelligence operations. Halfway around the world, the holdings of the Harry S. Truman Presidential Library and Museum at Independence, Missouri, gave me an inside look at high-level decision making on intelligence matters in the late 1940s. Many U.S. intelligence agencies have their own archives, and I must thank my colleagues across the federal government for their help in accessing, researching, and declassifying pertinent records of their organizations. At the Center for the Study of Intelligence of the Central Intelligence Agency (CIA) in Virginia, chief historian David Robarge granted me access to files on the agency's early years. Paul J. Isakson of the Defense Intelligence Agency's history office helped me review his agency's records at Landover, Maryland. At Fort George G. Meade, Maryland, the staff of the National Security Agency (NSA) history office and archives made available the operational records of the Army Security Agency (ASA), America's premier signals intelligence organization in the early Cold War. For their help in locating, reviewing, and declassifying these documents, I am grateful to former NSA senior historian Betsy Rohaly Smoot; the former head of NSA's Strategy and Policy, David J. Sherman; the chief of NSA's Center for Cryptologic History, John A. Tokar; archivists Amy B. Degroff and James P. Bauer; and NSA's mandatory declassification lead official, Patricia L. Bither.

Furthermore, I would like to acknowledge the support of the U.S. Army Intelligence and Security Command (INSCOM) at Fort Belvoir, Virginia. Joseph R. Frechette and Thomas N. Hauser of the INSCOM history office assisted me in locating and declassifying the annual ASA histories for the early years of the Cold War. Joe also verified information on various Army Intelligence units in Germany, and he procured several photographs illustrating Army Intelligence training and operations. INSCOM's Information Security Branch chief, Catherine M. Clary-Brown, expeditiously reviewed the entire manuscript for declassification.

Several retired intelligence officers and their families generously shared their recollections with me. Bruce McIntyre and Gerhardt Thamm corresponded with me about their work for the Counter Intelligence Corps (CIC) in postwar Germany. Jeffrey Van Davis and T.H.E. Hill (a pseudonym) discussed their tours of duty with the Army Security Agency, Europe. E. S. "Jim" Browning shared his memories of his father, Maj. Earl S. Browning, who served as chief of operations at CIC headquarters in Germany. Anne Sibert Buiter, Alan C. Sibert, and William C. Sibert Jr. helped me better understand the personality of their grandfather, Brig. Gen. Edwin L. Sibert, who served as the first director of Army Intelligence during the occupation. I am especially indebted to Peter M. F. Sichel, who served with the CIA and its precursor organizations in Berlin from 1945 to 1952. Over several years, Mr. Sichel patiently answered my questions on "what it was like" to be an American intelligence officer at such a momentous time and place. His vivid recollections and his photographic memory went a long way in illuminating the secret landscape of postwar Germany.

"Revising," notes E. B. White, "is part of writing."[3] To help this process along, a CMH review board discusses each draft with the author. Led by Jon Hoffman, the board for this volume included Don Carter, David Hogan, and Shane Story. I am grateful to all of them for their consistently sound feedback and for many seminal discussions. Their informed critiques helped me avoid factual errors, keep my narrative focused, and explore different points of view.

In December 2019, the Center convened a panel of subject matter experts to review the manuscript. Chaired by Jon Hoffman, the panel included Dave Hogan as well as U.S. Army War College professor Genevieve Lester, INSCOM command historian Lt. Col. (Ret.) Michael E. Bigelow, NSA senior historian David A. Hatch, CIA historian David A. Welker, former CIA historian Kevin C. Ruffner, and National Defense University professor Walter M. Hudson, who happens to be the grandson of Bavaria's second military governor, Brig. Gen. Walter J. Muller. I gratefully acknowledge their thoughtful comments, suggestions, and constructive criticism.

The Center of Military History is blessed with a superb production team. Headed by Cheryl L. Bratten, our Historical Products Division's editors, cartographers, and graphic designers worked wonders in turning my manuscript into a clean and appealing product. I am indebted to Matthew T. Boan for creating the maps; to Gene Snyder for designing the cover, the diagrams, and the layout; and to Deborah A. Stultz for her meticulous copyediting. Special thanks is due to senior editor Shannon L. Granville, who carefully reviewed each chapter and oversaw the entire production process. Her attention to detail, her command of the nuances of the English language, and her passion for the history of early Cold War intelligence have made this a better book.

Many more historians, journalists, archivists, curators, and intelligence veterans have provided information, encouragement, and feedback. I gratefully acknowledge the generous support of the late Matthew M. Aid, Richard Aldrich, Stephen F. Anderson, Nikolai Brandal, Richard D. Breitman, Robert Byer, Daniel Crosswell, Richard Cummings, Sarah K. Douglas, Nicholas Dujmovic, Walter F. Elkins, Benjamin B. Fischer, Jan Foitzik, Josef Foschepoth, James L. Gilbert, Norman J. W. Goda, Joseph C. Goulden, Solveig Gram Jensen, Daniel F. Harrington, William R. Harris, Bodo Hechelhammer, Enrico Heitzer, Bryan J. Hockensmith, the late Keith

---

3 William Strunk Jr. and E. B. White, *The Elements of Style*, 4th ed. (New York: Pearson, 2000), 74.

Jeffery, Eva Jobs, Gary Keeley, Peter Köpf, Bernd von Kostka, Wolfgang Krieger, Clayton D. Laurie, Peter Martland, Oliver Moody, Frank Myers, Christian Ostermann, Martin Otto, Susan M. Perlman, Mark J. Reardon, Steven P. Remy, Nicholas E. Reynolds, Thomas Rid, Michael R. Rouland, Allan A. Ryan, Bernd Schaefer, Richard E. Schroeder, Alaric Searle, Shlomo J. Shpiro, Patrick C. Stein, Gerald J. Steinacher, Lori S. Stewart, Wolfgang Stienes, Mark E. Stout, Dan Treado, Matthias Uhl, Karina Urbach, Andres Vaart, Armin Wagner, Michael Wala, Michael Warner, Florian Weiss, Rüdiger Wenzke, Klaus Wiegrefe, the late David Wise, and Richard I. Wolf.

Finally, I would like to express my deep gratitude to my family. I could not have completed this book without their loving support.

Contents

Foreword by Katrin Paehler —— VII

Foreword by Jon T. Hoffman —— IX

Preface —— XI

List of Maps, Charts and Illustrations —— XXI

The Author —— XXIII

Introduction —— 1

Part I: Intelligence In World War II

1 **Intelligence Goes to War —— 13**
   The Army's Wartime Intelligence Organization —— 14
   Personnel, Recruitment, and Training —— 21
   Army Intelligence in the European Theater —— 28
   Conclusion —— 36

2 **Operations in Wartime Germany —— 38**
   The Occupation of Aachen —— 39
   The Battle of the Bulge —— 44
   The *Werwolf* —— 52
   Intelligence Myths: The Alpine Redoubt and the Lost Race for Berlin —— 57
   Counterintelligence —— 66
   Army Intelligence and the Allies —— 71
   Conclusion —— 79

Part II: Intelligence Organization in Occupied Germany

3 **Intelligence Headquarters —— 83**
   The American Occupation of Germany —— 84
   The Intelligence Division at the Pentagon —— 89
   Army Intelligence Headquarters in Frankfurt and Heidelberg —— 91
   The Intelligence Organization of the Military Government —— 101
   Berlin Command —— 111

From OSS to CIA —— 119
U.S. Navy and U.S. Air Force Intelligence Efforts —— 129
Conclusion —— 130

4 Intelligence Field Agencies —— 131
The Counter Intelligence Corps —— 132
The Army Security Agency, Europe —— 143
The Intelligence Center in Oberursel —— 151
Intelligence Acquisition Through Censorship —— 155
The Intelligence School at Oberammergau —— 160
The Berlin Documents Center —— 164
The United States Military Liaison Mission —— 167
Conclusion —— 170

Part III: Intelligence Operations in Occupied Germany

5 The Long Shadow of the Third Reich —— 173
In Search of Adolf Hitler —— 174
Denazification —— 182
Nazi Subversion —— 191
War Crimes —— 201
The Breakdown of Inter-Allied Cooperation —— 211
Conclusion —— 216

6 Intelligence Exploitation —— 219
Wartime Intelligence Exploitation —— 221
Project PAPERCLIP —— 226
The Target Intelligence Committee —— 233
Operation RUSTY —— 243
Defectors, Informants, and Ratlines —— 258
Conclusion —— 266

7 New Challenges —— 268
Chaos, Corruption, and the Black Market —— 268
Displaced Persons —— 280
Soviet Espionage —— 288
Conclusion —— 304

8 Democratization —— 305
Shaping the Political Landscape in Postwar Germany —— 308
The Bavarian Challenge —— 317
The Communist Party of Germany —— 329
Intelligence and Politics in Berlin —— 337
Conclusion —— 348

9 The Soviet Zone —— 350
Economic Exploitation —— 351
Political Control —— 358
The SPD Ostbüro —— 368
The Red Army —— 376
Conclusion —— 394

10 The Berlin Blockade —— 396
War Scares —— 398
The Blockade —— 408
The Struggle for Berlin's Hearts and Minds —— 417
Covert Action —— 425
The Federal Republic of Germany —— 435
Conclusion —— 438

Conclusion —— 440

Bibliography —— 447

Abbreviations and Glossary of Terms —— 469

Index —— 477

List of Maps, Charts and Illustrations

Maps

Map 1 Army Intelligence Units, Germany, 1945–1949 (incl. map legend) —— **95**
Map 2 American CIC Regions, Germany, 30 November 1945–15 April 1949 —— **135**
Map 3 American CIC Regions, Germany, 15 April 1949 —— **142**

Charts

Chart 1 Army Intelligence in the European Theater of Operations at the End of World War II —— **17**
Chart 2 Army Intelligence, U.S. Forces in the European Theater, July 1945–March 1947 —— **103**
Chart 3 Army Intelligence, European Command, 1947–1949 —— **106**

Illustrations

Figure 1 Henry Kissinger with fellow U.S. soldiers and German children, 1946 —— **3**
Figure 2 Stefan Heym, 1944 —— **5**
Figure 3 Mock-up of a German village at Camp Ritchie —— **24**
Figure 4 Mock interrogation at Camp Ritchie —— **27**
Figure 5 Lt. Col. Leo A. Swoboda in Berlin, 1946 —— **40**
Figure 6 CIC Special Agent Dave Reisner interrogates four *Werwolf* members, April 1945 —— **53**
Figure 7 U.S. Army poster of the execution of *Werwolf* Richard Jarzcyk —— **58**
Figure 8 Polish evacuees from the Soviet Union —— **76**
Figure 9 29th Infantry Division officers toasting the defeat of Germany —— **80**
Figure 10 The IG Farben building in Frankfurt, U.S. Army headquarters in Europe —— **86**
Figure 11 Maj. Gen. Edwin L. Sibert, 1953.
Illustrations courtesy of the following sources: 1st Lt. Paul K. Whitaker, 27; Allied Museum, Berlin, 1, 2; Archiv der sozialen Demokratie, Friedrich-Ebert-Stiftung, Germany, 36; Bundesbeauftragter für die Unterlagen des Staatssicherheitsdienstes der ehemaligen Deutschen Demokratischen Republik (BStU), 13; Enrico Heitzer and BStU, Berlin, 45; Gedenkstätte und Museum Sachsenhausen, Germany, 37; *Life* magazine, 23 July 1945, 26; National Archives, College Park, Maryland (NACP), 5, 6, 7, 8, 9, 10, 11, 12, 22, 23, 24, 29, 31, 32, 33, 34, 35, 38, 40, 41, 42, 43, 44, 46, 47; Peter M. F. Sichel, 14; *Tägliche Rundschau*, 15 November 1947, 39; U.S. Army, 21; U.S. Army Intelligence and Security Command, 17, 18; U.S. Army Intelligence Center History Office, 3; U.S. Army Signal Corps, 4, 19, 20, 25, 28; *Washington Sunday Star*, 22 October 1950, 30; Yale University, 15, 16 —— **92**
Figure 12 Col. Robert A. Schow, April 1947 —— **99**

Figure 13 Col. Peter P. Rodes in Berlin, April 1949 —— **104**
Figure 14 Army Intelligence safe house in Berlin, Bogotastrasse 19 —— **112**
Figure 15 Peter M. F. Sichel —— **122**
Figure 16 The "Joe House," Promenadenstrasse 2, Berlin —— **123**
Figure 17 Agents dining inside the Joe House in Berlin —— **124**
Figure 18 Headquarters, Army Security Agency, Europe, IG Farben building —— **143**
Figure 19 An Army Security Agency operator at the Herzogenaurach field station —— **147**
Figure 20 The 7712th European Intelligence Command School in Oberammergau, January 1948 —— **161**
Figure 21 German instruction for Army Intelligence personnel, January 1948 —— **162**
Figure 22 Document storage at the Berlin Documents Center —— **165**
Figure 23 Executions of SS guards at Dachau concentration camp —— **174**
Figure 24 Capt. Edward Levy interviews Hans Goebbels, April 1945 —— **183**
Figure 25 The Stuttgart *Spruchkammer* courtroom after the bombing —— **197**
Figure 26 Capt. Curt Bruns, shortly before his execution —— **206**
Figure 27 Artist rendition of the Nazi space mirror, *Life* magazine, 23 July 1945 —— **220**
Figure 28 German prisoners of war prepare a replica of a Soviet cipher machine for shipment, June 1945 —— **236**
Figure 29 Reinhard Gehlen in U.S. captivity —— **245**
Figure 30 Col. Jack W. Durant and Capt. Kathleen B. Nash Durant arrive at Frankfurt airport for their trial, June 1945 —— **270**
Figure 31 Cartoon from the *Washington Sunday Star*, 22 October 1950 —— **278**
Figure 32 Five Soviet soldiers arrested on suspicion of espionage —— **295**
Figure 33 Fifteenth Army soldiers view Cologne Cathedral, April 1945 —— **306**
Figure 34 The American flag flies over Munich's *Rathaus* (city hall) —— **318**
Figure 35 Josef Müller —— **325**
Figure 36 Undercover photograph of communists Dora and Josef Angerer, January 1949 —— **331**
Figure 37 Willy Brandt with the Norwegian liaison mission in Berlin, 1946 —— **344**
Figure 38 A watchtower of the *Spezlager* Sachsenhausen, May or June 1949 —— **351**
Figure 39 Workmen prepare equipment for shipment to the Soviet Union, July 1946 —— **357**
Figure 40 Soviet propaganda cartoon against the Marshall Plan (*Tägliche Rundschau*, 15 November 1947) —— **373**
Figure 41 A Red Army convoy on the autobahn near Weimar, July 1945 —— **377**
Figure 42 A Soviet artillery unit on the island of Rügen in the Baltic Sea, August 1948 —— **379**
Figure 43 Army Intelligence estimate of the advance routes of Soviet forces in case of war in Europe, 1947 —— **392**
Figure 44 Sgt. Marvin E. Sanchez of the 7773d Signal Service Company operates a radio on a U.S. interzonal train, October 1951 —— **400**
Figure 45 Berlin-bound trucks blocked at the British-Soviet intrazonal border at Helmstedt, June 1948 —— **409**
Figure 46 *Reifentöter* (caltrops) used to incapacitate vehicles —— **433**
Figure 47 The end of the blockade, summer 1949 —— **439**

The Author

Thomas Boghardt was born in the Rhineland and grew up in Hamburg, Germany, and Venice, Florida. From 1990 to 1991, he served with the 183d Panzerbataillon of the German army. He received his master's degree in history from the University of Freiburg in 1996, and his Ph.D. in modern European history from the University of Oxford in 2002. Dr. Boghardt taught history at the University of Management Sciences in Lahore, Pakistan, in 2002 before joining Georgetown University's Edmund A. Walsh School of Foreign Service as the Fritz Thyssen Fellow from 2002 to 2004. For the next six years, he worked as a historian at the International Spy Museum in Washington, D.C. In 2010, he joined the U.S. Army Center of Military History as a senior historian.

Dr. Boghardt has published numerous articles and books on intelligence in the twentieth century, and he lectures frequently on this subject. He lives with his wife and two children in the Washington, D.C., area.

Introduction

In September 1944, American forces pierced the borders of the Third Reich. Eight months later, Germany surrendered unconditionally, and the victorious Allies occupied the defeated nation for the next four years.[1] Yet the wartime coalition of the United States, Great Britain, and the Soviet Union (USSR; Union of Soviet Socialist Republics) did not survive victory for long. By the late 1940s, the Grand Alliance had disintegrated into two hostile and ideologically opposed camps. The Soviet Union held sway over a vast communist empire stretching across Eurasia, and the United States led a group of capitalist states that ranged from the Pacific Rim to Western Europe. The front line between the two sides, known as the "Iron Curtain," ran straight through a now-divided Germany. Full of mistrust, competition, and proxy conflicts, the new Cold War order would remain in place for four decades.

Germany played a central role in the onset of the Cold War. Its defeat notwithstanding, the country remained the most populous and technologically advanced nation in Europe, and its strategic location at the center of the continent made it a coveted prize for East and West alike. Consequently, American policy toward Germany changed radically in the span of a few years. During the war, President Franklin D. Roosevelt had contemplated the draconian Morgenthau Plan. Named after its architect, Treasury Secretary Henry J. Morgenthau Jr., the plan would cede large areas of German territory to its neighbors to the east and west, break up the remaining country into smaller states, and completely deindustrialize the former Reich. People living in previously industrialized areas, Morgenthau proposed, "should be as widely dispersed as possible," and the German people as a whole should "be held down to a subsistence level."[2]

Roosevelt's successor, President Harry S. Truman, set the United States on a far different course. Dismissing Morgenthau as a "blockhead" who "didn't know s–t from apple butter," the new president quickly pushed the treasury secretary

---

[1] The term "military occupation" denotes the time period from September 1944 to September 1949 when the U.S. Army constituted the highest political authority in Germany. A formal U.S. military government organization existed from August 1944 to September 1949. Thereafter, the American occupation continued until 1955 under the authority of the U.S. Department of State, represented by a civilian high commissioner in the city of Bonn, the capital of the Federal Republic of Germany.
[2] Memo, Henry Morgenthau Jr., n.d. [1944], sub: Suggested Post-Surrender Program for Germany, Folder "PSF Germany 1944–45," President's Sec Files, Franklin D. Roosevelt Presidential Library, Hyde Park, NY (hereinafter Roosevelt Library); Henry Morgenthau Jr., Diary, book 768, 1–4 Sep 1944, 3, Henry Morgenthau Jr. Papers, Roosevelt Library.

https://doi.org/10.1515/9783110988550-001

out of his job.³ In 1948, Truman embraced the antithesis to Morgenthau's project of a punitive peace. The Marshall Plan, named after Truman's secretary of state, George C. Marshall, provided massive financial aid to Western Europe and to the western parts of Germany. As an internal U.S. document explained, this effort aimed at ensuring that pro-Western countries "do not pass under the influence of any potentially hostile nation"—a thinly veiled reference to the Soviet Union.⁴ The process of realignment between Germany and the United States concluded in May 1949 with the establishment of the Federal Republic of Germany, a state firmly embedded in the Western camp and a cornerstone of American Cold War strategy.

The principal instrument by which the United States waged the war and shaped the peace in Europe was the U.S. Army. Alongside British and Canadian troops, American soldiers fought their way from the beaches of Normandy to the heart of the Reich, and they served as occupation forces after the Allied victory in May 1945. General of the Army Dwight D. Eisenhower led the Western forces as supreme commander. Another Army officer, General Lucius D. Clay, represented the highest American authority as commander in chief in Europe and military governor of Germany. The Army was America's public face in Europe, and soldiers devised, interpreted, and executed American policies in Germany during those years.

In addition to combat troops, administrators, and logisticians, the Army sent scores of covert operatives to Germany. The Army's intelligence services collected, analyzed, and distributed to local commanders and military government officials information that could not be gleaned from openly available sources.⁵ The sheer size of the Army's intelligence organization suggests its significance. In 1949, the various Army Intelligence agencies employed well over 5,000 individuals in Germany.⁶ By comparison, only 2,500 soldiers and civilians worked for the U.S. military government.⁷

The Army's intelligence organization used a comprehensive set of collection techniques in their wide-ranging surveillance. Personnel of the Civil Censorship Di-

---

3 Michael R. Beschloss, *The Conquerors: Roosevelt, Truman, and the Destruction of Hitler's Germany, 1941–1945* (New York: Simon & Schuster, 2003), 249.
4 Benn Steil, *The Marshall Plan: Dawn of the Cold War* (New York: Simon & Schuster, 2018), 86. Technically, the Marshall Plan was open to all European nations, including the Soviet Union, but Moscow rejected it as an American attempt to gain influence over the communist countries.
5 The narrative refers to these services collectively as "Army Intelligence."
6 Most of those employed in this area worked for the Counter Intelligence Corps (CIC); the Army Security Agency (ASA); and in the mail, telegram, and telephone censorship offices. See Chapter 4 for more detailed information on the figures.
7 Lucius D. Clay, *Decision in Germany* (Garden City, NY: Doubleday, 1950), 66.

vision monitored thousands of phone calls, telegrams, and letters. Signal intelligence specialists of the Army Security Agency (ASA) listened in on radio traffic across Europe via intercept stations. Special agents of the Army's Counter Intelligence Corps (CIC) recruited informants across Germany and interviewed hundreds of thousands of Nazi officials, refugees, and defectors from the East. Uniformed officers of the United States Military Liaison Mission roamed across the Soviet occupation zone to assess the strength of Red Army units. As one Army Intelligence veteran recalled, "We were the CIA, FBI and military security all in one."[8]

Figure 1: Henry Kissinger (right) with fellow U.S. soldiers and German children, 1946. Allied Museum.

The top intelligence officer in the European Theater at the end of the war was Brig. Gen. Edwin L. Sibert. A career officer, Sibert had served as General Omar N. Bradley's intelligence chief in the 12th Army Group during the liberation of France and the invasion of Germany. Smart, level-headed, and mindful of diverging U.S.-Soviet interests, Sibert guided the transformation of the Army's intelligence apparatus from its war footing to occupation duties. For the most part, the

---

8 Ian Sayer and Douglas Botting, *America's Secret Army: The Untold Story of the Counter Intelligence Corps* (London: Fontana, 1990), 281.

commanding officers of individual agencies mirrored Sibert's profile. They were professional soldiers who inspired confidence in their subordinates and knew how to lead military units.

Below the leadership level served a diverse group of wartime veterans, postwar draftees, and civilian employees. The Army was especially keen on recruiting German émigrés and Americans with knowledge of the German language. During the war, nearly two thousand German-born soldiers went through Camp Ritchie in western Maryland, the Army's principal intelligence training facility for the European Theater. The polyglot, highly educated "Ritchie Boys" included the future East German writer Stefan Heym; Klaus Mann, the novelist and son of famed German writer Thomas Mann; and the future secretary of state and national security adviser Henry A. Kissinger. The American novelist J. D. Salinger also joined this illustrious group on account of his knowledge of German and French.[9]

Army Intelligence pursued many missions. Long before Allied armies entered Germany, intelligence supported military operations against the German forces in North Africa, Italy, and France through the interrogation of prisoners of war, the interception and decryption of the enemy's radio traffic, and aerial reconnaissance. When American troops crossed the border into the Reich, Army Intelligence added to its portfolio the fight against an underground Nazi organization, the so-called *Werwolf*.

As the Army seized German territory, the military's intelligence agencies broadened their mission in support of the occupation. During the summer of 1945, the removal of Nazi officials from office and the arrest of war crimes suspects ranked among intelligence officials' most urgent tasks. Within two months of the end of the war, 70,000 arrestees awaited their fate in American detention camps. As an official history noted, intelligence operations during that time "can be grouped largely under a single heading: De-Nazification."[10]

The Army's covert legions also served as Washington's chief instrument for the exploitation of the enemy's advanced scientific knowledge. Following closely on the heels of the conquering forces, intelligence personnel apprehended and interviewed German scientists, and captured large volumes of scientific records

---

[9] The four Ritchie Boys took divergent paths after the end of the war. Salinger and Mann returned to writing, while Kissinger entered the field of international relations. Heym briefly worked for the U.S. military occupation in Germany but became increasingly critical of American policy. In 1952, he returned all his military commendations in protest against American intervention in the Korean War, moved to Prague, and eventually settled in East Germany and continued his writing career.

[10] Maj. Ann Bray et al., ed., *The History of the Counter Intelligence Corps*, vol. 26, *German Occupation* (Fort Holabird, MD: U.S. Army Intelligence Center, 1959), 12.

Figure 2: Stefan Heym in 1944. Allied Museum.

and hardware. By the end of the war, Army Intelligence units had seized and shipped vast amounts of documents and equipment to the United States, including an entire chemical factory.

Yet even as the Americans conquered and occupied, they also reformed and rebuilt. Long before Allied forces crossed the borders of the Reich, U.S. intelligence had begun the process of identifying politically untarnished individuals, such as journalists, administrators, and politicians with anti-Nazi and prodemocratic backgrounds, who might be willing to work with the occupying forces. This process proved a critical moment in the formation of West Germany's political elite. Many of the local officials identified by Army Intelligence and appointed by American military officials to public office at the end of the war would move on to illustrious public careers in West Germany. The list included the first chancellor and the first president of the Federal Republic, Konrad Adenauer and Theodor Heuss.

To determine how to democratize Germany's authoritarian society, the occupying powers felt they would need to develop a deeper understanding of the occupied people's psyche. "The German mind," General Sibert noted, was "our greatest problem," and Army Intelligence analysts labored over unraveling its mysteries.[11] Against the backdrop of the war and the unspeakable atrocities committed by the Nazis, early American assessments did not look kindly on the average German. A report of the intelligence branch of the Seventh U.S. Army used the following narrative to explain what it termed the "schizophrenia of the German mind":

> Today the "little man" in Germany feels that he has reached the rightfully ordained end of the road that is in store for every German. The law said to him: "Go ahead, cross the street!", and upon executing this order, he was immediately run down. This did not come as a surprise. Rather than surprise, he feels a mixture of righteousness and self-pity; righteousness for having followed the letter of the law, self-pity for having been knocked out cold in so doing—a fate which he considers to be the traditional tragedy of the German people. By an infinitely complicated process of thought, the whole business is a matter of profound satisfaction to him.

The report then sought to explain the ideological fanaticism and the horrendous crimes by the Nazis as symptoms of the schizophrenia of the German psyche:

> A combination of the romantic with the unimaginative, coldly rational, and dull, was the reason why SS-men charted their wild blood-orgies in neat book-keeping of the daily numbers of corpses. It was the reason why Hitler, a mixture of potent lunatic and small *Beamter* (Civil Servant)[,] sent millions of Germans into a frenzy of adulation. It was the reason why German soldiers would fight fanatically at one minute, and, upon counting their last bullet, surrender quite reasonably the next.[12]

Within a few years, however, American sentiments toward Germany and its people made a volte-face. At the root of this remarkable shift stood the Cold War realignment, with Berlin as its fulcrum. In June 1948, the Soviets imposed a blockade on the western sectors of the city, a measure that forged a tight bond between local citizens and their Western occupiers. For almost a full year, the Western Allies supported the city with a round-the-clock airlift, bringing in supplies for the people of West Berlin in defiance of the Soviet restrictions. The monumental logistics effort of the Berlin Airlift awed the German population, and German endurance in the face of the blockade moved American officials. Brig. Gen. Frank L. Howley, the American commander in Berlin from 1945 to 1949, tells the following vignette about his departure from the former German capital in September 1949. As Howley

---

11 Brig. Gen. Edwin L. Sibert, "The German Mind: Our Greatest Problem," *New York Times*, 17 Feb 1946.
12 Rpt, HQ Seventh Army, G–2 Bull no. 94, 26 Dec 1945, sub: The German Mind, Folder "VI Corps G–2 Journals 26–30 Dec 45," Historical Div, Program Files, VI Corps, G–2 Jnls, 1945, Record Group (RG) 498, National Archives and Records Administration, College Park, Maryland (hereinafter NACP).

and his wife Edith prepared to get into the car that would take them to the airport, a large crowd gathered to cheer and shake hands with the departing commander. "Pushing her way through the crowd," Howley wrote in his memoirs,

> came a determined, hatless woman, her hair strained back from her face, her features pinched and wan, for Berlin rations were still very low. But the sparkle in her eyes transformed that face and hid the marks of suffering and privation. In her arms she carried a blue-eyed baby—as healthy a child as I've ever seen pictured in a baby contest. "This is my baby you saved when the Russians would not give us milk," she told me, tears filling her eyes. "We will never forget you, sir. Goodbye and good luck!"[13]

As Howley's car pulled away, he and his wife wiped tears from their eyes. "The German mother's tribute," he recalled, "was as high a reward as I will ever merit. I treasure it." What a difference a few years had made.

Dealing with the Nazi legacy, exploiting the enemy's technology, and democratizing German society were but a few of the missions pursued by America's covert warriors. Yet the central role of Army Intelligence in the occupation has remained largely unexplored in the historiography. Authors have not ignored the subject altogether, but most works dealing with the Army's covert operations in postwar Germany do so only peripherally, or focus on a few selected aspects.

One subject that has received ample attention is the collaboration of American intelligence with former Nazi officials and the moral implications of this questionable partnership. Historians and journalists have published a great deal about the Army's enlistment of Nazi scientists to further U.S. defense technologies (Project PAPERCLIP), the use of former *Wehrmacht* (German armed forces) officers to establish a German protointelligence service (Operation RUSTY), and the recruitment of former *Gestapo* (*Geheime Staatspolizei*, the Nazi secret police) officers to provide information on the German Communist Party (Kommunistische Partei Deutschlands; KPD).[14] These topics merit continued attention, but they represent only a small part of the Army's covert activities in postwar Germany. Viewed in isolation, they reveal little about the overall significance of intelligence for the American occupation and for U.S. policy during those years.

---

13 Frank L. Howley, *Berlin Command* (New York: G. P. Putnam's Sons, 1950), 5.
14 Examples include Brian E. Crim, *Our Germans: Project Paperclip and the National Security State* (Baltimore: Johns Hopkins University Press, 2018); Jens Wegener, *Die Organisation Gehlen und die USA. Deutsch-Amerikanische Geheimdienstbeziehungen, 1945–1949* [The Gehlen organization and the United States: German-American intelligence relations, 1945–1949] (Münster: Lit Verlag, 2008); and Richard Breitman, Norman J. W. Goda, Timothy Naftali, and Robert Wolfe, eds., *U.S. Intelligence and the Nazis* (Cambridge, UK: Cambridge University Press, 2005).

Historians have also explored the interception and decryption of foreign communications (signals intelligence) in the 1940s. Specifically, authors have examined Allied efforts to break German ciphers during the war (ULTRA) as well as the postwar endeavors of American cryptanalysts to decipher Soviet wartime intelligence messages (VENONA).[15] More recently, Anglo-American efforts to intercept and decrypt Soviet communications in the postwar era have come under scrutiny as well (BOURBON).[16] Yet the operations of the ASA in Germany have long remained shrouded in mystery.

Writers have discussed, at some length, the history of the Office of Strategic Services (OSS) and its eventual successor, the Central Intelligence Agency (CIA). The two organizations operated successively in Germany during the occupation. Memoirs and books on their exploits abound, and many works include treatments or references to OSS and CIA operations during the mid- to late 1940s in Germany.[17] But for the most part, these studies treat Army Intelligence cursorily, if at all. Usually left unsaid is the fact that the OSS and the CIA played only subordinate roles in the postwar U.S. intelligence system; the Army dominated and directed the American intelligence effort during those years.

This volume provides a comprehensive organizational and operational history of Army Intelligence in Germany from the time U.S. forces entered the country in September 1944 to the end of the military occupation five years later. Although it seeks to address all facets of this subject, it does so through the prism of the changing relationship between the United States and the Soviet Union. The U.S.-Soviet rivalry turned Germany into the principal battleground of the early Cold War. As such, it became the dominating factor of the American occupation and affected virtually every aspect of U.S. intelligence operations in central Europe.

Conservative and anticommunist, the U.S. Army's officer corps had long been skeptical of their country's alliance with the Soviet Union. During the war, some intelligence officers openly voiced their misgivings about Moscow's postwar intentions. Brig. Gen. Joseph A. "Mike" Michela, the American military attaché to

---

15 Examples include Stephen Budiansky, *Battle of Wits: The Complete Story of Codebreaking in World War II* (New York: Free Press, 2000); and Robert L. Benson, *The Venona Story* (Fort Meade, MD: Center for Cryptologic History, National Security Agency, 2001).

16 See, for example, Matthew M. Aid, *The Secret Sentry: The Untold History of the National Security Agency* (London: Bloomsbury Press, 2009).

17 Examples include Evan Thomas, *The Very Best Men: Four Who Dared: The Early Years of the CIA* (New York: Touchstone, 1995); David E. Murphy, Sergei A. Kondrashev, and George Bailey, *Battleground Berlin: CIA vs. KGB in the Cold War* (New Haven, CT: Yale University Press, 1997); and David Alvarez and Eduard Mark, *Spying Through a Glass Darkly: American Espionage Against the Soviet Union, 1945–1946* (Lawrence: University Press of Kansas, 2016).

Moscow, warned as early as February 1943 that the Soviets "intend to push their claims in Europe even to the extent of resorting to armed force, the day the war with Germany ends." Michela concluded his report to the War Department with the exhortation that a "stiffening in our attitude [toward the Soviets] is long past due."[18]

With the end of the war, concern about Soviet policies in central Europe mounted among Army Intelligence personnel. In the summer of 1945, General Sibert ordered his intelligence services to assess the strength of the Red Army in the Soviet occupation zone. Shortly thereafter, Army Intelligence began monitoring the KPD, a party that many American officials considered to be Moscow's Trojan horse in the Western occupation zones. By late 1946, Army Intelligence had zeroed in on the Soviets and their auxiliaries as its principal targets.

The demise of the Grand Alliance affected numerous intelligence operations that originally had no bearing on the U.S.-Soviet relationship. The Americans initially regarded Nazi officials as a threat to democratization, but eventually ended up taking a softer stance in view of their erstwhile enemies' avowed anticommunism. Over time, the occupation government eased up on denazification and prosecution for war crimes and tolerated the return of former Nazis to official positions. The same dynamics applied to intelligence exploitation. At first, the Army pursued the technology and individuals involved in Nazi Germany's scientific research programs solely as a means of improving its own military capabilities. But before long, denying this knowledge to the Soviets became one of the main drivers of these efforts.

The Cold War strengthened the ties between American officials and the emerging West German political elite, as illustrated by the case of the future mayor of West Berlin and chancellor of West Germany, Willy Brandt. Brandt agreed to become a CIC informant in 1948 out of concern over Soviet efforts to suppress his party, the Social Democratic Party of Germany (Sozialdemokratische Partei Deutschlands; SPD). In the years that followed, he provided his handlers with several hundred reports obtained from social democrats in the Soviet Zone about political, military, and economic conditions there. An idealist, Brandt refused payment for his services, but happily accepted a hard-to-come-by commodity in postwar Berlin: American whiskey. Brandt was one of the most notable contacts of Army Intelligence, but he was far from the only one.

*

---

18 Rpt, Brig. Gen. Joseph A. Michela, Mil Attaché to Moscow, to Mil Intel Div (MID), 18 Feb 1943, sub: Comments on Current Events No. 105, Folder "350.05 U.S.S.R. 6-4-44 thru 1-31-42," Army-Intel Project Decimal File 1941–1945, RG 319, NACP.

The book is divided into three parts. The first, consisting of Chapters 1 and 2, discusses Army Intelligence organizations and operations during the war. Part II, covering Chapters 3 and 4, examines the administrative structure of Army Intelligence in occupied Germany and gives an overview of the various headquarters organizations, the principal field agencies, and key personnel. Part III, spanning Chapters 5 through 10, explores the operations of Army Intelligence in Germany from Victory in Europe (V-E) Day to the end of the military occupation in September 1949.

Parts I and III form a narrative unit, covering the operations of Army Intelligence in Germany from 1944 to 1949 in a broadly chronological fashion. Part II provides an in-depth perspective on the structural makeup of the Army Intelligence organization in Germany during this period. This close examination of the Army's organizational structure is important for understanding how the Army did business in Germany, but readers interested chiefly in operational aspects of may want to consult Part II as a reference, rather than consider it an integral part of the narrative.

Geographically, this volume covers all areas under the American occupation, including the states (*Länder*) of Bavaria, Greater Hesse, and Württemberg-Baden, as well as the city of Bremen (which remained under American occupation even though the enclave was surrounded by the British occupation zone). The city of Berlin, divided into four occupational sectors, receives particular attention. Until 1945, Berlin was the capital of Germany. Thereafter, it served as the headquarters of the four Allied powers in the occupied country. The American military governor and, from 1947, the Army's top intelligence officer in Europe also worked in the city. Given its proximity to the Soviet Zone, Berlin became a hotspot of Soviet and Western intelligence. If Germany was the principal theater of the early Cold War, Berlin was its front line.

*

Many American officials shaped U.S. policy during the occupation, but Army Intelligence was an indispensable agent in this endeavor. America's covert legions served as Washington's eyes and ears as well as the first line defense of U.S. interests in central Europe. "Divided Germany during the Occupation was an intelligence jungle," recalled an American intelligence officer. "The two sides waged the largest, most concentrated and intense intelligence warfare in history on German soil."[19] The men and, in a few cases, women of Army Intelligence played a key part in this struggle. This is their story.

---

[19] James H. Critchfield, *Partners at the Creation: The Men Behind Postwar Germany's Defense and Intelligence Establishments* (Annapolis, MD: Naval Institute Press, 2003), 162.

Part I: **Intelligence In World War II**

1 Intelligence Goes to War

The journey of Army Intelligence to Germany started with the war on Japan. In December 1941, Col. Rufus S. Bratton was chief of the Far Eastern Section of the Military Intelligence Division in Washington, D.C. Bratton had graduated from West Point as well as from the Imperial Japanese Army Staff College in Tokyo, and he was fluent in Japanese. At the intelligence division, he was one of a handful of Army officers cleared to know that the United States had broken the cipher of the Japanese foreign ministry and its diplomats abroad. American codebreakers called the Japanese cipher machine PURPLE and referred to the resulting decrypts as MAGIC messages. It was Bratton's job to evaluate the contents of the decrypts and pass them up the chain of command.[1]

As relations between Washington and Tokyo deteriorated, U.S. intelligence officials were looking for indications of a Japanese surprise attack on the United States. The Army's and the Navy's signals intelligence services picked up tantalizing bits and pieces of operational traffic from MAGIC, but nothing in the messages provided definitive information about a time or place of attack. The two services seldom coordinated their work or shared their findings, a lapse that led to gaps in the intelligence coverage of Japan.

On 3 December 1941, the Army decrypted a message from Tokyo to the Japanese ambassador in Washington. It instructed the ambassador to destroy his codes, an act that Bratton interpreted as a sign of Japanese war preparations. He immediately sent one of his officers to the Japanese embassy on Massachusetts Avenue "to find out if they were burning any papers in their backyard." The officer confirmed that they were. Bratton ordered the Army's military attachés in East Asia to destroy their codes to prevent them from falling into Japanese hands in case of war.[2]

On the morning of 7 December, a MAGIC message arrived in Washington with instructions for the Japanese ambassador to break off relations with the United States. Convinced that this order indicated an imminent "attack on an American installation in the Pacific," Bratton grabbed the chief of the intelligence division, Brig. Gen. Sherman Miles. The two officers went to see the Army's chief of staff, General George C. Marshall, but a series of bureaucratic hang-ups delayed their meeting by several hours. As soon as Marshall read the message, he instructed Bratton to send out alerts to military stations across the Pacific. However, poor

---

[1] "Col. Bratton, 65, Army Expert," *Washington Post*, 21 Mar 1958; Roberta Wohlstetter, *Pearl Harbor: Decision and Warning* (Stanford, CA: Stanford University Press, 1962), 172, 176.
[2] Wohlstetter, *Pearl Harbor*, 308.

atmospheric conditions blocked radio communications with Hawai'i, delaying the warning. Hours before the message reached the territory, at 0748 Hawaiian time, the Japanese executed a surprise attack on the U.S. naval base at Pearl Harbor on the island of O'ahu, damaging or destroying twenty-one ships and killing more than 2,000 military personnel and civilians. Within a few days, Nazi Germany and Fascist Italy joined Japan in declaring war on the United States. America had entered World War II.[3]

The Army's Wartime Intelligence Organization

Many U.S. officials blamed faulty intelligence for the devastating attack on Pearl Harbor. Despite the MAGIC message and Bratton's frantic efforts to alert Marshall, America's spies had failed to produce a timely and unequivocal warning of the impending attack. The blemish of Pearl Harbor and the ensuing American mobilization for war put enormous pressure on Army Intelligence and forced profound reforms in how the service collected, processed, and analyzed the information it acquired. The need for change shaped the intelligence services throughout the war and prompted one Army historian to quip, "it would be easy to assume that the Military Intelligence Division did nothing but reorganize."[4]

The Military Intelligence Division stood at the apex of Army Intelligence. Its director served as Assistant Chief of Staff, G–2 (Intelligence) on the Army general staff. Between 1941 and 1944, the division had four different directors before entering a phase of leadership continuity. On 21 February 1944, Maj. Gen. Clayton L. Bissell replaced the ailing Maj. Gen. George V. Strong as director, and Bissell served as the assistant chief of staff through the remainder of the war.[5] The intelligence division had no direct role in field operations. Rather, it formulated policies, made plans, and coordinated intelligence activities with other U.S. and Allied organizations. It also oversaw the activities of the Army's various intelligence organizations and the military attachés, and it directed military intelligence train-

---

3 ohlstetter, *Pearl Harbor*, 310.
4 Bruce W. Bidwell, History of the Military Intelligence Division, Department of the Army General Staff, Part V: World War II, 8 December 1941–2 September 1945 (unpublished manuscript, Office of the Chief of Military History, Department of the Army, 1957–1958) (hereinafter MID History WWII), chap. 1, Functional Conflict, 5, Historians Files, U.S. Army Center of Military History (CMH) (hereinafter Historians Files, CMH).
5 John Patrick Finnegan and Romana Danysh, *Military Intelligence*, Army Lineage Series (Washington, DC: U.S. Army Center of Military History, 1998), 63; Bidwell, MID History WWII, chap. 8, Counterintelligence Operations, 44.

ing as well as the Army's historical program.⁶ In 1943, it established a propaganda branch to undermine enemy morale.⁷

To implement its policies, the division relied on its executive agency, the Military Intelligence Service. Brig. Gen. Hayes B. Kroner headed the service during the early war years, handing over to Brig. Gen. Russell A. Osmun from May 1944 to April 1945, and then to Brig. Gen. Paul E. Peabody through the end of the war.⁸ The service produced intelligence on enemy tactics, organization, and equipment, and it conducted censorship of potentially sensitive information in everything from press releases to soldiers' mail.⁹ Furthermore, the service established and directed the Military Intelligence Research Section with offices in London and Fort Hunt, Virginia. In collaboration with British analysts, the research section exploited captured German documents and developed estimates of enemy strength and capabilities. The London branch conducted short-range or tactically relevant assessments of German documents; the Fort Hunt branch, soon to be renamed the German Military Documents Section, developed long-range strategic assessments from the captured material.¹⁰ Many of the soldiers working in the documents section were of German descent and had command of the language.¹¹

At Fort Hunt and other locations in the United States, the Military Intelligence Service established special units to assist the escape attempts of downed Ameri-

---

6 Lt. Col. George J. Le Blanc, "History of Military Intelligence Training at Camp Ritchie, Maryland for the period 19 June 1942–1 January 1945," 4 vols. (Camp Ritchie, MD: G–2 Military Intelligence Training School, 1945), 1:30, Historians Files, CMH. The link between the Army's intelligence and historical branches dates back to 1903, and was grounded in a shared responsibility for handling military information matters: see Finnegan and Danysh, *Military Intelligence*, 67; Bidwell, MID History WWII, chap. 10, Historical Branch, 1.
7 Michael E. Bigelow, "A Short History of Army Intelligence," *Military Intelligence Professional Bulletin* 38, no. 3 (Jul-Sep 2012), 24.
8 iographical information on U.S. Army Generals, n.d., Historians Files, CMH; "War Experience of Alfred McCormack," 31 Jul 1947, Special Research History (SRH) 185, in *U.S. Army Signals Intelligence in World War II: A Documentary History*, ed. James L. Gilbert and John P. Finnegan (Washington, DC: U.S. Army Center of Military History, 1993), 127.
9 Bigelow, "A Short History of Army Intelligence," 24; and Intel Div, Army Service Forces, "History of Military Censorship: Activities of the War Department during World War II" (unpublished manuscript, War Department, 1946), Historians Files, CMH.
10 Bidwell, MID History WWII, chap. 5, Field Collection, 39; Derek R. Mallett, *Hitler's Generals in America: Nazi POWs and Allied Military Intelligence* (Lexington: University Press of Kentucky, 2003), 142; F. H. Hinsley with E. E. Thomas, C. A. G. Simkins, and C. F. G. Ransom, *British Intelligence in the Second World War*, vol. 3, part 2, *Its Influence on Strategy and Operations* (London: Her Majesty's Stationery Office, 1988), 27–28.
11 Gerhardt B. Thamm, "The Potsdam Archive: Sorting Through 19 Linear Miles of German Records," *Studies in Intelligence* 58, no. 1 (Mar 2014), 3.

can airmen (MIS-X) and to conduct in-depth interrogation of captured enemy personnel (MIS-Y).[12] The intelligence service employed a wide array of topical and geographic specialists who constantly grappled with the challenge of processing the vast and ever-increasing volume of information.[13]

Like the rest of the Army, the service grew substantially during the war, from 342 officers and 1,005 civilians in 1942, to a peak strength of 1,512 officers, 51 warrant officers, and 2,083 enlisted men in October 1944 (1.100).[14] During the same period, the combined budget of the intelligence service and the intelligence division soared from $360,000 to $13,960,000.[15]

In December 1944, the Military Intelligence Service assumed operational control of the Signal Security Agency from the Signal Corps.[16] Headed by Col. W. Preston Corderman, the agency was responsible for intercepting and decrypting enemy communications—signals intelligence—and for securing the Army's communications systems against cryptanalytic attacks by the enemy. Colonel Corderman doubled as commanding officer of the 9420th Technical Service Unit, which operated intercept stations around the globe and produced most of the material for decryption by the agency's codebreakers.[17]

Together, the director of the Signal Security Agency's Special Branch, Col. Alfred McCormack, and the deputy chief of the Military Intelligence Service, Brig. Gen. Carter W. Clarke, integrated signals intelligence into the Army's intelligence product.[18] As a mark of their organizations' elevated status within the Army, McCormack's and Clarke's offices occupied a series of outward-facing rooms on the ground floor of the Pentagon's E Ring, with a prized view of the lawn.[19] The

---

12 Marc B. Powe and Edward E. Wilson, "The Evolution of American Military Intelligence" (Fort Huachuca, AZ: United States Army Intelligence Center and School, 1973), 47.
13 Otto L. Nelson, *National Security and the General Staff* (Washington, DC: Infantry Journal Press, 1946), 522. In May 1942 alone, G–2 handled 125,779 communications.
14 Bidwell, MID History WWII, chap. 1, Functional Conflict, 7; chap. 7, Intelligence Production, 7.
15 Bidwell, MID History WWII, chap. 2, Unprecedented Growth, 3–4.
16 Finnegan and Danysh, *Military Intelligence*, 72. The Signal Corps retained administrative control.
17 The 9420th Technical Service Unit had been the 2d Signal Service Battalion until G–2 took operational control of the Signal Security Agency in 1942; see David Kahn, *The Codebreakers: The Comprehensive History of Secret Communication from Ancient Times to the Internet* (New York: Simon & Schuster, 1996), 576f. For a list of intercept stations, see George F. Howe, *American Signal Intelligence in Northwest Africa and Western Europe*, Sources in Cryptologic History, series iv, vol. 1 (Fort Meade, MD: National Security Agency, 2010), 113.
18 "War Experience of Alfred McCormack," SRH 185, in Gilbert and Finnegan, *U.S. Army Signals Intelligence*, 127.
19 Thomas D. Parrish, *The American Codebreakers: The U.S. Role in Ultra* (Chelsea, MI: Scarborough House, 1991), 180.

The Army's Wartime Intelligence Organization — 17

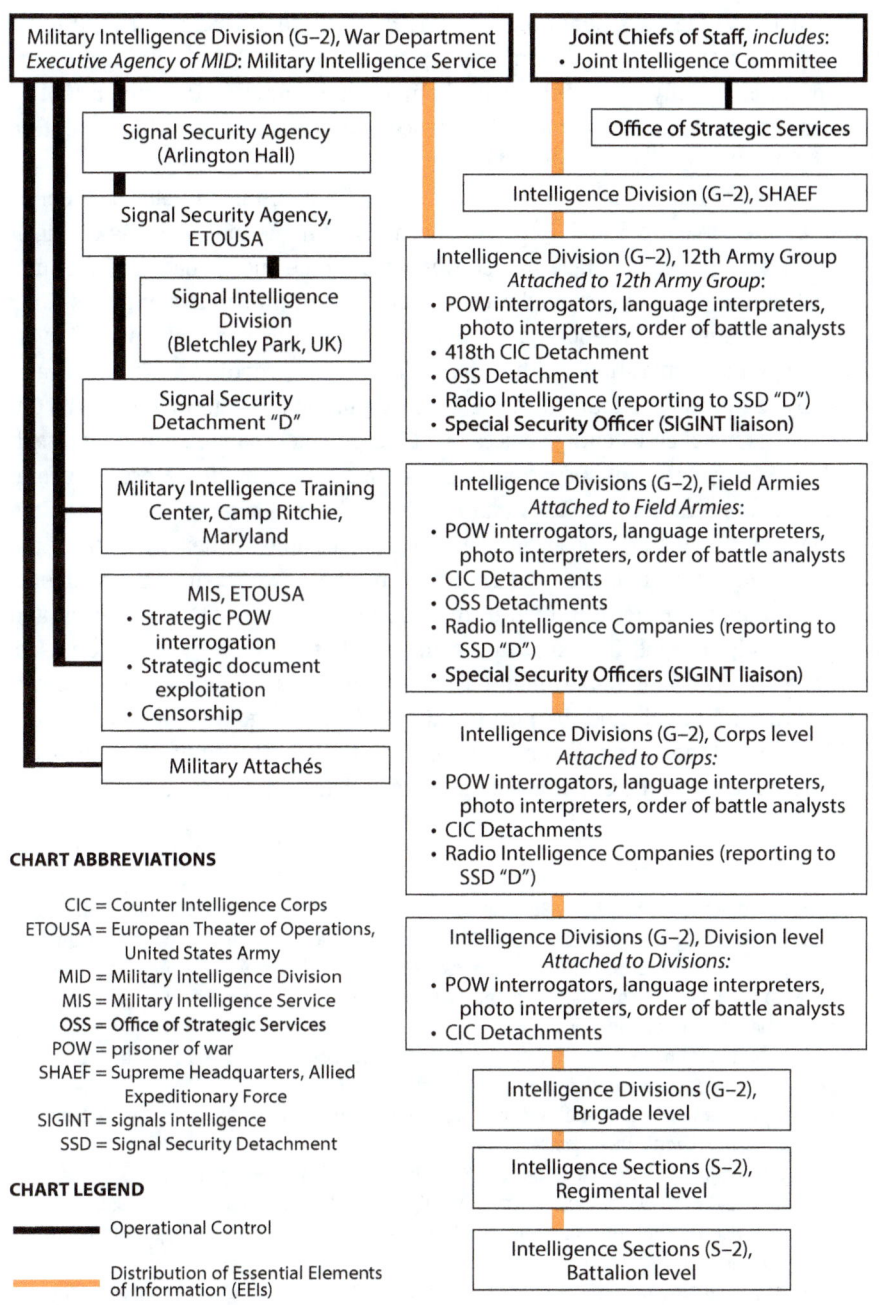

Chart 1: Army Intelligence in the European Theater of Operations at the End of World War II. U.S. Army Center of Military History.

Signal Security Agency's headquarters was in Arlington, Virginia, at Arlington Hall, a former girls' school taken over by the Army in 1942.[20] The agency expanded exponentially during the war, from 331 personnel in December 1941 to 10,371 in August 1945.[21] The volume of processed messages grew likewise, to a peak of 381,590 intercepts in July 1945.[22]

The Military Intelligence Service also managed the Counter Intelligence Corps, headed by the 34-year-old Maj. Henry G. Sheen. As its name indicates, the CIC dealt with foreign espionage, sabotage, and subversion at home and abroad.[23] By the summer of 1943, the CIC had recruited tens of thousands of informants and was filing hundreds of thousands of reports per month.[24] However, its wide-ranging and overzealous espionage operations within the United States provoked resentment and eventually led to the curtailment of the Corps' domestic mission. In early 1943, CIC special agents installed listening devices in a Chicago hotel room occupied by Joseph P. Lash, an Army sergeant suspected of communist ties. The CIC recorded several amorous encounters between Lash and his girlfriend. In a bizarre coincidence, the president's wife, Eleanor Roosevelt, concurrently occupied a nearby suite in the same hotel. Intentionally or not, the CIC mixed up these two separate facts, erroneously informing the Federal Bureau of Investigation (FBI) that "Mrs. Roosevelt and Mr. Lash [had] engaged in sexual intercourse."[25] The president was not amused. Later that year, the War Department terminated the CIC's domestic countersubversion program and abolished the post of CIC chief. The outgoing chief, Col. Harold R. Kibler, blamed the fall of his command on the enmity of the White House. For the remainder of the war, the CIC directed operations exclusively overseas.[26]

---

20 "The Achievements of the Signal Security Agency in World War II," SRH 345, in Gilbert and Finnegan, *U.S. Army Signals Intelligence*, 91. For a colorful description of the Army's takeover of Arlington Hall, see Parrish, *American Codebreakers*, 77–78. Key personnel at Arlington Hall included the director of its cryptanalytic team, William F. Friedman, and Frank B. Rowlett. Both worked on Japanese ciphers during the war.
21 "The Achievements of the Signal Security Agency in World War II," SRH 345, in Gilbert and Finnegan, *U.S. Army Signals Intelligence*, 88–89.
22 "The Achievements of the Signal Security Agency in World War II," SRH 345, in Gilbert and Finnegan, *U.S. Army Signals Intelligence*, 96.
23 ames L. Gilbert, John P. Finnegan, and Ann Bray, *In the Shadow of the Sphinx: A History of Army Counterintelligence* (Fort Belvoir, VA: U.S. Army Intelligence and Security Command, 2005), 24.
24 Powe and Wilson, "Evolution of American Military Intelligence," 49; Finnegan and Danysh, *Military Intelligence*, 73f.
25 Curt Gentry, *J. Edgar Hoover: The Man and the Secrets* (New York: Norton, 2001), 304–06.
26 Finnegan and Danysh, *Military Intelligence*, 76. Sheen, now promoted to colonel, became the top CIC officer in Europe, serving as chief of the Counter Intelligence Branch at SHAEF; see Gilbert, Finnegan, and Bray, *In the Shadow of the Sphinx*, 41.

The Military Intelligence Division appointed and supervised military attachés, who served as the War Department's principal collectors of foreign intelligence before the war.[27] In the 1920s and 1930s, attachés in American embassies in Berlin, Rome, and Tokyo submitted numerous reports on the military buildup of the three Axis nations.[28] After the United States and the Soviet Union established diplomatic relations in 1933, the Army dispatched a military attaché to Moscow as well. However, the Soviet authorities severely restricted the movements of foreign officials, making it difficult to collect accurate information. American military attaché reports tended to underestimate the Red Army's capabilities.[29] With the onset of war, the role of the attaché as an intelligence collector diminished. American embassies in Japan, Germany, and Italy closed, and the War Department converted the office of the U.S. military attaché in Moscow into a military mission whose members liaised and exchanged information with the Soviets, rather than gathering intelligence on them.[30]

The war begot two new military intelligence outfits. In June 1942, a presidential decree established a foreign intelligence agency, the Office of Strategic Services, under Col. William J. "Wild Bill" Donovan. The office was to gather information through agents; work with underground groups in Europe and Asia; conduct propaganda operations to support the Allies and denigrate the enemy; and collect and analyze openly available economic, political, and military information to aid the American war effort. Although many of its members, including Donovan, wore Army uniforms, the office did not report to the War Department, but rather to the newly created Joint Chiefs of Staff, who in turn advised the president.

The OSS was meant to operate above Army Intelligence and coordinate the espionage activities of the U.S. armed forces, but instead it became a parallel, paramilitary intelligence agency. Many regular military officers regarded it as an

---

27 Bidwell, MID History WWII, chap. 5, Field Collection, 1.
28 Scott A. Koch, "The Role of U.S. Army Military Attachés Between the World Wars," *Studies in Intelligence* 38, no. 5 (1995), 111. The attaché reports on military matters in Germany, Italy, and Japan were mostly accurate, but their observations on civilian and political matters tended to be off the mark.
29 Mary E. Glantz, *FDR and the Soviet Union: The President's Battles over Foreign Policy* (Lawrence: University Press of Kansas, 2017), 48–52. In April 1941, one month before Nazi Germany attacked the Soviet Union, U.S. military attaché Col. Ivan D. Yeaton estimated that the Red Army "can hold out for three months at the most" against a foreign invasion.
30 For the role of the U.S. military mission in Moscow, see below. Generally, for the role of the military attaché in intelligence, see Alfred Vagts, *The Military Attaché* (Princeton, NJ: Princeton University Press, 1967).

unwelcome competitor.[31] One Army Intelligence chief reportedly declared he did not "want a man from OSS, nor a dwarf, nor a pygmy, or a God-damned soul" in his command area.[32] The haughtiness of some OSS members fueled the rivalry. Donovan recruited heavily among the ranks of the East Coast establishment. Many OSS officials had attended exclusive private schools and Ivy League universities. They tended to look down on the Army's officer corps, which was heavily middle-class and Midwestern. The elitism exhibited by many OSS officers led to the quip that the service's acronym stood for "Oh So Secret," "Oh So Social," or "Oh Such Snobs."[33]

The rivalry between Army Intelligence and the OSS produced yet another intelligence agency. In October 1942, General Kroner of the Military Intelligence Service received orders—probably from the Army's intelligence director, General Strong—to establish "a perpetual, a far-seeing, a far-distant, continuing secret intelligence service." Strong likely issued this order as a direct response to the creation of the OSS.[34] The resulting agency, which changed official names frequently but assumed the enduring nickname "The Pond," was headed by a pugnacious National Guard officer, Col. John V. "Frenchy" Grombach.[35]

The conspiratorial origins of Grombach's organization as the product of intergovernmental rivalry cast a long shadow over the Pond. Grombach spent much of his time denigrating the "amateurish" OSS, dismissing it as "merely shingle intelligence played with a Cloak and Dagger."[36] In marked contrast to Grombach's combativeness on the home front, his organization collected little of value. The surviving files of the Grombach organization on Nazi Germany contain mostly trivia, and the Pond's informants operated on the fringes of society. Grombach's

---

31 For a history of the Office of Strategic Services (OSS), see R. Harris Smith, *OSS: The Secret History of America's First Central Intelligence Agency* (Berkeley: University of California Press, 1972).
32 Interv, Forrest C. Pogue with Brig. Gen. Edwin L. Sibert, 11 May 1951, Historians Files, CMH. Sibert quoted Colonel Dickson.
33 W. Thomas Smith Jr., *Encyclopedia of the Central Intelligence Agency* (New York: Facts on File, 2003), 179.
34 Mark E. Stout, "The Pond: Running Agents for State, War, and the CIA," *Studies in Intelligence* 48, no. 3 (2004), https://www.cia.gov/resources/csi/studies-in-intelligence/, Historians Files, CMH.
35 Matthew M. Aid, "John V. 'Frenchy' Grombach" (unpublished research paper, n.d.), Historians Files, CMH. Grombach was born in Louisiana, the son of the French consul in New Orleans, hence the nickname "Frenchy."
36 Memo, no author [almost certainly Grombach], n.d., Folder "monograph on the O.S.S., undated," Grombach Organization ("The Pond"), Subject and Country Files, 1920–1963, RG 263, NACP.

principal source in Nazi-occupied France was a deranged serial killer.[37] Frustrated with the poor quality of Grombach's information, an officer of the Military Intelligence Division once noted that it "mean[t] absolutely nothing."[38] After the war, the Army transferred the Pond to civilian control.[39]

Personnel, Recruitment, and Training

Before the war, the Army had relegated intelligence to a junior status within the general staff. The director of military intelligence was only a colonel, whereas the directors of the personnel, operations, logistics, and plans sections were all general officers. The inferior status of intelligence at the Army's highest levels extended throughout the service, with intelligence officers typically holding lower ranks than their colleagues in other branches. Many officers sought to avoid being transferred to intelligence because other branches offered better opportunities for promotion.[40] As intelligence work acquired the reputation of being a dead-end career, soldiers got into the habit of saying, "I wonder what's wrong with him that he is in G–2."[41]

Reforms gradually improved the quality of the Army's intelligence personnel, but the profession's prewar legacy was difficult to overcome. The wartime memoirs of military leaders are replete with complaints about the insufficient training and the low caliber of their intelligence staff. General Dwight D. Eisenhower recalled "a shocking deficiency that impeded all constructive planning in the field of Intelligence."[42] General Omar N. Bradley, commander of the 12th Army Group, averred, "Misfits frequently found themselves assigned to intelligence duties.. . .

---

37 For Grombach's sparse intelligence reports on Germany, see Rcds of the Grombach Organization ("The Pond"), Subject and Country Files, 1942–1955, RG 263, NACP. For Grombach's alleged use of French serial killer Marcel Petiot, see Grombach's memoirs, *The Great Liquidator* (Garden City, NY: Doubleday, 1980). Petiot feigned membership in the French Resistance in order to rob and murder more than twenty people who sought his help to escape the Nazis. He was tried and executed for his crimes in France in 1946.
38 Pol[itical] Br Comment on Intel Rpt, Info Gp [i.e., Grombach], 28 Mar 1945, sub: Harbor Report, Trondheim, Folder "1641 File, 1944–1945 (folder 2 of 2)," Rcds of the Grombach Organization, Subject and Country Files, 1942–1955, RG 263, NACP.
39 Stout, "The Pond."
40 Bruce W. Bidwell, *History of the Military Intelligence Division, Department of the Army General Staff: 1775–1941* (Frederick, MD: University Publications of America, 1986), 409.
41 Interv, Pogue with Sibert, 11 May 1951.
42 Dwight D. Eisenhower, *Crusade in Europe: A Personal Account of World War II* (New York: Doubleday, 1948), 32.

And in some stations G–2 became a dumping ground for officers ill-suited to line command."[43]

To be sure, some intelligence officers received their assignments for reasons that had little to do with their qualifications, as the case of Brig. Gen. Clayton L. Bissell illustrates. An aviation officer by training, Bissell served with General Joseph W. Stilwell's mission to China from 1942 to 1943. Pedantic and inflexible, Bissell antagonized America's principal ally, General Chiang Kai-shek, as well as the local United States Army Air Forces commander, Brig. Gen. Claire L. Chennault.[44] Chennault felt "that Bissell prized a snappy salute from a perfectly uniformed staff officer more than a Japanese plane shot down in flames."[45]

Eventually, General Marshall recalled Bissell and appointed him assistant chief of staff for intelligence to fill the vacant post. Here, too, Bissell failed to gain respect. Colonel McCormack of the Military Intelligence Service described his new boss as a micromanager who "lived in deadly fear that somebody would arrive at General Marshall's office with an item of news that he, Bissell, had not heard about." The new director put an inordinate emphasis on organizing the daily morning intelligence briefings, replete with neatly arranged maps, pictures, graphs, and properly formatted reports. In Bissell's world, McCormack mused, an intelligence analyst might be forgiven for missing a major German offensive, but "a man who clipped the summary sheets in the lower right-hand corner instead of the lower left-hand corner, was in a fair way of being sent to the Aleutians."[46]

Nonetheless, the war produced a number of highly qualified intelligence officers. The intelligence chief of the 12th Army Group, Brig. Gen. Edwin L. Sibert, had trained as an artillery officer but took to intelligence like a duck to water. His superior, General Bradley, praised Sibert as "extremely capable." Bradley also thought highly of Col. Benjamin A. "Monk" Dickson, intelligence chief of the First Army, who was a reservist and West Point graduate with a degree from the Massachusetts Institute of Technology, and a linguist in French and German.[47] The intelligence chief of General George S. Patton Jr.'s Third Army, the "hard-driving

---

[43] Omar N. Bradley, *A Soldier's Story* (New York: Holt, 1951), 33.
[44] Charles F. Romanus and Riley Sunderland, *Stilwell's Mission to China*, United States Army in World War II (Washington, DC: U.S. Army Center of Military History, 1987), 198, 252, 275, 285, 345, 346.
[45] Claire Lee Chennault, *Way of a Fighter: The Memoirs of Claire Lee Chennault*, ed. Robert Hotz (New York: G. P. Putnam's Sons, 1949), 210.
[46] Parrish, *American Codebreakers*, 232.
[47] Bradley, *A Soldier's Story*, 223, 464. Dickson had served with the American Expeditionary Forces in Siberia at the end of World War I, and served in Army Intelligence from 1940 through the end of the war.

and scholarly Colonel [Oscar] Koch," commanded respect inside and outside the Army.[48] Back in Washington, General Clarke of the Military Intelligence Service had a reputation for bluntness bordering on rudeness, but he also commanded respect for his ability to get things done, and he became the driving force behind the buildup of the Army's signals intelligence organization.[49]

Even as the military intelligence officers' corps expanded in size and gradually improved in quality, the biggest change to the composition of Army Intelligence personnel came from the influx of thousands of new recruits. One intelligence recruit recalled that many of his fellow soldiers "were better educated" and included members "of the most prominent families in the country."[50] CIC candidates had to score high on the Army's aptitude test, possess a college degree, and ideally have knowledge of a foreign language.[51] In one instance, an intelligence chief fired two officers on his staff for their lack of language skills.[52] Work in signals intelligence also required top-notch personnel, and recruiters always struggled to find enough suitable candidates.[53] The Army filled many slots with lawyers, whose profession involved complex and logical thinking. Soldiers joked that the signals intelligence organization was "the best law office in Washington."[54]

In its quest for highly skilled staff, Army Intelligence tapped into the diverse human reservoir of American society and actively recruited recent émigrés from Europe. This group included many German Jews who had fled Nazi persecution.[55] They filled a critical need for German-language speakers and received high marks in the field. The "[b]est source of information we had was [prisoners of war] interrogation," recalled one intelligence officer, "because of the horde of German Jewish soldiers we had who . . . could worm information out of Germans by talking to them about their homes."[56] These soldiers ran particular risks if cap-

---

48 William J. Casey, *The Secret War Against Hitler* (Washington, DC: Regnery Gateway, 1988), 153.
49 Parrish, *American Codebreakers*, 80.
50 Patricia Kollander with John O'Sullivan, *"I Must Be a Part of This War": A German American's Fight Against Hitler and Nazism* (New York: Fordham University Press, 2005), 72.
51 Maj. Ann Bray et al., ed., *The History of the Counter Intelligence Corps*, vol. 16, *To the German Frontier: Part I* (Fort Holabird, MD: U.S. Army Intelligence Center, 1959), 5.
52 Interv, G. E. Patrick Murray with Col. Benjamin A. Dickson, 22 Sep 1972, Historians Files, CMH. One of the dismissed officers was Strom Thurmond, postwar senator of South Carolina.
53 "The Achievements of the Signal Security Agency in World War II," SRH 345, in Gilbert and Finnegan, *U.S. Army Signals Intelligence*, 89.
54 "War Experience of Alfred McCormack," SRH 185, in Gilbert and Finnegan, *U.S. Army Signals Intelligence*, 119.
55 Kollander, *"I Must Be a Part of This War,"* 73; and Joachim von Elbe, *Witness to History: A Refugee from the Third Reich Remembers* (Madison: University of Wisconsin Press, 1998), 258f.
56 Interv, F. C. Pogue with Adolph G. Rosengarten, 22 Dec 1947, Historians Files, CMH.

tured: the Germans might execute them for treason or send them to a concentration camp.[57]

The integration of so many well-educated and intellectually curious young men into the rigid ways of the Army produced culture shocks. Colonel McCormack, a lawyer in prewar times, was baffled that Pentagon bureaucrats operated their organizations on rigid schedules and left the building every day "on the dot at 5 p.m." as if it were still peacetime.[58] Another junior officer quipped that "the quickest way to reform G–2 was to kill off all officers above the rank of Major, and to throw in half the Majors for good measure."[59] Over time, the war ironed out much of the cultural divide between Army old-timers and civilian newcomers. McCormack, for one, forged a formidable alliance with General Clarke, and the high-powered lawyer and the consummate Pentagon infighter turned signals intelligence into one of most productive elements of the Army Intelligence apparatus.

Figure 3: Mock-up of a German village at Camp Ritchie, Maryland. INSCOM.

---

57 Peter Hutchinson, *Stefan Heym: The Perpetual Dissident* (Cambridge, UK: Cambridge University Press, 1992), 46.
58 "War Experience of Alfred McCormack," SRH 185, in Gilbert and Finnegan, *U.S. Army Signals Intelligence*, 120.
59 "War Experience of Alfred McCormack," SRH 185, in Gilbert and Finnegan, *U.S. Army Signals Intelligence*, 124.

The expanding force required training. In 1942, the Signal Security Agency opened a cryptographic school at Vint Hill Farms Station near Warrenton, Virginia. Here, officers and enlisted students learned about cryptanalysis, traffic analysis, and cryptographic equipment maintenance. The facility also housed an intercept station for high-grade German radio traffic. In addition to Vint Hill, Army signals intelligence operated a civilian training school at Arlington Hall and conducted tactical training at Camp Crowder in southwestern Missouri and at Fort Monmouth, New Jersey.[60]

In the same year, the Army activated the Military Intelligence Training Center at Camp Ritchie, Maryland, "beautifully situated on a lake high in the Blue Ridge Mountains," as one recruit recalled.[61] Here, Army Intelligence personnel took various training courses, for eight weeks on average, before being shipped overseas. Classes included training for military interpreters, prisoner-of-war interrogators, aerial photographers, order of battle specialists, and counterintelligence personnel. The camp emphasized practical exercises, including the application of camouflage techniques; aircraft sorties for training aerial photography; and the dreaded night field exercise, where pairs of candidates were dropped off at unfamiliar locations and had to find their way to specified coordinates.[62] For the completion of the Indoor Combat Firing Course, popularly known as the "House of Horrors," students received twenty-four rounds of ammunition, a pistol, and a fighting knife. Then, the instructors sent them to the dimly lit basement of the building, where a series of remotely controlled targets popped up and other combat training situations occurred.[63]

Camp Ritchie went to great lengths to give recruits a realistic sense of contemporary Germany. The camp included a life-size replica of a village square in a German town, complete with a town hall, post office, and beer garden. The setup served as a venue for street fighting practice runs, as well as for raiding and searching techniques and booby-trap instruction. Many instructors at Camp Ritchie were German-born, and students regularly watched captured German newsreels to expose them to Nazi propaganda techniques. Prisoner-of-war interrogators honed

---

60 Lori Tagg, "A Brief History of Training in Army Intelligence," *Military Intelligence Professional Bulletin* 34, no. 3 (Jul-Sep 2012), 89.
61 Von Elbe, *Witness to History*, 259. The camp was named after a former Maryland governor, Albert C. Ritchie.
62 Le Blanc, "History of Military Intelligence Training," 1:18–19, 1:27; Kollander, *"I Must Be a Part of This War,"* 73.
63 Le Blanc, "History of Military Intelligence Training," 1:99.

their skills by cross-examining German-speaking soldiers dressed in German uniforms.[64] According to one trainee, "[w]e were told to act as if this were 'the real thing' and not to refrain from invectives if we thought that our opposites merited rough handling because of their behavior."[65]

According to one soldier, the Army sent "pretty much anybody" who had some familiarity with Germany or the German language to the Maryland facility. This group included German citizens. The Second War Powers Act of March 1942 allowed "enemy aliens" to become naturalized after serving in the armed forces for at least three months. During their naturalization ceremony, these men had to renounce "all allegiance and fidelity . . . particularly to Germany, of which I have heretofore been citizen."[66] Occasionally, the search for German-language speakers overrode the official U.S. policy of racial segregation in the armed forces. The African American classical singer William C. Warfield, who had studied multiple languages during his musical training, used his fluency in German to convince the Army to send him to military intelligence at Camp Ritchie rather than to his original assignment in a segregated ordnance unit.[67]

By the end of the war, Army Intelligence had trained approximately 20,000 "Ritchie Boys," including nearly 2,000 German-born recruits, many of whom were Jewish.[68] Their postwar careers testify to their intellectual brilliance. Ralph H. Baer worked as a television engineer and is remembered as a "father of video gaming" for his pioneering efforts in computer electronics.[69] John W. Kluge became a media mogul and by the mid-1980s was the second wealthiest man in the United States. Hermann F. Eilts joined the State Department and served as ambassador to Saudi Arabia and Egypt. After the war, many Ritchie Boys joined the new Central Intelligence Agency, including Henry D. Hecksher, Howard C. Bowman, and Capt. Henry P. Schardt. Others chose an academic path and became notable historians, including

---

64 Le Blanc, "History of Military Intelligence Training," 1:69, 1:100–101.
65 Von Elbe, *Witness to History*, 261.
66 Niall Ferguson, *Kissinger*, vol. 1, *1923–1968: The Idealist* (New York: Penguin, 2013), 114–15.
67 Christian Bauer and Rebekka Göpfert, *Die Ritchie Boys: Deutsche Emigranten im amerikanischen Geheimdienst* [The Ritchie Boys: German emigrants in the American secret service] (Munich: Hoffmann und Campe, 2005), 52. As Warfield later remarked, "I got into Military Intelligence because I fought for it." Interv, William C. Warfield, with Ruth Watanabe and John Braund, 23 Dec 1992, University of Rochester Living History Project, https://livinghistory.lib.rochester.edu.
68 Bidwell, MID History WWII, chap. 2, Unprecedented Growth, 26; Bruce Henderson, *Sons and Soldiers: The Untold Story of the Jews Who Escaped the Nazis and Returned with the U.S. Army to Fight Hitler* (New York: William Morrow, 2017), 393.
69 David Marino-Nachison, "Ralph H. Baer, a Father of Video Gaming, Dies at 92," *Washington Post*, 7 Dec 2014.

Figure 4: A mock interrogation at Camp Ritchie. U.S. Army, NACP.

Hans W. Gatzke, John E. Rodes, and Klemens von Klemperer. Several opted for professional Army careers.[70]

The high concentration of well-educated Americans of German background, teachers and professors of the German language, and German émigrés gave Camp Ritchie a distinctly unmilitary, almost bohemian atmosphere. One recruit reinterpreted the camp's official acronym, MITC, as "Military Institute of Total Confusion." Another captured the unconventionality of the camp in a humorous poem:

Was you ever in Camp Ritchie?
The very schönste [beautiful] *Camp of all!*
Where the sun comes up with Donner [thunder],
And recorded bugle call.

---

[70] Hayley L. Fenton, "Notable Ritchie Boys" (unpublished paper, U.S. Army Center of Military History, 2020). Among those who remained in the Army were Col. Ralph M. Hockley, Maj. Thomas O. Schlesinger, and Col. Franz X. Westermeier.

> *Where the Privates are professors*
> *And the Corporals write books*
> *And all of them scare Captains*
> *With their supercilious looks!*[71]

For many immigrant soldiers, the U.S. Army and Camp Ritchie became the quintessential American experience. A fellow soldier of perhaps the most famous Ritchie Boy recalled that Henry Kissinger "forgot about the past" in the Army. "He was fighting for America. He was fighting as a soldier against the Nazis not because the Nazis did something bad to the Jews, but because the Nazis were the enemy of America. He was more American than I have ever seen an American."[72]

Army Intelligence in the European Theater

The Americans coordinated their military and intelligence operations closely with the British. In 1942, the two nations integrated their command structure at the highest level, creating the Combined Chiefs of Staff as their supreme military staff. The combined chiefs had their own intelligence organization, the Combined Intelligence Committee. To represent the U.S. side, the Americans established the Joint Chiefs of Staff (JCS), made up of Army and Navy representatives. The joint chiefs, in turn, had their own Joint Intelligence Committee, headed by the director of the Army's Military Intelligence Division and the Navy's Office of Naval Intelligence.[73] Neither the combined chiefs nor the joint chiefs collected intelligence in the field. They relied on the Army's intelligence division for information from Europe.

The integration of the U.S. and British command structure continued in the European Theater, with the establishment, in February 1944, of the Supreme Headquarters Allied Expeditionary Force (Supreme Allied Headquarters, or SHAEF), a combined U.S.-British command under General Eisenhower. The Supreme Allied Headquarters' supranational character required careful balancing in its top positions. A British officer, Maj. Gen. Kenneth W. D. Strong, became chief of the Intelligence Division, and an American, Brig. Gen. Thomas J. Betts, served as Strong's deputy. Both had intelligence backgrounds. Strong had been an assistant military attaché in Berlin before the war and worked as Eisenhower's intelligence chief in

---

71 Bauer and Göpfert, *Ritchie Boys*, 53, 57.
72 Ferguson, *Kissinger*, 1:172.
73 Bidwell, MID History WWII, chap. 3, Joint (Combined) Committees, 3, 6, 8, 9, 12, 19, 28, 33.

North Africa, and Betts had served as a language officer in China in the 1920s and on the staff of the Military Intelligence Division in Washington until 1943.[74]

In July 1944, the SHAEF Intelligence Division established its own Joint Intelligence Committee to review the military and political situation in Europe.[75] The division had two subdivisions: one for analyzing information on the enemy, the other for counterintelligence. It also established a joint Anglo-American War Room in London to track the movements of leading Nazi officials.[76] The Intelligence Division produced estimates based on reports from American and British forces in the theater. The division processed the incoming information, kept the supreme commander abreast of developments in the European Theater, and passed on weekly intelligence summaries and estimates to subordinate headquarters.[77] By April 1945, the supreme commander's intelligence staff had 209 members, roughly half British and half American.[78]

The intertwining of the U.S. and British command structure promoted close cooperation between Army Intelligence and its British counterpart throughout the European and Mediterranean Theaters. Whenever the Allies created a combined organization, they staffed it with intelligence and counterintelligence personnel from both nations. At the Combined Services Detailed Interrogation Center in England, U.S. and British military personnel extracted information from prisoners of war. At the London Military Documents Center, they analyzed captured enemy documents.[79] The Army's cooperation with the British proved especially seminal in the realm of signals intelligence. In 1943, the Army set up the Signal Intelligence Service of the European Theater under Col. George A. Bicher, with its operating arm, the Signal Intelligence Division, in England. The British signals intelligence service, the Government Code and Cypher School at Bletchley Park

---

74 Forrest C. Pogue, *The Supreme Command*, United States Army in World War II (Washington, DC: U.S. Army Center of Military History, 1954), 71. For Betts, see General Officers' Bios, Historians' Files, CMH.
75 Pogue, *Supreme Command*, 72. The SHAEF Joint Intelligence Committee is not to be confused with the Joint Intelligence Committee of the joint staffs or with the Joint Intelligence Committee of the British Chiefs of Staff in London, although the American and British intelligence staffs regularly worked together.
76 Kenneth Strong, *Intelligence at the Top: Recollections of an Intelligence Officer* (Garden City, NY: Doubleday, 1969), 178–79.
77 Pogue, *Supreme Command*, 71.
78 Hinsley, *British Intelligence in the Second World War*, vol. 3, part 2, 751.
79 Helen Fry, *The London Cage: The Secret History of Britain's World War II Interrogation Centre* (New Haven, CT: Yale University Press, 2017), 19–20; and Mallett, *Hitler's Generals in America*, 6. For document samples, see the nearly twenty boxes archived under decimal files "350.09 Great Britain," War Department, MID, Project Decimal Files, 1941–1945, RG 319, NACP.

near Oxford, had broken the standard cipher machine of the German armed forces, called Enigma, early in the war. The British, therefore, were decrypting German military communications when American signals intelligence joined the battle. It was Bircher's job to work with the British.[80]

The two allies formalized their coordination on 17 May 1943 with the "Agreement between British Government Code and Cipher School and U.S. War Department," stipulating that they would "exchange completely" all signals intelligence on the Axis powers.[81] The Americans would take the lead in attacking Japanese ciphers, such as PURPLE, while the British would focus on German and Italian traffic. The agreement opened the door for Army Intelligence to participate broadly in the British cryptanalytic effort at Bletchley Park. The intelligence produced from the joint cryptanalytic attack on German traffic was called ULTRA.[82]

In July 1943, the Americans began sending intercept operators, machine processors, and cryptanalysts to work with the British in England (Operation BEECHNUT). By March 1944, this contingent numbered about 36 officers and 400 enlisted men.[83] Maj. Roy D. Johnson served as their commander and Maj. William P. Bundy as their operations officer.[84] In addition to supporting British cryptanalysts, the codebreakers of Arlington Hall began using their own high-speed protocomputers ("bombes"), which processed particularly sophisticated German encrypts received from Bletchley Park. In addition to the Enigma traffic, American and British cryptanalysts exchanged information on communications generated by a group of high-level German cryptographic machines code-named FISH. They also intercepted messages from the Vatican, the Jewish Agency for Palestine, and the French secret service of General Charles de Gaulle.[85] Special security officers disseminated ULTRA to

---

80 Robert L. Benson, *A History of U.S. Communications Intelligence in World War II: Policy and Administration* (Fort Meade, MD: Center for Cryptologic History, National Security Agency, 1997), 149.
81 For the full text of the Britain–United States of America agreement (BRUSA), see John Cary Sims, "The BRUSA Agreement of May 17, 1943," *Cryptologia* 21, no. 1 (1997): 30–38. One of Arlington Hall's leading cryptanalysts, William F. Friedman, played a key role in the drafting of BRUSA.
82 Lee A. Gladwin, "Cautious Collaborators: The Struggle for Anglo-American Cryptanalytic Cooperation 1940–43," *Intelligence and National Security* 14, no. 1 (1999): 140. ULTRA was the original security label used by the British to classify intelligence derived from Enigma decrypts; see F. W. Winterbotham, *The Ultra Secret* (New York: Harper & Row, 1974), 24.
83 Howe, *American Signal Intelligence*, series iv, 1:159.They were organized in the 6811th, 6812th, and 6813th Security Detachments.
84 Benson, *A History of U.S. Communications Intelligence in World War II*, 110–11. Bundy later served as a foreign affairs adviser to both Presidents John F. Kennedy and Lyndon B. Johnson.
85 Gladwin, "Cautious Collaborators," 142; Benson, *A History of U.S. Communications Intelligence in World War II*, 113.

commanders, but for security reasons, the Allies did not share the material below the field army level.⁸⁶ By the end of the war in Europe, Bletchley Park had sent about 25,000 ULTRA signals to western commands, and 1,375 special processing requests to Arlington Hall.⁸⁷ In July 1945, General Eisenhower stated that ULTRA "has been of priceless value to me. . . . It has saved thousands of British and American lives and, in no small way, contributed to the speed with which the enemy was routed and eventually forced to surrender."⁸⁸

Below the integrated Anglo-American command structure, Army commanders relied principally on their own units for the collection and processing of information on enemy forces. Between the Allied invasion of Normandy in June 1944 and the German surrender the following summer, two army groups, six field armies, fifteen army corps, and sixty-one divisions fought in the United States Army in the European Theater of Operations. Army Intelligence supported this force at every echelon of command.

The Military Intelligence Service of the European Theater served as the European counterpart to its parent organization in the United States and replicated several of its elements, including its MIS-X and MIS-Y sections. The former dealt with the problems created by the capture of U.S. personnel by the Germans. It sought to determine the location of enemy prisoners of war camps and planned for the rescue of captured Americans. It also provided American soldiers with codes they could use, if taken prisoner, to transmit information disguised in letters sent home. The latter interrogated high-ranking enemy prisoners of war. Its personnel conducted these interrogations in the United States as well as overseas.⁸⁹

The European Military Intelligence Service also conducted censorship to prevent dissemination of sensitive information to the enemy, and it oversaw all military intelligence specialists in the field, with the exception of counterintelligence personnel. These intelligence specialists operated in four types of teams—prisoner-of-war interrogation, language interpretation, photo analysis, and order of battle—each comprising three to six members. At least fifty specialists served with each combat division, where they operated under the control of the divisional intelligence section. Larger numbers of teams were allotted to corps, field

---

86 Adolph D. Rosengarten Jr., "With Ultra from Omaha Beach to Weimar—A Personal View," *Military Affairs* 42, no. 3 (Oct 1978), 128.
87 Ralph Bennett, *Ultra in the West: The Normandy Campaign 1944–45* (New York: Charles Scribner's Sons, 1979), xiii; Gladwin, "Cautious Collaborators," 142. Arlington Hall solved 413 of these requests.
88 Ltr, Gen. Dwight D. Eisenhower to Maj. Gen. Stewart Graham Menzies, Jul 1945, cited in Winterbotham, *The Ultra Secret*, 2.
89 Powe and Wilson, "Evolution of American Military Intelligence," 47.

armies, and army groups. Army headquarters included OSS detachments and intelligence specialist teams that studied captured enemy documents in depth, instructed troops in escape and evasion techniques, and interrogated high-level prisoners of war. Toward the end of the war, these specialist teams comprised 3,500 officers and men in the European Theater.[90]

In addition to the joint strategic intelligence effort with the British (ULTRA), Army signals intelligence provided tactical support in the field. At the corps level in the European Theater, small signal service companies with an organic detachment of analytical personnel intercepted, decrypted, and processed enemy communications for the use of local commanders. Signal security detachments monitored friendly communications to detect vulnerabilities. Field armies and army groups in Europe included radio intelligence companies that received analytical support from the Signal Security Detachment D, another field element of the England-based Signal Intelligence Division.[91] Army signals intelligence units based outside Europe contributed to the overall intelligence picture as well. The monitoring station of the Signal Security Agency at Vint Hill Farms in Virginia and special radio intelligence detachments in Iceland and Newfoundland, Canada, intercepted some German traffic, although they were too far away from the European Theater to collect much from the weak signals they detected. Another monitoring station in Asmara, Ethiopia, served as part of the PURPLE and MAGIC effort by intercepting communications between the Japanese foreign ministry and Tokyo's ambassador to Berlin.[92]

Unlike the Army's signals and military intelligence organizations, the CIC initially had no central administrative headquarters in the North African and the Mediterranean Theaters of Operations. For the first few years of the war, the Military Intelligence Service controlled counterintelligence personnel directly from the United States, but as more and more CIC units deployed overseas, oversight from 3,000 miles away created enormous problems. To the dismay of counterintelligence personnel, the arrangement also slowed promotion, and the CIC became known as the "Corps of Indignant Corporals."[93]

---

90 Oscar M. Koch with Robert G. Hays, *G–2: Intelligence for Patton* (Atglen, PA: Schiffer Publishing, 1999), 136; Finnegan and Danysh, *Military Intelligence*, 92.
91 Howe, *American Signal Intelligence*, series iv, 1:120–27, 1:169.
92 Benson, *A History of U.S. Communications Intelligence in World War II*, 103. For a narrative of the intelligence derived from the communications of the Japanese ambassador to Berlin, see Carl Boyd, *Hitler's Japanese Confidant: General Ōshima Hiroshi and Magic Intelligence, 1941–1945* (Lawrence: University of Kansas Press, 1993).
93 Gilbert, Finnegan, and Bray, *In the Shadow of the Sphinx*, 76.

With the invasion of Italy in mid-1943 and the Normandy landings in June 1944, control of CIC personnel in the European Theater shifted to local commanders, and CIC detachments became organized as cells attached to Army units in the field. At the highest echelon of command, the 418th Counter Intelligence Corps Detachment of the 12th Army Group was established in August 1944.[94] As American armies fought their way toward the borders of the Reich, CIC detachments began operating in rear areas. Divisional CIC detachments consisted of seventeen men, and larger detachments served at higher echelons of command. For greater mobility, every two counterintelligence soldiers shared a jeep. By the end of the war, 241 CIC detachments consisting of 3,000 officers and enlisted men served overseas.[95]

Regular officers and soldiers often disliked the CIC. Counterintelligence personnel held military ranks, but when pursuing an investigation, they assumed the title of "special agent" and often removed their insignia.[96] This practice obscured their status when they investigated higher-ranking officers, and these officers resented the fact that CIC special agents had the power to investigate them. The wide distribution of CIC reports also resulted in the dissemination of unverified derogatory information "based on hearsay, gossip, and innuendo."[97] Indiscreet and clumsy snooping also tarnished the Corps' image. CIC agents occasionally joined unsuspecting soldiers as they showered and then reprimanded them later for any verbal security breaches in their casual conversations. Soldiers did not take well to this practice.[98]

In addition to the personnel who specialized in signals intelligence, military intelligence, and counterintelligence, tactical units played a vital role in the Army's intelligence-gathering efforts. Each infantry and armored regiment contained an intelligence and reconnaissance platoon. Armored divisions had reconnaissance squadrons, and infantry divisions had organic reconnaissance troops. Assigned to each division were ten L–4 Grasshopper airplanes, light aircraft used for artillery spotting and general intelligence. Higher echelons of command could call on groups of mechanized cavalry for reconnaissance purposes, although in practice the Army used them mostly as combat elements in a screening role.[99]

---

94 Rpt, 12th Army Gp, Rpt of Opns (Final AAR), vol. iv, G–2 Section, parts vi through vii, 110, Historians Files, CMH.
95 Finnegan and Danysh, *Military Intelligence*, 91; Gilbert, Finnegan, and Bray, *In the Shadow of the Sphinx*, 43, 77.
96 Maj. Ann Bray et al., ed., *The History of the Counter Intelligence Corps*, vol. 2, *Chronology, 1775–1950* (Fort Holabird, MD: U.S. Army Intelligence Center, 1959), 43.
97 Gilbert, Finnegan, and Bray, *In the Shadow of the Sphinx*, 32.
98 Maj. Ann Bray et al., ed., *The History of the Counter Intelligence Corps*, vol. 18, *The Last German Offensive* (Fort Holabird, MD: U.S. Army Intelligence Center, 1959), 41.
99 Finnegan and Danysh, *Military Intelligence*, 98.

OSS detachments served with army groups, field armies, and occasionally below that level, and gathered information through collaboration with local resistance groups and agents behind enemy lines.[100] General Donovan later claimed that his organization provided 50 percent of the intelligence available to the Seventh Army in preparation for the invasion of southern France (DRAGOON), but this number remains unverifiable, and the office never became fully integrated into the Army's intelligence process.[101] According to General Sibert, prisoner-of-war interrogations provided 75 percent of intelligence to local commanders, but Donovan's organization obtained most of its information from civilians who were not trained military observers.[102] Some officers considered OSS communications rich in anecdotes but poor in useful information. As one Army Intelligence officer complained, the OSS sent out reports "by the pound ... and you would read through all the gossip of the world heard in saloons from Casablanca to Havana, and you would read through this stuff hoping that there would be something there. Well, there was nothing."[103]

Intelligence collection started at the front lines as Army units took prisoners, picked up deserters, and overran wounded enemy soldiers. Teams of interrogators conducted initial interviews with prisoners of war to obtain information of immediate tactical value. German émigrés played a central role in this effort. The common language introduced an element of familiarity, put the prisoners at ease, and made many eager to talk. When met with silence, interrogators used creative methods to encourage cooperation. "We used to tell the prisoners we had two internment camps, one in Florida and the other in Siberia," recalled Hans L. Trefousse, an interrogator born and raised in Frankfurt. "I would hang a sign around the neck of a prisoner that said 'Russia' and send him out into the yard. He would ask a guard what the sign meant. Nine times out of 10 the prisoner came right back in and told us everything we wanted to know."[104]

The Army then moved its prisoners into camps or "cages" in the rear. Here, those of special interest underwent further interrogation—for example, by signals intelligence personnel if the routine interrogation indicated that a particular

---

100 Powe and Wilson, "Evolution of American Military Intelligence," 74.
101 Douglas Porch, *The French Secret Services: From the Dreyfus Affair to the Gulf War* (New York: Farrar, Straus and Giroux, 2003), 258. Porch suggests that this number is inflated.
102 Interv, Pogue with Sibert, 11 May 1951; Koch, *G–2*, 135.
103 Interv, G. E. Patrick Murray with Col. Benjamin A. Dickson, former G–2, First Army, 22 Sep 1972, Historians Files, CMH.
104 Margalit Fox, "Hans L. Trefousse, Historian and Author, 88," *New York Times*, 5 Feb 2010.

enemy soldier had cryptologic knowledge.[105] Each field army and army group had Interrogation and Counter Intelligence Interrogation Centers for this purpose.[106] The CIC controlled special annexes with soundproof interrogation rooms to question subversive elements and individuals with knowledge of the German intelligence services. Rumor had it that the CIC tortured prisoners there to extract information, but a former special agent noted that "[i]t is not really economical to torture prisoners to obtain information."[107]

For prisoners of exceptional intelligence value, the Army had a special interrogation center at Fort Hunt, Virginia, which operated under direct control of the chief of Military Intelligence Service. Here, specialists interrogated more than 3,000 prisoners, including 55 captured German general officers.[108] The intelligence service housed the generals in lavish surroundings to make them feel comfortable and drop their guard during conversations with each other. Army Intelligence personnel secretly recorded their exchanges to gather additional information.[109] Prisoner-of-war interrogations first provided the Army with in-depth information on the launch sites of German V–1 flying bombs and V–2 supersonic rockets, poison gas plants, biological warfare plans, and details about the Siegfried Line defenses at the German border.[110]

Captured enemy documents constituted another important source of intelligence. Armies in the European Theater exploited records of tactical value as soon as they fell into American hands. General Patton, commander of the Third Army, noted that a captured document allowed the Americans to predict an attack on the city of Luxembourg in December 1944.[111] As American forces advanced into Germany, they also seized a growing volume of nonmilitary records, including numerous files of the Nazi Party and its affiliates. Some were of an arcane nature, such as a set of 200,000 investigative files on prospective brides of SS (*Schutzstaf-*

---

105 "Third Army Radio Intelligence History (excerpt, 1945): D. Prisoner of War Interrogations," SRH 042, in Gilbert and Finnegan, *U.S. Army Signals Intelligence*, 204.
106 Bray et al., *History of the Counter Intelligence Corps*, 16:34; Maj. Ann Bray et al., ed., *The History of the Counter Intelligence Corps*, vol. 19, *The Rhine Breached* (Fort Holabird, MD: U.S. Army Intelligence Center, 1959), 66.
107 Ian Sayer and Douglas Botting, *America's Secret Army: The Untold Story of the Counter Intelligence Corps* (London: Fontana, 1990), 203; John Schwarzwalder, *We Caught Spies: Adventures of an American Counter Intelligence Agent in Europe* (New York: Duell, Sloan and Pearce, 1946), 268.
108 Bidwell, MID History WWII, chap. 5, Field Collection, 33.
109 Mallett, *Hitler's Generals in America*, 53.
110 George S. Patton, *War as I Knew It: A Human and Eloquent Story Told by a Great Military Genius* (New York: Houghton Mifflin, 1947), 200.
111 George S. Patton, *War as I Knew It: A Human and Eloquent Story Told by a Great Military Genius* (New York: Houghton Mifflin, 1947), 200.

fel) men.[112] In another case, CIC agents recovered a set of SA (*Sturmabteilung*) records buried in a manure pile in a cloister yard in Blaubeuren.[113] CIC Special Agent George J. Novak scored one of the most historically significant coups in the European Theater when he discovered the records of the German foreign ministry hidden at a castle in the Harz Mountains in central Germany.[114]

Other sources of intelligence included air, visual, and photo reconnaissance, as well as information obtained from the local population.[115] In occupied Germany, the CIC developed good relationships with the police, who sometimes volunteered information that led to the arrest of wanted individuals.[116] Colonel Koch, intelligence chief of the Third Army, noted,[117] "[s]ources were limited only by the individual officer's ingenuity in exploiting them." Some intelligence officers became very creative indeed. The intelligence chief of the First Army, Colonel Dickson, hired several Belgian and Dutch prostitutes to gather information among the local population in occupied Germany. According to Dickson, the women produced valuable information on German resistance plans and on unauthorized collusion between Army personnel and enemy aliens. In return, he provided them with penicillin to cure them of sexually transmitted infections contracted in their line of work and passports to allow them to leave the country. One of the members of Colonel Dickson's unconventional spy ring ended up marrying a soldier and moved to America with him. In the words of one intelligence officer involved in this operation, "[i]t was a crazy way to make prostitution pay."[118]

Conclusion

During the war, the Army built a large and complex intelligence organization that emphasized collection from a wide range of sources and involved every echelon of command. At the battalion level, commanders issued Essential Elements of

---

112 Maj. Ann Bray et al., ed., *The History of the Counter Intelligence Corps*, vol. 20, *Germany Overrun: Part I* (Fort Holabird, MD: U.S. Army Intelligence Center, 1959), 83.
113 Rpt, 100th Inf Div, G–2 Period Rpt no. 166, 29 May 1945, Folder "VI Corps G-2 Journals 26–31 May 45," Historical Div, Program Files, VI Corps, G–2 Jnls, 1945, RG 498, NACP.
114 Bray et al., *History of the Counter Intelligence Corps*, 20:65. The records were indexed, microfilmed, and eventually returned to the German foreign office. The microfilms remain available to the public at the National Archives at College Park, Maryland.
115 Koch, *G–2*, 139.
116 Bray et al., *History of the Counter Intelligence Corps*, 20:132.
117 Koch, *G–2*, 135.
118 Benjamin A. Dickson, "Memoirs of World War II" (unpublished manuscript, n.d.), 160–65, Historians Files, CMH.

Information, or EEIs, to their intelligence staffs, or S–2.[119] EEIs pertained to a range of combat-related issues, including enemy capabilities, the physical condition of an area, and the weather. The intelligence staff would collect the required information and provide it to the commander as well as to the intelligence staff at the next higher echelon, the regimental S–2. Above the regimental level, commanders and G–2 intelligence divisions engaged in the same process, reaching all the way to the European Theater and Supreme Allied Headquarters. The Intelligence Division of the European Theater would share information from lower echelons with the Military Intelligence Division in Washington where intelligence officers collated information from intelligence units across the globe, produced assessments of strategic long-term significance, and provided them to the Army staff. In turn, the Army's G–2 issued its own EEIs downward to the theater as general guidelines on what lower echelons were expected to collect. Likewise, theater intelligence issued elements to subordinate intelligence staffs.

Ideally, the Army's military intelligence effort constituted a system of multiple interlocking cycles that continuously collected, analyzed, and distributed information up and down the chain of command. This, at least, was the theory. In practice, this system contended with different levels of access to secret intelligence, the personalities of individual commanders and intelligence chiefs, and the vagaries of war. Perfect or not, this was the intelligence process the Army had in place when Allied forces entered Germany. It was about to be tested by a battle-hardened enemy.

---

119 Koch, *G–2*, 134.

2 Operations in Wartime Germany

In the afternoon of 11 September 1944, a patrol of seven American soldiers from the 85th Cavalry Reconnaissance Squadron, Mechanized, 5th Armored Division, approached a blown-up bridge across the Our River. The river marked the border between Belgium and Germany, and the men were on a mission to reconnoiter the fortifications on the German side. They had instructions to proceed with caution, but should "probing indicate great weakness in some portion of the frontier line, penetration may become possible."[1] When they crossed the river at 1630, they became the first members of the Allied invasion force to set foot on German soil. Accompanied by a rifleman and a French interpreter, the patrol leader, Sgt. Warner W. Holzinger, carefully proceeded into enemy territory.[2]

Holzinger hailed from the German city of Heilbronn and had immigrated to the United States with his parents as a child. He still spoke the language, and he later recalled being "thankful many times I could speak German." He made use of his linguistic skills shortly after entering the country of his birth. Their first contact was not an enemy combatant, but a farmer who told them he had last seen *Wehrmacht* (German army) soldiers the previous day. He then gave them directions to nearby German fortifications. Holzinger forced the man to accompany his patrol, "in case he was lying," and the four men trekked about 1.5 miles into enemy territory. On the crest of a ridge, the patrol scanned the landscape with their field glasses, identifying twenty pillboxes. One had a chicken coop attached to it but none were occupied. The pillboxes were part of the so-called Siegfried Line, a series of supposedly formidable fortifications on Germany's western border. Holzinger and his men then made their way back to report their observations.[3] The findings of the patrol contributed to a growing body of intelligence indicating that the much-vaunted Siegfried Line posed no insurmountable obstacle to the advancing Allied armies. Shortly thereafter, Allied combat units launched the final assault on Hitler's Germany.

---

1 Rpt, Maj. Emerson F. Hurley, Historical Div, n.d. [1947], Folder "605-CAV RCN (85th)-0.20 Hist'l Info 5th Armd Div. Sep 44," World War II (WWII) Opns Rpt, 1941–48, RG 407, NACP.
2 5th Armored Division Association, *Paths of Armor: The Fifth Armored Division in World War II* (Nashville, TN: The Battery Press, 1985), 115.
3 Ltr, Warner Holzinger to Maj. Emerson F. Hurley, 18 Sep 1947, Folder "605-CAV RCN (85th)-0.20 Hist'l Info 5th Armd Div. Sep 44," WWII Opns Rpt, 1941–48, RG 407, NACP; Rick Atkinson, *The Guns at Last Light: The War in Western Europe, 1944–1945* (London: Picador, 2014), 248.

The Occupation of Aachen

After crossing the German border, Allied forces advanced only slowly into the Reich. In mid-September, Operation MARKET-GARDEN, an Anglo-American airborne and ground operation to establish a bridgehead across the Rhine, failed after the British 21st Army Group intelligence underestimated German resistance, missing a *Panzer Corps* near the most advanced drop zone. Rugged terrain and shortages of everything from gasoline to ammunition hampered Allied offensive operations for the rest of the fall, while the Germans seized the chance to strengthen their defenses. In October, the 21st Army Group cleared the river approaches to the Belgian supply port of Antwerp. Meanwhile, the Americans continued to push into northeastern France, as the Third Army in Lorraine battered against the German works near Metz and the 6th Army Group struggled through the Vosges Mountains in its drive toward the upper Rhine.

On 1 October 1944, the First Army under General Courtney H. Hodges attacked the medieval border city of Aachen. On the first two days, 300 American aircraft dropped 161 tons of bombs, and twelve artillery battalions fired nearly 10,000 rounds into the city. During the ensuing three weeks, American infantry cleared the streets of German defenders in fierce house-to-house fighting that cost each side approximately 5,000 casualties. When the city surrendered on 21 October, 85 percent of its buildings had been destroyed, and the city's population had shrunk to barely 10,000, most of its 163,000 citizens having left before the attack. An American eyewitness who drove through Aachen shortly after its fall described the ravaged city as "a fantastic, stinking heap of ruins."[4]

Aachen was the first major German city captured by American forces, and its occupation inaugurated a new phase of the war for the Army: military government. This task fell to the civil affairs, or G–5, sections of each Army staff and to military government detachments earmarked for specific towns and cities. The Aachen detachment, F1G2, moved in one day after the surrender. It comprised 35 officers and 48 enlisted men.[5] Initially, the Army and the military government officials dealt with elementary tasks such as clearing roads and restoring water and power. Soon, they moved on to the politically sensitive job of selecting capable

---

[4] For the battle of Aachen, see Charles B. MacDonald, *The Siegfried Campaign Line*, United States Army in World War II (Washington, DC: U.S. Army Center of Military History, 2001), 307–22. For casualties, see Stephen E. Ambrose, *Citizen Soldiers: The U.S. Army from the Normandy Beaches to the Bulge to the Surrender of Germany, June 7, 1944–May 7, 1945* (New York: Simon & Schuster, 1997), 151. Quote from Earl F. Ziemke, *The U.S. Army in the Occupation of Germany, 1944–1946*, Army Historical Series (Washington, DC: U.S. Army Center of Military History, 1975), 178.
[5] Ziemke, *U.S. Army in the Occupation of Germany*, 142.

Figure 5: Leo A. Swoboda, shown here as a lieutenant colonel in Berlin, 1946. U.S. Army, NACP.

local officials who would be willing to work with the Americans but were not tainted by affiliation with the Nazis. For this mission, the detachment relied heavily on the Counter Intelligence Corps. A contemporary Army Intelligence report noted that, with the occupation of Aachen, "the ultimate task of CIC in Europe has begun. The new German Civil Administration under American MG [military government] is the most crucial single factor for the short and long range security of our Army and for peace in the future."[6] Aachen thus became a "test tube" for military government and for the role of Army Intelligence agencies in the occupation.[7]

---

6 Rpt, Maj. James K. Dorsett, HQ, VII Corps, Ofc of the Asst Ch of Staff (ACoS), G–2, 14 Jan 1945, sub: CIC and MG-Exterminators, Folder "Counterintelligence Corps Det Reports Volume I of II—Folder 2 of 2," U.S. Army Intel and Security Cmd (INSCOM), Rcds of the Investigative Rcds Repository (IRR), Security Classified Intel and Investigative Dossiers, Impersonal Files, 1939–76, RG 319, NACP.
7 "AMG Role Is Set Up East of Rhine; Children a Problem in Reich Areas," *New York Times*, 17 Mar 1945.

Most of Aachen's Nazi officials had fled the city or gone underground, and so one of the detachment's first tasks was to appoint a lord mayor (*Oberbürgermeister*). Having received no instructions on how to go about this business, the military government officer in charge of the search, Maj. Leo A. Swoboda, consulted the local bishop, who recommended a lawyer with anti-Nazi credentials, Franz Oppenhoff, for the job. Oppenhoff accepted the offer hesitatingly, fearing Nazi retribution against him or his family. For his protection, the Americans did not publish his name when they swore him into office. Swoboda drove Oppenhoff around the ruins of Aachen in his jeep to seek out men to join his administration. Eventually, Oppenhoff recruited a team of nine assistant mayors.[8]

After Major Swoboda selected Oppenhoff and helped him assemble the heads of his administration, the CIC screened them for political suitability. The main tool in this process was a *Fragebogen* (questionnaire) that required candidates to list past membership in the Nazi Party and affiliated organizations.[9] After the CIC cleared Oppenhoff and his core staff, the mayor hired additional personnel, and the job of screening those individuals fell to the CIC as well. The corps cleared most but not all candidates. In the case of Gerhard Reusch, one of the prospective assistant mayors, the CIC discovered that he had served for two years in the brutal German administration of Russia. The Americans not only rejected his application but also arrested him for collaboration with the Nazis. In the case of Wilhelm Görres, proposed as head of the chamber of commerce, the CIC found that he had joined the Nazi Party as early as 1933, and rejected him as well. In most instances, however, the Americans approved the personnel choices of Oppenhoff's administration. Occasionally, the CIC granted exceptions to candidates who had questionable backgrounds but vital qualifications—as in the case of Adolf Zinnecke, a longtime Nazi Party member and local banker, who was allowed to join Oppenhoff's team owing to the "complete lack of native financial experts."[10]

Oppenhoff governed in an authoritarian fashion, and several citizens complained that the mayor's administration represented exclusively Catholic, conservative, and business circles. Looking at these complaints, the CIC found that Oppenhoff and his subordinates had indeed formed a closely knit clique that proved impervious to outside scrutiny and control. "Since this civil government is staffed almost

---

8 Klaus-Dietmar Henke, *Die amerikanische Besetzung Deutschlands* [The American occupation of Germany] (Munich: R. Oldenbourg Verlag, 2009), 274.
9 Ziemke, *U.S. Army in the Occupation of Germany*, 147.
10 Maj. Ann Bray et al., ed., *The History of the Counter Intelligence Corps*, vol. 16, *To the German Frontier, Part I* (Fort Holabird, MD: U.S. Army Intelligence Center, 1959), 23–24.

entirely according to the recommendations of one man," the CIC noted, "it is not dissimilar to a Tammany Hall machine."[11] By comparing Oppenhoff's administration to the notoriously corrupt Democratic Party brokers of New York City, the CIC highlighted the challenge facing American occupation authorities.

The chief of Aachen's military government, Maj. Hugh M. Jones, defended Oppenhoff. The politically conservative Jones noted, correctly, that Oppenhoff was neither a Nazi nor a communist, and he appreciated the mayor's efficient administration. Jones also took note of Oppenhoff's loyalty to the Americans during a German offensive in December 1944—the Battle of the Bulge—when German troops came dangerously close to recapturing Aachen. To critics noting that Oppenhoff's administration employed former Nazi officials, Jones replied nonchalantly, "Where would you find competent people who are not Nazis?" In his support for Oppenhoff, Jones clashed repeatedly with his own deputy, Maj. John P. Bradford, a liberal New Dealer who took issue with the mayor's authoritarian leadership style and his hiring of former Nazi officials.[12]

In early 1945, the Oppenhoff controversy came to a head when a small team of Psychological Warfare Division officers descended on Aachen to investigate the matter. General Dwight D. Eisenhower had set up the "sykewar" (psychological warfare) division at Supreme Allied Headquarters in February 1944 to conduct propaganda operations in Germany.[13] Its members were utterly committed to rooting out Nazism, as Oppenhoff and his supporters were about to discover. Led by the Austrian-born Capt. Saul K. Padover, the sykewarriors compiled a stridently worded report condemning Oppenhoff's administration. Even if Oppenhoff and his closest associates had not been members of the Nazi Party, the report contended, they had benefited from its reign. "None of them," the report averred, "ever suffered under the Nazi regime—or ever, by word or deed, opposed it. The record shows that they prospered under Hitler."[14] When military government officials defended the mayor, Padover leaked his findings to the press in the United States, and the ensuing backlash put pressure on the military government to tighten the screws.[15] The CIC renewed its push to weed out former Nazi officials.

---

11 Rpt, Dorsett, 14 Jan 1945, sub: CIC and MG-Exterminators.
12 Frederick Taylor, *Exorcising Hitler: The Occupation and Denazification of Germany* (London: Bloomsbury, 2012), 16.
13 Alfred H. Paddock Jr., *U.S. Army Special Warfare: Its Origins: Psychological and Unconventional Warfare, 1941–1952* (Washington, DC: National Defense University Press, 1982), 12–13.
14 Saul K. Padover, *Experiment in Germany: The Story of an American Intelligence Officer* (New York: Duell, Sloan and Pearce, 1946), 223; Ziemke, *U.S. Army in the Occupation of Germany*, 183.
15 Henke, *Amerikanische Besetzung*, 285.

Eventually, 10 percent of public officials in Aachen resigned under pressure or were dismissed. In early March, the 12th Army Group ordered all Nazis removed from public offices and other positions of trust and influence.[16] Oppenhoff and the majority of his staff, however, remained in office.

The Oppenhoff controversy brought to the fore an essential problem of military government: whether the Americans, when recruiting German administrators, should put a premium on efficiency or on democratic credentials. In Aachen, the conflict remained largely unresolved. The fence-straddling solution of removing some of Oppenhoff's staff while leaving the mayor and most of his aides in place satisfied neither side. The military government had become disenchanted with the mayor but still had to work with him. Padover, meanwhile, continued to regard Oppenhoff as "a self-confessed fascist and, therefore, a political enemy."[17]

Being intimately involved in the identification, selection, and screening of German collaborators, the CIC was caught in the middle of a political firestorm. On the one hand, the CIC conceded that "Unfortunately, the best men for official positions, those with long experience as civil servants, were most often Nazis."[18] On the other hand, the Corps had strict orders to screen out former Nazis. For the most part, special agents followed their orders to the letter, earning them the reputation of zealots and putting them at loggerheads with military government officers who tended to be older, socially conservative, and more pragmatic in their hiring choices. As two special agents noted at the end of the war: "There is always the matter of conflict with other sections. We are the tearer-downers and G–5 is the builder-uppers. In building up the utilities and setting up Military Government, G–5 wants to use the German civilians best qualified for certain jobs. In a lot of cases, the people that G–5 wants to use are the very ones with bad party records."[19]

In a postmortem analysis of the Aachen quagmire, the CIC identified Oppenhoff's autonomy in hiring his staff as one of the key problems in establishing a democratically minded administration that reflected the entire political spectrum outside Nazism. In the future, the CIC and military government concluded, the

---

16 Bray et al., *History of the Counter Intelligence Corps*, 16:23; Ziemke, *U.S. Army in the Occupation of Germany*, 184.
17 Padover, *Experiment in Germany*, 247.
18 Bray et al., *History of the Counter Intelligence Corps*, 16:20.
19 Interv, Special Agents Harold F. Knapp and James H. Bready, 222d CIC, 19 May 1945, Folder "Interviews 1945," XXII Corps Engr Section Instructions, Interv Rpts, Sums, and Terrain Studies, compiled 03/1945–09/1945, RG 165, NACP.

Americans would screen candidates for government jobs more carefully and more extensively.[20] As the Allies expanded control over Germany, this comprehensive approach to military government heralded a profound and long-term involvement of Army Intelligence in the occupation and in the political affairs of the conquered nation.

The Battle of the Bulge

As the Americans were setting up a military government in Aachen, Allied forces pushed eastward. In mid-November, the First Army attempted to use heavy bombers to blast an opening in the Aachen corridor leading to the Rhine and the industrial region of the Ruhr. But the Germans offered fierce resistance, particularly on the First Army's flank in the Hürtgen Forest. A dense, primordial wood of tall fir trees, deep gorges, high ridges, and narrow trails, the forest was ideally suited for defense. Through the rest of November and into December, the Americans ground their way forward, paying a heavy price in lives for every territorial gain.

The Germans also were on the move. In early September, Adolf Hitler hatched a plan to launch a massive strike against the Allied forces at the German-Belgian border in the Ardennes. Code-named HERBSTNEBEL (Autumn Mist), the offensive aimed to pierce the enemy lines, capture the Belgian seaport of Antwerp about 100 miles to the northwest, and force the Western Allies to the negotiating table. The newly created *Sixth Panzer Army* would lead the charge. The Germans devised elaborate deception operations to disguise the preparations for the offensive. To aid in the initial breakthrough, one of Hitler's favorite SS commandos, SS Lt. Col. (*Obersturmbannführer*) Otto Skorzeny, would deploy German troopers disguised as American soldiers behind Allied lines to sow confusion. Parachutists dropped into the Malmedy area would support Skorzeny's men in their mission, which would be known as *Operation GREIF* (Griffin). Hitler's generals considered HERBSTNEBEL overly ambitious and sought to scale it back, but the Führer brushed them aside. The Germans scheduled the attack for 16 December 1944 (Map 1).[21]

Allied signals intelligence picked up signs that something was afoot. A MAGIC intercept revealed that Hitler had told the Japanese ambassador to Berlin on

---

20 Bray et al., *History of the Counter Intelligence Corps*, 16:23.
21 Ian Kershaw, *Hitler, 1936–45: Nemesis* (London: Penguin Press, 2000), 741; Forrest C. Pogue, *The Supreme Command*, United States Army in World War II (Washington, DC: U.S. Army Center of Military History, 1954), 359–60. Skorzeny had gained international fame through his daring airborne liberation of Italy's fallen fascist dictator, Benito Mussolini, in 1943.

5 September that the Germans planned "to take the offensive in the West on a large scale" sometime after early November.[22] Later that month, ULTRA began producing a steady stream of decrypts suggesting German preparations for a major operation. Perhaps the most significant of these messages was an intercept of 18 September revealing the establishment of the *Sixth Panzer Army* under SS General (*Oberstgruppenführer*) Josef "Sepp" Dietrich.[23] A butcher by profession and a protégé of Hitler's, Dietrich had made his mark on the eastern front as a bold if not reckless Map 1 commander. His transfer to the western front as the head of a major new *Panzer* formation suggested aggressive German designs.[24]

In the following months, Allied intelligence picked up additional clues. German prisoners of war exuded a newfound sense of confidence, and in early November a deserter confirmed the buildup of the *Sixth Panzer Army*. A captured enemy order disclosed that the Germans were forming English-speaking units for raids and sabotage on American command posts, and an ULTRA decrypt placed Otto Skorzeny in the area. Aerial reconnaissance and decrypts of the German railway (Reichsbahn) suggested major troop movements behind enemy lines. Radio intelligence companies of the U.S. Army intercepted communications indicating preparations for a major offensive. On 10 December, ULTRA reported that the *Sixth Panzer Army* had received orders to maintain radio silence, usually a sure sign of an impending attack.[25]

Although the raw intelligence suggested German preparations for a major operation, no item detailed the precise location, time, and scale of the attack. Consequently, Allied intelligence chiefs struggled to produce an accurate forecast. In early December, Maj. Gen. Kenneth W. D. Strong, the British chief of intelligence at Supreme Allied Headquarters, revealed the possibility of a German attack in the Ardennes but listed it only as one of several possibilities.[26] At the 12th Army Group headquarters, Brig. Gen. Edwin L. Sibert was hedging his bets. He warned

---

22 Carl Boyd, *Hitler's Japanese Confidant: General Ōshima Hiroshi and Magic Intelligence, 1941–1945* (Lawrence: University of Kansas Press, 1993), 156–57.
23 Ralph Bennett, *Ultra in the West: The Normandy Campaign 1944–45* (New York: Charles Scribner's Sons, 1979), 192.
24 Hugh M. Cole, *The Ardennes: Battle of the Bulge*, United States Army in World War II (Washington, DC: U.S. Army Center of Military History, 1993), 76.
25 David W. Hogan Jr., *A Command Post at War: First Army Headquarters in Europe, 1943–1945* (Washington, DC: U.S. Army Center of Military History, 2000), 217; Pogue, *Supreme Command*, 363; Bennett, *Ultra in the West*, 195; Peter Caddick-Adams, *Snow & Steel: The Battle of the Bulge, 1944–45* (Oxford: Oxford University Press, 2017), 147, 154, 155.
26 Pogue, *Supreme Command*, 365, 371; Caddick-Adams, *Snow & Steel*, 159.

of the capabilities of the *Sixth Panzer Army*, yet he also suggested the Germans were keeping this force in reserve for a counterattack at a later point.[27]

The intelligence chief of the First Army, Col. Benjamin A. "Monk" Dickson, came close to pinpointing German intentions. On 10 December, he raised the specter of an "all-out counterattack" on the western front. Yet he identified an area well north of the Ardennes as the most likely point of attack, and he failed to give a probable time for the operation. On 14 December, he went on leave to Paris, something he would not have done had he correctly guessed at the German battle plan.[28] Neither Dickson's warning nor any other intelligence estimate provided conclusive information about potential enemy movements. Thus, the Army saw little need to reinforce the VIII Corps, its principal unit in the Ardennes. On the eve of the offensive, the corps' own intelligence section reported that the Germans intended to "have this sector of the front remain quiet and inactive."[29]

On 16 December, *Wehrmacht* and SS units launched their surprise attack. The Germans deployed more than 200,000 men in thirteen infantry and seven *Panzer* divisions, including nearly 1,000 tanks and almost 200 guns, along a front of 60 miles on the Belgium-Germany-Luxembourg border. Within ten days, armored units of the *Sixth Panzer Army* and the *Fifth Panzer Army* pushed back the defending First Army 50 miles, creating a dangerous bulge in the Allied front line, giving the battle its popular name. To intimidate their opponents, the Germans deliberately committed acts of brutality. Near the village of Malmédy in Belgium, a spearhead of the *1st SS Panzer Division "Leibstandarte Adolf Hitler"* overran a rest area filled with soldiers of the 99th Infantry Division and other American units. After the Americans surrendered, SS troops under the command of SS Lt. Col. Joachim Peiper murdered more than eighty of the prisoners. In the following days, Peiper's men continued killing spree. By 20 December, approximately 350 American prisoners of war and at least 100 unarmed Belgian civilians had perished at their hands.[30]

The German army also committed atrocities. Not far from Malmédy, at the small town of Schoenberg, a *Wehrmacht* unit accepted the surrender of 3,000 soldiers of the 422d and 423d Infantry. Two German soldiers, who had been prisoners of war of those units, notified the local *Wehrmacht* commander about two "Jews from Berlin" among the captured Americans. The commander, Capt. Curt Bruns, identified the two individuals as the German-born S. Sgt. Kurt R. Jacobs and T/5 (Technician Fifth Grade) Murray Zapler, who had trained at Camp Ritchie

---

27 Caddick-Adams, *Snow & Steel*, 158–59.
28 Hogan, *Command Post*, 297.
29 Pogue, *Supreme Command*, 365.
30 Cole, *Ardennes*, 261–62.

and served as prisoner-of-war interrogators with the U.S. Army. Jacobs and Zapler pleaded with Bruns that they be treated as prisoners of war, but Bruns declared, "Juden haben kein Recht, in Deutschland zu leben" (Jews have no right to live in Germany). He then had them executed by firing squad.[31]

Army counterintelligence played a prominent role during the battle. On the first day of the attack, soldiers of the 106th Infantry Division found a secret order outlining *Operation Greif* on a dead German trooper. The CIC immediately publicized the German deception plan, and enacted a number of security measures. These included a poster campaign, roadblocks, control points, spot-checks of all vehicles near the front line, and an alert to look out for fake U.S. Army uniforms.[32] The CIC suggested that guards at checkpoints hold suspicious-looking soldiers at gunpoint and ask them questions that supposedly only a red-blooded American could answer, such as "What is the price of an air mail stamp?" or "Who is Frank Sinatra?" Guards tested accents by ordering soldiers to say out loud words such as "wreath" or "with." Because the German language does not contain the sound *th*, native German speakers would be prone to pronounce it as *s*—and give themselves away.[33]

The counterintelligence effort quickly yielded results. On 18 December, a military policeman detained a U.S. jeep carrying three men who were unable to give the password. Wearing U.S. Army uniforms and equipped with fake documentation, they confessed to being members of *Einheit Stielau* (Stielau unit), a commando force named after its leader, 1st Lt. Lothar Stielau. Upon further interrogation by agents of the 301st Counter Intelligence Corps Detachment, they described their outfit as a force composed of 150 English-speakers, which belonged to the *150th SS Panzer Brigade*. They were part of *Operation Greif* under the command of Colonel Skorzeny. Their mission, the captives continued, was to "cause confusion among retreating American troops." One of the men claimed that the Germans had coerced him to join the unit, while another contended that he wanted to sabotage the mission "because I want the Americans to conquer." The third man simply said, "I admit that what I did was unfair." A military court tried them as unlawful combatants and found all three guilty. A firing squad executed them on 23 December 1944.[34]

---

31 Ziemke, *U.S. Army in the Occupation of Germany*, 391; Bruce Henderson, *Sons and Soldiers: The Untold Story of the Jews Who Escaped the Nazis and Returned with the U.S. Army to Fight Hitler* (New York: William Morrow, 2017), 275–77.
32 Maj. Ann Bray et al., ed., *The History of the Counter Intelligence Corps*, vol. 18, *The Last German Offensive* (Fort Holabird, MD: U.S. Army Intelligence Center, 1959), 2–3.
33 Benjamin A. Dickson, "The G–2 Battle of the Bulge" (unpublished manuscript, n.d.), 8, Historians Files, CMH.
34 Bray et al., *History of the Counter Intelligence Corps*, 18:9–11.

Only a few days after the capture of the first group of *Einheit Stielau* commandos, soldiers of the 30th Infantry Division apprehended a "Capt. Cecil Dryer" after determining that he was another German soldier in U.S. uniform. They handed him to the 30th Counter Intelligence Corps Detachment for interrogation. "Captain Dryer" turned out to be a minor celebrity. His real name was Otto R. Struller, a professional ballet dancer who had performed in England, Germany, and the United States before the war. The *Washington Post* described a National Theatre performance of his troupe as "gay and somber, cheerful and grimly dramatic, romantic and realistic."[35] During his interrogation, Struller denied membership in *Einheit Stielau* and disclaimed knowledge of an organized deception operation. Instead, he sought to "discuss his successes on the New York stage" with his captors. A military court tried, convicted, and executed him.[36] Two days before Christmas, seven members of the *Einheit Stielau* wearing U.S. uniforms sought to engage an Army gun crew in a conversation, but the artillerymen identified, detained, and handed them over to the 30th CIC Detachment. The Americans tried and executed all seven. After the war, Skorzeny stated that forty-four of the commandos had penetrated Allied lines. If so, a quarter of his men faced U.S. Army firing squads. Others ended up in captivity, and those who slipped back behind German lines failed to do much damage. The CIC had stamped out *Operation* GREIF.[37]

At the same time, the counterintelligence effort caused a great deal of confusion on the Allied side. Having heard a rumor that the Germans were impersonating the commander of Britain's 21st Army Group, Field Marshal Bernard L. "Monty" Montgomery, American guards promptly stopped and detained his car. When Montgomery sought to brush aside his would-be captors, they shot at his tires and arrested him. General Eisenhower and General Omar N. Bradley got a good laugh at their colleague's expense, but soon enough they found themselves in the same predicament. During a stop at another security checkpoint, a guard asked General Bradley to name the capital of Illinois. The general replied correctly, "Springfield." The guard, however, thought the capital was Chicago, and detained Bradley as a potential imposter.[38]

Eisenhower avoided the humiliation of arrest by his own troops, but he did not escape the fallout from the rumor mill. On 19 December, a captured *Einheit Stielau* commando told CIC agents that the unit's ultimate mission was to move on

---

35 "Ballets of Jooss Closely Follow Theme of Life," *Washington Post*, 16 Feb 1936.
36 Bray et al., *History of the Counter Intelligence Corps*, 18:19–20. Although Struller's military ID identified him as Captain Dryer, his dog tags bore the name of Pvt. Richard Baumgardner.
37 Bray et al., *History of the Counter Intelligence Corps*, 18:23; Caddick-Adams, *Snow & Steel*, 44.
38 Caddick-Adams, *Snow & Steel*, 363, 365.

to Paris and assassinate the supreme commander. This statement was, in all likelihood, false. After the war, Skorzeny's U.S. interrogators noted that the assassination story "was one of a continuous crop of fantastic rumors which sprang up around Skorzeny's personality after the Mussolini rescue had made him the German 'Buck Rogers.' In addition," the interrogation report noted, "the atmosphere of extreme secrecy surrounding all preparations for the Ardennes offensive was the ideal breeding ground for all sorts of wild stories which were spread by self-styled heroes in an effort to emphasize the importance of the mission in which they were to partake."[39] Nonetheless, the phantom mission partially immobilized the Allied leadership. The CIC immediately forwarded news of the "assassination plot" to Paris. Against Eisenhower's protest, his security personnel restricted his movements, and he became holed up at the Hotel Trianon for the duration of the battle. A look-alike, Lt. Col. Baldwin B. Smith, impersonated the general in public. In due course, all senior Allied commanders involved in the Battle of the Bulge suffered similar fates and became virtual prisoners at their headquarters out of concern over German assassination attempts. Their immobilization frustrated them personally and hindered their ability to communicate with each other and with their troops.[40]

Behind Allied lines, *Operation GREIF* wreaked havoc. Anyone who had an accent or a German-sounding last name fell under suspicion of being a German commando in disguise. British soldiers, with their distinctive intonation and their unfamiliarity with American culture, frequently were detained and harassed. American soldiers with Germanic surnames had a lot of explaining to do. German émigrés serving with Army Intelligence were regularly "arrested and brought in for interrogation simply because, naturally, they spoke much better German or French than English."[41] For many, the rumor mill proved deadly. Out of fear or anger, nervous GIs may have shot hundreds of fellow soldiers, Belgian civilians, and German prisoners of war.[42]

Thanks to their dogged defense, a reorganization of the chain of command, and the arrival of reinforcements, the U.S. Army halted the *HERBSTNEBEL* offensive and erased German gains. By the time the fighting subsided, the Americans had sustained 75,000 casualties. Yet the Germans lost close to 100,000 soldiers, and un-

---

[39] Memo, Col. T. J. Sands, Counterintel Br, G–2, United States Forces in the European Theater (USFET), to ACoS, G–2, 30 Aug 1945, sub: Alleged Plot to Assassinate General Eisenhower, Folder "Otto Skorzeny XE 000417. Vol. 1," INSCOM, IRR, Personal Name Files, 1939–1976, RG 319, NACP.
[40] Bray et al., *History of the Counter Intelligence Corps*, 18:14.
[41] John Schwarzwalder, *We Caught Spies: Adventures of an American Counter Intelligence Agent in Europe* (New York: Duell, Sloan and Pearce, 1946), 213.
[42] Caddick-Adams, *Snow & Steel*, 365.

like the Americans, the *Wehrmacht* had no reserves to make up for their losses.[43] For the remainder of the war, the Germans stayed on the defensive in the West as the better-equipped and numerically superior Allies pushed into the Reich. "The rest," General Sibert recalled after the war, "was relatively down-hill work."[44]

The American press promptly identified faulty intelligence as the culprit for the initial German successes in the Battle of the Bulge. At the height of the battle, on 4 January 1945, the *New York Times* accused the Allies of having committed "the cardinal sin of underestimating the enemy."[45] Many Allied intelligence officers accepted this verdict. As General Sibert conceded after the war, "There is not the slightest doubt that the Germans achieved complete surprise in their counter offensive in the Ardennes in December, 1944."[46] Over the following years, a lengthy debate ensued over the exact cause of this failure and of the individual responsibility for it.

For one, Allied intelligence was not omniscient. Bad weather kept aerial reconnaissance to a minimum, and the Germans had gone to great lengths to mask their preparations. Their strict adherence to radio silence deprived the Americans of meaningful tactical signals intelligence.[47] Also, as the Allies approached the German border, ULTRA's significance declined because the Germans switched from using wireless radio transmissions to landlines inside their borders, and these communications were immune to Allied interception efforts. The Allied mindset in late 1944 played a significant role as well. As the Anglo-American armies prepared for the final push into the Reich, intelligence officers did not want to rock the boat with pessimistic estimates that emphasized the need for defensive measures.

Interpersonal rivalries also prevented closer cooperation between the various intelligence sections. Field Marshal Montgomery's intelligence chief, Brig. Gen. Edgar "Bill" Williams, hated his counterpart at Allied headquarters, General Strong, and referred to him as the "Chinless Horror."[48] For his part, Colonel Dick-

---

[43] Richard W. Stewart, ed., *American Military History*, vol. 2 (Washington, DC: U.S. Army Center of Military History, 2005), 157.
[44] Edwin L. Sibert, "Outline, Lecture on G-2 Section—Hq. 12 AG," n.d., Folder "Sibert Lecture and Letter re Bulge," Anthony Cave Brown Papers, Lauinger Library, Georgetown University, Washington, D.C. (hereinafter Georgetown Library).
[45] Hanson W. Baldwin, "The German Blow: Question of Our Strategy in West—Why Did the Germans Surprise Us?," *New York Times*, 4 Jan 1945.
[46] Edwin L. Sibert, "Military Intelligence Aspects of the Period Prior to The Ardennes Counter-Offensive," n.d., Folder 2, part 4, Anthony Cave Brown Papers, Georgetown Library.
[47] George F. Howe, *American Signal Intelligence in Northwest Africa and Western Europe*, Sources in Cryptologic History, series iv, vol. 1 (Fort Meade, MD: National Security Agency, 2010), 189.
[48] Caddick-Adams, *Snow & Steel*, 141.

son of First Army called Montgomery a "shyster" and Strong a "jackass." Dickson had coveted the post of intelligence chief at the 12th Army Group and never forgave Sibert for getting the job. He squarely pinned the blame for the German surprise attack on his rival, who "was caught in such a colossal, embarrassing error, and it shattered the rest of poor Eddie Sibert's life, because he has a paper to be eaten with the paper clips."[49]

This was unfair. Sibert never minimized his part in the battle. In fact, he reflected on his role in it for decades. One of his grandsons recalls him speaking "rarely of the war. Like many, I think he wanted to move on. As years have passed, I suspect he was probably deeply affected by the missed intelligence before the Bulge."[50] Despite Dickson's personal attacks, Sibert graciously conceded that Dickson "visualized the weight of a German attack rather better than most of us."[51] The top Allied intelligence officer in Europe, General Strong, considered the disparagement of Sibert "unmerited and unfair. . . . He behaved throughout with cool deliberation and never to my knowledge gave me bad advice during the whole battle."[52]

Perhaps the Allies' biggest failure was one of imagination. As Sibert noted after the war, the Germans "did not achieve complete surprise as to their capabilities but they did as to their intentions."[53] Most Allied intelligence officers concurred that the Germans had augmented their forces, but they did not understand that Hitler was gambling on an all-out attack. For a rational mind, such an operation made little sense as it would waste precious German resources and accelerate the end of the war. Hitler's generals had argued in the same vein, but the Führer overruled them, bringing about precisely this outcome. "One wonders," Sibert mused, "if intelligent Intelligence can be expected to forecast the intentions of a maniac."[54] It was an understandable question, one whose relevance goes far beyond events on the Belgian-German border in the winter of 1944–1945.

---

49 Interv, B. A. Dickson, with F. C. Pogue, 22 Dec 1947, Historians Files, CMH.
50 Email, Alan Sibert to Thomas Boghardt, 28 Apr 2018, Historians Files, CMH.
51 Sibert, "Military Intelligence Aspects of the Period Prior to The Ardennes Counter Offensive," 10.
52 Kenneth Strong, *Intelligence at the Top: Recollections of an Intelligence Officer* (Garden City, NY: Doubleday, 1969), 243.
53 Sibert, "Military Intelligence Aspects of the Period Prior to The Ardennes Counter Offensive," 2. Emphasis in original.
54 Sibert, "Military Intelligence Aspects of the Period Prior to The Ardennes Counter Offensive," 3.

The *Werwolf*

As the Allies closed in on the Third Reich, their intelligence services agonized over the specter of a Nazi underground organization that would continue the struggle under the occupation. The CIC first picked up hints about such a resistance effort in early 1944.[55] However, much of the initial intelligence came from prisoners of war, who reported mere hearsay and tended to make wild claims. One report improbably described a "vast organization of 200,000 members . . . spread throughout EUROPE and some countries in SOUTH AMERICA, with the intent of preserving the ideology of Nazism over as wide an area as it can with the ultimate goal of preparing the way for the return of the Party to power."[56] Guerrilla activity had been widespread across German-occupied Europe, and the Allies would have been ill-advised to dismiss a similar effort by the Nazis.

Indeed, Nazi leaders began discussing the creation of an underground army in earnest as the Allies approached the German borders. In late 1944, SS chief Heinrich L. Himmler ordered the creation of the so-called *Werwolf*, an organization that was to operate in the eastern and western German borderlands facing imminent invasion. Under the direction of SS Lt. Gen. (*Obergruppenführer*) Hans A. Prützmann, the *Werwolf* recruited members from various Nazi organizations and trained them to spread propaganda, conduct sabotage and espionage behind enemy lines, and assassinate German collaborators.[57]

Yet when the Allies entered German territory, they encountered little opposition from organized partisan groups. Many soldiers found German civilians tired of the war and unwilling to prolong their misery by opposing the Americans.[58] Clashes between American soldiers and German guerrillas proved rare, and the few troublemakers almost always turned out to be young and ill-trained. In the city of Giessen, for instance, the CIC arrested four young alleged *Werwolf* operatives who had "only one pistol but many plans." Elsewhere, the Americans apprehended a boy who had undergone training to attack American tanks with a bazooka. But he had not carried out his mission "because his mother had forbidden him."[59] In

---

55 Bray et al., *History of the Counter Intelligence Corps*, 16:11.
56 Rpt, no originating agency, n.d., sub: Nazi Underground Plans, Folder [ill.], HQ Sixth Army Gp Gen Staff, G–2 Section, Numeric-Subject File 1944–45, RG 331, NACP.
57 Volker Koop, *Himmlers letztes Aufgebot: Die NS-Organisation "Werwolf"* [Himmler's last force: The Nazi organization "Werwolf"] (Vienna: Böhlau, 2008), 30.
58 Rpt, HQ, Seventh Army, 15 Dec 1944, sub: Operations in Germany—Counter-Intelligence, Folder "407, Allied CI Operations in Germany," HQ Sixth Army Gp Gen Staff, G–2 Section, Numeric-Subject File 1944–45, RG 331, NACP.
59 Maj. Ann Bray et al., ed., *The History of the Counter Intelligence Corps*, vol. 19, *The Rhine Breached* (Fort Holabird, MD: U.S. Army Intelligence Center, 1959), 26, 32, 37, 84.

Siegburg, near Cologne, Army Intelligence arrested a group of sixteen-year-old supposed *Werwolf* agents, who "looked like Hitler Youth and were scared." The soldiers found nails and wires in their pockets. Upon questioning, the boys confessed that they had received instructions for sabotage. The interrogating officer admonished the boys' parents and had them sign an agreement that they would punish the boys and confine them to their homes.[60]

Figure 6: CIC Special Agent Dave Reisner with the 102d Infantry Division interrogates four *Werwolf* members who damaged U.S. communication lines, April 1945. U.S. Army, NACP.

By spring 1945, Army Intelligence dismissed the *Werwolf* as a threat to the Allied forces. The Nazi guerrillas were, one intelligence officer noted, "neither organized, coordinated, nor [did they] appear to have an active central control."[61] It

---

60 Patricia Kollander with John O'Sullivan, *"I Must Be a Part of This War": A German American's Fight Against Hitler and Nazism* (New York: Fordham University Press, 2005), 99.
61 Memo, unidentified author for Gen Harrison, 29 Apr 1945, Folder "452/2/1 Werewolf Organization in Germany," HQ Sixth Army Gp Gen Staff, G–2 Section, Numeric-Subject File 1944–45, RG 331, NACP.

was an apt assessment. Vain and incompetent, Prützmann proved a poor leader. From its inception, the *Werwolf* struggled to procure supplies and materiel, and recruit and train partisans in sufficient numbers and quality. The organization probably never had more than 5,000 members, the bulk consisting of fanaticized Hitler Youth.[62]

Given its weakness, the *Werwolf* directed its operations away from the Allied forces to an easier target: German collaborators.[63] In the spring of 1945, *Werwolf* operatives—or individuals claiming to be such—assassinated about half-a-dozen mayors appointed by Allied commanders.[64] Victims included the American-appointed mayors of Krankenhagen and Kirchlengern in Westphalia.[65] Next to the latter's body, the police found a scrap of paper with the word "traitor" scrawled in red crayon and beneath, in ink, the inscription, "Die Werwölfe."[66] The killers were never found.

The *Werwolf* scored its most spectacular success in Aachen. As the first major German city captured by the Americans, Aachen held symbolic value for the Allies as well as for the Nazis. The SS newspaper *Das Schwarze Korps* vowed death to any collaborator. Aachen's mayor, Franz Oppenhoff, understandably feared for his life. He told Captain Padover that the Nazis "have threatened to kill me, and I am afraid they will." Padover, who considered the mayor a beneficiary of the Nazi regime, believed that Oppenhoff was exaggerating.[67] Although the Americans had withheld Oppenhoff's name from the press, news of his appointment filtered to Berlin. Enraged by this "betrayal," SS chief Himmler ordered Prützmann to have the mayor assassinated as an "educational lesson" to other would-be collaborators. Prützmann, in turn, ordered a local SS police chief, Karl M. Gutenberger, to "bump off . . . that swine." Gutenberger then assembled a hit squad of seven, including several SS men as well as a woman and a boy for scouting purposes. They received training for their mission at Hülchrath Castle, a *Werwolf* facility near the city of Grevenbroich. Using a captured B–17 Flying Fortress bomber, the *Luftwaffe* dropped the group over Belgium, whence they crossed back into Germany. On the evening of 25 March 1945, two of the assassins sought out Oppenhoff and shot him to death on

---

[62] Perry Biddiscombe, *Werwolf! The History of the National Socialist Guerrilla Movement, 1944–1946* (Toronto: Toronto University Press, 1998), 13–16.
[63] Koop, *Himmlers letztes Aufgebot*, 7, 61, 159.
[64] Biddiscombe, *Werwolf!*, 276. Henke emphasizes that it has been difficult to identify the assassins, let alone determine their potential *Werwolf* membership; see Henke, *Amerikanische Besetzung*, 950.
[65] Biddiscombe, *Werwolf!*, 45.
[66] Bray et al., *History of the Counter Intelligence Corps*, 19:85.
[67] Padover, *Experiment in Germany*, 247.

the doorstep of his home. The group then fled across the front lines into unoccupied Germany.[68]

Padover, who had attacked Oppenhoff so vehemently for his alleged pro-Nazi views, improbably speculated that the mayor had perished at the hands of one of his colleagues. Yet agents of the 203d Counter Intelligence Corps Detachment in Aachen ascertained that Oppenhoff had fallen victim to a Nazi hit squad parachuted behind U.S. lines.[69] Testifying to Allied intelligence's continuing obsession with Otto Skorzeny, they suspected his hand behind the assassination.[70] After the war, the British arrested Gutenberger, and his interrogation filled out the gaps in the story, including the exact composition of the group and the involvement of Himmler and Prützmann.[71]

Meanwhile, in April 1945 Nazi propaganda minister Joseph Goebbels established a radio station that broadcast alleged and actual incidents of successful *Werwolf* operations and called on Germans in the occupied territories to continue the fight.[72] The station touted Oppenhoff's assassination as evidence of the prowess of the *Werwolf* and urged listeners to follow its example. The Allies feared this type of propaganda might foment unrest in postwar Germany.[73] As the CIC noted, the *Werwolf* "could do vast damage by serving as a propaganda mill and creating a fear psychosis among the German civilians in occupied territory."[74] Near the end of the war, therefore, the CIC renewed its warnings about the *Werwolf*, and Army Intelligence assessed the prospect of German subversion into the

---

68 Wolfgang Trees and Charles Whiting, *Unternehmen Karneval: der Werwolf-Mord an Aachens Oberbürgermeister Oppenhoff* [Operation Carnival: The Werwolf murder of Aachen's Mayor Oppenhoff] (Aachen: Triangel, 1982), 119, 126, 184, 218. SS Sgt. Josef Leitgeb, who killed Oppenhoff, stepped on a mine and died during the escape. The group's leader, SS Maj. Herbert Wenzel, disappeared amid the chaos of postwar Germany. A German civil court later tried the others and handed down mild sentences.
69 Padover, *Experiment in Germany*, 247.
70 Maj. Ann Bray et al., ed., *The History of the Counter Intelligence Corps*, vol. 20, *Germany Overrun, Part I* (Fort Holabird, MD: U.S. Army Intelligence Center, 1959), 12.
71 Commandant, CSDIC/WEA [Combined Services Detailed Interrogation Centre/Western European Area], BAOR [British Army of the Rhine] [ill.], 5 Oct 1945, sub: "M" Weekly Intelligence Summary no. 4, Folder "925667," Rcds of the ACoS, G–2 (Intel), Formerly Top Secret Intel Documents, 1943–59, RG 319, NACP.
72 Koop, *Himmlers letztes Aufgebot*, 59.
73 MFR, Combined Intel Committee, MFR no. 62, 24 Apr 1945, sub: Subversive Organizations, Folder "ABC 381 (29 Jan 43) Sec 2-B," ABC Series, RG 165, NACP.
74 Bray et al., *History of the Counter Intelligence Corps*, 20:97.

postwar period. The CIC had received reports about Nazi plans to go underground after the defeat of the *Wehrmacht*, "and thereby cause the Allies the maximum of difficulty."[75] An Office of Strategic Services report considered the likelihood of postwar Nazi subversion "not debatable." There could be "no question that the enemy will make every effort to conduct underground operations on a large scale."[76] This OSS memorandum reached the chief of Army Intelligence, Maj. Gen. Clayton L. Bissell, who endorsed its stark assessment and asserted that the Nazis would go underground following military defeat. "Such activities," he informed the Joint Intelligence Committee, "will probably take the form of short term obstruction to Allied occupation and to a long term underground movement aimed at perpetuation of Nazi ideology, evasion of the terms of the Peace Treaty and eventual control of the Post-War German government at the conclusion of the Allied occupation."[77]

To nip German postwar resistance in the bud, the Army dealt harshly with alleged and actual spies, saboteurs, and guerrillas, even if few of them posed a military threat. In mid-April, a reconnaissance patrol noticed a sullen-looking group of young boys in Breitingen in the state of Württemberg. When a soldier checked one of the boy's coats, he found two hand grenades. The other boys now all began removing grenades from their coats. When "attempts to control the youths failed," the report noted, "they had to be killed to prevent loss of our men and equipment." Just a few days before war's end, soldiers clashed with a "group of six young German sabotage agents dressed in civilian clothes," killing one and taking the rest prisoner.[78]

In an effort to deter subversion in the postwar period, the Army used several captured *Werwolf* operatives and spies for propaganda purposes. On 29 March, agents of the 42d Counter Intelligence Corps Detachment in the town of Bruchweiler arrested a member of the local military government, a Polish-German man

---

75 Bray et al., *History of the Counter Intelligence Corps*, 16:11.
76 Memo, Lt. Thomas W. Dunn, OSS, to Capt. Percy Madeira, 2 Mar 1945, sub: German Intelligence Plans for Underground Operations, Folder "925461," Rcds of the ACoS, G–2 (Intel), Formerly Top Secret Intel Documents, 1943–59, RG 319, NACP.
77 Memo, Maj. Gen. Clayton L. Bissell for Sec, Joint Intel Committee, 2 Mar 1945, sub: Determination of Measures to be taken to assist in the Suppression of Underground Activity following the Defeat of the German Armed Forces, Folder "925461," Rcds of the ACoS, G–2 (Intel), Formerly Top Secret Intel Documents, 1943–59, RG 319, NACP.
78 Rpt, Immediate Rpt no. 135, HQ, European Theater of Opns, U.S. Army, 17 May 1945, Folder "VI Corps G–2 Journal 20–22 May 45," Historical Div, Program Files, VI Corps, G–2 Jnls, 1945, RG 498, NACP.

named Richard Jarczyk, who had aroused suspicion owing to his repeated attempts to acquire travel passes.[79] His interrogation revealed that he had obtained a job with the military government to conduct sabotage and espionage, even though apparently he had accomplished neither. Jarczyk was court-martialed and executed by firing squad on 23 April. Nearly a month after the German surrender, the Army executed several more spies captured at the end of the war, including a sixteen-year-old and a seventeen-year-old Hitler Youth.[80] In all cases, Army photographers carefully documented the executions. Psychological warfare personnel used the photographs of the tied and blindfolded Jarczyk to prepare a poster proclaiming that other spies and saboteurs would meet the same fate. The Army printed the poster in German and distributed it widely.[81]

As an organization, the *Werwolf* did not survive the end of the war. After Hitler's suicide, his successor, Grand Admiral Karl Dönitz, dissolved the *Werwolf*. Meanwhile, the British apprehended Prützmann, who followed his Führer by swallowing a capsule of prussic acid.[82] The *Werwolf*, however, endured into the postwar period as a rallying cry for die-hard Nazis, and it was this aspect that continued to preoccupy Army Intelligence officials. As the intelligence section of the 44th Infantry Division speculated, youths fanaticized by Nazi propaganda "might well become the nucleus of the German postwar underground movement."[83]

Intelligence Myths: The Alpine Redoubt and the Lost Race for Berlin

In early November 1942, Allen W. Dulles arrived at the American embassy in Berne as the OSS representative in Switzerland. He immediately got to work. From his perch near the German border, Dulles put out feelers to several high-level German officials. Code-named CROWN JEWELS, these men provided informa-

---

79 Rpt, 307th CIC Detachment, HQ, Seventh Army, to Commanding Gen (CG), Army Services Forces, attn: Director of Intel, Pentagon, 16 May 1945, Folder "Counterintelligence Corps Det Reports Volume I of II—Folder 2 of 2," INSCOM, IRR, Impersonal Name Files, RG 319, NACP.
80 Photographs with descriptions, Folder "Germany-Execution-(Spies)," Allies and Axis, 1942–1945, RG 208, NACP.
81 Bray et al., *History of the Counter Intelligence Corps*, 20:109.
82 Biddiscombe, *Werwolf!*, 113; Note, no author, 16 May 1945, Folder "OSS Archives London, Pruetzmann," London X-2 PTS Files, RG 226, NACP.
83 Secret Intel Bull, 44th Inf Div, 15 May 1945, Folder "G-2 Journals 13–16 May 45," Historical Div, Program Files, IV Corps, G-2 Jnls, RG 498, NACP.

Figure 7: Death of a Werwolf: After the execution of Richard Jarzcyk, the Army published this poster to deter imitators. U.S. Army, NACP.

tion from inside the Reich. Dulles also contacted members of the German military who were plotting against Hitler. Their OSS codename was BREAKERS.[84]

Because Switzerland was surrounded by Axis territory, the Germans and their allies could easily intercept messages between the American embassy and Washington, D.C. To secure his communications, Dulles used a special cipher with OSS headquarters. British intelligence, however, discovered that his cipher had been compromised and informed Dulles accordingly. When the American spymaster ignored this warning and continued using his cipher, an irate British agent vented to his station chief: "[C]ould you report to the fool [Dulles] who knows his code was compromised if he has used that code to report meetings with anyone, Germans probably identified persons concerned and use them for stuffing [disinformation]. He swallows easily."[85] With this act of carelessness, Dulles set in motion a series of events that culminated in the creation of one of the enduring intelligence myths of the war.

Maj. Hans Gontard directed the branch office of the SD (*Sicherheitsdienst*), the intelligence service of the SS, in Bregenz, an Austrian town close to the Swiss border. According to a statement Gontard made after his capture by the Allies, in the late summer of 1944 he obtained a copy of a report from an American diplomat called "Bracker," or some such name, of the U.S. embassy in Berne, Switzerland.[86] In it, "Bracker" expressed concern about the possibility of the Nazis fortifying an area in the Austro-Bavarian Alps for a last stand, an operation that could prolong the war by months, if not years. Gontard shared this report with the regional Nazi boss of Tyrol, *Gauleiter* Franz Hofer, who presented it to the Nazi leadership in Berlin.[87]

Thanks to Dulles's compromised cipher, the Germans had access to his communications, and one such intercept was probably the source of Gontard's information. In the summer of 1944, Dulles sent several messages to OSS headquarters

---

84 James Srodes, *Allen Dulles: Master of Spies* (Washington, DC: Regnery, 1999), 368.
85 Keith Jeffery, *The Secret History of MI6, 1909–1949* (New York: Penguin, 2010), 511.
86 Statement, Maj. Hans Gontard, "Nationale Gebirgsfestung, Erklärung des SS-Sturmbannführers Gontardt [sic] über 'Alpen-Reduit' bezw. 'nationale Gebirgsfestung" [National mountain fortress, statement by SS-Sturmbannführer Gontardt [sic] regarding the "Alpine Redoubt" or "National mountain fortress"], 2 May 1946, Annex # 2, MS# B-457, Folder "German Language Drafts of B-Series Manuscript Studies Conducted as a Component of U.S. Army Europe Foreign Military Studies, 8/1/1952–7/6/1959," RG 549, NACP. Gontard recalled the diplomat's name as "Bracker," "Barker," or "Parker."
87 Statement, Franz Hofer, "USA-Diplomatic Representation in Switzerland, Father of Germany's Alpine-Fortification, the 'Festung Alpen,'" n.d., MS# B-457, Folder "German Language Drafts of B-Series Manuscript Studies Conducted as a Component of U.S. Army Europe Foreign Military Studies, 8/1/1952–7/6/1959," RG 549, NACP.

in Washington about the likelihood of a "National Redoubt" in the Alps. By "stationing 1,000,000 troops on the Vorarlberg, Austrian and Bavarian Alps," he cabled in mid-August, the Nazis "could resist for a period extending from 6 to 12 months."[88] During the same time period, Dulles sent cables on the BREAKERS opposition group.[89] Although the two items were unrelated, an uninitiated observer like Gontard easily might have inferred that "Breaker" was a personal name and connect it to the idea of the redoubt.[90]

Hitler had no plans for a last stand in the Alps, but Nazi propagandists and the SD spotted an opportunity. If the Americans could be persuaded that the Nazis would hunker down in a National Redoubt, this disinformation might open a venue for separate peace negotiations and perhaps even an alliance against the Soviets. Consequently, the SD began feeding disinformation to OSS agents about preparations for a defensive effort in the Alps, while Goebbels's propaganda ministry planted stories in the German and neutral press.[91] Within weeks, rumors of a formidable German defense effort in the Alps made it across the Atlantic.[92] Gontard called the ensuing wave of rumors in the neutral and Allied press a "redoubt psychosis."[93]

The mirage of the National Redoubt would have remained a footnote in the history of the war had it not coincided with a momentous decision at Supreme Allied Headquarters in Paris. Eisenhower had orders to "undertake operations aimed at the heart of Germany and the destruction of her armed forces."[94] This deliberately vague wording left the major strategic decisions to the supreme commander. Until early 1945, Eisenhower had planned to use Field Marshal Montgomery's 21st Army Group in the north to make a push toward Berlin. In early March,

---

88 Telg, Allen Dulles to OSS HQ, 12 Aug 1944, doc. 4–60, in *From Hitler's Doorstep: The Wartime Intelligence Reports of Allen Dulles, 1942–1945*, ed. Neal H. Petersen (University Park: Pennsylvania State University Press, 1996), 366–67.
89 Telg, Allen Dulles to OSS HQ, 15 Aug 1944, in Petersen, *From Hitler's Doorstep*, 366–67.
90 At least on one occasion, the OSS referred to the Breakers group as "Brakers"; see Memo, unsigned, 2 Sep 1944, Folder "Dulles Files—Gaevernitz, Gero," Field Station Files, RG 226, NACP. Moreover, Hofer was known to Dulles and the OSS station in Berne; see Telg, 30 Jan 1945, Folder "Dulles Files—Austria (Molden)," RG 226, NACP.
91 Rodney G. Minott, *The Fortress That Never Was: The Myth of Hitler's Bavarian Stronghold* (New York: Holt, Rinehart and Winston, 1964), 25; F. H. Hinsley with E. E. Thomas, C. A. G. Simkins, and C. F. G. Ransom, *British Intelligence in the Second World War*, vol. 3, part 2, *Its Influence on Strategy and Operations* (London: Her Majesty's Stationery Office, 1988), 711.
92 Harry Vosser, "Hitler's Hideaway," *New York Times*, 12 Nov 1944.
93 "National Redoubt by Gauleiter Franz Hofer," n.d., MS# B-458, Microfilm Publication M1035, Foreign Mil Studies, B-Series, RG 338, NACP.
94 Stephen E. Ambrose, *Eisenhower and Berlin, 1945: The Decision to Halt at the Elbe* (New York: Norton, 1967), 104.

however, Eisenhower abandoned this strategy. Instead, he ordered General Bradley's 12th Army Group to lead the Allied advance through central Germany and link up with the Red Army at the Elbe River, well south of Berlin. The western Allies would leave the capture of the German capital to the Soviets (Map 2).[95]

Eisenhower had good reasons to change his strategy. In early March, Allied intelligence sources indicated that spearheads of the Red Army had come within 20 miles of Berlin. Meanwhile, the Anglo-American forces were 300 miles away. Thus, the Western Allies would have been hard-pressed to capture the German capital before the Soviets. Moreover, Eisenhower had more faith in the energetic Bradley than in the cautious Montgomery to lead the final push into Germany. A lucky break at the Rhine sealed the deal for the new strategy. In early March 1945, a task force belonging to General Hodges's First Army entered the city of Remagen, south of Cologne. As the Americans approached the Rhine, they spotted a bridge the Germans had failed to destroy, and they immediately seized it. Informed by Hodges about this coup de main, Bradley burst out: "Hot dog, Courtney. This will bust him wide open. . . . Shove everything you can across it."[96] Within a week, the Americans had established a solid beachhead on the right side of the Rhine, opening the way into the heart of the Reich.

The British were upset by Eisenhower's change of strategy, which put the concluding campaign of the European war into American rather than British hands. Prime Minister Winston Churchill appealed directly to Eisenhower and President Roosevelt to rethink the supreme commander's decision. In a telegram to the American president, Churchill put forth two reasons for holding on to the original plan. First, Berlin's fall would "be the supreme signal of defeat to the German people" and therefore accelerate the end of the war. Second, leaving the city's capture to the Red Army would unduly boost Joseph Stalin's ego. If the Soviets took Berlin, Churchill wondered, "will not their impression that they have been the overwhelming contributor to our common victory be unduly imprinted in their minds, and may this not lead them into a mood which will raise grave and formidable obstacles in the future?"[97]

Churchill's arguments cut no ice with the Americans. First, they reasoned, if the Allies sought to demoralize the Germans by capturing their capital, the task could best be accomplished by the Red Army, which was within striking distance of the city. Second, given the tremendous Soviet sacrifices during the war, their failure to conquer Berlin would hardly diminish their sense of being the "over-

---

95 Pogue, *Supreme Command*, 434.
96 Omar N. Bradley, *A Soldier's Story* (New York: Holt, 1951), 510.
97 Telg, Churchill to Roosevelt, 1 Apr 1945, in Ambrose, *Eisenhower and Berlin*, 102.

whelming contributor" to victory. And third, Churchill, Roosevelt, and Stalin had already decided on the postwar division of Germany and Berlin into zones and sectors.[98] No matter who captured the city first, the conqueror would have to give up the predesignated areas to the other two Allies, which is what the Soviets did in July 1945. Eisenhower therefore stuck with his decision to abandon the push for Berlin.[99]

As the Americans and the British bickered over the direction of the main thrust of the final campaign, Allied intelligence produced increasingly alarmist estimates of the National Redoubt. On 10 March, Supreme Allied Headquarters intelligence reported that "Hitler and the Nazi leaders, supported by SS units, young fanatics and Quislings [collaborators], are planning to make a last stand in the so-called redoubt in Western Austria." The Allies therefore should make a push into Southern Germany to pre-empt this effort.[100] Two weeks later, the intelligence branch of Seventh Army produced an estimate on the Redoubt based on "fairly reliable sources." In a massive misreading of German capabilities, the branch noted that Himmler had ordered provisions for 100,000 men to the Redoubt, which was to be defended by "eighty crack units of from 1,000 to 4,000 men each." Supposedly, the Germans were amassing guns, armaments, and even an entire Messerschmitt aircraft factory in the area.[101]

Most of this information originated with agents and prisoners of war—that is, human sources, who were liable to report rumors and hearsay. According to the official history of the Army's campaign in Germany, most Allied intelligence officers discounted the possibility of a well-fortified defense effort in the Alps.[102] Nonetheless, the 12th Army Group used the National Redoubt as one reason to justify the redirection of the Allied thrust from Berlin to the south. In a memorandum on the "Re-Orientation of [Allied] Strategy," the group's operations branch argued that Berlin had lost its importance for the German war effort as most Nazi government agencies had evacuated the city and moved to lower Bavaria. The Allies should therefore push southward to preempt the construction of a National Redoubt. Crouched in guarded language, an appendix by Sibert's intelligence divi-

---

98 Ziemke, *U.S. Army in the Occupation of Germany*, 115–26.
99 Ambrose, *Eisenhower and Berlin*, 57–59.
100 Rpt, Strong et al., SHAEF Joint Intel Committee, 10 Mar 1945, sub: Ability of the German Army in the West to Continue the War, Folder "381-10 National Redoubt," SHAEF, Gen Staff, G–2 Div, Intel Target ("T") Sub-Div, Decimal File, 1944–45, RG 331, NACP.
101 Col. William W. Quinn, ACoS, G–2, Seventh Army, 25 Mar 1945, sub: "Study of the German National Redoubt," roll 52, Microfilm Publication M1642, RG 226, NACP.
102 Charles B. MacDonald, *The Last Offensive*, United States Army in World War II (Washington, DC: U.S. Army Center of Military History, 1973), 407.

sion on the National Redoubt laid out "increasing evidence" of "possible plans" for a last stand in the Alps by "Nazi party leaders and war criminals."[103]

Army Intelligence officers may have deliberately played up reports on the National Redoubt to convince the British of the necessity of redirecting the Allied war effort southward. Churchill, for one, considered a last stand of the Nazis in the Alps a real possibility.[104] Yet these intelligence reports did not prompt Eisenhower to change strategies: he had already done so. Nonetheless, the dire SHAEF intelligence estimates found their way into the Western press by way of Drew Middleton, the *New York Times* correspondent accredited to Supreme Allied Headquarters.[105] Here, they fed into the nascent myth of Eisenhower having lost Berlin to the Soviets because of faulty intelligence about the National Redoubt.

On the ground, Bradley remained in charge of the final Allied offensive and began marching into central Germany. Eisenhower's decision to focus on destroying Germany's remaining military potential, rather than targeting a fixed location, promptly paid off. In early April, the advancing Allies encircled a massive pocket of German troops in the Ruhr Valley, just east of the Rhine. By the time all opposition ended in the "Ruhr pocket," the Allies had captured 325,000 German soldiers. Meanwhile, American forces raced toward the Elbe, making 30 miles a day and riding roughshod over any German opposition. On 12 April, elements of the Ninth Army under Lt. Gen. William H. Simpson reached the Elbe at Magdeburg, just 50 miles short of Berlin. Thirteen days later, the 69th Infantry Division linked up with the 58th Guards Infantry Division of the Red Army at Torgau, splitting in two what remained of Hitler's Reich.[106]

Eager to take advantage of an unexpected opportunity, Eisenhower asked Bradley what it might take to conquer Berlin, now that the Ninth Army was so close to the city. Bradley estimated 100,000 casualties.[107] On 12 April, Simpson flew to Bradley's headquarters to propose a lightning strike toward Berlin. The enthusiasm among his troops was great, and there "was no question in my mind," he later recalled, "that we could do it and do it economically with little loss."[108] After Simpson's operations officer, Col. Armistead D. Mead, had presented their

---

103 Memo, HQ, 12th Army Gp, 21 Mar 1945, sub: "Re-Orientation of Strategy," Folder "Reorientation of Strategy (The Redoubt) 21 Mar. '45," HQ, 12th Army Gp, Gen Staff, G–3 Section, Administration Br, Subject Corresp Files, 1944–45, RG 331, NACP.
104 Henke, *Amerikanische Besetzung*, 940–41; Ambrose, *Eisenhower and Berlin*, 74.
105 Drew Middleton, "Nazi Die-Hards Man Their 'National Redoubt,'" *New York Times*, 8 Apr 1945.
106 Edward N. Bedessem, *Central Europe*, U.S. Army Campaigns of World War II (Washington, DC: U.S. Army Center of Military History, 1995), 23, 26, 30.
107 Bradley, *A Soldier's Story*, 399.
108 Ltr to the editor, William H. Simpson, "The Halt at the Elbe," *New York Times*, 12 Jun 1966.

plan to Bradley, the latter called Eisenhower. "All right, Ike," Mead overheard Bradley reply to the supreme commander, "that's what I thought. I'll tell him. Goodbye." Bradley told a greatly disappointed Simpson to stand down.[109]

Contemporary press reports suggested that Roosevelt had ordered Eisenhower to refrain from capturing Berlin because of a secret wartime agreement between Stalin and the U.S. government, which supposedly had promised the city to the Soviets. This rumor originated with the muckraking journalist Drew R. Pearson.[110] It was false but added fuel to the smoldering "lost race for Berlin" fire. At the time of Simpson's proposal to take Berlin, the Americans had merely 50,000 troops along the Elbe, with very little air and logistical support. In other words, the number of expected casualties—100,000—exceeded the number of available soldiers.[111] The Soviets knew that a successful attack required overwhelming superiority in men and materiel. On 16 April, they launched their assault with 2.5 million troops.[112] It still took them more than two weeks of bitter fighting to seize the city, and they lost over 80,000 men. Aside from the likelihood of getting entangled with the attacking Red Army, the U.S. Army had neither the manpower nor the resources to conquer Berlin.

Meanwhile, as Allied forces drew closer to the Alps, intelligence reports began to paint a much more realistic picture of the National Redoubt. In early April, General Sibert noted that "very little has actually been done" to fortify the area.[113] The intelligence division at the Pentagon reported to General George C. Marshall that the "many rumors [about] the 'Alpine Redoubt' are believed to lack substance."[114] Marshall agreed with this assessment.[115] At the end of the month, SHAEF intelligence came around as well. The Redoubt, General Strong's analysts concluded, "is another 'too little too late' affair." Analysts based the new estimates of the Redoubt

---

109 MacDonald, *Last Offensive*, 399.
110 Drew Pearson, "Yanks, at Berlin Edge, Left to Please Reds," *Washington Post*, 22 Apr 1945; "Eisenhower Halted Forces at Elbe; Ninth Had Hoped to Storm Berlin," *New York Times*, 2 May 1945.
111 Ambrose, *Eisenhower and Berlin*, 943.
112 William Stivers and Donald A. Carter, *The City Becomes a Symbol. The U.S. Army in the Occupation of Berlin, 1945–1949*, U.S. Army in the Cold War (Washington, DC: U.S. Army Center of Military History, 2017), 29.
113 Rpt, Edwin L. Sibert, Annex no. 1, Weekly Intel Sum no. 34, 3 Apr 1945, Folder "T 608–1/3 Nos 33–41 27 Mar 45–22 May 45," G–2 Weekly Sums, 1/1/1945–12/31/1945, RG 498, NACP.
114 SHAEF, Weekly Intel Sum, G–2, 29 Apr 1945, SHAEF, Gen Staff, G–2 Div, Operational Intel Sub-Div, Intel Rpts 1942–1945, RG 331, NACP.
115 Msg, Gen. Marshall to Sec of War, 2 Apr 1945, sub: Probable Developments in the German Reich, Folder "Sub-Series 1944–45," Ofc of the Ch of Staff, Top-Secret Gen Corresp, 1941–1947, RG 165, NACP.

on more reliable sources, including aerial photography and signals intelligence. The assessments also may have reflected a sense that, now that the question of Berlin was settled, the Americans no longer needed to get the British on board with the new strategy. When the XXI Corps finally entered the area of the supposed redoubt in early May, they encountered little resistance and found few defensive fortifications. The corps' intelligence section concluded that the Alpine fortress "was only a concept in the minds and on the planning table of a few Nazis and high ranking officials. . . . As Voltaire might have said, it is neither a Redoubt, nor is it National."[116]

The defeat of Nazi Germany briefly ended the debate over Allied strategy in the closing months of the war, but the controversy over the "lost race for Berlin" thrived in the context of the Cold War. As West Berlin became an island engulfed in a sea of red, contemporaries wondered if perhaps the West had lost a chance at the end of the war to seize the entire city. British writers remained critical of Eisenhower's decision to forego Berlin. In their memoirs, both Churchill and Montgomery argued that, owing to Eisenhower's decision, the British and the Americans had lost an opportunity to end the war quickly and to impress upon the Soviets a sense that the Western Allies would not yield to Moscow's aggressive designs in central Europe.[117]

In West Germany, the notion of a "lost opportunity" gained traction as well. Franz Josef Strauss, a war veteran from Bavaria who served as West German defense minister under Konrad Adenauer in the late 1950s, wrote in his memoirs: "For the Americans Berlin was a pile of scrap, a worthless heap of rubble—they did not understand anything about the symbolic significance of a capital city. . . . I have never forgiven the Americans their calamitous hesitation before Berlin."[118] This was a clever piece of dissimulation. After 1945, international public opinion conceived of historical "guilt" and "forgiveness" in terms of Nazi atrocities. By linking these concepts to the Americans' supposed hesitation to capture Berlin, Strauss adroitly maneuvered the United States into the position of the morally guilty party, while Germany appeared the victim of Soviet aggression.

---

116 Rpt, XXI Corps, Annex "B" to G-2 Periodic Rpt no. 117, 10 May 1945, sub: "The National Redoubt," Folder "G-2 Journals 13–16 May 45," Historical Div, Program Files, VI Corps, G-2 Jnls, 1945, RG 498, NACP.
117 David W. Hogan Jr., "Berlin Revisited—and Revised: Eisenhower's Decision to Halt at the Elbe," in *Victory in Europe 1945: From World War to Cold War*, ed. Arnold A. Offner and Theodore A. Wilson (Lawrence: University of Kansas Press, 2000), 81–83.
118 Franz Josef Strauss, *Die Erinnerungen* [Memoirs] (Berlin: Siedler Verlag, 1989), 64.

None of these interpretations captures what actually happened. Eisenhower single-mindedly pursued a military strategy—winning the war.[119] That he could have snatched Berlin from the jaws of the Red Army, and that such an operation would have changed the course of the Cold War, is doubtful.[120] Gaming out alternative historical scenarios is always a dicey proposition, but there can be little argument that Eisenhower accomplished his mission. As General Hastings I. Ismay, Churchill's principal military adviser, aptly put it, "What might have happened is speculation. What did happen was overwhelming victory."[121]

Counterintelligence

According to a military intelligence field manual prepared at Camp Ritchie, "[c]ounterintelligence measures are designed to neutralize enemy intelligence activities."[122] This definition included operations against the German secret services and its agents as well as measures to protect Army units against enemy intelligence operations, such as espionage, sabotage, and propaganda. Most Allied and Army Intelligence branches as well as the OSS had counterintelligence sections, but the main effort rested on the shoulders of the organization specifically created for this purpose: the Counter Intelligence Corps.

The Germans operated a plethora of intelligence services. Agent operations were the responsibility of the *Abwehr* (literally, "defense") military intelligence service, the SD (intelligence service of the SS), and the *Gestapo*. By the summer of 1944, all three had come under the overall command of the *Reichssicherheitshauptamt*, the gargantuan security apparatus directed by SS leader Heinrich Himmler. In addition, the Germans had no less than nine signals intelligence organizations, both civilian and military. The German navy and air force directed their own intelligence efforts, while the *Wehrmacht* had two analytical organizations

---

119 Hogan, "Berlin Revisited," 92, 94.
120 Recent works suggesting that Eisenhower lost a massive opportunity include Antony Beevor, *The Fall of Berlin 1945* (New York: Viking, 2002), 196; and Roland Kaltenegger, *Die "Alpenfestung." Der Endkampf um das letzte Bollwerk des Zweiten Weltkrieges* [The "Alpine Fortress": The final battle for the last bulwark of the Second World War] (Würzburg: Flechs, 2015), 195–200.
121 Quoted in Minott, *Fortress*, 72.
122 Mil Intel Training Center, "Tentative Manual of Military Intelligence, U.S. Army" (Camp Ritchie, MD: War Department, n.d.), 10, Historians Files, CMH.

that produced estimates of the military situation on the eastern and western fronts, *Fremde Heere Ost* (Foreign Armies East) and *Fremde Heere West* (Foreign Armies West).[123]

By the time the Anglo-American forces crossed into the Reich, the Allied intelligence services had a good grasp of their counterpart's structure and modus operandi as well as its limitations.[124] At first glance, German intelligence appeared well-built, but constant reorganization and interpersonal rivalries hampered its efficiency. After the war, an OSS report noted that "in theory the structure [of German intelligence] was 'pyramidal' and centralised, [but] in fact the apex of the pyramid, or the centre of the circle, was not a unitary structure at all but a vortex of competing personal ambitions."[125]

German intelligence in general, and the *Gestapo* and the SS in particular, had a well-deserved reputation for ruthlessness and brutality. The intelligence branch of Supreme Allied Headquarters warned the CIC that German agents would employ devious "sabotage methods," including the "neutralization" of sentries and guards, and the use of antipersonnel bombs as well as poisoned aspirin tablets, chocolate bars, and sugar. One of the most fiendish devices, SHAEF intelligence officials asserted, was a cigarette lighter that could poison a cigarette smoker: "A small spherical pellet about one mm. in diameter of unknown chemical constitution was fixed on the cigarette lighter near the wick, so that when the wick burned, the pellet became heated and vaporized, giving off a deadly poison."[126] Expecting a hostile reception, CIC agents went "underground" by replacing their military uniforms with civilian clothes when their units entered Germany.[127]

These fears proved exaggerated. The Americans found German civilians generally docile and willing to comply with orders issued by the occupying forces. To the surprise of the CIC, local authorities were happy to work with Army counterintelligence in dealing with potential threats. Rather than battling enemy spies, CIC personnel spent much of their time screening hundreds of thousands of displaced persons, German refugees, and *Wehrmacht* soldiers for security and war crimes suspects who sought to escape Allied scrutiny.[128]

---

123 For a more detailed assessment of the Germany security apparatus, see David Kahn, *Hitler's Spies: German Military Intelligence in World War II* (New York: Macmillan, 1979).
124 Rpt, SHAEF, ACofS, G–2, CI-subdiv, 4 Oct 1944, sub: German Intelligence Services, Folder "XE 003641 German Int. Service Folder 1 of 3," INSCOM, IRR, Impersonal Name Files, RG 319, NACP.
125 Rpt, W.R.E., 1 Dec 1945, sub: The German Intelligence Service and the War, Folder "4563 W.R.E. Publications Section 1 of 3, Folder 1626," London X-2 PTS Files, RG 226, NACP.
126 Bray et al., *History of the Counter Intelligence Corps*, 20:3.
127 Bray et al., *History of the Counter Intelligence Corps*, 19:55, 19:84.
128 Bray et al., *History of the Counter Intelligence Corps*, 20:5.

The occupation dragged the CIC into operations that had little to do with counterintelligence. American troops had hardly crossed the German border when pictures appeared in the Allied press of smiling soldiers posing with German civilians, mostly women and young children. The Soviets, who had borne the brunt of the fighting against the Germans, complained to the U.S. military mission in Moscow about their allies' chumminess with the enemy. President Roosevelt, too, was furious and ordered Eisenhower to suppress fraternization between U.S. soldiers and German civilians.[129] For reasons that were all too human, however, the enforcement of nonfraternization proved difficult. Many American soldiers found the company of German women appealing, even though anyone caught fraternizing was subject to a $65 fine. Inevitably, the propositioning of a German woman became known among GIs as "the 65-dollar question."[130]

Intelligence work required dealing with locals, and so Army Intelligence officials were excluded from the nonfraternization policy.[131] Nonetheless, the CIC became involved in the fallout of the policy because the association of American soldiers with enemy civilians carried the risk of the unauthorized disclosure of information. Occasionally, the consequences of an investigation could be harsh. In the small town of Wissen in the Rhineland, CIC agents monitored a house where locals were meeting with several soldiers. After the agents overheard the soldiers reveal their unit designations, the names of their officers, and other sensitive information, they entered the house where "several soldiers were found drinking with a German family." The Germans got off with a stern warning to stay clear of U.S. soldiers, but the soldiers stood trial in a special court-martial.[132]

The CIC captured a number of genuine spies in Germany, but enemy agents generally did not pose much of a threat. Many turned themselves in to American authorities, as did a female agent in Mönchengladbach on 3 March 1945. She revealed to a member of the 29th Counter Intelligence Corps Detachment that she and four other women had trained as wireless operators and were supposed to keep in touch with the German forces from behind Allied lines. Within a few days, the CIC located and arrested the four other women. Army Intelligence used two of them to communicate disinformation to the Germans. The material was convincing enough for the *Wehrmacht* to award the two women the Iron Cross, Second Class, "for their work in furnishing much valuable information to the Ger-

---

129 Ziemke, *U.S. Army in the Occupation of Germany*, 98.
130 Ian Sayer and Douglas Botting, *America's Secret Army: The Untold Story of the Counter Intelligence Corps* (London: Fontana, 1990), 212.
131 Interv, Brewster Chamberlin with William F. Heimlich, ACofS, G–2, Berlin Cmd, 4 Aug 1981, 14, Landesarchiv Berlin.
132 Bray et al., *History of the Counter Intelligence Corps*, 20:31.

man Army and for their bravery in operations behind the American lines." Special Agent Gordon M. Anderson, who had located one of the four additional women, received the Bronze Star for his part in the investigation.[133]

Local citizens frequently assisted the CIC in their hunt for enemy agents. In the city of Neuss, agents of the 95th Counter Intelligence Corps Detachment learned in early April 1945 that the local *Gestapo* chief, before his departure, had instructed plant managers of area factories to appoint workers to commit sabotage after the arrival of the Allied forces. When interviewed, the manager of the local National Radiator Company promptly confirmed this information, adding that he had not complied with this order. He pointed the CIC to other plant managers in the area who might know the names of would-be saboteurs.[134]

At times, the mere arrival of Allied soldiers ended potential security threats. "A pleasing number of small fry Nazis have committed suicide after their districts had been overrun," reported General Strong in May 1945.[135] In some cases, the fry were not so small. At the end of the war, a special agent of the 89th Counter Intelligence Corps Detachment located the whereabouts of Martin H. Hammitzsch, the brother-in-law of Adolf Hitler. Rather than fall into American hands, Hammitzsch took his own life by shooting himself in the temple.[136]

Despite its name, counterintelligence was not a purely reactive discipline. In early 1945, CIC agent Capt. Ernest Sidney Baker of the intelligence branch of the 12th Army Group devised a plan to destroy German intelligence centers through aerial bombing. The Corps named the operation GISBOMB, after the American acronym for the German intelligence services. After assembling information on several targets, Baker submitted them to the XIX Tactical Air Command of the Ninth Army. In due course, Army Air Forces bombers destroyed several enemy radio schools and local intelligence headquarters buildings. After bombing Kloster Tiefenthal, a monastery that had been turned into a sabotage training center, the returning pilots reported "a formidable explosion, with smoke rising to 4,000 feet." Presumably, they had hit a depot storing sabotage materiel. The official report on GISBOMB stated that the operation "hit the enemy hard," and that the Germans would find it difficult to replace the lost personnel and facilities.[137]

---

133 Bray et al., *History of the Counter Intelligence Corps*, 19:43–46.
134 Bray et al., *History of the Counter Intelligence Corps*, 20:35.
135 Political Intel Rpt, Gen Strong, SHAEF, 15 May 1945, sub: Germany, General Security, Folder "ABC 381 Germany (29 Jan 1943) Sec 1-B," American-British Corresp Relating to Planning and Combat Opns, 1940–1948, RG 165, NACP.
136 Bray et al., *History of the Counter Intelligence Corps*, 20:133. Hammitzsch was married to Hitler's older half-sister Angela.
137 Bray et al., *History of the Counter Intelligence Corps*, 18:71–72.

Nonetheless, the Army had serious counterintelligence deficiencies. One of the most significant American security breaches in Europe occurred in early February 1945, when soldiers of the 28th Infantry Division in northern France turned in to their billets for the night. Against regulations, they left their truck, which was loaded with several safes containing classified material and a SIGABA ciphering machine, without a guard by the roadside. The U.S. equivalent to the German Enigma, the SIGABA machine was used by the Army and Navy for enciphering and deciphering communications. While the soldiers were sleeping, a thief stole the unguarded truck. When news of the missing SIGABA reached Washington, the Army had to change ciphers throughout the theater, and the CIC, under Col. David G. Erskine of 6th Army Group, started an all-encompassing investigation that lasted forty-four days. Eventually, they found the thief, who had been interested only in the truck, dumping the safes with the SIGABA in a river, where CIC agents later recovered them. Colonel Erskine received a Bronze Star for his part in the investigation, but the truck driver, the signal officer, and several others were court-martialed for dereliction of duty.[138]

The SIGABA caper was not an isolated incident. In early April 1945, German soldiers captured Col. Robert S. Allen, an officer on the intelligence staff of the Third Army, near Gotha in central Germany after his driver had taken a wrong turn. Allen remained in captivity for less than a week before the Americans liberated him.[139] Because Allen had been briefed on ULTRA, his capture was a highly sensitive matter.[140] Allen did not betray the secret to the Germans, but the possibility of such a breach nevertheless was real, and proper counterintelligence procedures should have kept him from venturing so close to enemy lines in the first place. In addition, Allen—who before the war had been a journalist and coauthor of Drew Pearson's syndicated "Washington Merry-Go-Round" column—had briefly been a paid Soviet agent in the early 1930s.[141] By the time the war started, Allen and the Soviets had long parted ways, but the fact remains that an Army officer inducted into one of the most sensitive Allied intelligence secrets had occasion to betray it to the Germans and the Soviets.

Although the Allies restricted ULTRA to a small circle of officials, security was not watertight. Lt. Col. Adolph G. Rosengarten, the First Army's special security

---

138 Bray et al., *History of the Counter Intelligence Corps*, 19:3–5; Interv, G. E. Patrick Murray, with Col. Benjamin A. Dickson, former G-2, First Army, 22 Sep 1972, Historians Files, CMH.
139 Koch, *G–2*, 125–32.
140 Thomas Parrish, *The Ultra Americans: The U.S. Role in Breaking the Nazi Code* (New York: Stein and Day, 1986), 275.
141 John Earl Haynes, Harvey Klehr, and Alexander Vassiliev, *Spies: The Rise and Fall of the KGB in America* (New Haven, CT: Yale University Press, 2009), 159–60.

officer who received ULTRA decrypts from Bletchley Park, remarked on the undue speculation at First Army headquarters about the precise nature of his job. He also accused the intelligence chief of the First Army, Colonel Dickson, of leaking information to the journalist Drew Pearson. Although Pearson did not give away any sensitive information, he commented repeatedly on the "stupidity" of Dickson's rival, General Sibert.[142] Because of the rumor mill and the interpersonal rivalries at First Army headquarters, Rosengarten noted, the "security of Ultra was not good" and "the secret got out." How exactly this occurred, he added coyly, "I do not know for certain, and my suspicions are not worth recording, as they are unquestionably founded on personal prejudice."[143] Fortunately for the Allies, the press never picked up on these rumors, and ULTRA remained secret for several decades after the war.

Army Intelligence and the Allies

"There is only one thing worse than fighting with allies and that is fighting without them," Winston Churchill once quipped.[144] France was a case in point. Many U.S. officials considered the Free French government a junior partner who contributed little to the war effort while strenuously asserting its national interests. President Roosevelt referred to the mercurial leader of the Free French, General Charles de Gaulle, as a "prima donna," and an OSS report bemoaned the Frenchman's "messianic complex and his intolerance toward those who do not agree with him."[145] While fighting under Allied command, French forces repeatedly ignored Eisenhower's orders, choosing instead to pursue national objectives. As one Army Intelligence officer recalled, General Hodges of the First Army issued a specific order to General Philippe Leclerc of the 2e Division Blindée, only to find that Leclerc then "did just what he was told not to do."[146] On several occasions,

---

142 Interv, F. C. Pogue with Adolph Rosengarten, 22 Dec 1947, Historians Files, CMH.
143 Memo, Lt. Col. Adolph Rosengarten, for Col. Telford Taylor, 21 May 1945, sub: Report on Ultra Intelligence at First U.S. Army, Historians Files, CMH.
144 Alex Danchev and Daniel Todman, eds., *Field Marshal Lord Alanbrooke: War Diaries 1939–1945* (Berkeley: University of California Press, 1957), 680.
145 Charles Williams, *The Last Great Frenchman: A Life of General de Gaulle* (New York: John Wiley & Sons, 2003), 197–98, 230; OSS Interoffice Memo, R. K. Gooch for Mr. Wilmarth Lewis, 4 Mar 1943, sub: attachment, Folder "X8197656 Charles de Gaulle," INSCOM, IRR, Personal Name Files, 1939–1976, RG 319, NACP.
146 Interv, Dickson with Pogue, 22 Dec 1947.

Eisenhower threatened to withdraw Allied logistical support from the French forces to get them back in line.[147]

Intelligence mirrored this antagonism. The Americans and the British never shared ULTRA with the French. As the Allies crossed the borders of the Third Reich, American and French intelligence often competed rather than collaborated with each other. At the end of the war, a pastor in Austria informed soldiers of the 307th Counter Intelligence Corps Detachment that the Germans had hidden two caches of gold bullion nearby. The area was then under French control. Yet rather than cooperate with the French, the CIC devised a plan to snatch the booty from under their unsuspecting allies' noses. The Germans had cached some of the gold bullion in the cellar of a house occupied by members of the French Women's Army Corps. Mustering all of his authority, CIC Special Agent Victor de Guinzbourg entered the house and ordered the women to leave. Having disposed of their allies, the Americans retrieved the gold, hoisted it into the waiting trucks, and sped to the U.S. Zone. The CIC turned almost eight tons of gold over to the finance officer of the Seventh Army.[148]

By contrast, Anglo-American intelligence coordination proved easy. The two countries shared not only an integrated military command, SHAEF, but also regularly exchanged large volumes of signals, military, and counterintelligence information. Frictions arose occasionally over the appropriate sharing of captured enemy materiel and Britain's initial reluctance to trust the Americans with the ULTRA secret.[149] Also, the upper-class attitude of some British officers occasionally rubbed American intelligence personnel the wrong way.[150] But such minor irritations hardly clouded the bigger picture of a close, cordial, and productive intelligence relationship between the two nations.

In the field, the Anglo-American partnership was uncomplicated, as the case of American journalist Robert Henry Best illustrates. Best reported from Vienna on central European affairs for United Press in the 1920s and 1930s. He gradually became an admirer of Hitler and during the war worked as an English-language broadcaster for the Nazis. In 1943, the United States indicted him for treason. Three years later, British forces arrested him in Austria. Best figured prominently

---

147 Pogue, *Supreme Command*, 459–61; Dwight D. Eisenhower, *Crusade in Europe: A Personal Account of World War II* (New York: Doubleday, 1948), 362–63, 413.
148 Bray et al., *History of the Counter Intelligence Corps*, 20:93–94.
149 R. V. Jones, "Anglo-American Cooperation in the Wizard War," in *In the Name of Intelligence: Essays in Honor of Walter Pforzheimer*, ed. Hayden B. Peake and Samuel Halpern (Washington, DC: NIBC Press, 1994), 309–10.
150 Benjamin A. Dickson, "Memoirs of World War II" (unpublished manuscript, n.d.), 180–81, Historians Files, CMH; Interv, Murray with Dickson, 22 Sep 1972.

on the CIC's wanted list, and at the request of the Americans, the British promptly handed him over to the U.S. Army. In 1948, a federal court in Boston sentenced him to life imprisonment, where he died in 1952.[151]

In contrast to their smooth cooperation with the British, Army Intelligence struggled to liaise closely with the Soviets. In this, intelligence reflected the complexity of the relationship between the two countries. Before the war, many Americans despised the Soviet totalitarian system and its goal of world revolution. This gloomy view improved during the war. President Roosevelt then included the Soviet Union in a "lend-lease" program, which provided large amounts of materiel to the Red Army without asking for anything in return. The liberal W. Averell Harriman, a close confident of Roosevelt's who had helped coordinate the lend-lease agreement with Moscow, became ambassador to the Soviet Union in October 1943. The War Department in 1943 also replaced the office of the military attaché, headed at the time by the anti-Soviet Col. Ivan D. Yeaton, with a military mission. The secretary of war explicitly instructed the new appointee, Maj. Gen. John R. Deane, not to engage in espionage, but rather to exchange information openly and "promote the closest possible coordination" of U.S. and Soviet military efforts.[152]

Deane embraced his mission. Flooded with requests for information on the Soviet Union by U.S. intelligence agencies, Deane promptly forwarded all inquiries to his contact at the Red Army staff, Maj. Gen. Nikolai V. Slavin, who "could answer them or not, as he liked."[153] Working patiently with the Soviets, Deane's office accomplished several of its goals, including the signing of an agreement to exchange meteorological data. The mission also obtained information from the Soviets on the Japanese and German armies' order of battle, as well as on demolition techniques employed by the retreating *Wehrmacht* and German preparations for chemical warfare. This type of intelligence was not of the same scope and caliber as that routinely provided by the British. Still, the chief of Army Intelligence, General Bissell, considered it "very helpful."[154]

---

[151] Msg, Col. L. R. Forney, Intel Div, War Dept, to CG, U.S. Army Forces, Austria, 10 Nov 1947, Folder "Best, Robert Henry XE003721," INSCOM, IRR, Digitized Name Files, RG 319, NACP; "United States v. Best," *The American Journal of International Law* 42, no. 3 (Jul 1948): 727–29; "R. H. Best, Traitor, Dies in Felon Ward," *New York Times*, 21 Dec 1952.
[152] John R. Deane, *The Strange Alliance: The Story of Our Efforts at Wartime Co-Operation with Russia* (New York: Viking, 1947), 49; Bradley F. Smith, *Sharing Secrets with Stalin: How the Allies Traded Intelligence, 1941–1945* (Lawrence: University Press of Kansas, 1997), 167.
[153] Deane, *Strange Alliance*, 83.
[154] Smith, *Sharing Secrets with Stalin*, 127, 148, 172, 189, 191.

Yet the military mission obtained most of this intelligence only after much haggling with their hosts. Deane complained to General Marshall that Moscow's concessions stood in no proportion to the value of the vast quantities of U.S. materiel provided to the Soviets.[155] Constant harassment, refusals to cooperate, and penetration efforts by the Soviet security service wore down the mission. The Soviets barred the Moscow-based American officers from visiting the battlefront and concealed the planning of major military operations from them.[156] Whenever a dispute upset U.S.-Soviet relations, the mission felt the repercussions: "When it was 'Kick-Americans-in-the-pants' week," Deane recalled, "even the charwoman would be sour."[157]

The Soviet security service spied on the mission through listening devices, local personnel, and the occasional honey trap. As Brig. Gen. Frank N. Roberts, Deane's deputy, remembered, he often received phone calls "by ladies of the evening." Roberts was certain the Soviet security service had engineered these calls. "A saccharine voice would say, when I answered, 'Are you lonely?' This always amused me, for it was so patently a come-on. I would reply, 'No, I'm not lonely.' 'Oh, but you must be lonely,' wouldn't you like to have company?"[158] Roberts claims that the approach never worked with him, but the Soviet femmes fatales may have had better luck in other cases. Military attaché Colonel Yeaton worried about his assistant, Col. (later Brig. Gen.) Joseph A. "Mike" Michela, who was living with his Russian girlfriend. Yeaton also considered the officer in charge of lend-lease, Col. Philip R. Faymonville, "a captive of the NKVD [Soviet security]."[159]

The mission's concerns about Soviet espionage were well founded. Army signals intelligence had intermittently intercepted Soviet diplomatic traffic since the 1930s. In early 1943, the Military Intelligence Service established a small, compartmented program to decrypt the accumulated Soviet messages.[160] After the war, Army cryptanalysts managed to break some of the encrypts (Project VENONA). The

---

155 Msg., Maj. Gen. John R. Deane to Army Ch of Staff, Gen George C. Marshall, 2 Dec 1944, Folder "ABC 336 Russia Sec 1-A," American-British Conversations Corresp Relating to Planning and Combat Opns, 1940–1948, RG 165, NACP.
156 Smith, *Sharing Secrets with Stalin*, 160.
157 Deane, *Strange Alliance*, 97.
158 Frank N. Roberts, unpublished memoirs manuscript, n.d., 144, 145, 157–58, Folder "Memoirs," Frank N. Roberts Papers, Harry S. Truman Presidential Library, Independence, MO (hereinafter Truman Library).
159 Donal O'Sullivan, *Dealing with the Devil: Anglo-Soviet Intelligence Cooperation in the Second World War* (New York: Peter Lang, 2010), 61.
160 Robert L. Benson and Michael Warner, eds., *Venona: Soviet Espionage and the American Response, 1939–1957* (Washington, DC: Central Intelligence Agency, 1996), xiii.

messages originated with Soviet intelligence and revealed that Moscow had systematically recruited spies in every major branch of the U.S. government, in the OSS, and in the Manhattan Project, the Army's secret program to develop an atomic bomb.[161]

The constant surveillance, pervasive secrecy, and lack of cooperation dispirited Deane. In frustration, he wrote to General Marshall: "I have sat at innumerable Russian banquets and become gradually nauseated by Russian food, vodka, and protestations of friendship. Each person high in public life proposes a toast a little sweeter than the preceding one on Soviet-British-American friendship. It is amazing how these toasts go down past the tongues in the cheeks. After the banquets we send the Soviets another thousand airplanes, and they approve a visa that has been hanging for fire for months. We then scratch our heads to see what other gifts we can send, and they scratch theirs to see what else they can ask for."[162] He would not be the last Army officer to complain about the Soviets.

In the European Theater, distrust between the Western Allies and the Soviets prevented close intelligence cooperation. As Anglo-American forces fought their way up the Italian peninsula, the Americans refrained from sending supplies to communist resistance groups.[163] When Dulles brokered the surrender of German forces in northern Italy in the spring of 1945, known as Operation SUNRISE, Stalin immediately suspected collusion between the Americans and the Germans.[164] Meanwhile, with the end of the war, communist parties reemerged across Western Europe, and U.S. intelligence grew concerned about the Soviets using them "as instruments of national policy."[165] The CIC spoke of "Moscow's other war," and suspected communist parties in newly liberated countries of seeking to overthrow, and replace the newly reinstated governments with regimes loyal to Moscow.[166]

---

161 Robert L. Benson, *The Venona Story* (Fort Meade, MD: Center for Cryptologic History, National Security Agency, 2001); Christopher Andrew and Vasili Mitrokhin, *The Sword and the Shield: The Mitrokhin Archive and the Secret History of the KGB* (New York: Basic Books, 1999), 111, 118.
162 J Msg, Deane to Marshall, 2 Dec 1944.
163 James V. Milano and Patrick Brogan, *Soldiers, Spies, and the Rat Line: America's Undeclared War Against the Soviets* (Washington, DC: Brassey's, 1995), 25.
164 Stephen P. Halbrook, "Operation Sunrise: America's OSS, Swiss Intelligence, and the German Surrender 1945," in *"Operation Sunrise." Atti del convegno internazionale, Locarno, 2 maggio 2005* ["Operation Sunrise": Proceedings of the international conference, Locarno, 2 May 2005], ed. Marino Viganò and Dominic M. Pedrazzini (Lugano: No publisher, 2006), 103–30.
165 Memo, Joint Intel Committee, 18 Jan 1945, sub: Estimate of Soviet Post-War Capabilities and Intentions, Folder "ABC 336 Russia Sec 1-A," ABC Series, RG 165, NACP.
166 Bray et al., *History of the Counter Intelligence Corps*, 19:25.

Figure 8: A photograph, taken by Colonel Szymanski, of emaciated Polish evacuees from the Soviet Union. U.S. Army, NACP.

Soviet actions did little to alleviate such fears. Shortly after the German invasion of Poland in 1939, the Red Army had occupied the eastern parts of the country in accordance with a secret understanding between Moscow and Berlin. In 1941, a mass grave discovered by German forces near the Katyn Forest indicated that the Soviets had killed over 20,000 Polish officers and intellectuals in a series of nightly executions. A year later, Lt. Col. Henry I. Szymanski, a U.S. Army officer attached to evacuated Polish forces in Iran, informed the Military Intelligence Division that large numbers of Polish officers had disappeared from Soviet prisoner-of-war camps. He included photographs of malnourished Polish prisoners in the Soviet Union, pictures that eerily resembled the images of emaciated Holocaust survivors that would proliferate at the end of the war.[167] The head of the

---

[167] Rpt, Lt. Col. Henry I. Szymanski to MID, 22 Nov 1945, sub: Polish-Russian Relations, Folder "(3–17–42)," G–2 Project Decimal Files, 1941–1945 (MID), RG 319, NACP.

Eastern Europe Section of the Military Intelligence Division, Colonel Yeaton, believed that Szymanski's material provided ample proof of Soviet crimes and apprised General Strong, the director of the division. Strong, too, took the reports seriously, but the Roosevelt administration chose to do nothing about them for fear of irritating Stalin.[168] At the end of the war, when the Red Army liberated Poland from the Nazis, Stalin ignored the legitimate Polish exile government in London. Instead, a Soviet-controlled Polish Committee of National Liberation (Polski Komitet Wyzwolenia Narodowego), based out of the recently liberated city of Lublin, proclaimed a provisional government in July 1944.

With regard to possible Soviet designs for postwar Germany, the Soviet-backed National Committee for a Free Germany (Nationalkomitee Freies Deutschland) drew particular attention from Army Intelligence. The Soviets had established the National Committee in 1943 and recruited its members from among German prisoners of war. The committee produced propaganda against the Third Reich and exhorted *Wehrmacht* soldiers on the eastern front to desert. In the summer of 1943, the OSS suspected Moscow of using the committee for secret negotiations with Berlin.[169] At the request of Assistant Secretary of War John J. McCloy, the Military Intelligence Division issued periodic reports on the committee's activities.[170] The division noted that the committee's leadership included communist as well as non-communist members, and concluded this mix would broaden its appeal in Germany. Moscow thus had at its disposal not only a powerful propaganda weapon, the division argued, "but the nucleus of a new German government capable of taking over the Russian occupied zone or of all of Germany."[171]

One of the most censorious Army Intelligence analysts was General Michela, the military attaché to Moscow from 1941. The American embassy viewed Michela

---

168 George Sanford, *Katyn and the Soviet Massacre of 1940: Truth, Justice and Memory* (London: Routledge, 2005), 161.

169 Heike Bungert, "Ein meisterhafter Schachzug: das Nationalkomitee Freies Deutschland in der Beurteilung der Amerikaner, 1943–1945" [A masterful maneuver: The National Committee for a Free Germany in the judgment of the Americans, 1943–1945], in *Geheimdienstkrieg gegen Deutschland: Subversion, Propaganda und politische Planungen des amerikanischen Geheimdienstes im Zweiten Weltkrieg* [The intelligence war against Germany: Subversion, propaganda, and political planning by American intelligence in World War II], ed. Jürgen Heideking and Christof Mauch (Göttingen: Vandenhoeck & Ruprecht, 1993), 94.

170 Memo, Brig. Gen. John Weckerling, MID, to Asst Sec of War, 30 Dec 1944, sub: Free German Committee (Moscow), Folder "ASW 380.8 Free Germany Committee," Formerly Security Classified Corresp of John J. McCloy, 1941–45, RG 107, NACP.

171 Memo, Brig. Gen. John Weckerling, MID, to Asst Sec of War, 18 Nov 1944, sub: Free Germany Committee (Moscow), Folder "ASW 380.8 Free Germany Committee," Formerly Security Classified Corresp of John J. McCloy, 1941–45, RG 107, NACP.

as too anti-Soviet and successfully lobbied to recall him to Washington in 1943.[172] There, he became a leading expert on Soviet affairs for the Military Intelligence Division. If Soviet intelligence had sought to influence him through his Russian girlfriend, as Colonel Yeaton had feared, they evidently failed. In the spring of 1945, he submitted a lengthy memorandum on "The Military Implications in Future U.S.-Soviet Relations" to General Bissell, the assistant chief of staff for intelligence. In it, Michela warned that the Soviet Union intended to keep control of the eastern European countries liberated by the Red Army. Moscow's ultimate goal, Michela wrote, was "to make the USSR the greatest military, air, naval, economic and political power in the world. 'POWER' is the keystone of Soviet policy and 'POWER' is the only god their leaders respect." The Soviet leadership, Michela asserted, "is cunning, but primitive in its thinking and . . . affected by an inferiority complex that has been practically national in scope. . . . Power in such hands is not conducive to world cooperation." Michela advised a policy of patient pushback. If one dealt with the Soviets, he counseled, one had to do so "always with FIRMNESS."[173]

Michela's wording may have been crude, but many military intelligence officials shared his skepticism about the long-term viability of the Grand Alliance. The Joint Intelligence Committee identified two factors that would drive Soviet foreign policy in the postwar era. On the one hand, it would take the Soviets several years, possibly until 1952, to recover from the war, and the need to rebuild their shattered country would temper a confrontational policy toward the West. On the other hand, a Marxist belief in an existential conflict between communist and capitalist states would inform all aspects of Soviet foreign policy. In concrete terms, Moscow would seek to create a large sphere of influence, or security zone, to its west, with the establishment of pro-Soviet regimes in eastern Europe, and the strengthening of communist parties and popular fronts in countries beyond the reach of the Red Army. Soviet methods to accomplish these goals "are likely to seem repugnant and aggressive to governments not under Soviet influence."[174]

---

172 Bert Andrews, "Faymonville Recall From Soviet [sic] Stirs Talk of Political Intrigue," *Washington Post*, 18 Nov 1943.
173 Memo, Col. Joseph A. Michela for G-2, 25 Apr 1945, sub: Additional Comments on Attached Memorandum, Folder "092. U.S.S.R. 1 Jan 44 thru," Project Decimal Files, 1941–1945 (MID), RG 319, NACP.
174 Memo, Joint Intel Committee, 18 Jan 1945, sub: Estimate of Soviet Post-War Capabilities and Intentions. To contain Soviet expansionism, the OSS had even discussed the possibility of turning Nazi Germany against the Soviet Union; see Joint Ch of Staff Memo for Info no. 121, 22 Aug 1943, sub: Strategy and Policy: Can America and Russia cooperate?, Folder "ABC 336 Russia Sec 1-A," ABC Series, RG 165, NACP. The paper's author was Gerard T. Robinson, professor of history at Columbia University, and the OSS's principal Soviet expert.

In Germany, the "most critical area" of postwar competition between Moscow and the West, the Soviets would face a number of possible choices. They could pursue a policy of balancing influence with the Western powers, of predominant Soviet influence over all of Germany, of permanent partition, or the "most unlikely" option of accepting Western dominance. In all probability, the memorandum suggested, Moscow would seek to gain influence in Germany by supporting the local communist party, and by using war crimes trials and denazification as a means to remove pro-Western officials. "In a very real sense," the Joint Intelligence Committee noted more than three months before Germany's surrender, this inimical "'postwar' foreign policy of the U.S.S.R. is already in effect."[175] The committee's assessment did not bode well for the joint Allied occupation of Germany.

Conclusion

Army Intelligence faced a steep learning curve during the war. Relegated to a backwater before 1941, intelligence experienced a dramatic overhaul and expansion after Pearl Harbor. By the time American forces reached Germany, the Army had transformed its intelligence apparatus into a large organization that emphasized all-source collection, quick processing, and wide dissemination. This system proved efficient in providing commanders with a steady stream of tactical information on the enemy. However, the sheer amount of raw intelligence produced by the various agencies, and the pressure to analyze this material quickly, occasionally obscured a clear view of the enemy.

Counterintelligence posed a particular challenge. The Army was by nature a large and highly visible organization. Yet security can be maintained best by small units operating covertly. The CIC had little trouble dealing with the German intelligence service, but this success can only partly be ascribed to American counterintelligence. The Germans had always directed their main intelligence efforts at the Soviets, and by the time the Allies entered the Reich, German intelligence was a spent force. The Americans were fortunate that the Germans did not take advantage of the obvious security breaches among U.S. forces.

---

175 Memo, Joint Intel Committee, 31 Jan 1945, sub: Estimate of Soviet Post-War Capabilities and Intentions, Folder "ABC 336 RUSSIA Sec 1-A," ABC Series, RG 165, NACP.

Figure 9: Officers of the 29th Infantry Division propose a toast to the defeat of Germany during a dinner party in the home of Nazi propaganda minister Joseph Goebbels in Mönchengladbach. U.S. Army, NACP.

Ominously, Army Intelligence assessments of the Soviets and of the reemerging communist parties at the end of the war pointed to future challenges. Contrary to the expectations and hopes of many, the Allied victory marked the beginning, not the end, of a sustained American involvement in Germany. The occupation of the defeated Reich would test American intelligence in far different ways than the war had.

Part II: **Intelligence Organization in Occupied Germany**

3 Intelligence Headquarters

On 8 May 1945, Nazi Germany surrendered unconditionally to the Allied forces. Two months later, President Franklin D. Roosevelt's successor, Harry S. Truman, met with the leaders of Great Britain and the Soviet Union, Winston Churchill and Joseph Stalin, to discuss the future of the defeated enemy. The "Big Three," as the press dubbed them, agreed to convene a conference in Potsdam, a town outside war-ravaged Berlin. As the president and his delegation set sail for Europe, intelligence officials of the U.S. Army worked quietly in the background to ensure that Washington's leaders had everything they needed to make TERMINAL, the Allied code name for the meeting, a success.[1]

On 22 June, Maj. Gen. Floyd L. Parks arrived at Tempelhof airport in Berlin with an advance party to prepare for the conference. His delegation included three officers and two special agents of the U.S. Army's Counter Intelligence Corps, which had been charged with the security of the American delegation. The CIC officials set up checkpoints, established a guard system, and negotiated conference participant screening procedures with the British and the Soviets.[2] They also managed to "snoop around" Soviet-occupied Berlin, despite the Red Army's efforts to control the Americans' movements in the city. Here, they glimpsed the grim reality of the Soviet occupation. "Russian soldiers looting homes and shops and loading women into trucks," the official CIC history records, "were a common sight."[3] Reports on depredations in Berlin considerably dampened sympathies for the Soviets among the American delegation.[4]

American signals intelligence was busy as well. A little over a week after General Parks arrived in Berlin, a unit of the Army's Signal Corps entered the city to set up secure communications for the American delegation. Over the next days, the soldiers installed about five hundred telephones, 70 miles of cables, and a central switchboard for the president's party.[5] Meanwhile, members of the Army's

---

[1] Michael Neiberg, *Potsdam: The End of World War II and the Remaking of Europe* (New York: Basic Books, 2015), 102.
[2] Msg, Maj. Thomas A. Gagan, 970/13 CIC Detachment, Berlin District, to ACoS, G–2, HQ Berlin District, 30 Jun 1945, sub: CIC Office and Billets, Folder "Screening and Security Surveys, Potsdam Conference D248977," INSCOM, IRR, Digitized Name Files, RG 319, NACP.
[3] Maj. Ann Bray et al., ed., *The History of the Counter Intelligence Corps*, vol. 26, *German Occupation* (Fort Holabird, MD: U.S. Army Intelligence Center, 1959), 105.
[4] Carolyn Eisenberg, *Drawing the Line: The American Decision to Divide Germany, 1944–1949* (Cambridge, UK: Cambridge University Press, 1996), 80.
[5] George R. Thompson and Dixie R. Harris, *The Signal Corps: The Outcome*, United States Army in World War II (Washington, DC: U.S. Army Center of Military History, 1991), 591.

Signal Security Agency tapped the transcontinental cables running through Berlin and carrying the messages of America's allies. By intercepting and decrypting these communications during the conference, the Army's signals intelligence specialists provided the U.S. delegation with directives, secret negotiations, and sub-rosa agreements of their Allied negotiating partners.[6]

The Potsdam Conference foreshadowed the mission of Army Intelligence in occupied Germany.[7] Even as the U.S. leadership devised policies and negotiated with the Allies, the military's secret warriors operated quietly behind the scenes to ensure the smooth implementation of these policies and to procure the information commanders needed to run the occupation. If the American military government constituted the overt aspect of the military occupation, Army Intelligence served as its indispensable covert counterpart and support.

The American Occupation of Germany

The Allies envisioned a harsh peace. At Potsdam, the Americans and British conceded to Stalin the loss of one-third of German territory. Most of the ceded land came under Polish administration; the exception was East Prussia, a separate German province on the Baltic Coast, which the Soviet Union annexed outright. The "Big Three" also agreed to implement a set of policies for Germany that the Allied leaders had drafted previously at Yalta in February 1945. These policies became known as "the four D's": the denazification, democratization, demilitarization, and decartelization of German society and industry. The American occupation would be guided by Joint Chiefs of Staff Directive 1067, issued in the spring of 1945. JCS 1067 stated as a basic U.S. objective that it "should be brought home to the Germans that Germany's ruthless warfare and the fanatical Nazi resistance have destroyed the German economy and made chaos and suffering inevitable and that the Germans cannot escape responsibility for what they have brought upon themselves."[8]

---

6 ASA, "Post War Transition Period. The Army Security Agency 1945–1948" (Washington, DC: ASA, 1952), 23–24, National Security Agency, Fort Meade, MD.

7 The U.S. military occupation of Germany lasted from 1944 to 1949. The Office of Military Government, United States (OMGUS) in Germany existed from 1945 to 1949. The occupation continued for several years after 1949 under a civilian high commissioner.

8 For the genesis of Joint Chiefs of Staff (JCS) Directive 1067, see Earl F. Ziemke, *The U.S. Army in the Occupation of Germany, 1944–1946*, Army Historical Series (Washington, DC: U.S. Army Center of Military History, 1975), 98–106.

The three Allies planned to govern Germany jointly yet occupy the country separately. They established an Allied Control Council, headquartered in Berlin, to make key decisions pertaining to all of Germany. Initially, they divided the defeated nation into three separate occupation zones. At the insistence of General Charles de Gaulle, the Americans and the British ceded some of their territory to the French, creating a fourth occupation zone in southwest Germany.[9] According to a contemporary adage, the Russians, who occupied the largely agrarian eastern portions of the former Reich, received the corn; the British, who administered the industrialized and heavily bombed north, received the ruins; the French, who oversaw the bucolic southwest, received the wine; and the Americans, who took charge of the picturesque south, received the scenery.[10] The Allies divided Berlin into four sectors, and the Americans additionally obtained the seaport city of Bremen, in the British Zone, providing them with access to the North Sea (Map 1).

The U.S. Army served as Washington's executive agency in the occupied territories, and its administrative structure evolved along two distinct chains of command: one for military government purposes and the other for the tactical forces. The Army's tactical organization developed out of its wartime structure. In July 1945, the Americans and the British broke up their joint supreme command. The American personnel of the command joined with the 12th Army Group and the Army's European Theater headquarters to form the United States Forces in the European Theater under General Dwight D. Eisenhower.[11] The European Theater organization was responsible for the logistics, training, and administration of American forces in Europe. In the immediate postwar era, the tactical forces also carried out occupation duties through their civil affairs (G–5) sections and military government detachments. The Third Army under General George S. Patton Jr. administered the Eastern Military District, comprising Bavaria, while the Seventh Army under Lt. Gen. Wade H. Haislip occupied the Western Military District, including the territories to the west of Bavaria and the port of Bremen.

The European Theater set up headquarters in the IG Farbenindustrie (or IG Farben) building in Frankfurt am Main. A futuristic-looking, 1,000-room complex with more than 10,000 windows, the building became popular with occupation forces for its size and comfort, and soldiers fondly called it "The Westchester Bilt-

---

9 Ziemke, *U.S. Army in the Occupation of Germany*, 307–08.
10 Ian Sayer and Douglas Botting, *America's Secret Army. The Untold Story of the Counter Intelligence Corps* (London: Fontana, 1990), 271.
11 Ziemke, *U.S. Army in the Occupation of Germany*, 317. The 21st Army Group became the British Army of the Rhine, assuming control of the British Zone.

more of Germany."[12] It survived the war largely undamaged, which gave rise to the rumor that Allied bombers had spared it intentionally because of its potential as the seat of Allied authorities after the war.[13] Thanks to the Army's choice of Frankfurt as its headquarters, the city developed into the nerve center of the U.S. occupation. Amid the ruins, the American compound around the IG Farben building quickly took on a boomtown appearance, teeming with tens of thousands of military and civilian personnel working for numerous Allied and international agencies.[14]

Figure 10: The IG Farben building in Frankfurt, U.S. Army headquarters in Europe. U.S. Army.

The administrative organization of the tactical forces had a long history, but the Army's military government branch was still in the making. In August 1944, the Joint Chiefs of Staff had authorized General Eisenhower to establish the U.S. Group

---

12 Julian Bach, *America's Germany: An Account of the Occupation* (New York: Random House, 1947), 51.
13 Joachim von Elbe, *Witness to History: A Refugee from the Third Reich Remembers* (Madison: University of Wisconsin Press, 1988), 281.
14 Forrest C. Pogue, *The Supreme Command*, United States Army in World War II (Washington, DC: U.S. Army Center of Military History, 1954), 513.

Control Council, Germany, for military government purposes, and in April 1945, Lt. Gen. Lucius D. Clay assumed command of the council as deputy military governor. In the summer of 1945, Clay and his staff joined the European Theater headquarters in Frankfurt, but eventually they moved on to Berlin. There, they set up headquarters at a 546-room German court building in the Schöneberg district of Berlin, the site where Nazi judge Roland Freisler had sentenced the leaders of the 1944 conspiracy against Adolf Hitler to death.[15] A raid by the U.S. Army Air Forces in February 1945 had damaged the complex and killed Freisler, but the main building remained intact. On 29 September 1945, the Group Control Council became the Office of Military Government, United States (OMGUS).

The military government was responsible for all nonmilitary aspects of the occupation, including policy coordination with the Allies, the supervision of local politics, reparations, and the economic recovery of Germany. It took the organization several months to become fully operational. In the summer of 1945, only one military government detachment under Col. Frank L. Howley in Berlin reported directly to Clay. Within a few months of the end of the war, however, military government assumed its proper functions. Clay organized the U.S. Zone into the three *Länder* (states) of Greater Hesse, Württemberg-Baden, and Bavaria. The military government set up offices in each *Land* and in Bremen, and Howley remained in charge of American military government affairs in Berlin. This administrative structure endured until 1949.

The tactical forces and military government organizations merged only at the very top echelon of command in the European Theater. General Eisenhower and his successor, General Joseph T. McNarney, served as theater commanders as well as military governors. De facto, both Eisenhower and McNarney principally acted as military commanders and left military government affairs to the deputy military governor, General Clay.

Over time, Clay assumed command of all Army affairs in Germany. On 15 March 1947, the War Department reorganized the European Theater as the European Command and McNarney left for Washington. Clay, promoted to full general, replaced McNarney as military governor in Germany and as commander in chief of all American forces in Europe. He remained at military government headquarters in Berlin, and Maj. Gen. George P. Hays served as his deputy military governor. The European Command retained the IG Farben building in Frankfurt, but its headquarters and the bulk of its personnel moved to Heidelberg into the Großdeutschland Kaserne, a for-

---

15 Lucius D. Clay, *Decision in Germany* (Garden City, NY: Doubleday, 1950), 35; Christoph Weisz, *OMGUS-Handbuch: Die amerikanische Militärregierung in Deutschland 1945–1949* [OMGUS handbook: The American military government in Germany, 1945–1949] (Oldenbourg: De Gruyter, 1995), 15–18.

mer German military installation. The Americans renamed it Campbell Barracks, after S. Sgt. Charles L. Campbell, a U.S. soldier killed in action near the end of the war. Lt. Gen. Clarence R. Huebner served as deputy commander in chief. Clay remained in charge of the European Command until 1949.

Focused, driven, and highly intelligent, General Clay was the dominant figure of the American occupation. An Army engineer by training, Clay had distinguished himself during the war by solving a major logistical logjam at Cherbourg in Normandy in the fall of 1944. Afterward, he became the second-in-command of the American war economy by serving as the deputy director of the Office of War Mobilization and Reconversion. Despite his Army background, Clay was by instinct a political animal. The son of a U.S. senator from Georgia, he possessed innate diplomatic skills that enabled him to handle American officials in Washington as well as his Allied counterparts in occupied Germany. Many of his subordinates worshipped him, and he commanded respect among the other Allies. A State Department official reverently called Clay "one of the most skillful politicians ever to wear the uniform of the United States Army."[16] Some descriptions of Clay's demeanor were a little less flattering, such as that of one British officer who remarked after a hard inter-Allied bargaining session: "He looks like a Roman emperor—and he acts like one."[17]

Clay worked closely with his political adviser, Robert D. Murphy, an accomplished career diplomat who was well connected in Washington. With his intelligence agencies, however, Clay had a more distant relationship. He generally kept them at arms' length and usually ignored intelligence that contradicted his own estimates of the situation. "General Clay, to us as to all, is aloof and Olympian," noted one intelligence officer.[18] Another described Clay as "hostile" to the intelligence headquarters staff in Germany.[19] As a result of Clay's disinterest, Army Intelligence officials had to find circuitous routes in Germany and in Washington to make themselves heard.

---

[16] Cited by Clay's preeminent biographer, Jean Edward Smith, *Lucius D. Clay: An American Life* (New York: Henry Holt, 1990), 2. For Clay's years in Germany, see also Wolfgang Krieger, *Genera Lucius D. Clay und die amerikanische Deutschlandpolitik 1945–1949* [General Lucius D. Clay and the American policy toward Germany, 1945–1949] (Stuttgart: Klett-Cotta, 1987).
[17] "Lucius Clay Dies; Led Berlin Airlift," *New York Times*, 17 Apr 1978.
[18] Rpt, Dana B. Durand, Ch, Berlin Opns Base (BOB), to Ch, Foreign Br M, 8 Apr 1948, sub: Transmittal of Report on Berlin Operations Base, in *On the Front Lines of the Cold War: Documents on the Intelligence War in Berlin, 1946 to 1961*, ed. Donald P. Steury (Washington, DC: Center for the Study of Intelligence, 1999), 32. The author viewed an unredacted copy of this document to ensure the account accords with relevant background information.
[19] James H. Critchfield, *Partners at the Creation: The Men Behind Postwar Germany's Defense and Intelligence Establishments* (Annapolis, MD: Naval Institute Press, 2003), 44.

On the ground, things looked brighter, as Army Intelligence operated within an exceptionally permissive legal framework. When the U.S. Army entered Germany in 1944, the conquered territories came under a "belligerent occupation." Military commanders had "supreme authority, i.e., the fullest measure of control, necessary to accomplish [their] military objective."[20] By definition, military operations included the conduct of intelligence and counterintelligence activities. Following the German surrender, a "peaceful occupation" technically succeeded the "belligerent occupation." Supreme authority for relations between American officials and the German population passed from military commanders to the American military government. For the intelligence agencies, little changed, as the Army remained in charge of regulating all clandestine operations in the occupied country. This meant that local laws did not interfere with the operations of Army Intelligence personnel who, in the pursuit of their missions, had the power to arrest German citizens, monitor German communications, and protect their agents from local authorities. As one intelligence official put it, the "Occupying Powers could, simply stated, conduct whatever intelligence activities they deemed advisable."[21]

The Intelligence Division at the Pentagon

The Military Intelligence Division at the Pentagon remained the Army's top-level intelligence organization after the war. The division was responsible for collecting and analyzing information on a broad range of subjects and for providing intelligence to the War Department. It also represented the War Department on intelligence and counterintelligence matters in its relations with other government departments and with foreign governments.[22]

In 1947, Congress passed the National Security Act, which established the Department of Defense, the U.S. Air Force, and the CIA, and converted the War Department into the Department of the Army. The Act also created the National Security Council (NSC), which served as a formal mechanism to coordinate U.S.

---

20 Judge Advocate Gen Sch, *Law of Belligerent Occupation*, J.A.G.S. Text 11 (Ann Arbor, MI: The Judge Advocate General's School, 1944), 35.
21 Memo, L. A. Campbell, Ofc of the Coordinator and Special Advisor, U.S. Embassy, Bonn, 15 Jun 1956, sub: Sketch of U.S. Formal Intelligence Relationships with West Germany (1945–56), Folder "GFA 10 – Intelligence (1956)," Office of German Affairs, Rcds Relating to the Negotiations of the Status of Forces Agreement (SOFA) with Germany, 1954–1959, RG 59, NACP.
22 Bruce W. Bidwell, History of the Military Intelligence Division, Department of the Army General Staff, Part VI: Cold War, 3 September 1945–25 June 1950 (unpublished manuscript, Office of the Chief of Military History, Department of the Army, 1958–1960) (hereinafter MID History Cold War), chap. 1, Postwar Reorganization, 27, Historians Files, CMH.

foreign policy among military and civilian agencies and departments. The council dealt extensively with intelligence matters, and Army Intelligence representatives regularly participated in its meetings, ensuring a wide distribution of the division's product throughout the U.S. government.[23]

As a result of postwar demobilization and organizational reshuffling, the Military Intelligence Division underwent several administrative and personnel changes. In January 1946, Maj. Gen. Clayton L. Bissell was replaced by Maj. Gen. Hoyt S. Vandenberg, who had been the assistant chief of air staff for the U.S. Army Air Forces.[24] A man on the move, Vandenberg left five months later to become the Director of Central Intelligence. Upon his departure, the War Department reorganized the division. In June 1946, the Army's top intelligence officer assumed the title Director of Intelligence, and the Military Intelligence Division merged with its executive agency, the Military Intelligence Service, into the new Intelligence Division. Maj. Gen. Stephen J. Chamberlin became the first Director of Intelligence in this newly organized division. Chamberlin divided the Intelligence Division into four main departments, the Executive, Security, Training, and Intelligence Groups. On 1 November 1948, Maj. Gen. Stafford LeRoy Irwin replaced General Chamberlin, and held the Army's top intelligence post until 1950.[25]

General officers frequently served in positions outside their expertise, and none of the Army's four postwar intelligence chiefs had professional backgrounds in this discipline. Bissell and Vandenberg had Army Air Forces backgrounds, Chamberlin was a logistician, and Irwin was an artillery officer. Therefore, all four faced a steep learning curve when they became intelligence chiefs. Chamberlin later conceded that he felt uncomfortable in his new position.[26] The division's permanent staff, however, included dedicated professionals, and the intelligence chiefs came to rely heavily on this second tier of regional and subject-matter experts.

The Intelligence Group served as the division's executive organization for the production of intelligence estimates and as liaison to Army Intelligence units across the world, including in Europe and Germany. Col. Riley F. Ennis became the group's first chief. An infantry officer by training, Ennis served as a military

---

23 Bidwell, MID History Cold War, chap. 2, Central Intelligence, 23.
24 Vandenberg achieved an added measure of fame when Marilyn Monroe included him in a list of three men with whom she would like to be stranded on a deserted island. Col. Michael J. Underkofler, "Marilyn Monroe and the General," *Federal Information & News Dispatch*, 14 Aug 2012.
25 Bidwell, MID History Cold War, chap. 1, Postwar Reorganization, 21–22, 27; chap. 7, Intelligence Training, 7; chap. 9, Summary and Conclusions, 21.
26 Email, William R. Harris to Thomas Boghardt, 12 Apr 2017, Historians Files, CMH. Harris interviewed General Chamberlin in the 1960s.

observer with British forces in England and in Egypt during the war. Later, he led Combat Command A, 12th Armored Division, in the European Theater. After the war, he became the director of the Military Intelligence Service, and after the creation of the Intelligence Division, he headed the Intelligence Group until 1948. Colonel Ennis regularly traveled to Frankfurt to meet with military attachés and top intelligence officers from the European Theater.[27]

In January 1949, Col. George S. "Budge" Smith succeeded Ennis as chief of the Intelligence Group. An artillery officer by training, Smith switched to the field of intelligence in 1940. During the war, he led an intelligence task force that seized critical targets in Rome. He prepared a similar endeavor for Berlin, but this operation did not materialize. After leaving the division, he went on to teach military science and tactics at Cornell University in the 1950s.[28] Both Ennis and Smith worked closely with their executive officer, Col. Richard Collins, who brought regional as well as intelligence expertise to the group. An artillery officer by training, Collins served with the intelligence division of the Supreme Allied Headquarters in London in 1943. Following its dissolution, he transferred to the American military government in Berlin as an intelligence specialist. In 1946, Collins returned to Washington, eventually joining the Intelligence Group.[29] A visitor to the Pentagon in 1949 described him as the "key man" for intelligence matters concerning Europe and Germany at the Pentagon.[30]

Army Intelligence Headquarters in Frankfurt and Heidelberg

The top U.S. intelligence officer in Germany at the end of the war was the intelligence chief of the 12th Army Group, Brig. Gen. Edwin L. Sibert. In a figurative sense, he was coming home. An ancestor of his, David Siebert, had emigrated from the German Empire to the British colonies in North America in the mid-eighteenth century. The family subsequently anglicized their surname by dropping the "e" after the "i."

---

[27] Department of Defense (DoD), Ofc of Public Info, News Br, "Major General Riley Finlay Ennis," Aug 1955, Historians Files, CMH; Thomas Boghardt, "'By All Feasible Means': New Documents on the American Intervention in Italy's Parliamentary Elections of 1948," Sources and Methods Blog, Cold War International History Project, Wilson Center, 1 May 2017, https://www.wilsoncenter.org/ blog-post/all-feasible-means, Historians Files, CMH.
[28] Obituary, "George S. Smith," West Point Association of Graduates, n.d., https://westpointaog.org/, Historians Files, CMH.
[29] DoD, Ofc of Public Info, News Br, "Major General Richard Collins," Jun 1963, Historians Files, CMH.
[30] Memo, Donald H. Cooper, for Mr. I. D. Harris, 31 Mar 1949, sub: Notes on visit to Pentagon, Folder "350.09 (6) Essential Elements of Intelligence," Director of Intel, Analysis and Research Br, General Corresp, 1945–49, RG 319, NACP.

Figure 11: General Sibert, shown as a major general in 1953. U.S. Army, NACP.

Sibert was born in 1897 in Little Rock, Arkansas. His grandson described him as "a man of his times" who had "the 'greatest generation' mindset of sacrifice, duty, service."[31] Both Sibert's father and his brother were major generals.[32] Following in his father's footsteps, young Sibert joined the Army, graduated from West Point in 1918, and trained as an artillery officer. He gained firsthand experience in occupation duties during the brief U.S. occupation of the Rhineland after World War I, and he had some exposure to intelligence work while serving as military attaché to Brazil from 1940 to 1941.[33] It was this assignment that led the Army to pick him for intelligence duties in the European Theater.[34]

Sibert perceived a dual threat to the occupation. Like many of his colleagues, he recognized the enduring legacy of Nazism and the need to thoroughly reform German society. With the removal of Hitler, Sibert wrote in early 1946, this task had only just begun. He described Germany as a "hierarchy of robots," conditioned by hundreds of years of authoritarianism, and he warned that reform would require a complete reeducation in a democratic spirit at all levels and ages, "a very difficult task but it is the only one that is rewarding in the end."[35] At the same time, he discerned the emerging Soviet threat earlier than many others, and he became a forceful advocate of shifting the Army's intelligence activities toward the Red Army and the communist party in Germany.[36]

Pearl Harbor and the Battle of the Bulge had exposed the corrosive effects of a splintered intelligence organization, and Sibert worked hard to build an efficient, centralized apparatus in occupied Germany. For the most part, he succeeded. A Berlin-based intelligence officer noted approvingly that "under the vigorous leadership of Brig. Gen. Edwin Sibert, the G–2 Section of [the U.S. Forces in the European Theater] blossomed into the principal intelligence agency of the European Theater, and took over virtually all of the operational functions."[37]

The Army's intelligence apparatus in occupied Germany evolved from the American components of the Allied wartime intelligence establishment. In July 1945, the

---

31 Email, Will Sibert to Thomas Boghardt, 31 Jan 2018, Historians Files, CMH. A driven professional, General Sibert was grounded by a large and loving family. His granddaughter recalls him as "quiet, self-assured, intellectual, not pretentious, rather formal, usually cheerful and always curious and busy." Email, Anne Sibert Buiter to Thomas Boghardt, 1 Feb 2018, Historians Files, CMH.
32 Email, Alan Sibert to Thomas Boghardt, 30 Jan 2018, Historians Files, CMH.
33 DoD, Ofc of Public Info, News Br, "Edwin L. Sibert," 3 Apr 1952, Historians Files, CMH.
34 Interv, Forrest C. Pogue with Brig. Gen. Edwin L. Sibert, 11 May 1951, Historians Files, CMH.
35 Brig. Gen. Edwin L. Sibert, "The German Mind," *New York Times*, 17 Feb 1946.
36 Maj. Ann Bray et al., ed., *The History of the Counter Intelligence Corps*, vol. 27, *Four Years of Cold War* (Fort Holabird, MD: U.S. Army Intelligence Center, 1959), 62.
37 Rpt, Durand to Ch, Foreign Br M, 8 Apr 1948, sub: Transmittal of Report on Berlin Operations Base, in Steury, *On the Front Lines of the Cold War*, 36.

American intelligence personnel of the dissolved Supreme Allied Headquarters and the European Theater of Operations of the United States Army merged with the intelligence division of the 12th Army Group to form the Intelligence Division of the newly created United States Forces in the European Theater. Physically, the division was collocated with the European headquarters at the IG Farben building in Frankfurt. In his position as chief of the new division, General Sibert coordinated all U.S. intelligence activities within the European Theater, centered on Germany (Map 2).[38]

Sibert divided the division into four branches. The Intelligence Branch, under Lt. Col. William M. Connor, kept the assistant chief of staff informed of all matters likely to affect the theater commander's mission. The Counterintelligence Branch, under Lt. Col. Richard D. Stevens, oversaw the division's counterespionage, countersabotage, and countersubversion program and supervised the arrest of war criminals and other suspects. The Censorship Branch, under Lt. Col. Robert G. Crandall, intercepted and reviewed all communications throughout the theater. Finally, the Operations Branch, under Col. Richard D. Wentworth, handled interrogations, personnel, and training. Separate from the four branches, Col. John L. Inskeep served as chief of the 970th Counter Intelligence Corps Detachment.[39] In addition, the division supervised a number of field intelligence agencies that conducted operations across the American zone of occupation.[40]

Sibert's talents did not go unnoticed. In the summer of 1946, the office that would soon become the CIA asked him to join their staff in Washington, D.C. The offer was tempting, and Sibert was eager to return stateside to join his family after several years in Europe. He accepted, but the arrangement did not work out for either side. The core of the new CIA consisted of Office of Strategic Services veterans who viewed Sibert as an undeserving outsider. Sibert was under the impression that he had been offered *the* deputy directorship of the new agency, but when he arrived in Washington, he found that he was merely one of several officials holding this title. The CIA never made full use of his talents, and in disappointment he rejoined the Army two years later.[41]

---

[38] Msg, Maj. Gen. S. J. Chamberlin, Director of Intel, to CG, United States Forces in the European Theater (USFET), Mil Governor, Germany, 22 Oct 1946, sub: Coordination of Intelligence Activities in Europe and the Middle East, Folder "Department of Army Intelligence Requirements," Director of Intel, Miscellaneous Rcds re. Intel and Document Policies, 1944–1948," RG 260, NACP.
[39] Ofc of the Ch Historian, EUCOM, *The Second Year of the Occupation*, vol. 6, Occupation Forces in Europe Series, 1946–1947 (Frankfurt: Office of the Chief Historian, EUCOM, 1947), 2–3, 5–7.
[40] For more on the field intelligence agencies, see Chapter 4.
[41] Ludwell L. Montague, *General Walter Bedell Smith as Director of Central Intelligence, October 1950–February 1953* (University Park: Pennsylvania State University Press, 1992), 185–87.

Army Intelligence Headquarters in Frankfurt and Heidelberg — 95

Map 1a: Army Intelligence Units, Germany, 1945–1949 (incl. map legend). U.S. Army Center of Military History.

Location	Symbol	Description
Berlin	★	HQ (Headquarters), OMGUS (Office of Military Government, United States)
		Office of the Director of Intelligence, EUCOM (European Command)
		Office of the Deputy Director of Intelligence (OMGUS)
		Berlin Command, Intelligence section
	♠	CIA (Central Intelligence Agency), Berlin Operations Base
	⚓	HQ, COMNAVFOR (Commander of Naval Forces for Germany), Intelligence division (1949)
	🛡	HQ, CIC (Counter Intelligence Corps) Region VIII
		Civil Censorship Division branch office
	⚡	Central repeater station monitored by ASAE (Army Security Agency, Europe) and Civil Censorship Division
	⛓	Allied war criminals prison
Frankfurt	★	HQ, USFET (United States Forces in the European Theater)
		Office of the Deputy Director of Intelligence (military intelligence)
		HQ, Communications Intelligence Service Detachment
	🛡	HQ, CIC Region II
		HQ, 970th CIC Detachment
	♠	HQ, CIA (1949)
		HQ, ASAE
		HQ, Civil Censorship Division
	⚡	Central repeater station monitored by ASAE and Civil Censorship Division
Allendorf	✗	Army Historical Program
Altötting	▦	Polish displaced persons camp
Asperg	⛓	Seventh Army POW (prisoner-of-war) camp (1945)
Auerbach	⛓	U.S. Army camp for SS POWs
Bad Aibling	⛓	Third Army POW camp (1945)
Bad Hersfeld	⛓	Army processing camp for German POWs
Bad Nauheim	🛡	HQ, CIC Region III
	★	OMGUS Intelligence office
Bad Vilbel	⚡	ASAE, 2d Army Air Forces Squadron, Mobile
Bamberg	🛡	HQ, CIC Region VI
	★	HQ, U.S. Constabulary
Bremen	♠	OSS (Office of Strategic Services)/CIA branch office
	⚓	HQ, COMNAVFOR
	🛡	HQ, CIC Region IX
Dachau	⛓	U.S. Army war criminals enclosure
Esslingen	⚡	Civil Censorship Division branch office
Fritzlar	⚡	ASAE mobile unit
Funk Kaserne	▦	Displaced persons camp
Garmisch-Partenkirchen	✗	Army Historical Program
Giessen	⛓	Army processing camp for German POWs
Gross-Gerau	⚡	ASAE, Detachment "A"
Heidelberg	★	EUCOM headquarters
		HQ, Intelligence Division
	♠	HQ, OSS and Strategic Services Unit
Heilbronn	▦	Displaced persons camp
Herzogenaurach	⚡	ASAE station, Herzo Base
Hof	⛓	Army processing camp for German POWs
Karlsruhe	♠	HQ, CIA (1948)
	✗	Army Historical Program
Kassel	♠	OSS/CIA branch office
Kransberg Castle	⛓	Dustbin detention center
Landsberg	▦	Jewish displaced persons camp
	⛓	War criminals prison
Mannheim	▦	Polish displaced persons camp
Mondorf	⛓	Ashcan detention center
	✗	Army Historical Program
Munich	♠	OSS/CIA branch office
	🛡	HQ, CIC Region IV
	⚡	Civil Censorship Division branch office
Neustadt	✗	Army Historical Program
Nuremberg	♠	OSS/CIA branch office
	⚡	Central repeater station monitored by ASAE and Civil Censorship Division
Oberursel		6824th Detailed Interrogation Center – Military Intelligence Service Center
	★	Camp King
	✗	Army Historical Program
Offenbach	⚡	Civil Censorship Division branch office
Pfaffenhofen	⚡	ASAE mobile unit
Potsdam	★	United States Military Liaison Mission
Prague	♠	OSS/CIA branch office
Regensburg	♠	OSS/CIA branch office
	🛡	HQ, CIC Region V
Rothwesten	⚡	ASAE mobile unit
Scheyern	⚡	ASAE, 116th Signal Service Company
Sontra	⚡	ASAE, 114th Signal Service Company
Stuttgart	🛡	HQ, CIC Region I
Treuenbrietzen	⚡	Telecommunications relay station linking Berlin with U.S. Zone
Wiesbaden	♠	HQ, OSS
Wildflecken	▦	Displaced persons camp
Zuffenhausen	▦	Soviet displaced persons camp

Map 1a (continued)

In September 1946, Maj. Gen. Withers A. "Pinky" Burress succeeded Sibert. An infantry officer who had seen combat in both world wars, Burress became known as the "fighting general."[42] Yet he had no background and little interest in intelligence. He served as the Army's top intelligence officer in Europe for less than a year, until May 1947. From an administrative point of view, the most significant event during his tenure was the transitioning of the intelligence division from the European Theater to the European Command in March 1947.[43]

Both Sibert and, until March 1947, Burress reported directly to the commanders of the European Theater, General Eisenhower and his successor, General McNarney. When the European Theater organization became the European Command, the Intelligence Division underwent a significant reorganization. Its chief, Burress, became the first Director of Intelligence, Office of the Commander in Chief, European Command, and moved to Berlin. In his role as director, Burress (and his successors) served as Clay's top intelligence officer in Germany and Europe, advising him on all intelligence matters pertaining to the occupation and coordinating American intelligence collection efforts throughout Europe. The director also headed the Intelligence Coordinating Committee, a council composed of various American agencies in Germany to coordinate intelligence- and security-related matters, and he liaised with the intelligence chiefs of the other Allies. The office had a small staff, including an executive officer, an assistant executive officer, an administrative section, and a special assistant who provided subject matter expertise to the director.[44]

The reorganization of Army Intelligence redirected the vertical flow of the collected information. By removing the director of intelligence from his staff organization in Frankfurt, he became more of a personal adviser to Clay than the chief of Army Intelligence in Europe. Sibert had been a mere brigadier, whereas his successors held the rank of major general. Yet they did not attain the same level of authority. None of them matched Sibert's forceful and perceptive personality. At the same time, their proximity to Clay and their physical separation from their staff limited their independence.

In May 1947, Maj. Gen. Robert L. Walsh succeeded Burress. On the face of it, Walsh was a solid choice for the job. He had served as an Army Air Forces intelligence officer from 1940 to 1942 and as a member of the U.S. military mission to

---

42 "General Burress Retires," *New York Times*, 29 Nov 1954.
43 DoD, Ofc of Public Info, News Br, "Withers A. Burress," Sep 1954, Historians Files, CMH.
44 Lt. Col. Robert J. Quinn, Ofc of the Director of Intel (ODI), to Ofc of the Ch Historian, HQ, European Command (EUCOM), 26 Mar 1948, sub: Historical Report, ODI, EUCOM, Historian's Background Files, 1947–1952, RG 549, NACP. During that time, Lt. Col. R. J. Quinn served as executive officer, Dr. H. J. Russo as special assistant, and 1st Lt. R. E. Rochefort as assistant executive officer.

Moscow during the war.[45] But Walsh cared little for intelligence. In a lengthy exit interview conducted by the U.S. Air Force after his retirement, he spoke passionately and extensively about aviation but glossed over his work as intelligence director of the European Command.[46] At his own request, he joined the headquarters of the newly created U.S. Air Force in October 1948.[47]

Maj. Gen. William E. Hall replaced General Walsh as the last director of intelligence during the military occupation.[48] Like Walsh, Hall had an Army Air Forces background but little previous exposure to intelligence. Upon his assignment to Berlin, he nonchalantly told the press, "I know where to hang my hat and that's about all as yet."[49] This was an understatement. By the time Hall arrived in Berlin, the Soviets had imposed a blockade on the city, and the Western Allies had responded by establishing a massive airlift to supply the population with food, fuel, and other essentials. Hall's aviation background made him an excellent choice to deal with intelligence matters during the crisis.

Meanwhile, the intelligence staff in Frankfurt marched on without its chief. With the establishment of the European Command, the Intelligence Division became the Office of the Deputy Director of Intelligence. Officially, the office was responsible only for the collection of militarily relevant information, such as order of battle intelligence on the Soviet forces. Given its wide-ranging capabilities and its large staff, however, the office continued to be involved in a number of nonmilitary intelligence matters in Germany, including political and economic assessments.[50]

Col. Robert A. Schow headed the new office as the deputy director of intelligence, serving in this function until March 1949. He proved one of the most capable American intelligence officials in Germany. An infantry officer by training, Schow had served as the military attaché to the pro-German government of Vichy France until 1942. Shortly after the United States entered the war, at the end of 1941, the French interned him. After his release in 1944, he served as an assistant intelligence officer at Supreme Allied Headquarters. In February 1945, he became an assistant to General Sibert at the 12th Army Group and saw combat in Belgium.

---

45 DoD, Ofc of Public Info, News Br, "Robert LeGrow Walsh," 1 Nov 1946, Historians Files, CMH.
46 Interv, Hugh N. Ahmann with Maj. Gen. Robert L. Walsh, 9–10 Jan 1984, 204–05, U.S. Air Force (USAF) Historical Research Center, Ofc of Air Force History HQ, USAF.
47 Telg, Clay to Lt. Gen. Edwards, Ch of Personnel, Air Forces, n.d. [late summer or early fall 1948], Folder "CC 5878," Gen Lucius D. Clay Personal Papers Apr 1945–May 1949, RG 260, NACP.
48 Weisz, *OMGUS-Handbuch*, 39.
49 "Gen. Hall Heads U.S. Intelligence in Germany," *Washington Post*, 23 Oct 1948.
50 Msg., Maj. Gen. Robert L. Walsh to Director of Intel, OMGUS, attn.: Col. Rodes, 20 Nov 1947, sub: Intelligence Reporting, Folder "350.09 (1) Tables of Organization—ODI, OMGUS," Director of Intel, Analysis and Research Br, Gen Corresp, 1945–49, RG 319, NACP.

Figure 12: Colonel Schow, April 1947. U.S. Army, NACP.

At the end of the war, he followed Sibert as the deputy of the intelligence division.[51] With Sibert's departure from Europe, and the move of the Office of the Director of Intelligence to Berlin, Schow continued to report to the director of intelligence, but his independence grew substantially under Burress and Walsh. He had direct access to General Clay, and his office stayed in close contact with the intelligence division at the Pentagon, which regularly issued Essential Elements of Information. One writer described Schow as "the real managerial powerhouse around the U.S. intelligence complex in Frankfurt."[52]

Schow reorganized the division to fit its postwar mission. A new Research and Analysis Branch under Lt. Col. William M. Connor collated, evaluated, and disseminated all intelligence-relevant information on a command-wide basis. An-

---

[51] DoD, Ofc of Public Info, News Br, "Major General Robert Alwin Schow," Oct 1956, Historians Files, CMH.
[52] Burton Hersh, *The Old Boys: The American Elite and the Origins of the CIA* (New York: Charles Scribner's Sons, 1992), 267, 269.

alysts rated the reliability of sources and information according to an alphabetic and numerical code, a system that officials used throughout the Army's intelligence organization.[53] The branch indicated its requirements through its own EEIs, and kept the deputy commander in chief current on all militarily relevant developments in Germany and Europe. The newly organized Control Branch under Lt. Col. Milton C. Taylor was responsible for all administrative matters, including the screening of U.S. and non-U.S. personnel who had access to classified information. The Plans, Policy, and Inspection Group under Lt. Col. George Artman coordinated all joint projects involving any two branches or another staff division. The Operations Branch under Col. Richard D. Wentworth exercised staff supervision over all field intelligence agencies operated by the deputy director of intelligence. Colonel Inskeep remained chief of the 970th CIC Detachment. Each branch had subsections that handled particular projects.[54]

By early 1948, the Army was looking toward and beyond the end of the military occupation, and Schow directed a final round of reorganizations to prepare his organization for a long-term presence in Germany. In April 1948, the office received a new name, the Intelligence Division, and it joined European Command headquarters in Heidelberg. It now consisted of five branches. Lt. Col. William M. Slayden headed the Research and Analysis Branch; Lt. Col. William R. Rainford, the Control Branch; Lt. Col. Cyril J. Letzelter, the Policy and Inspection Branch; and Lt. Col. Merillat Moses, the Operations Branch. The new Special Projects Branch under Lt. Col. Milton C. Taylor was in charge of training, organizational matters, special intelligence projects, and interrogation.[55] Subsections of each branch handled specific issues. The personnel strength at headquarters varied over the course of the four-

---

53 The reliability of a source was rated with letter grades: A (completely reliable), B (usually reliable), C (fairly reliable), D (not usually reliable), E (unreliable), or F (reliability cannot be judged). The reliability of the information provided was rated with number grades: 1 (confirmed by other sources), 2 (probably true), 3 (possibly true), 4 (doubtfully true), 5 (improbable report), or 6 (truth cannot be judged). A B–3 rating, for example, indicated that the information was provided by a usually reliable source and should be regarded as possibly true. Memo, Col. Robert A. Schow, Deputy Director of Intel (DDI), EUCOM, 4 Jun 1947, Folder "350.09-4 Intelligence – Requirements, Powers & Duties," Director of Intel, Analysis and Research Br, Gen Corresp, 1945–49, RG 260, NACP.

54 Ofc of the Ch Historian, EUCOM, *The Second Year of the Occupation*, 6:4; Ofc of the Ch Historian, EUCOM, *The Third Year of the Occupation*, Part 1, *The First Quarter, 1 July–30 September 1947*, vol. 2, Occupation Forces in Europe Series, 1947–48 (Frankfurt: Office of the Chief Historian, EUCOM, 1947), 47, 52.

55 Ofc of the Ch Historian, EUCOM, *The Third Year of the Occupation*, Part 4, *The Fourth Quarter, 1 April–30 June 1948*, vol. 2, Occupation Forces in Europe Series, 1947–48 (Frankfurt: Office of the Chief Historian, EUCOM, 1947), 25–26.

year occupation period. At its final reorganization in early 1948, the division's staff stood fixed at sixty-eight officers and ninety enlisted men.[56]

Schow's aptitude for intelligence made him an attractive target for recruitment by other agencies. In March 1949, he joined the CIA as assistant director for special operations. Eventually, he attained the rank of major general, serving as the Army's assistant chief of staff for intelligence from 1956 to 1958.[57] In Heidelberg, Col. Richard C. Partridge succeeded Schow as deputy director of intelligence. Partridge, too, was well qualified for the task. Born in Boston in 1899, he graduated from Harvard University in 1918 and from West Point two years later. He trained as an artillery officer. From 1938 to 1939, he attended the German Kriegsakademie (army war college) in Berlin, and he served as assistant military attaché to Germany the following year. During the war, Partridge participated in the Battle of the Bulge and the expansion of the Remagen bridgehead as chief of staff of the VII Corps. After the war, he served as military attaché to Belgrade, Yugoslavia. Partridge ably guided the Office of the Deputy Director of Intelligence through the end of the military occupation in September 1949.[58]

The Intelligence Organization of the Military Government

In addition to its tactical intelligence arm headquartered in Frankfurt and Heidelberg, the Army operated a small military government intelligence organization headquartered in Berlin. Because military government was a new mission for the Army, the intelligence office had to be built from scratch. In its early phase, it went through considerable organizational turmoil and personnel turnover as it sought to find its role in the occupation (Chart 1).

Military government intelligence originated with the Intelligence Section of the U.S. Group Control Council, Germany. Col. Charles C. Blakeney led the section initially, but he was soon replaced by Col. Theodore J. Koenig, an Army Air Forces officer. On 25 April 1945, the day Clay became deputy military governor to Gen-

---

56 Ofc of the Ch Historian, EUCOM, *The Third Year of the Occupation*, Part 3, *The Third Quarter, 1 January–31 March 1948*, vol. 2, Occupation Forces in Europe Series, 1947–48 (Frankfurt: Office of the Chief Historian, EUCOM, 1947), 58.
57 Kevin C. Ruffner, ed., *Forging an Intelligence Partnership: CIA and the Origins of the BND 1945–49: A Documentary History* (Washington, DC: Center for the Study of Intelligence, 1999), 1:xxxix–xl.
58 DoD, Ofc of Public Info, News Br, "Major General Richard Clare Partridge," Oct 1956, Historians Files, CMH; "Richard Clare Partridge Dies; Retired Army General Was 77," *New York Times*, 27 Jul 1976.

eral Eisenhower, the council established the Office of the Director of Intelligence under Brig. Gen. Thomas J. Betts, and Koenig became his deputy. Betts also continued to serve as deputy director for intelligence at Supreme Allied Headquarters. After the dissolution of the latter in July 1945, Brig. Gen. G. Bryan Conrad succeeded Betts as director of intelligence. Conrad had served as an intelligence staff officer at the headquarters of the 12th Army Group during the war. He retained Koenig as his assistant, and when Conrad retired in 1946, Koenig became director of intelligence.[59]

The director represented the United States on the Quadripartite Intelligence Committee in Berlin, which was supposed to promulgate Allied intelligence policies for all of Germany. In practice, this arrangement never worked. The French and the Soviets refused to share any sensitive information with the Americans and the British, and their "representatives discuss only insignificant incidents," as a U.S. intelligence official lamented.[60] The Soviets, in particular, "were never even close to cooperation," and their understanding of intelligence differed substantially from that of the Americans. As a history of the Office of the Director of Intelligence observed, "The word 'intelligence' to the Soviets connotes covert rather than overt work and savors of secret police activity."[61]

The lack of stability at the top of the office and the failure of the quadripartite committee almost extinguished military government intelligence as an independent organization during the first year of its existence. General Clay had little faith in its leadership and repeatedly denied requests for personnel. As a result, the military government intelligence organization could not replace most of the personnel who returned to the United States as the services demobilized after the war. In June 1945, the office had a staff of 345, but a year later that number had contracted to a mere 48. Meanwhile, in his quest for a centralized Army Intelligence organization in Europe, General Sibert proposed to eliminate the office altogether and attach its functions to the intelligence division in Frankfurt. In the end, the office survived because of bureaucratic inertia, but it retained only limited authority. Clay prohibited its staff from actively collecting information, limiting their work to the analysis of information provided by other agencies and to advising the military governor on specific issues.[62]

---

59 Weisz, *OMGUS-Handbuch*, 46, 96, 97.
60 Msg, Col. Peter P. Rodes to Deputy Mil Governor, OMGUS, 9 Jul 1947, sub: Functional Program, Folder "350.09 (1) Tables of Organization – ODI, OMGUS," Director of Intel, Analysis and Research Br, Genl Corresp, 1945–49, RG 260, NACP.
61 "History of the Office of Director of Intelligence," May 1945–Jun 1946, Director of Intel, Analysis and Research Br, Gen Corresp, 1945–49, RG 260, NACP.
62 "History of Office of Director of Intelligence," May 1945–Jun 1946.

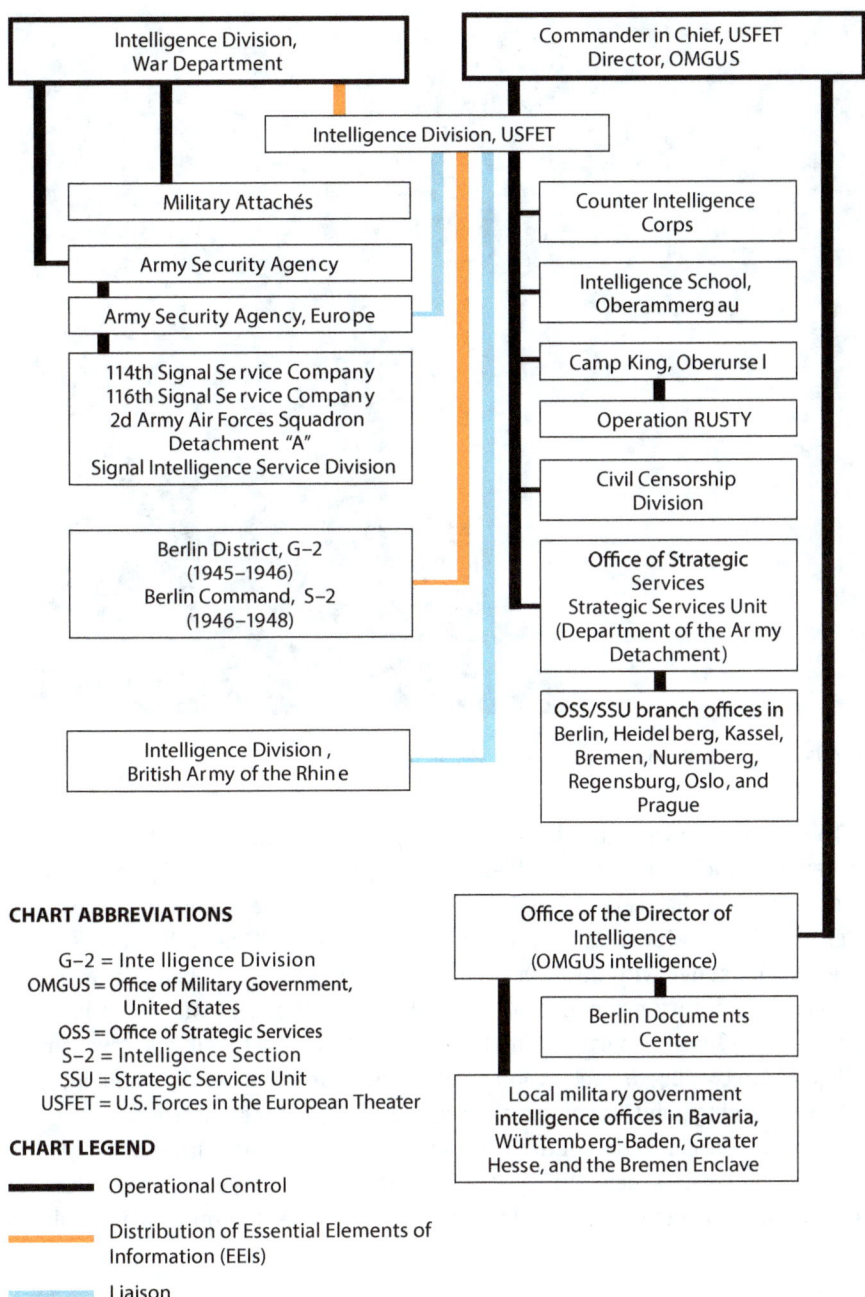

Chart 2: Army Intelligence, U.S. Forces in the European Theater, July 1945–March 1947. U.S. Army Center of Military History.

Figure 13: Colonel Rodes in Berlin, April 1949. U.S. Army, NACP.

The fortunes of the office began to change in November 1946 when Col. Peter P. Rodes succeeded Koenig as the chief of military government intelligence. An artillery officer, Rodes had served briefly with the American occupation forces in Bernkastel-Kues in the Rhineland in early 1919. During World War II, he had been an artillery commander with the 70th Infantry Division in the European Theater and received a temporary promotion to the rank of brigadier general. Rodes brought commitment, a sense of purpose, and much-needed stability to military government intelligence. According to a fellow intelligence officer in Berlin, Rodes's appointment marked a "turning point," as he "revitalized the nearly defunct" office.[63]

With the reorganization of the European Theater into the European Command and the creation of a new Office of the Director of Intelligence under General Walsh, Rodes became one of the director's two deputies, the other being Colonel

---

[63] War Department, "Peter Powell Rodes," 1 Apr 1946, Historians Files, CMH; Rpt, Durand to Ch, Foreign Br M, 8 Apr 1948, sub: Transmittal of Report on Berlin Operations Base, in Steury, *On the Front Lines of the Cold War*, 36.

Schow of the Office of the Deputy Director of Intelligence in Frankfurt (Chart 2). The new order put Rodes's organization formally in charge of collecting political, economic, and social intelligence, enabling Schow's office to focus on military intelligence. Rodes's organization adopted the designation "Office of the Deputy Director of Intelligence (military government)" or "Office of the Director of Intelligence, OMGUS." In theory, Rodes would report to Clay through Walsh, but in practice he retained direct access to Clay. Like Colonel Schow in Frankfurt, Rodes also exchanged information directly with the Army's intelligence division at the Pentagon. Rodes remained at the helm of military government intelligence in Berlin to the end of the military occupation in 1949.[64]

Rodes quickly expanded his staff as well as the purview of his office. Upon his arrival, he appointed Lawrence E. De Neufville as chief of the all-important Research and Analysis branch. Educated and worldly, De Neufville had a suitable background for the job. Born in London, he held degrees from Oxford and Harvard Universities, had worked as a foreign correspondent before the war, and joined the OSS after Pearl Harbor.[65] About a year later, Rodes added a Security Branch under Laughlin A. Campbell, formerly of the CIC. By 1949, Rodes had expanded the organization to seven branches: Research and Analysis, now under Innis D. Harris; Plans and Policy under Lt. Col. John D. Eason; European Command Requirements under Donald H. Cooper; Security under C. J. O'Connor; Liaison, for coordination with the Allies, under Jacques S. Arouet; Special Projects under Hans A. Kallmann; and Administration Personnel under Warrant Officer, Junior Grade (W1) Robert Baker. Harris, the chief of the Research and Analysis Branch, doubled as Rodes's deputy director.[66]

With this extensive reorganization, Rodes managed to turn operations around, but he struggled to find adequate replacements for soldiers who were demobilized or left Germany for another assignment. During the latter part of the military occupation, therefore, the office came to rely heavily on Swiss, Danish, and especially German citizens. Civilians were cheaper and easier to acquire than military person-

---

64 War Department, "Peter Powell Rodes," 1 Apr 1946; Rpt, Durand to Ch, Foreign Br M, 8 Apr 1948, sub: Transmittal of Report on Berlin Operations Base, in Steury, *On the Front Lines of the Cold War*, 36.
65 Obituary, "De Neufville, Lawrence E.," *Hartford Courant*, 14 Jul 1998, Historians Files, CMH.
66 Msg, Col. Peter P. Rodes, Director of Intel, to Ofc of the Deputy Director of Intel (ODDI), 29 Jul 1947, sub: Functional and Organizational Program for the Office of the Director of Intelligence, OMGUS, Folder "350.09 (1) Tables of Organization – ODI, OMGUS," Director of Intel, Analysis and Research Br, Gen Corresp, 1945–49, RG 260, NACP.

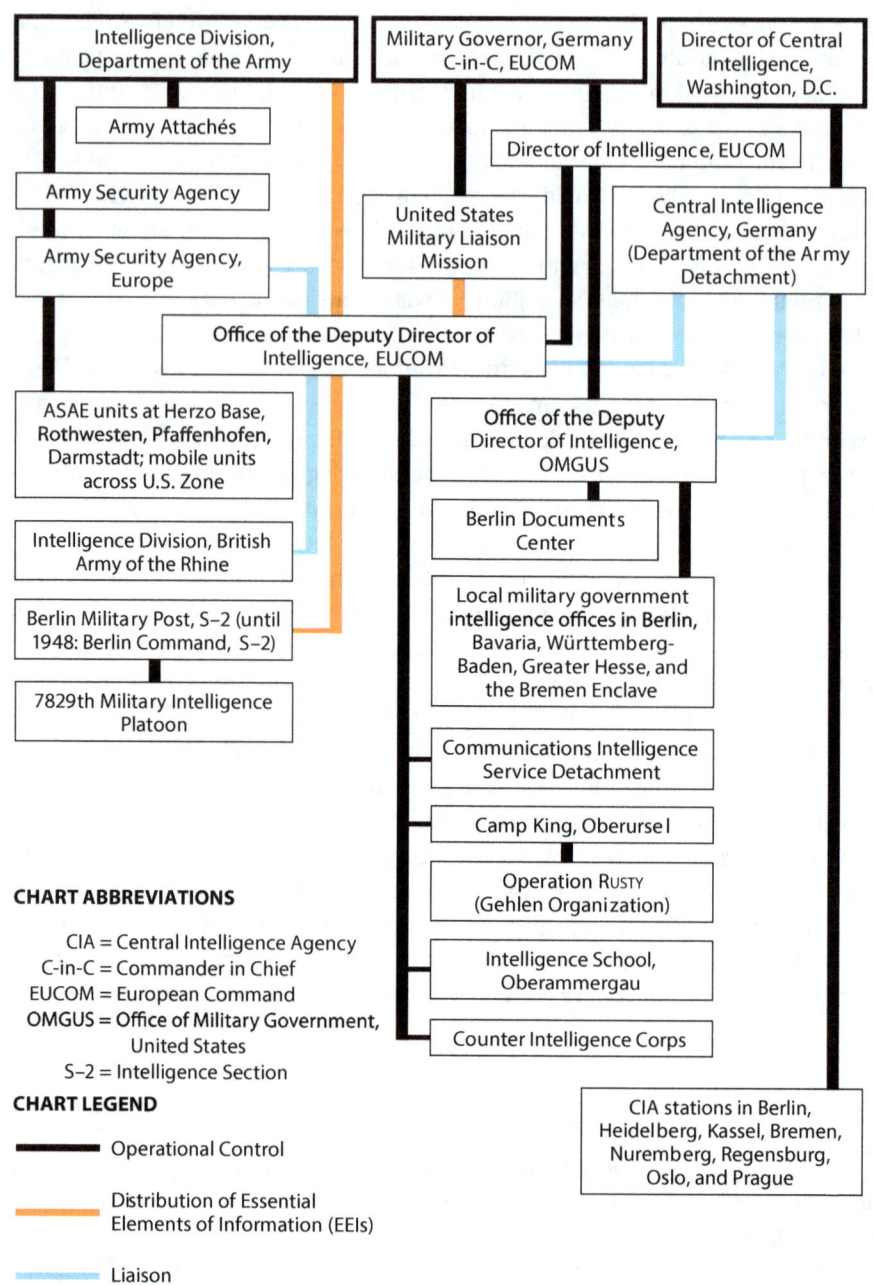

Chart 3: Army Intelligence, European Command, 1947–1949. U.S. Army Center of Military History.

nel, and often were more skilled.⁶⁷ Consequently, Rodes's outfit had a distinctly less military feel than the intelligence division in Frankfurt. Numerous military government intelligence officers became civilians in the course of the occupation, and by 1949, nonmilitary personnel held most of the office's key positions. Those who held military rank usually were draftees, not professional soldiers. Some, including Jacques Arouet and Harold E. Stearns, were former teachers or professors.⁶⁸ Rodes did not even consider military training an absolute requirement for his own position. "There is no reason," he noted, "why a civilian able to think clearly should not be appointed to this job."⁶⁹

As the wartime alliances fell apart, ushering in the Cold War, Rodes's heavy reliance on civilians hit a snag. The revelations of several espionage cases involving American citizens in the United States prompted President Truman in March 1947 to establish a federal loyalty program.⁷⁰ Henceforth, federal agencies had to screen their personnel for potential security risks, including links to foreign governments. Because several civilians working for Rodes's office were born and raised in Germany, the establishment of the loyalty program triggered a number of investigations.⁷¹

Hans A. Kallmann was a case in point. Born in Berlin in 1899, he worked as an editor for the prestigious *Frankfurter Zeitung* but left Germany for the United States in 1939 owing to his Jewish background. During the war, he became a U.S. citizen and served with the OSS in New York as an analyst of German politics and economics. In July 1946, he joined the Office of the Director of Intelligence in Berlin and quickly became one of Rodes's top analysts.⁷² As mandated by the fed-

---

67 Weisz, *OMGUS-Handbuch*, 97; OMGUS, Info Bull 158, 1 Apr 1949, Historians Files, CMH; Msg, Rodes to ODDI, 29 Jul 1947, sub: Functional and Organizational Program for the Office of the Director of Intelligence, OMGUS.
68 Daniel Lerner, *Sykewar: Psychological Warfare Against Germany, D-Day to VE-Day* (New York: George W. Stewart, 1949), 78.
69 Msg, Col. Peter P. Rodes, to Director of Intel, EUCOM, 15 Jul 1947, sub: Organization of Intelligence Agencies with the European Command, Folder "350.09 (1) Tables of Organization – ODI, OMGUS," Director of Intel, Analysis and Research Br, Gen Corresp, 1945–49, RG 260, NACP.
70 Harry S. Truman, Executive Order (EO) 9835, "Prescribing Procedures for the Administration of an Employees Loyalty Program in the Executive Branch of the Government," *Federal Register* 12 (21 Mar 1947), 1935–38.
71 Michael J. Hogan, *A Cross of Iron: Harry S. Truman and the Origins of the National Security State* (Cambridge, UK: Cambridge University Press, 1998), 254.
72 Rpt, Special Agent Wyatt J. Mitchell, Region VIII, CIC, 21 Jun 1949, Folder "XE 259448 Hans Albert Kallmann," INSCOM, IRR, Digitized Name Files, RG 319, NACP.

eral loyalty program, the CIC conducted a background check of Kallmann in 1949.[73] He passed with flying colors. The deputy director of the office, Innis D. Harris, praised Kallmann "as one of the most reliable and ethical persons in the present employ of ODI [Office of the Director of Intelligence]." Colonel Rodes told the investigating special agent that Kallmann was "probably the best political analyst in Military Government today. . . . I consider him a very fine individual and of great value to Military Government."[74] The CIC concluded that Kallmann was "definitely loyal to the U.S." and closed the investigation.[75] In fact, most investigations cleared personnel with similar backgrounds. Foreign-born intelligence officials contributed materially to the American intelligence mission and their chiefs were keen to retain them.

Geographically, the office expanded significantly under Rodes's aegis. The director resided in Berlin, but his deputy and the other branch chiefs and their staff set up shop in Bad Nauheim, north of Frankfurt. In addition, Rodes supervised regional intelligence offices in the three *Länder* of the U.S. Zone, as well as in the Bremen enclave and in the American sector of Berlin. A *Land* intelligence officer stood at the top of each of these five administrative units, and the offices organized along the same lines as headquarters in Berlin and Frankfurt. They monitored regional political developments and functioned as part of the local military government organizations. They coordinated operations closely with the peacetime successor of the Psychological Warfare Division, the Information Control Division, which oversaw the German media. Each office also worked with local Liaison and Security Detachments, which reported to the *Land* intelligence officer on a weekly basis. In July 1947, a total of 219 of these detachments operated across the U.S. Zone.[76]

Bavaria, the biggest *Land* in the U.S. Zone, had the largest intelligence office. More than half of all Liaison and Security Detachments, 141, operated here. At the end of the war, Maj. Peter J. Vacca headed this office. A former post intelligence officer at the Seneca Army Depot in central New York, Vacca had an affinity for

---

[73] Msg, Maj. Earl S. Browning, HQ, 7970th CIC Grp, to Commanding Ofcr (CO), Region VIII, CIC, 5 May 1949, sub: Kallmann, Hans Albert, Folder "XE 259448 Hans Albert Kallmann," INSCOM, IRR, Digitized Name Files, RG 319, NACP.

[74] Rpt, Mitchell, 21 Jun 1949.

[75] Msg, Special Agent Marvin L. Rissinger, Region VIII, CIC, to Maj. Earl S. Browning, CO, CIC 7970th CIC Gp, 28 Jun 1949, sub: Kallmann, Hans Albert, Folder "XE 259448 Hans Albert Kallmann," INSCOM, IRR, Digitized Name Files, RG 319, NACP.

[76] Msg, Rodes to ODDI, 29 Jul 1947, sub: Functional and Organizational Program for the Office of the Director of Intelligence, OMGUS; J. F. J. Gillen, "U.S. Military Government in Germany: American Influence on the Development of Political Institutions" (Karlsruhe: Historical Division, EUCOM, 1950), 101.

espionage and covert operations. Another military government intelligence officer, Col. Frank M. Potter Jr., described Vacca as a "character" who "is aggressive, likes to play around with 'side shows' and generally takes himself quite seriously. He is a 'cloak and dagger' type of operator." In April 1947, Harold E. Stearns, a civilian who held the rank of major during the war, replaced Vacca as the chief *Land* intelligence officer in Bavaria.[77] In 1948, Donald T. Shea became director of the Bavarian intelligence division, and he exercised this function until the end of the military occupation in 1949.[78]

Greater Hesse, the second largest *Land* in the U.S. Zone, included the city of Frankfurt, headquarters of the American forces in Europe. In October 1946, the intelligence office had only a staff of three. It expanded to sixteen by spring 1947, and shrank to two by the end of the military occupation. In addition, the office employed up to fifteen German citizens on short-term contracts. The office worked with forty-one local Liaison and Security Detachments. Lt. Col. James E. O'Steen served as chief from the end of the war through late 1948. Colonel Potter praised him as a "very brilliant, clear thinking Intelligence Officer and the strongest of the three" *Länder* intelligence chiefs. From late 1948, O'Steen's former deputy, Robert A. Cunningham, directed the office through the end of the military occupation.[79]

A small, rural, and generally quiet *Land*, Württemberg-Baden drew less attention from intelligence than either Bavaria or Hesse. Only three officers staffed the local military government's intelligence organization in July 1946. In January 1947, the office employed ten Americans and six Germans. It also worked with twenty-nine Liaison and Security Detachments. Maj. Harold E. Stearns, a former professor of German literature, served as its chief in 1946. Potter described him "as not as brilliant as O'Steen," and as "a plodder and quite thorough." He did not have an intelligence background, and "a couple of times has rather let us down by failing to report incidents to us here of a spot nature." In April 1947, Stearns and the chief of the intelligence office in Bavaria, Major Vacca, became civilians, and switched positions. In May 1948, J. Ward Starr succeeded Vacca, and directed the Württemberg-Baden intelligence office through September 1949.[80]

---

77 Memo, Lt. Col. Frank M. Potter Jr., Ch, Analysis and Rpts Section, for Col. Peter P. Rodes, 14 Oct 1946, Folder "Miscellaneous Reports & Memoranda 1946–48," Director of Intel, Miscellaneous Rcds re. Intel and Document Policies, 1944–1948, RG 260, NA; Weisz, *OMGUS-Handbuch*, 253.
78 Shea appears to have replaced Vacca in the summer of 1948. See Msg, Donald T. Shea, Acting Director, Ofc of Mil Government, Bavaria (OMGB), Intel Div, to Land Director, OMGB, 27 Jul 1948, sub: Bavarian Reaction to Western German State, Rcds of the OMGB, Rcds of the Intel Div, Intel Rcds of the Ofc of the Director, 1946–49, RG 260, NACP.
79 Memo, Potter for Rodes, 14 Oct 1946; Weisz, *OMGUS-Handbuch*, 385.
80 Memo, Potter for Rodes, 14 Oct 1946; Weisz, *OMGUS-Handbuch*, 540–41.

Completely enclosed by the British Zone, the smallish Bremen enclave barely registered on the radar of Colonel Rodes's office. Initially, the Americans relied on British intelligence and tactical intelligence personnel of the 29th Infantry Division for sensitive information from Bremen. For the remainder of the occupation, various military government agencies handled intelligence as part of a larger portfolio, and a proper *Land* intelligence office existed for only a few months in 1948. Merely two Liaison and Security Detachments operated there. In 1947, Rodes exhorted the director of the local OMGUS office to use Bremen as a platform for intelligence operations into the British Zone, but this effort did not get off the ground. Nicholas Metal, a civilian, served as the lone *Land* intelligence officer in Bremen from November 1946 to the end of the military occupation.[81]

In contrast to sleepy Bremen, the city of Berlin posed an extraordinary challenge to American intelligence. Initially, the military government expected to derive most intelligence in the city from liaison and coordination with the other Allied intelligence services. Therefore, its local intelligence office remained small, consisting of three Army officers in December 1945 and of four Americans and one German staff by September 1949. Louis Glaser, a former lieutenant colonel, served as chief in 1945, and Sidney M. Aronovitz was acting chief in the same year. Philip L. Barbour served from 1946 to 1948, and Harold E. Stearns from 1948 to 1949.[82] As relations between the Allies deteriorated and Berlin became an early Cold War battleground between Soviet and Western secret services, the diminutive and under-resourced U.S. intelligence apparatus in Berlin proved entirely inadequate. Colonel Rodes raised this issue repeatedly with intelligence and military leaders, including General Clay, and the need for reform of American intelligence in Berlin remained an ongoing concern for the American occupation authorities.[83]

---

[81] Weisz, *OMGUS-Handbuch*, 646–48; Msg, Col. Peter P. Rodes, Director of Intel, OMGUS, to Mr. Thomas F. Dunn, Director, Ofc of Mil Government for Bremen, 17 Sep 1947, Folder "350.09 (1) Tables of Organization – ODI, OMGUS," Director of Intel, Analysis and Research Br, Gen Corresp, 1945–49, RG 260, NACP.
[82] Weisz, *OMGUS-Handbuch*, 688–89.
[83] Note for record, Innis D. Harris, Executive Ofcr, ODI, OMGUS, 26 Apr 1948, Folder "350.09-4 Intelligence – Requirements, Powers & Duties," Director of Intel, Analysis and Research Br, Gen Corresp, 1945–49, RG 260, NACP. For a more detailed discussion of Army Intelligence organization and operations in Berlin, see Chapter 5.

Berlin Command

Members of a CIC Military Intelligence Interpreter Team were among the first American officials to enter Soviet-occupied Berlin. On 7 May 1945, the team left Wittenberge in Brandenburg for a one-day reconnaissance trip to the German capital. Upon their return, they reported finding the German population "completely intimidated and scared." Most Berliners would not talk to the team members, but one said the Americans "have come too late."[84] Lt. Col. John J. Maginnis, a civil affairs officer who reconnoitered Berlin on 26 June, echoed the grim findings of the CIC report: "Berlin was a mess. . . . It was almost completely ruined, much of it flattened but with skeletons of broken buildings emphasizing the desolation." The inhabitants, Maginnis noted, "looked beaten physically and in spirit."[85]

The Americans designated the Berlin District as the organization in charge of the U.S. sector (Map 3). It had its own intelligence (G–2) branch, headed by Col. Rufus S. Bratton, the officer in charge of the Far Eastern Section of Military Intelligence Division during the attack on Pearl Harbor. On 2 July, Bratton and his staff moved into the German capital.[86] The following day, the bulk of the District's intelligence personnel followed. On 4 July, the commander of Berlin District, Maj. Gen. Floyd L. Parks, officially took command of the American sector, which consisted of six *Bezirke* (administrative districts) in the southwestern area of the city: Zehlendorf, Steglitz, Schöneberg, Kreuzberg, Tempelhof, and Neukölln.[87] The Berlin District was subordinate to the European Theater in Frankfurt, and its intelligence branch coordinated its work closely with General Sibert.

In early August, Colonel Bratton left Berlin to testify before Congress about the intelligence failure to anticipate the Japanese attack on Pearl Harbor. His executive officer, Col. William F. Heimlich, succeeded him. Heimlich's outfit numbered nearly 200 officials, including prisoner of war interrogators, counterintelligence special-

---

84 Klaus-Dietmar Henke, *Die amerikanische Besetzung Deutschlands* [The American occupation of Germany] (Munich: R. Oldenbourg Verlag, 2009), 698. The team's official designation was MIIT 440-G ("G" stood for Germany). Their report noted: "In conclusion we would like to say that from all evidence, and from talking with many Red Army officers in Berlin it appears that we were the first U.S. Army men to enter the German capital since its capitulation." Henke, *Amerikanische Besetzung*, 698.
85 John J. Maginnis, *Military Government Journal: Normandy to Berlin* (Amherst: University of Massachusetts Press, 1971), 258.
86 Interv, Brewster Chamberlin with William F. Heimlich, ACofS, G–2, Berlin Cmd, 4 Aug 1981, 10, Landesarchiv Berlin.
87 William Stivers and Donald A. Carter, *The City Becomes a Symbol. The U.S. Army in the Occupation of Berlin, 1945–1949*, U.S. Army in the Cold War (Washington, DC: U.S. Army Center of Military History, 2017), 18, 47.

Figure 14: An Army Intelligence safe house located on Bogotastrasse 19. This photograph was taken clandestinely by East German intelligence in the early 1950s. BStU.

ists, and order of battle analysts. On his staff served several Camp Ritchie–trained German émigrés, such as Capt. Frederick Sternberg, a prewar graduate of Berlin University. For the purpose of liaison with the Soviets, who controlled the eastern third of the city, Heimlich commanded several Russian speakers, including Capt. George T. Gabelia, the son of a refugee who came to the United States after the 1917 Russian Revolution. Heimlich considered his team to be one of the best "units we had in American intelligence and I was awfully lucky to get them."[88]

Army Intelligence quickly put down roots. Along with Berlin District headquarters, the intelligence branch briefly occupied the *Luftgau* building, the German air defense headquarters on Kronprinzenallee.[89] Within a few days, however, the dis-

---

[88] Interv, Chamberlin with Heimlich, 4 Aug 1981, 20–21, 24, 52.
[89] Kronprinzenallee was renamed Clayallee, after General Clay, in June 1949.

trict had to make way for the U.S. Group Control Council, Germany, which set up headquarters at the former *Luftgau* building. The Berlin District headquarters moved into a compound of the Telefunken radio company.[90] Six CIC teams established offices in each administrative district and began operating on 5 July.[91] Meanwhile, the Signal Corps discovered that all of Berlin's long-distance lines terminated at the *Fernamt* (telephone exchange) in Schöneberg in the American sector. The district took possession of the building and restored the lines, allowing the Americans to eavesdrop on phone calls to and from many cities in Europe, including Warsaw, Prague, Moscow, Paris, and Frankfurt.[92]

In addition to their headquarters, Army Intelligence agencies in Berlin required local facilities or safe houses to meet with informants or debrief defectors. For this purpose, they tapped into the vast pool of private homes requisitioned by the Army. By September 1945, the Berlin District controlled 4,500 properties in the American sector. In the posh neighborhood of Steglitz, where many villas had survived the war intact, the Americans evacuated one-quarter of the local population to make room for Army personnel.[93] The intelligence branch used only up to a dozen safe houses at a given time, but they frequently changed location to keep their activities secret. Also for the purpose of secrecy, U.S. personnel working in safe houses wore civilian clothes and drove cars with German license plates.[94] Still, these measures may not always have accomplished their goal as some Berliners soon realized the purpose of their expropriation. One citizen remembered: "In early July, the Americans arrived in our neighborhood and immediately commandeered all halfway useful houses for their countless . . . offices. Our home was to house a secret service bureau, and we were given two hours to move out, but we were not allowed to take any furniture or material with us."[95]

---

90 Stivers and Carter, *City Becomes a Symbol*, 75.
91 U.S. HQ Berlin District and HQ First Abn Army, History and Rpt of Opns, 8 May–31 Dec 1945, Part 2, Rpt of Opns 1945–46, Historical Div OMGUS, Berlin District, RG 498, NACP.
92 U.S. HQ Berlin District and HQ First Abn Army, History and Rpt of Opns, 8 May–31 Dec 1945, Part 2, Rpt of Opns 1945–46, Historical Div OMGUS, Berlin District, RG 498, NACP; Interv, Chamberlin with Heimlich, 4 Aug 1981, 18.
93 U.S. HQ Berlin District and HQ First Abn Army, History and Rpt of Opns, 8 May–31 Dec 1945, Part 2, Rpt of Opns 1945–46.
94 Deposition, Capt. Joe W. Lang, court-martial of William T. Marchuk, 12 Apr–20 May 1955, Washington National Records Center, Suitland, MD (hereinafter WNRC); James V. Milano and Patrick Brogan, *Soldiers, Spies, and the Rat Line: America's Undeclared War Against the Soviets* (Washington, DC: Brassey's, 1995), 224–26.
95 Ferdinand Friedensburg, *Es ging um Deutschlands Einheit: Rückschau eines Berliners auf die Jahre nach 1945* [It was about German unity: Reminiscences of a Berliner on the years after 1945] (Berlin: Haude & Spener, 1971), 39.

Colonel Heimlich—whose German last name appropriately translates as "secretive" or "furtive"—pushed the intelligence branch to aggressively recruit informants in Berlin and in the adjacent Soviet Zone.[96] The environment benefited the Americans. In the summer of 1945, Berlin citizens lacked everything from food to clothes and shelter, and the Americans paid their sources handsomely with increased rations, gasoline, or relief from work details.[97] The Americans also offered the Germans something intangible: the GIs' comparatively benevolent attitude toward their former enemies contrasted sharply with the punitive, often vindictive treatment meted out by the Soviets. German civilians, especially women, had suffered heavily under the Soviet occupation.[98] An intelligence officer who entered Berlin in late July recalled, "[The Germans in Berlin] were really broken down and the Russians had been there and had taught them a very unpleasant lesson, rape and so on, and when the Americans came they were considered, after all, the best they could expect."[99] The mere fact that the Americans were not the Soviets gave Heimlich's men an edge in their recruitment efforts.

In spite of these fortuitous circumstances and his eagerness to get things done, Heimlich stumbled. He did not speak German and, despite his last name, he was not particularly discreet. Boastful, brash, and fond of living large, Heimlich made waves as well as enemies. He repeatedly crossed swords with General Clay's chief of staff, the balding Brig. Gen. Charles K. Gailey Jr., calling him "the fury with the fringe on top." He belittled Colonel Rodes's organization as the "so-called intelligence office in the Military Government" and sought to incorporate it under his command.[100] Rodes shot back that "Mr. Heimlich did not impress me favorably from the first time that I met him. I felt he was a fairly intelligent opportunist . . . that he was insincere and . . . perfectly capable of taking advantage of any situation which arose. He talked too freely."[101]

---

96 Heimlich's ancestors had immigrated to the United States from Alsace in the early nineteenth century; see Interv, Chamberlin with Heimlich, 4 Aug 1981, 1.
97 U.S. HQ Berlin District and HQ First Abn Army, History and Rpt of Opns, 8 May–31 Dec 1945, Part 2, Rpt of Opns 1945–46.
98 For a German woman's eyewitness account of the Soviet occupation of Berlin, see Anonymous [Marta Hillers], *A Woman in Berlin: A Diary: Eight Weeks in the Conquered City* (New York: Henry Holt, 2005).
99 Interv, Dr. Jürgen Wetzel and Brewster S. Chamberlin with John Backer, 14 May 1981, 7–8, Landesarchiv Berlin.
100 Inter, Chamberlin with Heimlich, 4 Aug 1981, 24, 39.
101 Msg, Henry W. Meinecke, Asst Inspector Gen to the Cdr in Ch, EUCOM, 15 Mar 1948, sub: testimony of Col. Peter P. Rodes, Folder "Goebbels Diary," Administrative Ofc Mail and Rcds Section Decimal File Jun 1947–Jun 1948, RG 159, NACP.

Heimlich was supposed to focus on military targets, but he threw himself into the emerging political scene. He worked closely with Clay's political adviser, Robert D. Murphy, and regularly hosted budding German politicians like Willy Brandt, Ernst Reuter, and Kurt Schumacher at his opulent villa at the Wannsee, a popular lakeside recreation area for Berliners. For his extracurricular activities, and perhaps also for his undiplomatic comportment and overly aggressive recruitment of informants, General Sibert reprimanded him sharply. In October 1946, Heimlich joined the political affairs branch of the military government in Berlin.[102]

Coincidentally with Heimlich's departure, the Berlin District merged with the city's U.S. military government organization to form a single administrative unit, the Berlin Command.[103] Technically, this reorganization amounted to a demotion of the G–2 branch, as the Army downgraded it to an S–2 section under a lieutenant colonel. On the ground, however, things changed very little. The S–2 section continued to supervise intelligence operations, censorship, and document collection in the city. It retained the right to communicate directly with the intelligence division in Frankfurt.[104] The section chief also temporarily assumed operational control of the local CIC, which until then had reported to the intelligence division in Frankfurt.[105]

The Telefunken building used by the Berlin District headquarters was too far away from military government headquarters at the former *Luftgau* building. On 15 November 1946, the new Berlin Command moved to the Kaiser Wilhelm Institute in Dahlem, an elegant district in Zehlendorf, closer to the military government office. The intelligence section seized this opportunity to establish a separate headquarters, first in a villa on nearby Gosslerstrasse and then in another villa at Ehrenbergstrasse 26/28. The building on Ehrenbergstrasse had housed the German entomological museum before the war. Spacious and conveniently located near command headquarters, it served as S–2 headquarters through the remainder of the 1940s.[106]

---

102 Interv, Chamberlin with Heimlich, 4 Aug 1981, 21, 26; Rpt, Durand to Ch, Foreign Br M, 8 Apr 1948, sub: Transmittal of Report on Berlin Operations Base, in Steury, *On the Front Lines of the Cold War*, 42. Because Durand disliked Heimlich and viewed the Army's intelligence effort in Berlin as competition, his judgment must be taken with a grain of salt.
103 Stivers and Carter, *City Becomes a Symbol*, 135.
104 HQ Berlin Cmd, Rpt of Activities, 1 Nov 1946–30 Jun 1947, OMGUS, Berlin Cmd, History of Activities 1946–1947, RG 260, NACP. In reality, the relationship between S–2 and CIC changed very little, and the Corps remained fairly independent.
105 Rpt, Durand to Ch, Foreign Br M, 8 Apr 1948, sub: Transmittal of Report on Berlin Operations Base, in Steury, *On the Front Lines of the Cold War*, 41.
106 HQ Berlin Cmd, Rpt of Activities, 1 Nov 1946–30 Jun 1947, OMGUS, Berlin Cmd, History of Activities 1946–1947; Msg, Special Agent Zoltan Weinberger, S–2 Br, to Ofcr in Charge, 29 Jan 1947, sub: Security Night Check on S–2 Building, Folder "Security Plan, Berlin (U.S. Sector) 233517," INSCOM, IRR, Digitized Name Files, RG 319, NACP.

In October 1946, Lt. Col. John P. Merrill became the first chief of the new intelligence section. According to a fellow intelligence official in Berlin, Merrill "delighted in playing a personal cloak and dagger role."[107] Despite his enthusiasm, his tour lasted less than a year and became clouded by a counterintelligence failure that occurred on his watch. One of his subordinates was Lt. Jacques Saunder, a "colorful operator in the gallery of motley figures in S–2."[108] Saunder had established a semi-independent espionage organization with several branches in Berlin. In January 1947, U.S. intelligence discovered that Soviet security officials had arrested several of Saunder's informants. Presumably, they revealed much about their employer. Consequently, Colonel Merrill shut down Saunder's unit. In the spring of 1947, Merrill relinquished his job as S–2 chief.[109]

Merrill's successor, Col. George W. Busbey, a staunch cavalry officer, had earned the respect of local law enforcement officials while serving as provost marshal in Berlin.[110] During his tour of duty, the S–2 branch received an important reinforcement. In the winter of 1946–1947, the European Theater had established the 7829th Station Complement Unit in Frankfurt. In the summer of 1947, the unit's name changed to the 7829th Military Intelligence Platoon, and it moved to the American sector of Berlin. After being briefly attached to the military government organization in Berlin, the platoon was transferred to the S–2 section, and Colonel Busbey became its first commander. The platoon was to support the overextended local Army Intelligence organizations. Initially, platoon interrogators debriefed Soviet defectors. Over time, the unit wove a large web of informants across the Soviet Zone and evolved into the Army's principal espionage arm in East Germany.[111]

---

107 Rpt, Durand to Ch, Foreign Br M, 8 Apr 1948, sub: Transmittal of Report on Berlin Operations Base, in Steury, *On the Front Lines of the Cold War*, 42.
108 Rpt, Durand to Ch, Foreign Br M, 8 Apr 1948, sub: Transmittal of Report on Berlin Operations Base, in Steury, *On the Front Lines of the Cold War*, 43.
109 Msg, Lt. Col. John P. Merrill, S–2 Berlin, to ACofS, G–2, USFET, 17 Feb 1947, sub: Compromise of Intelligence Facilities, Folder "350.11–1947," HQ, EUCOM, Ofc of the Ch of Staff, Intel Div, Administrative Br, Gen Corresp (Decimal File), 1947–1951, RG 549, NACP.
110 Rpt, Durand to Ch, Foreign Br M, 8 Apr 1948, sub: Transmittal of Report on Berlin Operations Base, in Steury, *On the Front Lines of the Cold War*, 43. According to Durand, Lt. Col. Wilbur Wilson briefly succeeded Merrill on an interim basis and resumed his tour after Merrill's departure.
111 Msg, Lt. Col. Harry H. Pretty, Berlin Mil Post, S–2, to S–1, 30 Sep 1948, sub: Report of Operations for the S–2 Branch from 1 July to 30 September 1948, Folder "350.09 Intelligence Book 1 1948," EUCOM, Mil Post Berlin, Classified Decimal File, 1948–1951, RG 549, NA; Rpt, EUCOM, Historical Div, Quarterly Rpt of Opns 1 Apr to 30 Jun 1948, Historian's Background Files, 1947–1952, RG 549, NACP; Testimony of Col. Merrill, court-martial of William T. Marchuk, Apr and May 1955, WRNC.

The successful integration of the new platoon into the S–2 organization notwithstanding, Busbey did not last long in his job. In May 1947, the CIC launched an investigation into the doings of Michael G. Stcherbinine, an S–2 liaison officer with the local military police. The son of Russian émigrés, Stcherbinine had provided information to U.S. intelligence about a supposed ring of dissidents within a local Soviet intelligence agency. Not only did this group turn out to be nonexistent, the CIC investigation also disclosed that Stcherbinine had never received a proper clearance and had revealed classified information to outsiders.[112] Although Busbey had not hired Stcherbinine, the investigation clouded the commander's reputation, and he left his job in the summer of 1947.

By now, the top job at the intelligence section had become a revolving door, and the transition of the European Theater into the European Command in 1947 added to the sense of organizational instability caused by the rapid leadership turnover. On 30 April, the Berlin Command became the Berlin Military Post, which moved to the grounds of the former Telefunken building, now renamed McNair Barracks. Under the new organizational chart, the S–2 section reported directly to the director of intelligence, General Walsh, rather than to the intelligence division in Frankfurt. On paper, the new chain of command made sense, as the director and the S–2 chief were colocated in Berlin. But Walsh had little interest in operational intelligence and provided little guidance to the S–2 section.[113]

Merrill's successor, Col. Wilbur Wilson, served only for a few months, and in the fall of 1947, Lt. Col. Harry S. Pretty assumed command of the S–2 section.[114] The constant reorganization took a toll. The branch was "in dilapidated condition," a fellow intelligence official noted, and Pretty had his hands full trying to stabilize the organization.[115] Shouldering "an excessive number of duties and re-

---

112 Rpt, Special Agent Ellis C. Graham, Region VIII, CIC, to CO, 28 Mar 1949, sub: Stcherbinine, Michael G., Folder "Tcherbinine, Michael XE224787," INSCOM, IRR, Digitized Name Files RG 319, NACP. For more on the Stcherbinine case, see Chapter 7.
113 Stivers and Carter, *City Becomes a Symbol*, 241; Rpt, Durand to Ch, Foreign Br M, 8 Apr 1948, sub: Transmittal of Report on Berlin Operations Base, in Steury, *On the Front Lines of the Cold War*, 44; Msg, Lt. Col. Harry S. Pretty, S–2 Br, Berlin Mil Post, to CO, Berlin Mil Post, 8 Feb 1951, sub: Punitive Action Under AW 104, Folder "Headquarters Berlin Military Post," HQ, EUCOM, Ofc of the Ch of Staff, Mil Posts Division, Berlin Mil Post, Classified Decimal File, 1948–51, RG 549, NACP.
114 Rpt, Durand to Ch, Foreign Br M, 8 Apr 1948, sub: Transmittal of Report on Berlin Operations Base, in Steury, *On the Front Lines of the Cold War*, 44.
115 Rpt, Durand to Ch, Foreign Br M, 8 Apr 1948, sub: Transmittal of Report on Berlin Operations Base, in Steury, *On the Front Lines of the Cold War*, 44.

sponsibilities with a limited number of personnel," he noted, "my working hours were unlimited with no leave from 1947 until June 1950."[116]

Shortly after becoming S–2 chief in Berlin, Pretty conducted one of the more unusual intelligence investigations. During the summer of 1947, numerous observers reported sightings of "flying saucers" in the United States, and U.S. Air Force intelligence launched an investigation.[117] Suspecting a link between the flying saucer phenomenon and an actual German wartime invention, the jet-powered Horten Ho 229 single-wing bomber, the European intelligence division asked Pretty to contact German air scientists to find out whether the *Luftwaffe* had ever built a "flying saucer." The sources contacted by Pretty agreed that, although a "flying saucer" design was "highly practical and desirable," Nazi Germany had never built such an aircraft.[118]

Pretty served as the chief of the intelligence section and as the commander of the 7829th Military Intelligence Platoon. By the summer of 1948, he had organized his outfit into three sections: an operational intelligence section, which handled defector interrogations and espionage; an economic intelligence section, which procured intelligence about the economic situation in Germany; and a scientific section, which dealt with the recruitment of German scientists for the United States (Project PAPERCLIP). The S–2 branch had an assigned strength of three officers, six enlisted men, and twelve civilians. The platoon, which supported the branch, had an assigned strength of twelve officers and thirty-three enlisted men. This organization remained in place through the end of the military occupation of Germany.[119]

In marked contrast to his short-term predecessors, Pretty led the intelligence section with a steady hand for three-and-a-half years, until the spring of 1951. He brought much-needed stability to U.S. intelligence in Berlin. Although he was not a trained intelligence professional, he learned quickly on the job. Unlike the flamboyant Heimlich or the secretive Merrill, the personable Pretty developed solid working relationships with other intelligence officials in the city.[120] Under his leadership, the Army's principal intelligence organization in Berlin evolved from a dysfunctional outfit into a disciplined unit that competently handled interrogations, espionage, and intelligence analysis.

---

116 Msg, Pretty to CO, 8 Feb 1951, sub: Punitive Action Under AW 104.
117 "Air Force Intelligence Joins Search for Flying Saucers," *Washington Post*, 8 Jul 1948.
118 Msg Lt. Col. Harry H. Pretty to DDI, 16 Dec 1947, sub: Horton [sic] Brothers (Flying Saucers), Historians Files, CMH.
119 Msg, Pretty to S–1, 30 Sep 1948, sub: Report of Operations for the S-2 Branch from 1 July to 30 September 1948. During the Berlin blockade, Pretty also supervised the local CIC.
120 Rpt, Durand to Ch, Foreign Br M, 8 Apr 1948, sub: Transmittal of Report on Berlin Operations Base, in Steury, *On the Front Lines of the Cold War*, 44.

From OSS to CIA

The Office of Strategic Services arrived in Germany in the wake of the conquering Allied forces. In May 1945, the office established its headquarters in the famous Henkell estate, a sparkling wine producer in a Wiesbaden suburb near Frankfurt.[121] Spacious and largely undamaged, the grandiose marble building had the added advantage that its new inhabitants "could drink unlimited quantities of green champagne," as one OSS veteran recalled. A nearby fourteen-room house served as residential quarters for twenty-two officers, "and we enjoyed the finest German featherbeds. Two polite German spinsters served as housekeepers." Living there "was an unforgettable experience."[122] Eventually, the Americans returned the building to its rightful owner, and OSS headquarters moved on to Heidelberg.

The first postwar OSS chief in Germany was Allen W. Dulles, who moved to Wiesbaden from his wartime post in Switzerland. Dulles's immediate concern was the well-being of the CROWN JEWELS—the high-level German officials, politicians, academics, and businessmen who had worked for him during the war. Dulles sought to convert his group into a postwar intelligence network, but this effort fell flat. His German contacts had little interest in spying for the Americans in peacetime and instead sought to get back into their erstwhile professions.[123]

The OSS had barely arrived in Germany when organizational turmoil threatened to end its efforts to establish an espionage organization in the conquered country. Concerned about the notion of an "American Gestapo," President Truman dissolved the office, effective 1 October 1945, and shifted its constituent parts to other government departments for liquidation.[124] The State Department assumed control of the research and analysis branch, and the War Department received its intelligence and counterespionage branches, and renamed them the Strategic Services Unit.[125]

---

121 Rpt, Capt. W. B. Kantack, to Director, OSS, 3 Aug 1945, sub: Report from OSS/Germany for June 1945, Folder "ETO – Germany June – 1945," OSS History Ofc, RG 226, NACP. The building had been identified by Col. Alfred D. Reutershan, and the OSS staff moved in between 19 and 21 May.
122 Richard Cutler, *Counterspy: Memoirs of a Counterintelligence Officer in World War II and the Cold War* (Washington, DC: Brassey's, 2004), 49–50.
123 Richard Helms with William Hood, *A Look Over My Shoulder: A Life in the Central Intelligence Agency* (Novato, CA: Presidio, 2004), 55; Rpt, Durand to Ch, Foreign Br M, 8 Apr 1948, sub: Transmittal of Report on Berlin Operations Base, in Steury, *On the Front Lines of the Cold War*, 7.
124 R. Harris Smith, *OSS: The Secret History of America's First Central Intelligence Agency* (Berkeley: University of California Press, 1972), 365; Michael Warner, "Salvage and Liquidation: The Creation of the Central Intelligence Group," *Studies in Intelligence* 39, no. 5 (1996), 112.
125 EO 9621, "Termination of the Office of Strategic Services and Disposition of Its Functions," 20 Sep 1945, doc. 14, in *Foreign Relations of the United States* (FRUS), *1945–1950, Emergence of the*

Many OSS veterans did not expect the rebranded outfit to last long and left. The exodus included Allen Dulles, who resigned from the Strategic Services Unit in early December to join his old law firm in New York.[126] His assistant, Lt. Col. William G. Suhling, served as chief of mission in Germany until January 1946 when Lt. Col. Crosby Lewis, a former CIC officer, took over.[127] Richard M. Helms, another OSS veteran who served in postwar Germany, remembered the period of the Strategic Services Unit as one marked by organizational turmoil and low morale.[128]

The Cold War breathed new life into the moribund espionage outfit. Against the backdrop of rising tensions between Moscow and Washington, the president changed his mind about the need for a central intelligence organization. In January 1946, he created a "Cloak and Dagger Group of Snoopers," as he called it, the Central Intelligence Group under a Director of Central Intelligence. A few weeks after its creation, the group assumed control of the Strategic Services Unit. With the passing of the National Security Act in 1947, the group became the CIA. The new organization was to coordinate all U.S. intelligence activities and produce strategic intelligence assessments. In addition, the agency actively collected information through human sources, including the recruitment of informants and the exploitation of defectors.[129]

Gordon M. Stewart, a former OSS officer, became the first CIA station chief in Germany, and he served in this function for the remainder of the military occupation.[130] Under his leadership, CIA headquarters moved twice. In 1948, when the Army relocated its European headquarters organization to Heidelberg and took over much of the available housing there, the CIA transferred its headquarters to Karlsruhe. At the end of the military occupation, it relocated again, this time into the IG Farben building in Frankfurt. By then, Stewart oversaw a staff of roughly two hundred personnel in all of Germany.[131]

Intelligence Establishment, ed. C. Thomas Thorne Jr. and David S. Patterson (Washington, DC: State Department, Office of the Historian, 1996), 44–45.
126 James Srodes, *Allen Dulles: Master of Spies* (Washington, DC: Regnery, 1999), 370–71.
127 Cutler, *Counterspy*, 54, 156n12; Ruffner, *Forging an Intelligence Partnership*, 1:xxxviii; Email, Kevin C. Ruffner to Thomas Boghardt, 10 Nov 2017, Historians Files, CMH.
128 Helms, *A Look Over My Shoulder*, 58.
129 Warner, "Salvage and Liquidation," 111.
130 Kevin C. Ruffner, "Eagle and Swastika: CIA and Nazi War Criminals and Collaborators" (Washington, DC: History Staff, Central Intelligence Agency, 2003), chap. 12, 8; Email, Ruffner to Boghardt, 10 Nov 2017.
131 Klaus Eichner and Andreas Dobbert, *Headquarters Germany: Die USA-Geheimdienste in Deutschland* [Headquarters Germany: The U.S. secret services in Germany] (Berlin: edition ost, 2001), 58; Matthew Aid, "The CIA in Germany: A Secret History," *Daily Beast*, 10 Jul 2014, https://www.thedailybeast.com/the-cia-in-germany-a-secret-history, Historians Files, CMH; Emails, Kevin C. Ruffner to Thomas Boghardt, 13 and 19 Nov 2017, Historians Files, CMH.

The military occupation and the Army's central role in it shaped the transformation of the OSS into the CIA in Germany. The OSS and its successor were subordinate to the Army's top intelligence officer in the European Theater, General Sibert.[132] Logistically, they depended on the Army for everything from support staff to gasoline. In order to fit into the Army's organization and to remain covert, the Strategic Services Unit adopted the cover name "War Department Detachment." When a *New York Times* story blew this cover in late 1947, the outed spies assumed a new name, "Department of the Army Detachment" or DAD.[133] Despite the name change, a CIA officer conceded, "we certainly fooled hardly anyone as to what our real associations were."[134]

The CIA's integration into the Army's occupational regime caused frictions. The CIA's creators had conceived of the agency as a national effort on top of the existing military intelligence organizations, but this notion sat ill with its need to report to Army authorities in Germany. In a telling aside, a CIA officer in Germany referred to Clay's director of intelligence, General Walsh, as representing a "competitive or at least divergent interest."[135] General Sibert's postwar efforts to create a centralized intelligence organization in Germany under his command probably had done little to endear the agency's leadership to the Army. Different organizational cultures and the old wartime rivalry between the OSS and Army Intelligence exacerbated the schism. Like the OSS, the CIA tended to recruit well-bred Ivy Leaguers who struck many outsiders as presumptuous and self-important. The Army officer corps, by contrast, remained middle American, practical, and mission driven. At the most basic level, the two groups simply did not speak the same language. When a CIA officer wanted to discuss one of his wordy memoranda with an Army general, the latter sighed, "Why can't you write in plain English?"[136]

The OSS established several branch offices in German cities, including Berlin, Bremen, Heidelberg, Kassel, Munich, Nuremberg, and Regensburg, as well as smaller

---

132 David Alvarez and Eduard Mark, *Spying Through a Glass Darkly: American Espionage against the Soviet Union, 1945–1946* (Lawrence: University Press of Kansas, 2016), 119.
133 "Mikolajczyk Got Secret Unit's Aid," *New York Times*, 4 Nov 1947; Rpt, Durand to Ch, Foreign Br M, 8 Apr 1948, sub: Transmittal of Report on Berlin Operations Base, in Steury, *On the Front Lines of the Cold War*, 2.
134 Email, Peter M. F. Sichel to Thomas Boghardt, 15 Sep 1017, Historians Files, CMH.
135 Rpt, Durand to Ch, Foreign Br M, 8 Apr 1948, sub: Transmittal of Report on Berlin Operations Base, in Steury, *On the Front Lines of the Cold War*, 32.
136 Evan Thomas, *The Very Best Men: Four Who Dared: The Early Years of the CIA* (London: Touchstone, 1997), 66.

Figure 15: Peter Sichel as a U.S. Army private. Courtesy of Peter Sichel.

units in Oslo and Prague.¹³⁷ Berlin received particular attention because the OSS had initially contemplated the German capital as its headquarters location.¹³⁸ An OSS advance party of fifteen officers and enlisted men under Lt. Col. Edwin F. Black entered the city on 13 July 1945.¹³⁹ Four days later, the rest of the OSS Berlin detachment followed. Initially, they joined the U.S. Group Control Council, Germany, in the *Luftgau* building, but the detachment was keen to find a more discreet facility nearby.¹⁴⁰ In August, they identified a villa formerly used by German Field Marshal Wilhelm Keitel on Föhrenweg 19, conveniently located only a few blocks from the *Luftgau* building. After fixing a number of security issues with the building, the detachment moved

---

137 Kevin C. Ruffner "Eagle and Swastika," chap. 3, 4–5.
138 Rpt, Durand to Ch, Foreign Br M, 8 Apr 1948, sub: Transmittal of Report on Berlin Operations Base, in Steury, *On the Front Lines of the Cold War*, 8.
139 Rpt, Kantack to Director, OSS, 3 Aug 1945, sub: Report from OSS/Germany for June 1945.
140 Msg, Lt. Col. Andrew H. Berding, Ch X–2/OSS, Germany, to Secretariat, OSS Mission for Germany, 7 Aug 1945, sub: Monthly Progress Report – X-2 Branch, July 1945, Folder "ETO – Germany July 1945, Folder 24," OSS History Ofc, RG 226, NACP.

Figure 16: The Joe House at Promenadenstrasse 2 in Berlin. Yale University.

into its new headquarters in September.[141] In December, it assumed the designation Berlin Operations Base.[142]

The Berlin base replicated the leadership revolving door of the headquarters in the U.S. Zone. Although Allen Dulles nominally headed the OSS presence in Berlin, he spent much of his time in Wiesbaden and winding down his affairs in Switzerland. In October, he turned over the Berlin station to his deputy, Richard Helms, a capable OSS veteran who had worked for several years in prewar Berlin as a journalist for United Press. In 1936, he had interviewed Adolf Hitler, who close up struck him as "shorter and less impressive than at a distance."[143] Helms

---

141 Msg, 2d Lt. Rene C. Champollion, Security Ofcr, to Lt. Col. Black, OSS, U.S. Gp Control Council (USGCC), 6 Sep 1945, sub: Physical Security, "Berlin – Lt. Champollion," Miscellaneous Washington Files; Budget, RG 226, NACP.
142 Peter M. F. Sichel, *Secrets of My Life: Vintner, Prisoner, Soldier, Spy* (Bloomington, IN: Archway Publishing, 2006), 161. The BOB designation was part of a reorganization of local elements of the Strategic Services Unit in December 1945.
143 Helms, *A Look Over My Shoulder*, 24.

Figure 17: Agents dining at the Joe House. Yale University.

stayed on until December 1945 when he turned things over to the chief of the secret intelligence, or espionage, section, Peter M. F. Sichel.

Sichel was a superb intelligence officer. The scion of a cosmopolitan German-Jewish wine merchant dynasty, he had come to the United States in 1941 and volunteered for the U.S. Army a week after Pearl Harbor. Intelligent, multilingual, and highly educated, he ended up with the OSS, serving in North Africa, Italy, and southern France. At the end of the war, he found himself in Heidelberg. In October, he transferred to Berlin where Helms picked him up at Tempelhof airport. "I shall never forget the first sight of Berlin," Sichel recalled. "It was a sunny day, and it was not cold, but the sight of the city—the mountains of debris and the forlorn, sad, and impoverished look of the population–was ghastly."[144]

The local OSS station was in a similarly sorry state. The rapid leadership turnover, widespread corruption, and the hemorrhage of capable personnel had taken its toll. Many OSS officials had become involved in the thriving black market. Not long after Sichel's arrival, he gained firsthand experience of the extent of this illegal

---

[144] Sichel, *Secrets of My Life*, 156.

activity among his own subordinates. Glancing at Sichel's watch, his deputy said he could sell it for him for $1,000. Sichel declined and gave the man the choice between an investigation of his financial activities or an immediate departure from Berlin and the OSS. The chastened official opted to vacate his position. "It was an appropriate introduction," Sichel noted, "and over the next couple of weeks, I cleaned house."[145] In January 1946, another OSS veteran, Dana B. Durand, took over from Sichel, but the latter continued to serve as deputy chief.

For operational purposes, the Berlin base took possession of a twelve-room villa in Lichterfelde, a district on the southern end of the American sector.[146] The "Joe House," as it became known, on Promenadenstrasse 2 was an oasis of luxury in war-ravaged Berlin. "I live in a house with a big radio, hot water, and heat," one occupant recalled. "I am even sleeping between sheets for the first time in five months. Besides a fairly good cook, we have maids and a handyman in this house (paid for by the German people). They do everything except read my mail and write letters. . . . When [my car] doesn't start in the morning, all the gals file out and push it down the drive."[147] The Joe House proved an attractive feature for prospective informants.

Former German intelligence officers constituted the first batch of OSS recruits in Berlin. The Americans used them to provide information on the Nazi secret service apparatus and to gather leads on other potential sources in the city. Over time, the Berlin base also sought to collect information on Soviet intelligence through these agents. Like the Americans, the Soviets recruited former German intelligence officers in Berlin, and many ended up working for both sides. In numerous cases, the OSS became aware of their informants' dual employment and sought to "double" them "back" against their Soviet spymasters. The German agents' true loyalty remains hazy, but because Soviet intelligence had been in the espionage business much longer than the Americans, one is left to wonder how many of them really were "a great find," as an OSS case officer noted about one his agents.[148] The following case illustrates the moral ambiguity of this cat-and-mouse game.

One of the earliest OSS recruits in Berlin was Heinz K. H. Krull, a former *Abwehr* and *Gestapo* officer, who began working for the Americans under the code

---

145 Helms, *A Look Over My Shoulder*, 58; Sichel, *Secrets of My Life*, 159.
146 Rpt, Durand to Ch, Foreign Br M, 8 Apr 1948, sub: Transmittal of Report on Berlin Operations Base, in Steury, *On the Front Lines of the Cold War*, 78.
147 Cutler, *Counterspy*, 106–07.
148 Cutler, *Counterspy*, 89.

name ZIGZAG in early 1945. An internal report praised him "as a walking encyclopedia" on German intelligence.[149] At Krull's suggestion, the Berlin base in late 1945 recruited another former *Abwehr* officer, Hans A. Kemritz, code-named SAVOY. His American handlers knew that Kemritz also spied for the Soviets, regularly pointing out German intelligence veterans to them. The Soviets arrested many of Kemritz's victims, executing several and sentencing others to years in prison. Eventually, the widows of some of the perished German officers joined forces and identified Kemritz as the culprit of their spouses' disappearance. When German authorities began legal proceedings against Kemritz for "aggravated deprivation of liberty" (*Schwere Freiheitsberaubung*) in connection with the missing Germans, the CIA resettled him in the Western Hemisphere. This intervention prevented the disclosure of American secrets in a public trial but it also cast a sinister light on U.S. intelligence in Germany.[150]

After the CIC and the Berlin District G–2 branch, the OSS became the third American intelligence outfit to operate in the former German capital. Within the narrow confines of the city, the latent rivalry between the Army and the fledgling CIA became more pronounced than in the rest of Germany. The CIA managed to establish a solid working relationship with the Army's counterintelligence operatives thanks to efforts of CIC Special Agent Severin F. Wallach, who served as the Corps' liaison with the agency.[151] The CIA and the Army's intelligence branch, by contrast, eyed each other warily, owing to their services' cultural differences and the fact that both organizations had the same basic mission: to collect intelligence by means of interrogation and informants.

Durand portrayed his outfit "in the true sense [as] an elite group," but this heroic self-image belied the agency's near-total dependence on the Berlin Command. Staff support, billets, operational facilities, military guards, air travel permits, and even furniture had to be requested from the Army. Payments for agents in the form of cigarettes (a vital substitute currency in struggling postwar Berlin), "operational liquor," and medicine came from Army supplies. In a city that was almost four times the size of the District of Columbia, any intelligence agency would need to have access to cars, gasoline, and technical support, and only the Army could provide these key assets. The organizational intertwining of the CIA and the Army necessitated frequent contact between the two sides, but many

---

[149] Index card, n.d., sub: ZIGZAG, Dr. Heinz Krull, Berlin, CIA Electronic Reading Room, https://www.cia.gov/readingroom.

[150] Arthur Smith, *Kidnap City: Cold War Berlin* (Westport, CT: Greenwood, 2002), 65–80; Cutler, *Counterspy*, 90–94.

[151] Rpt, Durand to Ch, Foreign Br M, 8 Apr 1948, sub: Transmittal of Report on Berlin Operations Base, in Steury, *On the Front Lines of the Cold War*, 48.

meetings ended on a discordant note. On one occasion, Maj. Gen. George P. Hays, the deputy military governor in Germany, lectured CIA officers in Berlin that "the Germans surrendered not because of OSS but because of the victorious advance of the ground troops."[152] The CIA, the Army felt, could not be allowed to forget who really ran the show in postwar Germany.

During the first two years of the occupation in Berlin, the CIA and the Army's intelligence branch frequently reported on each other to the Army's top intelligence officer in Germany about alleged security breaches. The chief of the Berlin base, Dana Durand, dismissed the Berlin District's chief of intelligence, Colonel Heimlich, as a "former radio executive" unsuited for intelligence work. According to Durand, Heimlich committed numerous "security lapses" of which civilian intelligence officials promptly informed General Sibert.[153] The ensuing reprimand contributed to Heimlich's decision to leave his post. A year later, Durand informed the intelligence chief that Heimlich's successor, Colonel Merrill, ran an amateurish spy network in Berlin. When notified, Merrill closed down the operation, although he disagreed with Durand's assessment.[154] Shortly thereafter, Merrill's successor, Colonel Wilson, gave Durand a taste of his own medicine. In the spring of 1947, the Soviets arrested a CIA agent who had neglected to destroy incriminating material in his possession. Wilson presented these facts to the director of intelligence "in a highly derogatory and colored report," an irate Durand wrote. He felt that Wilson's account of the incident was particularly hypocritical, considering that two recently arrested S–2 agents had been "guilty of at least equally great indiscretions."[155]

The relationship between the intelligence section and the Berlin Operations Base stabilized only in the summer of 1947. The unpretentious new S–2 branch chief, Colonel Pretty, received praise from Durand as "the most satisfactory" in comparison with his predecessors. Moreover, the Army developed its own collection capabilities to a degree that made it less reliant on the CIA. In the summer of 1946, General Sibert had ordered the Strategic Services Unit to collect order of battle information on the Soviet forces in Germany, but the largely civilian staff

---

152 Rpt, Durand to Ch, Foreign Br M, 8 Apr 1948, sub: Transmittal of Report on Berlin Operations Base, in Steury, *On the Front Lines of the Cold War*, 5, 72, 76, 78, 80, 81–83.
153 Rpt, Durand to Ch, Foreign Br M, 8 Apr 1948, sub: Transmittal of Report on Berlin Operations Base, in Steury, *On the Front Lines of the Cold War*, 42.
154 Rpt, Durand to Ch, Foreign Br M, 8 Apr 1948, sub: Transmittal of Report on Berlin Operations Base, in Steury, *On the Front Lines of the Cold War*, 43; Msg, Merrill to ACofS, G–2, USFET, 17 Feb 1947, sub: Compromise of Intelligence Facilities.
155 Rpt, Durand to Ch, Foreign Br M, 8 Apr 1948, sub: Transmittal of Report on Berlin Operations Base, in Steury, *On the Front Lines of the Cold War*, 43.

of the Berlin Operations Base felt uncomfortable with this "throwback to wartime operations" and fumbled the mission.[156] The transfer of the 7829th Military Intelligence Platoon to Berlin and the activation of the U.S. Military Liaison Mission in 1947 allowed the Army to collect the order of battle information it needed from the Soviet Zone without having to involve its unwilling civilian counterpart.[157]

For the Berlin Operations Base, this was a most welcome development. As the CIA leadership prepared for a briefing of General Clay in early 1947, Assistant Director Col. Donald H. Galloway emphasized the need to get away from "short-range tactical" targets and instead focus operations "toward a long-range strategic objective."[158] In practice, this meant the recruitment of local agents in eastern Germany who could provide inside information on the workings of the Soviet administration and on Soviet policy. Under the capable leadership of the agency's local espionage chief, Peter Sichel, the Berlin base did exactly that. His methodical approach earned him high praise from the CIA's German station chief, Gordon Stewart, who rated Sichel the "most experienced, most capable intelligence officer under my control."[159]

Tactical intelligence on the Soviet forces played only a minor role in Sichel's work, but by then, the Army felt confident in its abilities to procure this information through its own organizations. For their part, agency officials preferred to work with Clay's political adviser, Robert Murphy, rather than with the military leadership. A career diplomat with a soft spot for "cloak and dagger" work, Murphy was a kindred spirit who, Durand noted approvingly, "understands what we are doing and enjoys occasionally taking part in it himself."[160] The CIA in Germany continued to use its military cover name, Department of the Army Detachment, and the agency depended on the Army for logistical and administrative support. Yet its operational arm acted largely outside Army supervision. The CIA leadership was looking beyond the end of the military government.

---

156 David E. Murphy, Sergei A. Kondrashev, and George Bailey, *Battleground Berlin: CIA vs. KGB in the Cold War* (New Haven, CT: Yale University Press, 1999), 16. For intelligence operations in the Soviet Zone, see Chapter 9.
157 For more on the U.S. Military Liaison Mission to the Commander in Chief of the Soviet Occupied Zone of Germany (USMLM), see Chapter 4.
158 Memo, Donald H. Galloway, for Gen Vandenberg, 16 Jan 1947, sub: Points for discussion with General Clay, in Steury, *On the Front Lines of the Cold War*, 109–10.
159 Ruffner, "Eagle and Swastika," chap. 10, 9n24.
160 Rpt, Durand to Ch, Foreign Br M, 8 Apr 1948, sub: Transmittal of Report on Berlin Operations Base, in Steury, *On the Front Lines of the Cold War*, 32.

U.S. Navy and U.S. Air Force Intelligence Efforts

Besides the U.S. Army and the CIA, the U.S. Navy ran a small intelligence organization in occupied Germany. In late 1944, the Navy established the position of Commander of Naval Forces for Germany. The commander's intelligence division was to help disarm the *Kriegsmarine* (German navy) and exploit German naval technology. In April 1945, the division set up headquarters in the Bremen enclave. During the following months and years, it established branches and liaison offices across the U.S. Zone as its focus shifted to the Soviet navy. In 1949, division headquarters moved to Berlin under Capt. Arthur H. Graubart. A naval attaché to prewar Berlin, Graubart made a lasting impression on his fellow intelligence officers in the city. Peter Sichel remembered him as "a wonderful man" and "quite a character."[161] The U.S. Navy's intelligence effort remained small and relied heavily on its liaison with other agencies. By the late 1940s, Graubart commanded a staff of twenty-one in Berlin, Vienna, and seven cities in the U.S. Zone.[162]

In 1948, the newly created independent U.S. Air Force established two intelligence organizations, the U.S. Air Force Security Service for signals intelligence operations and the Office of Special Investigations (OSI) for operations involving agents and informants. The service activated a mobile radio squadron in Herzo Base, but the Air Force continued to rely heavily on the Army Security Agency for signal intelligence support.[163] The OSI conducted a wide range of espionage operations in East Germany in the course of the 1950s.[164] During the military occupation, the Air Force contributed to the U.S. intelligence effort chiefly by supporting the Army, and the two services remained closely intertwined. In fact, two out of three intelligence chiefs of the European Command, General Walsh and General Hall, were Air Force officers.

---

161 Interv, Peter M. F. Sichel with Thomas Boghardt, 7 Mar 2018, Historians Files, CMH.
162 Wyman H. Packard, *A Century of U.S. Naval Intelligence* (Washington, DC: Department of the Navy, 1996), 434–36.
163 USAF Intel, Surveillance and Reconnaissance Agency, "A Continuing Legacy: From USAFSS to AF ISR Agency, 1948–2012" (USAF Intel, Surveillance and Reconnaissance Agency History Ofc, no place, n.d.), 4.
164 Ministerium für Staatssicherheit (MfS; Ministry for State Security), HA II, "Dislokation, Strukturen und Methoden der imperialistischen Geheimdienste in Westdeutschland und Westberlin" [Dislocation, structures, and methods of the imperialist intelligence services in West Germany and West Berlin], 1 Jan 1956, MfS – HA II no. 43877, Der Bundesbeauftragte für die Unterlagen des Staatssicherheitsdienstes der ehemaligen Deutschen Demokratischen Republik (BStU; Federal Commissioner for the Records of the State Security Service of the former German Democratic Republic), Berlin. The archives of the BStU, or Stasi Records Agency, contain numerous references to USAF Office of Special Investigations espionage operations in the German Democratic Republic (East Germany) during the 1950s.

Conclusion

The Army successfully converted its wartime intelligence organization into an instrument of the occupation, though the sailing was far from smooth. To avoid organizational duplication and poor coordination between individual agencies, General Sibert sought to create a centralized intelligence organization under his command. His efforts inevitably aggravated those who had to cede authority. Administrative turmoil roiled U.S. intelligence for an extended period of time after the end of hostilities. As Army Intelligence and the OSS adapted to postwar conditions, their headquarters repeatedly moved to different locations, changed designations, underwent internal reorganizations, and rotated personnel in and out. Only by 1947, with the creation of the European Command and the passing of the National Security Act, had the Army and the CIA established semipermanent headquarters organizations in Germany, which guaranteed the steady management of the American intelligence effort. This task fell to a number of operational agencies, that conducted a wide range of activities in the U.S. Zone, the sectors of Berlin, and beyond.

4 Intelligence Field Agencies

The Grand Alliance between the Soviet Union and the Western Powers crumbled rapidly. Early disputes included Soviet leader Joseph Stalin's insistence on an all-communist government in Poland and his refusal to withdraw the Red Army from its wartime positions in Iran. In the summer of 1946, Moscow began to put pressure on the pro-Western Turkish government to permit a Soviet naval presence in the Dardanelles, a concession that would give the Red Fleet access to the Mediterranean Sea. Meanwhile, in neighboring Greece, pro-Soviet communist partisans were fighting the British-backed government.[1] Army Intelligence reports on Soviet troop concentrations in Rumania and Bulgaria, near the Greek and Turkish borders, underscored the seriousness of the threat.[2]

The U.S. government feared that if Greece and Turkey succumbed to Soviet pressure, neighboring countries would follow suit—a chain of events that U.S. officials would soon describe as the domino effect. Secretary of War Robert P. Patterson warned President Harry S. Truman of "communist infiltration" and "Soviet aggression," and urged the president to maintain a strong military and an effective intelligence organization to counter this growing threat. Patterson saw "only one real possibility of dealing with the policies at present pursued by the USSR. That is to be firm against any compromise of our fundamental ideals, the support of which is our responsibility to the world."[3] This advice matched Truman's own thinking. For some time, the president had been wary of what he regarded as Soviet recalcitrance and Stalin's efforts to expand his country's sphere of influence into Europe and the Middle East. "Unless Russia is faced with an iron fist and strong language," he told one of his cabinet members in 1946, "another war is in the making.... I'm tired of babying the Soviets."[4]

The crisis in the eastern Mediterranean sealed Truman's decision to adopt a hard policy toward Moscow. On 12 March 1947, the president asked Congress for aid to Greece and Turkey, but he emphasized that the issue at hand went beyond a regional conflict. "At the present moment in world history," he said, "nearly every nation must choose between alternative ways of life." One rested on freedom and democracy, the other relied "on terror and oppression." The United

---

1 John Lewis Gaddis, *The United States and the Origins of the Cold War, 1941–1947* (New York: Columbia University Press, 1972), 336.
2 Eduard Mark, "The War Scare of 1946 and Its Consequences," *Diplomatic History* 21, no. 3 (Summer 1997), 390, 402.
3 Ltr, Robert P. Patterson, Sec War, to President Harry S. Truman, 27 Jul 1946, Folder "Series 1946," Ofc of the Ch of Staff, Top-Secret Gen Corresp, 1941–1947, RG 165, NACP.
4 Gaddis, *United States and the Origins of the Cold War*, 289, 311–12.

States, Truman declared, could not stand by idly in this ideological struggle but "must support free people who are resisting attempted subjugation by armed minorities or by outside pressure."[5] With this speech, the president laid the foundations of the Truman Doctrine, a policy aimed at containing communism and Soviet power. It marked the beginning of what the British writer George Orwell coined the "cold war."[6]

The recalibration of U.S. policy from cooperation with the Soviet Union to the containment of communism had a profound effect on the Allied occupation of Germany. If the Potsdam agreement had emphasized dealing with the legacy of the Third Reich, the Cold War called for the close monitoring of communist and Soviet activities. The new mission constituted a sea change for intelligence officials in Germany. Some of the old hands who had hoped to exorcise Germany of its Nazi past felt demoralized that their assignment was now a lesser priority. "The changes that are taking place here are not at all pleasant," a member of the Information Control Division lamented in a letter home.[7] Others enthusiastically embraced the new policy. "The Soviet Union was the enemy, and the 'Soviet target' our intelligence mission," wrote a CIA official serving in Berlin.[8] Regardless of personal sentiments, everybody had to adapt.

The execution of intelligence operations in Germany fell to roughly half a dozen field agencies. The unexpected mission reset forced them to change their means of conducting business. To fight this emerging Cold War, field agencies would have to recruit new sources, develop new information-gathering techniques, and adopt a new outlook on the American presence in Germany. The operational and organizational transformation caused by this reorientation affected every agency and became the defining moment of Army Intelligence in postwar Germany.

The Counter Intelligence Corps

The Army's counterintelligence plans for postwar Germany took shape in the winter of 1944 to 1945. In early 1945, the 418th Counter Intelligence Corps Detachment of the 12th Army Group received additional personnel from tactical detachments

---

[5] Gaddis, *United States and the Origins of the Cold War*, 351.
[6] George Orwell, "You and the Atomic Bomb," *Tribune*, 19 Oct 1945.
[7] Arthur D. Kahn, *Experiment in Occupation: Witness to the Turnabout, Anti-Nazi to Cold War, 1944–1946* (University Park: Pennsylvania State University Press, 2004), 140.
[8] Harry Rositzke, *The CIA's Secret Operations: Espionage, Counterespionage, and Covert Action* (New York: Reader's Digest Press, 1977), 13.

in preparation for its peacetime mission. On 10 May 1945, the 418th CIC Detachment disbanded, and its personnel transferred to a new organization, established on the same day, the 970th CIC Detachment under Lt. Col. Norman J. Hearn with headquarters in Wiesbaden. After the establishment of the United States Forces in the European Theater, Hearn oversaw the relocation of his command to the IG Farben building in Frankfurt in mid-July 1945. This move united the CIC with the intelligence division to which it reported.[9]

The Counter Intelligence Corps served as the praetorian guard of the American occupation, and had wide-ranging powers and responsibilities. In addition to investigating potential threats to the military government, the Corps collected information on political, social, economic, and military issues. Special agents had the authority to arrest suspects, a right they exercised with abandon. In a typical week in July 1945, the Corps made 6,500 arrests.[10] Often operating in uniform and equipped with side arms, steel helmets, and armbands emblazoned with the letters "CIC," soldiers of the Corps represented the hard side of the occupation.[11] Germans often addressed letters to CIC offices to "the American Gestapo." Whether this word choice betrayed contempt or awe, the CIC took pride in it. According to the Corps' official history, it demonstrated "a clear token of German respect for the Americans' authority."[12]

The CIC headquarters organization adopted a traditional staff structure with three sections: S–1 for administration, S–3 for operations, and S–4 for supply. S–3, in turn, had two subsections: the Case Section, which processed information on individual operations, and the Central Registry, which acted as the repository of information on all individuals and organizations of intelligence interest. By late 1949, its Central Personality Index on individuals of intelligence interest included 1,350,000 cards, and its Impersonal File referenced 42,000 organizations. CIC headquarters managed confidential funds to pay informants, supervised radio direction facilities to intercept wireless communications, and had access to an intelligence laboratory to detect secret writing, covertly open mail, and analyze handwriting. In addition, headquarters supervised a Special Squad located at Camp King near Frankfurt. Until its dissolution

---

9 Maj. Ann Bray et al., ed., *The History of the Counter Intelligence Corps*, vol. 26, *German Occupation* (Fort Holabird, MD: U.S. Army Intelligence Center, 1959), 1–3, 6, 12; James L. Gilbert, John P. Finnegan, and Ann Bray, *In the Shadow of the Sphinx: A History of Army Counterintelligence* (Fort Belvoir, VA: U.S. Army Intelligence and Security Command, 2005), 87.
10 Bray et al., *History of the Counter Intelligence Corps*, 26:12.
11 Richard Bessel, *Germany 1945: From War to Peace* (New York: Harper, 2009), 188.
12 Bray et al., *History of the Counter Intelligence Corps*, 26:12.

in 1947, the squad handled "hot projects," such as the transfer of war criminals and urgent investigations.[13]

For operational purposes, the CIC established a regional structure (Map 1). On 30 November 1945, the Corps introduced eight regions covering the entire U.S. Zone and the American sector of Berlin: Region I, headquartered in Stuttgart; Region II (Frankfurt); Region III (Bad Nauheim); Region IV (Munich); Region V (Regensburg); Region VI (Bamberg); Region VIII (Berlin); and Region IX (Bremen). No Region VII existed at this point. In October 1946, the Corps reduced the eight regions to seven when Region III absorbed Region II.[14] Below the regional levels operated subregional offices, field offices, and resident agents assigned to individual counties (*Landkreise* or *Stadtkreise*). These lower-level agents carried out much of the routine work, such as checking local police blotters on a daily basis for any cases of counterintelligence significance.[15]

After V-E Day, the Army rapidly demobilized its forces in the European Theater and shifted troops to the Pacific to support the ongoing war against Japan. This transition resulted in a heavy personnel turnover at the CIC leadership level. At the end of the conflict, Lt. Col. H. E. Wilson replaced Colonel Hearn as the local CIC commander. Just a few months later, on 31 October 1945, Lt. Col. Richard D. Stevens replaced Colonel Wilson, but Stevens served for only one month. Lt. Col. Harold E. Marr Jr. headed the CIC from December 1945 to April 1946, and Col. Clarence M. Culp followed him from April to June 1946. Col. John L. Inskeep headed the Corps in Germany from June 1946 to January 1948, with Lt. Col. Louis DeRiemer serving as acting commander from April to October 1947. Col. David G. Erskine took charge from January 1948 to November 1950.[16]

Despite the Army's overall downsizing in the European Theater, the CIC managed to keep its personnel strength stable. In May 1945, the 970th CIC Detachment had an authorized strength of 1,400. By late 1949, when many other occupation units had been reduced or eliminated, the CIC had 361 officers, 107 warrant officers, 760 enlisted men, and 163 civilians.[17] Nonetheless, demobilization posed a challenge as experienced veterans left the Army. Men like Henry Kissinger, J. D. Salinger, and Stefan Heym returned stateside as soon as they were eligible

---

13 Maj. Ann Bray et al., ed., *The History of the Counter Intelligence Corps*, vol. 21, *Germany Overrun, Part II* (Fort Holabird, MD: U.S. Army Intelligence Center, 1959), 20–21, 86, 122; vol. 27, *Four Years of Cold War*, 2–4, 43, 45, 92.
14 Ofc of the Ch Historian, EUCOM, *The Second Year of the Occupation*, vol. 6, Occupation Forces in Europe Series, 1946–47 (Frankfurt: Office of the Chief Historian, EUCOM, 1947), 18.
15 Bray et al., *History of the Counter Intelligence Corps*, 26:3; 27:2, 27:5, 27:6, 27:38.
16 Bray et al., *History of the Counter Intelligence Corps*, 27:12, 27:37.
17 Bray et al., *History of the Counter Intelligence Corps*, 26:2; 27:21.

Map 2: American CIC Regions, Germany, 30 November 1945–15 April 1949. U.S. Army Center of Military History.

for demobilization. In their stead arrived young draftees who usually did not know German and often lacked motivation. Their training, too, was inadequate. The new CIC personnel fell short of the high standards set by the wartime Ritchie Boys.

After the closure of Camp Ritchie in October 1945, the CIC moved its training to Fort Holabird, located in Dundalk, an industrial suburb of Baltimore near the city's harbor.[18] Although "The Bird," as students called it, proved an ideal location for the practice of certain counterintelligence techniques such as shadowing suspects, its training staff did not teach recruits the skills required for operations in Germany, including the local language or the economic and political aspects of the occupation. As one graduate complained, the CIC training stateside proved "almost completely useless . . . for overseas CIC work and that is where most of us were going." A senior CIC officer noted in 1947 that he had to "untrain" his replacements before he could deploy them in the field.[19]

Complaints about CIC personnel in postwar Germany abounded. A theater-wide survey conducted by the director of intelligence found that 20 percent of CIC personnel were unqualified.[20] "I tried to stay away from the CIC," recalled one member of the occupation force, "because they were a bunch of bums as far as I was concerned. They were a bunch of hooligans."[21] Erhard Dabringhaus, a CIC member serving in Augsburg, recalled that only one among the fifteen agents stationed there spoke German, and that most of them "were paper pushers." As for the commander,

> he was a perfect example of an officer misplaced in his assignment. He had had no intelligence training. He never learned a word of German although he spent years of service in occupied Germany. I don't believe he could even say "*Gesundheit*." He had a total disregard for other cultures and considered all Germans living in Germany foreigners. He possessed no aptitude for intelligence. He was the kind of American who tended to create the false impression that all Americans are cowboys.[22]

---

18 Gilbert, Finnegan, and Bray, *In the Shadow of the Sphinx*, 82; Lori Tagg, "A Brief History of Training in Army Intelligence," *Military Intelligence Professional Bulletin* 34, no. 3 (Jul-Sep 2012), 90.
19 Memo, Lt. Col. Stephen J. Spingarn for Maj. Gen. Alfred W. Gruenther, JCS, 8 Apr 1948, sub: Memorandum Re United States Military Counter Intelligence and Related Papers Prepared for Major General Alfred M. Gruenther, Director, The Joint Staff, Joint Chiefs of Staff, Folder "Counter Intelligence Corps File Memos re U.S. military C.I. and related papers prepared for General Gruenther," The Papers of Stephen J. Spingarn, Truman Library.
20 Bray et al., *History of the Counter Intelligence Corps*, 27:17–21.
21 Ian Sayer and Douglas Botting, *Nazi Gold: The Story of the World's Greatest Robbery – And Its Aftermath* (New York: Granada, 1984), 261.
22 Erhard Dabringhaus, *Klaus Barbie: The Shocking Story of How the U.S. Used This Nazi War Criminal as an Intelligence Agent* (Washington, DC: Acropolis Books, 1984), 96.

The CIC responded in several ways to this unsatisfactory state of affairs. One measure included training at the regional level. Typically, incoming agents received a brief introduction, and would then spend several weeks in the file room of their regional office, reading up on cases and investigations. After that, training would continue on the job. A survey conducted in May 1947 suggested that CIC personnel needed additional training in the German language as well as in investigation and recruitment techniques. CIC headquarters authorized the regions to hire native Germans as language teachers, with instruction based on the Berlitz conversational method, a teaching style that uses real-life situations to present practical vocabulary and grammar.[23]

The CIC leadership shifted subpar personnel into positions where they could do less harm, such as jobs involving routine screening or administrative work. Another technique favored by CIC commanders involved sending unwanted subordinates to a training course at the intelligence school in Oberammergau. The school offered courses tailored to the needs of the CIC, but commanders were reluctant to spare their top personnel for a month or two, sending their more expendable soldiers instead. Unsurprisingly, the school complained to the senior leadership in Germany that even though they offered the CIC "cream" slots, most of the students "failed to meet even the lowered minimum standards for Counter Intelligence Corps personnel."[24]

Qualified personnel being a scarce commodity, the CIC assigned their top special agents to key regional posts. The best went to Region VIII in Berlin, which, against the backdrop of the U.S.-Soviet rivalry, developed into a hot spot for American intelligence.[25] Special Agent Severin F. Wallach was a case in point. Born in Vienna and trained as a lawyer, Wallach had immigrated to the United States when Germany annexed Austria in 1938. During the war, the Nazis wiped out nearly his entire family in Europe. In America, Wallach joined the Army, arriving in Berlin as a member of the intelligence branch of Berlin District at the end of the war.[26] Colleagues from those days described him as a brilliant if solitary man. Despite his biography, his main concern was the Soviet threat, not denazification.[27] By 1948, he headed Region VIII's special case section, which directed all CIC agent operations in

---

23 Bray et al., *History of the Counter Intelligence Corps*, 27:23–25.
24 Rpt, Ofc of the DDI, EUCOM, Quarterly Rpt of Opns, 1 Jan to 31 Mar 1948, Historian's Background Files, 1947–1952, RG 549, NACP.
25 Bray et al., *History of the Counter Intelligence Corps*, 27:16.
26 Testimony, Capt. George T. Gabelia, 15 Mar 1948, Folder "Hitler's Death Reports," Gen Staff, Intel Div, Administration Br, Misc. Items of Intel Interest, 1947–49, RG 549, NACP.
27 Gitta Sereny, *The Healing Wound: Experiences and Reflections, Germany 1936–2001* (New York: W. W. Norton, 2001), 214.

the city. At any time, Wallach ran thirty to sixty sources in Berlin. The region also employed a "really expert forger," a former *Abwehr* officer who was the envy of the American intelligence community in the city. Even Dana B. Durand, the CIA base chief who hardly spoke well of Army Intelligence, lauded Wallach and the local CIC for their professionalism and cooperation.[28]

These measures could not obscure the shortcomings of many of the newcomers. But they shifted sway to experienced veterans such as Lt. Col. Earl S. Browning, who joined the Corps in 1942 and served in Germany until August 1949. According to Browning, the quality of the average agent had improved perceptibly by 1949.[29] The CIC managed to make the best out of a situation that was less than ideal.

Two missions guided CIC operations in Germany: denazification and the containment of communism. The Counter Intelligence Directive, issued by the 12th Army Group on 10 April 1945, served as the Corps' principal mission statement during the first year of the occupation. The directive emphasized the destruction of the Nazi Party apparatus and the identification and arrest of former Nazi officials and war crimes suspects.[30] These tasks involved screening millions of Germans and locating and taking many thousands into custody. By the end of 1945, the CIC had apprehended more than 120,000 individuals suspected of having committed war crimes or having been members of dangerous Nazi organizations such as the SS or the *Gestapo*.[31]

Within a few months of the war's end, the focus of the CIC shifted. As early as November 1945, the CIC began investigating communist activity in Bremerhaven.[32] A month later, Brig. Gen. Edwin L. Sibert informed his staff that the CIC "must be an active and aggressive information gathering agency," including espionage operations ("positive intelligence") in the Soviet Zone.[33] A series of new directives and Essential Elements of Information issued by the intelligence division in Washington stressed the need to investigate Soviet and KPD activities in Ger-

---

28 Rpt, Dana B. Durand, Ch, BOB, to Ch, Foreign Br M, 8 Apr 1948, sub: Transmittal of Report on Berlin Operations Base, in *On the Front Lines of the Cold War: Documents on the Intelligence War in Berlin, 1946 to 1961*, ed. Donald P. Steury (Washington, DC: Center for the Study of Intelligence, 1999), 48, 85.
29 Bray et al., *History of the Counter Intelligence Corps*, 27:21.
30 Bray et al., *History of the Counter Intelligence Corps*, 26:5–7.
31 Bray et al., *History of the Counter Intelligence Corps*, 26:12.
32 Bray et al., *History of the Counter Intelligence Corps*, 27:36.
33 John Patrick Finnegan and Romana Danysh, *Military Intelligence*, Army Lineage Series (Washington, DC: U.S. Army Center of Military History, 1998), 110; Memo, Brig. Gen. Edwin L. Sibert for Brig. Gen. G. Bryant Conrad, 3 Dec 1945, sub: Comments by G–2 USFET, Folder "79 A," Director of Intel, Miscellaneous Rcds re. Intel and Document Policies, 1944–1948, RG 260, NACP.

many. By the summer of 1946, countering the communist threat replaced denazification as the CIC's focal mission.

In addition, the CIC handled an array of routine duties. Its staff protected Army facilities and personnel as well as military government organizations against espionage, sabotage, and subversion; operated border control stations and checkpoints; and made efforts to crack down on black market activity. Among its investigative activities, it screened emigrants and displaced persons, as well as German nationals intending to marry Americans, for potential security risks, and interrogated prisoners of war and security suspects. As part of its broader intelligence remit, the CIC's tasks included the procurement of intelligence from the French Zone and from the British secret services, the monitoring of Russian and Ukrainian émigré groups; and the surveillance of efforts by Jewish associations to recruit concentration camp survivors in Germany as prospective settlers for Palestine.

To pursue its mission effectively, the CIC developed liaison arrangement with several other organizations, including various U.S. intelligence and law enforcement units, the German police, and British intelligence. The U.S. Constabulary, an Army organization, became a particularly valuable partner. Established in the winter of 1944–1945 by the European Theater, the Constabulary was a lightly armed, highly mobile force designed to deter civilian unrest and perform police-type duties such as conducting raids and searches. In the course of its operations, the Constabulary became closely involved with and highly knowledgeable on German affairs.[34]

The Constabulary's intelligence section served as its principal link to the CIC and other Army Intelligence units. The Corps and the Constabulary regularly exchanged information of security interest.[35] General Sibert enjoined the CIC to serve as the Constabulary's "eyes and ears."[36] In return, the Corps routinely called on the Constabulary's support for so-called swoop operations: the coordinated arrest of multiple individuals in certain geographic areas. In July 1946, for example, the 303d Counter Intelligence Corps Detachment coordinated raids across the U.S. Zone by the Constabulary and other military units on railroad stations, overnight hotels, and railroad bunkers.

---

34 For a history of the U.S. Constabulary, see Kendall D. Gott, *Mobility, Vigilance and Justice: The U.S. Army Constabulary in Germany 1946–1953* (Fort Leavenworth, KS: Combat Studies Institute Press, 2005).
35 Memo, J. S. Arouet, Ch, Liaison Br, for Mr. I. D. Harris, 29 Sep 1949, sub: EUCOM Intelligence Agencies, Folder "350.05 Military Information-Collection, Dissemination," Director of Intel, Analysis and Research Br, Gen Corresp, 1945–49, RG 260, NACP.
36 Memo, Brig. Gen. Edwin L. Sibert for Brig. Gen. G. Bryant Conrad, 3 Dec 1946, Folder "79 A," Director of Intel, Miscellaneous Rcds re. Intel and Document Policies, 1944–1948, RG 260, NACP.

Other sources of information included telecommunications intercepts, the interrogation of individuals, and the use of informants. If special agents had the linguistic ability to pass for a German, they, in theory, could assume a false identity and personally monitor or seek access to the target of an investigation. Given that only a small number of agents possessed this skill, the CIC relied heavily on hired informants, or agents, for this type of clandestine work.[37] Special agents sought to recruit informants in every sphere of activity that affected the security of the occupation. As special agents and potential agents came to know each other at interrogation facilities, through investigations, or by references from a third party, the CIC could take advantage of these opportunities to recruit new sources of information. Trusted informants met with their handlers at safe houses for briefings and compensation. Personal chemistry between an agent and his informant was important for a successful working relationship, but operational requirements occasionally made these arrangements difficult to maintain. The CIC's practice of periodically rotating and redeploying personnel did not sit well with informants who suddenly had to deal with an unfamiliar handler.

The profile of CIC sources changed along with the Corps' shifting mission. Many informants of the immediate postwar period were denouncers, eager to identify former Nazi officials. Those who joined the ranks of CIC informants during the later years, by contrast, often did so out of an "intense hatred of communism and the Soviet Union." Regardless of ideological motivation, material compensation almost always played a role in an informant's decision to work for the CIC. Initially, the Corps paid informants with consumable or tradable commodities such as food, coffee, and cigarettes. Later, when the German economy had stabilized, hard currency became the standard payment.[38]

At first, the recruitment of sources proceeded with little coordination and oversight, which led to overpayment and a redundancy of information. In 1947, therefore, the CIC introduced Technical Specialist Sections at the regional level and at headquarters. Technical specialists set up and supervised standards of pay and discipline for informants, and kept track of their activities. Their efforts "proved an immense step forward in CIC operations." Under the new system, sources fell into four categories: Penetration ("P") agents obtained information on specific targets, such as a local branch of the KPD or a Nazi organization. Net leaders ("X") handled other agents or subinformants on behalf of the CIC. Investigative ("O") informants provided information from records or agencies to which

---

37 Bray e[38] Bray et al., *History of the Counter Intelligence Corps*, 27:31–33.
38 Bray et al., *History of the Counter Intelligence Corps*, 27:22, 27:33–34.

they had access. Automatic ("A") informants were regular employees in civilian, governmental, and semiofficial agencies.[39]

The work with local informants brought CIC members in contact with the seedier sides of postwar Germany. These activities could be dangerous, as 1st Lt. Jack D. Hunter learned firsthand. A disgruntled German followed Hunter from the IG Farben building to a bar, where Hunter waited to meet an informant. When the unsuspecting Hunter went to the toilets to relieve himself, his pursuer followed him, grabbed him from behind, shoved his face into the urinal, and beat him severely. Hunter's informant appeared just in time to rescue his handler, who had been too surprised to fend off the assailant. Shaken and bruised, but with his sense of humor intact, Hunter considered himself lucky merely to have his "head shampooed in a nightclub urinal."[40]

To put itself in a better position for continued operations after the military occupation, the CIC comprehensively restructured its organization in 1948 and 1949 (Map 2). On 20 June 1948, the 970th CIC Detachment inactivated in Germany, and its personnel and equipment transferred to the 7970th Counter Intelligence Group. This change would align the Corps with the new European Command. The CIC leadership then set out to reform the cumbersome regional structure. The regions had developed into personal fiefdoms that shared little information laterally. Local informants occasionally took advantage of the lack of interregional communication by selling the same information multiple times to different CIC offices. To tighten control, shorten lines of communication, and eliminate redundancy, the CIC in the winter of 1948–1949 eliminated the old regional structure, and had its subregions—now redesignated as regions—report directly to headquarters. When this reorganization completed on 15 April 1949, the CIC had twelve regions: Region I (Stuttgart), Region II (Heidelberg), Region III (Frankfurt), Region IV (Munich), Region V (Regensburg), Region VI (Nuremberg), Region VII (Bayreuth), Region VIII (Berlin), Region IX (Bremen), Region X (Bad Wildungen), Region XI (Würzburg), and Region XII (Augsburg).[41] In September 1949, the 7970th Counter Intelligence Group transferred its headquarters from Frankfurt to the Wallace Barracks, formerly known as the Reiter Kaserne, in Stuttgart.[42] This move completed the reorganization process of the military occupation period.

---

39 Scott Andrew Selby, *The Axmann Conspiracy: The Nazi Plan for a Fourth Reich and How the U.S. Army Defeated It* (New York: Penguin, 2012), 92.
40 *History of the Counter Intelligence Corps*, 27:22.
41 Bray et al., *History of the Counter Intelligence Corps*, 27:6–7.
42 Bray et al., *History of the Counter Intelligence Corps*, 26:1–3, 26:6, 26:12; Gilbert, Finnegan, and Bray, *In the Shadow of the Sphinx*, 87.

Map 3: American CIC Regions, Germany, 15 April 1949. U.S. Army Center of Military History.

The Army Security Agency, Europe

During the war, American signals intelligence had read the secret communications of several foreign governments, and American policymakers wanted to retain this valuable information-gathering tool in peacetime. Expressing a widespread sentiment among top U.S. officials, Assistant Secretary of War John J. McCloy demanded in August 1944 that "one of the chief pillars of our national security system after the war must be an extensive intercept service."[43] A month later, the chief of the Military Intelligence Service, Brig. Gen. Russell A. Osmun, proposed to Maj. Gen. Clayton L. Bissell the establishment of a globally operating, permanent postwar signals intelligence organization. This service, Osmun argued, ought to target not only

Figure 18: Gateway to the ASAE headquarters on the seventh floor, West Block, in the IG Farben building. INSCOM.

---

43 "Papers from the Personal Files of Alfred McCormack; Memorandum for General McNarney (1944)," 22 Aug 1944, SRH 141–2, in *U.S. Army Signals Intelligence in World War II: A Documentary History*, ed. James L. Gilbert and John P. Finnegan (Washington, DC: U.S. Army Center of Military History, 1993), 164.

"clandestine traffic throughout the occupied territories of Europe" but also those of "all [European] governments [currently] in exile." Moreover, Osmun submitted, "the question of studying and researching the traffic of some of our present Allies merits deep consideration."[44]

The Allied victory enabled the Army to realize this ambitious goal. On 15 September 1945, the War Department replaced the Signal Security Agency with the Army Security Agency under Brig. Gen. W. Preston Corderman. The new agency consolidated all Army signals intelligence elements under one roof and reported directly to the Army's intelligence division at the Pentagon. To bolster its global reach, the ASA coordinated its operations closely with the U.S. Navy's signals intelligence services, as well as those of Canada and Great Britain. In March 1946, the Army and the British signals intelligence service signed the UKUSA Agreement, extending their wartime cooperation into the postwar period. The ASA established a U.S. Combined Intelligence Liaison Center in London to coordinate operations with the British.[45] Thus, the end of the war hardly interrupted American signals intelligence operations. "Indeed," an annual ASA history noted, "wartime activity . . . differed [from peacetime activity] neither in volume nor urgency but merely in the direction of the attack."[46]

As Europe's foremost telecommunications hub, Germany was key in the Army's global signals intelligence enterprise. The occupation posed no legal barriers to eavesdropping operations, and the Army quickly asserted administrative control over the local communications networks. Because the Allied bombing campaign had destroyed much of Germany's infrastructure, the U.S. Army Signal Corps laid hundreds of miles of new telephone, teletype, and telegraph cables, all centered on Army headquarters in Frankfurt.[47] As a result, the Army found itself in an ideal position to consolidate and expand its signals intelligence presence in central Europe. Not surprisingly, the ASA intended to stay in Germany "as long as possible."[48]

On 25 November 1945, the ASA activated a regional theater headquarters in Frankfurt, the Army Security Agency, Europe (ASAE). Like many other Army agen-

---

44 Memo, Brig. Gen. Ross A. Osmun, Ch, Mil Intel Service, for Maj. Gen. Clayton L. Bissell, ACofS, G–2, 7 Sep 1944, Folder "350.01–385 (1944)," Rcds of the Army Staff, Ofc of the Asst Ch of Staff for Intel (OACSI), MID, Top Secret Decimal File, 1942–1952, RG 319, NACP.
45 ASA, "Post War Transition Period: The Army Security Agency 1945–1948" (Washington, DC: ASA, 1952), 14.
46 Annual Rpt, ASA, *Summary Annual Report of the Army Security Agency, Fiscal Year 1947* (Washington, DC: ASA, 1950), 24.
47 George R. Thompson and Dixie R. Harris, *The Signal Corps: The Outcome*, United States Army in World War II (Washington, DC: U.S. Army Center of Military History, 1991), 275.
48 ASA, "Post War Transition Period," 6.

cies, the headquarters of the new organization moved into the IG Farben building. Most of its staff resided in the Gutleutkaserne, a former *Wehrmacht* installation near the Frankfurt central railway station. Given its global outlook and its operational integration with ASA headquarters at Arlington Hall, the ASAE evolved more independently from the Army's intelligence apparatus in Germany than did other agencies. The ASAE operated under the command of the ASA director, rather than the European Theater commander, but the agency was attached to the European Command for administration and discipline. The ASAE coordinated its operations with the European Command intelligence division, and an ASAE representative regularly participated in the executive council meetings of the European Command.[49] Col. Earle F. Cook, a West Point graduate who directed the Army's Signals Intelligence Division in Europe during the war, became the agency's first chief. On 1 August 1947, another signals intelligence veteran, Lt. Col. Robert T. Walker, succeeded Cook and served through the remainder of the occupation.[50]

ASAE headquarters included two divisions, the Administrative Division and the Operations Division. The latter, in turn, consisted of two branches. The Security Branch was in charge of communications security for Army organizations throughout Europe and operated a cryptologic repair school to train staff on the maintenance of the agency's technical equipment. The Intelligence Branch was responsible for the collection of signals intelligence. It received intercepts from field stations in Germany and Europe, scanning them for items of immediate value. The ASAE then forwarded all intercepts to ASA headquarters at Arlington Hall, where analysts collated the messages from Army intercept stations from across the globe, sought to decrypt the encrypted ones, compiled summaries of the collected intelligence, and forwarded them to the Army's intelligence division at the Pentagon.[51]

The ASAE took over all Army signals intelligence units in Germany. In February 1946, the agency also temporarily assumed responsibility for signals intelligence in the Mediterranean Theater and Austria. At its inception, the ASAE had five operating units: the 114th Signal Service Company at Sontra in northeastern Hesse, the 116th Signal Service Company at Scheyern in central Bavaria, the 2d Army Air Forces Squadron Mobile at Bad Vilbel near Frankfurt, Detachment "A" at Gross-Gerau near Frankfurt, and the Signals Intelligence Service Division at

---

49 Annual Rpt, ASA, *Summary Annual Report of the Army Security Agency, Fiscal Year 1946* (Washington, DC: ASA, 1947), 27; ASA, "Post War Transition Period," 48.
50 Edwin C. Fishel and Robert S. Benjamin, eds., *ASA Review* 1, no. 2 (Jul-Aug 1947), 22.
51 Thomas Boghardt, "Semper Vigilis: The U.S. Army Security Agency in Early Cold War Germany," *Army History* 106 (Winter 2018), 10–11.

Caserta in Italy. Over time, the ASAE added and expanded units across the American zone. The ASAE units at Gross-Gerau moved to Herzo Base in Herzogenaurach, a former *Luftwaffe* base near Nuremberg. Toward the end of the occupation period, the agency deployed mobile units to Pfaffenhofen in Bavaria, to Darmstadt and Fritzlar in Hesse, and to Rothwesten, another former *Luftwaffe* base in Hesse near the border with the Soviet Zone. In August 1949, Rothwesten became a permanent ASAE station, principally serving the needs of the U.S. Air Force.[52]

As the ASAE expanded, its personnel strength increased as well. In November 1945, ASAE units in Germany outside headquarters had an authorized strength of 28 officers and 572 men. By the end of the occupation, the agency had a staff of 90 officers and 840 men, in addition to more than 500 German civilians working at Herzo Base, and over a hundred local employees working for the 116th Signal Service Company.[53] All signals intelligence personnel received specialized training before deployment to Germany. During the early years of the occupation, the cryptographic school at Vint Hill Farms in Warrenton, Virginia, trained enlisted men, and Arlington Hall trained officers in various signals intelligence disciplines. In 1948, the ASA consolidated training for all its personnel at Carlisle Barracks, Pennsylvania. The Army Language School at the Presidio of Monterey, California, provided language training.[54] Like other Army Intelligence agencies in Germany, the ASAE struggled to find adequate replacements for its highly qualified wartime personnel. In 1949, all ASAE units together had only 72.6 percent of operational strength because, as the ASA's annual history notes laconically, "[i]t was difficult to get the personnel for operative missions."[55]

The ASAE cast a wide net operationally. In late 1945 and in 1946, signals intelligence units in Europe intercepted German, Portuguese, French, Spanish, Russian, Swedish, Swiss, and even Syrian wireless traffic. In addition, the ASAE led the American exploitation effort of German signals intelligence personnel and technology.[56] In another "special activity," the agency worked closely with the European Theater command's Civil Censorship Division. Electronic signals, such as telegrams and phone calls, lost strength as they traveled, and had to be reinforced

---

52 Annual Rpt, ASA, *Summary Annual Report of the Army Security Agency, Fiscal Year 1946*, 27; Annual Rpt, ASA, *Summary Annual Report of the Army Security Agency, Fiscal Year 1948* (Washington, DC: ASA, 1950), 41; ASA, "Post War Transition Period," 65, 72.
53 Boghardt, "Semper Vigilis," 11.
54 Tagg, "Brief History of Training," 89.
55 Annual Rpt, ASA, *Summary Annual Report of the Army Security Agency, Fiscal Year 1949* (Washington, DC: ASA, 1952), 64.
56 Annual Rpt, ASA, *Summary Annual Report of the Army Security Agency, Fiscal Year 1946*, 29. For the operations of the Target Intelligence Committee—that is, the exploitation of German signals intelligence—see Chapter 6.

Figure 19: An Army Security Agency operator on duty at the field station in Herzogenaurach, Germany. U.S. Army.

periodically by technical personnel at repeater stations. Whoever had access to these stations could easily intercept the signals. In a joint effort, the ASAE and the Civil Censorship Division deployed intercept units to strategically located repeater stations in Berlin, Frankfurt, and Nuremberg. Because Germany remained a European communications hub after the war, with numerous international cables running through the country, this operation gave the Army access to international phone calls and telegraph traffic along with German communications.[57]

France emerged as the most important American signals intelligence target in the immediate postwar period. As a global power, France had diplomatic representations around the world, and the vulnerability of French encryptions—along with the chattiness of French officials—made their communications an easy and rewarding prey for American codebreakers. The ASAE became the primary agent in this signals intelligence operation. On 15 January 1946, the Army's assistant chief of staff for intelligence assigned "the French military cryptanalytical problem" to the ASAE.[58] The agency also regularly intercepted diplomatic communications between the French foreign ministry and its ambassador in Moscow, presumably by plucking them from international telegraph cables running through Germany.[59]

The reconfiguration of the global order in the wake of World War II generated a host of international conferences, and these gatherings presented rich targets for American codebreakers. In Europe, U.S. signals intelligence successfully intercepted communications from diplomatic delegations participating in the Potsdam Conference in July and August 1945, the Council of Foreign Ministers Conference in London in August 1945, and the Peace Conference in Paris from July through October 1946. As was the case with some of the intercepted French traffic, the Americans presumably gained access to these communications by picking them off international cables running through Germany. The ASA provided the diplomatic intercepts to the Department of State, and American diplomats praised this intelligence as being "of the highest importance in the conduct of foreign relations."[60]

The Army had not conceived the ASA as a Cold War agency, but the Soviet target loomed large from early on. In the summer of 1945, British and American signals intelligence embarked on BOURBON, a joint operation to intercept and de-

---

57 ASA, "Post War Transition Period," 33, 83; Annual Rpt, ASA, *Summary Annual Report of the Army Security Agency, Fiscal Year 1949*, 2.
58 Annual Rpt, ASA, *Summary Annual Report of the Army Security Agency, Fiscal Year 1946*, 29–30.
59 Sum, ACoS, G–2, 2 Jan 1946, sub: "MAGIC" – Diplomatic Summary, National Security Archive, https://nsarchive.gwu.edu.
60 ASA, "Post War Transition Period," 23, 24, 47, 51.

crypt Soviet ciphers. Initially, the ASAE contributed little to this effort. American signals intelligence resources in Europe were stretched thin, and the ASA obtained the bulk of the Soviet intercepts it processed at Arlington Hall in 1945 and 1946 from U.S. intercept stations outside Europe and from the British.[61] By the summer of 1947, however, the ASAE began producing a steady stream of intercepted Soviet military messages as well as Czechoslovak, Hungarian, Polish, and Yugoslav police traffic. In 1948, the agency completed a listening and direction-finding post at Herzo Base, which enabled the Americans to launch extensive eavesdropping operations in Soviet-controlled territory.[62]

Initially, the ASAE sent all encrypted messages to Arlington Hall for decryption, but eventually it developed the capabilities to decrypt some of the intercepts in Frankfurt. In addition to encrypted radio traffic, the ASA and the ASAE intercepted large volumes of unencrypted ("plaintext") commercial communications from Soviet-controlled territory. They also systematically analyzed undecipherable intercepts of the Soviet armed forces, and the militaries of Moscow's satellites in Eastern Europe, for patterns that might reveal something about their order of battle ("traffic analysis").[63] In 1947 and 1948, the Soviets tightened their communications security procedures, culminating in a massive change of virtually all their ciphers on 29 October 1948. This incident, referred to as "Black Friday" by American codebreakers, was an acute setback for U.S. signals intelligence, but thanks to plaintext intercepts and traffic analysis the ASAE managed to continue collecting vital information on Soviet activities in Europe.[64]

In addition to the procurement of signals intelligence, the ASAE was responsible for protecting and bolstering the security of the Army's communication systems. The agency regularly intercepted messages from other Army units in Europe to ascertain whether proper security procedures had been followed. Often, this was not the case: in the first half of fiscal year 1949 alone, the agency flagged 2,359 out of 3,745 intercepted messages for security violations. Occasionally, the agency examined unencrypted messages between the Pentagon and Army headquarters in Frankfurt to determine how much an adversary might be able to learn from this information.[65]

---

61 Annual Rpt, ASA, *Summary Annual Report of the Army Security Agency, Fiscal Year 1947*, 31.
62 Boghardt, "Semper Vigilis," 17.
63 Boghardt, "Semper Vigilis," 17.
64 Stephen Budiansky, *Code Warriors: NSA's Codebreakers and the Secret Intelligence War against the Soviet Union* (New York: Penguin Random House, 2016), 109–14; Annual Rpt, ASA, *Summary Annual Report of the Army Security Agency, Fiscal Year 1949*, 9–14.
65 Annual Rpt, ASA, *Summary Annual Report of the Army Security Agency, Fiscal Year 1949*, 17; Annual Rpt, ASA, *Summary Annual Report of the Army Security Agency, Fiscal Year 1948*, 25.

Communications security included providing assistance to General Lucius D. Clay, the Army's top commander in Europe. The ASA rendered this service through Capt. Richard R. Hallock, a World War II veteran, who had seen action in Sicily and southern France as well as during the Battle of the Bulge. In 1946, Brig. Gen. Carter W. Clarke picked Hallock for an assignment with the Intelligence Group in Washington. Later that year, Hallock joined Clay's staff in Berlin as the general's personal aide for intelligence. He served in this function until 1949. Hallock encrypted and decrypted especially sensitive messages that Clay sent to, or received from, the Pentagon by means of a separate signals intelligence channel operated by the ASA in Berlin, Frankfurt, and at Arlington Hall.[66]

To protect its organization and operations, the ASA strictly limited access to its products and carefully screened its employees. In September 1946, the agency introduced security clearance policies mandating that none of its military personnel must have an "intimate connection" to a foreigner. All employees working in sensitive positions had to be U.S. citizens, "preferably native born, with trustworthy character and unquestioned financial habits."[67] The agency strictly enforced these guidelines. As an ASAE veteran recalled, "ASA never trusted any German nationals. Absolutely no Germans were allowed in any ASA activities, duties, etc. The only jobs I ever saw where Germans worked were in security such as guarding outward perimeters of installations."[68] The rules applied to U.S. intelligence officials as well. Even Peter M. F. Sichel, the deputy chief of the CIA station in Berlin, faced these stringent restrictions because of his place of birth: "I was never cleared for signal intelligence, no one who was foreign born was at that time."[69] Though the Soviets did penetrate several American intelligence agencies in postwar Germany, the ASAE seems to have eluded Moscow's prying eyes. The agency's strict security measures may well have aided in this feat.[70]

---

[66] Emails, Daniel Crosswell to Thomas Boghardt, 7 Jun 2017, 14 Nov 2017, 15 Nov 2017, Historians Files, CMH. Richard R. Hallock must not be confused with Lt. Richard T. Hallock, a Signal Corps officer who participated in the decryption of wartime Soviet communications (Project VENONA).
[67] ASA, "Post War Transition Period," 51.
[68] Email, Jeffrey van Davis to Thomas Boghardt, 25 Jan 2017, Historians Files, CMH. Van Davis served as a voice intercept operator, Specialist 5th Class, with the Army Security Agency, Europe (ASAE).
[69] Email, Peter M. F. Sichel to Thomas Boghardt, 27 Jun 2017, Historians Files, CMH.
[70] Boghardt, "Semper Vigilis," 23.

The Intelligence Center in Oberursel

The collection of documents, photographs, and maps, as well as the interrogation of prisoners of war, constituted critical sources of intelligence during the war. It remained a priority for Army Intelligence during the occupation. During the war and through the early postwar years, numerous Army units roved through Germany, collecting large amounts of data. By 30 June 1947, the European Theater had shipped 279.5 tons of captured documents to the German Military Documents Section at the War Department.[71] Meanwhile, Army units in Germany arrested about 150,000 persons in the first year of the occupation.[72] The detainees ended up in one of a number of Army-operated prisoner-of-war and internment camps, including several camps for special intelligence purposes. A detention facility at Mondorf in Luxembourg, code-named ASHCAN, operated as an interrogation center for captured top Nazi officials. Another camp at Kransberg Castle, located 15 miles north of Frankfurt and code-named DUSTBIN, served as a collection point for German scientists.[73] As the American occupation settled in, the Army in the European Theater consolidated most of its camps, interrogation centers, and material collection points into one intelligence center located in the small town of Oberursel, about 10 miles northwest of Frankfurt.

During the war, the *Luftwaffe* operated a prisoner-of-war and interrogation center, the Durchgangslager der Luftwaffe (or Dulag Luft), for captured Allied pilots in Oberursel.[74] Its central location made the camp easily accessible from almost any point in Europe, and it had ample internment and interrogation facilities, so the Allies decided to use the camp for their own purposes. In June 1945, the U.S. element of the 6824th Detailed Interrogation Center, a joint agency operating under the Supreme Allied Headquarters, began transferring its functions from Givet, France, to Oberursel. After the dissolution of the supreme headquarters, the unit in Oberursel became the U.S. Forces, European Theater, Military Intelligence Service Center. On 1 November 1945, it was redesignated as the Military Intelligence Service Center. In September 1946, the installation itself officially assumed the name Camp King, after Col. Charles B. King, an officer who had been killed during

---

71 Ofc of the Ch Historian, EUCOM, *The Second Year of the Occupation*, 6:12.
72 Ofc of the Ch Historian, EUCOM, *The First Year of the Occupation, 1945–1946*, Part 5, *A Survey of Occupation Problems*, Occupation Forces in Europe Series, 1945–46 (Frankfurt: Office of the Chief Historian, EUCOM, 1947), 139.
73 Ziemke, *U.S. Army in the Occupation*, 221, 263, 277, 314.
74 Rpt, HQ, Third United States Army, Ofc of the ACofS, G–2, 18 May 1945, sub: interrogation report no. 4, Folder "ZF 011020 Auswertstelle West Oberursel," INSCOM, IRR, Impersonal Files, 1939–1980, RG 319, NACP.

the Normandy landings. Unofficially, the camp became known as "Camp Sibert," after the chief of the intelligence division in Frankfurt.[75] The intelligence division, through its Operations Branch, supervised, staffed, and formulated polices for the intelligence center. Col. William R. "Rusty" Philp served as Camp King's commanding officer from July 1945 to September 1947, Col. Roy M. Thoroughman was in charge until August 1949, and Col. Gordon D. Ingraham supervised the center until July 1951.[76]

The center's Documents Section collected, microfilmed, processed, and shipped captured German documents, maps, and photographs to the United States. It also coordinated the operations of the various American document collection activities in Germany, and responded to requests from other agencies for specific records. From Oberursel and other collection points in Germany, the material went to the German Military Documents Section in Washington, where analysts exploited it for military and intelligence purposes, or passed it on to other organizations, such as the Department of State, the Library of Congress, the National Archives, and the Hoover War Library at Stanford University. The processed material covered a wide range of topics, including official war crimes records, aerial photographs taken by the *Luftwaffe* during the war, and a collection of 100,000 German maps. The section also completed several photo intelligence projects, including a post-hostilities mapping program in Europe (Project CASEY JONES) and an analysis of captured postcards to identify military targets (Project PATRON). Early collection activities yielded a large amount of records pertaining to Nazi organizations and crimes, but over time the collectors recalibrated their effort on material that provided insights into the military and economic capabilities of the Soviet Union.[77]

Although the Army's collections of documents, photographs, and maps provided the Americans with information on the war itself, the interrogation of and collaboration with human sources promised to develop postwar knowledge on the Soviets. Because of the wide variety of interviews and the sensitive nature of the discussions, the intelligence officers at Oberursel needed a system with multiple lo-

---

75 James C. Spratt, "The History of Camp King" (Carlisle, PA: U.S. Army Military History Institute, n.d.), 98; Selby, *Axmann Conspiracy*, 213.
76 Spratt, "History of Camp King," appendix.
77 Information on the collected files can be found in Intel Div, Folder "Quarterly Report of Operations 1 October to 31 December 1948," Historian's Background Files, 1947–1952, RG 549, NACP; Folder "EUCOM G–2 Quarterly Report of Operations, 1 January to 31 March 1949," Historian's Background Files, 1947–1952, RG 549, NACP; Ofc of the Ch Historian, EUCOM, *The Second Year of the Occupation*, vol. 2, Occupation Forces in Europe Series 1946–47 (Frankfurt: Office of the Chief Historian, EUCOM, 1947), 12, 13, 15; Ofc of the Ch Historian, EUCOM, *The Third Year of the Occupation*, Part 4, *The Fourth Quarter, 1 April–30 June 1948*, vol. 2, Occupation Forces in Europe Series 1947–48 (Frankfurt: Office of the Chief Historian, EUCOM, 1948), 49.

cations that would allow them to interrogate inmates individually or in separate groups. To do so, they designated a series of properties named after U.S. states, including "Alaska House," the "House Virginia," the "House Vermont," the "House Mississippi," the "House Maine," the "House Ohio," the "House Utah," the "House Wyoming," and the "House Washington." These naming conventions allowed Army Intelligence to refer to specific interrogation projects by the name of the house where the interviews took place, rather than by their content.[78]

Finding and retaining qualified personnel to handle this mission posed a significant challenge. All interrogators assigned to the 7707th Military Intelligence Service Center in the summer of 1945 had graduated from the Military Intelligence Training Center in Camp Ritchie, Maryland, and almost all of them had served in prisoner-of-war interrogation teams during the war. They spoke a variety of languages, including German, Russian, and, in one case, even Japanese. Yet by the end of 1945, demobilization and assignment to other duty stations reduced the pool of interrogators to roughly forty.[79] The center hired a number of civilians, including German native speakers, as replacements for the departed staff. However, new security procedures—which mandated that any person involved in intelligence work had to have held U.S. citizenship for at least ten years—made it difficult to recruit either foreign citizens or recently naturalized Americans for these posts. Many of the center's interrogators had become U.S. citizens during the war, and in late 1947, the center had to let go six highly qualified interrogators because they had been U.S. citizens for less than a decade.[80]

As was the case for most intelligence units in Germany, the mission of the interrogation program in Oberursel changed markedly between 1945 and 1949. At the start, the vast majority of internees were former Nazi officials, SS men, and German prisoners of war, and interrogators screened them for crimes committed during the Third Reich. Oberursel also issued a regularly updated rogues' gallery, a list of persons wanted within the European Command for interrogation. Most were war crimes suspects. The center distributed the list to approximately a thousand U.S., British, and French intelligence and security organizations as well as

---

[78] Col. Gordon D. Ingraham, CO, 7707 European Cmd Intel Center, to Director of Intelligence, EUCOM, 8 Mar 1951, sub: Housing Held by ECIC, folder "Journals & Files – Intelligence Division, EUCOM Jan-Mar 1951," Army-AG Cmd Rpts 1949–1954, EUCOM/USAREUR (U.S. Army Europe), Staff Rpts, Jnls & Files G–2 (Jan-Jun) 1951, RG 407, NACP.
[79] Arnold M. Silver, "Questions, Questions, Questions: Memories of Oberursel," *Intelligence and National Security* 8, no. 2 (Apr 1993), 81.
[80] Ofc of the Ch Historian, EUCOM: *The Third Year of the Occupation*, Part 3, *The Third Quarter, 1 January–31 March 1948*, vol. 2, Occupation Forces in Europe Series 1947–48 (Frankfurt: Office of the Chief Historian, EUCOM, 1948), 75.

more than 700 local German police forces. The center estimated that Allied and German agencies arrested between 50 percent and 65 percent of the persons listed in the rogues' gallery.[81]

By early winter of 1945–1946, Nazi-related interrogations had for the most part ceased, and most internees from the immediate postwar period had moved on from Oberursel. German prisoners of war returning from the East and defectors from the Soviet Union and Eastern Europe promptly took their place. The Soviets began releasing German prisoners in November 1946, and those arriving in the Western zones passed through processing camps in Bad Hersfeld, Hof, Ulm, and Giessen. Local Army Intelligence teams screened the returnees and sent those of particular intelligence value for interrogation to Oberursel. In the second half of 1948 alone, the center screened 71,472 returning German prisoners of war. Interrogators interviewed approximately 9,050 of them for information on the economic, political, and military situation of the countries where they were held captive. The center produced 691 intelligence reports based on this work.[82]

In addition to the large-scale screening and interrogation of German prisoners of war, Army Intelligence agencies used Oberursel for a number of special projects and operations. One of these initiatives, the TRIANGLE Project, aimed at extricating specific military and economic information on the Soviet Union from returning German prisoners of war. This effort focused on factories where prisoners of war had worked, the transportation infrastructure they had observed, the location of military installations they might have noticed, and the identification of prisoners with communist sympathies.[83] The CIC, under its counterintelligence remit, also used the camp as an interrogation center for sources, captured enemy agents, and other persons of interest.[84] In 1945, the center housed a group of German officers who were writing military histories of the war for the U.S. Army.[85] An Intelligence Group, headed by Capt. Henry P. Schardt, collected information on intelligence agencies of other countries, with particular emphasis on Soviet-controlled nations.

---

[81] Ofc of the Ch Historian, EUCOM, *The Second Year of the Occupation*, 6:16; Ofc of the Ch Historian, EUCOM, *The Third Year of the Occupation*, Part 3, Third Quarter, 2:51.
[82] Spratt, "History of Camp King," 106; Rpt, Intel Div, Folder "Quarterly Report of Operations 1 October to 31 December 1948," Historian's Background Files, 1947–1952, RG 549, NACP.
[83] Rpt, HQ, 7707 Mil Intel Service Center, Counterintel Special Rpt no. 24, Triangle Project, 16 Dec 1946, Folder "926562," Rcds of the ACoS, G–2 (Intel), Formerly Top Secret Intel Documents, 1943–59, RG 319, NACP; Spratt, "History of Camp King," 106.
[84] Bray et al., *History of the Counter Intelligence Corps*, 27:92.
[85] James A. Wood, "Captive Historians, Captivated Audience: The German Military History Program, 1945–1961," *Journal of Military History* 69, no. 1 (Jan 2005), 133.

In 1948, the center used the Alaska House facility for the accommodation and interrogation of refugees from Czechoslovakia.[86] Other projects involved the exploitation of displaced persons, German scientists, and Soviet and Eastern European deserters.[87] The center also established a Resettlement Section, which protected compromised agents by providing them with new identities and homes.[88]

In 1949, the Army's intelligence center in Oberursel strengthened its joint interrogation efforts with other agencies and extended its reach to Berlin. Camp King activated a Joint Interrogation Center, where Army Intelligence interrogators exploited detainees jointly with personnel from U.S. Air Force intelligence, the Office of Naval Intelligence, and the CIA.[89] Army Intelligence also built on its existing ties with those who had helped it in the past. In the British sector of Berlin, a former Army Intelligence employee, the German progressive activist Marie-Elisabeth Lüders, helped set up a refugee center under the aegis of the city administration. To interview these refugees from the East, in September 1949 American and British intelligence authorities established an Anglo-American Interrogation Center in Berlin. The Army flew particularly valuable sources from Berlin to Oberursel for in-depth interrogation.[90] By the end of the occupation, Camp King had become the hub of American intelligence operations in Germany and Europe.

Intelligence Acquisition Through Censorship

The Army had been planning for the monitoring of civilian communications, or civil censorship, in occupied Germany since 1942. This program called for the control of all forms and types of postal, telegraphic, and telephonic communications as well as travelers' documents in order to obtain military, political, and eco-

---

86 Igor Lukes, *On the Edge of the Cold War: American Diplomats and Spies in Postwar Prague* (New York: Oxford University Press, 2012), 201f.
87 Spratt, "History of Camp King," 107.
88 Rpt, Historical Div, EUCOM, Folder "Quarterly Report of Operations 1 July to 30 September 1948," Historian's Background Files, 1947–1952, RG 549, NACP.
89 Spratt, "History of Camp King," 106.
90 Keith R. Allen, *Befragung, Überprüfung, Kontrolle: Die Aufnahme von DDR-Flüchtlingen in West-Berlin bis 1961* [Questioning, verification, control: The admission of GDR refugees in West Berlin through 1961] (Berlin: Ch. Links, 2013), 33; Paul Maddrell, *Spying on Science: Western Intelligence in Divided Germany, 1945–1961* (Oxford: Oxford University Press, 2006), 56.

nomic information.[91] Even before the German surrender, small teams of Allied specialists moved into the country and occupied vital communications centers.[92] The CIC followed quickly to ensure the loyalty of German personnel at repeater stations, which were critical parts of the communications infrastructure and convenient access points for interception efforts.[93]

In areas under American control, the U.S. Army Signal Corps took possession of the remaining communications infrastructure. The Allied bombing campaign had destroyed much of it, requiring the Signal Corps to lay more than 900,000 miles of field wire and rebuilt radio and teletype nets. Frankfurt, as the headquarters of the European Theater, became the center of this American-controlled communications system.[94] Meanwhile, Army censorship personnel pushed for the quick restoration of local communications to prevent the Germans from reverting to illegal channels and to facilitate the monitoring of the local population. Limited telephone service in Frankfurt resumed in June 1945, and over the following months, mail, phone, and telegraph services across the U.S. Zone followed suit.[95]

On 1 July 1945, the European Theater command activated the Civil Censorship Division with headquarters in Frankfurt. In March 1947, it became the 7742d Civil Censorship Division. The unit operated under the Censorship Branch of the Army's Intelligence Division and had the mission of exploiting German communications "as a valuable source of intelligence for the occupation authorities."[96] The director of the Censorship Branch, Lt. Col. Robert G. Crandall, temporarily headed the similarly named branch of the military government intelligence office, facilitating coordination between the two organizations.[97] Whereas the Censorship Branch of the Intelligence Division executed censorship functions, the significantly smaller OMGUS Censorship Branch set policies and was supposed to coordinate operations with the other Allies through a quadripartite agreement.[98] Collaboration with the British proved easy, but the Soviets showed no interest in

---

91 Ofc of the Ch Historian, EUCOM, *Censorship*, Occupation Forces in Europe Series, 1945–46 (Frankfurt: EUCOM, 1947), 8, 9, 22.
92 Sean Longden, *T-Force: The Race for Nazi War Secrets, 1945* (London: Constable, 2009), 90.
93 Rpt, HQ, Theater Service Forces European HQ, Ofc of the Ch Signal Ofcr, n.d., Rpt of Opns, Covering the Period 1 October through 31 December 1945, Folder "Report of Operations, OCSigO, Headquarters TSFET main 1. October – 31 December 1945," Historical Files, Program Files, USFET, Signal Section, Opns Rpts, 1945–1946, RG 498, NACP.
94 Thompson and Harris, *Signal Corps: The Outcome*, 173.
95 Ofc of the Ch Historian, EUCOM, *Censorship*, 22–24.
96 Ofc of the Ch Historian, EUCOM, *The First Year of the Occupation, 1945–46*, Part 5, 152.
97 Ofc of the Ch Historian, EUCOM, *The Second Year of the Occupation*, 6:3.
98 Msg, Col. Peter Rodes, OMGUS Director of Intel, to DDI, EUCOM, 29 Jul 1947, sub: Functional and Organizational Program for the Office of the Director of Intelligence, OMGUS, Folder "350.09

joining this effort. As an Army history noted, the Soviets "gain political intelligence from other channels."[99]

To cover communications in the entire U.S. Zone, the division established local groups in Munich ("A"), Offenbach ("B"), Berlin ("C"), and Esslingen ("D"). In Bremen, Army censorship relied heavily on British assistance. The German postal service (Reichspost) was required to deliver all mail items and telegrams to one of the groups where censorship personnel read them, deleted or paraphrased passages, destroyed objectionable letters and parcels, and passed documents suspected of containing coded messages or writing in secret ink to a special laboratory for further examination. Located at the building of the former Hoechst chemical company in Frankfurt, the lab provided services to other American intelligence agencies as well. In addition, mobile censorship units, dispatched on temporary duty for telephone monitoring, moved into positions "inconspicuously, in order to have their presence known by as few people as possible and their purpose by none."[100]

Meanwhile, the Signal Corps retained control of repeater stations at the two central communications nodes of postwar Germany, Frankfurt and Berlin. It also administered several stations in the Soviet Zone, which Moscow had granted to the Army for the maintenance of communications lines between the American sector of Berlin and the U.S. Zone. Access to these stations provided the Civil Censorship Division and the Army's signals intelligence service a unique opportunity to intercept a large volume of interzonal, intrazonal, and international telephone calls and telegraph traffic.[101]

In February 1945, the Army's Censorship Branch sent a team to the United States to recruit American personnel with censorship experience for duty in occupied Germany, and the first Americans from this new group arrived in Europe in April. The branch also sought to recruit personnel in France, Belgium, and Luxembourg, but had little success. Censorship, and especially the monitoring of telephone calls, required near-native language skills, which ruled out most individuals who had not grown up in a German-speaking country. As Colonel Crandall noted with regard to the analysis of telephone conversations:

---

(1) Tables of Organization – ODI, OMGUS," Director of Intel, Analysis and Research Br, Gen Corresp, 1945–49, RG 260, NACP.
99 Ofc of the Ch Historian, EUCOM, *Censorship*, 26.
100 Ofc of the Ch Historian, EUCOM, *Censorship*, 13.
101 Msg, Col. Peter Rodes, OMGUS Director of Intel, to DDI, EUCOM, 29 Jul 1947, sub: Functional and Organizational Program for the Office of the Director of Intelligence, OMGUS, Folder "350.09 (1) Tables of Organization – ODI, OMGUS," Director of Intel, Analysis and Research Br, Gen Corresp, 1945–49, RG 260, NACP.

When a telephone conversation is suspected of containing a hidden message, a transcript will be made and referred to the Research Section for analysis. As the inflection of the voice and the spacing of words are often very significant, it may be desirable for Research personnel to listen to the recording of the conversation in some cases.[102]

Evidently, native German speakers would be best suited for this job. In July 1945, the Civil Censorship Division obtained permission to hire 3,500 German citizens.[103]

Among the new recruits were numerous Jewish emigrants and Holocaust survivors, who were deemed politically more reliable than average Germans.[104] Nonetheless, the employment of a large number of German citizens by an American intelligence agency posed a significant security challenge. Local employees could work only in nonsensitive positions, and they were not allowed to see any papers classified Confidential or higher. Allied personnel closely monitored German employees who bore the brunt of the division's censorship workload, but initial concerns about the employment of Germans quickly dissipated. As the division noted, "German personnel proved efficient, their mail examination capacity being higher than that of Americans employed in the United States Office of Censorship." Moreover, the division found "virtually no evidence of willful attempts to conceal or let pass pernicious information."[105] Given their positive track record, Germans citizens became an indispensable part of the censorship workforce. By the end of September 1947, the division employed 2,319 civilians, including 325 Americans, 584 Allied citizens, and 1,410 Germans.[106]

The Civil Censorship Division worked closely with approximately 150 American user agencies, including several military government organizations, the CIC, the U.S. Constabulary, and the CIA. User agencies could request the monitoring of certain individuals or organizations by entering a submission slip to the division.

---

102 Msg, Lt. Co. R. G. Crandall, HQ, Civil Censorship Div, to CO, Gp "A," "B," "C" (Berlin District), "E", 24 Jun 1946, sub: Handling of Communications of Interest to Research, Folder "Censorship orders 1946," Director of Intel, Analysis and Research Br, Gen Corresp, 1945–49, RG 260, NACP.
103 Ofc of the Ch Historian, EUCOM, *Censorship*, 14.
104 Susanne Meinl, "'Our Headquarters in Bormann's Nest': Die US-amerikanische Zensurbehörde CCD in Pullach" ["Our Headquarters in Bormann's Nest": The US censorship agency CCD in Pullach], in *Geheimobjekt Pullach: Von der NS-Mustersiedlung zur Zentrale des BND* [Secret object Pullach: From the Nazi model housing estate to BND headquarters], ed. Susanne Meinl and Bodo Hechelhammer (Berlin: Ch. Links, 2014), 135.
105 Ofc of the Ch Historian, EUCOM, *Censorship*, 15. The United States Office of Censorship was the federal government agency established in 1941 to censor wartime communications in the United States.
106 Ofc of the Ch Historian, EUCOM, *The Third Year of the Occupation*, Part 1, *First Quarter: 1 July–30 September 1947*, vol. 2, Occupation Forces in Europe Series 1947–48 (Frankfurt: Office of the Chief Historian, EUCOM, 1948), 69.

The division then added the slips to a regularly updated watch list. Initially, the list consisted mostly of war criminals. German businesses, such as the Allianz and Münchener Rückversicherungs Gesellschaft insurance companies, also were censorship targets.[107] In January 1947, the division censored 194,517 phone calls, 1,492,055 telegrams, and nearly 3.5 million mail items.[108] Amid the chaos of postwar Germany, censorship produced a wealth of financial, social, and political data, including information on the movements and whereabouts of former Nazi officials, on subversive activities, on the black market, and even on the latest popular rumors. The intercepts also painted a rich, firsthand picture of German attitudes toward the occupation.

By 1947, American interest in denazification and the prosecution of war criminals had waned. Therefore, the Intelligence Division drew up plans to dissolve the 7742d Civil Censorship Division, which had worked principally on Nazi-related issues. In August, the division's headquarters moved from Frankfurt to Esslingen near Stuttgart for liquidation in December.[109] These plans changed, however, in view of intensifying rivalry between the Western Allies and the Soviet Union in Germany. American intelligence officers realized that censorship could be a valuable tool to collect information on Soviet and communist activities. On 10 November 1947, the European Command stood up the Communications Intelligence Service Detachment as a field agency under the supervision of the Operations Branch of the Army's European intelligence division. Headquartered in Frankfurt, the detachment deployed local censorship teams and intercept units to communications centers in Berlin, Bremen, Frankfurt, Munich, Nuremberg, and Stuttgart. Personnel from the Civil Censorship Division transferred to the newly established detachment.[110]

The detachment was smaller than its predecessor and adopted a narrower approach to censorship. As an Army Intelligence official noted, its "attention centers chiefly on a small number of extremist personalities of the Max Reimann type."[111] Max Reimann was a leading KPD politician who had been active in German communist circles since before World War I. Because of his communist back-

---

107 Msg, Theodore H. Ball, Director, Finance Div, OMGUS, to Civil Censorship Div, EUCOM, 18 Apr 1947, sub: Amendment to Censorship Watch List, Folder "311.7 Censorship Watch Lists (3)," Director of Intel, Analysis and Research Br, Gen Corresp, 1945–49, RG 260, NACP.
108 Ofc of the Ch Historian, EUCOM, *The Second Year of the Occupation*, 6:28.
109 Ofc of the Ch Historian, EUCOM, *The Third Year of the Occupation*, Part 1, *First Quarter*, 2:69.
110 Ofc of the Ch Historian, EUCOM, *The Third Year of the Occupation*, Part 2, *The Second Quarter: 1 October–31 December 1947*, vol. 2, Occupation Forces in Europe Series 1947–48 (Frankfurt: Office of the Chief Historian, EUCOM, 1948), 65.
111 Memo, Arouet for Harris, 29 Sep 1949, sub: EUCOM Intelligence Agencies.

ground, multiple American intelligence agencies kept him under surveillance. In spite of its reduced size, the detachment continued to produce intelligence on a significant scale. During the first quarter of 1948, Army censors monitored 329 telephone circuits and 13,211 telephone calls. They examined 692 postal communications and intercepted 175 that they deemed suspicious.[112] The detachment also expanded its laboratory, which now worked mostly on behalf of the rapidly expanding CIA.[113] By the end of the military occupation, the review of material afforded by the censorship process had become an indispensable tool for American intelligence.

The Intelligence School at Oberammergau

During the war, Army Intelligence personnel received their training in the United States. Although specialized training in interrogation techniques, photo reconnaissance, counterintelligence, and signals intelligence continued stateside during the postwar period, General Sibert realized the need for additional instruction in the European Theater. In August 1945, he directed the opening of a theater intelligence school in Germany for this purpose. General Order No. 310 of 16 November formally established the European Theater Intelligence School under the aegis of the intelligence division in Frankfurt. After extensive inspections of several facilities, the division selected the Kimmel-Kaserne in Oberammergau at the foot of the Bavarian Alps as the location for the new school. During the war, the barracks had housed a German mountain battalion. Units of the Seventh Army had captured it in April 1945, and the Americans initially used it as an interrogation site for local Nazi officials. On 14 December 1945, the first three instructors of the new intelligence school arrived.[114]

As General Sibert clarified in a letter of instruction, the mission of the school was "to support the intelligence agencies in the European Theater in carrying out their Occupational duties."[115] When the school opened, it offered courses in counterintelligence, interrogation techniques, photographic interpretation, order of battle analysis, and military government, including lessons on the German military and Nazi organizations. In early 1946, the school offered its first German and Russian language classes, the latter designed for intelligence officers on liaison

---

112 Ofc of the Ch Historian, EUCOM, *The Third Year of the Occupation*, Part 3, *Third Quarter*, 2:71.
113 Memo, Arouet for Harris, 29 Sep 1949, sub: EUCOM Intelligence Agencies.
114 Rpt, Ofc of the DDI, EUCOM, Quarterly Rpt of Opns, 1 Jan to 31 Mar 1948.
115 Rpt, Ofc of the DDI, EUCOM, Quarterly Rpt of Opns, 1 Jan to 31 Mar 1948.

Figure 20: The 7712th European Command Intelligence School, located in the former Nazi mountain division training and housing barracks in Oberammergau, January 1948. INSCOM.

duty with the Soviets. Classes were available to tactical troops as well as to members of the military government.

The nucleus of the school's personnel came from a similar school at Saint-Georges-Motel in France, which had closed at the end of the war. During the first year of operations, demobilization and redeployment made the administration of the school both difficult and wasteful. Oftentimes, the school could not retain qualified administrative staff and instructors who left for the United States, and replacements frequently did not have the necessary training or skills to be effective. The same could be said of many of the students, such as the CIC students mentioned earlier who failed to measure up to their instructors' expectations. "Ingenuity, initiative and aggressiveness were therefore primary requisites of the personnel who established the School," an official history notes. This initial phase of extreme turmoil lasted until the summer of 1946 when the personnel situation in the European Theater began to stabilize.[116]

---

[116] Rpt, Ofc of the DDI, EUCOM, Quarterly Rpt of Opns, 1 Jan to 31 Mar 1948.

Figure 21: Miss Buttner, a German instructor, lectures Army Intelligence personnel, January 1948. INSCOM.

Many German native speakers served as school instructors. This group included both German citizens and American intelligence personnel with a German background. In late 1945, staff from the school canvassed Oberammergau and surrounding towns, and identified potential German language teachers from the local population. Most had previously worked as teachers in German schools. After a careful security screening, the school hired eight of them as language instructors.[117] In addition to local recruits, the school drew personnel from across Germany. Its early staff included Marie-Elisabeth Lüders, a German women's rights activist and former parliamentarian who had been briefly jailed by the Nazis in the late 1930s. Another staff member, Fritz Gustav Anton Kraemer, was a German Jewish refugee who had joined Army Intelligence during the war and would become a key advisor on national security affairs at the Pentagon in later years.[118]

---

117 Rpt, Ofc of the DDI, EUCOM, Quarterly Rpt of Opns, 1 Jan to 31 Mar 1948.
118 "'Die Sauhund' hau'n wir wieder 'naus'" ["We'll knock the bastards off again"], *Der Spiegel*, 17 Nov 1980.

Kraemer, in turn, recruited several fellow Army Intelligence soldiers of German Jewish background. Helmut Sonnenfeldt, born in Berlin, had served in the Army during the war and joined the staff of the school shortly after its establishment. After teaching at Oberammergau, he worked for many years at the State Department and the National Security Council. The former Sgt. Henry A. Kissinger also joined the school as a civilian instructor for ten months at Kraemer's request. Kissinger earned the princely sum of $3,640 a year, plus a 25 percent "overseas differential" of $910—more than double the median U.S. income. He taught courses on "German History & Mental[ity]," "Intelligence Investigation," and "Eastern Europe." Kissinger was particularly interested in alerting his students to the Soviet and communist threats.[119] Although he was around the same age as most of his students, he felt perfectly comfortable teaching a class. One of the students, Henry Rosovsky, recalled years later: "Though he was not long out of high school, Henry had a very authoritative—and authoritarian—manner. He would lecture with great self-confidence and intellectual sophistication."[120]

In the course of 1947, the organization of the school underwent several changes. As the European Theater made way for the European Command organization in the spring of 1947, the school assumed a new name, the 7712th European Command Intelligence School. It came under the supervision of the Training and Organization Section of the Intelligence Division's Special Projects Branch. Headed by Col. Julian E. Raymond, the school had a military and civilian staff of 203 persons as well as 276 local resident employees by the end of March 1948.[121] In the second annual quarter of 1948, 360 students were enrolled in all courses, and the school produced 306 graduates.[122]

The European Command made instruction in the German language mandatory for all military officers who would serve one or more years in the theater. The school therefore began offering more courses taught in German and replaced its two-month German language course with a four-month course, titled "Military Intelligence, Language." It consisted of 320 hours of conversational German and of 233 hours of background subjects dealing with Germany, the Soviet Union, intelligence, and counterintelligence. Given the growing rift between the Western Powers and the Soviet Union, the school also made an effort to offer additional

---

119 Niall Ferguson, *Kissinger*, vol. 1, *1923–1968: The Idealist* (New York: Penguin, 2013), 198.
120 Walter Isaacson, *Kissinger: A Biography* (New York: Simon & Schuster, 1992), 55.
121 Ofc of the Ch Historian, EUCOM, *The Third Year of the Occupation*, Part 2, *Third Quarter*, 2:53, 2:73.
122 Ofc of the Ch Historian, EUCOM, *The Third Year of the Occupation*, Part 4, *Fourth Quarter*, 2:47.

courses tailored to the needs of Army Intelligence personnel dealing with Soviet issues, especially language training.[123]

In May 1947, the Intelligence Division at the Pentagon established Detachment "R" (Department of the Army detachment for Russian language and area training) at the intelligence school at Oberammergau to conduct a "War Department Area and Language Course (Russian)." The school lent logistical support and coordinated its own Russian language program with Detachment "R." To give students the ability to practice their Russian language skills, the intelligence division reached an agreement with the American ambassador to Moscow to have Army Intelligence officers enrolled at Oberammergau serve in groups of two as couriers between Berlin and Moscow. The division also proposed a plan to detach students for temporary service with the Constabulary on the U.S.-Soviet interzonal border to practice their Russian.[124] By the end of 1948, 68 out of a total 364 students had enrolled in Russian language classes at Oberammergau, more than in any other course. Also in late 1948, the school replaced its military government course with a course on combat intelligence, which dealt mostly with the Soviet order of battle in Eastern Europe.[125] By the end of the military occupation, the school had thoroughly revised its curriculum to meet the Army's Cold War needs.

The Berlin Documents Center

In 1944 and 1945, Army units captured reams of official German documents, including numerous records generated by the Nazi regime. The U.S. military government coordinated these collection efforts in Berlin, and shortly after the end of the war it established the 6889th Berlin Documents Center (BDC) as a central aggregation point for captured records of the Third Reich.[126] The new organization moved into a spacious private home located at Wasserkäfersteig 1 in the American sector of Berlin. A visitor described the site as "a largish suburban villa, like so many in [the Berlin district of] Zehlendorf," and noted the ample se-

---

[123] Ofc of the Ch Historian, EUCOM, *The Third Year of the Occupation*, Part 4, *Fourth Quarter*, 2:48.
[124] Rpt, Ofc of the DDI, EUCOM, Quarterly Rpt of Opns, 1 Jan to 31 Mar 1948; Ofc of the Ch Historian, EUCOM, *The Third Year of the Occupation*, Part 1, *First Quarter*, 2:55–56.
[125] Ofc of the Ch Historian, EUCOM, *The Fourth Year of the Occupation, 1 July–31 December 1948*, vol. 2, Occupation Forces in Europe Series, 1948 (Karlsruhe: Historical Division, EUCOM, 1949), 47.
[126] Astrid Eckert, *The Struggle for the Files: The Western Allies and the Return of German Archives after the Second World War* (Cambridge, UK: Cambridge University Press, 2012), 96; "News Notes," *The American Archivist* 10, no. 1 (Jan 1947), 105.

curity measures: "the high barbed-wire double fence around the periphery of its extensive grounds, the floodlights, and the armed, steel-helmeted sentries told me I had come to the right spot."[127]

Figure 22: Document storage at the Berlin Documents Center. U.S. Army.

The Office of the Director of Intelligence of the military government exercised operational control over the BDC.[128] Given the nature of its work, the center required leaders who were fluent in German. Its first commanding officer was Lt. Col. Hans W. Helm, "a tough German-American warhorse, a professional soldier in the Weimar Republic's Reichswehr [army] before he emigrated to the States in the twenties."[129] Helm's deputy was Sgt. Kurt Rosenow, a German Jewish lawyer born in Berlin. In 1940, Rosenow had immigrated to the United States where he worked as a butler. The Army drafted him in 1943, sent him for training to Camp Ritchie, and then assigned him to the document section of the Supreme

---

127 George Clare, *Before the Wall: Berlin Days, 1946–1948* (New York: Dutton, 1990), 198.
128 Memo, Col. Bruce Easley Jr., OMGUS, for Directors of Div and Staff Ofcs, 12 Oct 1945, sub: Organization Plan, Folder "17/57–3 (6)," Director of Intel, Miscellaneous Rcds re. Intel and Document Policies, 1944–1948, RG 260, NACP.
129 Clare, *Before the Wall*, 194.

Allied sHeadquarters' intelligence division, where he analyzed the correspondence of German prisoners of war. In August 1945, he returned to the city of his birth as an American soldier. In 1946, Rosenow left the Army, but he remained with the BDC as deputy director and curator. He and Helm supervised a small staff of thoroughly screened German employees.[130]

The center administered several hundred tons of captured Nazi records, including a near-complete set of membership records of the Nazi Party, described as the "nastiest 'Who's Who' in the world" by one soldier who worked with them.[131] The *Gestapo* had moved these records to a paper mill in the community of Freimann, north of Munich, at the end of the war, and ordered their destruction. The local staff, however, had not obliged. After the German surrender, CIC Special Agent Francesco S. Quaranta heard of the records, went to the mill, and found the entire second floor of the building filled with them. Immediately recognizing the files' value, he informed his superiors, who ordered them shipped to Berlin.[132] Rosenow, who collected and catalogued these and many other Nazi records at the center, remembered that he and his staff "were overwhelmed by the mass of paper that came in."[133]

The BDC supported military government operations by cataloging and making available the documents in its possession. Its collections quickly became a powerful tool in the identification and arrest of wanted Nazi officials, in the denazification effort, and in the investigation of suspected war criminals. The CIC considered the center's holdings "invaluable" in tracking down Nazis who had gone into hiding and routinely furnished the names of wanted officials to the local police.[134]

All Allied agencies in Germany had access to the BDC's research services. The Americans used this opportunity most liberally, filing more than 61,000 requests from 1 September to 30 November 1946. The British filed more than 12,000 requests during the same time period, while the French made merely three inquiries. The Soviets made none.[135]

When the Soviets blockaded the Western sectors of Berlin in 1948, the military government created a rear element of the center at Darmstadt, and flew 288 tons of documents to that city.[136] In addition, Army Intelligence shipped fifty tons

---

130 Biographical info, "Mr. Kurt Rosenow, Department of the Army Civilian, Retired (Deceased)," Historians Files, CMH; "News Notes," *American Archivist*, 105.
131 Clare, *Before the Wall*, 199.
132 Bray et al., *History of the Counter Intelligence Corps*, 26:69.
133 Mary Williams Walsh, "Who Owns the Nazi Paper Trail?" *Los Angeles Times*, 30 Jun 1994.
134 Bray et al., *History of the Counter Intelligence Corps*, 27:48.
135 Rpt, Col. Peter P. Rodes, 7 Dec 1946, Weekly Intel Rpt no. 30, Folder "OMGUS Intelligence Notes # 21–41, 9.14.46–2.22.47," Historian's Background Files, 1947–1952, RG 549, NACP.
136 Eckert, *Struggle for the Files*, 98.

of particularly sensitive records directly to the United States. These records included technical data, which the Army sought to prevent from falling into Soviet hands in case the Western sectors of Berlin succumbed to Moscow's pressure.[137] In 1949, the blockade ended, and the BDC remained in Berlin. Over the following years and decades, the center became a permanent feature of Cold War Germany and an important reference point for researchers seeking to understand the country's Nazi past.

The United States Military Liaison Mission

In September 1946, the Soviets reached an agreement with the British to accredit military missions of the other power at their respective headquarters in occupied Germany. The missions were to facilitate communications between the military forces of the two sides. General Clay pushed for a similar agreement with the Soviets. On 5 April 1947, the two sides signed the so-called Huebner-Malinin Agreement, after Clay's deputy, Lt. Gen. Clarence R. Huebner, and the deputy commander of the Soviet forces in Germany, Lt. Gen. Mikhail S. Malinin.[138]

The agreement provided for the accreditation of a Soviet Military Liaison Mission to European Command headquarters in Frankfurt and of a United States Military Liaison Mission (USMLM) in Potsdam, near the headquarters of the Group of Soviet Occupation Forces in Germany. Both missions had an authorized strength of fourteen officers and enlisted men. Reflecting the dominance of the Army's position and interests in Germany, the European Command staffed its contingent with twelve Army personnel and one Air Force and Navy officer each. An artillery officer, Brig. Gen. Walter W. Hess Jr., served as the mission's commander for the duration of the military occupation. The Soviets assigned the U.S. mission a spacious mansion that had belonged to a relative of the last German emperor, and came to be known as "Potsdam House." Brig. Gen. Charles K. Gailey Jr. of the U.S. military government, who inspected the proposed site in late 1946, was impressed by what he saw: "Apparently the Russians have gone to considerable trouble and pain to set this mission up in good style."[139]

As luxurious as the Potsdam House was by postwar standards, its location inside the Soviet Zone exposed it to surveillance and penetration attempts. The Amer-

---

137 Telecon 9807, 20 Jul 1948, Folder "#1 Telecons (1–1–48 thru TT-1156, 9–5–48)," ACoS, G–2 (Intel), "Top Secret" Incoming and Outgoing Cables, 1942–52, RG 319, NACP.
138 Dorothee Mußgnug, *Alliierte Militärmissionen in Deutschland 1946–1990* [The Allied military missions in Germany, 1946–1990] (Berlin: Duncker & Humblot, 2001), 19–21.
139 Mußgnug, *Alliierte Militärmissionen*, 22.

icans had to assume that the Soviets monitored all telephone calls, and the CIC uncovered an attempt by Soviet intelligence to insert a spy into the ranks of the local German maintenance staff.[140] The U.S. mission therefore billeted most of its personnel in nearby Berlin, using Potsdam House primarily for ceremonial activities and as a venue for the exchange of official communications with the Soviet military. For all administrative matters, briefings, and the storage and processing of classified documents, mission personnel used two rooms in the headquarters compound of the Berlin Command, just a few miles northeast of Potsdam.[141]

The United States Military Liaison Mission to the Commander-in-Chief of the Soviet Occupied Zone of Germany—the unit's official designation until 1 March 1948, when it was redesignated as the 7893d U.S. Military Liaison Mission to the Commander-in-Chief of the Soviet Occupied Zone of Germany—reported to the Director of Operations, Plans, Organization, and Training at the European Command.[142] The Huebner-Malinin Agreement defined the unit's principal mission as providing effective liaison with the Soviet military. Yet, as one intelligence officer noted, the Army "from the outset" established the USMLM with a view "to perform an intelligence function."[143] The Office of the Director of Intelligence had carefully reviewed the draft of the agreement and successfully pushed for the inclusion of language ensuring a minimum of travel restrictions.[144] As result, the agreement guaranteed mission members "complete freedom of travel" throughout the Soviet Zone, with the exception of designated militarily sensitive areas.

Some U.S. officials remained skeptical about the mission's intelligence value. "It is apparent," noted Dana Durand, the CIA chief in Berlin, "that an American officer in uniform cannot conduct espionage on anything but the most obvious

---

140 Msg, 1st Lt. Serge S. Coval, U.S. Military Liaison Mission (USMLM), to Historical Div, HQ, EUCOM, 31 Mar 1953, sub: Transmittal of Unit History, Folder "Unit History – 7893rd US Military Mission 1952," Army – AG Cmd Rpt 1949–1954, RG 407, NACP; Rpt, HQ, Region VIII, CIC, 10 Jun 1948, Folder "CIC Region VIII (Berlin) Periodic Counter Intelligence Reports," Director of Intel, Analysis and Research, Misc. Rpts and Publications, 1941–50, RG 260, NACP.
141 Paul G. Skowronek, "U.S.-Soviet Military Liaison in Germany, Since 1947" (PhD diss., University of Colorado, 1975), 70; James R. Holbrook, *Potsdam Mission: Memoir of a U.S. Army Intelligence Officer in Communist East Germany* (Carmel, IN: Cork Hill Press, 2005), 18.
142 Ofc of the Ch Historian, EUCOM, *A Survey of Soviet Aims, Policies, and Tactics*, Occupation Forces in Europe Series 1947–1948 (Frankfurt: Historical Division, EUCOM, 1948), 293.
143 Rpt, Durand to Ch, Foreign Br M, 8 Apr 1948, sub: Transmittal of Report on Berlin Operations Base, in Steury, *On the Front Lines of the Cold War*, 49.
144 Memo, Lawrence E. deNeufville, Ch, Analysis and Reporting, to Director of Intel, 12 Feb 1947, sub: Agreement on Military Missions, Folder "091.112 Military Missions," Director of Intel, Analysis and Research Br, Gen Corresp, 1945–49, RG 260, NACP.

and uninteresting targets."[145] Others seized on the opportunity offered by the new unit. Both the Navy and the Army attached trained intelligence officers to the mission, Navy Capt. Philip Schneider and Lt. Col. Oleg J. Pantuhoff. The latter was a Russia expert. Born in Tsarist Russia, the bilingual Pantuhoff had served as an interpreter for President Franklin D. Roosevelt at Tehran and Yalta and for General Dwight D. Eisenhower at Potsdam in May 1945. On account of his background and training, Pantuhoff, "was admirably qualified to carry out intelligence observation as a side line to his liaison work."[146]

The intelligence division provided the commander, General Hess, with a list of Essential Elements of Information concerning military targets in the Soviet Zone, and from the beginning, intelligence collection appears to have been the main purpose of trips undertaken by mission members.[147] In June 1947, General Hess, Captain Schneider, and their driver traveled from Potsdam to the Baltic coast and reported on naval facilities at Güstrow, Rostock, and Stralsund. They also received permission from the local Soviet commander to visit the former German V-2 supersonic rocket test site at Peenemünde. Schneider suspected that the Soviets did not object to their visit because "everything had been removed or destroyed. . . . What we saw at Peenemunde was actually a wilderness."[148] Both Schneider and Pantuhoff made several attempts to get a closer look at militarily interesting targets, but the Soviets detained them repeatedly in the process. Each time, mission headquarters quickly obtained their release, but the Soviets became wary of the two men. In early 1948, after Pantuhoff, at General Hess's request, had sought to gain entry to an officially barred factory, the Soviet commander declared Pantuhoff and Schneider personae non gratae and demanded their recall.[149]

The mission soon began coordinating their operations with its British counterpart.[150] As Moscow's relations with the West deteriorated over the status of Berlin in 1948, the Soviets tightened the screws on the mission. A little over a year after

---

145 Rpt, Durand to Ch, Foreign Br M, 8 Apr 1948, sub: Transmittal of Report on Berlin Operations Base, in Steury, *On the Front Lines of the Cold War*, 50.
146 Rpt, Durand to Ch, Foreign Br M, 8 Apr 1948, sub: Transmittal of Report on Berlin Operations Base, in Steury, *On the Front Lines of the Cold War*, 49. Pantuhoff later changed his name to John L. Bates.
147 Ofc of the Ch Historian, EUCOM, *A Survey of Soviet Aims, Policies, and Tactics*, 292.
148 Rpt, Capt. Philip Schneider to Ch, USMLM, 18 Jun 1947, sub: Field Report, Folder "TSC # 3901—4000," Top Secret Rpts of Naval Attaches, compiled Feb 1944–Aug 1947, RG 38, NACP.
149 Rpt, Durand to Ch, Foreign Br M, 8 Apr 1948, sub: Transmittal of Report on Berlin Operations Base, in Steury, *On the Front Lines of the Cold War*, 50. Pantuhoff left Germany shortly thereafter.
150 Anya Vodopyanov, "A Watchful Eye Behind the Iron Curtain: The U.S. Military Liaison Mission in East Germany, 1953–61" (master's thesis, Stanford University, 2004), 22; For the British

the Huebner-Malinin Agreement had been signed, General Huebner informed the director of intelligence at the Pentagon, Maj. Gen. Stephen J. Chamberlin, that Soviet commanders sometimes refused to issue travel passes, had repeatedly detained members, and exercised close supervision of USMLM teams traveling through East Germany. In the town of Meiningen in southwest Thuringia, the Soviet security service arrested a mission member and held him incommunicado overnight.[151] When protests failed to improve the situation, the Department of the Army authorized the European Command to retaliate by threatening to shut down the Soviet military liaison mission in Frankfurt.[152] Eventually, the two sides returned to the status quo and the USMLM continued to gather intelligence in the Soviet Zone. As the only U.S. organization authorized to travel with comparative freedom behind the Iron Curtain, it became one of the most effective collectors of intelligence on the Soviet military in Europe during the Cold War.

Conclusion

The story of the intelligence field agencies in occupied Germany is one of constant adaptation. Organizationally, they had to adjust to the Army's transformation from a war-fighting to an occupation force. Operationally, they shifted their focus from denazification and war crimes investigation to counterintelligence against the communist party in the West and information gathering in the Soviet Zone. And whereas most agencies managed to maintain or even expand their manpower, recruitment and staffing posed an ongoing challenge. Always in flux, this was the Army's machinery for dealing with the legacy of the Third Reich and the looming Soviet challenge.

---

mission, see Tony Geraghty, *Brixmis: The Untold Exploits of Britain's Most Daring Cold War Spy Mission* (London: HarperCollins, 1997).

151 Msg, Lt. Gen. Clarence R. Huebner to Maj. Gen. Stephen J. Chamberlin et al., 20 Apr 1948, Folder "#1 FR: 'S' Germany 1000–4000 1-1-48–6-9-48," ACoS, G–2 (Intel), "Top Secret" Incoming and Outgoing Cables, 1942–52, RG 319, NACP.

152 Msg, Lt. Gen. Daniel Noce, Civil Affairs Div, to Cdr in Ch, Europe (CINCEUR), 1 Jul 1948, Folder "19. To: Consolidated Outgoing 6\84000–85999 (6-30-48–7-15-48)," ACoS, G–2 (Intel), "Top Secret" Incoming and Outgoing Cables, 1942–52, RG 319, NACP.

Part III: **Intelligence Operations in Occupied Germany**

5 The Long Shadow of the Third Reich

For American soldiers fighting their way through Europe, perhaps no site epitomized Nazi cruelty as poignantly as Dachau. Established as a prison for political prisoners outside Munich in 1933, Dachau became the model for concentration camps across the Third Reich. By the end of the war, more than 30,000 inmates had perished there through forced labor, medical experiments, and executions by SS guards. When soldiers of the 45th Infantry Division liberated the camp on 29 April 1945, they encountered hundreds of decaying bodies as well as numerous sick and dying inmates subsisting in appalling conditions. Outraged GIs shot some of the captured SS guards on the spot. One soldier later commented on these extrajudicial killings: "We got all the bastards."[1]

Dachau made a lasting impression on the Army Intelligence personnel who passed through the camp. Maj. Earl S. Browning Jr. of the Counter Intelligence Corps, who visited Dachau two days after its liberation, told his son decades later that he never forgot the "dead bodies ... stacked outside the barracks like wood."[2] The intelligence division of the Seventh Army published a report documenting the atrocities committed by the Nazis at Dachau. The division chief, Col. William W. Quinn, noted in the foreword: "Dachau ... will stand for all time as one of history's most gruesome symbols of inhumanity. There our troops found sights, sounds and stenches horrible beyond belief, cruelties so enormous as to be incomprehensible to the normal mind. Dachau and death were synonymous."[3]

With these images in mind, Army Intelligence personnel embarked on an arduous reckoning with Germany's past. This mission included the apprehension of war criminals, the suppression of subversive groups such as the *Werwolf*, and the denazification of German society. Given that thousands of soldiers serving in intelligence units were refugees from the Third Reich and had lost family members

---

[1] Howard A. Buechner, *Dachau: The Hour of the Avenger* (Metairie, LA: Thunderbird Press, 1986), 96. For accounts of the liberation of Dachau, see Klaus-Dietmar Henke, *Die amerikanische Besetzung Deutschlands* [The American occupation of Germany] (Munich: R. Oldenbourg Verlag, 2009), 922–23; Jürgen Zarusky, "'That is not the American Way of Fighting': The Shooting of Captured SS-Men During the Liberation of Dachau," in *Dachau and the Nazi Terror 1933–1945*, vol. 2, Studies and Reports, ed. Wolfgang Benz and Barbara Distel (Dachau: Verlag Dachauer Hefte, 2002), 134–60. For the Army's official report on the killings of SS men by U.S. soldiers, see Rpt, Lt. Col. Joseph D. Whitaker, HQ Seventh Army, Ofc of the Inspector Gen, to CG, Seventh Army, 8 Jun 1945, sub: Investigation of Alleged Mistreatment of German Guards at Dachau, Seventh United States Army, Inspector Gen Section, Rpts of Investigations 1943–1945, RG 338, NACP.
[2] Email, Jim Browning to Thomas Boghardt, 10 Sep 2020, Historians Files, CMH.
[3] Rpt, Col William W. Quinn, ACoS, G-2, Seventh U.S. Army, Dachau, 1945, 2, online edition, Dwight D. Eisenhower Presidential Library, Abilene, KS (hereinafter Eisenhower Library).

Figure 23: Photograph taken shortly after U.S. soldiers shot SS guards at Dachau concentration camp. U.S. Army, NACP.

in the Holocaust, the Army's endeavor to make Germany face up to its crimes was for many an intensely personal affair.

In Search of Adolf Hitler

American intelligence had long been interested in the person and the personality of Adolf Hitler. During the war, the Office of Strategic Services commissioned the psychoanalyst Walter C. Langer to write a secret psychological profile on the Führer. Langer completed his work in late 1943 and later published it under the title *The Mind of Adolf Hitler*. The report portrayed Hitler as a mentally disturbed individual and sexual pervert, and predicted that he would probably take his own life at the end of the war, rather than surrender or try to escape. "The course he will follow," Langer wrote, "will almost certainly be the one which seems to him to be the surest road to immortality and at the same time drag the world down in flames."[4]

---

[4] Walter C. Langer, *The Mind of Adolf Hitler: The Secret Wartime Report* (New York: Basic Books, 1972), 249.

It was a prescient estimate. In January 1945, Hitler moved into the Führerbunker, a reinforced underground shelter under the Reich Chancellery in Berlin. Here, he spent the rest of the war with a small entourage, directing the forces of his ever-shrinking Reich. On 30 April, with the Red Army closing in on his hideout, Hitler shot himself in the head with his own pistol, and his newly wedded wife, Eva Braun, poisoned herself with cyanide. The following day, 1 May, propaganda minister Joseph Goebbels and his wife Magda also used cyanide to murder their six children and then kill themselves. The remaining staff placed the bodies of Hitler and his wife as well as those of the Goebbels family in bomb craters outside the bunker, doused them in gasoline, set them afire, and buried the remains. Shortly thereafter, German radio announced that Hitler had died in Berlin, "fighting to the last breath against Bolshevism."[5]

Army Intelligence had little reason to doubt Hitler's demise. "We were certain that he had committed suicide at his bunker," one CIC soldier recalled.[6] Nonetheless, the Allies wanted to confirm Hitler's death to bring home the finality of defeat to the Germans. Around V-E Day, Supreme Allied Headquarters ordered Col. Rufus S. Bratton, the designated U.S. Army Intelligence chief for Berlin, to its headquarters at Reims, France. Here, they handed him a sketch of the Führerbunker and instructed him as well as his British counterpart to investigate "the circumstances surrounding the death of Adolf Hitler" as soon as Allied forces moved into Berlin.[7]

For the time being, the only party in a position to confirm Hitler's fate were the conquerors of Berlin, the Soviets, who assumed control of the Führerbunker site on 2 May. Soviet intelligence officers immediately began interviewing the remaining members of Hitler's entourage and his doctors about their leader's fate, quickly piecing together the events of the final days in the bunker. On 9 May, they identified the burial site and secured the charred remains of Hitler, Goebbels, and their wives. Despite the damage inflicted by the fire, they positively identified the bodies. "Hitler's skull," one Soviet intelligence officer marveled, "was almost intact, as were the cranium and the upper and lower jaws."[8]

Red Army officers told General Dwight D. Eisenhower's staff in early June that they had identified Hitler's body with a fair amount of certainty, but the Soviets quickly changed their story. On 6 June, Joseph Stalin told Harry L. Hopkins, the top U.S. representative in Moscow, that Hitler was alive. On 9 June, Marshal

---

5 Richard Bessel, *Germany 1945: From War to Peace* (New York: Harper, 2009), 121.
6 Matthew Brzezinski, "Giving Hitler Hell," *Washington Post*, 24 Jul 2005.
7 Testimony, William Friel Heimlich, 11 Mar 1948, Folder "Hitler's Death Reports," Gen Staff, Intel Div, Administration Br, Misc. Items of Intel Interest, 1947–49, RG 549, NACP.
8 H. R. Trevor-Roper, *The Last Days of Hitler* (London: Cox & Wyman, 1972), 35.

Georgy K. Zhukov, the chief of the Soviet Military Administration and commander of the Soviet forces in Germany, told the press in Berlin: "We have not identified the body of Hitler. . . . He could have flown away from Berlin at the very last moment." At the same time, General Nikolai E. Berzarin, the Soviet commandant of Berlin, stated that Hitler had "gone into hiding and is somewhere in Europe, possibly with [Spanish dictator] General [Francisco] Franco." The notion that Hitler had survived the war and gone underground would remain the official Soviet position for the next quarter-century.[9]

By deliberately spreading disinformation about Hitler's fate, the Soviets hoped to keep the fear of a resurgent Nazi Germany alive, implicitly justifying their own military presence in central Europe. For the same reason, the uncertainty of Hitler's death posed a problem to the Western Allies. Shortly after the end of the war, Army Intelligence received reports about suspicious Hitler sightings. One had him living as a shepherd in the Swiss Alps, another as a croupier in a casino near Evian in France, and yet another as a fisherman off the Irish coast.[10] Local informants told their American handlers that subversive neo-Nazi radio stations claimed "that Hitler is alive and would return to save Germany."[11] As improbable as these reports were, they fed into a growing Hitler myth, which the Western Allies wanted to avoid at all costs. "Hitler will continue to have the respect of a large part of the population," noted the Army's chief of staff, General George C. Marshall, as early as April, and he warned of the threat Hitler's shadow might pose to the occupation.[12]

Consequently, Army Intelligence broadened its quest to confirm Hitler's death. Much of this effort centered on the identification and interrogation of Hitler's staff. On 25 May, Canadian forces arrested a bunker guard, Hermann Karnau, who told his captors that he personally witnessed the cremation of Hitler's body.[13] The following month, the Army interrogated several more bunker guards who confirmed the story. In July, the CIC interviewed Hitler's surviving sister, Paula, in Austria. She had not been in Berlin during the final phase of the war, so she could not contribute any details, but she did not doubt that her brother had died. Glossing over the appalling crimes that Hitler had perpetrated against humanity, she noted, "He

---

9 Donald M. McKale, *Hitler: The Survival Myth* (New York: Stein and Day, 1981), 51.
10 Ian Sayer and Douglas Botting, *America's Secret Army: The Untold Story of the Counter Intelligence Corps* (London: Fontana, 1990), 306.
11 Rpt, Ofc of the Ch of Naval Opns, 26 Jul 1945, sub: Germany – Subversive Activities, Folder "XE 049888 Werewolf Activities," INSCOM, IRR, Impersonal Name Files, 1939–1976, RG 319, NACP.
12 Msg, Gen George C. Marshall to Sec War, 2 Apr 1945, sub: Probable Developments in the German Reich, Ofc of the Ch of Staff, Top-Secret Gen Corresp, 1941–1947, RG 319, NACP.
13 Sarah K. Douglas, "The Search for Hitler: Hugh Trevor-Roper, Humphrey Searle, and the Last Days of Hitler," *Journal of Military History* 78 (Jan 2014), 168.

was still my brother, no matter what happened. . . . His end brought unspeakable sorrow to me, as his sister." At this point, she burst into tears, and the interview had to end.[14]

Supreme Allied Headquarters and the Army's top intelligence officer in Europe, Brig. Gen. Edwin L. Sibert, forwarded the reports concerning Hitler's death to Colonel Bratton, who launched his investigation upon the American forces' entrance into Berlin in early July.[15] Bratton approached Maj. Gen. Aleksei M. Sidnev, a high-ranking Soviet intelligence official, and asked him whether the Soviets had discovered Hitler's body. Sidnev replied evasively that he had not been present when the Red Army had captured the bunker and therefore could not answer the question. But he had no objection to the Americans' request to inspect the bunker, which was located in the Soviet sector of Berlin. Bratton then turned over the investigation to his executive officer and soon-to-be successor, Col. William F. Heimlich.[16]

In the middle of August, Heimlich and two fellow Army Intelligence officers made their way to the bunker. As the three men descended into the concrete shelter, they smelled the "stink of mold, rats, decay, and human excrement." Inside, they found the bunker thoroughly ransacked and the remaining furniture utterly destroyed. Outside, the Americans looked for signs of Hitler's charred body. To rule out the possibility that Hitler's body had completely dissolved in the fire, Heimlich and his men purchased a pig, killed it, poured gasoline over the carcass, set it on fire, and let it burn for several hours. "The smell of roasted pork reminded all of us of barbecue in the South," Heimlich recalled, yet "nobody suggested we eat the pig at the end of our experiment." To their relief, the Americans found that the fire had left the animal's body sufficiently intact to determine its features, and they continued their efforts to refute the Soviet claims.[17]

In September, the Allied quest to uncover the truth received a boost when the Soviets stated that the British were hiding Hitler and Braun in their zone. This contention was one of Moscow's early attempts to smear the Western powers with the taint of collaboration with the former enemy. In an effort to disprove the spurious claim and to put the matter to rest once and for all, British intelli-

---

14 Memo, no author, for Ofcr in Charge, 101st Abn Div, CIC Detachment, 12 Jul 1945, sub: Interrogation of Frau Paula WOLFF (Frl. Paula HITLER), U.S. Army Unit Rcds, 101st Abn Div, 1942–1949, Eisenhower Library.
15 Testimony, Heimlich, 11 Mar 1948.
16 Testimony, Heimlich, 11 Mar 1948; Interv, Brewster Chamberlin with William F. Heimlich, ACofS, G-2, Berlin Cmd, 4 Aug 1981, 51, Landesarchiv Berlin.
17 Tamara Domentat and Christina Heimlich, *Heimlich im Kalten Krieg: Die Geschichte von Christina Ohlsen und Bill Heimlich* [Heimlich in the Cold War: The history of Christina Ohlsen and Bill Heimlich] (Berlin: Aufbau-Verlag, 2000), 61, 63–67, 75.

gence instructed Maj. Hugh R. Trevor-Roper to conduct an expanded investigation into the circumstances of Hitler's death. An Oxford University–trained historian, Trevor-Roper carried out his mission methodically, speedily, and with great determination.[18]

On 19 September, the British Army of the Rhine formally requested American assistance for Trevor-Roper's investigation.[19] Army Intelligence promptly delivered. Beginning that month, Army interrogators conducted a series of interviews with Hitler's personal physician, Dr. Theodor G. Morell, who lingered in American captivity. Morell's mental and physical health were rapidly declining, and interviewing him brought its own challenges. One interrogator pronounced the doctor "physically decayed and mentally gaga." Another described "his hygienic habits as being those of a pig."[20] Even so, Morell shed light on numerous aspects of Hitler's life, including the much-discussed question of his sexual proclivities that had so intrigued the OSS. Morell had a mundane take on this issue. Although Hitler's sexual physiognomy was normal, Morell explained, the Führer was "not strongly inclined to sexual activity," especially during the war when his "libido was apparently sublimated with the increase in duties and responsibility." Morell's medical assessment suggested that Hitler had indeed perished in Berlin. Having left the bunker on the night of 22–23 April, Morell had not personally witnessed Hitler's suicide. However, he portrayed the Führer as a man suffering from multiple ailments, including symptoms of advanced-stage Parkinson's disease, who was neither willing nor able to make a last-minute escape.[21]

American intelligence produced two additional key witnesses. In Austria, the Army Air Division interviewed Hanna Reitsch, a Nazi test pilot. Reitsch and a companion had managed to fly a small aircraft into Berlin on 26 April. They found their way to the bunker, met with Hitler, and offered to take him out of Berlin. According to Reitsch, Hitler declined, and she and her companion then flew out of the besieged city on their own two days later. Reitsch confirmed Morell's assessment that Hitler was neither willing nor capable of leaving the bunker.

---

18 Trevor-Roper, *Last Days of Hitler*, 36; Douglas, "Search for Hitler," 165. In later life, Trevor-Roper gained notoriety for vouching for the authenticity of the forged Hitler diaries. See Robert Harris, *Selling Hitler: The Extraordinary Story of the Con Job of the Century* (New York: Pantheon, 1986).
19 Douglas, "Search for Hitler," 169.
20 Rpt, HQ, USFET, MISC, Consolidated Interrogation Rpt no. 4, 29 Nov 1945, sub: Hitler as seen by his doctors, Folder "926363," Rcds of the ACoS, G–2 (Intel), Formerly Top Secret Intel Documents, 1943–59, RG 319, NACP.
21 Rpt, Brig. Gen. Edwin L. Sibert, ACofS, G–2, to MID, 2 Jan 1946, sub: Request for Interrogation Report, Folder "926363," Rcds of the ACoS, G–2 (Intel), Formerly Top Secret Intel Documents, 1943–59, RG 319, NACP.

"Hitler is dead!" she told her interrogators. "The man I saw in the shelter could not have lived. He had no reason to live and the tragedy was that he knew it well; knew it better than perhaps anybody else."[22]

On 26 September 1945, Lt. Col. Oron J. Hale, a professor of German history at the University of Virginia in civilian life, interrogated Hitler's personal driver, Erich Kempka, at the Third Army Interrogation Center at Bad Aibling. Kempka had remained at the bunker until after Hitler's suicide. He told Hale that he had personally delivered the gasoline to burn the bodies of Hitler and the others, and he described the exact location of the crater where Hitler and Braun had been buried.[23] The interrogators forwarded a sketch made by Kempka of the bunker area to Colonel Heimlich's intelligence branch in Berlin.[24]

Heimlich turned the sketch and the responsibility for the search over to one of his officers, Capt. George T. Gabelia. Technically, the enterprise had become a four-power operation. Yet the French sent a naval officer "who could not speak English and who did not speak Russian and who was almost totally intoxicated every day." The Soviets formally went along with the project but never participated actively. Under Gabelia's leadership, the search essentially remained an Anglo-American effort.[25] His U.S. team included four members: Severin F. Wallach and 2d Lt. Charles H. Lehman of the Berlin District intelligence branch, and Special Agent Daniel W. Montenegro and Capt. Anthony A. Schepsis of the CIC.[26]

Gabelia hired fifty local workers to dig systemically through the site where the occupants of the bunker supposedly had burnt and buried the bodies. Initially, the Soviets granted him and his party permission to access the site, with work beginning on 10 December. The Americans found little besides a silken hat bearing the initials "A. H.," and at the end of the month, the Soviets declared the site closed. According to Heimlich, "the Russians said they simply had reached the

---

22 Rpt, Capt. Robert E. Work, Air Corps, Interrogation Sum, Hanna Reitsch, 8 Oct 1945, sub: The Last Days in Hitler's Air Raid Shelter, Folder "24 to 40 USDIC/AIU/IS," G–2 Section, Prisoner of War Interrogation Section (MIS-Y), Air Interrogation Unit (Austria), Interrogation Sums, 1944–1945, RG 498, NACP; Kelsey Mullen, "American Intelligence and the Question of Hitler's Death" (undergraduate research thesis, Ohio State University, 2014), 30. Mullen was the first researcher to identify pertinent records on the U.S. intelligence investigation of Hitler's death.
23 Interrogation Rpt, Lt. Col. Oron J. Hale, 26 Sep 1945, sub: Oberstrumbannführer Erich Kempka, chief driver and head of the Führer's motor pool, Folder "Interrogation Summaries, 1945–1945," Historical Interrogation Commission Interrogation Rpts, RG 498, NACP.
24 Testimony, Capt. George T. Gabelia, 15 Mar 1948, Folder "Hitler's Death Reports," Gen Staff, Intel Div, Administration Br, Misc. Items of Intel Interest, 1947–49, RG 549, NACP.
25 Interv, Chamberlin with Heimlich, 52.
26 Testimony, Gabelia, 15 Mar 1948.

decision that they were going to destroy the building and they saw no point in pursuing [the search] any further."[27]

Based on evidence produced by Army Intelligence as well as by his own efforts, Trevor-Roper presented his findings to the public at the Berlin Hotel am Zoo. Even without having seen Hitler's body, and without having spoken to key witnesses under Soviet control, he made a compelling case for the Führer's demise. According to one journalist present at the briefing, Trevor-Roper "managed to disperse the propaganda miasma that had been rolling in from the east for weeks. As of that evening, 1 November 1945, most of the international press stationed in Berlin was finally convinced that Hitler was indeed dead." Trevor-Roper submitted his official report to the Quadripartite Intelligence Committee, which considered it on 10 November. The report explicitly dismissed "incorrect versions" claiming that Hitler had survived the war. Even though a Soviet representative served on the committee, the Soviet-controlled press responded to Trevor-Roper's findings with complete silence.[28]

The report, however, did not mark the end of the search for Adolf Hitler. On Christmas Eve, Trevor-Roper requested the assistance of the CIC to locate a certain Wilhelm Zander in southern Bavaria. A personal adjutant to Hitler's secretary, Martin L. Bormann, Zander had left the bunker on 29 April. Zander was believed to have in his possession Hitler's personal and political testament, as well as the certificate of his marriage to Eva Braun. The CIC assigned the case to Special Agent Arnold H. Weiss, a war veteran and Ritchie Boy. It turned out to be an inspired choice. In a matter of days, Weiss tracked down Zander with the help of local informants in the small town of Aidenbach near Passau. There, he lived under an alias with his girlfriend, Bormann's former secretary Ilse Unterholzner, and worked as a gardener. Weiss and Trevor-Roper arrested Zander early in the morning of 28 December. Under cross-examination, Zander revealed his true identity, and confessed that he had left the documents with Unterholzner's sister, where the local CIC retrieved them.[29] An Army officer delivered the findings to General Sibert, who was "extremely concerned and impressed with the Hitler

---

27 Testimony, Heimlich, 11 Mar 1948; Interv, Chamberlin with Heimlich, 57.
28 Douglas, "Search for Hitler," 165–66, 178, 198; Trevor-Roper, *Last Days of Hitler*, 39.
29 Memo, Special Agent Arnold H. Weiss, CIC Munich Subregional Ofc, for Ofcr in Charge, 30 Dec 1945, sub: Zander, Wilhelm, alias Paustin, Friedrich Wilhelm, Folder "Willi Zander D011874," INSCOM, IRR, Digitized Name Files, 1939–1975, RG 319, NACP; Maj. Ann Bray et al., ed., *The History of the Counter Intelligence Corps*, vol. 26, *German Occupation* (Fort Holabird, MD: U.S. Army Intelligence Center, 1959), 26.

documents."[30] The material suggested, yet again, that Hitler had died by suicide in the bunker.

For nearly two years, the Americans received little additional information on the subject. In late 1947, a former Army interrogator named Fox Mathews approached the European Command, claiming that in late 1945 Hitler's dentist had told him that the Soviets had asked him to identify Hitler's jawbone.[31] By 1947, Mathews was working for William Heimlich in the Political Affairs Branch of the American military government in Berlin.[32] Heimlich's reminiscences of his search for Hitler's body in 1945 may have prompted Mathews to report the interview to the European Command.

Although Mathews's recollections were hazy, he provided important leads. In Berlin, Special Agent Severin Wallach, now working for the CIC, tracked down and interviewed a Bulgarian dentist, Dr. Michael Arnaudow, who was working at the Charité, Berlin's leading research hospital, in the Soviet sector. Because Arnaudow had acted as a translator for the Soviets in the summer of 1945, he hesitated to speak about the subject of Hitler's death for fear of Soviet reprisals. However, Wallach convinced him to cooperate. Arnaudow told Wallach that he had identified Hitler's jawbone "with a great degree of certainty," based on drawings made available to him by the Soviets. Wallach recommended that the Americans resettle Arnaudow and his wife in one of the Western zones to protect him from the Soviets.[33]

For the Army, the investigation ended with this revelation, but the lack of positive evidence of Hitler's fate, which only the Soviets could provide, kept the rumor mill churning. The Federal Bureau of Investigation, which assumed responsibility for tracking Hitler sightings, followed up on a series of outlandish reports over the following years. In 1951, a concerned citizen informed FBI director J. Edgar Hoover that Hitler had spent the previous winter in Miami Beach bussing tables in order to learn

---

30 Rpt, Maj. William T. Gleason, HQ, Third Army, 8 Jan 1946, sub: Report of Mission to G–2, USFET and Inspection Trip, Folder "3rd Army G–2 Security Control 371.2," Third United States Army, G–2 Section, Decimal Files 1944–1947, RG 338, NACP.
31 Msg, ODDI to Director of Intel, Washington, 24 Mar 1948, sub: Fedor Bruck, Folder "Hitler, Death of D206014," INSCOM, IRR, Selected Printouts of Digital Intel and Investigative Dossiers, Impersonal Files, 1933–1958, RG 319, NACP.
32 Telg, Maj. Earl S. Browning Jr., CO, CIC, EUCOM, to CO, Region VIII, CIC, 21 Nov 1947, Folder "Hitler, Death of D206014," INSCOM, IRR, Selected Printouts of Digital Intel and Investigative Dossiers, Impersonal Files, 1933–1958, RG 319, NACP.
33 Rpt, Severin Wallach, Region VIII, CIC, to CO, 8 Sep 1948, sub: Death of Adolf Hitler, Folder "Hitler's Death Reports," EUCOM, Gen Staff, Intel Div, Administration Br, Misc Items of Intel Interest, 1947–49, RG 549, NACP.

English.³⁴ Four years later, the FBI interviewed a man in Dayton, Ohio, in response to his claim that he had seen Hitler in Buenos Aires several years earlier.³⁵ In the 1960s, the Hitler survival myth underwent another twist when individuals claiming to be the Führer's children came forward. Only in 1968, when the Soviets at last released their investigative report of Hitler's death, did the rumor mill stop.³⁶

The search for Adolf Hitler provided important lessons to Army Intelligence. For one, it highlighted the continued usefulness of interrogation as an information-gathering technique in postwar Germany. The investigation also validated the Army's close relationship with British intelligence. If the Soviets had sought to sow division between the Americans and the British by claiming that Hitler was hiding in the British Zone, their attempt fell flat. But the search for Hitler also highlighted Western unpreparedness in dealing with a deliberate Soviet disinformation campaign. In the context of the joint Allied occupation of Germany, the difficulties encountered while working with the Soviets on an issue that should have been uncontroversial, alerted Army Intelligence to keep a watchful eye on their wartime ally.

Denazification

At the Yalta and Potsdam Conferences, the Allies agreed to purge German society of vicious Nazi ideology. This effort became known as denazification, a term coined by the Army's Civil Affairs Division in 1943.³⁷ The policy of denazification included the dissolution of the Nazi Party, the removal of Nazi officials from public life, the suppression of Nazi propaganda, and the reeducation of Germans in a democratic spirit. Each ally was to implement denazification in its own zone of occupation. In territories under U.S. control, Joint Chiefs of Staff Directive 1067 provided general guidance. Army Intelligence agencies spearheaded the American denazification effort.³⁸

---

34 Ltr, Anonymous to J. Edgar Hoover, 30 Nov 1951, Folder "65–53615 Section 3, 2 of 4," Investigative Rcds, Classified Subject Files, Released Under the Nazi & Japanese War Crimes Disclosure Acts, Classification 65: Espionage, RG 65, NACP.
35 Memo, Special Agent in Charge, Cincinnati, for FBI Director, 19 Jan 1955, sub: W. A. Voice, Folder "65–53615 Section 3, 1 of 4," Investigative Rcds, Classified Subject Files, Released under the Nazi & Japanese War Crimes Disclosure Act, Classification 65: Espionage, RG 65, NACP.
36 McKale, *Hitler*, 152, 180.
37 Memo, Maj. Gen. John H. Hilldring, Ch, Civil Affairs Div, for Brig. Gen. Edward S. Greenbaum, 17 Nov 1943, sub: Dr. Herbert Schatian, Folder "CAD 014 Germany (7–10–42) (1) Section 2," Civil Affairs Div, Gen Rcds, Security Classified Gen Corresp, 1943–44, RG 165, NACP. General Hilldring here discusses the "de-Nazification of the German laws."
38 Frederic Taylor, *Exorcising Hitler: The Occupation and Denazification of Germany* (London: Bloomsbury, 2012) 253–54.

For the CIC, operations began in earnest two months before the German surrender. The Army leadership sought to arrest any leading Nazi personnel immediately for security and denazification purposes. The Counter Intelligence Directive for Germany, issued by the 12th Army Group on 10 April 1945, spelled out in detail the categories of officials wanted for arrest. These "automatic arrestees" included all members of Nazi police and intelligence services like the SD and the *Gestapo*, Nazi paramilitary forces such as the SS and the SA, and top functionaries of the Hitler Youth and of various other Nazi auxiliary organizations.[39]

Figure 24: Capt. Edward Levy of the 94th Counter Intelligence Corps Detachment interviews Hans Goebbels, the brother of Nazi propaganda minister Joseph Goebbels, in April 1945. U.S. Army, NACP.

---

39 For a complete copy of the counterintelligence directive, see Maj. Ann Bray et al., ed., *The History of the Counter Intelligence Corps*, vol. 21, *Germany Overrun, Part II* (Fort Holabird, MD: U.S. Army Intelligence Center, 1959), appendix 1, 1–126.

For the most part, the Americans found it easy to identify and apprehend automatic arrestees. Captured Nazi documents as well as monitored mail and telephone calls provided a wealth of information on the identity and location of wanted individuals, and security or "swoop" operations netted thousands of suspects. In the early days of the occupation, local denouncers flooded the CIC with tip-offs on the whereabouts of automatic arrestees. Some informants had a genuine desire to help the Americans; others were driven by less altruistic concerns. In Berlin, for example, a hairdresser denounced her boss as an SS veteran. Army Intelligence noted that the woman had been motivated by a desire to "gain control of [the] subject's prosperous business" as well as by "slighted affections."[40] For American authorities, the woman's intentions made no difference; they promptly arrested the man. By mid-July, the Americans had apprehended 70,000 Nazi officials, and by fall the bulk of automatic arrestees lingered in detention centers across the U.S. Zone.[41]

The apprehension of hardcore Nazis constituted merely one element of the denazification effort. As the occupation consolidated, the military government launched a broad operation to screen all German officials in the U.S. Zone and remove those compromised by their Nazi past. The Public Safety Division screened statewide institutions, such as the police and firefighter agencies. At the county or *Kreis* level, special branch or denazification officers distributed questionnaires, known as *Fragebogen*, to German officials, demanding information about the individual's activities and organizational memberships during the Third Reich. Based on their answers, each subject received a classification depending on their degree of complicity with the Nazi regime: category I (*Hauptschuldige*; major offenders), II (*Belastete*; incriminated), III (*Minderbelastete*; less incriminated), IV (*Mitläufer*; fellow travelers), and V (*Entlastete*; exonerated).[42]

The denazification officers forwarded the *Fragebogen* to the CIC and to other agencies for verification. The CIC then checked an individual's questionnaire against its own files and against information obtained from the Berlin Documents Center. If an answer looked suspicious, agents made further inquiries. Once the agents completed the check, the denazification officer decided whether to keep or discharge the official.[43] To determine the efficiency of denazification and to re-

---

40 Rpt, Berlin District Interrogation Center, G–2 Div, HQ Berlin District, 20 Aug 1945, sub: Diezmann, Willi, Folder "BDIC/CI # 1–105 2 of 2," G–2 Section, PW Interrogation Rpts (MIS-Y), Berlin District Interrogation Center, Counter Intel Rpts, 1945, RG 498, NACP.
41 Walter M. Hudson, "The U.S. Military Government and Democratic Reform and Denazification in Bavaria, 1945–47" (master's thesis, Command and General Staff College, Fort Leavenworth, Kansas, 2001), 109; Bray et al., *History of the Counter Intelligence Corps*, 26:51.
42 Taylor, *Exorcising Hitler*, 261.
43 Hudson, "U.S. Military Government," 121–23.

move officials who had slipped through the cracks, the Seventh Army in July 1945 launched a large-scale swoop screening operation code-named LIFEBUOY, after a popular brand of disinfectant soap. With heavy support from the CIC, Army units vetted more than 93,000 German officials and arrested over 2,000.[44]

The initial phase of denazification delegated implementation to local commanders, and some pursued the effort only half-heartedly. This was especially true for the commander of the Third Army, General George S. Patton Jr., who considered the economic revival of Germany and the country's fortification against the Soviet Union his most important task. Patton publicly belittled the denazification effort. As he told a group of American journalists, "the Nazi thing is just like a Democrat and Republican election fight."[45] This attitude did not sit well with the Army leadership. Patton's boss, General Eisenhower, told Patton to "get off [his] bloody ass and carry out the denazification program . . . instead of mollycoddling the goddamn Nazis."[46] Eventually, Eisenhower replaced the obstinate Patton with the more traditionalist Lt. Gen. Lucian K. Truscott Jr.

Meanwhile, General Lucius D. Clay centralized and broadened the denazification campaign. On 26 September, the Americans promulgated Military Government Law No. 8, which prohibited employment in public office or private business of any member of the Nazi Party or an affiliate organization.[47] The new law exponentially increased the administrative burden on Army Intelligence personnel, who now had to screen virtually every German adult in the U.S. Zone. In the winter of 1945–1946, the CIC and other Army agencies reviewed almost 1.6 million questionnaires. Eventually, the Americans registered more than 13.4 million Germans and charged nearly 3.7 million with some type of Nazi affiliation. In addition to screening and investigating employees and job-seekers, CIC agents served on local review boards established to give Germans a chance to appeal a negative finding. During this period, the official history of the CIC noted, operations in Germany "can be grouped largely under a single heading: De-Nazification."[48]

---

44 Earl F. Ziemke, *The U.S. Army in the Occupation of Germany, 1944–1946*, Army Historical Series (Washington, DC: U.S. Army Center of Military History, 1975), 382–83; Rpt, Consolidated Rpt on Opn "Lifebuoy," n.d. [Oct 1945], Folder "Operation 'Lifebuoy,' Folder No. 1, VII, October 1945," Seventh Army, G–2, Subject Files 1942–1946, RG 338, NACP.
45 Raymond Daniell, "Patton Belittles Denazification; Holds Rebuilding More Important," *New York Times*, 23 Sep 1945.
46 Perry Biddiscombe, *The Denazification of Germany: A History 1945–1950* (London: Tempus, 2006), 56.
47 Hudson, "U.S. Military Government," 133; Ziemke, *U.S. Army in the Occupation of Germany*, 386.
48 Hudson, "U.S. Military Government," 135; Bray et al., *History of the Counter Intelligence Corps*, 26:16.

Military Government Law No. 8 roiled the U.S. Zone. By early 1946, the military government had removed more than 42 percent of Germany's public officials. Such dismissals often threatened the material existence of entire families and occasionally had tragic consequences—as happened in the town of Kempten in southwestern Bavaria. There, the CIC had removed from office and interned the city treasurer, Dr. Bernhard Wagner, in October 1945. After his conditional release, Wagner was asked to come in for another interview with the CIC. Assuming that he was about to be rearrested, he and his wife administered a lethal dose of morphine to their child before taking the substance themselves. When the morphine killed only the child, Mrs. Wagner opened the veins on her husband's wrist, and he died the next day at the local hospital. She survived and was charged with murder.[49]

Army Intelligence closely monitored German reactions to denazification. In the immediate postwar period, many Germans applauded American efforts to remove and punish former Nazis. In June 1945, the military government intelligence office in Bavaria reported that, if anything, local inhabitants felt that too many culprits remained "in comfortable positions as ever."[50] This attitude changed markedly later that year. An informant told the CIC that the Germans considered a "blanket arrest policy" unjust, and the intelligence staff of Seventh Army reported that many Germans criticized "the strictness of Public Law No. 8."[51] Germans griped that the removal of local officials or business owners punished not only that particular individual but also those who depended on their services. If military government officials were to close the shop of a shoemaker in a small village, an informant explained to his case officer, the entire "village goes without shoes."[52]

The CIC also noted that many Germans scorned American efforts to educate them about the evils of National Socialism. In the summer of 1945, the Information Control Division of the U.S. military government produced a documentary film titled *The Death Mills* (*Die Todesmühlen*). Codirected by the Austrian-born

---

49 Maj. Peter Vacca, Annex, OMGB, n.d. [Nov 1945], sub: Intelligence Annex to Weekly Report of the Office of Military Government of Bavaria for the Period 8–15 November 1945, Folder "Intelligence Annexes to Weekly Reports 1945–1946," Rcds of the OMGB, Rcds of the Intel Div, Weekly Intel Rpts, 1945–1947, RG 260, NACP.
50 Hudson, "U.S. Military Government," 128.
51 Bray et al., *History of the Counter Intelligence Corps*, 26:52; Sum, HQ Seventh Army, G–2 Weekly Intel Sum no. 23 for Period Ending 19 Dec 1945, Folder "VI Corps G–2 Journals 20–25 Dec 45," Historical Div, Program Files, VI Corps, G–2 Jnls, 1945, RG 498, NACP.
52 Rpt, HQ USFET, Info Control Div, Daily Intel Digest #72, 13 Dec 1945, Folder "ICD OMGUS Daily Intelligence Digest, Nos. 1–72, 31 August 1945–13 December 1945," Historical Div, Program Files, OMGUS, Daily Intel Digests, 1945–46, RG 498, NACP.

Hollywood director Billy Wilder, the 22-minute film showed footage of recently liberated German concentration camps, including mass burials, piles of corpses, and naked and emaciated survivors. The military government released the film in the western zones in January 1946, and the CIC sent undercover agents to screenings to gauge its reception. "The reactions were extremely varied," the CIC reported. In the city of Ulm, for example, "some of the people left the movie speechless with expressions of shame and visible moral depressions." Others, however, "were not too much impressed and said it was just another poor form of Allied propaganda."[53]

In some areas, denazification bogged down amid defiance and passive resistance, as happened in the case of Heidelberg University. In April 1945, shortly after the Seventh Army occupied the town, the 307th Counter Intelligence Corps Detachment began removing and arresting university staff on charges of membership in the SS and for other offenses.[54] Yet in July, with Germany facing a pressing demand for physicians, the military government allowed the university to reopen its medical school. As the university's leadership lobbied for the lifting of restrictions across all faculties, the promulgation of Military Government Law No. 8 prompted the Americans to renew the denazification of the university. In October, the CIC assigned Special Agent Daniel F. Penham to lead this effort.[55]

Within a few weeks, Penham determined that the denazification of Heidelberg University had been less than thorough. He found that numerous faculty members had endorsed or benefited from the Nazi regime. The university *Rektor* (president), Karl Heinrich Bauer, had been an advocate of *Rassenhygiene* ("racial hygiene" or eugenics), which promoted the sterilization of individuals with intellectual disabilities, mental illness, or other medical conditions, or racial backgrounds that the Nazis considered detrimental to their social order. Penham recommended closing the university until the Americans had fully investigated the faculty and staff. The local CIC supported their agent and arranged for the removal of several faculty members, but these efforts met fierce resistance. The faculty members, including those not tainted by Nazism, closed ranks against Penham. Karl Jaspers, the famous Swiss philosopher and psychiatrist who taught at Heidelberg, attacked Penham as pathological (*"das Krankhafte des CIC-Agenten"*),

---

53 Sum, HQ, Seventh Army, Weekly Intel Sum No. 35, 15 Mar 1946, Folder "7th Army, G–2 Weekly Summaries, 1946," Seventh Army, G–2, Subject Files 1942–1946, RG 338, NACP.
54 Memo, Special Agent Thomas A. Emmet et al., 307th CIC Detachment, for Ofcr in Charge, 9 Apr 1945, sub: Heidelberg University, Folder "CIC [Counter Intelligence Corps] Reports, 3 Apr to 30 July 1945," Seventh United States Army, G–2 Section, Rpts Files 1944–1946, RG 338, NACP.
55 Ralph W. Brown III, "Removing 'Nasty Nazi Habits': The CIC and the Denazification of Heidelberg University, 1945–1946," *The Journal of Intelligence History* 4 (Summer 2004), 38, 43.

implying that the investigation of the university was driven by Penham's personal obsession rather than concrete evidence. The military government officer in charge of Heidelberg, Maj. Earl Le Verne Crum, was keen on reopening Heidelberg as soon as possible and sided with the Germans. The military government censured the CIC for overstepping its bounds, and shortly thereafter the Army recalled Penham to the United States.[56]

The Heidelberg controversy contained subtext that would become more prominent as denazification efforts progressed: Penham's German-Jewish background. Born Sigfrid Oppenheim in the Hessian town of Bad Hersfeld, Penham had left Europe during the Third Reich and joined Army Intelligence.[57] Many Germans regarded the second phase of American denazification as an overreach and ascribed its excessive implementation to the vindictiveness of German-Jewish Army Intelligence personnel, such as Penham. "The Americans," a Berlin politician opined, "used the services of former German emigres, whom they had brought along with them. Not a few of the émigrés—understandably, though it wasn't helpful—vented their bitter resentments on us."[58]

Undoubtedly, German-Jewish émigrés regarded denazification as a deeply personal issue. Many had lost family members in the Holocaust, and some openly advocated a harsh application of denazification.[59] However, many non-Jewish Americans felt the same way. For a short period, the U.S. government had envisioned the punitive deindustrialization of Germany, as seen in the draconian policy proposal put forward by Treasury Secretary Henry J. Morgenthau Jr. The unforgiving attitude toward the Nazis held by some German-Jewish émigrés dovetailed with the postwar mission of the Army. It also reflected the attitudes of intelligence personnel at large, certainly in the immediate postwar period. For example, a report from the intelligence section of the VI Corps, dated 15 May 1945, exhorted the Army to keep the Germans "cowed," and demanded that the defeated nation "must be made to taste to

---

56 Uta Gerhardt, "Die Amerikanischen Militäroffiziere und der Konflikt um die Wiedereröffnung der Universität Heidelberg 1945–1946" [American military officers and the conflict over the reopening of Heidelberg University, 1945–1946], in *Heidelberg 1945*, ed. Jürgen Heß, Hartmut Lehmann, and Volker Sellin (Stuttgart: Franz Steiner Verlag, 1996), 49, 53.
57 "Daniel Penham, Columbia Professor and Scholar of Budé, Dies at Age 86," *Columbia News*, 21 Jul 2001.
58 Ferdinand Friedensburg, *Es ging um Deutschlands Einheit: Rückschau eines Berliners auf die Jahre nach 1945* [It was about German unity: Reminiscences of a Berliner on the years after 1945] (Berlin: Haude & Spener, 1971), 145–46.
59 Taylor, *Exorcising Hitler*, 272.

the dregs the full bitterness of humiliation and defeat." If this approach seemed vindictive, it was by no means unique to German-Jewish émigrés.[60]

Moreover, many émigrés displayed sympathy for the plight of the German people. According to a U.S. military government official, German-Jewish intelligence officials "considered Germany as their home, notwithstanding the holocaust. . . . [Their] main concern was to root out the Nazis and see Germany become a democratic state to which they could one day return as their rightful homeland."[61] If anything, they ran the risk of being too sympathetic. One of the sternest advocates of denazification, Capt. Saul K. Padover of the Psychological Warfare Division, complained that German-born interrogators "tended to too much familiarity with the Germans and . . . were inclined to identify themselves with their interlocutors." For this reason, Padover urged, U.S. intelligence should not employ German-born U.S. citizens. As Padover himself had been born in Austria, his was a curious stance, but it indicates that German-Jewish émigrés had not embarked as a group on a crusade of vengeance.[62]

An Army officer in Germany compared the American denazification effort to one of the twelve labors of Hercules. In the ancient myth, the Greek hero cleans the prodigiously filthy Augean stables by rerouting two rivers through them.[63] In his quest to denazify Germany, General Clay could not call on nature for help, yet the growing resistance to Military Government Law No. 8 and the Americans' eagerness to hand over government responsibilities to the Germans prompted him to rethink the U.S. approach. Eventually, the military government rid itself of the thorny issue of denazification by handing over responsibility for this policy to the Germans.

On 5 March 1946, Clay and the minister presidents of the three German *Länder* in the U.S. Zone signed the Law for Liberation from National Socialism and Militarism. Under the new law, local denazification tribunals (*Spruchkammern*) staffed by German citizens assumed responsibility for screening and determining the guilt of individuals. A year later, in the summer of 1947, the Joint Chiefs of Staff replaced JCS 1067 with JCS 1779, a directive that emphasized eco-

---

60 Rpt, Appendix "A" to VI Corps G–2 Rpt No. 342, 15 May 1945, Folder "VI Corps G–2 Journal 20–22 May 45," Historical Div, Program Files, VI Corps, G–2 Jnls, 1945, RG 498, NACP.
61 Ian Sayer and Douglas Botting, *Nazi Gold: The Story of the World's Greatest Robbery – And Its Aftermath* (New York: Granada, 1984), 261.
62 Saul K. Padover, *Experiment in Germany: The Story of an American Intelligence Officer* (New York: Duell, Sloan and Pearce, 1946), 308.
63 Eugène Jolas, *Man from Babel*, ed. Andreas Kramer and Rainer Rumold (New Haven, CT: Yale University Press, 1998), 217.

nomic reconstruction over retribution. For all intents and purposes, active American involvement in denazification came to an end.[64]

The CIC and military government intelligence offices, aided by the Civil Censorship Division, closely monitored the German handling of the denazification effort. For those keen on purging German society, it proved a disappointing exercise. Phone and mail intercepts revealed many tribunals as lenient and incompetent. They routinely issued exonerating statements, derisively nicknamed *Persilscheine* ("soap certificates") after a popular laundry detergent. When the Americans handed off denazification to the Germans, hundreds of thousands of former Nazi officials came flooding back into local and regional offices. A military government report from Greater Hesse from September 1948 suggested that 85 percent of persons removed earlier by the Americans were now back at their jobs.[65]

Henceforth, Army Intelligence agencies grew less concerned with the effectiveness of the tribunals than with their political makeup. Average German citizens were reluctant to serve on a *Spruchkammer* board, fearing ostracism within their communities for passing judgment on their neighbors. Members of the German Communist Party, however, generally had few reservations about negative local reactions, and Army Intelligence agencies nervously tracked the growing KPD representation on the tribunals. One report suggested that communist preponderance was the result of a deliberate strategy. Another concluded that communist overrepresentation resulted merely from noncommunists' reluctance to participate, rather than being part of a wider KPD plot. Either way, the Army's European intelligence division suspected that communists were using their influence on the *Spruchkammern* to blackmail former Nazis into joining the KPD.[66] This allegation seemed like a stretch, and the division did not follow up on it. Yet the communist presence on the tribunal boards fed into larger American fears of a burgeoning German communism, which by this time had replaced concerns over the persistence of the National Socialist ideology.

---

64 Biddiscombe, *Denazification*, 78.
65 Biddiscombe, *Denazification*, 72, 211.
66 Msg, 1st Lt. A. C. Moe, HQ, ODDI, EUCOM, to Director of Intel, OMGUS, attn. Lt. Col. Murphy, 30 Jan 1948, sub: KPD Interest in Former Nazis, Folder "security section-McGreevy, G," Director of Intel, Analysis and Research Br, Gen Corresp, 1945–49, RG 260, NACP; Rpt, Ofc of Mil Government, Württemberg-Baden (OMGWB), Rpt No. 2, 21 Jan 1948, Folder "23a Resistance & Subversive Activity (U.S. Zone) Jan '48–Dec '48," ODI, Excerpts of Miscellaneous Rpts & Publications, Analysis & Research Br, 1947–48, RG 260, NACP.

Nazi Subversion

While the denazification of German society absorbed a large share of intelligence resources, the suppression of Nazi subversion remained a core responsibility of Army counterintelligence. In the immediate postwar period, occupation authorities had little to concern them in this regard. American officials recognized that the original *Werwolf* organization had not survived the end of the war, and that the German populace appeared too apathetic to engage in organized resistance.[67] Supreme Allied Headquarters described resistance and sabotage activities as "insignificant" and "scattered," and one Army Intelligence officer noted that the Germans "looked whipped . . . beaten physically and in spirit."[68]

Actual *Werwolf*-type incidents were few and far between in the immediate postwar period. In early June, an informant of the 206th Counter Intelligence Corps Detachment reported a rare instance. In Schwäbisch Gmünd near Stuttgart, a small group of former Hitler Youth who called themselves "werewolves" had collected arms and talked about building a paramilitary organization. Although the group's members were teenagers—their parents had forbidden some of them to attend the meetings—and had not perpetrated any subversive acts, the Americans decided to act decisively. In early July, the CIC and military police raided a meeting of the group in an orchard, mortally wounded their seventeen-year-old leader, and retrieved rifles, machine pistols, a machine gun, and 10,000 rounds of ammunition.[69]

To keep the German population pacified through a show of strength and to nip any neo-Nazi resistance movement in the bud, the CIC orchestrated several swoop operations. In late July 1945, 160,000 soldiers participated in the zonewide Operation TALLY HO. This two-day endeavor netted several thousand German security suspects as well as more than 300,000 items of contraband, including prohibited weapons such as bazookas. In October, a similar operation, code-named DOUBLE CHECK, yielded another 150 security suspects. In early 1946, the CIC sealed off a crowded passenger train that ran from Bamberg to Nuremberg in Bavaria,

---

[67] Volker Koop, *Himmlers letzte Aufgebot: Die NS-Organisation "Werwolf"* [Himmler's last force: The Nazi organization "Werwolf"] (Vienna: Böhlau, 2008) 246; Interv, Col. Thomas L. Crystal Jr., G–2, 21 May 1945, Folder "Interviews 1945," XXII Corps Engr Section Instructions, Interview Rpts, Sums, and Terrain Studies, compiled 03/1945–09/1945, RG 165, NACP.

[68] Msg, SHAEF to USFET, 10 Jun 1945, Folder "Germany E, UA, FWD & CC Series 1945," ACoS, G–2 (Intel), "Top Secret" Incoming and Outgoing Cables, 1942–52, RG 319, NACP; Maj. Gen. John J. Maginnis, *Military Government Journal: Normandy to Berlin* (Amherst: University of Massachusetts Press, 1971), entry for 26 Jun 1945, 258.

[69] VI Corps History July – 1945, Annex # 2, Ofc of the ACofS, G–2, 2 Aug 1945, Folder "VI Corps History July –1945," Historical Div, Program Files, VI Corps, History, 1945–1946, RG 498, NACP.

and carefully screened every single one of the 1,200 passengers. Appropriately dubbed Operation Choo Choo, this effort unmasked several security suspects.[70]

To gauge German reactions to these security operations and toward the military government in general, the CIC sometimes inserted covert agents into the mass of civilians during screening. In the course of Operation Choo Choo, two CIC agents rode the train pretending to be "disgruntled passengers" while eavesdropping on comments from fellow travelers about the American screening effort. They later reported that the Germans had largely taken Operation Choo Choo in stride. Operation Double Check, the CIC noted, "resulted in a greater respect . . . toward the Occupation forces." Likewise, the CIC concluded that the deliberate display of American might in Operation Tally Ho had a "highly beneficial effect on the German people." Through the winter of 1945–1946, the security situation in U.S.-occupied Germany remained stable and posed no threat to the military government.[71]

About half a year after the end of the war, the tide started to turn. The Germans recovered somewhat from the shock of defeat, and Army Intelligence agencies began reporting on the activities of various Nazi-inspired organizations from across the U.S. Zone. In Göppingen near Stuttgart, German women seen in the company of American soldiers received anonymous letters signed with a drawing of a black hand, noting that they were being watched.[72] In Dieburg, Hesse, the intelligence section of the Third Army reported on a paramilitary organization called the "Eagle Eye" whose members conducted drills, carried weapons, and traded in alcohol, guns, and ammunition.[73] In Berlin, members of groups called the "Cross and Chain" and "Germany for the Germans" had allegedly formed gangs to carry out acts against "anti-Nazis who are cooperating with the occupational forces and to harassing [sic] Military Government."[74] And in the town of Hofgeismar in northern Hesse, the 78th Counter Intelligence Corps Detachment

---

70 Bray et al., *History of the Counter Intelligence Corps*, 26:14–16, 26:26.
71 Bray et al., *History of the Counter Intelligence Corps*, 26:15, 26:27–28.
72 Msg, Col. C. P. Bixel, HQ, Seventh Army Western Mil District, Ofc of the ACofS, G–2, to G–2, XXI Corps, 15 Sep 1945, sub: Possible Resistance Organizations, Folder "CI [Counter Intelligence] Reports, Information, 26 Jun 1944 to 27 Sep 1945 [2]," Seventh United States Army, G–2 Section, Rpts Files 1944–1946, RG 338, NACP.
73 Memo, "Edelweisspiraten," n.d., Folder "3rd Army G-Operation Valentine 380.4," Third United States Army, G–2 Section, Decimal Files 1944–1947, RG 338, NACP.
74 G–2 Bull no. 93, HQ, Seventh Army Western Mil District, Ofc of the ACofS, G–2, 19 Dec 1945, Folder "VI Corp [sic] G–2 Journals 20–25 Dec 45," Historical Div, Program Files, VI Corps, G–2 Jnls, 1945, RG 498, NACP.

suspected a local football (soccer) team, the TSG 1884 Hofgeismar, of serving as a cover for subversive activities.[75]

Upon closer examination, however, these groups hardly posed a real threat to American soldiers and occupation authorities. To the extent that Army Intelligence agencies managed to track down individual subversives, they turned out to be very young and pursued their plots in isolation. Their overriding grievance, the CIC noted, was a "frustrated desire for female companionship." In fact, many subversives had come to the attention of the occupation authorities after threatening or physically attacking German women accused of "fraternizing" with American soldiers.[76] When interviewed, the suspected soccer subversives from Hofgeismar admitted that they, too, had discussed the unwelcome competition of U.S. soldiers for female companionship during their biweekly practice sessions.

Very little genuine sabotage activity occurred during this time. Army Intelligence recorded scattered acts of sabotage and violence against U.S. forces, although most were "unorganized and often ridiculously amateurish."[77] In Munich, for example, soldiers found sugar in the gas tank of a jeep.[78] In Westerstetten near the city of Ulm, a *Wehrmacht* veteran attempted to stab an American soldier with a pitchfork.[79] Occasionally, a sniper would shoot at American soldiers from a safe distance, and U.S. forces regularly found leftover booby traps and arms caches from the war. Army Intelligence units reported several instances of "decapitation wires" strung across roads, but these improvised devices caused little damage.[80] The most common form of reported sabotage was the cutting and removal of telephone wires, but in most cases civilians had taken the wires for personal use.[81] In one case, soldiers managed to arrest a wire cutter in Neckarsulm near Stuttgart. The perpetrator turned out to be a 12-year-old boy who confessed

---

75 HQ, Seventh Army, Weekly Intel Sum no. 18, 18 Nov 1945, Folder "Weekly Intelligence Summary, October–December 1945," Seventh Army, G-2, Subject Files, 1942–1946, RG 338, NACP.
76 Msg, T/3 [Technician Third Grade] Walter Ullman, to Intel Ofcr, Würzburg, 15 Oct 1945, sub: Stringing of Decapitation Wires in Würzburg, Folder "3rd Army G-2 Sabotage 000.5," Third United States Army, G-2 Section, Decimal Files 1944–1947, RG 338, NACP.
77 OMGUS, Monthly Rpt of Mil Governor U.S. Zone no. 4, Intel and Confidential Annexes, 20 Nov 1945, Historians Files, CMH.
78 HQ, XV Corps, G-2 Intel Bull no. 2, 14 May 1945, Folder "G-2 Journals 13–16 May 45," Historical Div, Program Files, VI Corps, G-2 Jnls, 1945, RG 498, NACP.
79 VI Corps History, Jun 1945, Historical Div, Program Files, VI Corps, 1945–1946, RG 498, NACP. The German was arrested and held for trial.
80 VI Corps History, 20 Jul–30 Sep 1945, Historical Div, Program Files, VI Corps, History, 1945– 1946, RG 498, NACP.
81 Annex #3, ACofS, G-2, Section History, 12 Oct 1945, Historical Div, VI Corps, History, 1945–1946, RG 498, NACP.

that "he was acting on orders from the station master who had told him the wire was no longer in use."[82]

One group stood out from among the restless youth gangs in postwar Germany. Beginning in late 1945, Army Intelligence received reports about a subversive youth movement called "Edelweiss pirates" (*Edelweisspiraten*) who supposedly boasted thousands of members.[83] *Edelweisspiraten* youth groups traced their origins to the Nazi era, when their membership consisted of antiregime working-class youth. The postwar pirates, however, assumed a distinctly nationalist outlook. They chanted nationalist slogans, beat up Polish displaced persons, and harassed German women dating American soldiers.[84] As a common identifier, the pirates sported edelweiss flowers in their jacket buttonholes.

To learn more about the composition and aims of the *Edelweisspiraten*, the Army in early 1946 launched Operation VALENTINE, a zonewide dragnet that delivered hundreds of pirates into American hands.[85] The resulting interrogation reports produced little evidence of a large-scale subversive movement. Instead, they painted a sobering picture of postwar German society. Most of the detainees, one CIC report noted, were very young, homeless, had no family, and lived "in a state of complete deterioration morally, spiritually and even in external appearance." Most were males, but a number of females had joined their ranks as well. Although many had served in the *Wehrmacht* or were former Hitler Youth members, and espoused a crude nationalistic creed, their principal motivations centered on survival and a desire for a sense of community. Loosely organized in small gangs, they wandered from railway station to railway station, looking for opportunities "to steal, rob and deal on the black market."[86] Some Army personnel expressed exasperation at having expended so much time and resources on what turned out to be a false alarm: "FANTASTIC," one scribbled at the bottom of

---

82 VI Corps History, Jun 1945.
83 Thomas Boghardt, "America's Secret Vanguard: U.S. Army Intelligence Operations in Germany, 1944–1947," *Studies in Intelligence* 57, no. 2 (Jun 2013), 7.
84 Perry Biddiscombe, "'The Enemy of Our Enemy': A View of the Edelweiss Piraten from the British and American Archives," *Journal of Contemporary History* 30, no. 1 (1995), 49.
85 Memo, Special Agent Frank B. Crippen, Region IV, CIC, for Ofcr in Charge, 3 Apr 1946, sub: Comprehensive Report re: Operation "Valentine," Folder "E.P. Valentine Region IV XE-111873," INSCOM, IRR, Impersonal Files, RG 319, NACP.
86 Memo, Special Agent J. Thomas Dale, Region II, CIC, for Ofcr in Charge, 4 Mar 1946, sub: Edelweiss Piraten, Folder "E.P. Valentine Region IV XE-111873," INSCOM, IRR, Impersonal Files, RG 319, NACP.

a report, "a bunch of kids are taking us for a sleighride!"[87] Others took the findings with a sense of humor and, perhaps, relief. "We are closing the famous 'VALENTINE' case," noted one official. "It was fun while it lasted."[88]

As Operation VALENTINE was winding down, the CIC zeroed in on what appeared to be a real Nazi conspiracy. About a month after the end of the war, a former SS officer and Hitler Youth leader, Siegfried Kulas, had turned himself in to American authorities in Munich. During his interrogation, he told the CIC that he knew about a large subversive Nazi organization that operated under the cover of a transportation company, Christian Tessmann & Sons at Bad Tölz in Bavaria. After vetting Kulas, the CIC recruited him as an informant under the cover name "Karl" and sent him to infiltrate Tessmann & Sons.[89] Over the next few months, the investigation broadened. The Corps recruited several more informants, and the officer in charge, 1st Lt. Jack D. Hunter, took an active part in the penetration effort. Fluent in German, he approached Tessmann & Sons in the guise of a shady black marketer named "Hans Jäger" (the German translation of "Jack Hunter") and established a business relationship with the company.[90] The initial investigation revealed that Tessmann & Sons employed a large number of former Hitler Youth. The CIC christened the operation NURSERY, probably in acknowledgment of the fact that so many young men and boys made up the target group. According to a participating agent, General Sibert considered the operation of such importance that he personally took over its direction and authorized "unlimited supplies, funds and any other assistance we might ask for."[91]

Operation NURSERY affirmed that, in the dying days of the war, the last chief of the Hitler Youth, Artur Axmann, had instructed his deputies to gather in Bad Tölz and prepare for a postwar Nazi resurgence. Axmann told one of his associates, Willi Heidemann, to withdraw over one million Reichsmark from Hitler Youth funds to establish a commercial enterprise for this purpose. While Axmann

---

87 Memo, Special Agent Erwin Jost, Region IV, CIC, to Ofcr in Charge, 1 Feb 1946, sub: Operation Valentine, ref. Spot Report 30 Jan 46, Third United States Army, G–2 Section, Decimal Files 1944–1947, RG 338, NACP.
88 Office Memo Slip, HQ, Third U.S. Army, 18 Feb 1946, Folder "3rd Army G–2 Operation Valentine 380.4," RG 338, NACP.
89 Bray et al., *History of the Counter Intelligence Corps*, 26:20; Scott Andrew Selby, *The Axmann Conspiracy: The Nazi Plan for a Fourth Reich and How the U.S. Army Defeated It* (New York: Penguin, 2012), 94–102; Rpt, Capt. Dewey M. Campbell, HQ, Third United States Army, to CG, 1st Inf Div, 25 Mar 1946, sub: Operation Nursery, Folder "3rd Army G–2 Operation Nursery 380.4," Third United States Army, G–2 Section, Decimal Files 1944–1947, RG 338, NACP.
90 Hunter later worked his experience into a novel, *The Expendable Spy* (New York: E. P. Dutton, 1965).
91 Selby, *Axmann Conspiracy*, 162–63.

was lying low in northern Germany, Heidemann established Tessmann & Sons, quickly turning it into a commercial success. He hired many former Hitler Youth members, expanded the company, acquired several competitors, and even did business for the U.S. military government.[92]

By early 1946, the CIC had managed to identify the leading personalities connected with Tessmann & Sons, and had purloined from two of Heidemann's associates' lists with names of more than 2,500 prospective Nazi sympathizers. Most were former Nazi officials who fell into the automatic arrest category.[93] When Tessmann & Sons expanded into the British Zone, the CIC enlisted the cooperation of the British Army of the Rhine. Operation NURSERY thus became a joint U.S.-British counterintelligence effort.[94] In a series of raids in the spring of 1946, the CIC apprehended approximately 1,000 individuals associated with the scheme, including Axmann, Heidemann, and other top leaders.[95] Agents also confiscated over one million Reichsmark. Operation NURSERY, an official report noted, "closed the history of the organization, which is not expected to offer any future threat to the occupation."[96]

Virtually all subversive activity in the immediate postwar period had emanated from former Hitler Youth who were fanatical but had little practical sabotage or combat experience. This changed somewhat in the middle of 1946 when the Americans began releasing large numbers of detained SS men. Many awaited their release in a special camp for SS inmates at Auerbach in Bavaria. In the company of like-minded veterans, the inmates reaffirmed their ideological commitment to Nazism and promised each other mutual assistance in the future. Information received by the CIC indicated that, once released, former SS men planned to recognize and help each other by using the code word ODESSA, which stood for *Organisation der Ehemaligen SS Angehörigen* (Organization of Former SS Members). As SS veterans settled into postwar society, references to the ODESSA code word popped up across southern Germany.[97]

---

92 Selby, *Axmann Conspiracy*, 101.
93 Rpt, G–2 Div, 1 Apr 1946, Folder "G–2 Notes for General Council Meeting," Corresp, Rpts, Dirs, and Other Rcds Relating to the Activities and Functions of the Intel Gp, 1943–1947, RG 165, NACP.
94 Special Interrogation Rpt no. 28, British Army of the Rhine, 18 Apr 1946, sub: Secret Report on Nursery, Folder "CSDIC-WEA-BAOR-SIR," Rpts Relating to POW Interrogations 1943–1945, RG 165, NACP.
95 Bray et al., *History of the Counter Intelligence Corps*, 26:25.
96 Monthly Rpt, Mil Governor, U.S. Zone, Intel and Confidential Annexes, 20 Apr 1946, Historians Files, CMH.
97 Memo, Special Agent Otto R. Urbach, HQ, CIC, USFET, for Ofcr in Charge, 3 Jul 1946, sub: Subversive Organization of Released SS Prisoners "Odessa," Folder "Odessa Organization ZF 015116," INSCOM, IRR, Impersonal Name Files, 1939–1976, RG 319, NACP; Guy Walters, *Hunting Evil: The*

Figure 25: A photograph of the Spruchkammer courtroom in Stuttgart after the bombing. U.S. Army, NACP.

A 23-year-old former SS trooper, Siegfried Kabus, gained inspiration from ODESSA. A die-hard Nazi who harbored delusions of grandeur, Kabus had fled from a prisoner-of-war facility in France, forged his discharge papers, and settled near the city of Stuttgart. He recruited several former Hitler Youths as well as a 57-year-old former concentration camp guard to form a small group of malcontents. They quickly got to work. On 9 August 1946, Kabus tossed a bomb at a church whose pastor had made anti-Nazi remarks. Two months later, one of Kabus's recruits threw a hand grenade at an American car parked outside the home of the driver's German girlfriend. Meanwhile, Kabus prepared for a more spectacular act of defiance.[98]

In the evening of 19 October 1946, two fragmentation bombs exploded at the *Spruchkammer* buildings in Backnang and Stuttgart. German police informed the local CIC office in Stuttgart, and the two organizations began a widespread investigation. Initially, all leads ended in blind alleys. However, in early November, a

---

Nazi War Criminals Who Escaped and the Quest to Bring Them to Justice (New York: Broadway Books, 2009), 140.
98 Koop, *Himmlers letztes Aufgebot*, 261.

man named Franz Hummel informed the CIC that he had worked as a courier for a Nazi underground organization led by a certain Siegfried Kabus, and that he suspected Kabus as the instigator of the *Spruchkammer* bombings. The CIC recruited Hummel as an informant. Equipped with a false letter from a denazification court that accused him of Nazi sympathies, Hummel approached one of Kabus's associates and requested readmission to the organization. Meanwhile, Stuttgart's lord mayor offered a reward of 25,000 Reichsmark for information leading to the arrest of the perpetrators. Shortly thereafter, a local man identified Kabus's mother and his girlfriend to the CIC and the police. By mid-November, the CIC had enough evidence to arrest their prime suspect.[99]

On 19 November, CIC special agents surrounded Kabus's house in Stuttgart. On a signal from the raid commander, the men, with pistols drawn, broke into the house through the doors and windows. They caught Kabus and some of his associates, ranged along a dining room table, in the act of manufacturing more bombs. The CIC arrested Kabus and his gang. Upon searching the house, they found eleven pistols, two hundred rounds of ammunition, shells, delayed action fuses, and a number of detonators.[100]

The ensuing investigation and military government court trial, which took place in January 1947, confirmed that Kabus was an unrepentant, violent Nazi. The CIC dug up his SS personnel evaluation form, which praised his "very energetic, upright" bearing and applauded his "cold-bloodedness," especially "in moments of danger."[101] CIC special agents also determined that Kabus and his men had planned additional bombings of *Spruchkammer* courts as well as the abduction of the denazification minister of Württemberg-Baden, Gottlieb Klamm. Kabus planned to have the minister tried by a "military court martial."[102]

Yet the findings also indicated the limits of Kabus's mental capabilities. His SS personnel form cautioned that Kabus's judgments were "not yet entirely objective," and the CIC confirmed the psychological issues the SS evaluators had noticed. During the war, Kabus had feigned his own death and arranged for the news to be delivered to his family so they would be proud of his sacrifice for the Reich. At his trial, Kabus boasted he had "absolute knowledge" that Hitler was still alive and hid-

---

99 Maj. Ann Bray et al., ed., *The History of the Counter Intelligence Corps*, vol. 27, *Four Years of Cold War* (Fort Holabird, MD: U.S. Army Intelligence Center, 1959), 59; "Bomben auf Spruchkammern" [Bombs in the local tribunals], *Der Spiegel*, 1 Nov 1947.
100 Bray et al., *History of the Counter Intelligence Corps*, 27:60.
101 Rpt, Personal-Bericht, SS-Unterscharführer Siegfried Kabus, 16 Apr 1943, Folder "Kabus, Siegfried D168988C," INSCOM, IRR, Digitized Name Files, 1939–1976, RG 319, NACP.
102 Perry Biddiscombe, *The Last Nazis: SS Werewolf Guerrilla Resistance in Europe, 1944–1947* (Charleston, SC: Tempus, 2000), 203.

ing in Spain. Because the Führer was paralyzed, Kabus explained, "it became necessary for me to assume the job of leader."[103] His coconspirators were surprised to learn that Kabus held the lowly rank of sergeant, rather than major as he had told them. Special Agent Sidney Stecher described Kabus as "a pathological liar."[104] Nonetheless, on 21 January, Judge Marshall Herro sentenced Kabus to death by hanging. His associates received lengthy prison sentences.

During his interrogation, Kabus informed the CIC about his familiarity with the ODESSA code word, and the trial acquainted a broader public, for the first time, with the notion of a large underground organization with this name.[105] Prompted by the unexpected publicity, the CIC renewed its investigation of the alleged ODESSA organization at the Auerbach camp. Over the spring and summer of 1947, the CIC recruited several former SS men as informants to penetrate the organization. Most reports ended inconclusively, but one informant suggested the existence of a vast SS conspiracy. Upon further investigation, however, the informant's mind-boggling claims turned out to be entirely invented, and the local CIC office concluded that "his fantastic stories" seemed "completely unreliable," and that he should be "prosecuted if there is a recurrence of his activities." The CIC concluded that no ODESSA organization existed and closed the investigation in September 1947.[106]

Even though Kabus had been a delusional fanatic and ODESSA did not exist, the broader question of the subversive potential of former SS men remained. In early 1947, the CIC and the Intelligence Division of the British Army of the Rhine launched a major joint operation, code-named SELECTION BOARD, to prevent subversive SS veterans from joining forces in larger organizations.[107] The CIC used mail censorship,

---

103 Win Fanning, "Hitler Rules from Spain, Kabus Tells Stuttgart Court," *Stars and Stripes*, European edition, 16 Jan 1947.
104 Memo, Special Agent Sidney Stecher, for Ofcr in Charge, 28 Oct 1947, sub: Beck, Josef, re: Kabus, Siegfried, Folder "Kabus, Siegfried D168998V2," INSCOM, IRR, Digitized Name Files, 1939–1976, RG 319, NACP.
105 Confession of Siegfried Kabus, 19 Dec 1946, Folder "Kabus, Siegfried D168998V2," INSCOM, IRR, Digitized Name Files, 1939–1976, RG 319, NACP; "Bomben auf Spruchkammern," *Der Spiegel*, 1 Nov 1947.
106 Memo, CIC Special Agent William E. Larned Jr., HQ, Region VI, CIC, for CO, 18 Sep 1947, sub: Organization ODESSA, Folder "XE 180 07.3 Odessa Movement, Coburg Movement," INSCOM, IRR, Impersonal Name Files, 1939–1976, RG 319, NACP. Based on conversations with the Nazi hunter Simon Wiesenthal, the British writer Frederick M. Forsyth later popularized the myth of the *Odessa* as a vast and powerful network in his best-selling novel, *The Odessa File* (New York: Viking Press, 1971). See also Walters, *Hunting Evil*, 139.
107 Msg, C. J. W. Legry, Sec, [British] Joint Intel Committee (Germany), to Foreign Ofc (German Section), 25 Jul 1947, sub: Right Wing Movement curtailed by Operation "SELECTION BOARD," Folder "Operation Selection Board Vol I of II Vols ZF 016151," INSCOM, IRR, Impersonal Name Files, 1939–1976, RG 319, NACP.

phone surveillance, and informants to identify potentially dangerous suspects. In Munich, two German CIC informants attended a performance of the Wespennest cabaret group in Munich, where they met two SS veterans who were recruiting men for "a large organization . . . hidden out in the mountains." Giving fictitious names, the two informants joined this organization, after which the SS veterans took them to their headquarters at a farmhouse. There, a former SS officer warned them that "they would die" in case of betrayal. The informants learned that the group had plenty of American supplies, including arms, and that they intended to "blow up supply trains, gas dumps and the like." Upon their return to Munich, the informants reported promptly to the local CIC office.[108]

On the night of 22–23 February 1947, the Allies arrested forty-four suspects in the U.S. Zone and eighty-nine in the British Zone.[109] The Americans delivered their arrestees to the intelligence center in Oberursel where CIC personnel interrogated them. The interrogations revealed that some of the men were former high-ranking SS officers living under assumed names, who had established informal networks of "a potential underground movement." Yet the CIC found no evidence that any of them had actively engaged in subversion. The center concluded that, whatever the potential threat emanating from these networks, their growth had been "nipped in the bud."[110]

By early 1947, the Army's leadership in Germany concluded that Nazi subversion posed no viable threat to the military government. Only one day after the conclusion of Operation SELECTION BOARD, General Clay stated that he did not attach "great significance to the movement whose leaders have just been arrested."[111] Occupation authorities imposed notably lax sentences on the SS veterans in U.S. custody. American and British military courts tried only thirty-five of the arrestees, and none received a lengthy sentence.[112] Meanwhile, the execution of Kabus's sentence stalled. Local authorities had managed to find an executioner willing to do the job for 250 Reichsmark, but they had been unable to procure a functioning gallows or guillotine. The German press, meanwhile, suggested that the sentence was too harsh, as Kabus

---

108 Memo, Special Agent Frank B. Crippen, CIC, Region IV, for Ofcr in Charge, 27 Feb 1946, sub: SS Organization in the Bavarian Mountains, Folder "3rd Army Operation Gopher 380.4," Third United States Army, G–2 Section, Decimal Files 1944–1947, RG 338, NACP.
109 Perry Biddiscombe, "Operation Selection Board: The Growth and Suppression of the Neo-Nazi 'Deutsche Revolution,' 1945–47," *Intelligence and National Security* 11, no. 1 (Jan 1999), 73.
110 Counter Intel Section, Rpt of Opns, 1 Jan 1947 to 31 Mar 1947, Folder "7707 Military Intelligence Service Center, Operations Reports," Historian's Background Files, 1947–1952, RG 549, NACP.
111 Dana Adams Schmidt, "Round-up Thwarts Budding Nazi Plot for War on Soviet," *New York Times*, 23 Feb 1947.
112 Biddiscombe, "Operation Selection Board," 74.

had merely caused damage to property. In April 1948, Clay commuted Kabus's sentence to life in prison. German courts released him as well as his accomplices in the early 1950s.[113]

The decline of the subversive threat did not mean that potentially dangerous Nazi officials disappeared entirely from the radar of Army Intelligence. Rather, the rationale for monitoring such individuals underwent a Cold War metamorphosis. In the late 1940s, the CIC investigated reports that Soviet intelligence directed an organization named "Theo" to recruit SS veterans for covert operations against the West. Special agents went to considerable lengths to establish the veracity of such claims. In the city of Bamberg, they even checked "on the most prominent Pissorts [public toilets] in this Area," albeit "with negative results."[114] Theo proved elusive, as ODESSA had earlier, but American suspicions of Soviet recruitment of former SS men persisted.[115]

War Crimes

Nazi Germany waged a war of terror and annihilation aimed at the racial and territorial remaking of Europe. European Jewry, eastern European nations, and the Soviet Union bore the brunt of Nazi brutality, but American soldiers had been the subjects of war crimes as well, most notably during the Battle of the Bulge. On 30 October 1943, the American, British, and Soviet governments issued the Moscow Declaration, denouncing the "atrocities, massacres and cold-blooded mass executions" committed by the Nazi forces. The Allies also vowed that the German perpetrators would be "judged and punished." In American-controlled territories, the U.S. Army took the lead in the investigation and prosecution of war crimes.[116]

In November 1944, Secretary of War Henry L. Stimson directed the Army's judge advocate general to establish a war crimes office. The judge advocate general, in turn, created a War Crimes Group in the European Theater as his executive agency. As the group collected evidence and prepared the trials, its staff struggled with what turned out to be a monumental task. Consequently, war

---

113 Koop, *Himmlers letztes Aufgebot*, 263.
114 Memo, Special Agent Henry V. McCalla, HQ, Region VI (Bamberg), CIC, for Ofcr in Charge, 5 Nov 1946, sub: Alleged Soviet Sponsored Organizations to Recruit Former SS Personnel, INSCOM, IRR, Impersonal Name Files, 1939–1976, RG 319, NACP.
115 Perry Biddiscombe, "The Problem with Glass Houses: The Soviet Recruitment and Deployment of SS Men as Spies and Saboteurs," *Intelligence and National Security* 15, vol. 3 (2000), 141.
116 Frank M. Buscher, *The U.S. War Crimes Trial Program in Germany, 1946–1955* (New York: Greenwood Press, 1989), 9.

crimes investigators relied heavily on the cooperation of other organizations, including Army Intelligence.[117]

In the fall of 1945, the assistant chief of staff for intelligence in the European Theater formally assumed responsibility for the capture of war crimes suspects and unfriendly witnesses. The principal agencies involved in this effort included the tactical intelligence units of the occupation forces, the CIC, and the Civil Censorship Division. To help local agencies identify war crimes suspects, Supreme Allied Headquarters created the Central Registry of War Criminals and Security Suspects, or CROWCASS, in April 1945. CROWCASS constituted a "living document" that eventually grew into a mammoth registry containing more than 100,000 names.[118]

Some Army Intelligence personnel may have engaged in extrajudicial acts of retribution. Arnold Weiss, the CIC agent involved in capturing Hitler's testament, told a journalist sixty years after the war that he and his colleagues had disposed of "about a dozen" former concentration camp guards. They did not kill the SS men personally, Weiss said, but instead delivered them "for additional debriefing" to displaced persons camps. Many displaced persons had personally experienced Nazi brutality. It was understood, according to Weiss, that the SS guards handed over to them would simply disappear. One U.S. lawyer, who worked as a prosecutor in several war crimes trials in postwar Germany, reported witnessing such acts: "I once saw DPs [displaced persons] beat an SS man and then strap him to a gurney of a crematorium. They slid him in the oven, turned on the heat and took him back out. Beat him again, and put him back until he was burnt alive. I did nothing to stop it."[119]

To the extent that this type of personal vengeance happened, it remained confined to a short period at the end of the war. For the most part, Army Intelligence personnel in postwar Germany followed orders to track down war crimes suspects and collect evidence for trials. Of the many individuals wanted by the U.S. judiciary, American citizens who had collaborated with the Nazis were high on the list. As the war ended, Army Intelligence sought to locate and return them stateside for trial. The FBI attached agents to CIC detachments to lend assistance in the quest.

---

117 Rpt, Lt. Col. C. E. Straight, Deputy Judge Advocate for War Crimes, EUCOM, to Judge Advocate, EUCOM, n.d. [1947 or after], sub: Report of the Deputy Judge Advocate for War Crimes, European Command, June 1944 to July 1948, 2, 4, Historians Files, CMH.
118 Rpt, Straight, n.d., sub: Report of the Deputy Judge Advocate, 19, 20, 22, 27; Thomas Boghardt, "Dirty Work? The Use of Nazi Informants by U.S. Army Intelligence in Postwar Europe," *Journal of Military History* 79 (Apr 2015), 399.
119 Matthew Brzezinski, "Giving Hitler Hell," *Washington Post*, 24 Jul 2005.

One of the most notorious of these American collaborators was Mildred E. Gillars. Dubbed "Axis Sally" by the soldiers, Gillars broadcast Nazi propaganda to the Allied forces from Berlin. She sought to demoralize American soldiers by highlighting the dangers of war, suggesting the infidelity of their wives and girlfriends back in the United States, and attacking President Roosevelt. At the end of the war, she disappeared amid the ruins of bombed-out Berlin. By identifying and interviewing acquaintances of hers, and by tracking furniture she had sold to a store on Berlin's Kurfürstendamm, the CIC eventually discovered her whereabouts. Special agents arrested her and detained her in Oberursel for interrogation. Occupation authorities then sent her to the United States, where a court tried and convicted her for treason. During her trial, she complimented the CIC agents for their acumen: "I will take off my hat to U.S. investigators," she said. "They certainly knew a lot about me."[120]

On a few occasions, the CIC also participated in the transfer of Nazi sympathizers, accused traitors, and enemy agents from the United States to Germany. One such case was that of Fritz J. Kuhn, the leader of the German American Bund, the principal prewar Nazi organization in the United States. Born in Germany, Kuhn had become a naturalized U.S. citizen in 1934 but lost his citizenship in 1943 while serving a sentence for embezzlement. In 1945, American authorities deported him to Germany and detained him in the Seventh Army Internment Camp in Asperg. A CIC agent who interrogated Kuhn in January 1946 believed that the detainee was politically "discredited and spiritually broken," and recommended his release.[121] The Americans handed him over to German authorities for denazification, and the Germans eventually released him. Through the Civil Censorship Division, the CIC continued to monitor Kuhn, confirming his harmlessness save for a brief incident in 1952. In that year, the division intercepted a letter from Kuhn to the Czechoslovak consulate general in Frankfurt in which Kuhn offered to work for the communist nation's "Information Service"—likely a euphemism for Czechoslovak intelligence.[122] Whatever motivated Kuhn to contemplate spying for the Czechs, his effort came to naught. He died shortly thereafter, "a poor and obscure chemist, unheralded and unsung."[123]

---

120 Bray et al., *History of the Counter Intelligence Corps*, 27:51–52.
121 Rpt of Preliminary Interrogation, 1st Lt. Herman Roselinsky, 9 Jan 1946, sub: Kuhn, Fritz Julius, Folder "Fritz Julius Kuhn D003351," INSCOM, IRR, 1939–1976, Digitized Name Files, RG 319, NACP.
122 Msg, Lt. Col. Robert A. Van Houten, CO, Region III, CIC, to HQ, 66th CIC Detachment, 15 Dec 1952, sub: Czech Trade Mission, Folder "Kuhn Fritz XE 003351," INSCOM, IRR, 1939–1976, Digitized Name Files, RG 319, NACP.
123 "Fritz Kuhn Death in 1951 [sic] Revealed," *New York Times*, 2 Feb 1953.

War crimes trials constituted the principal venue for justice in postwar Germany, with the International Military Tribunal commanding the most attention. In 1945 and 1946, the four Allies jointly tried the surviving Nazi leaders for war crimes. The trial took place in the old Palace of Justice in Nuremberg. The accused group included twenty-four individuals, most of whom had surrendered or fallen into Allied hands at the end of the war. As preparations for the Nuremberg trial got underway, the chief of Nazi Germany's intelligence services, Ernst Kaltenbrunner, was still at large. The CIC launched an investigation, and Special Agent Robert E. Matteson tracked down and apprehended Kaltenbrunner in an isolated hut in the Austrian Alps. He joined the ranks of Nazi Germany's erstwhile leadership at Nuremberg. Sentenced to death, Kaltenbrunner was hanged on 15 October 1946, along with eleven other defendants.[124]

Army Intelligence support of the International Military Tribunal included the physical security of the Palace of Justice. In January 1946, the CIC learned that a group of SS veterans planned to sabotage the court proceedings. Supposedly, the saboteurs would be dressed in U.S. uniforms and equipped with forged papers and an American jeep. Consequently, the CIC tightened security around the palace, and the trial proceeded undisturbed.[125]

Disagreement among the four Allies led to the breakup of the joint International Military Tribunal in 1946. The Americans then proceeded on their own to try another batch of war crimes suspects in Nuremberg over the next three years. The so-called subsequent Nuremberg trials targeted the second tier of the Nazi regime and included arraignments of Nazi doctors, judges, corporate leaders, the German high command, and the notorious SS *Einsatzgruppen*, the mobile killing squads that operated in the rear of the *Wehrmacht* in Eastern Europe and the Soviet Union. Owing to their expertise and language skills, Army Intelligence personnel contributed to many aspects of the trials, including the location and apprehension of suspects, the gathering of evidence, and the interrogation of witnesses and defendants. The German-born Ralf Wartenberg, for example, had trained at Camp Ritchie as a prisoner-of-war interrogator and applied his skills as the chief interrogator in the *Einsatzgruppen* trial.[126]

---

[124] Robert E. Matteson, "The Last Days of Ernst Kaltenbrunner: Personal Recollections of the Capture and Show Trial of an Intelligence Chief," *Studies in Intelligence* 4, no. 2 (Spring 1960): 9–29.

[125] Memo, HQ, Third U.S. Army, 30 Jan 1946, sub: Counter-measures to be Adopted Against Suspected Resistance Organization, Folder "3rd Army G–2 Operation Valentine 380.4," Third United States Army, G–2 Section, Decimal Files, 1944–1947, RG 338, NACP.

[126] Steven P. Remy, *The Malmedy Massacre: The War Crimes Trial Controversy* (Cambridge, MA: Harvard University Press, 2017), 294n14.

The Nuremberg trials focused on the Nazi elite—a mere fraction of German war criminals. Between 1945 and 1947, the Army tried some 1,700 additional war crimes suspects in over 400 trials by military commission court. These trials focused on the mass murders committed by concentration camp personnel, the killings of Allied airmen shot down over Germany, and war crimes committed during the Battle of the Bulge. The Army conducted most of the trials at Dachau. The former concentration camp provided sufficient space to hold such a large number of defendants while serving as a constant reminder of the monstrous reality of the Third Reich.[127] As they did at Nuremberg, Army Intelligence personnel contributed to the proceedings in a number of ways.

The largest Dachau trial involved the prosecution of more than sixty SS personnel of the Mauthausen concentration camp in Austria. The Americans were particularly keen to get their hands on August Eigruber, the *Gauleiter* (local Nazi Party governor) of upper Austria. Eigruber had been in charge of Mauthausen and was rumored to have instigated some of the most brutal atrocities there. At the end of the war, he went underground, but the CIC managed to insert one of their agents into Eigruber's inner circle. The CIC man gained Eigruber's confidence and lured him into a trap. As the prosecution prepared their case, 2d Lt. Paul C. Guth, formerly serving with an Army Intelligence unit, interrogated Eigruber and his codefendants. Guth put his training to good use. "If you want to get confessions from Germans," he had learned at Camp Ritchie, "imitate a Prussian officer. Behave like Herr Doktor Guth and watch what happens. There will be no need to shout." Guth's approach worked like a charm. He extracted numerous confessions, and the court found all of the defendants guilty. On 27 May 1947, the Army hanged forty-nine of them, including Eigruber, in the largest mass execution of the American war crimes trials program.[128]

For Army Intelligence, the Battle of the Bulge held particular significance because of the fate of two of their own: S. Sgt. Kurt R. Jacobs and T/5 Murray Zapler. Local *Wehrmacht* commander Capt. Curt Bruns had executed Jacobs and Zapler when he learned of their German-Jewish background, even though both men should have been protected by their status as prisoners of war.[129] Shortly after the battle, an American interrogator, Guy Stern, interviewed a German prisoner of war who had witnessed the shootings. The German prisoner told Stern about Bruns's role in the murder. Stern filed a report, and Army Intelligence personnel initiated a theaterwide search for Bruns.

---

127 Tomaz Jardim, *The Mauthausen Trial: American Military Justice in Germany* (Cambridge, MA: Harvard University Press, 2012), 2.
128 Jardim, *Mauthausen Trial*, 83–84, 89, 104, 106, 197.
129 See Chapter 2 for additional details of the execution.

When units of the Third Army apprehended Bruns in early February, they quickly identified him as a war crimes suspect and sent him to the First Army headquarters for interrogation and trial. Initially, Bruns denied giving the order to shoot the two captives, and blamed his regimental commander for their deaths. Army Intelligence then placed another prisoner of war, who worked for the Americans as an informer, in the cell next to Bruns. Posing as a tough paratrooper who had killed several Belgian civilians, the informant quickly gained the trust of Bruns, who boasted to his newfound confidant that he had the two prisoners "mowed down." This inadvertent confession doomed Bruns. On 7 April 1945, a military commission tried him, found him guilty, and sentenced him to death. Bruns faced the firing squad on 14 June. He died in the same uniform he had worn the day he ordered the executions of Jacobs and Zapler.[130]

Figure 26: Capt. Curt Bruns, about to be executed for war crimes. U.S. Army, NACP.

---

130 Bruce Henderson, *Sons and Soldiers: The Untold Story of the Jews Who Escaped the Nazis and Returned with the U.S. Army to Fight Hitler* (New York: William Morrow, 2017), 307, 308, 346, 350–51.

In the Army's investigation of German war crimes committed during the Battle of the Bulge, the Malmédy massacre took center stage. On 17 December 1944, German soldiers murdered more than eighty American prisoners of war in the fields near the Belgian town of Malmédy. Reports and photographs of the dead U.S. soldiers, some found with their arms still raised above their heads, enraged the American public and prompted the Army to redouble its efforts to search for and prosecute the perpetrators.[131] In the summer of 1945, Army Intelligence personnel began scanning U.S. internment camps for men who had served in the *Kampfgruppe Peiper*, the SS unit believed to be responsible for the murders. The search lasted for several months. By the end of the year, intelligence personnel had located most of the wanted men, including the group's leader, Lt. Col. Joachim Peiper, and his commander, General Josef "Sepp" Dietrich. The court indicted seventy-three SS men, and their trial began on 16 May 1946.[132]

Army interrogators had questioned Dietrich on his role in the Malmédy massacres at the Seventh Army Interrogation Center on 11 June 1945. Dietrich claimed to know "nothing about the shooting of American PW [sic]" at the time of the battle. "If it happened at all," he told his interrogator, "it must have been in the sector of [*Wehrmacht* General Hasso E. von] Manteuffel's army."[133] Peiper, for his part, admitted having received written orders from Dietrich "that prisoners of war must be shot where the local conditions of combat should so require it," but he remained evasive about his own role.[134] He implied that Lt. Col. Otto Skorzeny's men, rather than his own unit, may have had something to do with the killings.[135] But Dietrich's and Peiper's obfuscations and denials failed to sway the court. Army interrogators had taken pains to separate the inmates, preventing them from coordinating their stories. In multiple cases, interrogators gained the defendants' trust and persuaded them to implicate their fellow soldiers. On 16 July 1946, the court found all of the defendants guilty. Forty-three men, including Peiper, received death sentences. Dietrich was sentenced to life imprisonment.

---

131 "Slain U.S. Captives Found in Belgium," *New York Times*, 4 Jan 1945.
132 Patricia Kollander with John O'Sullivan, *"I Must be a Part of this War": A German American's Fight against Hitler and Nazism* (New York: Fordham University Press, 2005), 139; Rpt, Counter Intel Br, Weekly Program Rpt, 7 Dec to 14 Dec 1945, Folder "3rd Army G–2 Operation Gallop 21 Oct. 45–31 Jan. '46 000.5," Third United States Army, G–2 Section, Decimal Files 1944–1947, RG 338, NACP.
133 Rpt, Seventh Army Interrogation Center, 11 Jun 1945, sub: Josef ("Sepp") Dietrich, Folder "D-000932 Sepp Dietrich," INSCOM, IRR, Digitized Name Files, 1939–1976, RG 319, NACP.
134 Remy, *Malmedy Massacre*, 59–81.
135 James J. Weingartner, "Otto Skorzeny and the Laws of War," *Journal of Military History* 55 (Apr 1991), 216.

A year later, the trial of Otto Skorzeny for his role in the Battle of the Bulge marked one of the first major setbacks for the Dachau prosecutors. Skorzeny had been high on the Army's wanted list. A CIC-generated poster distributed to Army units in Europe described him as an "extremely clever and very dangerous" spy, saboteur, and assassin.[136] On 16 May 1945, Skorzeny surrendered to U.S. forces in Austria. The atmosphere of the ensuing interrogation differed markedly from the typically frosty reception reserved for most captured SS personnel. As Skorzeny regaled agents of the 307th CIC Detachment with his day-to-day challenges of running an intelligence organization, the Americans found his "complaints had a familiar ring" and that they had much in common with the German commando. In August, the Army transferred Skorzeny to Oberursel for further interrogation. A month later, the Americans moved him to Nuremberg to serve as a witness during the ensuing trials.[137]

On 18 August 1947, a Dachau military court charged Skorzeny and nine of his officers with war crimes during the Battle of the Bulge. Initially, the arraignment included charges for the murder of American prisoners of war, but the prosecutors later dropped these for lack of evidence. For the most part, the trial revolved around the question of whether Skorzeny had violated international laws of war by obtaining and using American uniforms in the course of *Operation GREIF*. Skorzeny's defense counsel argued that both sides had used enemy uniforms as ruses, and produced a star witness in the person of Wg. Cdr. Forest F. E. Yeo-Thomas, a Royal Air Force intelligence officer. Yeo-Thomas testified that his own men routinely donned German uniforms and were prepared to "bump off the other guy" while in disguise.[138] If this behavior was acceptable on the Allied side, the defense argued, Skorzeny had not breached international law by outfitting his men with American uniforms. This argument carried the day, and on 9 September the tribunal acquitted all of the defendants.[139] The verdict stood in stark contrast to the Army's swift execution of several of Skorzeny's men who had been caught wearing U.S. uniforms during the Battle of the Bulge.

The weakness of the prosecution's case against Skorzeny and the respect shared by many American military men for the dashing German commando cer-

---

136 Poster, "Wanted, Skorzeny, Spy, Saboteur, Assassin," n.d., Folder "Otto Skorzeny XE 000417. Vol. 1," INSCOM, IRR, Personal Name Files, 1939–1976, RG 319, NACP.
137 Molly R. Ricks, "After Acquittal: Otto Skorzeny's Postwar Life" (unpublished research paper, U.S. Army Center of Military History, 2018), Historians Files, CMH; Bray et al., *History of the Counter Intelligence Corps*, 26:30.
138 Weingartner, "Otto Skorzeny and the Laws of War," 218.
139 Ricks, "After Acquittal." Skorzeny then worked briefly for the Army's Historical Program, writing about his rescue of Mussolini during the war. Subsequently, the Army transferred him to a German internment camp for denazification. In 1948, he escaped from the camp and eventually settled in fascist Spain, where he lived until his death in 1975.

tainly contributed to his acquittal. But if these factors were unique to Skorzeny's case, the rules for war crimes trials began to change in favor of other defendants as well. Two years into the occupation, many Germans started to resent the large-scale trials of their compatriots, and their sentiments gained weight as the military government sought to establish a politically stable, pro-Western German state. Peiper, Dietrich, and the other Malmédy defendants benefited from the new political climate.

While the Dachau court tried and acquitted Skorzeny, the Malmédy defendants filed an appeal. Several of them argued that the court should rescind their confessions because they had signed them under duress. The U.S.-appointed lawyer for the defense, Col. Willis M. Everett, became an ardent advocate for his clients.[140] He launched a public relations campaign that sought to discredit the verdict on the grounds that interrogators supposedly had used mock trials, starvation, and physical torture to obtain statements from the defendants. These allegations were factually inaccurate but politically explosive. A CIC agent noted in early 1948 that the defendants' affidavits must "be regarded as an attempt to discredit the entire War Crimes Court, as well as the American Occupation forces as a whole" and recommended that military government prohibit their publication.[141]

Eventually, the appeals landed on the desk of General Clay. He recognized the torture allegations for what they were: deliberate falsehoods to overturn the initial guilty verdicts. Still, Clay had to be mindful of public opinion in Germany, which had become a significant factor in American decision-making by the late 1940s. Clay's intelligence agencies informed the governor that a campaign for the release of the prisoners was stoking anti-American sentiments. Carefully navigating the legal and political landscape, Clay in 1948 commuted some death sentences into lifetime prison sentences. He confirmed others, including the verdict of the chief perpetrator, Joachim Peiper. By this time, however, the torture allegations had become so toxic that Secretary of the Army Kenneth C. Royall ordered all executions stopped, pending further investigation.[142]

The publicity campaign for the defendants caught on in the United States where pro-German sympathizers, right-wing newspapers, and conservative politicians used the allegations as a battering ram against the Truman administration's handling of the occupation. It was in response to the rising chorus of outrage over the supposed use of torture by interrogators that Royall created a commission to investigate the allegations. In March 1949, the U.S. Senate's Committee on

---

140 For Everett's role in the trial, see James J. Weingartner, "Unconventional Allies: Colonel Willis Everett and SS-Obersturmbannfuehrer Joachim Peiper," *The Historian* 62, no. 1 (1999): 79–98.
141 Remy, *Malmedy Massacre*, 209–10.
142 Remy, *Malmedy Massacre*, 209–10.

Armed Services formed a subcommittee to look into this issue. The committee consisted of three senators—including Republican senator Joseph R. McCarthy of Wisconsin—who traveled to Dachau to investigate the allegations.[143]

Motivated by a combination of anti-Semitism, anticommunism, and a proclivity for grandstanding that would become his trademark, McCarthy vociferously took up the cause of the Malmédy defendants and their supporters. He dismissed the accusations against the SS soldiers as "fantastic," "unbelievable," and "incredible," and denounced the judges as "brainless" and "imbecilic." With his characteristic bigotry, he lambasted the Army Intelligence personnel of Jewish background as "non-Aryan refugees" and asked rhetorically: "If you were a German would you feel that you would be willing to have a matter of life and death decided by this man [Judge Col. Abraham H.] Rosenfeld?"[144]

Army personnel in Germany strongly repudiated the torture claims. When questioned by McCarthy, the prosecutor of the Malmédy trial, Col. Burton L. Ellis, dismissed them as "utterly ridiculous."[145] Much of McCarthy's "evidence" had been provided by Rudolf Aschenauer, a German lawyer involved in the campaign to undermine the court's credibility. In September 1949, therefore, the CIC and the Civil Censorship Division began monitoring Aschenauer and his communications.[146] The surveillance, which continued into the 1950s, revealed that he had extensive ties with organizations that sought to assist and rehabilitate former Nazis, and that "Aschenauer's political tendencies are very near that of National Socialism."[147] Later, rumors surfaced that Aschenauer had exploited the Malmédy trial on behalf of Soviet intelligence to discredit the Americans. Although these rumors could not be proven, they prompted the journalist Drew R. Pearson to pen a column in the *Washington Post* under the provocative title "Communists Love McCarthy."[148]

When West Germany gained limited sovereignty in late 1949, the Malmédy defendants remained in prison, but pressure for their liberation continued. In the polarized political climate that emphasized anticommunism over denazification,

---

143 Remy, *Malmedy Massacre*, 209.
144 David M. Oshinsky, *A Conspiracy So Immense: The World of Joe McCarthy* (Oxford: Oxford University Press, 2005), 78.
145 Remy, *Malmedy Massacre*, 225.
146 Request for CIS coverage, Capt. Lloyd W. Rausch, Tech Specialist, Region IV, CIC, 2 Sep 1949, Folder "Rudolf Aschenauer XE 260416 vol. 4," INSCOM, IRR, 1939–1976, RG 319, NACP.
147 Msg, Lt. Col. Alfred C. Scherer, CO, Region IV, CIC, to CO, 66th CIC Gp, 28 May 1953, sub: Aschenauer, Rudolf, Dr., Folder "Rudolf Aschenauer XE 260416 vol. 2," INSCOM, IRR, 1939–1976, RG 319, NACP.
148 Oshinsky, *A Conspiracy So Immense*, 77, note; Drew Pearson, "Communists Love McCarthy," *Washington Post*, 15 Jun 1954.

the Army gradually released all of them. In 1956, Colonel Peiper became the last Malmédy defendant to gain his freedom. However, the long shadow of his crimes caught up with him in the end. In the early 1970s, he retired quietly in France, but the public eventually became aware of his presence. Following weeks of thinly veiled anonymous warnings, in July 1976 a group of assailants set fire to Peiper's house, killing him. French authorities never charged anyone in the attack.[149]

The Breakdown of Inter-Allied Cooperation

In the Moscow Declaration of 1943, the Allies had stated their intention to deliver war criminals for trial to the authorities of those countries where the atrocities had been committed. In Germany, this approach required inter-Allied cooperation, as the four powers had to move many war crimes suspects from one occupation zone to another for trial. Allied Control Council Law No. 10, passed on 20 December 1945, created a legal basis for the extradition of war criminals across occupation zones. The law vested ultimate authority for extradition in the military governors, but it did not spell out the mechanics of inter-Allied cooperation.[150] For the most part, the mission of locating war criminals across occupation zones and coordinating extraditions among the Allies fell to their intelligence services. In the U.S. Zone, the CIC played a leading role in this mission.

Anglo-American cooperation on war crimes investigations proved uncomplicated. Usually, each side complied with extradition requests from their Allied partner. Franco-American cooperation on war crimes investigations encountered some difficulties. Political disagreements between Washington and Paris in the immediate postwar era carried over into their relationship during the occupation, and therefore Army Intelligence personnel did not work as closely with their French counterparts as they did with the British. Yet the French occupation zone was small and housed comparatively few war criminals of interest to the Americans. Hence, the tracking and extradition of wanted persons represented just a small aspect of intelligence relations between France and the United States.

War crimes investigations played a significantly larger role in the context of American dealings with the Soviets. The Germans had committed most of their war crimes in Poland and in the western areas of the Soviet Union. Fearing retri-

---

149 Remy, *Malmedy Massacre*, 272.
150 Bogdan Musial, "NS-Kriegsverbrecher vor polnischen Gerichten" [Nazi war criminals before Polish courts], *Vierteljahrshefte für Zeitgeschichte* 47, no. 1 (Jan 1999), 26–27. For Everett's role in the trial, see James J. Weingart.

bution, many perpetrators had fled to the Western occupation zones at the end of the war, and Polish and Soviet authorities now demanded their extradition. In 1945 and 1946, American authorities complied liberally with these requests and delivered 1,315 war crimes suspects to the east.[151] In several cases, however, cooperation between Army Intelligence and the Soviets stalled soon after the end of the war.

American authorities in Berlin were particularly keen on capturing Frederick W. Kaltenbach, an American from Iowa who had settled in the German capital in the 1930s. Under the call name "Lord Hee-Haw"—itself a spin on "Lord Haw-Haw," the moniker given to a number of English-speaking propagandists on German airwaves—Kaltenbach had broadcast radio propaganda for the Nazis during the war. Ten days after American forces entered Berlin, two Army officers sought out Kaltenbach's German wife Dorothea, who informed them that the Soviets had picked up her husband a month earlier.[152] The Soviets subsequently told the Americans that they did not have Kaltenbach in their custody and that they considered the matter "officially closed."[153]

The Americans remained skeptical. In June 1946, the CIC took up the issue directly with Soviet intelligence in Berlin. Two CIC special agents met with two NKVD (Naródnyy Komissariát Vnútrennikh Del; People's Commissariat for Internal Affairs) officers at the Berlin Police headquarters (Präsidium) near Alexanderplatz and gave them photographs of Kaltenbach for identification. The Soviets suggested a quid pro quo. Handing the Americans a list of "Russian traitors" residing in the U.S. Zone, they requested that Kaltenbach be exchanged for those. Pointing to a particular name on the list, one of the Soviets said emphatically, "This man is for us as Kaltenbach is for you."[154] The CIC's search for Kaltenbach went nowhere. Eventually, the Soviets informed the Americans that he had died in the Soviet Zone in October 1945.[155]

By "this man," the Soviet secret service officer meant Stepan A. Bandera, a Ukrainian nationalist and sometime Nazi collaborator who had settled in postwar Munich.[156] Numerous Ukrainian nationalists and Nazi collaborators had fled to

---

151 Musial, "NS-Kriegsverbrecher," 30.
152 Maginnis, *Military Government Journal*, entry for 10 Jul 1945, 270.
153 Clayton D. Laurie, "Goebbels's Iowan: Frederick W. Kaltenbach and Nazi Short-Wave Radio Broadcasts in America, 1939–1945," *The Annals of Iowa* 53, no. 3 (1994): 243.
154 Memo, Special Agent Robert R. Reeder Jr. and Special Agent Stephen C. Rostan, HQ, Region VIII, CIC, USFET, for Ofcr in Charge, 10 June 1946, sub: CIC-NKVD Liaison, Folder "XE 152 738 CIC NKVD Liaison," INSCOM, IRR, Impersonal Files, RG 319, NACP.
155 Laurie, "Goebbels's Iowan," 244.
156 Memo, Reeder and Rostan for Ofcr in Charge, 10 Jun 1946, sub: CIC-NKVD Liaison.

the U.S. Zone at the end of the war, and U.S. intelligence regarded them as potentially valuable sources of information on the Soviet Union.[157] For their part, the Soviets regarded all Ukrainians as Soviet citizens and demanded their repatriation under an inter-Allied agreement struck at the Yalta Conference. In particular, they demanded Bandera's extradition for war crimes. Army Intelligence, however, considered him too valuable an asset to hand him over, so in 1946 the CIC launched an operation to hide him from Moscow's prying eyes. Named after a Dick Tracy character who could change his appearance at will, the CIC's Operation ANYFACE successfully shielded Bandera from Soviet extradition requests.[158]

Army Intelligence rebuffed Soviet requests for the extradition of other Ukrainians as well. In late 1947, the Soviets notified the U.S. military government that the Army newspaper *Stars and Stripes* had written about former Ukrainian partisans in American detention centers and demanded their repatriation. At the behest of the Army's Intelligence Division in Heidelberg, the U.S. military government replied that they were unaware of any "Banderists" in their zone.[159] The Soviet-controlled press, in turn, angrily denounced the "fascist organizations of the Ukrainian nationalists" who "continued to operate in the British and American zones of occupation."[160] Embarrassingly for the United States, these charges were partly true, in that Bandera and others like him held ultranationalist views and occasionally had collaborated with the Nazis during the war.

The Ukrainian controversy prompted American occupation authorities in the spring of 1947 to begin limiting the extradition of suspected war criminals to Soviet-controlled nations. Army Intelligence played an active part in the recalibration of U.S. policy. For one, intelligence personnel did not want to lose access to sources with knowledge about the Soviet Union. They also suspected Soviet and Polish authorities of using extradition requests specifically to deny the Americans this source of information. Their concern had some basis: as early as April 1946, Polish authorities were arguing among themselves to demand extraditions of war crimes suspects as a means of "reducing the number of potential American friends" among the ranks of Germans with intelligence value.[161]

---

157 Kevin C. Ruffner, "Cold War Allies: The Origins of CIA's Relationship with Ukrainian Nationalists," *Studies in Intelligence* (1998), 19.
158 Bray et al., *History of the Counter Intelligence Corps*, 27:97. Eventually, the Soviets caught up with Bandera. In 1959, a KGB assassin killed him in Munich with a cyanide gun.
159 Ofc of the Ch Historian, EUCOM, *A Survey of Soviet Aims, Policies, and Tactics*, Occupation Forces in Europe Series 1947–1948 (Frankfurt: Historical Division, EUCOM, 1948), 310.
160 "Faschistische Geheimgruppen" [Fascist secret groups], *Neues Deutschland*, 15 Nov 1946.
161 Boghardt, "Dirty Work?," 407; Musial, "NS-Kriegsverbrecher," 30–31.

In the fall of 1947, Director of Intelligence Maj. Gen. Robert L. Walsh intervened directly with the U.S. Department of State to fend off a Polish extradition request for five German generals, including Heinz W. Guderian, a famous tank commander and one of the architects of the German "blitzkrieg" tactics during the war.[162] At this time, Guderian was writing a study of the eastern front for the Army's Historical Program at Camp Neustadt in Greater Hesse. Soviet intelligence was vaguely aware of Guderian's activities there.[163] This information stoked Moscow's fears about the reconstitution of the German general staff under American auspices and rendered the Polish extradition request even more urgent from the Soviet perspective. Walsh strongly advised against "delivering to Poles an officer of such exceptional talent as Guderian, in view of the possibility that Eastern powers might seek to use him for military intelligence" purposes.[164] The Americans promptly denied the Polish request, and on 1 January 1948 the U.S. military government effectively put an end to any further extraditions to Poland and the Soviet Union.[165]

If the contentiousness of the extradition question accelerated the unravelling of the wartime alliance, the controversy over Soviet war crimes committed in Poland formally terminated it. The dispute had its origins in the early days of the war. In 1939, the Red Army invaded the eastern parts of Poland, taking many Polish soldiers as prisoners. On the direct orders of Joseph Stalin, the Soviet security service in 1940 executed approximately 5,000 Polish officers and noncommissioned officers, as well as several hundred lawyers, doctors, and teachers, in an effort to decimate the Polish elite and facilitate a communist takeover of the country. In a series of mass executions, the Soviets killed and buried their victims near the Katyn Forest in western Russia.[166]

When the Germans discovered the mass graves at Katyn in 1943, they denounced the Soviets as the responsible party. Moscow denied the accusations, blaming the Germans for the murders instead. To bolster their claims, the Germans brought international observers as eyewitnesses to Katyn, including several American prisoners of war. The ranking officer among the captive Americans was Col.

---

[162] Thomas O'Toole, "U.S. Used Many Ex-Nazis Early in Cold War," *Washington Post*, 28 Mar 1983. The other four officers were *Wehrmacht* Generals Heinrich F. von Lüttwitz and Nikolaus von Vormann, and SS Generals Heinz Reinefarth and Ernst A. Rode.
[163] David E. Murphy, Sergei A. Kondrashev, and George Bailey, *Battleground Berlin: CIA vs. KGB in the Cold War* (New Haven, CT: Yale University Press, 1999), 71.
[164] Msg, Sec State (signed Lovett), to U.S. Political Adviser, 23 Oct 1947, Folder "1–1–47 thru 12–31–47," ACoS, G–2 (Intel), "Top Secret" Incoming and Outgoing Cables, 1942–52, RG 319, NACP.
[165] Musial, "NS-Kriegsverbrecher," 32.
[166] Benjamin B. Fischer, "The Katyn Controversy: Stalin's Killing Field," *Studies in Intelligence* (Winter 1999/2000), online edition, https://www.cia.gov/resources/csi/studies-in-intelligence/.

John H. Van Vliet, a fourth-generation West Pointer. At the end of the war, Van Vliet regained his freedom and returned to the United States. On 22 May 1945, he personally informed the director of intelligence, Maj. Gen. Clayton L. Bissell, about his observations at Katyn.[167]

Van Vliet had no doubt about Soviet responsibility for the Katyn murders and Bissell asked him to dictate a formal report on this issue. As soon as Bissell received the document, he classified it "top secret," effectively removing it from circulation. Seven years later, in 1952, Bissell told a congressional committee investigating Katyn that he saw in the report "great possibilities of embarrassment" to the Soviet Union, and that he was merely carrying out "the spirit of the Yalta agreement" with his decision. The report vanished, and it remains unclear what happened to it. Bissell told the committee that he forwarded the report to the State Department, but the diplomats stated they never received it. Eventually, the committee concluded that "the Van Vliet report was either removed or purposely destroyed in Army Intelligence (G–2)" and pinned responsibility on Bissell.[168] The following year, the U.S. Air Force reprimanded Bissell because he had not offered "an acceptable explanation" for the disappearance of the document.[169]

When the Allies set up the International Military Tribunal, this venue potentially offered an opportunity to establish responsibility for the Katyn murders. Because the investigation of war crimes committed in eastern Europe rested with the Soviets, Katyn ironically fell within their remit. Against the advice of his Allied colleagues, the Soviet chief prosecutor Roman A. Rudenko charged the German army with responsibility for Katyn, but his case quickly fell apart as German witnesses demolished this thesis. Because the Soviets had no interest in investigating the matter further, the Katyn murders disappeared from the Nuremberg proceedings.[170]

The issue rested until 1948, when Army Intelligence in Germany became directly involved in the Katyn controversy. On 12 March, the Office of the Deputy Director of Intelligence asked all major intelligence units in Germany to report

---

167 Rpt, *The Katyn Forest Massacre, Final Report of the Select Committee to Conduct an Investigation and Study of the Facts, Evidence, and Circumstances of the Katyn Forest Massacre*, 22 Dec 1952, Folder "Investigation 403. General Bissell (Katyn Forest Massacre), 5/25/1954," Case Files 1950–1955, RG 340, NACP (hereinafter Katyn Forest Massacre Report).
168 George Sanford, *Katyn and the Soviet Massacre of 1940: Truth, Justice and Memory* (London: Routledge, 2004), 163; Katyn Forest Massacre Report, 6–9.
169 Msg, Gen. Nathan F. Twining to Maj. Gen. Clayton L. Bissell, 4 May 1953, sub: Administrative Reprimand, Katyn Forest Massacre Report, appendix.
170 Sanford, *Katyn*, 140–41.

any "information which might be available concerning the Katyn Forest murders." The office specifically suggested that Army Intelligence personnel seek out and interview German military personnel who had served in the vicinity of Katyn.[171] The German interviewees confirmed Soviet responsibility. General Guderian, the commander of the *Second Panzer Army* in Russia during the war, told the CIC that "there was no doubt in his mind, but that the murders had been committed by the Soviet forces."[172]

The CIC also reached out to Polish refugees living in Germany. Many had been near the murder site or knew someone who had been there, and their testimony added to the growing body of evidence of Soviet responsibility. As part of the investigation, CIC agents interviewed several Polish officers who had visited Katyn under German supervision. As one CIC agent commented at the end of a report based on these interviews, "All evidence . . . seems to point to the Soviets as the perpetrators of this massacre. It follows their policy of making a country ready for Communist dictatorship by 'removing' most of the intelligentsia of the country, leaving only the Communistic elements and others not capable of organizing resistance."[173]

For several years, Katyn remained too controversial a topic for U.S. officials to raise in an open forum. Only in late 1951, when the United States was locked in mortal combat with communist forces in Korea, did Congress begin to conduct an official investigation of the atrocities. The final report squarely assigned responsibility to the Soviets.[174]

Conclusion

Ridding Germany of its Nazi legacy was a core mission of the American military government. To execute this mission, it needed specialized personnel to gather evidence, track down suspects, and operate independently amid the ruins of the

---

[171] Memo, Intel Collection Memo no. 28, 12 Mar 1948, Folder "D 229548 Katyn Forest Murders," INSCOM, IRR, Digitized Name Files, 1939–1976, RG 319, NACP.
[172] Memo, Special Agent Thomas H. Evans, for Ofcr in Charge, Region III, CIC, 14 Apr 1948, sub: Katyn Forest Murders, Folder "D 229548 Katyn Forest Murders," INSCOM, IRR, Digitized Name Files, 1939–1976, RG 319, NACP.
[173] Rpt, Special Agent Norman T. Woods, Region III, CIC, 28 Jul 1948, Folder "D229548 V2 Katyn Forest Murders," INSCOM, IRR, Digitized Name Files, 1939–1976, RG 319, NACP.
[174] The hearings began before the House of Representatives in October 1951. For the final report, see *Final Report of the Select Committee to Conduct an Investigation and Study of the Facts, Evidence, and Circumstances of the Katyn Forest Massacre*, 82d Cong. (Washington, DC: U.S. Government Printing Office, 1952).

Third Reich. With their wartime training in investigation and interrogation techniques, and their familiarity with the German language and culture, interrogators of the Military Intelligence Service and special agents of the CIC were uniquely qualified for this task. Although many agencies contributed to the wide-ranging endeavors of denazification, war crimes investigations, and countersubversion, Army Intelligence participated in virtually all of them.

Nonetheless, from the early days of the occupation, denazification and its corollaries clashed with American efforts to rebuild Germany and to delegate administrative responsibilities to local officials. As Army officers looked for competent bureaucrats and businessmen to put the defeated German nation back on its feet, they often found that the most qualified individual for a job had political baggage. As Maj. Gen. Ernest N. Harmon, commander of the XXII Corps, explained to a group of war correspondents in June 1945, "Everybody in the area had to be affiliated with the Nazi Party or he wouldn't have been able to hold his job. This made it extremely difficult to find non-Nazis to hold important jobs."[175] Through national trials and local tribunals, backed by reams of questionnaires and the clandestine work of informants, the American military government sought to weed out the worst offenders while accommodating those whose skillsets outweighed their potential culpability under the Nazi regime. From the perspective of some Germans, this extensive vetting went too far; in the minds of others, it did not go far enough.

The nascent Cold War did not create this contradiction, but it tipped the scales in favor of a softer U.S. approach to denazification. For one, the U.S.-Soviet rivalry prompted both sides to regard Germany as a potential asset and partner, rather than a nation requiring punishment and reeducation. Moreover, the combined threat of international communism and Soviet military might commanded an ever greater share of intelligence resources and personnel who were then unavailable for other tasks. Over time, German authorities assumed greater responsibility for denazification and war crimes investigations, but their enthusiasm for these tasks remained limited.

In spite of these challenges, Army Intelligence personnel doggedly pursued their mission of dealing with Germany's Nazi past through the end of the military occupation. Occasionally, their dedication earned them the opprobrium of those who sought to tamp down or end these efforts, and unfairly denounced them as

---

[175] Interv, Maj. Gen. Ernest H. Harmon, 4 Jun 1945, Folder "Interviews 1945," XXII Corps Engr Section Instructions, Interv Rpts, Sums, and Terrain Studies, compiled 03/1945–09/1945, RG 165, NACP.

overzealous or un-American. In the span of four years, Army Intelligence personnel vetted millions of Germans, contributed to the trials of hundreds of war criminals, and investigated dozens of subversive movements. Regardless of how one evaluates the U.S. military government's attempts to deal with Germany's Nazi past, the Americans could not have carried it out without the aid of their intelligence services.

6 Intelligence Exploitation

On 12 June 1945, Lt. Col. John A. Keck, a technical intelligence officer in the European Theater's ordnance division, gave a press briefing in Paris. Keck told the assembled journalists that the Army was detaining approximately 1,200 enemy scientists who had information about a series of special weapons and inventions the Germans had been developing during the war. One of the devices was "the biggest gun in the world," a 32-inch railroad gun that supposedly had fired a 16,450-pound shell 81,000 yards against Soviet forces at Sevastopol'. The prisoners also talked about the advanced state of German rocket technology, and predicted that in the next fifteen to twenty-five years further developments in this field would enable humans to cross the Atlantic in less than an hour. Yet none of the innovations revealed by Colonel Keck compared in boldness and imagination to the Germans' plans to create a massive space-based weapon that would harness the power of the sun to wreak havoc on earth.

As Keck told the astonished journalists, the scientists had discussed plans to craft a gigantic mirror, about 3 kilometers (1.86 miles) in diameter, and lift it 5,100 miles above earth where "gravity is neutral." They would pair it with a "space station" from which astronomers would operate the outsized mirror to focus the sun's rays and direct them at a target on earth. This mechanism could be used for peaceful purposes, such as the production of steam or electric power, but it also could be used to kill humans instantly by focusing the sun's rays on its unfortunate victims. The generated heat, Keck explained, would be sufficient "to set the ocean boiling and to burn large land areas in a flash." The first nation to own and operate this enormous "space gun," Keck added, "will rule the world."[1]

The German scientists' fantastic concept captured the public imagination. A month after Keck's press conference, *Life* magazine published a feature story on "The German Space Mirror," accompanied by a series of evocative illustrations drawn by the artist James Lewicki.[2] In 1948, the British novelist George Orwell published *1984*, a dystopian vision of a future world ruled by three warring totalitarian superpowers. Like the Nazi scientists captured by the Army, Orwell's scientists sought to focus "the sun's rays through lenses suspended thousands of

---

[1] Gladwin Hill, "Nazis' Scientists Planned Sun 'Gun' 5,100 Miles Up," *New York Times*, 28 Jun 1945; "U.S. Army Reveals Secrets of Nazis' 'Screwball' Weapons," *Washington Post*, 28 Jun 1945; Clarence G. Lasby, *Project Paperclip: German Scientists and the Cold War* (New York: Athenaeum, 1975), 42–43, 49.

[2] "The German Space Mirror," *Life*, 23 Jul 1945.

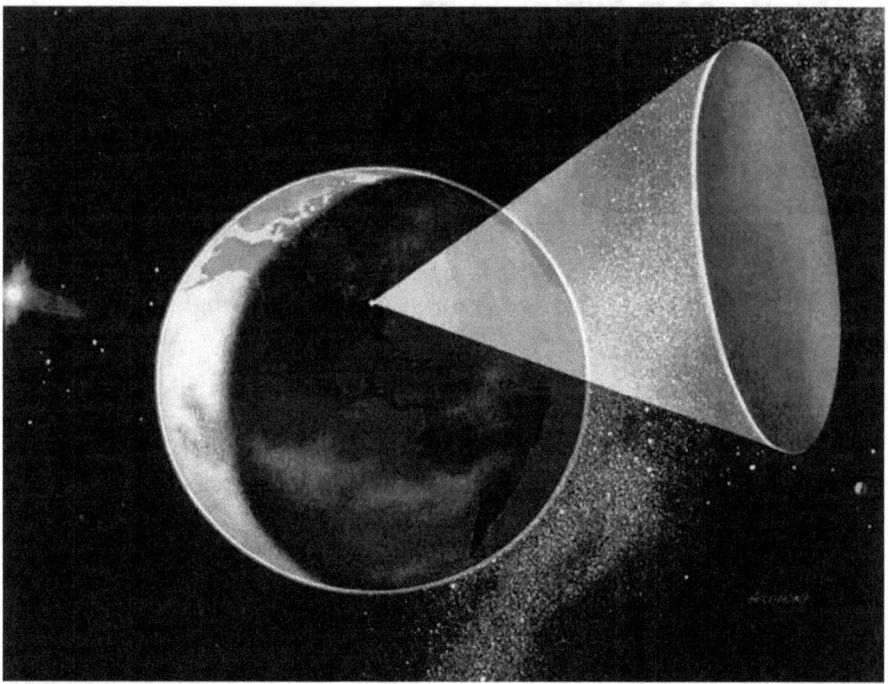

Figure 27: Artist James Lewicki's rendition of the Nazi space mirror, as seen in Life magazine, 23 July 1945. *Life magazine.*

kilometers away in space."[3] Nearly a quarter of a century later, the "space gun" became a central plot element in a James Bond movie. In *Diamonds Are Forever* (1971), the screen villain builds a space-mounted laser weapon to blackmail the world.[4]

The U.S. Army never built a "space gun," but the revelations about the captured German scientists and their plans hinted at the knowledge that the Allies might be able to gain from the defeated enemy. If the idea of harnessing the power of the sun seemed fantastic at the time, more practical German explorations in fields like rocket technology and cipher machines were believed to be easily transferable to other nations. Germany's collapse therefore offered the Allies a unique opportunity to catch up with their enemy's inventions.

---

[3] George Orwell, *1984* (New York: Signet, 1950), 194.

[4] Jeremy Black, *The Politics of James Bond: From Fleming's Novels to the Big Screen* (London: Praeger, 2001), 126. The diamond-powered space laser was a creation of the film version; it does not appear in Ian Fleming's original 1956 novel.

Wartime Intelligence Exploitation

Even before the war, the U.S. Army had been interested in foreign military developments, or "technical intelligence." However, America's entry into the conflict greatly increased the need for information on enemy weaponry. The arrival of Anglo-American forces in the Mediterranean and European Theaters offered the Allies an unprecedented opportunity to exploit the military technology developed by Germany, one of the most scientifically advanced nations in the world. In short order, a plethora of technical intelligence units and coordinating bodies, designed to gather and process information on enemy technology, sprang up across the Allied military forces. As early as 1942, the Army's Ordnance Department sent specially briefed teams to combat areas to collect enemy equipment samples and ship them to Aberdeen Proving Ground in Maryland.[5] On 5 December 1943, a combined Allied "S" or Security Force, including fifty Counter Intelligence Corps agents, accompanied the first combat troops of the Fifth Army into Rome, seizing documents, apprehending enemy agents, and arranging for the long-term exploitation of the city for intelligence purposes.[6] Meanwhile, the Army Air Forces launched Operation LUSTY (short for *Luftwaffe* Secret Technology) to capture German air force technology and personnel.[7]

A key player in this wide-ranging effort, Army Intelligence focused its operations on unconventional German war technology, such as atomic, biological, and chemical weapons, as well as rocketry. When Allied intelligence agencies received disquieting reports that the Germans were deploying secret weapons on the English Channel coast, Secretary of War Henry L. Stimson established the Crossbow Committee in the winter of 1943–1944. Led by the Army's Military Intelligence Division, the committee collected and processed all pertinent information on this issue. After the Allied invasion of Normandy and the dissolution of Crossbow in the summer of 1944, the Military Intelligence Service in Washington established a Scientific Branch. This new office put the Army's intelligence gathering activities for unconventional German weapons on a more permanent footing. The branch

---

5 Lasby, *Project Paperclip*, 18.
6 James L. Gilbert, John P. Finnegan, and Ann Bray, *In the Shadow of the Sphinx: A History of Army Counterintelligence* (Fort Belvoir, VA: U.S. Army Intelligence and Security Command, 2005), 37; Msg, Col. George S. Smith to CG, Rome Area Cmd, 17 Jun 1944, sub: Final Report of "S" Force Operations, Gen Staff Divs, G–2 Intel Target ("T") Sub-Div, Subject File, 1944–45, RG 331, NACP.
7 Dik Alan Daso, "Operation LUSTY: The U.S. Army Air Forces' Exploitation of the Luftwaffe's Secret Aeronautical Technology, 1944–45," *Aerospace Power Journal* 16, no. 1 (Spring 2002): 28–40.

included Chemical and Biological Warfare Sections, as well as a New Weapons Section for collecting intelligence on "weapons of a radically different nature."[8]

Shortly after the Allied invasion OF Italy in September 1943, Army Intelligence had taken the lead in creating the ALSOS mission, code-named after the Greek word for "grove." Under the direction of counterintelligence officer Lt. Col. Boris T. Pash, ALSOS personnel followed the advancing Allied forces in the European Theater and collect intelligence on Axis atomic bomb development, bacteriological and chemical warfare, and aeronautical research.[9] Dr. Samuel A. Goudsmit served as Pash's chief adviser on scientific matters. The Army chose Goudsmit because of his professional qualifications as a prominent nuclear physicist but also because he had not been involved in the U.S. effort to produce the atomic bomb. If captured by the enemy, the Military Intelligence Division reasoned, "no secrets of that vital nature could be pried out of him."[10]

Army Intelligence soon dispelled Allied concerns about Germany's atomic capabilities. In late 1944, the Military Intelligence Division received information from a source inside Germany that the Nazis were seven to eight years from producing an atomic bomb.[11] In the first half of 1945, the ALSOS mission confirmed this intelligence. Having searched a number of universities and research facilities across central and southwest Germany to assess the state of the German nuclear weapons program, Goudsmit recalled that "the whole German uranium set up was on a ludicrously small scale."[12] Nonetheless, the Americans secured several German nuclear scientists for their own purposes. During the war, several Nazi research institutes had moved from Berlin to the safety of the Black Forest area of southwest Germany. Here, an ALSOS team lead by Colonel Pash narrowly beat the advancing French forces to round up a group of German nuclear scientists, including Otto Hahn, Werner K. Heisenberg, and Carl Friedrich von Weizsäcker.[13] Pash's team also recovered a stash of documents hidden in a cesspool, three drums of heavy water (deuterium oxide, a form of water used to moderate nuclear reactions), and a collection of uranium ingots that constituted nearly the en-

---

8 Bruce W. Bidwell, MID History WWII, chap. 6, "Technical (Scientific) Intelligence," 23–24.
9 Vincent C. Jones, *Manhattan: The Army and the Atomic Bomb*, 2nd ed., United States Army in World War II (Washington, DC: U.S. Army Center of Military History, 1985), 287.
10 Bidwell, MID History WWII, chap. 6, "Technical (Scientific) Intelligence," 27–28.
11 Msg, Maj. Arthur Conradi Jr., Asst Mil Air Attaché, to MID, 29 Dec 1944, sub: Weapons – Research and Development, Folder "925611," Rcds of the ACoS, G–2 (Intel), Formerly Top Secret Intel Documents, 1943–59, RG 319, NACP.
12 Cited in Jones, *Manhattan*, 291.
13 Charles B. MacDonald, *The Last Offensive*, United States Army in World War II (Washington, DC: U.S. Army Center of Military History, 1973), 427–30.

tire core of the Nazi atomic pile.[14] The ALSOS mission concluded in October 1945. In the words of the official history of the Military Intelligence Division, ALSOS was "the crowning governmental achievement in connection with scientific intelligence during World War II."[15]

The Army conducted the ALSOS mission alone, but in many other areas the Americans coordinated and integrated their exploitation forces with the British. For this purpose, the Combined Chiefs of Staff created the Combined Intelligence Objectives Agency in August 1944. A binational agency, it received support from the Washington-based Technical Industrial Intelligence Committee and its British counterpart, the London-based British Intelligence Objectives Subcommittee.[16] At the direction of the deputy intelligence director of the Allied Supreme Command, Brig. Gen. Thomas J. Betts, the agency developed comprehensive target lists of technology and military research establishments across Europe. Known as "blacklist" or "black books," they were invaluable reference materials for Allied intelligence exploitation teams and operations in Europe.[17]

To carry out the Anglo-American collection effort in the European Theater, General Dwight D. Eisenhower's chief of staff, Lt. Gen. Walter B. Smith, in July 1944 ordered the establishment of special units that would seize and safeguard targets. Attached to each Army Group but independent of the combat troops, these "T" or Target Forces consisted of British and American soldiers specifically trained for intelligence exploitation missions. (Cdr. Ian L. Fleming, the creator of James Bond, directed a Royal Navy "T" Force unit and later incorporated many details of their operations into his spy thriller novels.)[18] Recognizable by the large red "T" painted on their helmets, these soldiers closely followed the combat troops, entered designated areas within a few hours after resistance had ceased, and searched and secured the targets identified by the Combined Intelligence Objectives Agency. Key intelligence locations investigated by the T Forces included post offices, power stations, factories, Nazi Party offices, and research laboratories.[19] By the end of the war, the T Forces and other intelligence exploitation units had seized several hundred tons of documents and shipped 700,000 pounds of equipment to the United States. They even dismantled an entire IG Farben synthetic fuel production plant and transferred it stateside. One contemporary expert estimated that the captured

---

14 Boris Pash, *The Alsos Mission* (New York: Charter Books, 1969), 217.
15 Bidwell, MID History WWII, chap. 6, "Technical (Scientific) Intelligence," 25.
16 John Gimbel, *Science, Technology, and Reparations: Exploitation and Plunder in Postwar Germany* (Stanford, CA: Stanford University Press, 1990), 6.
17 Sean Longden, *T-Force: The Race for Nazi War Secrets* (London: Constable, 2009), 42.
18 Longden, *T-Force*, 310.
19 Longden, *T-Force*, 37, 46; Lasby, *Project Paperclip*, 19.

material would save American industry billions of dollars and advance U.S. research by several years.[20]

In addition to technological hardware, the T Forces sought out and interrogated German scientists. A few weeks before the end of the war, Army Intelligence hit a proverbial gold mine when an exploitation team led by Maj. R. A. Fisher captured Werner Osenberg, a leading official of the German Research Council (Reichsforschungsrat), in Lindau near Göttingen.[21] Osenberg gave the Americans information about virtually every German scientist of significance. Maj. Robert B. Staver of the Army's Ordnance Department used Osenberg's data to compile an exhaustive list of human exploitation targets. The Osenberg file became the key instrument of American intelligence in their efforts to locate, interrogate, and recruit German scientists over the next decade.[22]

To process the scientists systematically, Supreme Allied Headquarters established a detention center in Paris, code-named DUSTBIN. Later, the camp moved to Kransberg Castle near Frankfurt. The interviews of German scientists quickly yielded results. As one interrogator recalled: "I think we found out more about what had been going on in the war in a few days conversations with some of these key German leaders, than all the running around and digging for drawings and models . . . could bring."[23] Only now, after talking to the captured scientists, did the Allies realize the enormous extent of Germany's war-related research programs. The interviews generated an exploitation effort that would endure for more than a decade.

The victory in Europe and the breakup of General Eisenhower's Supreme Allied Headquarters in July 1945 heralded the end of the integrated Anglo-American exploitation effort. The Combined Intelligence Objectives Agency and the Technical Industrial Intelligence Committee dissolved. In their place, the Joint Intelligence Committee of the Joint Chiefs of Staff established the Joint Intelligence Objectives Agency. Col. Ernest W. Gruhn became the first director of the new agency. In early 1946, Col. Thomas R. Ford replaced Gruhn.[24] Navy Capt. Bouquet

---

20 Lasby, *Project Paperclip*, 26.
21 Bidwell, MID History WWII, chap. 6, "Technical (Scientific) Intelligence," 38.
22 Brian E. Crim, *Our Germans: Project Paperclip and the National Security State* (Baltimore: Johns Hopkins University Press, 2018), 41. Some of the lists are preserved in Osenberg's surviving CIC file: "Osenberg Werner Ewald D004947," INSCOM, IRR, Digitized Name Files, 1939–1976, RG 319, NACP.
23 Daso, "Operation LUSTY," 32.
24 Crim, *Our Germans*, 72, 102; Annie Jacobsen, *Operation Paperclip: The Secret Intelligence Program That Brought Nazi Scientists to America* (New York: Little, Brown, 2014), 247; Linda Hunt, *Secret Agenda: The U.S. Government, Nazi Scientists and Project Paperclip, 1944–1990* (New York: St. Martin's Press, 1991), 26, 36.

N. Wev represented naval interests. The joint agency assumed overall control of the coordination and execution of U.S. exploitation efforts.

In the European Theater, the end of the war and the creation of the new military government also prompted the United States to reorganize its scientific exploitation program. Under the guidance of the designated deputy military governor of Germany, Lt. Gen. Lucius D. Clay, the Allies created the Field Information Agency, Technical (FIAT) at the end of May. The new agency absorbed the wartime T Forces as well as the DUSTBIN interrogation center.[25] With the dissolution of the Supreme Allied Headquarters, FIAT came under exclusive American control. Headed by Col. Ralph M. Osborne, the agency henceforth reported to the OMGUS Office of the Director of Intelligence.[26]

The new field agency pursued the same mission as the T Forces, albeit under peacetime conditions. "Through FIAT," General Clay wrote in a message to Washington, "we are taking from Germany all information we can obtain relative to trade processes and advanced scientific thought . . . and refashioning it to our own purpose."[27] During the first year of the occupation, the agency processed more than 23,000 reports, collected 53 tons of documents, and shipped large amounts of hardware to the United States.[28] The agency also continued the wartime interrogation program, but it proved ill-equipped at handling this aspect of the exploitation effort. Thousands of German scientists ended up at the DUSTBIN detention center at Kransberg Castle and at other camps. Subjected to repetitive interviews, and with no professional prospects, many became discouraged, slipped out of the poorly guarded enclosures, and quietly returned to their homes. Making productive use of scientists in occupied Germany required a new approach, which prompted the Army to launch a separate program to secure the United States' continued access to this valuable resource.[29]

---

25 Earl F. Ziemke, *The U.S. Army in the Occupation of Germany, 1944–1946*, Army Historical Series (Washington, DC: U.S. Army Center of Military History, 1975), 315f.; Crim, *Our Germans*, 54.
26 Rpt, History of the ODI, OMGUS, May 1945–Jun 1946, Director of Intel, Analysis and Research Br, Gen Corresp, 1945–49, RG 260, NACP.
27 Msg, Gen Lucius Clay to Gen Daniel Noce, 22 Jan 1947, sub: Use of German Technical Information, doc. 186, in *The Papers of General Lucius D. Clay, Germany 1945–1949*, vol. 1, ed. Jean Edward Smith (Bloomington: Indiana University Press, 1974), 305–06.
28 Ziemke, *U.S. Army in the Occupation of Germany*, 316. When SHAEF dissolved, the Field Information Agency, Technical (FIAT) came under USFET and the USGCC. FIAT continued its activities until September 1947.
29 Lasby, *Project Paperclip*, 76.

Project PAPERCLIP

In July 1945, the War Department approved a new exploitation plan, code-named Project OVERCAST, to bring German scientists and engineers to the United States on short-term visas to continue their research in American facilities. The Army hoped to use the results from this project in the war against Japan, but as the Army's chief of staff, General George C. Marshall noted, "some aid to our post-war research will result inevitably from such exploitation" as well.[30]

The War Department instructed General Eisenhower to "locate, screen, contract, and ship" up to 350 scientists to the United States. The theater commander, in turn, assigned the practical execution of the task to his intelligence agencies. Based principally on information from the Osenberg file, CIC special agents and other Army Intelligence personnel located and offered contracts to promising candidates. Subsequently, they transferred recruits with their families to Camp Overcast, a housing project at Landshut 40 miles northeast of Munich. From there, the scientists traveled to the United States while their families awaited their return.[31]

Several problems hobbled OVERCAST. For one, the end of the war with Japan in August 1945 deprived the program of its ostensible rationale. Also, many officers involved in the project took a long-term view of exploitation and regarded the number of 350 recruits as too low. Major Staver, who recruited German rocket scientists for the Ordnance Department, wanted to obtain that number for his organization alone. Yet many scientists hesitated to sign up for a short-term contract that did not guarantee them a professional career, and they were loath to leave their dependents behind at Camp Overcast. Security, too, became an issue when the idle chatter of family members at Camp Overcast spread word of the supposedly secret program among the local population. In the end, the Army recruited less than two hundred candidates for Project OVERCAST.[32]

As OVERCAST struggled to attract German scientists in sufficient numbers, the exploitation operations of the other Allies prompted the Americans to overhaul their own effort. Anglo-American coordination in this area proved uncomplicated, but the United States came to view both the Soviet Union and France as competitors in a race to secure the most valuable German assets. The issue of de-

---

30 Ziemke, *U.S. Army in the Occupation of Germany*, 315; Memo, G. C. Marshall, Ch of Staff, for Air Marshal D. Colyer, 3 Jul 1945, sub: Employment of German Civilian Scientists and Technicians in the United States, Folder "925245," Rcds of the ACoS, G–2 (Intel), Formerly Top Secret Intel Documents, 1943–59, RG 319, NACP.
31 Lasby, *Project Paperclip*, 88–89.
32 Ziemke, *U.S. Army in the Occupation of Germany*, 315; Lasby, *Project Paperclip*, 89.

nying German know-how to a wartime ally arose first in the summer of 1945. By the end of the war, U.S. and British forces had conquered a large swath of land in central Germany, which was earmarked for Soviet occupation. This area, including Thuringia and Saxony, housed numerous weapons installations, armament factories, and research facilities. Top Allied officers considered it "undesirable that any equipment of vital importance for the security" of the United States and Great Britain "should be left behind in the Russian zone" upon the withdrawal of Western forces. Hence, they recommended its removal.[33] In due course, the Western Allies aggressively targeted German scientists for evacuation. The British relocated 250 individuals while the Americans moved ten times that number into the future U.S. Zone. Although many scientists jumped at the chance to escape from the Soviets, the Army had to remove others by force.[34]

As the Allied occupation consolidated, the restored French government's aggressive pursuit of German scientists added urgency to American thinking about exploitation. In June 1946, Brig. Gen. Edwin L. Sibert alerted the assistant political adviser for Germany, Carmel Offie, that Army Intelligence had tracked several French attempts to recruit and remove scientists in the U.S. Zone.[35] Offie, in turn, informed his boss that "we have caught the French red-handed again stealing scientists out of our zone."[36] Eventually, General Clay broached the subject with his French counterpart, Maj. Gen. Roger Noiret, who brushed off the complaint by noting that he did "not have sufficient data to settle this question immediately."[37]

Meanwhile, Army Intelligence registered a large-scale Soviet exploitation effort. The CIC launched Operation MESA "to divulge Soviet activities in the forceful repatriation" of German scientists. In due course, special agents managed to re-

---

[33] Memo, Combined Chs of Staff, 9 Jun 1945, sub: Disposition of Secret Weapon Installations and Armament Factories in Ultimate Russian Zone of Occupation – Treatment of Underground Factories and Installations, Folder "Intelligence Objectives in Soviet Zone of Occupation in Germany," Central Decimal File 1942–45, RG 218, NACP.
[34] Longden, T-Force, 241; Klaus-Dietmar Henke, *Die amerikanische Besetzung Deutschlands* [The American occupation of Germany] (Munich: R. Oldenbourg Verlag, 2009), 749.
[35] Ltr, Edwin L. Sibert to Carmel Offie, 10 Jul 1946, Folder "Top Secret – 1946 – Amb. Murphy's Correspondence," Germany, Ofc of the U.S. Political Adviser for Germany, Berlin, Top Secret Rcds, 1944–1949, RG 84, NACP.
[36] Ltr, Carmel Offie to Robert D. Murphy, 11 Jun 1946, Folder "Top Secret – 1946 – Amb. Murphy's Correspondence," Germany, Ofc of the U.S. Political Adviser for Germany, Berlin, Top Secret Rcds, 1944–1949, RG 84, NACP.
[37] Ltr, Gen Lucius Clay to Maj. Gen. Roger Noiret, 20 Jul 1946, and Ltr, Maj. Gen. Roger Noiret to Gen Lucius Clay, 3 Jul 1946, Folder "Top Secret – 1946 – Amb. Murphy's Correspondence," Germany, Ofc of the U.S. Political Adviser for Germany, Berlin, Top Secret Rcds, 1944–1949, RG 84, NACP.

cruit from the technical bureau of the Soviet Military Administration an employee who provided insider information on Soviet exploitation efforts.[38] The CIC also discovered that the Soviet liaison mission at the IG Farben building in Frankfurt was covertly recruiting scientists in the U.S. Zone. In one case, the Soviets offered a jet-propulsion engineer "good food, good pay, and good living conditions" for a three-year contract in the Soviet Union.[39] Army Intelligence also received numerous reports about large-scale arrests of German scientists in the Soviet Zone and their shipment to the USSR.[40]

Partly in response to Soviet exploitation efforts, in March 1946 the War Department merged Project OVERCAST with a similar civilian-managed endeavor to form a larger and more ambitious exploitation program, code-named PAPERCLIP. The name derived from the habit of Army officers attaching paperclips to the folders of scientists they wished to recruit.[41] The new project sanctioned the recruitment of up to a thousand German and Austrian scientists, offering them long-term contracts in the United States and allowing them to bring their families. The project fell under the authority of the Joint Intelligence Committee of the Joint Chiefs of Staff, and the Joint Intelligence Objectives Agency directed the program from Washington.[42] In the European Theater, the Army's intelligence agencies continued to locate, vet, recruit, and transfer suitable candidates to collection points in Germany and onward to the United States.[43]

Whereas OVERCAST had attempted to recruit scientists purely on the basis of merit, the Joint Chiefs of Staff included a new provision in the directive for Project PAPERCLIP, making the denial of scientists "to a foreign power" an additional selection criteria.[44] The term "foreign power" applied to France and especially to

---

38 Draft ltr, Lt. Col. Dale M. Garvey, to Ch, CIC, n.d. [mid-1946], sub: Soviet Liaison Mission at Headquarters, USFET, Folder "Soviet Repatriation Mission Frankfurt, FRG ZF 010111," INSCOM, IRR, Impersonal Name Files, 1939–1976, RG 319, NACP; Msg, Lt. Col. W. R. Reinford, Intel Div, HQ, EUCOM, to Director of Intel, Washington, 18 Jun 1948, sub: Medjeslav Gudakowsky, Folder "926604",Rcds of the ACoS, G–2 (Intel), Formerly Top Secret Intel Documents, RG 319, NACP.
39 Draft ltr, Garvey to Ch, CIC, n.d. [mid-1946], sub: Soviet Liaison Mission at Headquarters, USFET.
40 See, for example, Draft ltr, Garvey to Ch, CIC, n.d. [1946], sub: Soviet Liaison Mission at Headquarters, USFET.
41 John Gimbel, "German Scientists, United States Denazification Policy, and the Paperclip Conspiracy," *International History Review* 12, no. 3 (Aug 1990), 448; Lasby, *Project Paperclip*, 155; Hunt, *Secret Agenda*, 115.
42 Bruce W. Bidwell, MID History Cold War, chap. 9, "Conclusions," 10.
43 Ofc of the Ch Historian, EUCOM, *The Second Year of the Occupation*, vol. 6, Occupation Forces in Europe Series, 1946–1947 (Frankfurt: Office of the Chief Historian, EUCOM, 1947), 8.
44 Memo, Maj. Gen. W. A. Burress, ACofS, G–2, 28 Oct 1946, sub: Surveillance of Scientists, Folder "XE 065587 Project 'Paperclip' Folder 1 of 6," INSCOM, IRR, Impersonal Files, RG 319, NACP.

the Soviet Union. In an internal memorandum, the Joint Intelligence Committee spelled out explicitly the scientific fields the Americans should deny to Moscow. They included nuclear physics, chemical and biological warfare, and guided missiles.[45] In 1949, the Joint Intelligence Objectives Agency even suggested "the use of physical restraint" of key scientists "to prevent them from leaving the US-UK Zones."[46] In any event, coercion proved unnecessary, as many German scientists wanted to move to the United States and work for the Americans. As one of them summed up the view of many of his colleagues in postwar Germany: "We despised the French, we were afraid of the Russians and we didn't think the British could afford us. That left the Americans."[47]

Although PAPERCLIP targeted scientists from a wide range of fields, the Army had a particular interest in acquiring German rocket technology, including the V–1 flying bomb and the V–2 supersonic rocket. In 1944, Col. Gervais W. Trichel of the Army Ordnance Department's Rocket Branch instructed Col. Holger N. Toftoy, chief of the Army Ordnance Technical Intelligence teams assigned to Europe, to launch "Special Mission V–2," a plan to obtain components of one hundred rockets. The plan came to fruition in April 1945 when the First Army liberated Nordhausen, an underground facility where the Nazis used enslaved foreign laborers to manufacture V–2 rockets. T Forces secured the site. The CIC captured Albin Sawatzki, a leading V–2 scientist, and transferred him to an Army technical intelligence unit for further interrogation.[48] On 2 May, Wernher von Braun, the inventor of the V–2, and several of his team members surrendered to soldiers of the 44th Infantry Division in Austria.[49]

Von Braun was arguably the biggest prize among the surviving German scientists. The Army was eager to bring him and his team to the United States and put them to work on developing guided missiles for the military. Before the Army could offer von Braun and his colleagues a contract, however, the scientists had to pass a background check. A Project PAPERCLIP directive mandated specifically that individuals "with Nazi or militaristic records" be excluded from

---

45 Memo, Joint Intel Committee, 12 Jul 1946, sub: Soviet Exploitation of German and Austrian Scientists and Technicians, Folder "ABC 476.1 (7 Oct 43) Sec 1-C," American-British Conversations Corresp Relating to Planning and Combat Opns 1940–1948, RG 165, NACP.
46 Msg, Lt. Gen. Clarence R. Huebner to Ch of Staff, Joint Intel Objectives Agency (JIOA), 15 Feb 1949, Folder "Top Secret Out Jan 1949 to 30 June 1949 Book III," EUCOM, Ofc of the Ch of Staff, Sec of the Gen Staff, Msg Control Center, Outgoing Msgs, top secret section, 1948–1951, RG 549, NACP.
47 Thomas O'Toole, "W. R. Dornberg Dies, German Rocket Expert," *Washington Post*, 2 Jul 1980.
48 Maj. Ann Bray et al., ed., *The History of the Counter Intelligence Corps*, vol. 20, *Germany Overrun, Part I* (Fort Holabird, MD: U.S. Army Intelligence Center, 1959), 44.
49 Lasby, *Project Paperclip*, 38–40.

recruitment.⁵⁰ The Joint Intelligence Objectives Agency exercised overall supervision of the screening process. In the European Theater, the responsibility fell to the Intelligence Division and the CIC.⁵¹

The famed German rocket scientist and his team did not make a good first impression on the Americans. The first CIC agent to interview von Braun, 2d Lt. Walter Jessel, found him deceptive and opportunistic, and in his report he warned against bringing von Braun to the United States. The CIC came down even more harshly against some of von Braun's colleagues. Special agents described von Braun's brother Magnus, also a rocket scientist, as a "dangerous German Nazi" who is "a worse threat to security than a half dozen discredited SS generals." A report on another team member, Arthur Rudolph, described him as "100% Nazi, dangerous type, security threat . . . !! Suggest internment." A third associate, Georg J. Rickhey, "was [considered] a strong Nazi" who reportedly had instigated the hanging of twelve foreign laborers at Nordhausen.⁵² Despite these alarming assessments, the Army offered von Braun and his team contracts to work in the United States. The Army flew the men to New Castle Airport near Wilmington, Delaware, in September 1945 without putting them through the normal visa application process or having them go through standard denazification procedures. Von Braun and several of his colleagues, along with their families, then remained in the United States and continued to work on ballistic missile technology for the U.S. government. Eventually, von Braun and several other members of the original V–2 rocket team became U.S. citizens.⁵³

Not every PAPERCLIP candidate fared as smoothly as the rocket men. In 1947, for example, the Joint Intelligence Objectives Agency requested that the intelligence division in Frankfurt make inquiries regarding one of Europe's top experts in shale oil, the Austrian geologist, paleontologist, and petrochemical scientist Karl Krejci-Graf. Intelligence personnel duly located Krejci-Graf in Kleegarten, a small town in Bavaria, but cautioned that he "is considered an ardent Nazi having been a Hauptsturm Fuehrer [captain] in the SS." Army Intelligence barred him from leaving Kleegarten and advised the joint agency that "his entry into the United States would be considered a security threat." Krejci-Graf remained in Europe.⁵⁴

---

50 Memo, Dean Acheson to President Harry S. Truman, 30 Aug 1946, sub: Exploitation of German and Austrian Specialists in the United States, Folder "ABC 471.6 (7 Oct 43) Sec 1-D," ABC File, RG 165, NACP.
51 Ofc of the Ch Historian, EUCOM, *The Second Year of the Occupation*, 6:10–11.
52 Crim, *Our Germans*, 36, 40, 44–47. See also Jessel's autobiography, *Class of '31: A German-Jewish Émigré's Journey Across Defeated Germany* (Brookline, MA: Academic Studies Press, 2017).
53 Lasby, *Project Paperclip*, 88; Hunt, *Secret Agenda*, 56.
54 Msg, Intel Div, EUCOM, to War Department, Intel Div, for JIOA, 14 Apr 1947, Folder "1. Fr: 'S' Germany 1000–5999 1-1-47–6-30-47," ACoS, G–2 (Intel), "Top Secret" Incoming and Outgoing Cables. 1942–52, RG 319, NACP.

But time and again, the military's desire to harness German scientific thought overrode concerns regarding the problematic background of potential recruits. When State Department officials raised objections to granting visas to certain scientists, Captain Wev of the Joint Intelligence Objectives Agency complained they were "beating a dead Nazi horse." He advocated for a speedier process that disregarded Nazi affiliations as a factor in the screening process.[55] In several instances, the Joint Intelligence Objectives Agency altered security evaluations, as happened in the case of Arthur Rudolph. The original military government background review categorized him as "an ardent Nazi," but the joint agency reversed this assessment simply by inserting the word "not" before "an." Rudolph received a PAPERCLIP contract.[56]

In the United States, the immigration of former Nazis so soon after the end of the war ignited a controversy. When the War Department informed the public about Project PAPERCLIP in November 1946, forty distinguished individuals, including Albert Einstein, expressed their "profound concern" about the program in an open letter to President Harry S. Truman. The Army defended the practice by highlighting the exigencies of the Cold War. "The fact is, of course, that a great many German scientists had been taken by the Russians, and their protest makes no mention of this fact," argued Secretary of War Robert P. Patterson in response to a complaint by the Federation of American Scientists.[57] In the case of Georg Rickhey, von Braun's colleague in V–1 and V–2 rocket production, public pressure forced the Army to release him to Germany, where he faced trial for war crimes at Dachau in 1947. Although Rickhey was acquitted for lack of evidence, he did not return to the United States.[58]

Army Intelligence played an ambivalent role in the controversy over the importation of German scientists. In Germany, CIC agents and other military government personnel carefully screened recruits and in several cases raised red flags,

---

55 Memo, Capt. Bosquet N. Wev for Maj. Gen. Stephen J. Chamberlin, 2 Jul 1947, sub: Exploitation of German and Austrian Scientists and Technicians in Science and Technology in the United States, Folder "1443/02 400.112 Research/014.32 Undated (14 May 45)," Army-Intel Decimal File 1941–1948, RG 319, NACP.
56 Crim, *Our Germans*, 46–47.
57 Lasby, *Project Paperclip*, 193, 204.
58 "Mass Trial in Germany: Engineer Taken to U.S. Heads 19 Nordhausen Defendants," *New York Times*, 7 Aug 1947; Michael Löffelsender, "'A particularly unique role among concentration camps.' Der Dachauer Dora-Prozess 1947," in *Zwangsarbeit im Nationalsozialismus und die Rolle der Justiz. Täterschaft, Nachkriegsprozesse und die Auseinandersetzung um Entschädigungsleistungen* [Forced labor under National Socialism and the role of justice: Culpability, post-war processes and the dispute over compensation payments], ed. Helmut Kramer, Karsten Uhl, and Jens-Christian Wagner (Nordhausen: Nordhausen Fachhochschule, 2007), 162–64.

as they had with Rickhey. Eager to exploit German knowledge for the benefit of the military, however, intelligence chiefs often dismissed these warnings. The director of intelligence in Berlin, Maj. Gen. Robert L. Walsh, advocated for the transfer of German technical personnel to the United States even if the individuals in question had close ties to the Third Reich.[59] Likewise, the director of the Intelligence Division in Washington, Maj. Gen. Stephen J. Chamberlin, pushed the State Department to grant visas for controversial PAPERCLIP recruits.[60] If the perspectives of personnel at the bottom and at the top of the Army Intelligence pyramid appeared diametrically opposed, this contradiction reflected overall American policy toward exploitation.

By early 1948, 475 PAPERCLIP scientists had entered the United States. Most stayed permanently and assumed U.S. citizenship.[61] The program continued for several years, and recruitment declined only in the 1950s when improved employment opportunities in Germany made it more viable for scientists to remain in their home country. Many "Paperclippers" made valuable contributions to American science and technology. Von Braun and his team developed the Jupiter-C missile, which launched the first Western satellite into space in 1958, and the Apollo booster rocket, which put the first human on the moon in 1969.[62] "Perhaps some mistakes were made," one Army Intelligence officer noted in retrospect, "but . . . we knew that these people were invaluable to us." With some exaggeration, he added, "Just think what we have from their research—all our satellites, jet aircraft, rockets, almost everything else."[63]

The U.S. government's "mistakes" in recruiting former Nazis, however, continued to undercut the official success story of Project PAPERCLIP. In 1982, for example, a member of von Braun's original V–2 team, Arthur Rudolph, had to renounce his U.S. citizenship and return to Germany after the Department of Justice confronted him with evidence that he had availed himself of slave labor at Nordhausen.[64] The communist press was only too happy to exploit the PAPERCLIP controversy for its decades-long propaganda campaign, portraying the West as morally compromised for its apparent eagerness to embrace figures from Germany's Nazi past. The official newspaper of the East German communist party, *Neues Deutschland*, disparaged PAPERCLIP recruits as a "technological Foreign Legion" and denounced Rudolph

---

59 Hunt, *Secret Agenda*, 101.
60 Jacobsen, *Operation Paperclip*, 315–16.
61 Lasby, *Paperclip*, 270.
62 J. Y. Smith, "Dr. Wernher von Braun, 65, Dies," *Washington Post*, 18 Jun 1977.
63 Hunt, *Secret Agenda*, 110.
64 Jacobsen, *Operation Paperclip*, 428.

as a "fascist desk murderer" (*faschistischer Schreibtischmörder*).[65] Project PAPERCLIP thus constituted a double-edged sword. Although the program yielded tangible results, it also ignited an intense debate over the ethics of intelligence exploitation and handed America's Cold War antagonists a powerful propaganda weapon.

The Target Intelligence Committee

Rocket technology was the principal focus of the PAPERCLIP recruitment efforts. In addition, Army Intelligence also managed a specialized program aimed at exploiting German signals intelligence. Both the British and the American signals intelligence services sought to learn more about the German achievements in this arena. In the summer of 1944, Col. George A. Bicher, the director of the U.S. Army's Signal Intelligence Division at Bletchley Park, suggested that the U.S. Navy and the British join forces with his own organization to exploit German cryptologic organizations and personnel. Two months after D-Day, Army chief of staff General Marshall formally instructed General Eisenhower to form an American team to coordinate efforts with the British and send him a list of specific subjects of inquiry.[66] In October, the Army, the Navy, and the British intelligence community formally established the Target Intelligence Committee, or TICOM, to coordinate and supervise their exploitation efforts in this field.[67]

The committee originally planned an airdrop on Berlin. In November 1944, Supreme Allied Headquarters completed ECLIPSE, an operations plan contingent on a sudden collapse of Nazi Germany. The First Allied Airborne Army would seize an airhead in the city and paratroopers would secure important signals intelligence facilities in the city.[68] Cryptanalytic specialists from Bletchley Park would then move

---

65 "Westdeutsche Monopole über ihren wissenschaftlich-technischen Rückstand alarmiert" [West German monopolies alarmed about their scientific-technical backwardness], *Neues Deutschland*, 26 Feb 1969; "'New York Times' stellt betreten fest: Faschistischer Schreibtischmörder diente als Raketenspezialist dem Pentagon" [New York Times embarrassed: Fascist "desk murderer" served as a missile specialist in the Pentagon], *Neues Deutschland*, 27 Oct 1984.
66 Msg, Gen. George C. Marshall to Gen. Dwight D. Eisenhower, 7 Aug 1944, in ASA, "European Axis Signal Intelligence in World War II as Revealed by 'TICOM' Investigations and by other Prisoner of War Interrogations and Captured Material, Principally German," 9 vols. (ASA, 1 May 1946), vol. 8, Miscellaneous, 55, National Security Agency (NSA) Online Archive, https://www.nsa.gov.
67 ASA, "European Axis Signal Intelligence in World War II," vol. 1, Synopsis, 2, NSA Online Archive, https://www.nsa.gov.
68 William Stivers and Donald A. Carter, *The City Becomes a Symbol. The U.S. Army in the Occupation of Berlin, 1945–1949*, U.S. Army in the Cold War (Washington, DC: U.S. Army Center of Military History, 2017), 26.

in, photograph documents, seize technical equipment, and round up German personnel. Thereafter, one author mused, "a flying tank column was supposed to be smashing its way into the city and carry everybody westward into the sunset." However, the Germans kept on fighting, and so Army planners shelved ECLIPSE. For a time, American and British TICOM members feared they would have to conduct the airdrop and their exfiltration without the support of major Allied forces. "Oh, my gosh," a team member thought. "Why me?"[69]

Toward the end of the war, the Nazis dispersed their signals intelligence headquarters from Berlin to northern and southern Germany where they would be less exposed to Allied bombing and to the advancing Red Army. Consequently, the Target Intelligence Committee dropped the idea of an advance mission to Berlin. Instead, the Allies in March 1945 activated six U.S.-British teams who were to follow the advancing Allied armies into Germany and secure the enemy's signals intelligence technology and personnel (Map 1).[70] Their mission was threefold: first, to learn about the extent of the German cryptanalytic effort against Great Britain and the United States; second, to prevent the Germans from destroying their equipment or letting it fall into the wrong hands; and third, to uncover items of signals intelligence value for the war against Japan.[71]

Despite its designation, Team 6 was the first team activated, beginning its mission in mid-April. Under the command of a Royal Navy officer, the team included fifteen U.S. and British target reporting officers who had completed a two-month course on recognition of enemy signals intelligence material. Equipped with a Dodge six-wheel personnel carrier, a jeep, and two British vehicles, the team linked up with a T Force at Venlo, Netherlands. From there, they followed the advance of the British 21st Army Group into northern Germany. On 19 May, they reached Flensburg, the seat of the last Nazi government under Grand Admiral Karl Dönitz. In the course of their operations, Team 6 apprehended several cryptologists of the German Army High Command signals intelligence service (*Oberkommando der Wehrmacht Chiffrierabteilung; OKW/Chi*). The arrestees included the service's commanding officer and his deputy, Col. Hugo Kettler and Lt. Col. Werner Mettig, as well two key scientists, Dr. Erich Hüttenhain and his assis-

---

[69] Thomas Parrish, *The American Codebreakers: The U.S. Role in Ultra* (Chelsea, MI: Scarborough House, 1991), 272.
[70] ASA, "European Axis Signal Intelligence in World War II," 1:3.
[71] James Bamford, *Body of Secrets: Anatomy of the Ultra-Secret National Security Agency* (New York: Anchor Books, 2002), 9.

tant Dr. Walter E. Fricke. Across northern Germany and in Flensburg, Team 6 secured a wealth of German naval signals intelligence equipment.[72]

Meanwhile, a second team embarked on a mission in the future Soviet zone of occupation. On 13 April, a U.S. military government officer, 2d Lt. Alfred G. Fenn, inspected a baroque castle in the village of Burgscheidungen, 30 miles north of the city of Jena. There, he discovered the castle housed the personnel and equipment of the cryptographic section of the German foreign office. Fenn warned the Germans that any destruction of files or equipment would be punished by death, and he alerted his superiors who sent forces to secure the site. He also phoned Colonel Bicher at Bletchley Park, who immediately dispatched a team of signals intelligence experts under Lt. Col. Paul E. Neff of the Signal Intelligence Division and Lt. Col. Geoffrey H. Evans of the British Army's Intelligence Corps. This team, known as Team 3, arrived at Burgscheidungen on 27 April and began securing equipment and interviewing the Germans. On 8 May, the Allied soldiers celebrated V-E Day by raiding the castle owner's wine cellar, "with additional toasts and additional fireworks with materials available."[73]

Team 3 flew out valuable documents and cryptomaterial, and destroyed the remainder. When interrogating the Germans, team members sought to conceal their own identities by assuming cover names. Unaccustomed to this type of cloak-and-dagger routine, however, they often slipped, "and it is likely that the Germans knew our right names at all times and were probably deriving a little quiet amusement from the attempt to conceal them." Some of the German officials provided information only reluctantly, but most did so freely. The interrogators surmised that the imminent arrival of the Red Army motivated many of the Germans to cooperate with their captors.

Absorbed by their mission, the Allied soldiers gave little thought to the fact that the Soviets would soon assume control of the castle and might discover traces of the Anglo-American exploitation effort. Higher authorities therefore informed them of "the necessity of screening the pinch from the Russians." To deprive the Soviets of witnesses to their activities, the team decided to evacuate almost all civilians from the castle and from the village of Zschepplin in Saxony to Marburg in the U.S. Zone. "The standard used was a rough and ready one to some extent," their final report conceded, noting that "wives were taken but the mistress of one of those evacuated to England was left in Zschepplin."[74]

---

72 Rpt, Target Intel Committee (TICOM), 5 Sep 1945, "Narrative and Report of Proceedings of TICOM Team 6, 11th April–6th July 1945," 5 Sep 1945, Historians' Source Files Relating to Target Intel Committee (TICOM), 1944–1946, RG 457, NACP.
73 Rpt, TICOM, 8 Jun 1945, Final Report of TICOM Team 3 on exploitation of Burgscheidungen, Archival and Historian's Source Files, 1809 [sic]–1994, RG 457, NACP.
74 Rpt, TICOM, 8 Jun 1945, Final Report of TICOM Team 3 on exploitation of Burgscheidungen,.

Figure 28: German prisoners of war in Zell prepare a replica of a Soviet cipher machine (Fish) for shipment, June 1945. 1st Lt. Paul K. Whitaker.

Team 2 ventured even further afield. At the end of the war, the V Corps of General George S. Patton Jr.'s Third Army briefly moved into western Czechoslovakia and liberated the city of Pilsen.[75] Here, the Americans captured 350 personnel of a signals intelligence unit of the *Wehrmacht*'s *Heeresgruppe Mitte* (*Army Group Center*), which had operated in the Soviet Union. The prisoners were of particular interest to the Western Allies because they had worked on Soviet ciphers. On 23 May, members of Team 2 arrived in Pilsen to start screening and interrogating the Germans and to begin preparations for their transportation to Camp King in Oberursel. By 2 June, they had transferred all prisoners. Despite the logistical challenges of feeding and housing the prisoners along the way, the team managed to keep the Germans "in a cheerful and consequently informed mood. They found the situation ausgezeichnet [excellent] and produced at Oberursel the bulk of the documents which formed the basis for later interrogations."[76]

---

75 MacDonald, *Last Offensive*, 466.
76 Rpt, TICOM, 5 Jul 1945, Final Report of TICOM Team 2, Archival and Historian's Source Files, 1809 [*sic*]–1994, RG 457, NACP.

The remaining teams struck gold in southern Bavaria, where the Germans had relocated some of their headquarters organizations toward the end of the war. In the Zell area, Team 1 recovered several intact models of the Siemens T–52 Geheimschreiber, a teleprinter cipher machine used by the German army. Near Berchtesgaden on the Austrian border, a U.S. Army officer handed over a captured convoy with models of another high-level German cipher machine, the Lorenz SZ–42. The Allies also discovered the remnants of the Nazi Party's cryptologic service (*Forschungsamt*) in Bavaria and picked up two former members.[77]

The Third Army headquarters at Bad Aibling included a prisoner-of-war enclosure where the Americans detained personnel of the German supreme army command's signal intelligence service.[78] Team 1 interviewed the Germans and discovered that they were specialists in the interception of Soviet radioteleprinter traffic. On 22 May, the prisoners led the team to a spot in nearby Rosenheim where they unearthed 7.5 tons of equipment, which turned out to be parts of a machine used to intercept high-level Soviet radio communications. The Germans reassembled the device and, according to the recollections of one TICOM member, proceeded to intercept "Russian traffic right while we were there."[79] Team 1 then packed up the material and left Rosenheim with four diesel trucks, the captured equipment, and twenty-eight prisoners.[80]

Though they had succeeded in gaining some equipment and information, the Allies still sought the crown jewels of the German signals intelligence apparatus: the records of the army high command's cryptanalytic organization. Its commander, Colonel Kettler, told his interrogators that the Germans had evacuated the archives of his service to Schliersee, a picturesque village in southern Bavaria by a lake of the same name. Under U.S. Navy Lt. Cdr. Howard H. Campaigne, TICOM Team 4 set out to retrieve the material. After having searched all the public buildings in vain, the Allies suspected that the Germans had dumped the archives in the lake. Campaigne recommended a systematic search of the lake, but the endeavor posed major logistical challenges, and Army authorities did not execute his proposal at the time. On 30 June, Campaigne and his men moved on to other targets.[81]

---

77 Randy Rezabek, "TICOM and the Search for OKW/*Chi*," *Cryptologia* 37, no. 2 (Apr 2013), 144.
78 Patricia Kollander with John O'Sullivan, *"I Must Be a Part of This War": A German American's Fight Against Hitler and Nazism* (New York: Fordham University Press, 2005), 130; Rpt, TICOM, 16 Jun 1945, Final Report of TICOM Team 1, 16 Jun 1945, Archival and Historian's Source Files, 1809 [sic]–1994, RG 457, NACP.
79 Parrish, *American Codebreakers*, 283.
80 Rpt, TICOM, 16 Jun 1945, Final Report of TICOM Team 1.
81 Interv, Robert D. Farley with Dr. Howard Campaigne, 29 Jun 1983, online archive, National Security Agency; Rezabek, "TICOM and the Search for OKW/*Chi*," 143, 146, 147.

The archives would have been lost entirely had it not been for a personal tragedy. On 17 July 1945, Pfc. Gerald E. Storie drowned in the Schliersee.[82] While dragging for the body, Army officials retrieved a waterproof box containing some of the documents Commander Campaigne's team had been looking for. Local authorities alerted TICOM headquarters, which then arranged for a team—now designated Team 5—of Army engineers and divers to resume the search. Eventually, the Army recovered nineteen boxes of German signals intelligence documents and transferred them to Bletchley Park for evaluation.[83]

The Americans rarely encountered deception efforts when interviewing German signals intelligence personnel. Most interviewees realized the war was over and shared information freely, at times even enthusiastically. Wilhelm F. Flicke, a signals intelligence officer of the German army supreme command, served at a German intercept station in the small town of Lauf in Bavaria at the end of the war. When the Americans captured Lauf, they promptly appointed Flicke *Landrat* (county head). Over the ensuing years, Flicke cooperated "whole-heartedly" with the Army Security Agency, produced numerous reports on his wartime work, and became "the largest single contributor to the TICOM files."[84] Eventually, the intercept station at Lauf would resume its duties under Flicke, who now worked for the so-called Gehlen Organization, West Germany's U.S.-financed protointelligence agency.[85]

ASA personnel questioned the Germans extensively about their cryptanalytic attacks on Allied systems. The interviewees confirmed that the Germans had failed to break the Army's principal cipher machine, the SIGABA.[86] One prisoner noted that the Germans had envisaged using submarines to tap the long-distance cables between Great Britain and North America off the Irish coast but apparently never enacted the plan.[87] Nonetheless, the interrogations revealed that German signals intelligence had succeeded in breaking several U.S. diplomatic codes

---

82 Rpt of Burial, Pfc. Gerald E. Storie, 31 Jul 1945, Historians Files, CMH.
83 Interv, Farley with Campaigne, 29 Jun 1983; Rezabek, "TICOM and the Search for OKW/*Chi*," 147–48.
84 Note, Armed Forces Security Agency, Jul 1951, sub: biographical note: Wilhelm F. Flicke, Folder "Critical Reflection of the German Intercept Service in WWII," Historians' Source Files Relating to TICOM, 1944–1946, RG 457, NACP.
85 Erich Schmidt-Eenboom, "The Bundesnachrichtendienst, the Bundeswehr and Sigint in the Cold War and After," *Intelligence and National Security* 16, no. 1 (2001), 132; Rezabek, "TICOM and the Search for OKW/*Chi*," 149n16.
86 Rezabek, "TICOM and the Search for OKW/*Chi*," 152.
87 Rpt, TICOM, interrogation of Oberpostrat Kurt Vetterlein (18 Dec 1945), 4 Feb 1946, Folder "Attempted Tapping of Trans-Atlantic Cable," Historians' Source Files Relating to TICOM Interrogation Rpts, 1945–1945 [sic], RG 457, NACP.

and were reading messages between the State Department and the American legations in Cairo, Egypt, and Berne, Switzerland.[88] A German intercept station in the Netherlands had monitored AT&T's New York–London circuit and recorded thirty to sixty phone conversations per day, including calls between President Franklin D. Roosevelt and Prime Minister Winston Churchill. Though the Germans could not break the SIGABA, they had managed to decipher about 10 percent of the traffic generated in the European Theater by the Army's portable cipher machine, the M–209.[89]

The breaking of the German Enigma had been the greatest signals intelligence coup of the war, and TICOM interrogators were eager to find out whether the Germans had ever suspected the machine's vulnerability. The Germans told them that they knew a massive cryptanalytic effort might break the Enigma, but they dismissed this possibility as purely theoretical.[90] The cryptanalyst Hüttenhain told his captors haughtily, "The English of course are notoriously stupid."[91] "The Enigma," he declared categorically, "cannot be solved."[92] For good reason, the TICOM interrogators did not tell him and his colleagues otherwise. In 1947, the Army Security Agency, Europe, discreetly researched the contemporary activities of German companies that had built Enigma machines during the war to determine if the device was still in production and in operation.[93] As it turned out, it was. In the 1950s, the East German police used the Enigma for internal communications. Because Anglo-American signals intelligence had kept their wartime breakthrough a secret from Germans and Soviets alike, the Americans could now decipher the communications of the unsuspecting East Germans.[94]

---

88 Randy Rezabek, "TICOM: The Last Great Secret of World War II," *Intelligence and National Security* 27, no. 4 (2012), 519; Interrogation Rpt, Dr. Erich Huettenhain, 10 Jun 1945, Folder "Interrogation of Dr. Huettenhain and Dr. Fricke at Flensburg 21 May 1945," Historians' Source Files Relating to TICOM Interrogation Rpts, 1945–1945 [sic], RG 457, NACP; Interrogation Rpt, Liselotte Gebert of OKW/Chi, 12 Feb 1946, Historians' Source Files Relating to TICOM Interrogation Rpts, 1945–1945 [sic], RG 457, NACP; Msg, Maj. Earl S. Browning, Jr., to CO, Region IV, CIC, 1 Jul 1949, sub: Oswin Fritz Menzer, Folder "Menzer, Fritz Oswin 261111," INSCOM, IRR, Digitized Name Files, RG 319, NACP.
89 Rezabek, "TICOM: The Last Great Secret," 519, 526.
90 Bamford, *Body of Secrets*, 17.
91 Rezabek, "TICOM and the Search for OKW/*Chi*," 152.
92 Interrogation Rpt, Huettenhain, 10 Jun 1945.
93 Msg, DDI, EUCOM, to DDI, OMGUS, 20 Aug 1947, sub: Location of Former German Firms (Enigma-Cipher-Device), Folder "Former German Enigma Cypher Firms D190213," INSCOM, IRR, Impersonal Name Files, RG 319, NACP.
94 Stephen Budiansky, *Code Warriors: NSA's Codebreakers and the Secret Intelligence War against the Soviet Union* (New York: Penguin Random House, 2016), 225.

By the end of 1945, TICOM teams had interrogated scores of key German signals intelligence personnel and captured more than 4,000 separate documents weighing over five tons. Using this information, the ASA within a few months produced nine volumes on the history of European Axis signal intelligence in World War II. Originally designated "Top Secret Cream," this publication remained classified for over half a century.[95] TICOM's initial mission had been accomplished, and the breakup of the Supreme Allied Headquarters earlier in the summer heralded the winding-down of other Anglo-American wartime collaboration efforts. The binational TICOM organization officially dissolved on 25 November 1945.[96] The American signals intelligence exploitation effort, however, continued unabated.

The ASAE took over the U.S. element of TICOM and directed it until 1949.[97] Army interrogators continued to process signals intelligence personnel. At first, they transferred persons of interest to the DUSTBIN detention center at Kransberg Castle for this purpose. After the dissolution of the original TICOM organization in late 1945, they interviewed German signals intelligence personnel at Camp King.[98] One of their prize catches was Wilhelm Fenner, a key figure in the establishment of the *Wehrmacht*'s cipher bureau. At the camp's Alaska House, he provided his interrogators with details about his career and the inner workings of his former employer. ASAE produced reports based on his information until 1950.[99]

When the Allies initially conceived the creation of TICOM, they had not considered Soviet ciphers as a target. But in the context of rising tensions between the erstwhile allies, this aspect assumed critical importance. During the war, the Germans had directed much of their signals intelligence effort toward the eastern front, and TICOM officers learned a great deal about Soviet codes and ciphers from captured German documents and personnel. The Germans had mostly broken low-level ciphers, but the materiel and individuals captured at Rosenheim provided TICOM with insights into the workings of high-level Soviet encryptions as well. "Through TICOM," a U.S. cryptanalyst recalled, "I had my first contact with the Soviet SIGINT [signals intelligence] problem when we interrogated members of the

---

[95] Rezabek, "TICOM and the Search for OKW/*Chi*," 151n18. "Cream," in this context, is a specific classification level.
[96] Rezabek, "TICOM and the Search for OKW/*Chi*," 149, 151.
[97] Thomas Boghardt, "Semper Vigilis: The U.S. Army Security Agency in Early Cold War Germany," *Army History* 106 (Winter 2018), 14; Ltr, Col. George A. Bicher, Signal Corps, to Chairman, TICOM, Government Communications HQ (GCHQ), 1 Aug 1945, Folder "TICOM administrative correspondence," Archival and Historian's Source Files, 1809–1994, RG 457, NACP.
[98] Boghardt, "Semper Vigilis," 14.
[99] ASA, "Post War Transition Period: The Army Security Agency 1945–1948" (Washington, DC: Army Security Agency, 1952), 110.

several SIGINT organizations of the Third Reich."[100] When the ASA embarked on a joint effort (BOURBON) with the Navy and the British in August 1945 to intercept and decrypt Soviet communications, the German TICOM material proved valuable to their effort.[101]

For the remainder of the military occupation, the ASAE focused its TICOM activities on the Soviet cipher problem. In October 1946, the head of the Berlin bureau of the Associated Press, Louis P. Lochner, informed the American authorities that he had heard about a stash of German signals intelligence documents buried in the Austrian town of Glasenbach. The material supposedly included "name keys and code methods employed by the USSR" as well as a "complete file of economic intelligence reports on the USSR." Within a few weeks, an Army Intelligence officer from Austria tracked down Rudolf Hentze, a German signals intelligence veteran then teaching at a school in Kassel. In December, Hentze helped the Americans identify the exact location of the buried documents in Glasenbach. ASAE headquarters assumed control of the material.[102]

The postwar odyssey of another German signals intelligence veteran pitted the Americans directly against the Soviets. During the war, the Allies had developed an interest in Ostwin Fritz Menzer, an inventor and cryptologist who worked directly for Colonel Kettler and subsequently for Admiral Wilhelm F. Canaris, the head of the German *Abwehr* intelligence service.[103] Menzer had invented the so-called *Schlüsselkasten* (cipher box), the designated successor of the Enigma below the division level. For lack of resources, however, the Germans did not make the substitution, leaving the compromised Enigma in place.[104] At the end of the war, the Third Army briefly detained Menzer as a prisoner of war at Bad Aibling without apparently recognizing his signal intelligence value. In late 1945, Menzer settled with his family in the city of Zschopau in Saxony in the Soviet Zone.[105]

---

100 Oliver R. Kirby, "The Origins of the Soviet Problem: A Personal View," *Cryptologic Quarterly* 2, no. 4 (Winter 1992), 52.
101 Michael L. Peterson, "BOURBON to Black Friday: The Allied Collaborative COMINT Effort Against the Soviet Union, 1945–1948" (Fort Meade, MD: Center for Cryptologic History, National Security Agency, 1995), 39, 41.
102 Msg, Col. Earle F. Cook, Signal Corps, to Ch, ASA, 24 Apr 1947, sub: Circumstances of Discovery of TICOM Material, Historians' Source Files Relating to TICOM, 1944–1946, RG 457, NACP.
103 Msg, Browning to CO, Region IV, CIC, 1 Jul 1949, sub: Oswin Fritz Menzer.
104 David P. Mowry, "Regierungs-Oberinspektor Fritz Menzer: Cryptographic Inventor Extraordinaire," *Cryptologic Quarterly* 2, nos. 3–4 (Autumn/Winter 1983–1984), 21.
105 Msg, Lt. Col. James F. Ritter, Ch, Opns Div, to Director of Intel, EUCOM, 2 Feb 1950, sub: Biography of Fritz Menzer, Folder "Menzer, Fritz Oswin D 261111," INSCOM, IRR, Digitized Name Files, RG 319, NACP.

In the summer of 1947, the ASAE requested that the European Command Intelligence Center set up an interview with Menzer. The Americans had interrogated one of his former colleagues and learned that Menzer sometimes visited Berlin, and so they decided to try to meet with him in the American sector of the city. They contacted him through another former coworker, Siegfried Uhlig, who also lived in Saxony. Menzer readily agreed and met with Capt. Eugene V. Valic, an Army Intelligence veteran, in Berlin. Valic then took Menzer to Oberursel, where several interrogators, including Valic, Capt. Hermann Halle and Capt. Mary C. Lane, interviewed him. The Americans wanted to bring Menzer permanently to the U.S. Zone, especially after he told Lane that he kept a *Schlüsselkasten* at his home in Zschopau. Yet after Menzer made demands for specific living and working conditions, as well as the transfer of his family, that would have cost the ASA $2,500, the Americans declined to meet his requirements and the deal fell through.[106]

As soon as Menzer returned to Zschopau, the Soviet authorities arrested and interrogated him on his trip to the U.S. Zone. Apparently, they knew about his contacts with American intelligence, and Menzer later claimed that his associate Uhlig had betrayed him. Menzer was released only after he had signed an agreement to spy for the Soviets. In constant fear of arrest and deportation, Menzer and his family fled to Berlin in the summer of 1949 and contacted the American authorities. The local CIC, in turn, informed the ASA in Frankfurt of Menzer's arrival.[107] The agency arranged for Menzer and his family to move to Oberursel, and paid him 500 deutsche marks (DM) for his resettlement. At Camp King, he became a "voluntary source" for the ASA. After Menzer expressed a desire to move to the United States with his family, the Intelligence Division began vetting him for immigration under the auspices of Project PAPERCLIP.[108]

The prospect of Menzer's recruitment for PAPERCLIP raised the larger question of whether the ASA should employ German signals intelligence veterans directly. At the end of the war, Lt. Gen. Heinrich Aschenbrenner, a *Luftwaffe* signals intelligence officer, told his captors that many of his men were ready to conduct radio

---

[106] Rpt, ASA, "Description of Contacts of Fritz Menzer with American and Soviet Authorities and Summary of Career," Sep 1949, Historians' Source Files Relating to TICOM, 1944–1946, RG 457, NACP.
[107] Rpt, ASA, "Description of Contacts of Fritz Menzer with American and Soviet Authorities and Summary of Career," Sep 1949.
[108] Msg, Col. David G. Erskine, HQ, 66th CIC Detachment, to Director, Intel Div, EUCOM, 17 Mar 1950, sub: Menzer, Fritz, Folder "Menzer, Fritz Oswin D 261111," INSCOM, IRR, Digitized Name Files, RG 319, NACP.

intercept operations for the Americans against the Soviets.[109] But signals intelligence remained a highly compartmentalized area within the Army, and a foreign background generally precluded access.[110] After some debate, the ASA advised against the idea of hiring former enemy personnel.[111] Menzer remained in Germany.[112] When it came to exploiting German espionage veterans, however, Army Intelligence had fewer reservations.

Operation RUSTY

By 1945, Army Intelligence had launched a wide-ranging effort to mine information from captured documents and intelligence personnel on the Soviet Union. One early target of these efforts were Russian soldiers who had fought for the Germans as members of the so-called Vlasov Army. The *Wehrmacht* had captured Soviet Lt. Gen. Andrey A. Vlasov on the eastern front in 1942. Disillusioned with Stalin, Vlasov agreed to collaborate with the Germans and establish a military auxiliary force recruited from Soviet prisoners of war. Eventually, the Russian Army of Liberation, colloquially known as the Vlasov Army, numbered roughly 50,000 men.[113]

At the end of the war, many of Vlasov's soldiers sought to escape the wrath of the Red Army by entering American-controlled territory in Czechoslovakia and southern Germany. At Yalta, the Americans had agreed to return any Russian soldiers captured in German uniform to the Soviets, but local American commanders exercised considerable leeway in handling this matter. Some abided by the Yalta agreement and turned Vlasov's men over to the advancing Red Army. In May 1945, Vlasov himself met this fate when he and his senior officers fell into Soviet hands in western Czechoslovakia while riding in a U.S. convoy. The Soviets court-martialed and executed Vlasov the following year. In other instances, however, local Army

---

109 Rpt, G. R. Treviranus, n.d. sub: Lt. General Heinrich Aschenbrenner suggests use of German intercept operators to cover Russian targets, Historians' Source Files Relating to TICOM, 1944–1946, RG 457, NACP.
110 Boghardt, "Semper Vigilis," 23.
111 Memo, TICOM Conference, 24 Sep 1947, sub: ASA Interests and Policy in regard to Employment of Former Enemy Signal Intelligence Personnel by the United States, Historians' Source Files Relating to TICOM, 1944–1946, RG 457, NACP.
112 Name Trace Request Form, Fritz Menzer, 25 Jan 1961, Folder "Fritz Oswin Menzer XE 261111," INSCOM, IRR, Digitized Name Files, RG 319, NACP. Menzer's greed, seen in his list of demands, also militated against his recruitment.
113 For a history of the Vlasov Army, see Joachim Hoffmann, *Die Geschichte der Wlassow-Armee* [The history of the Vlasov Army] (Freiburg: Rombach, 1986).

commanders let the fleeing Russians pass through their lines to spare them the harsh fate that awaited them under the Soviets.[114]

Within a few months, the captured Vlasov veterans became prized intelligence targets. In October 1945, Army Intelligence moved some of Vlasov's surviving officers to Camp King, where interrogators asked them to write down their knowledge about the Soviet Union.[115] The following year, the Intelligence Division transferred a handful of Vlasov veterans to Fort Hunt in Virginia for further exploitation.[116] Eventually, the Central Intelligence Agency recruited some Russian collaborators as informants and as covert agents for operations inside the Soviet Union.[117]

In addition to the use of the Vlasov soldiers, Army Intelligence participated in two programs that exploited the resources of the *Luftwaffe* and the *Wehrmacht*. In a project code-named DICK TRACY, the Americans and the British analyzed captured *Luftwaffe* photographs taken over Eastern Europe and the Soviet Union. This material provided strategic target intelligence to the air forces of both countries for several years.[118] Concurrently, the U.S. Army Historical Section of the Military Intelligence Division supervised a large project involving German officers to write histories of their wartime campaigns. Led by the former *Wehrmacht* chief of staff, General Franz Halder, the Germans turned out roughly 200,000 manuscript pages analyzing *Wehrmacht* operations on the western and eastern fronts.[119]

Eventually, the Army's thirst for information on the Soviet military led them to Brig. Gen. Reinhard Gehlen, the chief of the *Wehrmacht*'s analytical intelligence unit on the eastern front, *Fremde Heere Ost* (*Foreign Armies East*). In April 1945, Gehlen met with Lt. Col. Hermann Baun, the head of the *Abwehr*'s espionage organization on the eastern front. Anticipating Germany's imminent defeat, they dis-

---

114 Hoffmann, *Wlassow-Armee*, 270–324.
115 Hoffmann, *Wlassow-Armee*, 322.
116 Msg, Maj. Gen. Stephen J. Chamberlin, War Department, Intel Div, to CG, USFET, 14 Nov 1946, Folder "3. Consolidated Outgoing 11-6-46–12-3-46 (85000–86999)," ACoS, G–2 (Intel), "Top Secret" Incoming and Outgoing Cables, 1942–52, RG 319, NACP.
117 Kevin C. Ruffner, "Eagle and Swastika: CIA and Nazi War Criminals and Collaborators" (Washington, DC: History Staff, Central Intelligence Agency, 2003), chap. 8, 3–7.
118 Richard J. Aldrich, *The Hidden Hand: Britain, America, and Cold War Secret Intelligence* (New York: Overlook Press, 2001), 207.
119 Much of this work had a self-serving intent, as the German officers sought to protect the reputation of the *Wehrmacht* and distance it from Hitler and the Nazi Party. See James A. Wood, "Captive Historians, Captivated Audience: The German Military History Program, 1945–1961," *Journal of Military History* 69, no. 1 (Jan 2005): 123–47.

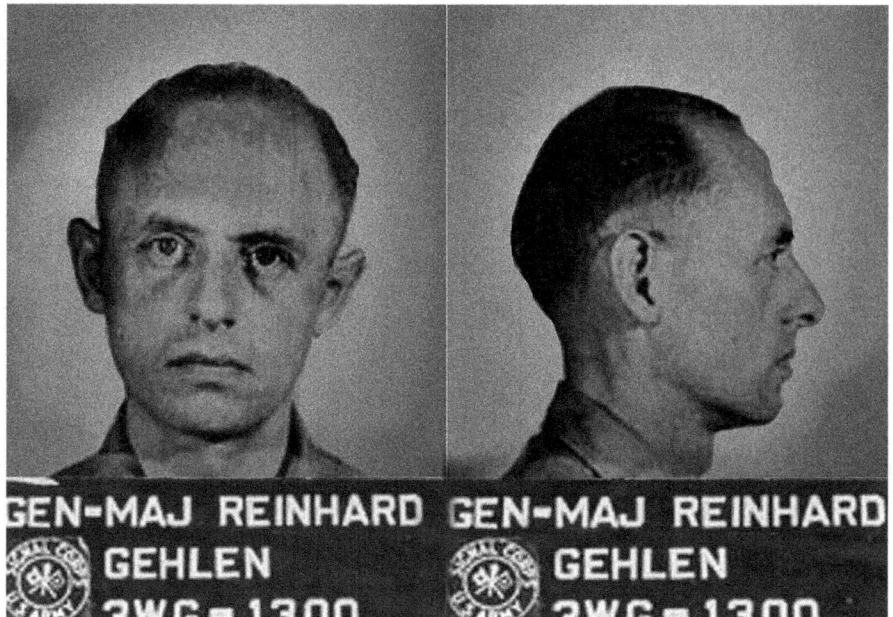

Figure 29: Mugshot of Reinhard Gehlen in U.S. captivity. U.S. Army.

cussed plans for the postwar world. Gehlen later insisted that working with the Americans had been his sole motive since early 1945.[120] Other German prisoners, however, stated that Gehlen had entertained the idea of joining a postwar guerrilla effort against the Allies.[121] In any event, Gehlen and a group of his close associates retreated to southern Bavaria, where they crated and buried photocopies of their organization's archives. On 23 May, he surrendered to an American officer in Fischhausen, a small town at the southern tip of the Schliersee in Bavaria.[122]

---

[120] John R. Boker Jr., Report of initial contact with General Gehlen's Organization, 1 May 1952, doc. 6, in *Forging an Intelligence Partnership: The CIA and the Origins of the BND, 1945–1949: A Documentary History*, vol. 1, ed. Kevin C. Ruffner (Washington, DC: Center for the Study of Intelligence, 1999), 23; Reinhard Gehlen, *Der Dienst: Erinnerungen, 1942–1971* [The service: Memoirs, 1942–1971] (Mainz-Wiesbaden: Hase & Koehler, 1971), 120–24.

[121] Wolfgang Krieger, "U.S. Patronage of German Postwar Intelligence," in *A Handbook of Intelligence Studies*, ed. Loch Johnson (London: Routledge, 2007), 94. See also Statement of General Gehlen on Walter Schellenberg Story (Post Defeat Resistance), n.d., doc. 5, in Ruffner, *Forging an Intelligence Partnership*, 1:17–18.

[122] Jens Wegener, *Die Organisation Gehlen und die USA: Deutsch-amerikanische Geheimdienstbeziehungen, 1945–1949* [The Gehlen Organization and the United States: German-American intelli-

When the 12th Army Group's intelligence division learned of Gehlen's capture, it sought to bring him under its control. Sibert's men initially had difficulty tracking him down. A handwritten note on a cable from Supreme Allied Headquarters to Sibert stated that Gehlen was "requested from Third Army" on 27 May.[123] Instead, Gehlen's local captors transferred him to the Seventh Army Interrogation Center in Augsburg, where he provided information on the Soviet army, intelligence, and security forces. He also lectured his interviewer on the importance of understanding the "discordant Russian psychology, as presented in Dostoievski's novels." The interview files indicate that Gehlen sought to position himself as someone who could be of use to the Americans; his interrogator commented that the prisoner "talked freely and gave all information willingly; he is anti-Communist and anticipates a Russo-Allied conflict." Based on the interviews, the commanding officer of the center, Maj. Paul Kubala, compiled two detailed reports, dated 21 and 24 June.[124] The reports did not mention the buried *Fremde Heere Ost* archives, but Gehlen evidently informed his captors about them soon after his surrender at Fischhausen. On 25 June, the Military Intelligence Division at the Pentagon and the Intelligence Section of the Supreme Allied Headquarters agreed to evacuate the records to Washington via London. "These are strategic documents," Maj. Gen. Clayton L. Bissell noted, "which can best be exploited" at the Pentagon.[125] A few days later, on 29 June, General Bissell informed General Sibert and Supreme Allied Headquarters that "Gehlen was desired [by the] War Department after Theater Interrogation."[126] Bissell's decision to transfer Gehlen to the United States set up a tug-of-war with General Sibert's intelligence division over the control of the materiel from *Fremde Heere Ost*.

Meanwhile, the Seventh Army had released Gehlen to the 12th Army Group on 17 June.[127] The group's intelligence division transferred Gehlen to a villa for special prisoners in Wiesbaden, administered by Camp King under Col. William

---

gence relations, 1945–1949] (Münster: Lit Verlag, 2008), 57; Ruffner, *Forging an Intelligence Partnership*, 1:xliii.

123 Incoming Cable, SHAEF to G-2, COM Z, 12th Army Gp, 3 Jul 1945[?], Folder "Von Gehlen, Reinhard XE282 212," INSCOM, IRR, Digitized Name Files, RG 319, NACP.

124 Seventh Army Interrogation Center, Notes on the Red Army – Intelligence and Security, 24 Jun 1945, doc. 10, in Ruffner, *Forging an Intelligence Partnership*, 1:51–56; Rpt, Seventh Army Interrogation Center, Notes on the Red Army – Leadership and Tactics, 21 Jun 1945, Folder "Gehlen, Reinhard," Rcds Relating to Prisoners of War, 1943–1945, RG 165, NACP.

125 Msg, Maj. Gen. Clayton L. Bissell to CG, USFET, 7 Aug 1945, Folder "#1 to Germany 90804 & 10207 thru 54917," ACoS, G-2 (Intel), "Top Secret" Incoming and Outgoing Cables, 1942–52, RG 319, NACP.

126 Incoming Cable, SHAEF to G-2, COM Z, 12th Army Group, 3 Jul 1945[?].

127 Incoming Cable, SHAEF to G-2, COM Z, 12th Army Group, 3 Jul 1945[?].

R. "Rusty" Philp.[128] There, Gehlen met Capt. John R. Boker, an American of German descent who had already interrogated numerous German officers about their insights on Soviet issues. Boker recalled that Gehlen "was very anxious to cooperate with the Americans." With Philp's backing, Boker identified members of Gehlen's staff in various U.S. prisoner-of-war camps and transferred them to Wiesbaden. He also removed their names from Allied wanted lists to protect them from Soviet demands for extradition.[129] Boker and Philp probably acted under direct orders of General Sibert, who regarded Gehlen and his men as sources of intelligence on the Soviet forces.[130] Based on information provided by the Germans, Sibert's interrogators on 16 August produced a report on Soviet radio procedures and forwarded it to the intelligence division at the Pentagon.[131]

While Gehlen and his men settled in at Camp King, General Bissell sought to sideline Sibert in the exploitation of German intelligence personnel. In early July, Bissell reached an agreement with British Maj. Gen. Kenneth W. D. Strong and General Betts of Supreme Allied Headquarters that "German PW [prisoners of war] with knowledge of Russian Armed Forces should be sent for interrogation to cities US or UK according to nationality of captors."[132] On 24 July, General Sibert met with the Supreme Allied Headquarters intelligence staff. Probably at Bissell's urging, headquarters informed Sibert to limit his intelligence-gathering activities on the Soviets and promptly forward to Washington all intelligence his agencies were producing on the USSR. On 4 August, Eisenhower and Marshall formally notified Sibert of this decision.[133]

A few days later, Bissell reminded Eisenhower of the 26 June agreement to the effect that the *Fremde Heere Ost* archives were to go to London and thence to

---

128 Ruffner, *Forging an Intelligence Partnership*, 1:xliii. The address of Villa Pagenstecher in Wiesbaden was Bodenstedtstrasse 2a; today, it is the Konservatorium on Parkstrasse 16.
129 Wegener, *Organisation Gehlen*, 60.
130 NFR, Maj. Gen. Clayton L. Bissell to Brig. Gen. John Weckerling, Ch, Mil Intel Service, 8 Sep 1945, sub: USSR Research, Folder "'Lansisky,–' Courier of the Soviet Embassy," INSCOM, IRR, Impersonal Name Files, RG 319, NACP.
131 Msg, Col. C. F. Fritzsche, G–2, USFET, to ACofS, G–2, War Department, 16 Aug 1945, Folder "925184," Rcds of the ACoS, G–2 (Intel), Formerly Top Secret Intel Documents, 1943–59, RG 319, NACP.
132 Msg, Maj. Gen. Clayton L. Bissell to CG, USFET, 14 Aug 1945, Folder "#1 to Germany 90804 & 10207 thru 54917," ACoS, G–2 (Intel), "Top Secret" Incoming and Outgoing Cables, 1942–52, RG 319, NACP.
133 NFR, Bissell to Weckerling, 8 Sep 1945, sub: USSR Research; Msg, Gen Dwight D. Eisenhower to Brig. Gen. Edwin L. Sibert, signed Marshall, 4 Aug 1945, Folder "#1 to Germany 90804 & 10207 thru 54917," ACoS, G–2 (Intel), "Top Secret" Incoming and Outgoing Cables, 1942–52, RG 319, NACP.

Washington. In an apparent dig at Sibert, Bissell emphasized that this should be done "as soon as practicable and without local examination."[134] Eisenhower passed the message on to Sibert, who replied to Bissell three days later with a counterproposal to send the records to London for two weeks and then return them to Germany "for necessary local exploitation." Only when his team was done with them, Sibert suggested, should the material go to Washington.[135] Sibert did not mention the Gehlen group in his proposal. If he assumed that the Germans would remain at Camp King regardless of what happened with the records, he was in for a rude awakening.

On 14 August, Bissell instructed Eisenhower to send the records via London to the War Department and asked him to ship the Gehlen group "direct to Washington accompanied by Capt Boker at earliest practicable date." In the United States, Gehlen and his men were to join another group of some 400 German officers. All of them would work on a historical project (Project HILL) at Camp Ritchie in Maryland.[136] On 21 August, Boker gathered Gehlen, five of his officers, and the *Fremde Heere Ost* records, and they flew to Washington, D.C., aboard the aircraft of General Eisenhower's chief of staff, Maj. Gen. Walter B. Smith.[137] To conceal the trip from the Soviets, who were looking for Gehlen, the Army assigned the Germans cover names. Gehlen traveled under the pseudonym "Richard Garner."[138] At this time, the European Theater code-named intelligence on the Soviet armed forces BOLERO, and the U.S.-bound German veterans therefore received the code name BOLERO GROUP.[139] By design or by accident, neither Bissell nor Eisenhower shared the decision to move Gehlen stateside with Sibert, who learned about it only after the fact. Within a couple of weeks, Sibert traveled to Washington and met with Bissell at his office in the Pentagon on 8 September. As Bissell

---

134 Msg, Bissell to CG, USFET, 7 Aug 1945.
135 Msg, Brig. Gen. Edwin L. Sibert to Maj. Gen. Clayton L. Bissell, 10 Aug 1945, Folder "S91027 thru S 96761 'S' Germany – S 12365 thru S 20404," ACoS, G–2 (Intel), "Top Secret" Incoming and Outgoing Cables, 1942–52, RG 319, NACP.
136 Statement of Lt. Col. Gerald H. Duin on Early Contacts with the GEHLEN Organization, n.d., doc. 7, in Ruffner, *Forging an Intelligence Partnership*, 1:35–37.
137 Boker, Report of initial contact with General Gehlen's Organization, 1 May 1952, doc. 6, in Ruffner, *Forging an Intelligence Partnership*, 1:30.
138 Bodo Hechelhammer, "Unter amerikanischer Flagge: Die 'Bolero Group' um Reinhard Gehlen" [Under the American flag: The "Bolero Group" around Reinhard Gehlen], in *Achtung Spione: Geheimdienste in Deutschland 1945–1956* [Attention spies: Secret services in Germany 1945–1956], ed. Magnus Pahl, Gorch Pieken, and Matthias Rogg (Dresden: Sandstein Verlag, 2016), 47.
139 Msg, CG, USFET, to War Department, 13 Sep 1945, sub: Reference BOLERO, Folder "From Germany S-20405 thru S-39481," ACoS, G–2 (Intel), "Top Secret" Incoming and Outgoing Cables, 1942–52, RG 319, NACP.

noted diplomatically, the two officers discussed the matter of Gehlen's abrupt departure "frankly and openly." Sibert complained that the Gehlen group "had been ordered away from his Theater without his knowledge or concurrence," and he "objected to the principle of pulling people away without letting people know what was going on." Bissell emphasized that his division had overall responsibility for the collection of intelligence on the Soviets, but he conceded that he should not have removed Gehlen without informing Sibert. In the end, the two generals reached a compromise. For the time being, Gehlen and his group would remain in the United States, retain access to the *Fremde Heere Ost* records, and work on Soviet issues for Bissell. In Germany, Sibert would be allowed to "build up another little group for his purposes." According to Bissell, this solution closed the matter "in an attitude of friendliness and understanding."[140]

Sibert's "little group" referred to a handful of German intelligence veterans at Camp King, including Lt. Col. Gerhard Wessel of *Fremde Heere Ost*, who had surrendered to the Americans on 20 May 1945, and Colonel Baun of the *Abwehr*, who had been arrested by the Third Army on 29 July 1945.[141] According to Wessel, he and Baun met in Oberursel, where they agreed to work for the Americans.[142] The Army moved them to the Blue House, a villa outside Camp King, where the Germans worked under the supervision of the camp's operations officer, Lt. Col. John R. "Jack" Deane Jr.[143] Unlike the various historical exploitation projects that engaged in purely analytical work, this group was to engage in espionage. Baun's outfit assumed the cover name Operation RUSTY.[144]

Baun depended on the Army for material support. In order to recruit and pay agents, Baun in early 1946 asked for a monthly allowance of 300 kilograms of coffee, 25,000 cigarettes, and 10,000 match boxes.[145] He used this largesse, he told the Americans, to recruit sources in the Soviet Zone. By the fall of 1946, he informed his handlers, he had established a radio monitoring service to intercept low-level

---

140 NFR, Bissell to Weckerling, 8 Sep 1945, sub: USSR Research.
141 Preliminary Interrogation Report, HQ, Third U.S. Army Intelligence Center, 16 Aug 1945, sub: Baun, Hermann, doc. 11, in Ruffner, *Forging an Intelligence Partnership*, 1:57.
142 Statement of Gerhard Wessel on Development of the German Organization, n.d., doc. 1, in Ruffner, *Forging an Intelligence Partnership*, 1:5.
143 Ruffner, "Eagle and the Swastika," chap. 9, 7.
144 Ruffner, "Eagle and the Swastika," chap. 9, 8n15. The cover name "Rusty" derives either from Colonel Philp's nickname or from the name of Lt. Col. John R. Deane Jr.'s son (who was born around that time).
145 Thomas Wolf, *Die Entstehung des BND: Aufbau, Finanzierung, Kontrolle* [The creation of the BND: Development, financing, control] (Berlin: Ch. Links Verlag, 2018), 74.

Soviet communications, and he handled "500 to 600 agents" there.[146] This claim was exaggerated. In fact, many of his sources were either nonexistent or yielded very little intelligence of value.[147]

Meanwhile, Col. Demitri B. Shimkin of the Military Intelligence Service arranged to transfer the BOLERO GROUP to "P.O. Box 1142," a code name for Fort Hunt in Virginia.[148] After an initial period of strict confinement, Gehlen and his men settled in two blockhouses near the Potomac River. Here, they lived in relative comfort. Boker left the group shortly after arrival at the airport, and Shimkin replaced him with 1st Lt. (later Capt.) Eric Waldman, an officer of the Russian Order of Battle Section of the Military Intelligence Service. An Austrian by birth, Waldman had left his country in 1938 after its forcible annexation by Germany and joined Army Intelligence during the war. Even though the *Gestapo* had murdered his father, Waldman worked harmoniously with Gehlen and his men, and he became an early champion of the Germans.[149]

Under Waldman's supervision, the BOLERO GROUP became part of "a systematic plan [of the Military Intelligence Service] for the exploitation of German sources with regard to USSR Armed Forces."[150] The group had access to the *Fremde Heere Ost* records as well as some current intelligence material on the Soviet armed forces from the intelligence divisions in Washington and Frankfurt.[151] They also received assistance from three Soviet officers, possibly Vlasov men, who had defected to the Germans during the war.[152] Eleven prisoners from Proj-

---

146 Msg, Maj. Gen. W. A. Burress, G-2, to Lt. Gen. Hoyt S. Vandenberg, Director of Central Intelligence (DCI), sub: Operation RUSTY – Use of the Eastern Branch of the Former German Intelligence Service, 1 Oct 1946, doc 19, in Ruffner, *Forging an Intelligence Partnership*, 1:103.
147 Magnus Pahl, "Hermann Baun (1897–1951): Der gescheiterte Spionagechef" [Hermann Baun (1897–1951): The failed espionage chief], in *Spione und Nachrichtenhändler: Geheimdienstkarrieren in Deutschland 1939–1989* [Spies and news traders: Intelligence careers in Germany, 1939–1989], ed. Helmut Müller-Enbergs and Armin Wagner (Berlin: Ch. Links Verlag, 2016), 38–77.
148 Wegener, *Organisation Gehlen*, 62–63.
149 James H. Critchfield, *Partners at the Creation: The Men Behind Postwar Germany's Defense and Intelligence Establishments* (Annapolis, MD: Naval Institute Press, 2003), 37; Debriefing of Eric Waldman on the U.S. Army's Trusteeship of the Gehlen Organization during the years 1945–1949, 30 Sep 1969, doc. 9, in Ruffner, *Forging an Intelligence Partnership*, 1:47.
150 Lt. Stanley Wilcox, Lt. Eric Waldman, Intel Research Project, 16 Jan 1946, Folder "926375," FTSI Documents, RG 319, NACP; Debriefing of Eric Waldman, 30 Sep 1969, doc. 9, in Ruffner, *Forging an Intelligence Partnership*, 1:45–50.
151 Msg, Lt. Col. John R. Deane Jr., Mil Intel Service Center, USFET, to ACofS, G-2, USFET, 2 Jul 1946, sub: Plan for the Inclusion of the Bolero Group in Operation Rusty, doc. 17, in Ruffner, *Forging an Intelligence Partnership*, 1:96.
152 Msg, Chamberlin to CG, USFET, 14 Nov 1946.

ect HILL at Camp Ritchie became attached to Gehlen and his men as well.[153] The BOLERO GROUP remained at Fort Hunt until July 1946, prepared several studies on the Soviet military potential and on the German experience on the eastern front, and briefed visiting American officers on issues pertaining to the Red Army.[154]

In June 1946, the Department of State demanded that the War Department repatriate all German prisoners of war by the end of the month.[155] Consequently, Captain Waldman traveled to Germany to prepare for the BOLERO GROUP's return. Colonel Deane proposed attaching the group to Operation RUSTY "to increase the efficiency and value of the work carried on at the present time at" Camp King. Lt. Col. Gerald H. Duin, an Army Intelligence interrogator, accompanied Gehlen and his associates on a troop transport to Brest, France, where Waldman received the group and escorted them to Oberursel.[156]

While Gehlen and his men returned to Germany, General Sibert had been preparing for his departure to Washington to join the Central Intelligence Group. On 30 August 1946, the day before he left Germany, he met Gehlen in person for the first time. On this occasion, Gehlen wrote in his memoirs, the two men reached a "gentlemen's agreement": RUSTY would remain a quasi-German organization financed by the Army, and it would provide intelligence to the Americans but would not be beholden to them.[157] These terms would have signified sweeping American concessions to the Germans. Sibert remembered the meeting quite differently. In an interview conducted just before Gehlen's memoirs appeared, he described the encounter as a mere courtesy, one which did not go beyond a brief "hello and goodbye."[158] As RUSTY was merely an appendix to the Army's vast intelligence machinery, Sibert's version appears to be the likelier of the two.

---

153 Derek R. Mallett, *Hitler's Generals in America: Nazi POWs and Allied Military Intelligence* (Lexington: University Press of Kentucky, 2003), 163.
154 Statement of Heinz Danko Herre, 8 Apr 1953, doc. 4, in Ruffner, *Forging an Intelligence Partnership*, 1:11–15.
155 Mallett, *Hitler's Generals in America*, 164.
156 Msg., Deane to ACofS, G–2, USFET, 2 Jul 1946, sub: Plan for the Inclusion of the Bolero Group in Operation Rusty, doc. 17, in Ruffner, *Forging an Intelligence Partnership*, 1:93–97; Statement of Lt. Col. Gerald Duin on Early Contacts with the GEHLEN Organization, n.d., doc. 7, in Ruffner, *Forging an Intelligence Partnership*, 1:35–41; Hechelhammer, "Unter Amerikanischer Flagge," 54–55.
157 Gehlen, *Der Dienst*, 149–50.
158 Report of Interview with General Edwin L. Sibert on the Gehlen Organization, 26 Mar 1970, doc. 8, in Ruffner, *Forging an Intelligence Partnership*, 1:44. The CIA's liaison officer with Operation Rusty, Col. James H. Critchfield, wrote in his memoirs that Sibert told Gehlen at their meeting about his plans to relocate Rusty to the United States because "I must be able to guarantee that the organization works for and not against America." Critchfield, *Partners at the Creation*, 38.

At Oberursel, the Americans divided Operation RUSTY into two separate groups. The Intelligence Group under Gehlen would provide analysis and evaluation of the Soviet forces, whereas the Information Group under Colonel Baun would continue procuring intelligence from agents in the Soviet zone of occupation. For the purpose of supervision, the Army employed a small U.S. staff, including Colonel Philp; Colonel Deane; Deane's assistant Captain Waldman; Waldman's wife Jo-Ann, who served as secretary and typist; and a few clerks and translators. Deane and Waldman were to provide intelligence targets to the Germans and receive their reports.[159]

Gehlen had no experience running agents, but he was a capable administrator and a keen empire builder. He was also "as clever as a fox," according to an American intelligence officer, and he quickly outmaneuvered his less wily counterpart, Baun.[160] During his sojourn in the United States, Gehlen had methodically built personal relationships with Army Intelligence officers, such as Waldman, and he skillfully played up his pro-American credentials at Camp King. Baun's overt nationalism and his inability to speak English aided Gehlen in his efforts to sideline his competitor. In early 1947, Gehlen became sole chief of Operation RUSTY. Under the leadership of "Dr. Schneider," the cover name Gehlen chose for himself, the organization expanded its espionage operations. In May 1947, it set up a radio intercept section at the former DUSTBIN detention center, Kransberg Castle.[161]

Just as Gehlen consolidated his hold on RUSTY and expanded operations, American supervision of the project receded. When Sibert left the Army, he wanted to transfer Operation RUSTY to the Central Intelligence Group's executive agency, the Special Services Unit. He asked the head of the unit in Germany, Crosby Lewis, whether his organization was prepared to take over Gehlen and his men. With some caveats attached, Lewis replied in the affirmative.[162] On 1 October, Sibert's

---

159 Wegener, *Organisation Gehlen*, 73; Schmidt-Eenboom, "The Bundesnachrichtendienst, the Bundeswehr and Sigint in the Cold War and After," 131; Msg, Deane to ACofS, G-2, USFET, 2 Jul 1946, sub: "Plan for the Inclusion of the Bolero Group in Operation Rusty," doc. 17, in Ruffner, *Forging an Intelligence Partnership*, 1:95–96; Susanne Meinl, "'Our Headquarters in Bormann's Nest': Die US-amerikanische Zensurbehörde CCD in Pullach" ["Our Headquarters in Bormann's Nest": The US censorship agency CCD in Pullach], in *Geheimobjekt Pullach: Von der NS-Mustersiedlung zur Zentrale des BND* [Secret object Pullach: From the Nazi model housing estate to BND headquarters], ed. Susanne Meinl and Bodo Hechelhammer (Berlin: Ch. Links Verlag, 2014), 154.
160 Email, Peter M. F. Sichel to Thomas Boghardt, 27 Jun 2017, Historians Files, CMH.
161 Wegener, *Organisation Gehlen*, 73–74; Armin Müller, "Die Technische Nachrichtenbeschaffung der Organisation Gehlen," in Pahl, Pieken, and Rogg, *Achtung Spione*, 227.
162 Msg, Crosby Lewis, Ch, Strategic Services Unit Mission to Germany, to Brig. Gen. Sibert, ACofS, G-2, USFET, 6 Sep 1946, sub: Operation KEYSTONE, doc. 18, in Ruffner, *Forging an Intelligence Partnership*, 1:100–101.

successor in Germany, Maj. Gen. Withers A. "Pinky" Burress, recommended to Lt. Gen. Hoyt S. Vandenberg Jr. "that SSU [Special Services Unit] take over Operation RUSTY and conduct it from the United States."[163] Yet the transfer of Operation RUSTY from the Army to the Central Intelligence Group quickly stalled. A representative of the group, Col. Donald H. Galloway, conducted an initial review of RUSTY on behalf of General Vandenberg. He criticized the operation as too expensive and too independent of American control. He also noted that the Germans produced only low-level intelligence and pointed to signs that the group had been penetrated by the Soviets. Therefore, he recommended against its transfer to the Central Intelligence Group.[164] When Sibert met with high-ranking representatives of the Central Intelligence Group in New York City on 19 December, he encountered similar objections. Two special advisers to the director of central intelligence, Allen W. Dulles and William H. Jackson, pointed out "the dangers of the operation," and recommended an extensive survey before any decision be taken. As a result of this meeting, a group representative, Samuel B. Bossard, traveled to Oberursel and reviewed Operation RUSTY for two months.[165]

In May 1947, Bossard submitted his findings. His comprehensive report revealed that Operation RUSTY had grown into a vast organization of 3,000 staff and informants spread across Germany and beyond, costing the Army more than $47,000 per month. Sibert's departure had left the low-ranking Deane and Waldman in charge of the sprawling organization. Both were sympathetic to Gehlen and lacked the wherewithal to keep him under tight control. As a result, Bossard reported, RUSTY had evolved from an instrument of the Army to a semi-independent German intelligence agency that assisted the Americans on its own terms. Its employees included numerous unvetted former Nazi and SS officials. RUSTY's cryptographic section, Bossard worried, might be attacking not only Soviet codes but those of other countries as well. Bossard also pointed out that the Soviets and other nations had become aware of Operation RUSTY, raising the specter of penetration by Soviet intelligence.[166]

---

163 Msg, Maj. Gen. Withers A. Burress to Lt. Gen. Hoyt S. Vandenberg Jr., 1 Oct 1946, sub: Operation RUSTY – Use of the Eastern Branch of the former German Intelligence Service, doc. 19, in Ruffner, *Forging an Intelligence Partnership*, 1:104.
164 Memo, Donald H. Galloway, Asst Director Special Opns, Central Intel Gp, for DCI, 17 Oct 1946, sub: Operation Rusty, doc. 22, in Ruffner, *Forging an Intelligence Partnership*, 1:167.
165 MFR, Richard Helms, 19 Dec 1946, sub: Operation RUSTY, doc. 25, in Ruffner, *Forging an Intelligence Relationship*, 1:195.
166 Memo, Samuel B. Bossard, for Director, Central Intel Gp, 29 May 1947, sub: Operation Rusty, doc. 43, in Ruffner, *Forging an Intelligence Relationship*, 1:369.

Indeed, by the time Bossard submitted his report, Gehlen's organization had become a major Soviet target. In November 1947, the Soviets arrested an agent of Operation RUSTY, Rudolf Harnisch, in Leipzig. Faced with either a lengthy internment in Siberia or becoming a Soviet double agent, Harnisch chose the latter. He identified roughly thirty of Gehlen's Soviet Zone agents, who were promptly arrested.[167] In another incident of suspected penetration, a phone intercept ordered by the CIC revealed that information from "some American intelligence agency" had been leaked to Soviet intelligence. The CIC filed the report in a folder designated "Soviet penetration of Operation Rusty."[168]

The discovery of the so-called Chikalov ring served as the starkest reminder yet of RUSTY's vulnerability. In early 1947, a Russian émigré named Alexander F. Chikalov offered his services to one of Gehlen's officials. The Germans promptly recruited Chikalov as a source, but he seemed more interested in learning about Operation RUSTY than in providing information to Gehlen's outfit. In the fall of 1947, the CIC launched Operation HAGBERRY to determine Chikalov's true motives. They discovered that he had served in Soviet intelligence before the war but had joined General Vlasov's army as a top intelligence officer after his capture by the Germans. After the war, he remained in Germany, recruiting a network of Russian émigrés as sources.[169] Chikalov paid his informants handsomely and told them he collected information on behalf of "American intelligence agencies." The CIC, however, concluded that "there has been no indication that these reports have been forwarded to any American intelligence agency."[170] Suspecting that Chikalov was a Soviet operative, Army Intelligence warned Gehlen's organization to sever ties with

---

167 Stefan Appelius, "Rudolf Harnisch und die Verhaftung der Pinckert-Gruppe" [Rudolf Harnisch and the arrest of the Pinckert Group], *Zeitschrift des Forschungsverbundes SED-Staat* 38 (2015), 156–59; Msg, Col. B. L. Hardick, Intel Div, EUCOM, to Deputy Asst Director, 15 Dec 1950, sub: Rudolf Herbert Harnisch, Folder "Harnisch, Rudolf Herbert XE 286167," INSCOM, IRR, Digitized Name Files, RG 319, NACP.
168 Msg, Special Agent G. W. Greer Jr., CIC Regensburg, to CO, 7970th CIC Gp, 18 Oct 1948, sub: EEI's Concerning Uranium Mines, Folder "Soviet Penetration of Operation Rusty XE 202539," INSCOM, IRR, Digitized Name Files, RG 319, NACP.
169 Memo, CIC [badly legible], 12 Dec 1947, sub: Chikalow, Alexander, Folder "Chikalow Alexander D 153518," INSCOM, IRR, Digitized Name Files, RG 319, NACP.
170 Rpt, Special Agent Frederick O. Schnackenberg, Region IV, CIC, to CO, 8 Dec 1947, sub: Operation Hagberry; cross reference: Alexander Chikalow, Folder "Chikalow Alexander D 153518," INSCOM, IRR, Digitized Name Files, RG 319, NACP.

him. In December 1947, the CIC ended Chikalov's suspicious activities by apprehending multiple members of his network.[171]

In light of the group's numerous security issues and the lack of American control, Bossard recommended that the War Department liquidate Operation RUSTY. The Central Intelligence Group would then quietly vet and take over those elements that were most promising. Rather than dissolve it entirely, however, the new director of the Army's Intelligence Division in Washington, Maj. Gen. Stephen J. Chamberlin, decided to keep Operation RUSTY under Army control. Chamberlin then directed Maj. Gen. Robert L. Walsh, the incoming director of the Army's European intelligence division, to continue to manage and finance Operation RUSTY. Walsh, for his part, intended to inspect the operation personally with a view to reducing it in size, splitting up its activities, and exerting greater control over it.[172]

This effort fell flat. When Walsh visited Operation RUSTY, the Germans put on an elaborate show to demonstrate their intelligence prowess, which left the American general spellbound. "They were awfully good," he later stated. "They were the best of all. I went down to see them many times and to talk with them, and they briefed me many times. They were the best intelligence you could possibly get."[173] Had Walsh consulted his own men at Camp King, he might have developed a more realistic view of Operation RUSTY. General Clay was of little help in the matter. According to Col. James H. Critchfield, a former Army counterintelligence officer who joined RUSTY as a CIA liaison in 1948, Clay "had taken a uniquely hostile position toward all members of the German Army General Staff" and "had never shown the slightest interest in Gehlen and his project."[174] Although Clay knew of Operation RUSTY and sought to ensure continued funding for it in a conversation with Secretary of Defense James V. Forrestal, he left the day-to-day management of the Germans to the sympathetic Walsh.[175]

---

171 Msg, EUCOM, G–2, Intel Div (ECGID) to Ch of Staff, G–3, Plans and Opns Div (CSGPO), 1 Dec 1947, Folder "2. Fr: 'S' Germany 1000–4741 7-1-47–12-31-47," ACoS, G–2 (Intel), "Top Secret" Incoming and Outgoing Cables, 1942–52, RG 319, NACP.
172 Donald H. Galloway, Samuel B. Bossard, and Richard Helms, Report of Meeting at War Department, 26 June 1947, 26 Jun 1947, doc. 50, in Ruffner, *Forging an Intelligence Partnership*, 1:398.
173 Interv, Maj. Gen. Robert L. Walsh with Hugh N. Ahmann, USAF Historical Program, 9–10 Jan 1984, Washington, D.C., 205, Historians Files, CMH.
174 Critchfield, *Partners at the Creation*, 44.
175 Sum, [James V. Forrestal,] summary of conversations with General Clay in Berlin, 13–15 Nov [1948], Folder "Clay, Lucius D. 100-13," The President's Sec Files, Papers of Harry S. Truman, Truman Library.

In September 1947, Walsh replaced the easygoing Colonel Deane with Col. Willard K. Liebel as RUSTY's supervisor. A tough combat veteran, Liebel had previously served as the chief of staff of the 17th Airborne Division in the European Theater.[176] On 6 December, he moved the organization, now officially codenamed the 7821st Composite Group, from its cramped quarters at Camp King over 200 miles to the south to a spacious new location at Pullach near Munich. At the so-called Camp Nikolaus ("Camp Santa Claus"), the German intelligence personnel and their families lived in a fenced-in compound that included a hospital, a school, and a kindergarten, all intended to make the organization independent of the outside world.[177] The move made sense from a logistics and security perspective, but it isolated Liebel and his small staff of twenty-five Americans from the larger Army Intelligence organization at Camp King.

As a liaison officer, Liebel turned out to be a poor choice. Brash and authoritarian, he quickly ran into a wall of resentment and passive resistance. Gehlen later complained that Liebel treated the Germans "as subordinates of the U.S. Army who had to follow orders."[178] Captain Waldman, who joined the organization in Pullach, recalled that his new boss made no attempt to gain the Germans' confidence: "Col. Liebel spoke no German, did not like Germans, and did not hesitate to show it." Waldman remembered "sitting in Liebel's office and hearing him lecture Gehlen and [former German General Staff commander in chief Adolf] Heusinger, fortissimo, on how stupid the German General Staff had been."[179] Isolated from his American superiors and resented by the Germans, Liebel failed to impose the Army's authority over RUSTY. When evidence of his involvement in illegal currency speculation surfaced, Liebel's opponents skillfully exploited his transgressions. In November 1948, the intelligence division replaced Liebel as the U.S. supervisor with the commander of Camp King, Colonel Philp.[180] The latter focused on his main job at Camp King and spent little time on RUSTY. Liebel's departure marked the end of the Army's effort to reintegrate Operation RUSTY into its intelligence apparatus. For the remainder of the military occupation, the Army funded Gehlen's outfit but exerted little control over

---

176 DoD, Ofc of Public Info, News Br, "Major General Willard Koehler Liebel," Oct 1956, Historians Files, CMH.
177 Heinz Höhne and Hermann Zolling, *The General Was a Spy: The Truth About General Gehlen and His Spy Ring*, trans. Richard Barry (New York: Coward, McCann & Geogheghan, 1972), 84–85.
178 Gehlen, *Der Dienst*, 162.
179 Debriefing of Eric Waldman, 30 Sep 1969, doc. 9, in Ruffner, *Forging an Intelligence Partnership*, 1:48.
180 Wegener, *Organisation Gehlen*, 80.

it. In an acknowledgment of Gehlen's de facto independence, the Americans began referring to Operation RUSTY as the "Gehlen Organization."[181]

Budgetary constraints prompted the Army to transfer American supervision of the Gehlen Organization to the newly established and well-funded CIA. General Clay and top Army and CIA intelligence officers on both sides of the Atlantic discussed this subject repeatedly in 1948 and 1949. The deputy chief of the CIA's Berlin station, Peter M. F. Sichel, considered a takeover "a danger to our security [and] a waste of time" and counseled against it.[182] But other intelligence officials feared that RUSTY had grown too big to go away quietly. As Bossard had pointed out earlier, unemployed former Gehlen officials might defect to the Soviets, a hazard that could prove "highly embarrassing or compromising."[183] Moreover, American withdrawal of support might not end Gehlen's efforts, but rather "set in motion a powerful machine over whose course and driver we relinquish control."[184] Colonel Critchfield acknowledged the organization's unwieldy size, its loose security, and its resemblance of "a re-established GIS [German intelligence service]." Nonetheless, he favored a takeover, and the CIA relieved the Army of the Gehlen Organization on 1 July 1949.[185]

For Army Intelligence, Operation RUSTY was a mixed bag. By late 1946, Gehlen's men claimed to run between 500 and 600 sources in the Soviet Zone, and they had sent approximately 400 intelligence reports to the Army.[186] The Army praised Operation RUSTY as "one of its most prolific and dependable sources," but this encomium must be viewed in the context of the Army's efforts to persuade the Central Intelligence Group to assume control of Gehlen's organization.[187] Another official dismissed such accolades, contending instead that Gehlen's intelligence product was "comparatively low-level and entirely tactical. Other than in the field of unit identification little new or particularly valuable information . . . has been obtained."[188]

---

181 Wegener, *Organisation Gehlen*, 5.
182 Email, Peter M. F. Sichel to Thomas Boghardt, 26 Jun 2017, Historians Files, CMH.
183 Rpt, Samuel B. Bossard, Central Intel Gp, to General Vandenberg, DCI, 29 May 1947, doc. 43, in Ruffner, *Forging an Intelligence Partnership*, 1:367, 1:369.
184 Rpt, Samuel B. Bossard, Central Intel Gp, to Lt. Gen. Hoyt S. Vandenberg Jr., DCI, 5 May 1947, doc. 41, in Ruffner, *Forging an Intelligence Partnership*, 1:339–61.
185 Ruffner, *Forging an Intelligence Relationship*, 1:xxvi–xxvii; Ch, MOB [Munich Opns Base] [Critchfield] to Ch, OSO [Ofc of Special Opns], 17 Dec 1948, sub: Report of Investigation—RUSTY, doc. 72, in Ruffner, ed., *Forging an Intelligence Partnership*, 1:45–123.
186 Msg, Burress to Vandenberg, 1 Oct 1946, sub: Operation RUSTY, doc. 19, in Ruffner, *Forging an Intelligence Partnership*, 1:112–15.
187 Msg, Burress to Vandenberg, 1 Oct 1946, sub: Operation RUSTY, doc. 19, in Ruffner, *Forging an Intelligence Partnership*, 1:103.
188 Memo, Galloway for DCI, 17 Oct 1946, sub: Operation Rusty, doc. 43, in Ruffner, *Forging an Intelligence Partnership*, 1:371.

One of the earliest in-depth studies of the Gehlen Organization concluded that Operation RUSTY provided 70 percent of the American government's information on the Soviet forces.[189] This figure probably came directly from Gehlen or one of his associates. It has long influenced appraisals of Operation RUSTY, but it is not supported by archival evidence. The early espionage efforts of Baun and Gehlen were decidedly modest.[190] The records of the Army's intelligence divisions in Europe and Washington detail the input from its various organizations and sources in Europe, but they contain little evidence of information provided by Operation RUSTY.[191] Although the Germans produced a good deal of low-level tactical information on the Soviets, Army Intelligence had plenty of sources capable of producing similar data. At the highest echelon of Army Intelligence analysis, Operation RUSTY was notable by its absence.

More important for the Army's and the CIA's decision to support Gehlen was RUSTY's "Potential Future Value."[192] The Americans rightly anticipated that Gehlen would be a key figure in the intelligence and military affairs of a future West German state, and they wanted to keep him on their good side. Some intelligence officers also suspected Gehlen of using his organization primarily as a means to "offer shelter and support for a future German General Staff." This, too, proved an apt assessment.[193] With an eye on a future West German state allied with the United States, American intelligence preferred loose supervision of RUSTY to none at all. Weak American oversight, the growing Soviet threat, and Gehlen's organizational skills and determination thus conspired to produce a semiautonomous German espionage organization that had obvious security issues and resembled Hitler's intelligence apparatus. In the context of the Cold War, this was a price both the Army and the CIA were willing to pay.

Defectors, Informants, and Ratlines

Defectors from the Soviet forces constituted a valuable and abundant source of information for U.S. intelligence. The Office of the Deputy Director of Intelligence estimated that 60,000 soldiers had deserted from the Red Army in the first three

---

189 Höhne and Zolling, *The General Was a Spy*, 88.
190 Pahl, "Hermann Baun (1897–1951)," in Müller-Enbergs and Wagner, *Spione und Nachrichtenhändler*, 59.
191 For Army Intelligence sources on and estimates of the Soviet forces, see Chapter 9.
192 Draft to Deputy A, Operation Rusty, 16 Oct 1946, doc. 21, in Ruffner, *Forging an Intelligence Partnership*, 1:159–62.
193 Email, Sichel to Boghardt, 26 Jun 2017.

years of the postwar period.[194] Most fled not because of ideological opposition to communism but because of the dismal conditions in their units and in search of a better life in the West. As one Army Intelligence official observed, "Stalin made two big mistakes in this war; first, he let Western Europe see the Soviet Army and second, he let the Soviet Army see Western Europe."[195]

For would-be defectors in Europe, Austria and Germany offered the most obvious path to the West.[196] In Berlin, where one could simply hop on a local train and cross the sectoral border, defection was particularly easy. In late 1945, the intelligence branch of the Berlin District established a formal exploitation program for defectors. According to Col. John P. Merrill, the Army's tactical intelligence chief in Berlin in 1946, the program "began from a very small beginning . . . and gradually in a very, almost haphazard way, seemed to grow."[197]

The information provided by defectors turned out so valuable that Army Intelligence launched an effort to induce desertions. The promise of adequate medical care proved a particularly powerful lure. Colonel Merrill related a story that may have been apocryphal, but nonetheless highlighted how the Americans exploited Red Army brutality and the rampant spread of sexually transmitted infections among Soviet soldiers to encourage defections. According to Merrill:

> [the] Soviet Army had a particularly savage method of treating venereal disease in which people who were infected—whether they were officers or enlisted—were thrown into a very barren sort of prison camp, with no beds and no normal medical facilities of any sort, or normal cooking or amenities of life, and given injections of milk in their veins which raised their temperature to 104 or 105 or more and threw them into these terrible fevers and delirium not unlike malaria, but which created so much body heat that these germs were killed; and that was a particularly brutal treatment but very effective. It was greatly

---

194 Msg, Lt. Col. W. R. Rainold, ODDI, to Director of Intel, OMGUS, 12 Feb 1948, sub: Report on Soviet Military Espionage Activities, Folder "383.4-1 Espionage," Director of Intel, Analysis and Research Br, Gen Corresp, 1945–49, RG 260, NACP.
195 Rpt, Lawrence E. deNeufville, to Director of Intel, 21 Feb 1948, sub: Weekly Intelligence Report No. 93, Folder "OMGUS ID Wkly Intelligence Rpts 01–94 Feb 48," Rpts of the ODI, 1947–1949, RG 260, NACP.
196 Msg, Capt. N. W. Malitch, Capt. Victor Koenigsberg, 307th CIC Detachment, HQ, Seventh Army, to ACofS, G-2, Seventh Army, 4 Jan 1946, sub: Subversive Action of USSR Officers, Folder "Subversive Activities of USSR Officers ZF 011636," INSCOM, IRR, 1939–1976, Impersonal Name Files, RG 319, NACP; Maj. Ann Bray et al., ed., *The History of the Counter Intelligence Corps*, vol. 25, *Occupation Austria and Italy* (Fort Holabird, MD: U.S. Army Intelligence Center, 1959), 37.
197 Deposition, Col. John P. Merrill, court-martial of William T. Marchuk, 12 Apr–20 May 1955, WNRC.

feared by all of the Soviet soldiers and they would do almost anything to avoid it, and consequently, we used to find that penicillin was one of the most valuable incentive supplies we had in the business.[198]

In wartime Europe, Army Intelligence occasionally recruited local prostitutes by providing vital medical treatments they could not obtain on their own. In the postwar period, this same incentive worked equally well to induce defections among the Soviet ranks.

Desperate to stem the flow of defectors to the West, the Soviets in 1946 persuaded the Americans to sign the Clay-Sokolovsky agreement, named after the deputy commanders of the U.S. and Soviet forces in Germany, General Clay and General Vasily D. Sokolovsky.[199] The agreement required each side to return defectors immediately. American intelligence officials abhorred the agreement, and the Army complied with its terms only in exceptional cases, such as a defector being the subject of a criminal investigation. In the winter of 1946–1947, for example, an interpreter for Soviet intelligence, Alexander Bassubenko, defected to the U.S. Zone, bringing files from his office. The intelligence division in Frankfurt made copies of the documents and forwarded them to the Pentagon. Meanwhile, Soviet authorities claimed that Bassubenko was wanted for murder and demanded his release. The Americans complied and he "was returned to Soviet custody on 17 January 1947," as the intelligence division noted laconically.[200]

By the late 1940s, not even implied criminal activity could sway the Army to abide by the Clay-Sokolovsky agreement. In the summer of 1949, a Soviet private named Filin sought refuge with the Americans. As Lt. Gen. Clarence R. Huebner informed Clay's deputy, Maj. Gen. George P. Hays, "Filin is not a political refugee nor a disgruntled deserter but an escaped criminal by his own confession." The Soviets demanded his return, but by this time the Cold War had obliterated the spirit if not the letter of the Clay-Sokolovsky agreement. Huebner instructed the

---

198 Deposition, Merrill, 12 Apr–20 May 1955. This alleged method may have been a crude form of "fever therapy" (pyrotherapy), which was an accepted treatment—even in the United States—for sexually transmitted infections such as syphilis up until antibiotic treatments became more widespread in the 1940s. For a contemporary U.S. Navy medical account of the practice, see Davis H. Pardoll and Robert L. Dennis, "Chemotherapy, Pyrotherapy and Penicillin in the Treatment of Gonorrhea," *United States Naval Medical Bulletin* 43, no. 5 (Nov 1944): 988–96.
199 Ruffner, "Eagle and the Swastika," chap. 12, 6–7.
200 Msg, Col. M. C. Taylor, ODDI, EUCOM, to Director of Intel, War Department, Gen Staff, 8 Apr 1947, sub: Transmittal of MGB files, Folder "926058," Rcds of the ACoS, G–2 (Intel), Formerly Top Secret Intel Documents, 1943–59, RG 319, NACP.

U.S. Constabulary that Filin should be "immediately released without further processing in the United States Zone in civilian clothing." Meanwhile, he ordered the U.S. Military Liaison Mission in Potsdam to tell the Soviets that Filin "is not under our control and we know nothing of his whereabouts."[201]

The flow of deserters to the West continued unabated. In one of the most high-profile defections of the early Cold War, two Soviet Air Forces officers, lieutenants Peter A. Pirogov and Anatoly Barsov, flew 800 miles from their airbase in the Soviet Union to crash-land their plane in the U.S. Zone of occupied Austria in October 1948. The incident became an intelligence windfall for the Americans and a public relations disaster for Moscow. The two men lamented the oppression in their home country and said that listening to broadcasts of the U.S. foreign news service Voice of America had enticed them to defect. The CIC interrogated them on their military background and U.S. Air Force personnel disassembled the plane to learn more about Soviet aviation technology. The Soviets demanded the return of the crew and the plane, but U.S. authorities transferred both to the United States. In 1950, Pirogov published his memoirs, *Why I Escaped*, a powerful indictment of Stalinist rule.[202]

Most defectors arrived in a less spectacular fashion, usually by crossing the interzonal or the intersectoral border. After an initial screening, Army Intelligence transferred most of them to Camp King for in-depth interrogation.[203] Upon the completion of this process, the Americans quietly released them. Many defectors subsequently settled in the U.S. Zone and mingled with various émigré groups.[204] Some joined labor service battalions, auxiliary formations consisting

---

201 Msg, Lt. Gen. Clarence R. Huebner, EUCOM, to Maj. Gen. George P. Hays, OMGUS, 8 Jul 1949, Folder "Top Secret Out's 1948 01 Jul to 31 Dec Book IV," EUCOM, Ofc of the Ch of Staff, Sec of the Gen Staff, Msg Control Center, Outgoing Msgs, top secret section, 1948–1951, RG 549, NACP; Msg, Lt. Gen. Clarence R. Huebner to Maj. Gen. George P. Hays, OMGUS, 11 Jul 1949, Folder "Top Secret Out's 1948 01 Jul to 31 Dec Book IV," EUCOM, Ofc of the Ch of Staff, Sec of the Gen Staff, Msg Control Center, Outgoing Msgs, top secret section, 1948–1951, RG 549, NACP.
202 Bray et al., *History of the Counter Intelligence Corps*, 25:38; James V. Milano and Patrick Brogan, *Soldiers, Spies and the Rat Line: America's Undeclared War Against the Soviets* (Washington, DC: Brassey's, 2000), 127; Albion Ross, "2 Soviet Officers Flee to Austria, Landing Bomber at U.S. Army Base," *New York Times*, 21 Oct 1948; Peter A. Pirogov, *Why I Escaped: The Story of Peter Pirogov* (New York: Duell, Sloan and Pearce, 1950). The crew also included a gunner who voluntarily returned to the Soviet Union from Austria.
203 James C. Spratt, "The History of Camp King" (Carlisle, PA: U.S. Army Military History Institute, n.d.), 107. Army Intelligence had established a formal defector interrogation program at Camp King in September 1948.
204 Memo, Special Agent Edward G. Zimmerman, Region I, CIC, for Ofcr in Charge, 19 Apr 1948, sub: Disability of Josef Stalin, Folder "Stalin, Joseph," INSCOM, IRR, Selected Printouts of Digital Intel and Investigative Dossiers – Personal Files, 1933–1958, RG 319, NACP.

mostly of Eastern European nationals performing guard and other housekeeping duties for the Army. The CIA recruited particularly valuable or motivated defectors for operations behind the Iron Curtain.[205]

Meanwhile, the Soviets moved aggressively to deal with the defector problem. In February 1949, a Soviet intelligence agent fired several shots at a deserter in the American sector of Berlin. The agent sought to force the defector in a car and drive him to the Soviet sector, but the defector managed to escape, and American military police arrested the agent.[206] A few months later, Soviet intelligence tried to carry out an even more brazen abduction in the heart of downtown Washington, D.C., mere blocks away from the White House. In mid-1949, Soviet officials contacted one of the defected pilots, Lieutenant Barsov, and persuaded him to return to the USSR. Before his departure, Barsov met with his former comrade, Pirogov, at a restaurant on Connecticut Avenue near the Soviet embassy. There, Pirogov later testified, several men attacked and handcuffed him—an apparent kidnapping attempt—but other patrons came to his rescue.[207] Barsov duly returned to the Soviet Union alone. According to CIC informants, upon his arrival the Soviets imprisoned and interrogated him. Although the embassy had promised the unfortunate pilot his freedom, Soviet troops "were assembled to watch the execution of Barsov by a firing squad as a lesson to anyone else who might decide to defect to the West."[208]

In the face of these aggressive Soviet measures, American intelligence sought to transfer their more vulnerable assets outside Europe. Between 1945 and 1949, the CIA evacuated a total of thirty-eight defectors and former agents from Germany.[209] The CIC aided in resettlement efforts, too, especially in Austria where the Clay-Sokolovsky agreement did not apply. Because Austria was comparatively smaller than Germany, the local CIC found it difficult to hide their evacuees from the Soviets. In the summer of 1947 the intelligence division of the U.S. Forces in Austria issued instructions for the 430th Counter Intelligence Corps Detachment to "establish a means of disposition" for compromised agents and defectors.[210]

---

[205] Ruffner, "Eagle and the Swastika," chap. 12, 20.
[206] Memo, Special Agent Severin F. Wallach, Region VIII, CIC, for CO, 13 Feb 1949, sub: Soviet Intelligence Activities in the U.S. Sector of Berlin, Folder "Confidential Operation Control of CIC Region VIII XE 232591," INSCOM, IRR, Impersonal Name Files, RG 319, NACP.
[207] "Resumed Testimony of Peter Pirogov, Washington, D.C., June 13, 1956," CIA-RDP58-00597A000200140045-9, CIA Electronic Reading Room, https://www.cia.gov/readingroom.
[208] Bray et al., *History of the Counter Intelligence Corps*, 25:39.
[209] Ruffner, "Eagle and the Swastika," chap. 12, 8.
[210] Milano and Brogan, *Soldiers, Spies and the Rat Line*, 224.

The CIC commander in Austria, Col. James V. Milano, chose an unorthodox method for moving his charges out of the country. He availed himself of a "ratline"—an escape route established at the end of the war by former Nazis and fascists to help fugitive Axis officials and war criminals evade trial. With the support of a network of sympathizers, these escapees traveled from Austria to Italy and on to South America. In Italy, profascist elements of the Catholic clergy obtained false documentation and made travel arrangements for fascists and Nazis on the run. A Croatian priest ensconced in Rome, Father Krunoslav S. Draganović, served as the Americans' principal contact. The CIC noted that Draganović "is known and recorded as a Fascist, war criminal, etc.," but once again, Cold War concerns trumped moral scruples.[211] At the price of $1,000 to $1,400 per head, the Austrian CIC resettled a number of Soviet defectors and compromised German informants in South America via the Italian ratline.[212]

At the time, the CIC in Germany had been unaware of their Austrian colleagues' use of the ratline.[213] In fact, special agents investigated illegal escape routes as part of their mission to track the activities of former Nazi officials. South America was not the only destination for those fleeing their pasts; for some, an equally friendly nation was much closer to home. In early 1947, an informant of the CIC in Munich reported that "high ranking [Third Reich] officials and SS officers" were traveling on falsified papers via Austria and Italy to fascist Spain.[214] Over time, the CIC compiled additional information on this escape network. The CIC in Frankfurt reported that the Horcher restaurant in Madrid served as a contact for Nazi refugees. During the war, the Horcher family had run a luxury restaurant in Berlin catering to Nazi bigwigs like Hermann W. Göring. In 1943, the family relocated to the Spanish capital and continued to support their fascist clientele under cover of Spanish neutrality.[215] American intelligence also learned that Otto Skorzeny had settled under a false name in Madrid. He report-

---

211 Milano and Brogan, *Soldiers, Spies and the Rat Line*, 226.
212 Gerald Steinacher, *Nazis on the Run: How Hitler's Henchmen Fled Justice* (Oxford: Oxford University Press, 2011), 202.
213 Rpt, Allan A. Ryan Jr., *Klaus Barbie and the United States Government: A Report to the Attorney General of the United States* (Washington, DC: U.S. Department of Justice, 1983), 136 (hereinafter Barbie Report).
214 Memo, Special Agent Peter R. Renno, Munich, Region IV, CIC, for Ofcr in Charge, 13 Feb 1947, sub: Escape organization in Spain, Folder "Illegal Emigration to Spain," INSCOM, IRR, Impersonal Name Files, RG 319, NACP.
215 Memo, Special Agent Peter Nadsen, Frankfurt, Region III, CIC, for Ofcr in Charge, 18 Apr 1948, sub: Spanish Activity, Folder "Illegal Emigration to Spain," INSCOM, IRR, Impersonal Name Files, RG 319, NACP; Giles Macdonogh, "Otto Horcher, Caterer to the Third Reich," *Gastronomica* 7, no. 10 (Winter 2007): 31–38. The Horcher restaurant remains in Madrid to this day.

edly met on a regular basis with other former Nazi officials, local fascists, and like-minded individuals at the Horcher restaurant.[216] The escape of Skorzeny and other Nazis may partially account for the proliferation of the Hitler survival myth around the globe.

The CIC's information on the Spanish ratline was accurate if incomplete. Masterminded by a Catholic priest, José La Boos, and run by a naturalized Spanish citizen, Clarita Stauffer, the "Iberian Way" helped thousands of former Nazis and war criminals escape from the authorities in Germany and Austria.[217] In June 1947, Special Agent Richard H. Weber requested authority from CIC headquarters to send an informant to Spain to investigate "the presence of large German Nazi element" there.[218] But the operations officer of the 970th CIC Detachment, Maj. Earl S. Browning Jr., turned down the request because the detachment's mission was "confined to the U.S. Zone of Germany."[219]

The Spanish ratline reveals the dilemma of many intelligence officials in postwar Germany. Browning knew of the monstrosity of the Nazi regime. He had fought in the European Theater, and he never forgot the horrors he had witnessed at Dachau.[220] At the same time, he had to consider the legal perils involved in sending a CIC agent to Spain, a sovereign country outside the U.S. security umbrella. Nor could he ignore the diminishing American interest in denazification and war crimes investigations. These factors all played a part in his decision not to expend CIC resources on the Spanish ratline.

During the war and in the immediate postwar period, the occasional use of former Nazis by the U.S. military government prompted pushback from many American officials. Against the background of the U.S.-Soviet rivalry, however, such pangs of conscience subsided. For its part, Army Intelligence began recruiting former Nazi officials for their supposed expertise in combating communism. "In selecting informants," the official CIC history noted, "CIC agents had to adopt the rule of thumb of the 'right man for the right job.' At times, this meant that former Ge-

---

216 Molly R. Ricks, "After Acquittal: Otto Skorzeny's Postwar Life" (unpublished research paper, U.S. Army Center of Military History, Washington, DC, 2018), 28, Historians Files, CMH; Rosa Belmonte, "Horcher, de Hermann Göring a Ferran Adrià" [Horcher, from Hermann Göring to Ferran Adrià], *ABC*, 25 May 2014.
217 Guy Walters, *Hunting Evil: The Nazi War Criminals Who Escaped and the Quest to Bring Them to Justice* (New York: Broadway Books, 2010), 131.
218 Memo, Special Agent Richard H. Weber, CIC Region IX, Bremen, 3 Jun 1947, sub: Illegal Emigration to Spain, Report No. 1, INSCOM, IRR, Impersonal Name Files, RG 319, NACP.
219 Msg, Maj. Earl. S. Browning Jr., 970th CIC Detachment, to CO, CIC Region IX, 18 Jul 1947, Folder "Illegal Emigration to Spain," INSCOM, IRR, Impersonal Name Files, RG 319, NACP.
220 Email, Jim Browning to Thomas Boghardt, 10 Sep 2020, Historians Files, CMH.

stapo agents and other individuals with Nazi backgrounds had to be utilized, because they were the only ones who could develop the desired information."[221]

In a particularly notorious case, this forgiving attitude came back to bite the Corps. In April 1947, the CIC in Bavaria recruited a former *Gestapo* officer, Klaus Barbie, as a source, and directed him to collect information on French and Soviet intelligence operations in Germany. Even when compared with other former Nazi officers exploited by the Americans, Barbie's wartime record stood out. During the war, he headed the *Gestapo* office in German-occupied Lyon, where he personally tortured and killed numerous suspected resistance fighters, earning him the nickname "Butcher of Lyon." At the time of his recruitment, the CIC had been aware of Barbie's unrepentant pro-Nazi views but not of his involvement in specific crimes. This changed in April 1949, when French authorities requested that the U.S. military government extradite Barbie to face charges for his war crimes. To avoid public embarrassment, as well as to keep Barbie from revealing sensitive information about American intelligence to the French, the Corps decided to help him escape from Europe rather than turn him over to France.[222]

To resettle Barbie, the CIC in Germany approached their counterparts in Austria. In December 1950, a technical specialist of CIC headquarters at Heidelberg met with a group of special agents in Austria. "The 430th CIC Detachment," the specialist reported, "has been operating what they term a 'Ratline' evacuation system to Central and South America without serious repercussions."[223] With the help of their Austrian colleagues, the CIC in Germany hired the services of Father Draganović. Under the false name of Klaus Altman, Barbie and his family traveled safely via Italy to Bolivia in 1951.

Morally and legally, the CIC's decision to help Barbie evade trial was highly problematic, and the collaboration with former Nazi officials made some Army Intelligence personnel distinctly uneasy. One intelligence official recalled that he felt "uncomfortable among colleagues who never discussed German denazification or democratization but were obsessed with finding ways to thwart and weaken the Soviet Union."[224] Nor did Barbie's disappearance via the ratline make the issue go away. Twenty years after Barbie's resettlement, French Nazi hunters discovered his whereabouts in South America and demanded his extradition. In 1983, Bolivia expelled him to France. A French court sentenced Barbie to life in

---

221 Maj. Ann Bray et al., ed., *The History of the Counter Intelligence Corps*, vol. 27, *Four Years of Cold War* (Fort Holabird, MD: U.S. Army Intelligence Center, 1959), 31.
222 Barbie Report, 38–39, 84.
223 Barbie Report, 141.
224 Arthur D. Kahn, *Experiment in Occupation: Witness to the Turnabout; Anti-Nazi War to Cold War, 1944–1946* (University Park: Pennsylvania State University Press, 2004), 79.

prison, where he died in 1991.[225] Meanwhile, the U.S. Department of Justice conducted an inquiry into the CIC's involvement with Barbie and the ratline, which shone a bright light on an unsavory aspect of CIC operations in postwar Europe.[226] The Soviet-controlled press, for their part, covered the revelations about Barbie in detail and hammered American intelligence for their use of Draganović's ratline and their protection of a notorious Nazi torturer.[227] The reporting of the communist press on Barbie fit neatly into the larger Soviet-orchestrated propaganda campaign of accusing the West of colluding with former Nazi officials and war criminals.

The exploitation of Soviet defectors, Nazi informants, and the infamous ratline illustrates how the Cold War reshaped American intelligence operations in occupied Germany. Initially, U.S. intelligence employed the ratline exclusively to help Soviet defectors escape the long arm of Moscow, but the Americans ended up using it for a heavily compromised Nazi informant in order to save face and protect their own secrets. The murky triangle of defectors, informants, and ratlines became a Cold War exercise of achieving an end by questionable means and left a black mark on the reputation of American intelligence.[228]

Conclusion

The American intelligence exploitation of Nazi Germany was an exercise in contradiction. On the one hand, it delivered precious scientific knowledge and provided much-needed information from behind the Iron Curtain. On the other hand, it allowed many Nazis to reinvent themselves as useful Cold Warriors and elude questions about their past. The role of Army Intelligence in the exploitation

---

225 Boghardt, "Dirty Work?," 387–88.
226 The result of this investigation was the Barbie Report.
227 Klaus Steiniger, "Wie das CIC einen Henker übernahm" [How the CIC took over an executioner], *Neues Deutschland*, 16 Jul 1983.
228 Journalists and historians have explored numerous aspects of American intelligence cooperation with former Nazi officials. Authoritative accounts include Richard Breitman, Norman J. W. Goda, Timothy Naftali, and Robert Wolfe, eds., *U.S. Intelligence and the Nazis* (New York: Cambridge University Press, 2005); and Richard Breitman and Norman J. W. Goda, *Hitler's Shadow: Nazi War Criminals, U.S. Intelligence, and the Cold War* (Washington, DC: National Archives and Records Administration, 2010).

effort was as ambiguous as the program itself. Many intelligence officials in Germany pointed to the dubious backgrounds of potential recruits, but decision-makers generally brushed these concerns aside. If the response of Army Intelligence to the exploitation program was contradictory, it mirrored American policy at large.

7 New Challenges

From the moment American forces crossed the border, they faced surprising challenges that had not factored into any wartime intelligence assessment. The travails of the 218th Counter Intelligence Corps Detachment exemplify the experience of many intelligence units. The CIC soldiers arrived at Appelhülsen, a small town to the west of Münster, shortly after its capture in March 1945. They intended to identify politically reliable individuals, but the utter chaos they encountered upon arrival upended their original mission. The American unit occupying the town had locked up the citizenry in a school building, and some of the soldiers appeared to be looting with impunity. In the absence of a military government agency, the detachment had to restore control over the undisciplined soldiers, screen the population for Nazi officials and sympathizers, and work with the local priest, who assumed interim responsibility for the townspeople. In the days ahead, additional duties fell into the CIC's lap. As the detachment commander, Capt. Albin P. Dearing, lamented in his weekly report:

> A day spent carrying women (three days locked up in a school building without food or water); helping midwife a cow (the farm labor was also interned and the droves of fine stock left untended); doctoring a young girl who had lacerations on her face from shelling; settling the problems of sorting out and shipping 78 Poles, Dutch, Italians, and French [i.e., recently liberated forced laborers], while at the same time finding white bread for a dying diabetic; putting out fires; chasing drunken GI's out of the Headquarters; and finding details to bury dead Jerries . . . is a far cry from the intelligent, systematic search for the dissident elements whom we have come here to find.[1]

The CIC's experience in Appelhülsen foreshadowed the trials of Army Intelligence during the occupation. The Army did not have the luxury of focusing its intelligence resources on only a few prioritized tasks. A host of new concerns would test the agencies' adaptability and redefine their mission as the American military occupation evolved from a postwar pacification effort to a forward base of the Cold War.

Chaos, Corruption, and the Black Market

In early April 1945, Army Intelligence personnel at the village of Merkers in Thuringia encountered several displaced persons who told them that the German

---

[1] Maj. Ann Bray et al., ed., *The History of the Counter Intelligence Corps*, vol. 20, *Germany Overrun: Part I* (Fort Holabird, MD: U.S. Army Intelligence Center, 1959), 56.

Reichsbank (central bank) had recently moved its gold reserves from Berlin to a nearby potassium mine. At the request of the intelligence section of the 90th Infantry Division, the local Army commander sealed off the area, and on 7 April the assistant division commander descended into the mine, accompanied by small group of Army personnel and German mining officials. At the bottom, they found more than 8,000 bars of gold bullion and approximately 2.76 billion Reichsmarks (German currency).[2] In addition, they discovered more than 2,000 bags of assorted foreign currency and a vast collection of artwork looted by the Nazis from all over Europe. Three days later, Generals George S. Patton Jr., Omar N. Bradley, and Dwight D. Eisenhower entered the mine to see the treasure for themselves. As the rickety elevator descended into the mineshaft, Patton looked at the single cable attached to their carriage and quipped that "promotions in the United States Army would be considerably stimulated" if it snapped. An unamused Eisenhower replied, "Ok, George, that's enough. No more cracks until we are above ground again."[3] After the generals' visit, the next steps included moving the valuables to a more secure location. Within a few days, the Army transferred its massive find in a heavily guarded convoy of thirty-two trucks to a bank vault in Frankfurt. The operation, code-named Task Force WHITNEY, unfolded flawlessly. The discovery and evacuation of the Nazi gold deprived Adolf Hitler's faltering regime of any hope of using these precious resources in its final struggle against the Allies. Yet the Americans had an ulterior motive for securing the treasure with all speed: the Merkers mine was in the future Soviet Zone. The operation kept the gold from falling into Moscow's hands.

The fortunes secured at Merkers constituted merely a part of the vast holdings of the Reichsbank, and their acquisition was only the beginning of the Army's embroilment with the economic turmoil brought about by the collapse of the Third Reich. At the end of the war, several German government and Nazi Party organizations transferred their valuables from war-torn Berlin to the seemingly more secure central and southern parts of Germany. Much of this fortune disappeared amid the postwar disorder. Over the following years, the Army's intelligence agencies sought to track down the elusive Third Reich assets. By 1947, the CIC search for Nazi gold took agents as far away as Spain.[4] Often, the chase proved quixotic, chaotic, and futile. As one frustrated investigator later uttered, "It was a f–ked-up mess."[5]

---

2 In 2020 U.S. dollars, this find would be worth nearly $500 million.
3 Greg Bradsher, "Nazi Gold: The Merkers Mine Treasure," *Prologue Magazine* 31, no. 1 (Spring 1999), online edition, Historians Files, CMH.
4 MFR, Col. [illegible], Criminal Investigation Div, 4 Apr 1947, sub: Reichsbank gold, Folder "Reichsbank Gold D 153767," INSCOM, IRR, Digitized Rcds, RG 319, NACP.
5 Ian Sayer and Douglas Botting, *Nazi Gold: The Story of the World's Greatest Robbery – And Its Aftermath* (London: Granada, 1984), 262.

Figure 30: Col. Jack W. Durant and his wife, Women's Army Corps Capt. Kathleen B. Nash Durant, arrive at Frankfurt airport for their trial, June 1945. U.S. Army.

Even as the Allies sought to impose order over the areas they occupied, Army personnel also became perpetrators. The widespread involvement of American soldiers in the stealing and selling of German property added to some German perceptions that the U.S. military government could be as crooked and rapacious as the regime it had replaced. "Looting," according to the official historian of the early occupation period, "had become something of an art."[6] A spectacular jewel theft at the end of the war highlighted the issue and brought it home to the American public. In late 1944, Princess Sophia of Hesse hid her family's jewels, estimated at $1.5 million, in the cellars of the family castle in Kronberg, located 2 miles east of Oberursel.[7] In April 1945, the Army requisitioned the castle, and thirsty soldiers

---

6 Earl F. Ziemke, *The U.S. Army in the Occupation of Germany, 1944–1946*, Army Historical Series (Washington, DC: U.S. Army Center of Military History, 1975), 250.
7 Princess Sophia (also known as Sophie) was the widow of Prince Christoph of Hesse, who had died in a plane crash in 1943. She was the older sister of Prince Philip of Greece and Denmark,

stumbled across the treasure while looking for a secret wine cache. The local commander, Capt. Kathleen B. Nash of the Women's Army Corps, took ownership of the find. Together with her lover, Col. Jack W. Durant, and a few other soldiers, Nash decided to sell the collection. Meanwhile, Princess Sophia approached Nash and asked her to return the jewels. When Nash deflected her inquiries, the princess contacted the American authorities in Germany in April 1946 and reported her property stolen. The Army's Criminal Investigation Division quickly identified Nash and Durant, who had married after returning to the United States with their loot, as the culprits. In early June, military police arrested them in a hotel in Chicago.[8] Following trials in U.S. civil courts and a court-martial in Germany, the two suspects received sentences of five and fifteen years in prison, respectively.[9] American authorities recovered barely half of the jewels and returned them to the Hesse family. The press widely reported on the case, and the War Department's director of public relations, Maj. Gen. Floyd L. Parks, stated that the Army was "mortified" over the affair.[10]

Looting subsided by the end of 1945, but the black market posed an enduring challenge to U.S. authorities. The Reichsmark had collapsed along with the Nazi regime, and many Germans reverted to bartering. Cigarettes emerged as a convenient substitute for hard currency, as they were widely coveted and easy to trade. American soldiers, with ready access to cigarettes and other goods through the Army, found themselves ideally positioned to take advantage of the new economic reality. For example, a soldier could buy a pack of cigarettes for fifty cents at the local U.S. military post exchange and sell it on the black market for the equivalent of $10 to $20.[11] With their comparative wealth, some soldiers found it difficult to resist the potential profits to be gained through such illicit activities.

The black market boomed in two areas of the American occupation: Bavaria and Berlin. In southern Germany, the illegal sale of Reichsbank gold bullion and other Nazi-era assets and the smuggling of goods such as antiques and jewelry across the borders fueled illegal bartering activities.[12] As late as March 1949, the

---

who in 1947 would become Duke of Edinburgh upon his marriage to then Princess Elizabeth of the United Kingdom.
8 Rpt, Special Agent William L. Mulcaheny and Special Agent Aviv Blackman, Criminal Investigations Div, to CO, 23 Apr 1946, sub: Capt. Kathleen B. Nash, L-918024, Mess Section, HQ Cmd, USFET, APO 757, Folder "1947 Cables and Orders Pertaining to Kronberg Case – Durant, Nash, Watson," HQ Commandant: Classified Records Re Disappearance of Hesse Family Jewels from Kronberg, Germany, 1946–47, RG 498, NACP.
9 "Durant Given 15 Years for Jewels Theft," *Washington Post*, 1 May 1947.
10 Sidney Shalett, "Colonel, Wac Captain Held in German Royal Gem Theft," *New York Times*, 8 Jun 1946.
11 Julian Bach, *America's Germany: An Account of the Occupation* (New York: Random House, 1947), 57.
12 Sayer and Botting, *Nazi Gold*, 179.

intelligence division of the Office of Military Government, Bavaria, reported that a single police raid had confiscated a large illegal cargo of more than 120 tons of coffee, 18 tons of chocolate, and 6 tons of cocoa.[13]

In Berlin, the black market boomed with the help of the Soviets. Following Germany's defeat, the Allies had issued a new currency, the Occupation Mark, to replace the worthless Reichsmark. To produce the Occupation Mark, the Americans shared a set of printing plates with the Soviets, who immediately started issuing reams of bills to pay their occupation forces. The Red Army soldiers flooded the market with this new currency by buying goods and services from Germans and Americans at the two major trading sites in the city, Alexanderplatz and Tiergarten.[14] As the resulting inflation eroded the value of the occupation government's official currency, Berliners and Allied forces alike turned to the city's underground economy for their wants and needs. With the benefit of regular wages and comparatively easy access to the scarce necessities and rare luxuries available in postwar Germany, many U.S. soldiers made a fortune from the black market. However, such activities undermined morale and tainted the image of the occupation. The military government repeatedly sought to clamp down on those who sought to profit from ill-gotten gains.[15]

The problem of the black market involved Army Intelligence in two ways. First, it caused security concerns for the military at all levels. The intelligence division in Frankfurt feared that subversive groups might use black market activities to finance their operations, and the CIC in Kassel reported that agents of the local communist party (KPD) organization sought to recruit informants at black market sites in railroad stations.[16] A Soviet defector told the CIC that Soviet intelli-

---

13 Msg, OMGB, Field Opns Div, Nuremberg, to Br Ch, 22 Mar 1949, sub: Alleged Black-Market Activity, Folder "2 Black Market," Rcds of the OMGB, Rcds of the Intel Div, 1946–49, RG 260, NACP.

14 William Stivers and Donald A. Carter, *The City Becomes a Symbol: The U.S. Army in the Occupation of Berlin, 1945–1949*, U.S. Army in the Cold War (Washington, DC: U.S. Army Center of Military History, 2017), 118.

15 Msg, Gen. Lucius D. Clay to Brig. Gen. Edward H. White, Ofc of the Comptroller, USFET, 2 Nov 1946, re: Barter Market in Berlin, doc. 166, in *The Papers of General Lucius D. Clay, Germany 1945–1949*, vol. 1, ed. Jean Edward Smith (Bloomington: Indiana University Press, 1974), 276–79; Msg, Clay to Lt. Gen. David Noce, sub: Cigarettes and the Black Market, 14 Apr 1947, doc. 211, in Smith, *The Papers of Lucius D. Clay*, 1:335–36.

16 Ofc of the Ch Historian, EUCOM, *The First Year of the Occupation, 1945–1946*, vol. 2, Occupation Forces in Europe Series, 1945–46 (Frankfurt: Office of the Chief Historian, EUCOM, 1947), 166; Msg, Special Agent William W. Eitner, Region III, CIC, to CO, 4 Aug 1947, sub: KPD urging SS members to go to Soviet Zone, Folder "Alleged Soviet Sponsored Organizations to Recruit Former SS Personnel," INSCOM, IRR, Impersonal Name Files, RG 319, NACP.

gence sought to enlist black marketers and smugglers as agents.[17] The CIC conducted several raids to take out black market rings but, by its own admission, failed to root out the problem.[18] Second, Army Intelligence personnel occasionally had to investigate within their own ranks to crack down on those who had succumbed to the allure of black market profits. Intelligence officials often dealt with German informants and typically paid them in black market currency such as cigarettes or liquor. Operating in a shroud of secrecy, they had many opportunities to abuse their privileged positions for financial gain.[19] The situation was particularly acute in Berlin, where some intelligence personnel appeared to spend the bulk of their time wheeling and dealing. Corruption and illegal trading had become so pervasive within the city's Strategic Services Unit that General Lucius D. Clay reportedly complained to Allen W. Dulles: "How the hell can you expect those guys to catch spies when they can't smell the stink under their own noses?"[20]

The corruption issue came to the attention of the U.S. public in 1946 when an intelligence officer leveled a series of accusations against the military government. A member of the wartime Office of Strategic Services, Col. Francis P. Miller, was disappointed when General Clay failed to appoint him head of a large postwar espionage organization in occupied Germany. He also nursed personal grudges against several of Clay's leading staff officers, especially Brig. Gen. James B. Edmunds, the director of administrative services.[21] With the assistance of Col. Henry G. Sheen, the top counterintelligence officer in Germany, Miller collected evidence of personal misconduct among Army officers and intelligence personnel. The charges included corruption, black market activities, and the failure of Army commanders to curb the alleged misbehavior of American soldiers. The son and grandson of Presbyterian ministers, Miller particularly despised what he regarded as "lecherous living";

---

17 Rpt, [CIC] to ACofS, G–2, USFET, 31 Jan 1947, sub: Counterintelligence Report no. 154, Operation Rusty, Folder "Operation Rusty ZF010807W Volume I, 1 of 2," INSCOM, IRR, Impersonal Name Files, RG 319, NACP.
18 Maj. Ann Bray et al., ed., *The History of the Counter Intelligence Corps*, vol. 27, *Four Years of Cold War* (Fort Holabird, MD: U.S. Army Intelligence Center, 1959), 98.
19 Msg, Donald T. Shea, Director, Intel Div, OMGB, to Asst Land Director, 28 Feb 1949, sub: Operational Cigarettes, Folder "A Cigarettes," Rcds of the OMGB, Rcds of the Intel Div, Ofc of the Director: Administrative Rcds, 1948–49, RG 260, NACP.
20 Leonard Mosley, *Dulles: A Biography of Eleanor, Allen, and John Foster Dulles and Their Family Network* (New York: The Dial Press/James Wade, 1978), 225.
21 Kevin C. Ruffner, "The Black Market in Postwar Berlin: Colonel Miller and an Army Scandal," *Prologue Magazine* 34, no. 3 (Fall 2002): 1–20.

he accused several officers, including General Edmunds, of "having illicit relations with one or more German frauleins."[22]

The Army's leadership in Germany had little sympathy for Miller. When Clay learned of the investigation, he ordered it ceased. Miller then approached the inspector general in the European Theater, Maj. Gen. Withers A. "Pinky" Burress, who dismissed the claims as lacking foundation. Stymied in Europe, Miller contacted the office of Senator James M. Mead, the New York Democrat who headed the Special Committee to Investigate the National Defense Program. The committee, established in 1941 under the leadership of then Senator Harry S. Truman, looked into claims of fraud, waste, and abuse in war production industries and within the U.S. defense establishment. Called to testify before the committee, Miller reiterated his charges against the U.S. military government in Germany, and the committee ordered an investigation. The resulting report dismissed Miller's more sweeping charges but confirmed the existence of specific problems. When it came to the issue of "lecherous living," for example, the report conceded that many "American wives have joined their husbands, only to find that their places had been usurped, or at least temporarily occupied by other women." The report suggested that General Edmunds had indeed engaged in an extramarital affair and that Clay "relied too much" on his flawed director of administrative services. Although it recommended the promulgation of new regulations for the purchasing of goods by U.S. soldiers, the report essentially exonerated the military government. In a final twist, the report's authors suggested that "a prominent notation be made" on Miller's personnel file to consider his actions "in the event of any future evaluation of" his services—a mark that effectively would hobble Miller's future Army career.[23]

Unsurprisingly, conditions in the European Theater did not change. It was only a question of time before someone else would raise anew the issue of corruption in Army Intelligence. It happened the following year when a colorful individual, Guenther P. Reinhardt, precipitated another investigation. In 1925, the German-born Reinhardt had immigrated to the United States, where he developed a flair for the world of intelligence. Before the war, he worked as an investigator for the Federal Bureau of Investigation while simultaneously extending feelers to Soviet intel-

---

22 Memo, Col. Eugene L. Wilder, for Under Sec War, 21 Nov 1946, sub: Inquiry regarding certain phases of the Army's Administration of the United States Zone of Occupied Germany, Folder "333.9-Army of Occupation (Germany)," Gen Corresp 1939–1947, RG 165, NACP. For Miller's biography, see Martin Weil, "Francis Pickens Miller Dies at Age 83, Father of Va. Senatorial Nominee," *Washington Post*, 5 Aug 1978.
23 Memo, Wilder for Under Sec War, 21 Nov 1946, sub: Inquiry regarding certain phases of the Army's Administration of the United States Zone of Occupied Germany.

ligence.²⁴ In May 1947, the CIC in Germany hired him as a civilian employee on account of his FBI experience and his knowledge of German. Yet his tour did not go well. Insecure, paranoid, and depressive, Reinhardt discussed classified information in public to impress others, became heavily involved in the black market, and used his official position to try to pressure a female employee of the Civil Censorship Division into sleeping with him. His superior stated that Reinhardt "has embarrassed the CIC" and discharged him in November 1947.²⁵

But Reinhardt did not go quietly. "When I got back to the United States," he wrote a friend, "I was so damn mad I wanted to blow my top."²⁶ In short order, he submitted two memoranda to the Army leadership, accusing members of the CIC and other U.S. personnel in Germany of corruption, black marketeering, "scandals in connection with German mistresses," and several other transgressions.²⁷ In response, the inspector general of the Army launched an investigation, but Reinhardt's personal involvement in questionable activities undermined his credibility. As the assistant inspector general, Maj. Robert B. Hensley, pointedly stated, Reinhardt seemed guilty of "some of the same shortcomings he so freely ascribes to others." On the one hand, Hensley acknowledged the existence of disciplinary and ethical problems in the European Theater. "It is realized," he noted, "that some individuals take literally and practice assiduously the precept of, 'To the victor belong the spoils' and elements of greed can be found which are not praiseworthy in themselves." On the other hand, the assistant inspector general

---

24 "Guenther Reinhardt, 63, Dies; Was a Writer and Investigator," *New York Times*, 3 Dec 1968; Alexander Vassiliev and John Earl Haynes, eds., "Translation of original notes from KGB archival files by Alexander Vassiliev (1993–1996), Yellow Notebook #4" (trans. Steve Shabad), 33, Vassiliev Notebooks, Digital Archive, Cold War International History Project, Wilson Center, Washington, D.C., https://digitalarchive.wilsoncenter.org/.
25 Memo, Col. F. J. Pearson, Inspector Gen Department, to Cdr in Ch, EUCOM, 22 Apr 1948, sub: Reports of Investigation of Allegations made by Mr. Guenther P. Reinhardt, Folder "333.9 Reinhardt. Guenther P. to Reis, David F.," Administrative Ofc Mail and Rcds Section Decimal File, June 1947–June 1948, RG 159, NACP; Certificate, Capt. Frederick C. Schnackenberg, 7 Jan 1948, Folder "333.9 Reinhardt. Guenther P. to Reis, David F.," Administrative Ofc Mail and Rcds Section Decimal File, June 1947–June 1948, RG 159, NACP; Rpt, Capt. I. F. Bennett, Neuropsychiatric Section, 98th Gen Hospital, 21 Jan 1948, sub: Psychiatric examination of Mr. Guenther P. Reinhardt, Folder "333.9 Reinhardt, Guenther P. to Reis, David F.," Administrative Ofc Mail and Rcds Section Decimal File, June 1947–June 1948, RG 159, NACP.
26 Ian Sayer and Douglas Botting, *America's Secret Army: The Untold Story of the Counter Intelligence Corps* (London: Fontana, 1990), 284.
27 Memo, Pearson, Inspector Gen Department, for Cdr in Ch, EUCOM, 22 Apr 1948, sub: Reports of Investigation of Allegations made by Mr. Guenther P. Reinhardt.

refuted the overall charges as too "broad and malicious."[28] As had been the case with the Miller investigation the previous year, the one triggered by Reinhardt had little impact on the military government in Germany.

As the Reinhardt investigation wound down, yet another scandal hit the military government. In 1947, former U.S. president Herbert C. Hoover visited Berlin on a humanitarian mission. He also used his sojourn in the city to acquire valuable documents for the Hoover War Library, his collection of war-related papers and other materials housed at Stanford University. Frank E. Mason, a member of the mission, arranged for Hoover to meet with William F. Heimlich, the Army's former assistant chief of intelligence. In 1946, Heimlich had purchased a set of manuscript pages of the diary of the Nazi propaganda minister Joseph Goebbels from a local junk dealer in Berlin. At their meeting, Heimlich offered Hoover the Goebbels manuscript. The two men agreed that Heimlich would donate the manuscript to Hoover's library and that the Pulitzer Prize–winning journalist Louis P. Lochner would translate it for a U.S. commercial publisher. Heimlich would receive a third of the proceeds from the book's sales.[29] In early 1948, Doubleday published *The Goebbels Diaries, 1942–1943*, which quickly became a bestseller and within a few months generated over $150,000 in revenue.[30]

The publication of the *Goebbels Diaries* triggered investigations by the Office of Alien Property and by the Army's inspector general. The manuscript evidently originated in occupied Germany, and Military Government Law No. 161 prohibited the removal of German documents having a property value without proper authorization. Investigators quickly zeroed in on Heimlich, who claimed to have given the manuscript to Hoover only after having offered it to various military government organizations. By Heimlich's account, none of the proper authorities had been interested in it. When interviewed, however, no military government official corroborated Heimlich's assertions. The inspector general concluded that the former intelligence officer had transferred the manuscript without authority and with the intention of profiting from its eventual publication. In late 1950, the

---

28 Rpt, Maj. Robert B. Hensley, Asst Inspector Gen, to Cdr in Ch, EUCOM, n.d. [March 1948], sub: Alleged Black Market Activities of American Personnel, Folder "333.9 Reinhardt. Guenther P. to Reis, David F.," Administrative Ofc Mail and Rcds Section Decimal File, June 1947–June 1948, RG 159, NACP.
29 Bertrand M. Petanaude, "Curse of the Goebbels Diaries," *Hoover Digest* 3 (2012), https://www.hoover.org/research/curse-goebbels-diaries. As a journalist with the Associated Press, Lochner had won the 1939 Pulitzer Prize for correspondence for his reporting from Berlin on Nazi Germany.
30 Rpt, Ofc of Inspector Gen, Report of investigation concerning the publication of "The Goebbels Diaries" by Doubleday & Company, Inc., 28 Jul 1948, Folder "Goebbels Diary," Administrative Ofc Mail and Rcds Section Decimal File June 1947–June 1948, RG 159, NACP.

Office of Alien Property reached an agreement with Heimlich, Lochner, and Mason to the effect that the three men would transfer their copyrights to the office in exchange for $55,000 of the proceeds of book sales.[31] Presumably, the agreement left Heimlich with one-third of this sum.

Clay endorsed the findings of the Goebbels diaries investigation and acknowledged Heimlich's guilt. Summarizing the investigation for Lt. Gen. Daniel Noce, the chief of the Civil Affairs Division, Clay wrote that Heimlich had purchased the diaries, lied about offering them to military government repositories, and tendered them to Hoover to enrich himself.[32] Nonetheless, Clay refrained from reprimanding the former intelligence officer. One reason for his reluctance may have been his need for Heimlich to serve as the new director of Radio in the American Sector (RIAS; Rundfunk im amerikanischen Sektor), the American broadcasting station that had become a potent weapon in the escalating propaganda war with the Soviets over the status of Berlin.[33] Another reason may have been Clay's concern that punishing Heimlich would make him a scapegoat for a common crime in postwar Germany, and could have a demoralizing effect on other military government officials. Thus, Heimlich's transgression did not derail his career in Germany. He served as the head of RIAS until 1949.

Rumors about illegal transactions reached the highest levels of military government and Army Intelligence, even implicating some of the family members of top American personnel in Germany. According to an agent of the Criminal Investigation Division, "it was common gossip that Mrs. [Marjorie] Clay was engaged in . . . extensive black market trading."[34] In the case of the Army's former chief of intelligence, Maj. Gen. Clayton L. Bissell, similar rumors led to a formal investigation. Bissell had served as the military and air attaché in London from May to July 1948 when the U.S. Air Force ordered him to Washington at the request of the American ambassador. Allegedly, Bissell had used his personal aircraft to fly coffee into Germany, where it was sold on the black market.[35] In March 1949, the Air Force opened an investigation and spent just over a year following up on these allegations.[36] Eventually, the investigators cleared Bissell of all charges, but

---

31 Patricia Kollander with John O'Sullivan, *"I Must Be a Part of This War": A German American's Fight Against Hitler and Nazism* (New York: Fordham University Press, 2005), 191.
32 Ltr, Gen. Lucius D. Clay to Maj. Gen. Daniel Noce, Director, Civil Affairs Div, 18 Apr 1948, Folder "Goebbels Diary," Administrative Ofc Mail and Rcds Section Decimal File June 1947–June 1948, RG 159, NACP.
33 Nicholas J. Schlosser, *Cold War on the Airwaves: The Radio Propaganda War Against East Germany* (Champaign: University of Illinois Press, 2015), 19f.
34 Sayer and Botting, *Nazi Gold*, 315.
35 Drew Pearson, "Air Forces Black-Market Probe Goes On," *Charlotte News*, 14 Aug 1948.
36 Jack Raymond, "Gen. Bissell Faces U.S. Army Inquiry," *New York Times*, 31 Mar 1949.

the Air Force never made its findings public. Reporters who inquired about details were informed that Air Force personnel were under "strictest orders" to release no information on the case.[37]

The transgressions of the "wine, women, and song boys," as one Army historian called them, corroded the morale of the occupation forces and defied remediation efforts.[38] For the intelligence agencies, whose members were supposed to operate with a minimum of visibility, the investigations and exposures were jarring. In its official history, the CIC vehemently refuted the "attack" on its reputation.[39] The investigations also may have confirmed General Clay's reservations about the trustworthiness of his intelligence agencies—their inability to "smell the stink under their own noses," as he put it to Dulles—and perhaps persuaded him to disregard their advice.

Figure 31: A U.S. journalist ridiculed Army Intelligence personnel in Germany as greedy, easy to spot, and "an embarrassing cross-section between an all-American Rover Boy and a more moronic member of the old Gestapo." Cartoon from the *Washington Sunday Star*, 22 October 1950. *Washington Sunday Star*.

---

37 "Air Force Investigation Clears Bissell of Undisclosed Charges," *Washington Post*, 14 Apr 1950.
38 Ziemke, *U.S. Army in the Occupation of Germany*, 76.
39 Bray et al., *History of the Counter Intelligence Corps*, 27:19.

Likewise, the drumbeat of scandals involving intelligence personnel created bad press for the Army and politicized the occupation back in the United States. In December 1946, the Army Intelligence veteran Col. Robert S. Allen published a major exposé in the *New York Times* about the "immorality" of U.S. forces in Germany.[40] The article suggested that the misbehavior of African American troops posed a particularly grave problem to the occupation and lowered its prestige among the Germans. This charge, which reflected the prejudices of many White American soldiers at the time, said more about the accuser than it did about the accused. In contrast to Allen's claims, one contemporary report noted that Germans generally regarded Black soldiers "as very friendly, polite and helpful."[41] Even the die-hard Nazi Otto Skorzeny remarked in his memoirs on the Army guards in Nuremberg: "I always got along well with the blacks, who proved to be much more humane than the whites."[42]

Nonetheless, Allen's larger point about the negative effect of crimes and corruption among the occupation forces on American prestige in Germany holds true. A weekly intelligence summary from late 1945 observed that the Germans "consider the GI's and Officers as men who drink to excess; who do not wear uniforms as they should; who make a great deal of noise on the streets at night; who beat civilians without reason; who engage in black marketing." The summary went on to describe several examples, including an incident near Stuttgart of an officer allegedly raping a German woman repeatedly before turning her over to the military police for having improper papers. Such reports, the summary concluded, "have become very numerous and are certainly to be considered detrimental to the prestige of the American Army."[43]

In early 1948, Army Intelligence became a target of the well-known journalist Drew R. Pearson. Following a visit to the European Theater, Pearson penned a stinging piece on the CIC in his "Washington Merry-Go-Round" column for the *Washington Post*. Pearson lamented that CIC agents were constantly snooping on him. "Just what these mysterious gentlemen do is not exactly known," Pearson wrote, but if members of Congress wanted "to save some money, [they] might cast

---

40 Col. Robert S. Allen, "Suppressed Report on Germany Lays Immorality to U.S. Forces," *New York Times*, 2 Dec 1946.
41 Stivers and Carter, *City Becomes a Symbol*, 125. On the subject of African American soldiers in Germany, see also Margaret L. Geis, *Negro Personnel in the European Command, 1 January 1946–30 June 1950*, Occupation Forces in Europe Series (Karlsruhe: Historical Division, EUCOM, 1952).
42 Otto Skorzeny, *My Commando Operations: The Memoirs of Hitler's Most Daring Commando* (Atglen, PA: Schiffer Publishing, 1995), 440.
43 G–2 Weekly Intel Sum no. 10, 26 Nov 1945, Folder "VI Corps G–2 Intel Sums Nov 45," Historical Div, Program Files, VI Corps, G–2 Intel Sums, 1945–1946, RG 498, NACP.

an eye on the so-called Counter Intelligence Corps."[44] Concerned about the impact of such a widely syndicated critique, the Army's chief of public information, General Parks, contacted Pearson directly in an effort to diffuse the situation.[45]

When a member of the Hoover mission suggested to Clay that the CIC was wasting taxpayer money by monitoring even the most innocuous visitor, Clay laughed off the issue. "Oh, I can't control those fellows," he said. "They even spy on me."[46] Behind this congenial façade, however, Clay understood the problems plaguing the military government and intelligence agencies, and the negative press coverage they generated. "During this period," he lamented in his memoirs, "charges of almost every kind appeared to be a part of the daily fare—loose living by officers, luxurious living, black marketing, looting, cruelty toward the Germans." The constant distraction of the various scandals and investigations diluted the focus of the military government. In his memoirs, Clay downplayed the issue somewhat. "It was regrettable," he wrote, "that the actions of a small minority in the early days of the occupation should discredit the efforts of the whole."[47] That he felt compelled to mention the unpalatable subject at all goes to show how unsettling he found it and how much it tainted the occupation in the eyes of his contemporaries.

Displaced Persons

Soon after American forces crossed the German border, they encountered groups of so-called displaced persons, consisting mostly of Eastern Europeans whom the Nazis had brought to Germany as forced laborers. With the collapse of the Third Reich, many of these laborers broke free from their factories and concentration camps, congregating in cities or roaming the countryside. Most displaced persons were Russians or Poles, but their ranks also included Balts, Belgians, French, and many others from countries formerly under German rule, as well as liberated concentration and extermination camp survivors. At the Yalta Conference in 1945, the Allies agreed to assume responsibility and care for the displaced persons

---

44 Drew Pearson, "The Washington Merry-Go-Round: Generals Rate Expensive Spies," *Washington Post*, 18 Jan 1948, Folder "Pearson, Drew XA 165948," INSCOM, IRR, Digitized Name Files, RG 319, NACP.
45 Ltr, Maj. Gen. Floyd L. Parks, Ch, Public Info Div, to Lt. Gen. Geoffrey Keyes, CG, U.S. Forces in Austria, 18 Feb 1948, Folder "Pearson, Drew XA 165948," INSCOM, IRR, Digitized Name Files, RG 319, NACP.
46 Pearson, "Generals Rate Expensive Spies."
47 Lucius D. Clay, *Decision in Germany* (Garden City, NY: Doubleday, 1950), 63–64.

and to work toward their repatriation. In the U.S. Zone, the Army established special camps to register and process them. In their effort to care for and repatriate the various foreign nationals, Army authorities worked closely with the United Nations Relief and Rehabilitation Administration (UNRRA).[48]

The Americans tackled the task of repatriation vigorously. Most displaced persons from France, Belgium, and other Western European countries yearned to return to their homes, and the Army provided the necessary means of transport to help them leave Germany. Many of the Russians, however, feared mistreatment— including execution or imprisonment in the Soviet Union's own extensive system of forced labor camps—if they returned to their homeland. Several threatened to resist repatriation "by all means including suicide."[49] Nonetheless, the Army managed to return most of the displaced Russians by the end of the summer of 1945. Within two months of the end of the war, the Americans had repatriated more than four million displaced persons. Yet over two million others, mostly from Eastern Europe, remained in the U.S. Zone and refused to return home because of dismal political and economic conditions there. Moreover, the Americans quickly developed a reputation among displaced persons for providing better care than that offered by the other Allies. Consequently, displaced persons from the other three zones as well as refugees from Eastern Europe streamed into the U.S. Zone. Even with the best repatriation efforts of the Army and UNRRA, a large number of displaced persons remained in the U.S. Zone throughout the military occupation period.[50]

Displaced persons posed significant security and intelligence challenges to the occupation authorities. In the spring of 1945, the Army established two large displaced persons camps near Trier and Aachen. Discipline among the camps' mostly Russian inhabitants deteriorated quickly. Many went on looting sprees near Aachen, as one report noted, and "murders, rapes, and robberies abounded." Sanitary conditions within the camp near Trier were "appalling," recorded another observer. "I myself witnessed occupants of the camp who in plain view were defecating in the shrubbery in their barracks." Russian displaced persons often reacted violently to the visits of Soviet liaison officers who sought to establish their nationality and speed up their repatriation. In the displaced persons camp near Aachen, a group of Russians murdered a liaison officer.[51] In another

---

48 Ziemke, *U.S. Army in the Occupation of Germany*, 200, 413.
49 Ziemke, *U.S. Army in the Occupation of Germany*, 414.
50 Clay, *Decision in Germany*, 231; Rpt, MID, *Review of Europe, Russia, and Middle East* 1, no. 12, 15 Jan 1946, Folder "Review of Europe, Russia, and Middle East," Corresp, Rpts, Dirs, and Other Rcds Relating to the Activities and Functions of the Intel Gp, 1943–47, RG 165, NACP.
51 Ziemke, *U.S. Army in the Occupation of Germany*, 202–03.

instance, the intelligence staff of the Seventh Army reported that the visit of a Soviet military delegation provoked a camp-wide riot.[52]

By late 1945, Poles had replaced Russians as the dominant nationality group of displaced persons, but the security situation did not improve. Like the Russians, the Poles had suffered heavily at the hands of the Germans during the war, and local citizens and displaced persons clashed regularly near the camps. A Third Army intelligence report for January 1946 recorded a "gun fight" between German police and Polish displaced persons in Mannheim, the arrest of a displaced person for the murder of a woman in Schorndorf, and the rape of two young girls by two displaced persons.[53] The previous month, a Seventh Army Intelligence report noted wearily that "the murder of an elderly woman by two Polish DPs [displaced persons] highlights this week's series of depredations, which sounds like 'The Song I've heard before.'"[54] As late as March 1949, a local official in southern Bavaria reported the theft of swine and fowl by inmates of a nearby displaced persons camp.[55] Germans resented the Army's perceived lack of willingness to restore order. "What are you going to do about it?" asked the author of an anonymous letter to the public safety officer in Schwäbisch Gmünd. The question was rhetorical; to the writer, the answer seemed obvious: "Nothing!"[56]

That was an exaggeration. Army Intelligence carefully monitored the displaced persons situation and repeatedly took action. As part of the multiagency Operation SYNDICATE, the CIC recruited sources in displaced persons camps to gain advance information of potential security issues.[57] In Operation BLACKJACK, the intelligence division of the Third Army directed a raid on a camp in Heilbronn and confiscated illegal weapons.[58] But intelligence operations involving displaced persons resem-

---

52 Sum, HQ, Seventh Army, Weekly Intel Sum no. 35, 15 Mar 1946, Folder "7th Army, G–2 Weekly Summaries, 1946," Seventh Army, G–2, Subject Files 1942–1946, RG 338, NACP.
53 Msg, HQ, Seventh Army to G–2, Third Army, 7 Feb 1946, sub: Security Incidents within Seventh Army Area during Month of January 1946, Folder "3rd Army G–2 Security Control 371.2," Third United States Army, G–2 Section, Decimal Files 1944–1947, RG 338, NACP.
54 Sum, HQ, Seventh Army, Weekly Intel Sum no. 21, 7 Dec 1945, Folder "Weekly Intelligence Summary, October–December 1945," Seventh Army, G–2, Subject Files 1942–1946, RG 338, NA.
55 Monthly Rpt, Strauss, Landratsamt Schongau, 29 Mar 1949, Folder "Civil Administration," Rcds of the OMGB, Rcds of the Field Opns Div, Gen Rcds of Schongau Resident Liaison & Security Ofc, 1945–49, RG 260, NACP. The author of this report probably was Franz Josef Strauss, later West German defense minister and minister-president of Bavaria.
56 Sum, HQ, Seventh Army, Weekly Intel Sum no. 15, 24 Oct 1945, Folder "Weekly Intelligence Summary, October–December 1945," Seventh Army, G–2, Subject Files 1942–1946, RG 338, NACP.
57 Ofc of the Ch Historian, EUCOM, *The First Year of the Occupation, 1945–1946*, 2:167.
58 Msg, HQ, 349th Arty Gp, to CG, 31st Anti-Aircraft Bde, 1 Apr 1946, sub: Operation Blackjack, Folder "3rd Army G–2 'Blackjack' 370," Third United States Army, G–2 Section, Decimal Files 1944–1947, RG 338, NACP.

bled the futile labors of Sisyphus. In late 1945, the CIC learned that inhabitants of the Wildflecken displaced persons camp at the Bavaria-Hesse border had been "terrorizing the neighborhood." The camp authorities forcibly repatriated several offenders to Poland, but within weeks "these same individuals returned to this camp with additional arms, and they are now continuing to plunder."[59] Other Polish displaced persons became "professional repatriates." After receiving UNRRA food rations for several months, the CIC noted, voluntary repatriates left for Poland only to return to the U.S. Zone shortly thereafter "to make another try at free provisions."[60]

Jews, who had been the principal target of Nazi brutality, came to play a central role in the efforts of American authorities to deal with displaced persons. At the end of the war, fewer than 100,000 Jewish survivors, mostly Polish nationals, remained in Germany. Over the next months, their numbers soared as numerous Jews from Eastern Europe joined them. Seeking to escape persistent anti-Semitism and the rise of communist rule in their home countries, many saw the U.S. Zone as a gateway for emigration to Palestine, the United States, or South America.[61]

Initially, Army authorities separated displaced persons purely along national lines, which meant that Jewish survivors ended up in camps established for Poles and other nationalities. Considering that many Eastern Europeans harbored anti-Semitic sentiments, and some inmates had actively assisted the Germans during the war, Jewish survivors often found themselves subjects of discrimination and harassment. Likewise, Jews from Axis nations such as Germany or Hungary were technically "enemy nationals" and were not entitled to special treatment. Sympathetic to the Jewish plight, President Truman instructed General Eisenhower to rectify the situation.[62]

Eisenhower embraced the mission. He came from a family that did not share the anti-Semitism common at the time. Owing to their German-sounding name, the Eisenhowers occasionally were assumed to be Jewish. When a Washington society dame told Eisenhower's brother Milton what "a pity it is that you Eisenhowers are Jewish," the latter sighed unhappily and replied: "Ah, madame, what a pity it is that we aren't!" Eisenhower himself once said, "The Jewish people couldn't have a better friend than me." True to his word, he arranged for Jewish displaced persons to be housed in designated camps, receive higher rations, and

---

59 Ltr, Lt. Col. Harold E. Marr Jr., HQ, CIC, USFET, to Ch, Region VI, CIC, 18 Dec 1945, sub: Control of Displaced Persons, Folder "Displaced Persons Camp I," INSCOM, IRR, Impersonal Name Files, RG 319, NACP.
60 Bray et al., *History of the Counter Intelligence Corps*, 27:85.
61 Judah Nadich, *Eisenhower and the Jews* (New York: Twayne Publishers, 1953), 30.
62 Mel Schiff, "President Truman and the Jewish DPs, 1945–46: The Untold Story," *American Jewish History* 99, no. 4 (Oct 2015), 334; Nadich, *Eisenhower and the Jews*, 33–34, 43.

have a special status that acknowledged the centrality of their faith regardless of their ostensible nationality.[63]

The establishment of all-Jewish displaced persons camps resolved frictions with other Eastern Europeans, but it also highlighted the Jewish presence to the local population. Many Germans remained anti-Semitic and resented the special treatment that the Americans gave to Holocaust survivors. On 28 April 1946, a large-scale riot occurred at a Jewish displaced persons camp at Landsberg in southwestern Bavaria. Apparently triggered by false rumors that locals had kidnapped several Jewish youths, some five thousand camp residents rioted for several hours and assaulted German citizens who passed by the camp. Eventually, military police and tactical troops arrived and restored order.[64] Fearing another outbreak of violence, occupation authorities deployed troops to guard the camp, but the security situation continued to deteriorate. On more than one occasion, the soldiers themselves attacked camp residents. In the fall of 1946, the CIC sent a special agent, Ernst S. Valfer, to investigate the serious disturbances at Landsberg. The camp commander told Valfer that the "misbehavior" of some of his men was due to immaturity, nervousness, inebriation, and provocations by the displaced persons. From his own observations, Valfer added a fifth reason: "inciting influence of some German girl-friend on US soldier."[65] The tensions at Landsberg improved gradually as Jewish displaced persons left the camp and emigrated. The facility closed in 1950.

Unlike many other displaced persons from Eastern Europe, Jewish survivors were eager to leave Germany. Many wanted to immigrate to Palestine, but this desire put them at odds with the British, who controlled Palestine as a mandate. For years, the British authorities in Palestine had discouraged and restricted legal Jewish immigration for fear of inflaming local Arab sentiments, and Jews who attempted to immigrate illegally ran the risk of internment in British detention camps in the region. American authorities in Germany, however, supported Jewish emigration. Under Eisenhower, Supreme Allied Headquarters worked closely with Jewish organizations facilitating this effort. In May and June 1945, the Supreme Allied Headquarters oversaw the transfer of a group of 1,500 Jewish survivors, including several hundred orphans from the Buchenwald concentration camp, to

---

63 Nadich, *Eisenhower and the Jews*, 11, 13.
64 Rpt, G–2 Div, 5 May 1946, Folder "G–2 Notes for Central Council Meeting, prepared by the Military Intelligence Service," Corresp, Rpts, Dirs, and Other Rcds Relating to the Activities and Functions of the Intel Gp, 1943–47, RG 165, NACP.
65 Memo, Special Agent Ernst S. Valfer, Region IV, CIC, for Subregional Cdr, 4 Oct 1946, sub: General Security Situation at the Landsberg DP Camp, Folder "ZF 015115 Landsberg, DP Camp Riot," INSCOM, IRR, Impersonal Name Files, RG 319, NACP.

Marseilles in southern France. There, an American troopship took them to Naples in Italy, and from there another troopship took them to Haifa in Palestine.[66]

The exodus of Eastern European Jews to Palestine via Germany steadily increased. By early 1947, four to five thousand Jews per month left Europe to immigrate illegally to Palestine. The intelligence division in Frankfurt was "aware of possibility that this may develop into mass movement" but did nothing to stop it.[67] When the CIC learned that Jewish agencies had recruited insurgents in German displaced persons camps to fight for a Jewish state in Palestine, it launched Operation RUMMAGE to investigate these activities. Although such efforts were illegal and offensive to the British, the CIC merely monitored them and their agents "made no attempt to break them up." The CIC ceased its covert surveillance efforts in May 1948 when the establishment of the state of Israel rendered immigration to the new country legal.[68]

Immigration to Palestine had barely receded as a political issue when a new challenge arose. On 25 June 1948, President Truman signed the Displaced Persons Act, which allowed for the admission of 205,000 displaced persons to the United States. In order to qualify for immigration, individuals had to meet certain criteria, such as a clean criminal record and no Nazi affiliations. The eligibility process therefore required large-scale screening. On 30 August 1948, Under Secretary of the Army William H. Draper Jr. designated the CIC as the responsible agency for investigating all persons in Germany and Austria who applied to the United States under the act.[69] The screening process involved checking an applicant's file against the records of the CIC registry, the Berlin Documents Center, and local criminal and intelligence agencies. Agents also had to conduct neighborhood interviews. American authorities screened roughly 12,500 persons each month, and the CIC dedicated 30 percent of its force to the vetting process. The program ended in the middle of 1950 when the quota set under the act had been met.[70]

Meanwhile, Army Intelligence had begun investigating reports of Soviet intelligence activities in displaced persons camps in the American zone. In July 1945, a

---

66 Msg, Lt. Col. Ernest F. Witte, SHAEF, G–5, to American Red Cross, 26 Jun 1945, sub: Request for Orders for Trip, Folder "23. Red Cross," SHAEF, SHAEF Mission (France), Gen Staff, G–5 Div, Executive Section, Subject File, May 1944–Sept 6, 1945, RG 331, NACP; Alan Swarc, "Illegal Immigration to Palestine 1945–1948: The French Connection" (PhD diss., University College London, 2006), 45–46.
67 Msg, Intel Div, EUCOM, to Intel Div, War Department, 31 Mar 1947, Folder "1. Fr: 'S' Germany 1000–5999 1-1-47–6-30-47," ACoS, G–2 (Intel), "Top Secret" Incoming and Outgoing Cables, 1942–52, RG 319, NACP.
68 Bray et al., *History of the Counter Intelligence Corps*, 27:86–87.
69 Bruce W. Bidwell, MID History Cold War, chap 6, "Security Function," 48.
70 Bray et al., *History of the Counter Intelligence Corps*, 27:88–90.

riot broke out at a Polish displaced persons camp at Fritzlar in northern Hesse. The camp commander informed a special agent of the 307th Counter Intelligence Corps Detachment that he believed Soviet intelligence had recruited an inmate who initiated the riot by circulating the rumor "that American authorities intended to force all Poles to work in the USSR or be returned to their former masters."[71] The investigation remained inconclusive. In March 1946, another CIC penetration of a Polish displaced persons camp at Altötting in southern Bavaria equally failed to turn up evidence of Soviet subversion. Most of the inmates, the CIC reported, were "too apathetic and lacking in initiative to engage in any other activities than eating, drinking, and sleeping."[72]

A few months later, Army Intelligence discovered hard evidence of Soviet espionage activities among displaced persons in the American zone. In August 1946, the European Theater announced the arrest of Lena Herz-Krupenko, a Soviet citizen who posed as a German and gained employment with UNRRA as a displaced persons camp doctor. From her strategic position, she observed the political activities of the camp residents, especially of Ukrainians; issued false papers to certain inmates; and reported to her Soviet spymasters. According to European Theater headquarters, she had also "attempted to undermine American authority and prestige among displaced persons." After obtaining her confession, the Americans turned her over to the Soviets.[73]

As U.S.-Soviet relations deteriorated, the Army's concerns about Moscow's intelligence operations involving displaced persons and refugees increased. In the fall of 1945, the Army became aware that Soviet liaison officers at displaced persons camps in the U.S. Zone frequently repatriated displaced persons to the Soviet Union against their will. A Polish resident of the Funk Kaserne, a major displaced persons camp near Munich, reported to Army authorities that Soviet officers had threatened him with a pistol and told him to claim Soviet citizenship. When the ranking Army officer at the Funk Kaserne, Col. Olan A. Nelson, reviewed conditions at the installation, he found that Soviet officers roamed the camp at will and had armed several Russian displaced persons without authorization. Nelson con-

---

71 Memo, Special Agent Henry H. Romney, 307th CIC Detachment, to Ofcr in Charge, 17 Sep 1945, sub: Undercover Activities in Polish DP Camp at Fritzlar, Folder "Report of Investigations, 10 Aug to 16 Oct 1945," Seventh United States Army, G–2 Section, Report Files 1944–1946, Decimal File, RG 338, NACP.

72 Msg, 1st Lt. Thomas H. Buckley, Bad-Reichenhall Sub-Region, CIC, to CO, Region IV, CIC, 25 Mar 1946, sub: POLECAT, Folder "Displaced Persons Camp I," INSCOM, IRR, Impersonal Name Files, RG 319, NACP.

73 Ofc of the Ch Historian, EUCOM, *A Survey of Soviet Aims, Policies, and Tactics*, Occupation Forces in Europe Series 1947–1948 (Frankfurt: Historical Division, EUCOM, 1948), 302; "Spied on Americans in American Zone," *New York Times*, 23 Aug 1946.

cluded that the Soviets and their auxiliaries used "unethical" methods to repatriate the displaced persons, even though many did not want to go and some may not even have been Soviet citizens. He requested the recall of the camp's Soviet liaison officer.[74]

Soviet transgressions at the Funk Kaserne prompted the CIC in early 1946 to launch Operation BINGO, a systematic, zonewide effort to document illegal activities of Soviet liaison personnel and of displaced persons. BINGO not only confirmed that the Soviets used heavy-handed tactics to repatriate displaced persons to the USSR, but also produced evidence that Soviet intelligence was recruiting displaced persons for espionage operations in the U.S. Zone. In one instance, CIC informants discovered that Soviet repatriation officers focused their recruitment efforts on Ukrainian displaced persons who had collaborated with the Germans during the war and therefore had good reason to fear returning to the Soviet Union. According to the CIC informants, a Soviet liaison officer would approach the wary Ukrainians by telling them that they could "straighten out their mistakes" by working for the Soviet Union. If the candidate wavered, the officer would offer him a large amount of money to close the deal. Soviet intelligence would have the men sign an oath of silence, assign them cover names, and send them on espionage missions.[75]

In early 1947, a Soviet defector told the Americans that Soviet intelligence sought to recruit displaced persons of Russian, Ukrainian, and Baltic origin, as well as German refugees who knew Slavic languages. The Soviets would forgive the agents any wartime collaboration with Axis authorities in exchange for their services.[76] Following the communist coup in Czechoslovakia in February 1948, a wave of refugees crossed into Bavaria. Over 5,000 individuals fled during the first two months. The CIC screened them to assess their potential intelligence value and to weed out embedded Soviet agents.[77] Even larger numbers of refugees streamed into the U.S. Zone from Soviet-occupied Germany, and these new arrivals also had to be checked for possible Soviet intelligence connections.[78] If dis-

---

74 Msg, Col. Olan A. Nelson, HQ, 68th Anti-Aircraft Arty Gp, to CG, USFET, 16 Oct 1945, sub: Lt. Colonel Alexander K. Oreskin, USSR Liaison Officer, Folder "Operation BINGO D169023," IRR, Selected Printouts, Impersonal Files, RG 319, NACP.
75 Msg, Lt. Col. Dale M. Garvey, HQ, CIC, USFET, to Lt. Col. Russo, Ch, Research & Rpts, 30 Mar 1946, sub: Recruiting methods for Soviet agents, Folder "Operation BINGO D169023," INSCOM, IRR, Selected Printouts, Impersonal Files, RG 319, NA.
76 Rpt to ACofS, G–2, 31 Jan 1947, sub: Counterintelligence Report No. 154, Operation Rusty, Folder "Operation Rusty ZF010807W Volume I, 1 of 2," INSCOM, IRR, Impersonal Name Files, RG 319, NACP.
77 Ofc Ch Historian, EUCOM, *A Survey of Soviet Aims, Policies, and Tactics*, 227–29.
78 Historical Div, EUCOM, Quarterly Rpt of Opns 1 July to 30 September 1948, Historian's Background Files, 1947–1952, RG 549, NACP.

placed persons presented security issues in 1945, by the end of the military occupation, Army Intelligence had come to regard them as a major source of concern—and information—about Soviet espionage activities.

Soviet Espionage

Soviet espionage posed a serious challenge to Army Intelligence. For Moscow, intelligence operations were an integral part of its foreign policy, and the Soviets initiated them as soon as their forces entered the Third Reich. "The conventional wisdom is that the Cold War started with Winston Churchill's 'iron curtain' speech in Fulton, Missouri, on March 6, 1946," wrote Soviet intelligence officer Lt. Gen. Pavel A. Sudoplatov in his memoirs. But "for us," he continued, "the confrontation with the Western allies had begun when the Red Army liberated Eastern Europe."[79]

A plethora of Soviet intelligence and security services descended on Germany in the wake of the Red Army. During the first year of the occupation, the NKVD (People's Commissariat for Internal Affairs) under General Ivan A. Serov became the chief organization responsible for espionage and counterespionage operations. Headquartered in Potsdam, the NKVD had 2,230 staff members for security operations and 399 for espionage in the Western zones.[80] In 1946, the MGB (Ministerstvo Gosudarstvennoy Bezopasnosti; Ministry for State Security) under Lt. Gen. (later General) Nikolai K. Kovalshchuk assumed most functions from the NKVD. Headquartered on Luisenstrasse 46 in Berlin, the MGB's intelligence apparatus in Soviet-occupied Germany had a latticework of regional offices, including a soon-to-be notorious prison in Berlin Hohenschönhausen. The office also took charge of the dreaded counterespionage agency, SMERSH, a telling acronym that stood for "Death to Spies" (*smert' shpionam*). In 1949, the MGB had 4,000 personnel.[81] Eventually, the bulk of the Soviet intelligence and security personnel in Germany moved into the large compound of the Soviet Military Administration in Karlshorst and in 1954 reorganized as the KGB (Komitet Gosudarstvennoy Bezopasnosti; Committee for State Security).[82]

---

[79] Pavel Sudoplatov and Anatoly Sudoplatov, *Special Tasks: The Memoirs of an Unwanted Witness— A Soviet Spymaster* (Boston: Little, Brown, 1994), 221.
[80] Jan Foitzkik and Tatjana W. Zarewskaja-Djakana, eds., *SMAD-Handbuch: Die Sowjetische Militäradministration in Deutschland 1945–1949* [SMAD-Handbook: The Soviet Military Administration in Germany, 1945–1949] (Munich: Oldenbourg, 2009), 69.
[81] Foitzkik and Zarewskaja-Djakana, *SMAD-Handbuch*, 70–71; 66th CIC Detachment, 1 Mar 1951, sub: MGB Workbook, CIA Electronic Reading Room, https://www.cia.gov/readingroom/.
[82] Ilko-Sascha Kowalczuk and Stefan Wolle, *Roter Stern über Deutschland: Sowjetische Truppen in der DDR* [Red star over Germany: Soviet troops in the GDR] (Berlin: Ch. Links, 2010), 126.

Military, trade, and diplomatic representations formed an important component of the Soviet espionage effort.[83] The Soviets established several liaison missions in the American zone of occupation to coordinate their policies with the Americans and to expedite the repatriation of Russian displaced persons. These included liaison missions at European Theater headquarters in Frankfurt; near the Seventh Army headquarters in Karlsruhe; and near Zuffenhausen, just outside Stuttgart, the Russian displaced persons camp at Helmut-Hirth-Strasse 1. Within a few months of the end of the war, the surveillance of Russian displaced persons, reports from local CIC offices, and observations by American liaison officers convinced the Army's European intelligence division that these missions constituted "important centers in the net of Soviet Russian" espionage agencies in the U.S. Zone.[84]

The Army used several techniques to determine the nature and extent of espionage activities emanating from the Soviet missions. Phone calls intercepted by the Civil Censorship Division identified certain Soviet officers as spymasters and revealed that Soviet liaison personnel in Frankfurt used their billet at Holzhausenstrasse 25 as an espionage hub. A CIC special agent observed the suspicious arrival of civilian automobiles "about two or three times every week, usually during the hours of darkness." The civilians typically left the house early in the morning, and an "attempt was made to follow those vehicles, but due to the empty streets at those hours a discreet tail was not possible, and the attempt was dropped."[85] American intelligence personnel also sought to engage the Soviets socially and solicit information about their covert assignments. These engagements yielded little specific intelligence but sometimes revealed a hostile attitude toward the United States. "After many more drinks," one American counterintelligence officer reported, "the Russian officers started talking without any restraint whatsoever." One of them "said Russia would soon fight America and [would] defeat us as they defeated Germany."[86]

---

83 Rpt, Clark Clifford to President Truman, "American Relations with the Soviet Union: A Report by the Special Counsel to the President," 24 Sep 1946, Subject File, "American Relations with the Soviets," Rose A. Conway Papers, Truman Library.
84 Rpt, Col. T. J. Sands, HQ, USFET, G–2, Counter Intel Br, 30 Nov 1945, Folder "Subversive Activities of USSR Officers ZF 011636," INSCOM, IRR, Impersonal Name Files, RG 319, NACP; Draft ltr, Lt. Col. Dale M. Garvey, for Ch, CIC, n.d., sub: Soviet Liaison Mission at Headquarters, USFET, Folder "Soviet Repatriation Mission Frankfurt, FRG ZF 010111," INSCOM, IRR, Impersonal Name Files, RG 319, NACP.
85 Draft ltr, Garvey for Ch, CIC, n.d., sub: Soviet Liaison Mission at Headquarters, USFET.
86 Rpt, Col. T. J. Sands, HQ, USFET, G–2, Counter Intel Br, 8 Jan 1946, Folder "Subversive Activities of USSR Officers ZF 011636," INSCOM, IRR, Impersonal Name Files, RG 319, NACP.

Shortly after the war, an opportunity arose for the CIC to recruit a spy inside the Soviet espionage apparatus at Zuffenhausen. In October 1945, a German citizen named Helmuth Kuebler approached the American military government office in Stuttgart. The 24-year-old Kuebler claimed that he was involved with the National Committee for a Free Germany, an organization of pro-Soviet German war veterans, and that he knew the Soviet intelligence officers at Zuffenhausen who oversaw the committee's activities in the West. For a price, Kuebler offered to report on the Germans and their Soviet masters. The military government office referred the case to the local 307th CIC Detachment.[87]

Special Agent Henry W. Kemp, who reviewed Kuebler's offer, was skeptical. He pointed out a number of discrepancies in Kuebler's statements and suspected the Soviets had sent Kuebler to penetrate the CIC. "Before anything else is done," Kemp concluded in his lengthy report, "Subject should be interrogated thoroughly."[88] Kemp's colleague, Special Agent Robert W. Maxwell, did so for three days in late November. He found Kuebler "intelligent and resourceful" but noted that he "is not above lying if he thinks he can get away with it." Nonetheless, Maxwell concluded, "Subject can be used under pressure for a short while." Based on Maxwell's recommendation, the 307th CIC Detachment recruited Kuebler as a penetration agent. He received a camera, 700 Reichsmarks, and the code name MARS.[89]

Over the following months, MARS produced numerous reports about the propaganda activities of the national committee and detailed descriptions of the facilities and personnel of the liaison mission at Zuffenhausen, including photographs of individual Soviet officers.[90] The chief of the intelligence division's counterintelligence branch in Frankfurt, Col. Thomas J. Sands, considered Kuebler's reports sufficiently valuable to relay excerpts directly to Brig. Gen. Edwin L. Sibert in Berlin. Sands's report to Sibert included Kuebler's dramatic assertion of having overheard Soviet officers at Zuffenhausen discussing the possibility of a war against the United

---

87 Memo, Special Agent Henry W. Kemp, 307th CIC Detachment, for Ofcr in Charge, 6 Nov 1945, sub: Kuebler, Helmuth, Penetration Agent, alias MARS, Folder "Kuebler, Helmuth 194180," INSCOM, IRR, Digitized Name Files, RG 319, NACP.
88 Memo, Kemp for Ofcr in Charge, 6 Nov 1945, sub: Kuebler, Helmuth, Penetration Agent, alias MARS.
89 Memo, Special Agent Robert W. Maxwell, 307th CIC Detachment, for Ofcr in Charge, 13 Dec 1945, sub: MARS (Penetration Agent), Folder "Subversive Activities of USSR Officers ZF 011636," INSCOM, IRR, Impersonal Name Files, RG 319, NACP.
90 Memo, Special Agent Ernest A. Jaffray, 21 Apr 1946, sub: Translation of description of personnel at Russian Camp, Folder "Kuebler, Helmuth 194180," INSCOM, IRR, Digitized Name Files, RG 319, NACP.

States. "Russia would succeed where Germany had failed," the Soviets supposedly boasted, "carrying the war—if it should break out—to American soil."[91]

But MARS proved demanding, mercurial, and troublesome. He complained that Maxwell showed up late to meetings, and he badgered his American handlers to "send me some cigarettes and, if possible, chocolate."[92] In December, German police arrested Kuebler for carrying unauthorized papers. He sent several sharp notes to Special Agent Maxwell, clamoring for the American to intervene. Eventually, Maxwell arranged for Kuebler's release. MARS continued to send in reports, but the CIC repeatedly noticed inconsistencies and falsehoods in his statements. In the spring of 1946, the Americans stopped working with him.[93] MARS may have been a double agent or, more likely, an opportunist who sold, embellished, and perhaps fabricated information for personal gain. Regardless of the veracity of his information, he provided the CIC an early opportunity to operate against a Soviet target and confirmed the reality of the new espionage threat.

Over time, the CIC took increasingly imaginative approaches to gather information on Soviet liaison missions. Agents of the CIC office in Stuttgart recruited an "attractive girl" and sent her to seduce a member of the local Soviet reparations mission. She succeeded, and the Soviet officer fell in love with her. At the instructions of her handlers, she persuaded him to go out with her in civilian clothes, which was illegal under a law passed by the European Theater. When the officer complied, the CIC promptly stopped him and told him that they would have to turn him over to Soviet liaison headquarters in Frankfurt. The Soviet officer replied that he would be in "hot water" if they did so and begged the agents to let him go. The CIC relented, but only after interviewing the Soviet officer in detail about his office. To retain leverage over him after his release, the agents made the officer sign a statement to the effect that he had been arrested by the CIC and had provided information on the liaison mission.[94]

The CIC also sought to penetrate the Soviet military mission at Army headquarters in Frankfurt, but this target proved impervious. As an American CIC defector told his Soviet interviewers, the mission "caused us a lot of work, but this

---

91 Msg, Col. T. J. Sands, HQ, USFET, G–2, Counter Intel Br, to Brig. Gen. Edwin L. Sibert, 8 Jan 1946, sub: National Committee for Free Germany and Activities of USSR Liaison Officers, Folder "Subversive Activities of USSR Officers ZF 011636," INSCOM, IRR, Impersonal Name Files, RG 319, NACP.
92 Memo, Special Agent Ernest A. Jaffray, 23 Apr 1946, sub: Translation of routine report, Folder "Kuebler, Helmuth 194180," INSCOM, IRR, Digitized Name Files, RG 319, NACP.
93 Memo, Special Agent Ernest A. Jaffray, for Ofcr in Charge, 23 Apr 1946, sub: Kuebler, Helmuth, Penetration Agent, alias MARS, Folder "Kuebler, Helmuth 194180," INSCOM, IRR, Digitized Name Files, RG 319, NACP.
94 Bray et al., *History of the Counter Intelligence Corps*, 27:78–79.

work yielded few results. Day after day we were looking for ways to infiltrate the military mission, but our operations only resulted in the collection of information [*Nachrichtensammlung*]. . . . We built devices to eavesdrop on telephone conversations. When I left Germany, at the end of July 1956, we still had not managed to penetrate the Soviet military mission."[95]

Nonetheless, by early 1946, Army Intelligence had collected enough information to conclude that Moscow had embarked on a broad, systematic espionage effort in U.S.-occupied Germany. As Lt. Col. Wilbur Wilson, the chief of Army intelligence in Berlin, wrote in a special intelligence report, "it can be stated unqualifiedly that there is a long-term and aggressive espionage against the U.S. forces by Soviet Intelligence agencies."[96]

In response, the Americans launched several swoop operations to investigate and crack down on Soviet intelligence.[97] Operation BINGO and Operation FLYPAPER focused on various Soviet liaison missions in the U.S. Zone, their attempts to recruit displaced persons as agents, and their sponsorship of communist propaganda.[98] Another CIC project, Operation BASKET or BASKET CASE, resulted in the arrest of four Polish and Russian displaced persons in Stuttgart. Posing as members of the "Russian Secret Police," the quartet had used crudely forged credentials to obtain food and gasoline from Army and Red Cross facilities. The four had not engaged in genuine espionage, but as the Army's counterintelligence section pointed out to General Sibert, the ease with which they moved through the U.S. Zone, obtained supplies, and persuaded American personnel of their status laid bare the Army's vulnerability to security threats.[99]

For the most part, Army Intelligence dealt with low-level agents, but in one instance the CIC in Berlin managed to catch a group of Soviet spy handlers in the act. This counterespionage operation began in the spring of 1946 when an Army private, Claude W. Whidby of the 3d Infantry, informed his unit's intelligence officer that a female German friend of his, Sunihild Pfeiffer, was involved with the Soviets. Because Pfeiffer had studied at the American military government's German stenographer school, the CIC in Berlin took over the investigation. The Corps

---

95 Rpt, MfS, HA II, "Übersetzung aus dem Russischen, Auszug aus dem Bericht vom 5. Januar 1961" [Translation from the Russian, excerpt from the report of 5 Jan 1961], 17 Apr 1961, 168–74, MfS-HA II, no. 44666, BStU, Berlin.
96 Rpt, Lt. Col. Wilbur Wilson, Director, S–2 Br, Berlin, 30 Sep 1947, sub; "Espionage by Soviet Intelligence Against U.S. Forces in Berlin," Folder "960045," Rcds of the ACoS, G–2 (Intel), Formerly Top Secret Documents, 1943–1959, RG 319, NACP.
97 Ofc of the Ch Historian, EUCOM, *A Survey of Soviet Aims, Policies, and Tactics*, 301.
98 Draft ltr, Garvey for Ch, CIC, n.d., sub: Soviet Liaison Mission at Headquarters, USFET.
99 Rpt, 1st Lt. George Wenzel, Ch, Counter Intel Section, HQ, USFET, 17 Jun 1946, sub: The Basket Case, Folder "Operation Basket ZF 010433," INSCOM, IRR, Impersonal Name Files, RG 319, NACP.

assigned several special agents as well as a civilian special investigator, Severin F. Wallach, to the case. The CIC code-named the ensuing effort Operation SAND.

Wallach started his investigation by interviewing Pfeiffer. She told him that Soviet military police, having determined that she was affiliated with the American military government, had arrested her while she was visiting a café near the Brandenburg Gate in March. They brought her to Potsdam, she said, where a Soviet officer interrogated her on her work for the Americans. He gave her copious amounts of food, chocolate, and cigarettes. In exchange, she agreed to become a Soviet informant with the code name VICTORIA. After her release, she met several more times with the Soviets who encouraged her to seek a job at the military government headquarters and report on American troop units in Berlin. Having confessed to her recruitment by the Soviets, she now agreed to start working as a double agent for the CIC, and the Corps enlisted her under the code name SUNNY. She was to continue her liaison with her Soviet handlers while CIC special agents secretly observed their meetings and took photographs.[100]

CIC surveillance confirmed that Pfeiffer regularly met with Soviet intelligence officers in Berlin and received espionage instructions from them. At Wallach's suggestion, the CIC resolved to arrest her Soviet contacts during their next rendezvous. Wallach then met with General Clay's deputy, Maj. Gen. Frank A. Keating; Capt. Joseph M. Stewart of the CIC in Berlin; and Col. William F. Heimlich of Berlin's intelligence branch, to discuss the details of the operation. They enlisted the assistance of the U.S. Constabulary, and when Pfeiffer met again with three of her Soviet handlers in the American sector on 14 June, soldiers of the Constabulary lay in wait for them. They apprehended her and the Soviets the moment the four of them entered a car to drive away. The CIC evacuated the three Soviets to Camp King where a special agent interrogated them.[101]

On 19 July, the Soviet deputy military commander in chief of the Soviet Military Administration in Germany, General Pavel A. Kurochkin, formally protested to General Clay about "the outrageous case of arrest" of the three Soviet officers

---

100 Memo, Special Agent Severin F. Wallach, HQ, Region VIII, CIC, for Ofcr in Charge, 18 May 1946, sub: Russian Espionage Activities in the U.S. occupied Sector of Berlin – Pfeiffer, Sunihild, Folder "Operation Sand ZF 015114," INSCOM, IRR, Impersonal Name Files, RG 319, NACP.
101 Msg, Special Investigator Severin F. Wallach, HQ, CIC, Berlin Region, to Ch, CIC, USFET, 15 Jun 1946, sub: Pfeiffer, Sunihild, Folder "Operation Sand ZF 015114," INSCOM, IRR, Impersonal Name Files, RG 319, NACP; Special Agent Albert Poll, HQ, USFET, Ofc of the ACofS, G–2, extracts from CIC interrogation rpt, 21 Jun 1946, Folder "Operation Sand ZF 015114," INSCOM, IRR, Impersonal Name Files, RG 319, NACP.

"who were detained for no reason at all."[102] Clay remained unimpressed. "I think we should point out quite clearly why we arrested these people," he wrote to Maj. Gen. Harold R. Bull, the Army's chief of staff in Europe. In his response to Kurochkin, Clay explained matter-of-factly that the Americans had arrested the three Soviets because "they were engaged in the mission of forcing employees of the U.S. Army to deliver certain information to your Intelligence Service."[103]

Bent on obtaining the arrestees' release, the Soviet occupation authorities increased the pressure. In early July, they arrested four Americans—two Army officers as well as a warrant officer and his wife—who had traveled into the Soviet Zone. When the American military government inquired about their whereabouts, Lt. Gen. Mikhail I. Dratvin of the Soviet Military Administration responded that the Americans had entered their zone unauthorized and were apprehended because they had acted suspiciously. "I cannot avoid taking advantage of this opportunity to ask you to release our officers," Dratvin added, effectively suggesting a swap.[104] Although the Army later denied any such arrangement, this is precisely what happened. Later that month, both sides released their arrestees.[105]

Even after the conclusion of Operation SAND, some questions lingered about Pfeiffer's true loyalties. To keep her out of reach of the Soviets, the CIC resettled her in Bad Nauheim, a small town a few miles north of Frankfurt. She moved in with her uncle, who happened to live across the street from the Region III CIC headquarters. A local special agent, Albert Poll, interviewed her and concluded that she was holding back on her involvement with the Soviets. Pfeiffer, for her part, suggested that she and Poll spend the evening together. Poll declined her offer, noting to his commanding officer: "It seems that SUNNY does not lose any opportunity of being friendly with any Counter Intelligence Corps agent." He suspected that Pfeiffer was "now on a special mission for the Russians" and sought to use her proximity to the CIC for espionage purposes.[106]

---

102 Ltr, Gen. Pavel A. Kurochkin, SMAD (Sowjetische Militäradministration in Deutschland; Soviet Military Administration in Germany), to Gen. Lucius D. Clay, OMGUS, 19 Jul 1946, Folder "Operation Sand ZF 015114," INSCOM, IRR, Impersonal Name Files, RG 319, NACP.
103 Ltr, Gen. Lucius D. Clay, OMGUS, to Maj. Gen. H. R. Bull, Ch of Staff, USFET, 21 Jul 1946, Folder "Operation Sand ZF 015114," INSCOM, IRR, Impersonal Name Files, RG 319, NACP; Ltr, Gen. Lucius D. Clay, OMGUS, to Gen. Pavel A. Kurochkin, July 1946, Folder "Operation Sand ZF 015114," INSCOM, IRR, Impersonal Name Files, RG 319, NACP.
104 Ltr, Lt. Gen. Mikhail I. Dratvin, SMAD, to Maj. Gen. Robert W. Harper, 11 Jul 1946, Folder "Operation Sand ZF 015114," INSCOM, IRR, Impersonal Name Files, RG 319, NACP.
105 "Russians Release Two 'Lost' Americans," *New York Times*, 31 Jul 1946.
106 Memo, Special Agent Albert Poll, for Ofcr in Charge, Region III, CIC, 1 Jul 1946, sub: Operation Sand, Folder "Operation Sand ZF 015114," INSCOM, IRR, Impersonal Name Files, RG 319, NACP.

Figure 32: Five Soviet soldiers, arrested on suspicion of espionage in Stuttgart in February and March 1946. U.S. Army, NACP.

In Berlin, Severin Wallach and his colleague Theodor Hans investigated the stenographer school Pfeiffer had attended. They found that the Soviets had targeted not only Pfeiffer but also a fellow student and friend of hers, Dorothea Dominik. In July, they had kidnapped Dominik and detained her at a prison in Potsdam, but she escaped and went into hiding in the American sector. When the CIC learned of her fate, they took her into protective custody. The Soviets, in turn, ratcheted up the pressure on Dominik by arresting her father, who lived in the Soviet Zone. When Hans suggested to Dominik that she settle in the American sector of Berlin, she "suffered a nervous break-down and assumed an attitude of desolate helplessness." The Soviets, she told the agent, would get their hands on her anywhere in Berlin. Hans concluded that Dominik's fright was real, that the Soviets were indeed after her, and he recommended she be resettled in a small town in the U.S. Zone.[107]

Dominik's case was not exceptional. The Soviets routinely kidnapped individuals in Berlin. City employees and officials who posed a challenge to Moscow's rule constituted the majority of the victims. Although most kidnappings occurred in the Soviet sector, they occurred frequently in the three Western sectors as well. As the Berlin criminal police reported to the CIC in July 1946, in the previous month alone the Soviets had kidnapped 337 individuals, including 254 from the Soviet sector, 40 from the American sector, 26 from the British sector, and 17 from the French sector.[108]

The American view on the Soviet practice of kidnapping changed over the course of the occupation. During the immediate postwar period, when inter-Allied cooperation functioned fairly well in Germany, U.S. officials tolerated Soviet efforts to locate and arrest individuals in the American sector. The four-power statute over Berlin gave the Soviets the right to operate across the city, and initially the Americans had no objection to Moscow's search for war criminals.[109] Against the backdrop of deteriorating relations with the Soviets, however, the Americans came to resent and push back against kidnappings in their sector, especially when they involved U.S. interests. In March 1948, for example, Soviet agents tried and failed to kidnap an archivist, Edith Bankisch, of the S–2 section

---

[107] Memo, Special Agent Theodor Hans, Region VIII, CIC, for CO, 5 Dec 1946, sub: Pfeiffer, Sunihild; Dominik, Dorothea, Folder "Operation Sand ZF 015114," INSCOM, IRR, Impersonal Name Files, RG 319, NACP.
[108] Rpt, L-1589, 24 Jul 1946, Folder "Soviet Apprehension of German Nationals in U.S. Zone XE 182800," INSCOM, IRR, Impersonal Name Files, RG 319, NACP.
[109] Arthur Smith, *Kidnap City: Cold War Berlin* (Westport, CT: Greenwood, 2002), 29.

in Berlin.¹¹⁰ Two months later, they succeeded when they chloroformed the female acquaintance of a *Christian Science Monitor* correspondent in a public phone booth in Berlin. The kidnappers drove their unconscious victim to the Soviet sector. After three hours of interrogation, she was made to sign an agreement to become an informant before releasing her. She reported the incident to American officials, and the CIC immediately evacuated her from Berlin.¹¹¹

By 1947, Army Intelligence grasped the extent, methods, and objectives of Moscow's intelligence operations in U.S.-occupied Germany. The Americans noted that the Soviets used three different approaches for their espionage operations. First, Soviet liaison missions served as early espionage centers in the U.S. Zone. Second, the Soviets flooded the West with low-level spies who collected bits and pieces of information, which analysts in eastern Germany and Moscow would then use to assemble a comprehensive picture of the American occupation. In June 1947 alone, the intelligence division in Frankfurt reported the arrest of 516 Soviet agents, including 309 German citizens, 98 Soviets, and 36 Czechoslovakians. The Americans kept another 583 suspected agents under surveillance.¹¹² Third, the Soviets systematically sought to infiltrate the institutions and facilities of the American military government. The case of the stenographer school uncovered in the course of Operation SAND had not been an isolated incident. In another case, the Soviets had repeatedly interrogated a telephone operator in Treuenbrietzen, a relay station servicing the communications link between the American sector in Berlin and the U.S. Zone. The CIC recommended her removal to a nonsensitive position.¹¹³ Likewise, a British officer in Berlin told the Americans that the Soviets had embarked on a policy of forcing household help in the billets of prominent military government personnel to act as informants. He cited the case of a kitchen maid whom the Soviets had arrested and forced to sign a

---

110 Rpt, Region VIII, CIC, Counter Intel Rpt no. 92, 19 Mar 1948, Folder "CIC Region VIII (Berlin) Periodic Counter Intelligence Reports," Director of Intel, Analysis and Research Br, Misc. Rpts and Publications, 1941–50, RG 260, NACP.
111 Rpt, Region VIII, CIC, Counter Intel Rpt no. 101, 22 Jul 1948, Folder "CIC Region VIII (Berlin) Periodic Counter Intelligence Reports," Director of Intel, Analysis and Research Br, Misc. Rpts and Publications, 1941–50, RG 260, NACP.
112 Msg, Intel Div, EUCOM, to War Department, Intel Div, 7 Jun 1947, Folder "1. Fr: 'S' Germany 1000–5999 1-1-47–6-30-47," ACoS, G–2 (Intel), "Top Secret" Incoming and Outgoing Cables, 1942–52, RG 319, NACP.
113 Rpt, Region VIII, CIC, Counter Intel Rpt no. 90, 19 Feb 1948, Folder "CIC Region VIII (Berlin) Periodic Counter Intelligence Reports," Director of Intel, Analysis and Research Br, Misc. Rpts and Publications, 1941–50, RG 260, NACP.

statement agreeing to work as a spy.[114] European Theater headquarters instructed all major commands to interrogate non-American civilian employees, and this security measure yielded further evidence of Soviet infiltration attempts.[115]

The Soviets generally paid their agents very little. An exceptionally valuable and productive agent might make $100 to $120 per month, but the average low-level informant received merely $10 to $15.[116] By comparison, an American source would receive a starting salary of over $50 per month in the early 1950s.[117] Given the low pay, the Soviets relied heavily on blackmail and other coercive measures to recruit and run their agents. Often, they threatened former members of Nazi organizations with arrest if they refused to become spies.[118] Many of these coerced agents turned themselves over to the Americans at the first opportunity. In Rudolstadt in Thuringia, for example, Soviet officials took a former Nazi official to the local security office, where they advised him to "expiate" his criminal past by becoming an informant and thus avoid incarceration. He agreed, but as soon as the Soviets released him, he contacted Army Intelligence—who doubled him back against his erstwhile spymasters.[119]

Other Soviet intelligence techniques included "dangles" and "honey traps." In the case of the former, Soviet agents would masquerade as Red Army deserters seeking employment with American intelligence. If recruited, they would report back to the Soviet Zone on the inside machinations of U.S. intelligence.[120] A "honey trap" operation would involve the use of a sexual liaison to gain information. In one case, a Soviet agent kept a woman "under control through the use of narcotics" and used her to extract information "from American military person-

---

114 Msg, Lawrence E. deNeufville, ODDI, to Director of Intel, 2 Jul 1947, sub: Notes re Conversation with Brigadier Stawell, Folder "383.4–1 Espionage," Director of Intel, Analysis and Research Br, Gen Corresp, 1945–49, RG 260, NACP.
115 Ofc of the Ch Historian, EUCOM, *A Survey of Soviet Aims, Policies, and Tactics*, 301.
116 David Dallin, *Soviet Espionage* (New Haven, CT: Yale University Press, 1955), 333.
117 Transcript, MfS, HA II, "Vernehmungsprotokoll der Beschuldigten Ilenda, Charlotte, 5 Jun 1956" [Interrogation record of the accused Ilenda, Charlotte, 5 Jun 1956], MfS-HA II, no. 10, 41895, 32–34, BStU, Berlin.
118 Msg, Capt. A. H. Graubart, U.S. Navy, to ODI, 15 Apr 1947, sub: Russia/Germ. People & Social Forces. Espionage, Folder "14c Policy and General Activity of Occupying Powers (Soviet Zone) Jan '47 to Dec '47 Inc.," ODI, Excerpts of Miscellaneous Rpts and Publications, Analysis and Research Br, 1947–48, RG 260, NACP.
119 Counterintel Rpt no. 114, 10 Dec 1946, sub: Operation Rusty, to ACofS, G–2, HQ, USFET, Folder "Operation Rusty ZF010807W Volume I 1 of 2," INSCOM, IRR, Impersonal Name Files, RG 319, NACP.
120 Bray et al., *History of the Counter Intelligence Corps*, 27:77.

nel from PFC's [sic] to colonels." When the CIC eventually arrested the Soviet agent, a military court tried and sentenced him to ten years in prison.[121]

Moscow also enlisted the aid of satellite services to do their bidding. The intelligence service of Czechoslovakia became the Soviets' most important auxiliary for operations in American-occupied Germany.[122] In the wake of the communist coup in Prague in February 1948, thousands of refugees, including many German speakers, streamed across the border into Bavaria. Directed to vet the new arrivals, the CIC found that the Czechoslovak intelligence service had embedded a number of agents among them. Copying Soviet espionage methods, the Czechoslovaks pressed large numbers of low-level informants into service; as one Army Intelligence officer pointed out, many "got cold feet after they come over and turn themselves in."[123] Nonetheless, Czechoslovak espionage absorbed precious U.S. intelligence resources.

Beyond espionage, the Soviets engaged in several eavesdropping operations. In June 1949, an Army Intelligence source reported that Soviet officials working from a building in Berlin's Prinz-Heinrich-Strasse were tapping the telephone lines of various Allied offices and intercepting and decoding radio messages in the city. Moreover, the Soviets sought to install miniature microphones in the facilities of the Western powers. One method, U.S. counterintelligence personnel suspected, included the planting of a microphone into a radio set, where it would transmit conversations through a relay into the antenna. The Soviets would capture the conversations by tapping the antenna from the outside. When the intelligence division consulted with Lt. Col. Robert T. Walker, the chief of the Army Security Agency, Europe, he confirmed: "Yes, this is feasible."[124] A few months later, a discharged police officer from the Soviet Zone informed the CIC that the Soviets were tapping into the interzonal telephone lines. This revelation probably did not shock the Americans, who had been doing the same thing since 1945.[125]

---

121 Ofc of the Ch Historian, EUCOM, *The Second Year of the Occupation*, vol. 6, Occupation Forces in Europe Series, 1946–47 (Frankfurt: Office of the Chief Historian, EUCOM, 1947), 20.
122 Msg, Col. Henry G. Sheen, to G–2, USFET, 20 Mar 1946, Folder "3rd Army G–2 Security Control 371.2," Third United States Army, G–2 Section, Decimal Files 1944–47, RG 338, NACP.
123 Msg, Donald T. Shea, Intel Div, OMGB, to Director of Intel, OMGUS, 19 Oct 1948, sub: Intelligence Coordinating Meeting, Folder "23a Resistance & Subversive Activities (U.S. Zone) Jan. '48– Dec. '48," ODI, Excerpts of Miscellaneous Rpts and Publications, Analysis and Research Br, 1947–48, RG 260, NACP.
124 Msg, Lt. Col. Robert T. Walker, Ch, ASAE, to DDI, 6 Jul 1949, Folder "311 10 Mar–30 Dec '49," HQ, EUCOM, Ofc of the Ch of Staff, Intel Div, Administrative Files, Gen Corresp (Decimal File), 1947–1951, RG 549, NACP.
125 Msg, Special Agent Thomas H. Evans, Region X, CIC, to CO, 13 Sep 1949, sub: Tapping of U.S. Zone Telephone Lines by Soviet Soldiers, Folder "333.5 3 Jan 49–21 Sep 49," HQ, EUCOM, Of-

Army Intelligence noted that Moscow's spies sought information on a wide range of subjects. These included American reparations policy, the recruitment of German scientists, U.S. economic plans, the organization and operations of U.S. intelligence agencies, and American opinion toward the Soviets. Most of all, Moscow's agents sought to determine U.S. troop strength, the location of units and airfields, the state of training and discipline, and the condition of equipment and communications.[126] Over time, the Office of the Deputy Director of Intelligence estimated, the order of battle intelligence came to dominate Soviet intelligence requirements almost to the exclusion of everything else.[127]

In December 1947, Clay's deputy, Lt. Gen. Clarence R. Huebner, discussed the problem of Soviet espionage with the director of intelligence, Maj. Gen. Robert L. Walsh, as well as with several other top Army and civilian officials. Having just concluded a tour of CIC posts in Hesse, Walsh expressed his surprise at the large number of Soviet spy rings operating there. Huebner replied that he, for his part, was not surprised at all and recommended "greater care in security matters by United States personnel." When it came to Army counterespionage, however, the two generals agreed that "our record was really pretty good in this respect."[128]

Huebner and Walsh may have been overconfident in the Army's counterespionage capabilities. The Soviets had managed to recruit more than a few strategically placed agents. In August 1947, for instance, the Frankfurt military post hired a German named Gerhard Poss as a reception clerk at the Army's Victory Guest House in Königstein near the headquarters of the European Command. A year later, the post promoted Poss to be the guest house's assistant manager.[129] At some point, Soviet intelligence recruited him as a spy. Because numerous visiting American officers, diplomats, and dignitaries stayed at the Victory Guest House, Poss's position gave him access to a great deal of material. U.S. counterintelligence

---

fice of the Ch of Staff, Intel Div, Administrative Files, Gen Corresp (Decimal File), 1947–1951, RG 549, NACP.
126 Msg, HQ, USFET, to G-2, War Department, 27 May 1946, Folder "#2 from 'S' Germany 1945 thru 5-4870," ACoS, G-2 (Intel), "Top Secret" Incoming and Outgoing Cables, 1942–52, RG 319, NACP.
127 Msg, Lt. Col. W. R. Rainold, HQ, ODDI, EUCOM, to Director of Intel, OMGUS, 12 Feb 1948, sub: Report on Soviet Military Espionage Activities, Folder "383.4-1 Espionage," Director of Intel, Analysis and Research Br, Gen Corresp, 1945–49, RG 260, NACP.
128 Ltr, Robert F. Corrigan, Acting Political Ofcr, to [no name] Murphy, 5 Dec 1947, Folder "Top Secret–1947–Amb. Murphy's Correspondence," Office of the U.S. Political Adviser for Germany, Berlin, Top Secret Rcds, 1944–1949, RG 84, NACP.
129 Rpt, Special Agent Edwin R. Woods, 66th CIC Detachment, 11 Mar 1952, Folder "Poss, Gerhard XE 321618," INSCOM, IRR, Digitized Name Files, RG 319, NACP.

did not catch him until 1952, after he photographed the diary of a visiting Army general and passed the images to his Soviet handlers.[130]

In Berlin, the Soviets succeeded in gathering information through multiple channels on the Army's elite intelligence unit, the 7880th Military Intelligence Detachment. Michael G. Stcherbinine first popped up on the U.S. intelligence radar as a potential security threat in 1947. Nonetheless, he obtained a job as a Military Police liaison officer serving with the detachment in 1948 and 1949. He had access to sensitive information, including the whereabouts of Soviet defectors in the detachment's care. Stcherbinine, a gay man, was living openly with his German lover, who went by the name of Walter Vogt. As the CIC subsequently discovered, Vogt was not his real name. Nor, for that matter, was he a German. He was a Russian-born refugee named Valentin Losowsky, and in 1950 he disappeared from Berlin. The CIC suspected that the Soviets had used him to collect information on the 7880th Military Intelligence Detachment through Stcherbinine.[131]

On 1 February 1949, a member of the detachment, Pfc. William T. Marchuk, defected to the Soviet sector. The Army had assigned Marchuk to the unit in 1948 because of his supposed mastery of Russian, but his language skills turned out to be inadequate for the interrogation of Soviet deserters. Moreover, his superior considered him "lazy and lackadaisical" and unable to "pull his load," and assigned him to menial tasks.[132] Frustrated, Marchuk got drunk, crossed the sector border, and complained of his fate to a Soviet officer, who arranged for his transfer to Karlshorst. Over the next two months, Marchuk told the Soviets everything he knew about the detachment, including its operations and intelligence requirements, the names and descriptions of personnel, and the location of safe houses, including floor plans and phone numbers.[133] After the Soviets debriefed Marchuk, they sent him to a labor camp in Siberia. Following his release in 1955, an Army court-martial in Berlin sentenced him to twelve years of hard labor.[134]

In another case, the Soviets ran an undercover agent for over a decade in postwar Germany. Born in Moscow in 1902, Leo Blidin immigrated to Germany in the 1930s. In August 1946, Soviet intelligence recruited him to "work on" (*bear-*

---

130 George F. Hofmann, *Cold War Casualty: The Court-Martial of Major General Robert W. Grow* (Kent, OH: Kent State University Press, 1993), 65.
131 Info Sum, HQ, 66th CIC Gp, 21 Mar 1955, sub: Losowsky, Valentin, defense exhibit R, court-martial records of William T. Marchuk, WNRC.
132 Deposition, Maj. George T. Gabelia, court-martial of William T. Marchuk, Berlin, 12, 13, 14 April, and 16, 17, 18, 19, and 20 May 1955, WNRC.
133 Handwritten statement, William T. Marchuk, 11 Jan 1955, court-martial of William T. Marchuk, Berlin, 12, 13, 14 April, and 16, 17, 18, 19, and 20 May 1955, WNRC.
134 "Army Sentences U.S. Soldier Freed From Soviet Prison Camp," *New York Times*, 21 May 1955.

beiten) British and American agents. The Soviets later informed the East German intelligence service that they appraised Blidin's work as "positive." In 1951, Blidin recruited Michael R. Rothkrug, a civilian employee of the 7880th Military Intelligence Detachment.[135] The detachment had employed Rothkrug because he was a native German speaker. Information procured by Rothkrug allowed the Soviets to identify, apprehend, and try numerous American sources in the Soviet occupation zone in the early 1950s. Thanks to Rothkrug's espionage, the Soviets caught and executed forty-six informants of the detachment.[136] Eventually, the Soviets suspected that U.S. intelligence had become aware of Blidin's espionage activities and stopped working with him in 1957.[137] In fact, the CIC kept a file on Blidin, but it contained merely one entry: "Open Case, 5 Nov 60."[138]

The cases of Stcherbinine, Poss, Marchuk, and Rothkrug indicate that insufficient vetting and low-quality personnel were the weakest points of the Army, military government, and U.S. intelligence agencies in Germany. During the war and in the immediate postwar period, German émigrés had provided crucial language and cultural expertise to the Army. By and large, the émigrés' personal experience and their military service during the war guaranteed their unwavering loyalty to the United States. But when many of them returned to civilian life, Army Intelligence struggled to find adequate replacements. In several cases, the Army placed local citizens or second-generation Americans in sensitive positions. The loyalty and dedication of the émigrés' replacements, however, remained untested, making them attractive targets for Soviet recruitment efforts.

Soviet intelligence appears to have excelled at collecting tactical information. One Soviet report, available by translation through the East German intelligence service, includes several pages of names and descriptions of individual U.S. intelligence members in Germany. It also adds comments on their potential for recruitment. A certain intelligence analyst in Heidelberg, for example, supposedly did not advance as quickly in his career as he would have liked. Therefore, he was

---

135 Rpt, MfS, HA II, "Auskunftsbericht, betr.: Blidin, Leo, geb. 1902 in Moskau" [Information report, re: Blidin, Leo, born in Moscow in 1902], 10 Jun 1961, MfS-HA II, no. 41402, 145, BStU, Berlin.
136 Thomas Boghardt, "Betrayal in Berlin: The Riddle of the 'Walter Affair,'" Sources and Methods, Cold War International History Project, Wilson Center, 17 Aug 2020, https://www.wilsoncenter.org/ blog-post/betrayal-berlin-riddle-walter-affair; Enrico Heitzer, *Affäre Walter: Die vergessene Verhaftungswelle* [The Walter affair: The forgotten wave of arrests] (Berlin: Metropol, 2008), 71, 146; Enrico Heitzer, *Die Kampfgruppe gegen Unmenschlichkeit (KgU): Widerstand und Spionage im Kalten Krieg 1948–1959* [The Fighting Group against Inhumanity: Resistance and espionage in the Cold War, 1948–1959] (Cologne: Böhlau Verlag, 2014), 210.
137 Rpt, MfS, HA II, "Auskunftsbericht, betr.: Blidin, Leo, geb. 1902 in Moskau," 10 Jun 1961, 145.
138 Index card, n.d. [5 Nov 1960], Folder "Blidin, Leo GE 008141," INSCOM, IRR, Digitized Name Files, RG 319, NACP.

unhappy, and "any intelligence service would be able to recruit him."[139] Another Russian intelligence document gives a generally accurate description of the organization of the CIC in Germany.[140] However, the totalitarian structure of the Soviet state prevented rational analysis. Joseph Stalin despised analytical reports and demanded only raw intelligence. The Soviet dictator notoriously rejected information that contradicted his preconceptions. After concluding a nonaggression pact with Hitler in August 1939, Stalin refused to credit intelligence obtained from an informant inside the German military, indicating preparations for an assault on the Soviet Union. "Your source," Stalin thundered at his intelligence chief, "can go to his f–king mother. That is not a 'source,' but a disinformant."[141] Understandably, Soviet intelligence chiefs were loath to tell their boss things he did not want to hear.

The Soviets should have had little difficulty assessing the U.S. Army's order of battle because, the intelligence division noted, "no attempts are made to conceal it."[142] Nonetheless, the available evidence suggests that the Soviets grossly overestimated the American presence. A report from June 1948 assessed American troop strength in Germany at 160,000.[143] This erroneous number resulted from bad intelligence or, more likely, from Soviet intelligence officers who worried about reporting the military weakness of the supposedly belligerent United States. The Soviet leadership routinely emphasized the aggressive and militaristic nature of the West, and intelligence that questioned American prowess may not have received a warm reception in Moscow. Either way, the assessment was badly skewed. The Army had less than 100,000 soldiers in Germany at the time.[144]

By the end of the military occupation, Soviet intelligence and Army counterintelligence had settled into a stalemate. Although the Soviets flooded the U.S. Zone and the American sector in Berlin with spies, the CIC detected and apprehended

---

139 Rpt, MfS, HA II, "Verzeichnis der Mitarbeiter des amerikanischen Geheimdienstes, Übersetzung aus dem Russischen" [Directory of American Secret Service employees, translation from Russian], n.d., MfS-HA II, Nr. 44666, 181–87, BStU, Berlin.
140 Rpt, MfS, HA II, "Übersetzung aus dem Russischen, Auszug aus dem Bericht vom 5. Januar 1961," 17 Apr 1961, 168–74.
141 Matthias Uhl, *Krieg um Berlin? Die sowjetische Militär-und Sicherheitspolitik in der zweiten Berlin-Krise 1958–1962* [War over Berlin?: Soviet military and security policy in the second Berlin crisis, 1958–1962] (Munich: Oldenbourg, 2008), 73.
142 Teletype, EUCOM teletype message no. 13, n.d. [early 1949] re: DA-1, EUCOM, Ofc of the Sec of Staff, Sec of the Gen Staff Msg Control Center, Classified Teleconference Msgs, 1945–1951, 1948–1951, RG 549, NACP.
143 Victor Gobarev, "Soviet Military Plans and Actions During the First Berlin Crisis, 1948–49," *The Journal of Slavic Military Studies* 10, no. 3 (Sep 1997), 12.
144 U.S. War Department, Adjutant Gen Ofc, *Strength of the Army* (Washington, DC: Government Printing Office, 1 Jul 1948), 14.

many (if not most) of them. In the late 1940s, the Soviets successfully inserted several agents into sensitive positions, but Soviet intelligence analysis of the American military occupation remained mediocre. The Army's counterintelligence record may not have been "really pretty good," as Generals Walsh and Huebner claimed, but may have been good enough to keep the Soviets at bay.

Conclusion

Army Intelligence had prepared for specific occupation missions, but from early on the agencies had to confront a series of unanticipated challenges. Their record in meeting them proved uneven. Intelligence personnel succumbed to the temptations of the black market as easily as many regular soldiers and officers did, and the concomitant press coverage cast an unwelcome light on the supposedly secret world of America's clandestine warriors. The fate of the displaced persons was primarily a political and security problem, but no other U.S. agency in occupied Germany had the personnel and the capabilities to deal with them, and thus the job fell to the Counter Intelligence Corps. Overall, the CIC acquitted itself well, but the enormous task of overseeing and vetting several million individuals absorbed an inordinate amount of time and resources.

The activities of Soviet spies posed a major obstacle for the American military government. On the one hand, the Army's counterintelligence arm managed to detect this threat early; identified and apprehended large numbers of spies; and warned leaders in Berlin, Frankfurt, and Washington consistently about it. On the other hand, Soviet operations gained in sophistication over time, and several important foreign agents remained undetected for several years. If Army Intelligence managed to constrain the activities of Moscow's secret agents during the military occupation, the state of Soviet intelligence in the late 1940s suggested that this challenge would continue to test the Army's counterespionage organization in the years to come.

8 Democratization

In the spring of 1945, the political life of Konrad Adenauer seemed to be over. He had entered politics in 1906 as a representative of the Catholic Center Party (Deutsche Zentrumspartei), and had served as mayor of Cologne from 1917 until 1933. When the Nazi Party came to power, he lost his office, and the Nazis arrested him twice on suspicion of opposing their regime. By early 1945, he was a 69-year-old pensioner living quietly in a small town south of Cologne. Like other Rhinelanders, he eagerly awaited the end of the war. In mid-March, his sister Lilli, who lived in a nearby village, called him, gushing, "We are free, the Americans are here. By the way, they are pretty nice people."[1] The next day, these "pretty nice people" showed up at Adenauer's doorstep and reignited his political career.

As American forces moved into Germany, Nazi-appointed officials fled, perished, or went to prison. The task of finding replacement for hundreds of mayors, county executives (*Landräte*), and governors fell to military government detachments. The Americans carried with them blacklists of compromised Nazi officials as well as whitelists of politically reliable individuals, the latter compiled by U.S. intelligence to identify potential administrators. In his memoirs, Adenauer prided himself on being number one on the whitelist "for all of Germany, which means, I was judged especially trustworthy."[2] This was a bit of an exaggeration. The whitelists were organized regionally, and each list was arranged in alphabetical order. Because his last name started with the letters "a" and "d," Adenauer automatically floated to the top of the list. Nonetheless, it is true that he had his own entry, which noted: "Worth contacting by Allies for cooperation according to anti-Nazi [prisoner of war]."[3]

In all likelihood, the Americans tracked down Adenauer with the help of his sister Lilli and her husband, Willi Suth. Members of military government detachment E1H2 interviewed Suth on 15 March, and this interaction may have prompted Lilli to call her brother to tell him the Americans had arrived.[4] The following day, the detachment interviewed Adenauer and offered him a job in the new administration of Cologne. As the military governor of Cologne, Lt. Col. John K. Patterson,

---

1 Konrad Adenauer, *Erinnerungen 1945–1953* [Memoirs, 1945–1953] (Stuttgart: Deutsche Verlags-Anstalt, 1965), 18.
2 Adenauer, *Erinnerungen 1945–1953*, 23.
3 Henric L. Würmeling, *Die Weiße Liste und die Stunde Null in Deutschland 1945* [The whitelist and zero hour in Germany, 1945] (Munich: Herbig, 2015), 68.
4 Daily MG [Mil Government] Rpt, Lt. Col. John K. Patterson, to CO, First U.S. Army, 16 Mar 1945, Folder "MG Detachment Daily Reports 9 Mar–12 May 1945," Historical Div, Program Files, Fifteenth U.S. Army, Station Lists, Sums, and Rpts, 1945, RG 498, NACP.

Figure 33: Two soldiers of the U.S. Fifteenth Army view the Cologne Cathedral from under an arch of the wrecked Hohenzollern Bridge in Cologne, Germany, April 1945. U.S. Army, NACP.

noted, "Adenauer has three sons in the German army" and was therefore "hesitant about taking an active part in the government. As he was one of the most highly respected oberburgermeister [lord mayor] in the pre-Hitler days, he may be used in an advisory capacity."[5] Consequently, Adenauer entered American service as an adviser, rather than mayor. In an effort to protect Adenauer and his sons from reprisals, Patterson arranged for a censorship stop of all news radio releases connecting Adenauer to the occupation forces.[6]

A month later, an intelligence officer with the 12th Army Group, Capt. Ulrich E. Biel, visited Adenauer to take the measure of the man. Although Biel found the

---

[5] Daily MG Rpt, Lt. Col. John K. Patterson, to CO, First U.S. Army, 17 Mar 1945, Folder "MG Detachment Daily Reports 9 Mar–12 May 1945," Historical Div, Program Files, Fifteenth U.S. Army, Station Lists, Sums, and Rpts, 1945, RG 498, NACP.

[6] Msg, Lt. Col. John K. Patterson, Co H, 2d European Civil Affairs Rgt to Supreme Cdr, SHAEF, 22 Mar 1945, sub: Censorship Stop, Folder "Censorship + Communications, German," Gen Staff Div, G–2 Counter-Intel Sub-Div, Civil Security Section, Decimal Corresp File, 1943–45, RG 331, NACP.

elderly gentleman "slightly lacking the rigor one would expect from a political leader," he considered Adenauer a "man with . . . an important past and potential future." Despite his age, Biel noted, Adenauer was fully alert and only regretted his poor knowledge of the English language. The former mayor had little sympathy for Nazi officials and advised the Americans to "eliminate" all Nazi Party members from public office, "whatever their excuses may be." Overall, Biel considered Adenauer "too big a man" for the role of mere counselor, and he advised military government to use him for a leading position in the future administration of Germany.[7]

Adenauer, for his part, was impressed with the amount of information the Americans had accumulated on him and the speed with which they had located him. Likewise, he never forgot the favorable treatment he received at their hands. The U.S. officers he encountered "were all smart and sensible people," he recalled, "and soon we got along well." As a patriotic Rhinelander, he was charmed by the display of regional pride exhibited by one of Patterson's staff officers. Unfolding a map of his home state, the officer declared proudly, "This is Texas. Texas is the most beautiful, biggest, and richest place in the world, and I am a Texan!" In his memoirs, Adenauer acknowledged, "I have to admit, after visiting Texas in person, I understand his pride."[8]

The Americans formally appointed Adenauer mayor of Cologne at the war's end, restoring him to the office he had held before the rise of Nazism. With this promotion, one Counter Intelligence Corps officer noted, "we returned him to history."[9] Over the next four years, Adenauer used his unexpected reentry into public life to position himself as the preeminent politician of the Western zones. With the establishment of the Federal Republic of Germany in 1949, he became the country's first chancellor, a job he held for the next fourteen years. Under his leadership, West Germany became a staunch ally of the United States. Adenauer's postwar career exemplified the significance of Army Intelligence in molding the careers of German politicians and politics in the U.S. Zone. Many followed the same trajectory.

---

7 Martin Otto, "Adenauers Entdecker" [Adenauer's discoverer], *Frankfurter Allgemeine*, 16 May 2007; Memo, Ulrich E. Biel for [illegible], 23 Apr 1945, Historians Files, CMH. The latter document comes from the private files of Dr. Martin Otto.
8 Adenauer, *Erinnerungen 1945–1953*, 20.
9 Ian Sayer and Douglas Botting, *America's Secret Army: The Untold Story of the Counter Intelligence Corps* (London: Fontana, 1990), 220.

Shaping the Political Landscape in Postwar Germany

For Brig. Gen. Edwin L. Sibert, identifying and empowering suitable public figures was the key to the successful democratization of German society. "We must select," he wrote in the *New York Times*, "a German 'intellectual aristocracy,' which we can charge with the task of transforming every aspect of German life into a democratic mold. These 'intellectual aristocrats' should be found in every county, a small number of men very carefully screened whom we can back to the hilt in their work among their countrymen."[10] Army Intelligence agencies in Germany followed their chief's exhortation to the letter.

As early as 1942, the CIC had begun to interrogate German prisoners of war for the names of officials, journalists, and political figures who had not been compromised by relationships with the Nazi regime. Later, the Office of Strategic Services contributed to this endeavor. In December 1944, shortly after American forces had entered Germany, the Psychological Warfare Division of Supreme Allied Headquarters published the final edition of this wide-ranging effort: the "White List of persons in Germany who are believed to be anti-Nazi or non-Nazi." It included around 1,500 names of individuals presumed to reside in the designated U.S. zone of occupation and Berlin. To minimize the risk of Nazi retribution against potential Allied collaborators, the division classified the list "top secret," strictly limited its distribution, and prohibited the transfer of copies into combat areas. The White List was not the only source of information of military government detachments for the selection of local officials, but it served as an important tool in several notable cases such as Adenauer's.[11]

The White List also featured the name of Reinhold Maier, a politician of the left-of-center Democratic Party (Deutsche Demokratische Partei) and minister of economics of the state of Württemberg in pre-Nazi Germany. As Maier's entry noted, the Nazis had forced him to retire in 1933 because of his opposition to the new regime.[12] A U.S. informant in June 1945 confirmed Maier's anti-Nazi credentials and praised his "excellent administrative and financial qualities."[13] A subsequent CIC report noted that Maier's Jewish wife Gerta and his children had fled to Great Britain during the Third Reich, and that he enjoyed "a good reputation

---

10 Brig. Gen. Edwin L. Sibert, "The German Mind: Our Greatest Problem," *New York Times*, 17 Feb 1946.
11 Würmeling, *Weiße Liste*, 21, 26, 27.
12 Würmeling, *Weiße Liste*, 162.
13 Klaus-Jürgen Matz, *Reinhold Maier (1889–1971): Eine politische Biographie* [Reinhold Maier (1889–1971): A political biography] (Düsseldorf: Droste Verlag, 1989), 181.

among old Democratic and parliamentary circles."[14] In August 1945, the military government appointed him minister-president (*Ministerpräsident*; governor) of Württemberg-Baden, and he would lead the southwestern German *Land* for the next eight years. Thanks in part to Maier's steady hand, the military government of Württemberg-Baden experienced few problems. The Office of the Director of Intelligence came to regard it as "the least 'explosive' of the three Länder."[15]

Another politician who launched his postwar career with the assistance of Army Intelligence was Theodor Heuss.[16] A Reichstag deputy of the Democratic Party until 1933, Heuss had to suspend his political career when the Nazis came to power. He published a few nonpolitical articles during the Third Reich but stayed out of politics. His White List entry described him as an "Uncompromising Democrat."[17] In late April 1945, Sgt. John H. Boxer of the Psychological Warfare Division sought out Heuss, who promptly invited the American to celebrate the end of the war with a bottle of wine. Boxer's driver initially greeted the offer with skepticism: "Don't drink that, it's poisoned," he warned the sergeant. Boxer, however, dismissed these concerns, and the two Americans ended up sitting down with Heuss and his wife Elly Heuss-Knapp and emptied the bottle. Boxer and Heuss became lifelong friends, and the former warmly recommended the latter as a valuable asset to his boss, Maj. Shepard Stone.[18]

Heuss talked frequently with CIC officials, and he may have worked temporarily as an informant for the Stuttgart branch of the Corps.[19] When allegations about his journalistic work during the Third Reich threatened to derail his budding postwar career, a CIC investigation cleared his return to public life by concluding that Heuss had "made no compromise with the Nazis."[20] The Americans issued him a

---

14 Personality Rpt, no author, n.d., sub: Maier, Dr. Reinhold, Folder "Maier, Reinhold XE 179423," INSCOM, IRR, Digitized Name Files, RG 319, NACP.
15 Memo, Lt. Col. Frank M. Potter Jr., Ch, Analysis and Rpts Section, for Col. Peter P. Rodes, ODI, 14 Oct 1946, Folder "Miscellaneous Reports & Memoranda 1946–48," Director of Intel, Miscellaneous Rcds re. Intel and Document Policies, 1944–1948, RG 260, NACP.
16 For the following, see Thomas Boghardt, "The American Candidate: U.S. Intelligence, Theodor Heuss, and the Making of West Germany's First President," *Studies in Intelligence* 64, no. 2 (Jun 2020): 1–12.
17 Würmeling, *Weiße Liste*, 154.
18 Joachim Radkau, *Theodor Heuss* (Munich: Carl Hanser Verlag, 2013), 261. Elly Heuss-Knapp was a liberal politician in her own right, both before and after the war, and served as Württemberg-Baden *Landrat* (state legislature) member from 1946 to 1949.
19 Rpt, MfS, HA II, "Übersetzung aus dem Russischen, Auszug aus dem Bericht vom 5. Januar 1961" [Translation from the Russian, excerpt from the report of 5 Jan 1961], 17 Apr 1961, 168–74, MfS-HA II, no. 44666, BStU, Berlin.
20 Rpt, G.P. [German Personalities] no. 50, 20 Sep 1945, Folder "Theodor Heuss D078263," INSCOM, IRR, Digitized Name Files, RG 319, NACP.

coveted newspaper license for the *Rhein-Neckar-Zeitung* and in September 1945 appointed him minister of culture in Württemberg-Baden. His anti-Nazi credentials, his easy manners, and his pragmatic views endeared him to American officials and to the German public alike. Within a few years, he emerged as a leading liberal politician, first of the newly established Democratic People's Party (Demokratische Volkspartei) and later of its successor, the Free Democratic Party (Freie Demokratische Partei; FDP). In September 1949, the Bundestag (West German parliament) elected him as the first president of the Federal Republic—the official head of state. Special Agent Edward W. Hoffer, who assessed the political implications of Heuss's election for the CIC, described him as "a man of high character, personal integrity and excellent reputation." Heuss was known to be "friendly and open-minded towards Anglo-Saxon views of democracy," Hoffer concluded, and should be considered "the wisest choice" for the job.[21]

The Allies did not always choose as adroitly as in the cases of Adenauer, Maier, and Heuss. For example, the Americans had to remove from office the mayor of Bremen, Erich Vagts, within a few months of his appointment. A hand-me-down from the brief British occupation of Bremen, Vagts turned out to be pro-Nazi and "utterly incompetent," according to an American military government official.[22] The CIC confirmed his Nazi sympathies, described him "as an extremely clever opportunist," and put him in the "automatic arrest" category designated for key Nazi Party functionaries. Subsequently, Vagts spent six months in an internment camp.[23] Yet the majority of U.S.-appointed German officials proved competent and democratically minded.[24] Vagt's replacement, the social democrat Wilhelm Kaisen, was a case in point: he turned out to be an extremely capable mayor who would run Bremen's affairs for the next twenty years.

With a functioning administrative machinery in place, the military government set about the next task, the restoration of democracy in the U.S. Zone. This

---

21 Msg, Special Agent Edward W. Hoffer, Region I, CIC, to CO, 15 Sep 1949, sub: Heuss, Professor Dr. Theodor, folder "31 Jan 1884 Theodor Heuss XE 2009782," INSCOM, IRR, Personal Name Files, RG 319, NACP.
22 Walter L. Dorn, *Inspektionsreisen in der US-Zone: Notizen, Denkschriften und Erinnerungen aus dem Nachlass überetzt und herausgegeben von Lutz Niethammer* [Inspection trips in the U.S. Zone: Notes, memoranda and memories from the estate, translated and edited by Lutz Niethammer] (Stuttgart: Deutsche Verlags-Anstalt, 1973), 41f.
23 Rpt, Special Agent Brookes Friebolin, 970/110 CIC Detachment, HQ Enclave Mil District, n.d., Folder "Vagts, Erich Johannes XE 002324," INSCOM, IRR, Digitized Name Files, RG 319, NACP.
24 Walter Mühlhausen, *Demokratischer Neubeginn in Hessen 1945–1949: Lehren aus der Vergangenheit für die Gestaltung der Zukunft* [Democratic new beginning in Hesse, 1945–1949: Lessons from the past for shaping the future] (Wiesbaden: Hessische Landeszentrale für Politische Bildung, 2005), 13.

process began with the authorization of political activities in August 1945 and the licensing of local chapters of democratic parties. In short order, the military government sanctioned four parties in the U.S. Zone: the conservative Christian Democratic Union (Christlich Demokratische Union Deutschlands; CDU) with its Bavarian variant, the Christian Social Union (Christlich-Soziale Union; CSU); the right-of-center liberal party (FDP, or LDP [Liberal-Demokratische Partei; Liberal Democratic Party] in Hesse), the left-of-center Social Democratic Party (SPD), and the German Communist Party (KPD).

The licensing of these four parties, and the denial of licenses to any other group at the time, had major implications for the emerging political scene in the U.S. Zone. In Weimar Germany, the splintering of the political center-right into numerous smaller parties diluted the strength of their popular support and abetted the rise of National Socialism. By artificially limiting this segment of the political spectrum to two parties, the CDU/CSU and FDP/LDP, the Americans set the stage for a structural conservative majority in postwar Germany.[25] Especially in rural southern Germany, conservative parties could be expected to do well among the electorate.

At the same time, the liberals and especially the Christian democrats amalgamated a number of disparate elements, which weakened their cohesion and forced them to broaden their political platform to preserve their internal unity. An intelligence report of the military government in Bavaria commented repeatedly on the CSU's "inner dissension" and its "heterogeneous elements."[26] Some military government officials, including General Lucius D. Clay, had doubts about the new conservative alignments; they regarded the CDU as a haven of former Nazis.[27] It thus remained to be seen whether the Christian democrats could turn their structural advantage into political dominance.

In contrast to the conservative regrouping, Germany's social democrats and communists could fall back on established organizations and a cadre of experienced functionaries who had survived the Third Reich, often in exile or in concentration camps. Moreover, the Americans thought, the left-wing parties' documented opposition to the Nazis likely would give them an edge with German voters and the

---

25 Rebecca Boehling, "U.S. Military Occupation, Grass Roots Democracy, and Local German Government," in *American Policy and the Reconstruction of West Germany, 1945–1955*, ed. Jeffrey M. Diefendorf, Axel Frohn, and Hermann-Josef Rupieper (Cambridge, UK: Cambridge University Press, 1994), 297–98.
26 Rpt, OMGB, Periodic Rpt for Week ending 23 Oct 1946 and Periodic Rpt for Week ending 27 Nov 1946, Folder "Periodical Intelligence Reports, 25 Oct 46–6 Dec 46," Rcds of the OMGB, Rcds of the Intel Div, Weekly Intel Rpts, 1945–47, RG 260, NACP.
27 J. F. J. Gillen, *U.S. Military Government in Germany: American Influence on the Development of Political Institutions* (Karlsruhe: Historical Division, EUCOM, 1950), 67.

occupation authorities alike. The wartime military government handbook therefore predicted "a pronounced swing to the left, the Socialist and Communist Parties gaining many adherents" in postwar Germany.[28]

In the face of the complexity and the contradictions of the emerging party system, American officials were unsure of how it would evolve and relied heavily on Army Intelligence to monitor political developments. The new parties faced their first test in 1946. In a series of elections, voters chose representatives at the local, regional, and *Land* level. The intelligence division of the military government of Bavaria reported that, as expected, communist and social democratic candidates campaigned "very actively" while the CSU remained largely passive.[29] Nonetheless, the conservative parties prevailed in large parts of Bavaria and Württemberg-Baden, bolstered by the rural Catholic vote. The social democrats did well in Greater Hesse, one of the party's traditional strongholds, while the liberals and communists trailed the two major parties in most places. Turnout on average was over 80 percent, but Army Intelligence cautioned that "the heavy vote was more indicative of interest in the selection of local administrative officials than it was of enthusiasm for political issues."[30] If so, the elections amounted to a ringing endorsement by German voters of the choices that Army officials had made at the end of the war. In Bavaria alone, intelligence reported, more than three-fourths of the American-appointed mayors won reelection.[31]

Over time, the three noncommunist parties coalesced around nationally recognized leaders, and Army Intelligence kept a close eye on the key personalities. In the liberal party, the lawyer Thomas Dehler played a central role alongside the chairman, Theodor Heuss. Early on, Dehler became something of a golden boy of U.S. intelligence. His White List entry noted that his wife Irma was Jewish and that he "often defended at great personal risk Jews and other people persecuted by the Nazis. He was arrested several times by the Nazis because of his activities, but when in prison did not yield to requests made by high party officials. He is

---

28 SHAEF, *Handbook for Military Government in Germany Prior to Defeat or Surrender: Incorporating Revision 1-20 Dec. 1944* (SHAEF, 1945), Part ii, para. 245, Historians Files, CMH.

29 Rpt, OMGB, Periodic Rpt for Week Ending 17 April 1946, Folder "Periodical Intelligence Reports, 19 April 46–18 Oct 46," Rcds of the OMGB, Rcds of the Intel Div, Weekly Intel Rpts, 1945–47, RG 260, NACP.

30 *Review of Europe, Russia, and Middle East* 1 (22 Jan 1946), 13, Folder "Review of Europe, Russia, and the Middle East," Corresp, Rpts, Dirs, and Other Rcds Relating to the Activities and Functions of the Intel Gp, 1943–47, RG 165, NACP.

31 Rpt, Maj. Peter Vacca, Intel Br Ch, Weekly Mil Government Rpt no. 38, for week ending 31 Jan 1946, Folder "OMG Bavaria Wkly MG Rpts. (Summaries), Nos. 27–42, 15 Nov 45–28 Feb 46," Historical Div, Program Files, OMGUS, OMGB, Weekly Mil Government Rpts, 1945–47, RG 498, NACP.

unreservedly reliable."[32] The CIC's biographical file described him exuberantly as "good-looking; blond; blue eyes . . . a good speaker; a good writer; intelligent; courageous; well-balanced; dignified; has a social conscience."[33] The Army appointed him to various positions in 1945, and he quickly rose to prominence in the newly established FDP, becoming West Germany's first minister of justice in 1949.[34]

Within the CDU, the staunchly pro-Western Konrad Adenauer gradually emerged as the party's national leader. Well-known to the Americans since the liberation of Cologne, he remained a high-priority target for Army Intelligence during the following years. That his wife Auguste was a distant relative of Ellen McCloy—the wife of the future American high commissioner in Germany, John J. McCloy—certainly did not hurt Adenauer's prospects.[35] Because Adenauer resided in the British zone of occupation, the Americans had to route their collection efforts through Berlin. The intelligence section of the Berlin Command recruited the director of the city's St. Francis Hotel, Clemens Kleinschmidt, who personally knew and had access to Adenauer. An anti-Nazi who had suffered heavily at the hands of the *Gestapo*, Kleinschmidt served as a "very reliable and valuable contact source," producing information "on high level political matters" concerning Adenauer and the inner circle of the CDU.[36] Later, the CIC managed to recruit a friend of Adenauer's son Kurt as an informant in Munich.[37] By the summer of 1949, the military government's intelligence office praised the man from the Rhineland: "Adenauer has managed to keep the divergent groups [of the CDU] together. Adenauer, a man of high personal culture and education, extremely intelligent, and a master in tactics and negotiations, has accomplished this task through mere personal skill."[38]

---

32 Würmeling, *Weiße Liste*, 210.
33 Excerpt, no author, 31 Jul 1943, sub: U.S. Biographical Records, Folder "XE 223672 Thomas Dehler," INSCOM, IRR, Personal Name Files, RG 319, NACP.
34 Udo Wengst, *Thomas Dehler, 1897–1967: Eine politische Biographie* [Thomas Dehler, 1897–1967: A political biography] (Munich: Oldenbourg, 1997), 82.
35 Kai Bird, *The Chairman: John J. McCloy and the Making of the American Establishment* (New York: Simon & Schuster, 1992), 320.
36 Msg, HQ, USFET, to ACofS, G–2, 14 Feb 1947, sub: Penicillin Issued for Intelligence Purposes, Folder "400–1947," HQ, EUCOM, Ofc of the Ch of Staff, Intel Div, Administrative Br, Gen Corresp (Decimal File), 1947–1951, RG 549, NACP.
37 Msg, Lt. Col. Alfred C. Scherer, Region IV, CIC, to 66th CIC Gp, 12 Jan 1954, sub: Kurt Adenauer, Folder "XE 8004427 Konrad Adenauer Fldr. 1 of 2," INSCOM, IRR, Personal Name Files, RG 319, NACP.
38 Rpt, Innis D. Harris, ODI, OMGUS, 28 May 1949, sub: Weekly Intelligence Report no. 159, Folder "OMGUS Weekly Intelligence Reports May 1949," Historians' Background Files, 1947–1952, RG 549, NACP.

Adenauer was by no means the only American intelligence target in the CDU. During the war, the OSS contacted Eugen Gerstenmaier, a Protestant theologian and staunch opponent of the Third Reich. Thrown in jail for his involvement in an anti-Nazi conspiracy, he was liberated by American forces in Bayreuth in April 1945.[39] After the war, he assisted German refugees from the east and joined the CDU. In 1954, the Bundestag elected him president. Meanwhile, the CIA secretly subsidized his Hilfswerk der Evangelischen Kirche in Deutschland, the welfare agency of the Lutheran church with ties to Protestants in East Germany.[40] The agency's deputy chief of station in Berlin, Peter M. F. Sichel, described Gerstenmaier as an important liaison and good friend: "He continued to work with the CIA for many years."[41]

The military government had a more complicated relationship with the SPD and its leader, Kurt Schumacher, who had been a socialist organizer and SPD member in the Reichstag during the interwar years. Thanks to the White List, the Americans knew that Schumacher had staunchly opposed the Nazis and had spent ten years in various concentration camps.[42] His internment left him with severe disabilities, compounding his existing physical hardships (including the loss of his right arm in World War I), and he had to undergo an additional amputation of one leg in 1948. Yet within months of his liberation from the camps, Schumacher had established himself as the leader of the SPD in Hanover in the British Zone. The recently elected Labour government in London sympathized with his advocacy for strong unions and the socialization of key industries, and tacitly supported his rise. Because he had rejected overtures from communist-aligned SPD elements in the Soviet Zone, when he traveled to Berlin to consult with local social democrats an armed British soldier accompanied him for personal protection from Moscow's henchmen. In late 1946, Schumacher visited London at the invitation of the Labour Party to meet with Britain's own social democratic and socialist politicians.[43]

The Americans, for their part, found Schumacher's political views troublesome and regarded his closeness to the British with skepticism. The CIC had managed to recruit a personal acquaintance of Schumacher's as an informant. According to this

---

39 "Eugen Gerstenmaier," *Der Spiegel*, 16 Sep 1964.
40 Kevin Ruffner, "Eagle and Swastika: CIA and Nazi War Criminals and Collaborators" (Washington, DC: History Staff, Central Intelligence Agency, 2003), chap. 9, 14.
41 Interv, Peter M. F. Sichel with Thomas Boghardt, 7 Mar 2018, Historians Files, CMH.
42 Würmeling, *Weiße Liste*, 162.
43 Peter Merseburger, *Der schwierige Deutsche: Kurt Schumacher. Eine Biographie* [The difficult German: Kurt Schumacher. A biography] (Stuttgart: Deutsche Verlags-Anstalt, 1995), 203–04, 351–52.

source, code-named CHICAGO, Schumacher had returned from London claiming that the British had agreed to help him turn the SPD into the dominant party in Germany. The SPD leader, CHICAGO contended, "is very anti-American."[44] Moreover, Schumacher was a staunch nationalist who rejected the notion of German collective guilt. Given his principled opposition to Hitler, no one could accuse Schumacher of harboring pro-Nazi sentiments, but his lack of humility toward the Allies rubbed many U.S. officials the wrong way.[45] Yet Schumacher's avowed anticommunism and his unwillingness to compromise with the Soviets made him a potential partner of U.S. intelligence. The Pentagon's intelligence division recognized as early as October 1945 that a strong social democratic party "could be a powerful force in checking the spread of Communism."[46] The Strategic Services Unit used a German emigrant and wartime intelligence officer, 1st Lt. Siegfried Höxter, to reach out to Schumacher and other social democrats.[47] When Schumacher traveled to Berlin, he occasionally met with the CIA's deputy chief of station, Peter Sichel, to discuss anti-communist and anti-Soviet tactics. These gatherings had none of the warmth that sometimes developed between intelligence officers and their liaisons or informants in postwar Germany. Though Sichel was impressed with Schumacher's drive and focus, he regarded the German politician as "a cool customer."[48]

Schumacher's aloofness made Western intelligence keen to cultivate someone close to him. Fritz Heine fit the bill. A dedicated social democrat and fervent opponent of the Nazis, Heine had spent the war years in London, where he helped the British secret service handle German double agents.[49] After the war, Heine returned to his city of birth, Hanover, and became the revived SPD's press and propaganda chief as well as a close confidant of Schumacher. Fluent in English, he served as a liaison with the British occupation authorities as well as the Americans. In September 1947, Heine accompanied Schumacher on an official visit to the United States.[50] At some point, the CIA established a confiden-

---

44 Rpt, Chisel Rpt no. 620, source: Chicago, subsource: Schumacher, 3 Mar 1947, Folder "Schumacher, Kurt XE 058524," INSCOM, IRR, Digitized Name Files, RG 319, NACP.
45 Merseburger, *Der schwierige Deutsche*, 225.
46 *Review of Europe, Russia, and Middle East* 1 (29 Oct 1945), 1, Folder "Review of Europe, Russia, and Middle East," Corresp, Rpts, Dirs and Other Rcds Relating to the Activities and Functions of the Intel Gp, 1943–47, RG 165, NACP.
47 Memo, Special Agent Robert E. Hallowell, Region II, CIC, for Subregional Ch, 8 Aug 1946, sub: Background of 1st Lt. Hoexter, Siegfried, Folder "Hoexter, Siegfried XE 219424," INSCOM, IRR, Digitized Name Files, RG 319, NACP.
48 Interv, Boghardt with Sichel, 7 Mar 2018.
49 Index card, Heine, Fritz, 12 Oct 1949, Folder "Heine, Fritz D236313," INSCOM, IRR, Digitized Name Files, RG 319, NACP.
50 "Quisling Nr. 2 – Fritz Heine," *Neues Deutschland*, 22 Nov 1947.

tial relationship with him, and Heine came to serve as the SPD's unofficial contact with the agency.[51]

American intelligence assessments of the SPD at large mirrored the ambivalent relationship with Schumacher and his inner circle. Many intelligence officials did not take kindly to the SPD representatives. In 1946, a CIC contact dismissed the first elected minister-president of Greater Hesse, Christian Stock of the SPD, as a "very colorless fellow, nothing special about him."[52] The following year, the CIC investigated Greater Hesse's minister of justice, Georg A. Zinn, for anti-American utterances. Zinn had told a gathering of SPD members that U.S. society consisted of two classes: "Rich and poor, and the poor live in shacks made of gasoline tanks."[53] Nevertheless, the military government found several reliable allies among the social democrats. General Clay praised Wilhelm Kaisen, the longtime SPD mayor of Bremen, as "practical and realistic, essentially a man of action."[54] And in Berlin, social democrats became vital partners of U.S. intelligence against the Soviets and the KPD.

As West Germany gained conditional independence in late 1949, Army Intelligence had spun a large web over the political scene. The Bundestag, elected in August 1949, constituted the highest legislative body of the new state. In a testimony to the thoroughness of Army Intelligence, the CIC compiled dossiers on 340 of the 402 deputies, including members of every party.[55] As the Army released control over the political affairs of its former occupation zone, it did so knowing that its intelligence agencies remained well informed about the decision-making processes and the internal politics of the new state.

---

51 Susanne Meinl and Bodo Hechlhammer, "Kurz und Wichtig: Politiker-Besuche in der Zentrale" [Short and significant: Politicians visits to headquarters], in *Geheimobjekt Pullach: Von der NS-Mustersiedlung zur Zentrale des BND* [Secret object Pullach: From the Nazi model housing estate to BND headquarters], ed. Susanne Meinl and Bodo Hechlhammer (Berlin: Ch. Links Verlag, 2014), 222.
52 MFR, Biographical info, Christian Stock (SPD), n.d., Folder "Stock, Christian XE 204566," INSCOM, IRR, Digitized Name Files, RG 319, NACP.
53 MFR, Biographical info, sub: Zinn, Georg August, n.d., Folder "Zinn, Georg August XE 207841," INSCOM, IRR, Digitized Name Files, RG 319, NACP.
54 Lucius D. Clay, *Decision in Germany* (Garden City, NY: Doubleday, 1950), 96.
55 Molly R. Ricks, "CIC Records on Members of the First West German Parliament" (unpublished research paper, U.S. Army Center of Military History, Washington, DC, 2018), Historians Files, CMH.

The Bavarian Challenge

Bavaria absorbed the lion's share of American personnel and resources. It was by far the largest *Land* in the U.S. Zone, and its extensive borders with Austria, Czechoslovakia, and the Soviet Zone added an international dimension to local events. Politically, the Americans deemed Bavaria particularly sensitive. Munich had been the cradle of the National Socialist movement, and the Bavarian population remained deeply anti-Semitic.[56] Military government officials feared the effect of this legacy on postwar democratization. "Hitler's erstwhile supporters live here, and they still enjoy widespread sympathy," a weary official observed. "So do German nationalists, arch-Catholics, old army officers and bureaucrats, the mayors and county executives of old times, incorrigible elements of the Hitler youth—in one word: all the enemies of democracy."[57]

U.S. officials brought their own preconceptions and sometimes their personal interests to bear on local politics. Relationships between soldiers and local women were common, and some Army personnel used their positions to collude with Germans in black market activities. At the center of these nefarious activities stood Garmisch-Partenkirchen, a resort town near the Austrian border. It was, according to two investigative journalists, "the worst-run town in Germany and the Dodge City of Bavaria."[58]

Some military government officials sympathized with Bavaria's political and social conservatism. The state's first military governor, General George S. Patton Jr., became something of a local hero for his disregard for denazification and his reluctance to dabble in nonmilitary matters. Allegedly, he believed that the grateful citizenry would elect him "President of Bavaria" any time he wished.[59] Instead, his cavalier attitude toward denazification prompted Eisenhower to boot him out of office. Patton's successor, Brig. Gen. Walter J. Muller, lamented to an associate that in Bavaria he "was surrounded by knaves!"[60]

---

56 According to a March 1947 military government survey, 59 percent of Bavarians held racist or anti-Semitic views. Constantin Goschler, "The Attitude towards Jews in Bavaria after the Second World War," *The Leo Baeck Institute Year Book* 36, no. 1 (Jan 1991), 443.
57 Dorn, *Inspektionsreisen in der US-Zone*, 82.
58 Ian Sayer and Douglas Botting, *Nazi Gold: The Story of the World's Greatest Robbery – And Its Aftermath* (New York: Granada, 1984), 365.
59 Lutz Niethammer, "Die Amerikanische Besatzungsmacht zwischen Verwaltungstradition und politischen Parteien in Bayern 1945" [The American occupation forces between administrative tradition and political parties in Bavaria, 1945], *Vierteljahrshefte für Zeitgeschichte* 15, no. 2 (1967), 185.
60 Sayer and Botting, *Nazi Gold*, 332.

Figure 34: The original caption of this photograph, taken by the U.S. Army Signal Corps on 10 May 1945, reads: "Munich, badly battered cradle of the Nazi beast. Here, the American flag flies from the corner of the Rathaus, Munich city hall, now used by Military Government." U.S. Army, NACP.

U.S. officials intent on democratizing Bavarian politics faced stiff resistance, and local resentment often was mixed with anti-Semitism. Military government officials and intelligence personnel of German Jewish background often incurred the wrath of the locals. A journalist from Munich claimed that the Americans "sent only émigrés from Berlin, who were out for silent revenge on Bavaria."[61] A young deputy *Landrat* (county executive) from Schongau in upper Bavaria, Franz Josef Strauss, denounced Public Safety Branch officer 2d Lt. David B. Trott as "a Jewish lawyer and notorious German-hater."[62] Behind closed doors, many Bavarians complained about "Clay's Jews" (*Clay-Juden*) who supposedly conspired against local interests.[63] In his memoirs, Clay mused diplomatically: "All in all, Bavarian politics, though varied, are never dull."[64]

Unlike other German territories under U.S. control, Bavaria had survived the war geographically intact (Map 1). Because no territorial reform was needed, the Americans immediately reestablished the state's administration and appointed local officials. For many thus chosen, collaboration with the Americans heralded the beginning of a long-lasting career in public service. The aforementioned Franz Josef Strauss, for instance, served as a translator for the American forces and was appointed deputy *Landrat* in June 1945. From there, he climbed the ladder of Bavarian and West German politics as a central figure of the CSU, and his career highlights included holding office as minister of defense under Konrad Adenauer in 1956 and minister-president of Bavaria in 1978.[65] For the Americans, Strauss's derogatory remarks about a military government official had not disqualified him from future participation in German politics. Yet in their rush to install local officials, the military government often chose expediency over careful vetting. The top post of the Bavarian administration was a case in point.

On 22 May 1945, a unit of the 101st Airborne Division arrested the last Nazi-appointed governor of Bavaria, Franz Ritter von Epp. The prisoner promptly fell ill, and his captors transferred him to a military hospital in Bad Nauheim. An Army doctor found Epp's condition "by no means serious" and diagnosed the patient as "neurotic" and "suffering from mental depression as a result of the situation he is in." The Americans intended to try the ex-governor for war crimes, but

---

61 Peter J. Kock, *Bayerns Weg in die Bundesrepublik* [Bavaria's path to the Federal Republic] (Stuttgart: Deutsche Verlags-Anstalt, 1983), 179n40.
62 Franz Josef Strauss, *Die Erinnerungen* [Memoirs] (Munich: Siedler Verlag, 1989), 74.
63 Kock, *Bayerns Weg in die Bundesrepublik*, 179n40.
64 Clay, *Decision in Germany*, 93.
65 Rpt, Mil Govt Detachment E-368, Landkreis Schongau, Annual Historical Report 1945/46, n.d., Folder "Schongau E-368," Rcds of OMGB, Rcds of the Intel Div, Detachment Historical Rpts, Rpts Control Br, 1945–48, RG 260, NACP.

Epp died in prison before his trial.[66] Only a few days after Epp's arrest, on 28 May, military government officers in Bavaria appointed Fritz Schäffer as minister-president. It seemed like a good choice at the time. A leading member of the Catholic conservative Bavarian People's Party (Bayerische Volkspartei) before 1933, Schäffer had been removed from office and briefly imprisoned by the Nazis, a fact noted in his entry on the White List. The local cardinal highly recommended him, and at age fifty-three he was comparatively young for a prewar politician.[67] But Schäffer quickly drew criticism when he stacked his cabinet with former Nazis and ultraconservatives. His appointment, an American journalist wrote in the *New Republic* in an article titled "Bavarian Scandal," proved "the worst fears of those who expected American use of reactionary clerical forces in the administration of the defeated enemy country."[68] In September, the Americans dismissed Schäffer.

Following a recommendation from military government official Walter Dorn, General Dwight D. Eisenhower replaced Schäffer with Wilhelm Hoegner. Dorn personally knew and vouched for Hoegner, a former SPD politician who had fled Germany shortly after the Nazi takeover and spent the war in exile. At times, he served as an OSS source. As a social democrat, Hoegner did not condone rightwing elements, but his party affiliation put him outside the political mainstream in conservative Bavaria. Just a few weeks after Hoegner's appointment, the CIC learned that a group of former Nazis planned to assassinate him, and the Corps inserted five agents as "private secretaries" into his staff for protection.[69] Hoegner worked loyally with the military government, but some of his subordinates complained that he executed the wishes of U.S. military government all too eagerly, "humbly taking notes on the wishes of any American captain."[70] On a personal level, Hoegner could be idiosyncratic; for his autobiography, he chose the telling title "The Difficult Outsider" (*Der schwierige Außenseiter*).[71] Bavarians voted him

---

66 Memo, Special Agent Samuel J. Roumeles, CIC Detachment 219, for Ofcr in Charge, 6 Jun 1945, sub: Interrogation of Franz Ritter von Epp, Folder "Franz von Epp 16 Oct 68 XE 00067," INSCOM, IRR, Personal Name Files, RG 319, NACP.
67 Edward N. Peterson, *The American Occupation of Germany: Retreat to Victory* (Detroit: Wayne State University Press, 1977), 217; Würmeling, *Weiße Liste*, 218.
68 Walter M. Hudson, "The U.S. Military Government and Democratic Reform and Denazification in Bavaria, 1945–47" (master's thesis, U.S. Army Command and General Staff College, 2001), 129.
69 Msg, Col. Edward M. Fickett, ACofS, G-2, Third Army, to ACofS, G-2, USFET, 26 Jan 1946, Folder "Hoegner, Dr. Wilhelm XE 65583," INSCOM, IRR, Digitized Name Files, RG 319, NACP.
70 Peterson, *American Occupation*, 227.
71 Wilhelm Hoegner, *Der schwierige Außenseiter: Erinnerungen eines Abgeordneten, Emigranten und Ministerpräsidenten* [The difficult outsider: Memoirs of an MP, emigrant and prime minister] (Munich: Isar Verlag, 1959).

out of office at the first opportunity in December 1946. A CSU politician, Hans Ehard, succeeded him.

The Schäffer crisis cast a shadow over the American practice of appointing top officials, and it prompted Clay to press for "relaxing the ban on political activities as promptly as possible."[72] In short order, the Americans authorized local chapters of the four major political parties in Bavaria: CSU, FDP, KPD, and SPD. At the same time, military government officials denied licenses to the prewar Bavarian People's Party and a proposed monarchist party.[73] According to an American informant, the prohibition pleased CSU leaders because they feared electoral competition from the political right.[74] As the only licensed conservative party, the CSU now had a lock on the rural Catholic vote, preordaining its dominance in the agrarian *Land*. The Bavarian intelligence division predicted that the CSU would gain at least 45 percent at the first postwar elections to the Bavarian parliament on 1 December 1946. In the event, the party gained more than 52 percent statewide, scoring significantly higher in the most conservative counties of central and southern Bavaria.[75]

With the complex Bavarian political landscape limited to one conservative party, the CSU ended up incorporating numerous political subcurrents, including Catholic, Protestant, agrarian, monarchist, and separatist interests. In early 1946, Maj. Peter J. Vacca of the local intelligence division described the CSU as a "'catch-all' vehicle for many political elements."[76] In fact, the party included a number of shady characters. As an American informant noted, some CSU members referred to their own party in the earthy Bavarian dialect as "a bunch of swine" (*Sauhaufen*).[77] American officials frequently accused the CSU of being "a haven for Nazis."[78]

---

72 Earl F. Ziemke, *The U.S. Army in the Occupation of Germany, 1944–1946*, Army Historical Series (Washington, DC: U.S. Army Center of Military History, 1975), 61.
73 Gillen, *U.S. Military Government in Germany*, 74.
74 Klaus-Dietmar Henke and Hans Woller, *Lehrjahre der CSU:Eine Nachkriegspartei im Spiegel vertraulicher Berichte an die amerikanische Militärregierung* [Apprenticeship years at the CSU: A postwar party as reflected in confidential reports to the American military government] (Stuttgart: Deutsche Verlags-Anstalt, 1984), 53.
75 Rpt, Intel Div, OMGB, Periodic Rpt for Week Ending 20 Nov 1946, Folder "Periodic Intelligence Reports, 25 Oct 46–6 Dec 46," Rcds of the OMGB, Rcds of the Intel Div: Weekly Intel Rpts, 1945–47, RG 260, NACP.
76 Maj. Peter Vacca, Weekly Intel Rpt no. 11, for week ending 14 Feb 1946, Folder "Weekly Intelligence Reports Military Government for Bavaria, Nos. 8–16, 24 Jan 46–21 Mar 46," Historical Div, Program Files, OMGUS, OMGB, Periodic Intel Rpts, 1946, RG 498, NACP.
77 Henke and Woller, *Lehrjahre der CSU*, 16.
78 This state of affairs, the report noted philosophically, was "unfortunate but: The road to democracy is far from smooth." Rpt, OMGB to Director of Intel, OMGUS, sub: Periodic Report for

The CSU's internal fragility showed in March 1946 when the military government licensed the Economic Reconstruction Union (Wirtschaftliche Aufbau-Vereinigung; WAV) as an approved political party. Its nebulous, populist platform appealed to millions of German refugees from the east as well as to middle-class Bavarians. The WAV revolved entirely around its mercurial firebrand chairman, Alfred Loritz. "As a born intriguer," a CIC agent reported, Loritz "possesses the necessary eloquence and indefinite, all-embracing program for political remedies and the indisputable capability to unite ill-tempered Germans very closely in beer cellars."[79] According to the Bavarian intelligence division, CSU leaders considered Loritz one of their greatest enemies and embarked on a "get Alfred Loritz" campaign.[80] This intrigue proved unnecessary. Loritz's dictatorial leadership style and his "hysterical, supercilious and abnormal personality," in the words of a CIC report, led to the demise of the WAV in the early 1950s.[81] Nonetheless, Loritz's meteoric rise and fall highlighted the vulnerability of the nascent democratic order.

Given the outsized significance of the CSU in Bavarian politics, Army Intelligence agencies devoted substantial resources to monitoring the party and its personnel. The Bavarian intelligence division regularly interviewed leading CSU members, and Hoegner recalled an incident when a CSU politician was "sweating bullets" in a conversation with division director Vacca.[82] The Civil Censorship Division intercepted the mail and phone calls of numerous Bavarian politicians, including those made to and from the CSU's central office in Munich.[83] Several agencies used informants. For example, Annelore Ehard, the wife of Minister-President Hans Ehard, produced numerous reports about the internal politics of the CSU to an agent of the Information Control Division.[84] And a high-ranking of-

---

Week Ending 24 hours 24 Apr 1946, Folder "Periodical Intelligence Reports 19 April 46–18 Oct 46," Rcds of OMGB, Rcds of the Intel Div, 1945–47, RG 260, NACP.

[79] Rpt, Special Agent James R. Morgan, Region XII, CIC, 26 Dec 1950, re: Bavarian Landpolice Chief von Godin, Folder "Loritz, Alfred XE 267047," INSCOM, IRR, Personal Name Files, RG 319, NACP.

[80] Rpt, Donald T. Shea, Intel Div, OMGB, to Director of Intel, 27 Jul 1949, sub: Weekly Situation Report, Folder "Loritz, Alfred XE 267047," INSCOM, IRR, Personal Name Files, RG 319, NACP.

[81] Rpt, Morgan, 26 Dec 1950, re: Bavarian Landpolice Chief von Godin.

[82] Hoegner, *Der schwierige Außenseiter*, 233.

[83] Intercepted telecon, Civil Censorship Div, 21 Jan 1947, Folder "Hoegner, Dr. Wilhelm XE 65583," INSCOM, IRR, Digitized Name Files, RG 319, NACP.

[84] "Die Sauhund hau'n wir wieder 'raus: Die Akten der US-Militärregierung in Bayern 1945 bis 1949" [We'll knock the bastards out again: The files of the U.S. military government in Bavaria, 1945–1949], *Der Spiegel*, 17 Nov 1980.

ficial of the Bavarian ministry of culture, Otto Graf, provided the CIC with a wealth of "political material regarding the Bavarian situation."[85]

The Americans particularly valued a local intelligence network that went by the name of TURICUM.[86] The group included about a dozen democratically minded and pro-American individuals under the leadership of the Munich-based journalist Hans Georg Bentz. During the war, Bentz and his colleagues provided information to Allied intelligence, and when U.S. forces entered Bavaria, the two sides quickly struck a deal. The Americans set up TURICUM in a large mansion in a posh Munich suburb and provided them with cigarettes, roast beef, and whiskey, which gave the Germans the feeling of "living on an island" amid the postwar chaos. In return, TURICUM provided information to the OSS, the CIC, the Information Control Division, and the Bavarian intelligence division. Not all of this intelligence proved useful, and one U.S. official dismissed the TURICUM reports as "pretentious" and "meaningless."[87] Indeed, TURICUM conveyed a good deal of gossip and rumors; however, the organization also managed to insert an informant into two groups of CSU politicians who met confidentially once a week in Munich. The reports of this source, a man named Kurt Heinrich Heitzmann, gave the Americans continuous access to the internal deliberations of Bavaria's dominant party. The CIC considered TURICUM's intelligence "priceless."[88]

One key figure of postwar Bavarian politics became a source as well as a target of Army Intelligence. A prewar representative of the conservative Bavarian People's Party, Josef Müller had been ambivalent toward the Nazis in the 1930s. During the war, he came to cooperate with the anti-Hitler conspirators of Admiral Wilhelm F. Canaris's *Abwehr*, which sent him to Rome. Using Vatican officials as a conduit, Müller was to feel out the Western Allies for a separate peace. When the Nazis discovered the plot, they arrested the conspirators, including Müller, sending him to a concentration camp. The silver-tongued Müller survived this ordeal by sowing doubt about his involvement in the minds of his interrogators. At the

---

85 Memo, Special Agent J. Thomas Dale, for Ofcr in Charge, Region III, CIC, 9 Mar 1948, sub: Ministerialrat Otto Graf, Munich, Folder "Graf, Otto XE 230193," INSCOM, IRR, Digitized Name Files, RG 319, NACP. The CIC dropped Graf as an informant in 1948 over concerns that he had communist sympathies.
86 For Turicum, see Henke and Woller, *Lehrjahre der CSU*, 27–32. The designation "TURICUM" derived from the Latin name for the city of Zurich, Switzerland, the home of a member of Turicum's wartime organization.
87 Ltr, Ralph Brown, Intel Br, Info Control Div, OMGB, to Mr. Isenstead and Mr. Moeller, 16 Dec 1947, Folder "Reports 'T' Unit [Unit 4]," Rcds of OMGB, Rcds of the Intel Div: Intel Rcds of the Info Control Div, 1946–47, RG 260, NACP.
88 Henke and Woller, *Lehrjahre der CSU*, 30.

end of the war, American forces liberated him in South Tyrol and transferred him to the picturesque island of Capri off the coast of Naples for interrogation.[89]

The eloquence that had saved Müller in the camps helped him charm his new captors as well. Dale D. Clark, a naval officer who joined the military government after the war, called Müller his "hero friend."[90] Special Agent Joe B. Cox of the CIC praised Müller's anti-Nazi credentials and personally accompanied him back to Munich.[91] Clark and Cox ensured that Müller received permission to convene meetings even before the military government lifted the ban on political activities.[92] He became a founding member of the CSU, the party's first chair, and a preeminent figure in Bavarian politics. Meanwhile, he carefully cultivated his ties to U.S. intelligence. According to a CIC report from 1946, Müller personally knew the wartime chief of the OSS, William J. "Wild Bill" Donovan, and had "excellent connections" with Bavaria's intelligence division chief Peter Vacca.[93] The Strategic Services Unit formally recruited Müller as a source under the codename ROBOT.[94]

Despite his anti-Nazi credentials and his close ties to U.S. intelligence, the U.S. military government was of two minds about the Bavarian powerbroker. The Americans appreciated Müller's democratic convictions, his staunch opposition to the state's secessionist tendencies, and the confidential information he provided, such as a 1947 report on a separatist plot involving French intelligence and the right wing of the CSU.[95] Some also admired the wiliness of "this bluff Bavarian buccaneer."[96] At the same time, military government officials resented his leadership style, which involved wheeling, dealing, and spreading malicious rumors about political opponents.[97] Neither American officials nor German politicians could ever be sure about Müller's sincerity on a given issue, and this lack of trust

---

89 For Müller's biography, see Friedrich Hermann Hettler, *Josef Müller ("Ochsensepp"): Mann des Widerstandes und erster CSU-Vorsitzender* [Josef Müller ("Ochsensepp"): Man of the resistance and first CSU chairman] (Munich: Kommissionsverlag Uni-Druck, 1991).
90 Interv, Dale D. Clark with Robert Zigler, 14 Oct 1998, The Association for Diplomatic Studies and Training, Foreign Affairs Oral History Collection, Library of Congress, Washington, D.C.
91 Msg, Special Agent Joe B. Cox, HQ, CIC, Allied Forces HQ, for Ofcr in Charge, 10 Jun 1945, sub: Mueller, Josef, Folder "XE 138121 27 Mar 1898 Josef Mueller (Vol 3 of 4)," INSCOM, IRR, Personal Name Files, RG 319, NACP.
92 Josef Müller, *Bis zur letzten Konsequenz: Ein Leben für Frieden und Freiheit* [To the last consequence: A life for peace and freedom] (Munich: Süddeutscher Verlag, 1975), 304.
93 Memo, Capt. Victory J. Layton, HQ, CIC, USFET, for D. Benjamin, 8 Jun 1946, sub: Request for information on Josef Mueller, Folder "XE 138121 27 Mar 1898 Josef Mueller (Vol 3 of 4)," INSCOM, IRR, Personal Name Files, RG 319, NACP.
94 Ruffner, "Eagle and Swastika," chap. 3, 37.
95 Kock, *Bayerns Weg in die Bundesrepublik*, 184n67.
96 Rpt, Intel Div, OMGB, Periodic Rpt for Week ending 20 Nov 1946.
97 Hettler, *Josef Müller*, 265.

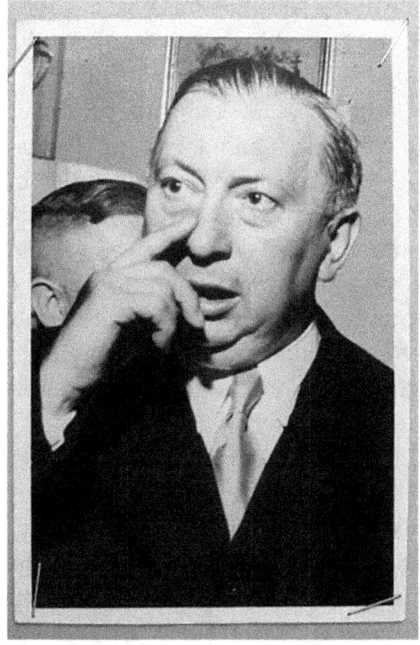

Figure 35: A photograph of Josef Müller from his CIC file. U.S. Army, NACP.

eroded his reputation. According to Turicum's Heitzmann, a CSU member lamented, "If one only knew when Dr. Müller is telling the truth."[98]

In the summer of 1947, the CIC took a closer look at Müller's private life. Walter Dreifuss, a special agent and Ritchie Boy, had two informants spy on Müller's wife Maria. They discovered some "highly embarrassing" information. According to the two agents, Mrs. Müller was "a narcotics addict . . . involved in a love affair" with a local sculptor. Dreifuss explained that he collected this information because Josef Müller "may at some time in the future be of CI [counterintelligence] interest."[99] Specifically, the CIC may have kept the derogatory reports on file in case the Americans ever needed to force Müller to resign. As Dreifuss explained in a separate message: "These reports are being collected in an effort to obtain as accurate as possible a true picture of subject. These reports may never be needed, and yet . . . ??!!!"[100]

---

98 Henke and Woller, *Lehrjahre der CSU*, 13.
99 Rpt, [Special Agent Walter Dreifuss,] Garmisch Subregion, CIC, 6 Aug 1947, sub: Dr. Mueller, Josef, Folder "XE 138121 27 Mar 1898 Josef Mueller (Vol 3 of 4)," INSCOM, IRR, Personal Name Files, RG 319, NACP.
100 Rpt, Special Agent Walter Dreifuss, 5 Jun 1947, sub: Mueller, Dr. Josef, Folder "XE 138121 27 Mar 1898 Josef Mueller (Vol 3 of 4)," INSCOM, IRR, Personal Name Files, RG 319, NACP.

More damaging to Müller's status with the Americans than this type of gossip was evidence of his dalliance with the Soviets. During his captivity under the Nazis, he had befriended several high-ranking Soviet fellow prisoners, including the nephew of Moscow's foreign minister, Vyacheslav M. Molotov. After the war, Müller had no qualms about mingling with communist and Soviet representatives. In 1947, he visited the headquarters of the Soviet Military Administration in Karlshorst, where he met with Col. Sergei I. Tulpanov, Moscow's propaganda chief in Germany. Müller's principal motivation for these discussions appears to have been a desire to close the growing rift between the Soviet and the Western zones, but in the context of the early Cold War, his contacts with Soviet officials looked sinister.[101] He did not help his cause by shrouding his trips to Berlin in mystery while at the same time boasting "frequently of his pleasant relations with the Soviets in Karlshorst."[102]

Army Intelligence thoroughly investigated Müller's relationship with the Soviets. One CIC informant reported that Müller stayed at Karlshorst whenever he visited Berlin, and that the Soviet commandant of the city was "a good friend of his." Another source claimed that Müller was "a very dangerous person and it is dangerous for the Americans to tangle with him."[103] The CIC found no concrete evidence suggesting that Müller was beholden to Moscow but noted that "there is much room for speculation." Overall, his relationship with the Soviets reinforced American concerns about his sincerity and commitment to the West. His "background and erratic career," the CIC stated, "does not reflect favorably on his character since, in almost every instance, he has travelled along the center lane with feelers extended in both directions."[104] Another report warned that if Müller were to become minister-president, "his government will probably have Eastern Zone sympathies."[105]

The Müller controversy came to a head over the "chicken feed" affair. On 6 January 1948, a protégé of Joseph Müller's, Johannes F. Semler, made a fiery speech to a closed meeting of CSU members at Erlangen in northern Bavaria. Semler was a director of the bizonal economic council, which was preparing a German currency reform in the Western zones. In his speech, he attacked Allied

---

101 Hettler, *Josef Müller*, 270–72; Müller, *Bis zur letzten Konsequenz*, 325–26.
102 Rpt, HQ, 66th CIC Gp, 12 Aug 1954, sub: Mueller, Josef Dr., Folder "XE 138121 27 Mar 1898 Josef Mueller (Vol 1 of 4)," INSCOM, IRR, Personal Name Files, RG 319, NACP.
103 Rpt, Special Agent Walter Dreifuss, 26 May 1947, sub: Mueller, Dr. Josef, Folder "XE 138121 27 Mar 1898 Josef Mueller (Vol 3 of 4)," INSCOM, IRR, Personal Name Files, RG 319, NACP.
104 Rpt, no author, 7 Dec 1956, Folder "XE 138121 27 Mar 1898 Josef Mueller (Vol 4 of 4)," INSCOM, IRR, Personal Name Files, RG 319, NACP.
105 Rpt, Special Agent Lowell C. Henry, Region V, CIC, 26 Oct 1950, Folder "XE 138121 27 Mar 1898 Josef Mueller (Vol 2 of 4)," INSCOM, IRR, Personal Name Files, RG 319, NACP.

economic policy and lambasted the Americans for supposedly sending the Germans only "chicken feed" (*Hühnerfutter*).[106] Within a few days, the text of the speech appeared in the press, and his vitriolic remarks prompted a backlash. "Apparently western German politicians believe the time has come when they can complain about the Allied occupation," the *Washington Post* noted.[107] Clay was understandably upset and called Semler's remarks "malicious lies."[108] Although Semler apologized personally to Clay, the British and the Americans dismissed him from the economic council at the end of the month.

On the face of it, Semler's speech and his subsequent dismissal seemed a straight-forward case of action and reaction, but the political reality was more complex. For one, the CIC considered Semler to have been "an active functionary" of the Nazi Party during the Third Reich, and in 1947 the Corps had opened an investigation into his role in the expropriation of Jewish property in wartime Austria.[109] For this reason alone, the Americans may have been happy to see him go. Furthermore, the Bavarian intelligence division noted, Semler was known as a close associate of the ubiquitous Josef Müller, which raised questions about the latter's role in the affair.[110]

According to Turicum's informant, CSU leaders considered Semler's speech and its subsequent publication an "accident" (*Panne*). Semler had intended his words exclusively for the benefit of CSU members and was baffled upon learning that they had reached the press.[111] This chain of events raised the question of how journalists had learned of the speech in the first place. Army Intelligence found the answer in an intercepted letter from Semler to Müller. In it, Semler wrote that he was "rather angry" at "your" CSU headquarters in Munich for forwarding "the stenographic record of my speech to [military government] without

---

106 John Gimbel, *The American Occupation of Germany* (Stanford, CA: Stanford University Press, 1968), 191–92.
107 Edwin Hartrich, "German Food Crisis Tests Rule by U.S.," *Washington Post*, 25 Jan 1948.
108 Msg, Clay to Noce, 9 Jan 1948, doc. 312, in *The Papers of General Lucius D. Clay*, ed. Jean Edward Smith (Bloomington: Indiana University Press, 1974), 2:528.
109 Draft msg, 23 Oct 1947, sub: Dr. Johannes Semler, Director of Economics Bizonal Council, Folder "50.501 Dr. Johannes F. Semler," Ofc of the Finance Div and Finance Adviser, Finance Adviser Recs of Subordinate Agencies, Gen Recs of the Financial Intel Gp, 1945–49, RG 260, NACP; Msg, Maj. Earl S. Browning Jr., HQ, 970th CIC Detachment, EUCOM, to CO, 20 Jan 1948, Folder "Semler, Johannes XE 191876," INSCOM, IRR, Digitized Name Files, RG 319, NACP.
110 Msg, R. C. Martindale, Intel Div, OMGB, to Land Director, 19 Feb 1948, Folder "Semler Investigation Part I," Rcds of OMGB, Rcds of the Land Director: Investigative Corresp and Rpts, 1945–49, RG 260, NACP.
111 Rpt, M-Group: Monatsbericht Nr. 4, 18 Jan 1948, Folder "Reports 'T' Unit," Rcds of OMGB, Rcds of the Intel Div: Intel Rcds of the Info Control Div, 1946–47, RG 260, NACP.

giving me an advance opportunity to read it, but the text reached the press from there."[112]

Müller's apparent involvement led to speculation on the part of Army Intelligence about his motivation. One CIC informant reported that "absolutely reliable press sources" had told him that Müller had arranged the speech and its publication at the behest of Colonel Tulpanov. In return for this verbal attack on the Americans, Tulpanov supposedly had promised Müller to treat the CDU in the Soviet Zone more leniently. Another informant alleged that Müller had masterminded the entire affair to discredit the occupation policies of the Democratic Truman administration. Presumably, this effort would lead the Republican Party to gain votes in the 1948 presidential and congressional elections, which somehow would then benefit the Germans.[113] U.S. officials remained in the dark about Müller's rationale, but the affair accelerated his political demise. Special Agent Marie T. Clair of the CIC opined that "Dr. Josef Müller knows that his reputation is so undermined by his activities, personal politics and attitude that he finds it practical and the only way to save face before his German and CSU followers is to oppose the Military Government and perhaps lose his position and then be considered a martyr."[114]

An unintended consequence of the Semler affair—but a fortunate one from the Americans' point of view—was the rise of Ludwig W. Erhard, a CSU man from northern Bavaria. At the end of the war, a military government detachment had appointed Erhard economic adviser in Nuremberg, and an intelligence investigation found him to be politically uncompromised by the Third Reich.[115] Jovial and easygoing, Erhard got along well with the occupiers, to the point of irritating his German colleagues. A fellow CSU politician called him "flesh of their flesh, spirit of their spirit. He had their informality, their happy self-confidence and said, quite openly, 'I like the American style.'"[116] But Erhard lacked Müller's vigor and slyness, which was required to prevail in the rough-and-tumble world of Ba-

---

112 Ltr [translated], [Johannes F. Semler] to Josef Mueller, 16 Jan 1948, Folder "50.501 Dr. Johannes F. Semler," Ofc of the Finance Div and Finance Adviser, Finance Adviser Recs of Subordinate Agencies, Gen Recs of the Financial Intel Gp, 1945–49, RG 260, NACP.
113 Rpt, Special Agent T. Schulz, Region IV, CIC, to S-2, 24 Jan 1948, sub: Rumors Concerning Dr. Mueller, re: to Dr. Semler Speech, Folder "XE 138121 27 Mar 1898 Joseph Mueller (Vol 4 of 4)," INSCOM, IRR, Personal Name Files, RG 319, NACP. For contemporary press speculation, see "Der Mann mit dem Hühnerfutter" [The man with the chicken feed], *Der Spiegel*, 17 Jan 1948.
114 Rpt, Special Agent Marie T. Clair, Region IV, CIC, 9 Aug 1948, Folder "XE 138121 27 Mar 1898 Josef Mueller (Vol 4 of 4)," INSCOM, IRR, Personal Name Files, RG 319, NACP.
115 Rpt, Charles K. Goldner, HQ, 7707 Mil Intel Service Center, to HQ, G-2, USFET, 29 Jan 1947, sub: Interrogation of Glass manufacturers in Alsace-Lorraine on Dr. Ludwig Erhard, Folder "Erhard, Ludwig D-106430," INSCOM, IRR, Digitized Name Files, RG 319, NACP.
116 Peterson, *American Occupation*, 227–28.

varian politics. By early 1948, his political career seemed over, but then Semler's position on the economic council opened, and Erhard replaced him. An economist by training, Erhard had found the "job of his life" and became the public face of the massively successful currency reform of 1948.[117] Catapulted to national fame, he became West Germany's first minister of economics and oversaw the critical early years of the country's postwar economic recovery. In 1963, he succeeded Adenauer as chancellor. The Americans had every reason to be pleased. An entry in Erhard's CIC file described him as "extremely pro-American, he has taken pride in his American association since 1945 . . . and has always spoken with admiration of the U.S."[118]

By 1949, the Army had helped establish a democratic, pro-Western political framework in Bavaria. Although the CSU remained vulnerable to conservative competitors such as the WAV, the star of the scheming Müller was fading, and one of his rivals, Minister-President Hans Ehard, had solidified his hold over the party. To some observers, Ehard could appear dull and uninspiring, but he impressed the Bavarian intelligence division as "capable," "honest," and "personally above suspicion."[119] As an old-line conservative, he had no illusions about the Soviets, and the West could expect his support in its confrontation with Moscow. In addition, the *Land* had produced a number of other democratically minded, pro-American politicians who would shape West German politics in the years to come. For four years, Army Intelligence had provided military government with a steady stream of confidential information on Bavarian politics, and these insights made the Americans cautiously optimistic about the future of this key *Land*.

The Communist Party of Germany

At the end of the war, the Americans viewed German communism with ambivalence. On one hand, officials respected communists' wartime opposition to the Nazis and the travails many activists endured during the Third Reich. To some, communists seemed natural partners in the Allied effort to root out National So-

---

117 Volker Hentschel, *Ludwig Erhard: Ein Politikerleben* [Ludwig Erhard: A political life] (Lech: Olzog, 1996), 51.
118 Rpt, Walter J. Muller, High Commission for Occupied Germany (HICOG), 27 May 1952, sub: Biographic Data, Ludwig Erhard, Folder "Erhard, Ludwig AC 854915," INSCOM, IRR, Personal Name Files, RG 319, NACP.
119 Peterson, *American Occupation*, 232.

cialism, and in one case, a CIC unit shared an office with a local KPD branch.[120] On the other hand, Americans regarded Marxist ideology as intrinsically undemocratic and considered all communist parties to be beholden to Moscow. This bond would not pose a challenge to the occupation as long as U.S. and Soviet policies remained aligned. Should rifts between the two wartime allies develop, however, "it is already clear that this would have immediate repercussions on the Communist estimate of the whole occupation problem."[121]

Despite its discipline and activism, the reestablished KPD fared badly at the polls. An Army Intelligence official noted gleefully in January 1946 that "the Communists were a poor third" in local elections in Greater Hesse.[122] Nonetheless, American worries about the party increased. Less than a year after the end of the war, intelligence noted that German communists openly criticized the U.S. occupation. Reports about the party's supposed involvement in strikes, espionage, pro-Soviet propaganda, the preparation of violent resistance, and attempts to infiltrate local political organizations added to American concerns. Making heavy use of censorship and informants, the CIC embarked on a wide-ranging effort to monitor and contain communist activities.[123]

The CIC launched one of its earliest operations against the communists in the Bremen enclave. The city's dockworkers constituted a traditional stronghold of left-of-center parties. In late 1945, a special agent began receiving numerous reports from his informants that the KPD sought to infiltrate local trade unions. When the CIC brought the matter to the attention of General Sibert in 1946, he authorized the Corps to penetrate the KPD. This effort, code-named Operation SUNRISE, yielded some evidence that the communists toed Moscow's line and sought to push the Western Allies out of Germany. At the same time, SUNRISE documented the limits of KPD activism and cast doubt on the party's ability to accomplish these ends through violence.[124]

---

[120] Maj. Ann Bray et al., ed., *The History of the Counter Intelligence Corps*, vol. 27, *Four Years of Cold War* (Fort Holabird, MD: U.S. Army Intelligence Center, 1959), 33.

[121] Rpt, Annex A, G–2 Periodic Rpt no. 136, XXI Corps, 30 May 1945, sub: The Pattern of German Communist Thinking, Folder "VI Corp [sic] G–2 Journal 1–4 Jun 45," Historical Div, Program Files, VI Corps, G–2 Jnls, 1945, RG 498, NACP.

[122] *Review of Europe, Russia, and Middle East* 1 (22 Jan 1946), 13.

[123] Sum, HQ, Seventh Army, Weekly Intel Sum no. 35, 15 Mar 1946, Folder "7th Army, G–2 Weekly Summaries, 1946," Seventh Army, G–2, Subject Files 1942–1946, RG 338, NACP; Bray et al., *History of the Counter Intelligence Corps*, 27:61.

[124] Bray et al., *History of the Counter Intelligence Corps*, 27:62–63; Patrick Major, *Death of the KPD: Communism and Anti-Communism in West Germany, 1945–1956* (New York: Oxford University Press, 1998), 241.

Figure 36: An undercover photograph taken in January 1949 of Dora and Josef Angerer, two communists who operated a print shop in Munich for propaganda material from the Soviet Zone. U.S. Army, NACP.

The following year, Army Intelligence agencies embarked on Project HAPPINESS, a zone-wide effort to assess the threat posed by the KPD.[125] In several cases, the resulting reports proved negative, vague, or ambivalent. In the fall of 1947, Army Intelligence ruled out the KPD's ability to conduct "guerilla-warfare" or "to seize the political control."[126] Intelligence officials also reported on "Planned Communist Activity among American Negro Troops," but the effort never gained much traction.[127] Another officer concluded that the KPD did not serve as an espionage vehicle for the Soviets because Moscow was concerned about compromising its local

---

125 Rpt, ODDI, for Maj. Gen. Robert L. Walsh, 10 Feb 1948, Folder "Project HAPPINESS, vol. 1 D137900," INSCOM, IRR, RG 319, NACP.
126 Major, *Death of the KPD*, 245.
127 Ofc of the Ch Historian, EUCOM, *A Survey of Soviet Aims, Policies, and Tactics*, Occupation Forces in Europe Series 1947–1948 (Frankfurt: Historical Division, EUCOM, 1948), 306.

auxiliary.[128] In other areas, however, the collected information suggested illegal or threatening activities and prompted the military government to take action.

Army Intelligence agencies produced abundant evidence of the KPD's subservience to the Socialist Unity Party (Sozialistische Einheitspartei Deutschlands; SED), the communist party in the Soviet Zone. In February 1947, the two parties announced the establishment of a joint working group, and the military government's intelligence office inferred that this group "intended to serve as a preparatory step for the extension of the SED over all four zones."[129] The fusion project did not come to fruition, but a year later, the European intelligence division reported on a secret coordinating meeting between communist officials from the east and the west at the former Buchenwald concentration camp.[130] And in early 1949, the European Command discovered KPD and SED plans to establish a conspiratorial joint "Western European Bureau."[131]

Over time, Army Intelligence picked up on a number of operational links between the two parties. In March 1947, a government official from the Soviet Zone defected to the Americans. He told the CIC that an SED courier regularly visited the "Communist infected newspaper *Frankfurter Rundschau*" in Frankfurt with instructions from East Berlin.[132] The *Rundschau* was the first U.S.-licensed newspaper in postwar Germany. A CIC investigation pointed to one of the paper's editors, KPD member and "fanatical communist" Emil Carlebach, as the recipient of the messages. In August, the military government removed Carlebach from the *Rundschau*'s editorial board, and General Clay personally ordered the CIC to

---

128 Msg, 1st Lt. Anne C. Moe, HQ, ODDI, EUCOM, to Director of Intel, OMGUS, 8 Jun 1948, sub: Transmittal of Speech Delivered at Military Attaché Conference, Folder "security section—McGreevy, G," Director of Intel, Analysis and Research Br, Gen Corresp, 1945–49, RG 260, NACP; Major, *Death of the KPD*, 244.

129 Rpt, Col. Peter P. Rodes, ODI, Weekly Intelligence Rpt no. 41, 22 Feb 1947, Folder "OMGUS Intelligence Notes # 21–41, 9.14.46–2.22.47," Historian's Background Files, 1947–1952, RG 549, NACP; Major, *Death of the KPD*, 54.

130 Msg, 1st Lt. Anne C. Moe, HQ, ODDI, EUCOM, to Director of Intel, OMGUS, 3 Mar 1948, sub: Secret Meeting of KPD Functionaries at Buchenwald, Folder "security section—McGreevy, G," Director of Intel, Analysis and Research Br, Gen Corresp, 1945–49, RG 260, NACP.

131 Msg, Lt. Gen. Clarence R. Huebner, EUCOM, to Ch of Staff, Director of Intel, 25 Jan 1949, Folder "Top Secret Out Jan 1949 to 30 June 1949 Book III," EUCOM, Ofc of the Ch of Staff, Sec of the Gen Staff, Msg Control Center, Outgoing Msgs, Top Secret Section, 1948–1951, RG 549, NACP; Major, *Death of the KPD*, 68.

132 Msg, Special Agent Carl J. Kuehnert to DDI, EUCOM, 26 Aug 1947, sub: Counterintelligence Report No. Z-53, Folder "Carlebach, Emil XE 53339," INSCOM, IRR, Digitized Name Files, RG 319, NACP.

maintain "a discreet investigation of Herr Carlebach."[133] The latter, in turn, protested the revocation of his newspaper license in a sharply worded open letter to Clay. But this initiative merely confirmed his subjection to the East. By means of censorship, the CIC intercepted a written communication from the Soviet Zone, indicating that Carlebach had run a draft of his open letter by the SED's central secretariat for approval.[134]

Carlebach was only one of many Soviet Zone contacts in the West. The SED leadership had good reason to suspect censorship of their communications to and from the Western zones, and so they established a large network of couriers who covertly delivered propaganda material, directives, and financial subsidies to KPD leaders. The man in charge of this endeavor, Arthur Illner, was a veteran communist operative who had served the party in Europe and China in the 1920s and 1930s. Illner went by the alias "Richard Stahlmann," perhaps in reverence to Soviet leader Joseph Stalin (both Stalin and Stahlmann translate as "man of steel.") A true believer, Illner obeyed orders with unquestioning loyalty and had no qualms about coordinating the execution of opponents who deviated from orthodox Marxist doctrine.[135]

In spite of Illner's efforts at hiding his network from the prying eyes of the U.S. military government, the CIC amassed a thick dossier on him and his operation. According to this record, Illner neatly fit contemporary notions of a communist villain. One report described him as an almost cartoonishly sinister figure, having "dark, almost black" eyes with a "slight slant," a feature that supposedly gave him a "Mongolian appearance." He had a "nervous twitch of lips," "two gold teeth," a "fleshy, reddish nose," and a "corpulent" body.[136] Another entry noted his "ruthless and extremely brutal" reputation.[137] In September 1947, a source informed U.S. intelligence about Illner's role in overseeing the couriers from the Soviet Zone, and the Americans quickly discovered his alias, "Stahlmann." Rather than roll up the network, the CIC closely monitored the operation through censor-

---

133 Memo, no author, for Col. Carl F. Fritzsche, Info Control Div, 30 Aug 1947, Folder "Carlebach, Emil XE 53339," INSCOM, IRR, Digitized Name Files, RG 319, NACP.
134 Rpt, Special Agent Gustav Bard, 13 Jan 1948, sub: Emil N. Carlebach, Folder "Carlebach, Emil XE 53339," INSCOM, IRR, Digitized Name Files, RG 319, NACP.
135 Major, *Death of the KPD*, 69–70.
136 Memo, Special Agent George B. Swerdlin, Region VIII, CIC, for Ofcr in Charge, 7 Apr 1948, Folder "Stahlmann, Richard XE 199249," INSCOM, IRR, Digitized Name Files, RG 319, NACP.
137 Memo, Special Agent Gustav Bard, for Ofcr in Charge, 19 Apr [year illegible], sub: Illner, Arthur, Folder "Stahlmann, Richard XE 199249," INSCOM, IRR, Digitized Name Files, RG 319, NACP.

ship and informants, gaining an accurate and comprehensive picture of the communists' interzonal lines of communication.[138]

As Soviet-Western relations deteriorated, American concerns over communists serving in military government positions grew. Officials feared that KPD members intended to infiltrate U.S. organizations in order to sabotage operations or leak sensitive information to the Soviets. Army Intelligence did not determine whether communists had been hired as a direct result of a KPD infiltration effort or whether they simply had been looking for a job. Either way, a certain number of communists served in military government positions, and given the political ramifications of the early Cold War, American officials had reason to be concerned.

In March 1948, the European Command issued "EUCOM Civilian Personnel Memo no. 16," which allowed U.S. authorities to discharge anybody "classed as [a] Communist or [a] Communist sympathizer."[139] The CIC determined who fell into these categories. By February 1949, the Corps had nearly completed the process of screening German employees in sensitive positions against lists of known communists, and the military government had dismissed most of them. The European Command consequently reported to the intelligence division at the Pentagon that the KPD had lost the ability to harm the military government through espionage or obstruction.[140]

The Cold War realignment fostered anticommunist sentiments among German politicians and American officials alike and infused both sides with a sense of common purpose. In November 1947, the chairman of the SPD in Giesenau in Bavaria, Hans Schröder, submitted an anticommunist pamphlet to Special Agent Albert L. Wroblewski at the CIC office in Marburg. The pamphlet accused the Eastern zone SED of running "concentration camps" for arrested social democrats in the Soviet Zone. Schröder's plan to distribute the brochure to embarrass the local communist party met with the special agent's hearty approval. "This pamphlet," Wrobleski stated, was "one of the most effective ever published."[141]

---

138 Msg, Silas B. Knight, Department of the Army Detachment (DAD), to 7970th CIC Gp, 15 Sep 1949, Folder "Stahlmann, Richard XE 199249," INSCOM, IRR, Digitized Name Files, RG 319, NACP.

139 Msg, Donald T. Shea, Intel Div, OMGB, to Director of Intel, OMGUS, sub: Intelligence Coordinating Meeting, 19 Oct 1948, Folder "23a Resistance & Subversive Activities (U.S. Zone) Jan. '48–Dec. '48," ODI, Excerpts of Miscellaneous Rpts and Publications, Analysis and Research Br, 1947–48, RG 260, NACP.

140 Msg, HQ, EUCOM, to Ch of Staff, Director of Intel, 18 Feb 1949, Folder "Top Secret Out Jan 1949 to 30 June 1949 Book III," EUCOM, Ofc of the Ch of Staff, Sec of the Gen Staff, Msg Control Center, Outgoing Msgs, Top Secret Section, 1948–1951, RG 549, NACP.

141 Rpt, Special Agent Albert L. Wrobleski, Region III, CIC, to CO, 20 Nov 1947, sub: Anti-KPD-SED Propaganda, Folder "Anti Communist Activities (CHISEL Reports) D 137903," INSCOM, IRR, Selected Printouts of Digital Intel and Investigative Dossiers–Impersonal Files, RG 319, NACP.

Occasionally, American soldiers and German civilians joined hands in containing communism. On the evening of 3 July 1948, Pfc. Joseph Presecan and Pfc. Arthur J. Carnicelli went for drinks to the Stardust Club at Camp Lindsey in the city of Wiesbaden. As they discussed their mutual dislike for communism, they decided to do their part in stemming the red tide by breaking into and setting fire to the local KPD branch. Having procured five gallons of gasoline and a sledgehammer from Presecan's nearby office, they proceeded to the neighborhood where the KPD bureau was located. Here, they ran into a group of like-minded Germans who agreed to help them. Despite their strength in numbers, the combined U.S.-German posse failed to break into the office. Not to be deterred, Presecan poured gasoline around the door and set it ablaze. Unfortunately for the soldier, he had accidentally splashed some of the gasoline on his body. He ended up with severe burns, forcing him to seek out the local military hospital. Here, the CIC special agent assigned to investigate the case, Thomas D. Fox, tracked him down. After some initial evasion, Presecan confessed his involvement in the attack but "could give no special motives for wishing to destroy the KPD offices other than a general dislike for the Communist Party" and "the fact that some of his relatives are living under Communist rule."[142]

By early 1948, the Americans considered communist penetration of German agencies, especially the police, one of the few remaining threats posed by the party, but a comprehensive investigation of this issue by the military government's intelligence office produced ambivalent evidence. The police department of Heilbronn, for example, employed 201 personnel. Out of these, the Americans had identified ten individuals—less than 5 percent of the total—as KPD members. This number was probably close to the percentage of KPD members in the city at large. In addition, however, the office described thirty police officers vaguely as "KPD sympathizers," raising the overall percentage in the force to twenty. Similarly, in the city of Ludwigslust, 5 KPD members served in a total force of 159 police officers. This amounted to a little over 3 percent, but when fifteen "sympathizers" were included, the total went up to 13 percent.[143]

To discuss future courses of action regarding the KPD, the military government created a committee consisting of representatives from the Civil Affairs Di-

---

142 Rpt, Special Agent Thomas D. Fox, 7970th CIC Gp, 6 Jul 1948, sub: KPD Kreisleitung Fire, Wiesbaden, Folder "Anti Communist Activities (CHISEL Reports) D 137903," INSCOM, IRR, Selected Printouts of Digital Intel and Investigative Dossiers–Impersonal Files, RG 319, NACP.
143 Rpt, Edward N. Litchfield, Civil Affairs Div, to Ch of Staff, Civil Affairs Div, 29 Apr 1948, sub: Report of OMGUS Committee on Extent of Communist Influence in U.S. Zone, Folder "23a. Investigation of Communist Penetration in the US Zone 1948," ODI, Excerpts of Miscellaneous Rpts and Publications, Analysis and Research Br, 1947–48, RG 260, NACP.

vision, the Political Affairs Division, the Manpower Division, and the Office of the Director of Intelligence. In April 1948, the committee presented four options to military government, ranging from an outright ban on the KPD to a proposal to dispose of the problem by "directing the Germans to clean their own house." The committee recommended the latter course, with some caveats.[144] The director of intelligence, Col. Peter P. Rodes, concurred with most of the findings but sought a more active role for his agency in detecting and removing "the evil" of communism.[145] In the end, the military government abstained from a ban, partly out of concerns that the party would be more dangerous if it went underground.[146] At the same time, intelligence agencies continued to dedicate significant personnel and resources to monitor the KPD.

Against the backdrop of the deepening Cold War, Army Intelligence became more aggressive in its operations against the KPD. In July 1949, CIC special agents detained Grete K. Schoofs, a member of the Frankfurt KPD, and confronted her with evidence that she had betrayed a fellow communist to the *Gestapo* during the Third Reich. If she agreed to spy on her party, the agents proposed, they would keep this information under wraps.[147] Confirming the limited reach of blackmail as a recruiting technique, however, Schoofs refused to go along and promptly denounced the CIC's ham-fisted effort in a press conference shortly after her release. The KPD and the Soviet Zone press had a field day reporting on Schoofs's "hijacking" (*Menschenraub*) by "CIC snitches" (*Spitzeln*), and her attempted recruitment through "constant threats" (*dauernden Drohungen*). To add insult to injury, Emil Carlebach, the communist activist who had clashed with

---

144 Draft memo, H. Kallmann, ODI, for Col. Peter P. Rodes, ODI, 29 Apr 1948, sub: Report and Recommendations of Committee on Communistic Penetration, Folder "security section—McGreevy, G," Director of Intel, Analysis and Research Br, Gen Corresp, 1945–49, RG 260, NACP.
145 Note, Col. Peter P. Rodes, ODI, 5 May 1948, Folder "security section—McGreevy, G," Director of Intel, Analysis and Research Br, Gen Corresp, 1945–49, RG 260, NACP.
146 Ofc of the Ch Historian, EUCOM, *The Third Year of the Occupation*, Part 2, *The Second Quarter, 1 October–31 December 1947*, vol. 2, Occupation Forces in Europe Series 1947–48 (Frankfurt: Office of the Chief Historian, EUCOM, 1948), 64.
147 Memo, Lt. Col. Cyril J. Letzelter, Ch, Opns Br, for Col. Charles M. Adams, 16 Aug 1949, sub: Desirability of Obtaining Policy Clarification Re Covert Dissemination by CIC of Derogatory Information Obtained on KPD Members for Purpose of Political Embarrassment, Folder "ID files 008," HQ, EUCOM, Ofc of the Ch of Staff, Intel Div, Administrative Br, Intel Rpts, 1948–51, RG 549, NACP. The communist Alfred List was in fact arrested by the *Gestapo* shortly after Schoofs allegedly had denounced him. See Hermann Weber and Andreas Herbst, eds., *Deutsche Kommunisten. Biographisches Handbuch 1918 bis 1945* [German communists: Biographical handbook, 1918–1945] (Berlin: Karl Dietz Verlag, 2008), entry for "List, Alfred."

General Clay two years earlier, demanded that the responsible CIC personnel be put on trial.[148]

By the end of the occupation, Army Intelligence regarded the KPD as a fierce if largely ineffectual foe. In the run-up to the first West German parliamentary elections in August 1949, the communists campaigned heavily on the issue of the division of Germany, assigning responsibility squarely to their political rivals and the military government. The campaign failed, with the KPD garnering 5.7 percent of the vote, which amounted to a meager 15 parliamentary seats out of a total of 402. "Obviously," an American intelligence official commented dryly, "the German electorate was not susceptible to KPD propaganda."[149]

As the election results demonstrated, communism in the U.S. Zone had been contained. Army Intelligence agencies may have spent an excessive amount of their resources on a threat that turned out hollow. Against the background of the Cold War and growing fears of international communism across the West, however, no responsible official could have afforded to disregard this issue. Indeed, intelligence provided the military government with detailed reports that helped American officials to understand the limited nature of the communist appeal and to gain confidence about the Federal Republic's democratic future.

Intelligence and Politics in Berlin

Nowhere in Germany were intelligence and politics more tightly intertwined than in Berlin. The joint Allied administration of the city ensured that the growing rift between the Soviet Union and the West would translate directly into local affairs. Military government personnel, German politicians, and intelligence officials all sought to monitor, comprehend, and shape this process. Consequently, U.S. intelligence became heavily involved in areas outside its traditional purview. As the CIA station chief reported to Washington in the spring of 1948, "because of the unique political

---

148 "Menschenraub auf offener Straße" [Abduction on the street], *Neues Deutschland*, 21 Jul 1949; "KPD beschuldigt CIC der Entführung" [KPD accuses CIC of kidnapping], *Frankfurter Rundschau*, 22 Jul 1949; "Verhaftung durch CIC 'normale Sache,'" [Arrest by CIC a "normal thing"], *Neues Deutschland*, 24 Jul 1949.
149 Msg, Innis D. Harris, ODI, to Col. Peter P. Rodes, 26 Aug 1949, sub: Quarterly Estimate of the Situation, Folder "350.05 Military Information – Collection, Dissemination," Director of Intel, Analysis and Research Br, Gen Corresp, 1945–49, RG 260, NACP.

situation in Berlin, the classic distinctions between clandestine and overt political intelligence, between truth and deception, have broken down completely."[150]

Between early May and early July 1945, when the Western Allies took over their sectors, the Soviets had the city to themselves. While Red Army soldiers raped and plundered at will, Soviet occupation authorities sought to staff the city administration with loyalists. The person responsible for this job was Walter Ulbricht, a long-time KPD activist from Leipzig who had been in exile in the Soviet Union since the late 1930s. At the end of the war, Ulbricht and his group of fellow German communist exiles in Moscow returned to Germany. The Soviets were especially keen on ensuring the loyalty of the Berlin police force, and Ulbricht appointed one member of his group, Paul Markgraf, as chief of police.[151] Numerous noncommunists served below Markgraf, and the violent removal of one of them became an early flashpoint between the Soviets and the Western powers in the city.

Karl Heinrich was a professional police officer and staunch social democrat. His opposition to the Nazis had brought him to the attention of U.S. intelligence as early as 1944.[152] He became the first postwar chief of Berlin's uniformed police force (Schutzpolizei), but he quickly found himself at loggerheads with his communist masters over their political differences. In early August, the Soviet security service arrested Heinrich on a flimsy charge, and he disappeared from public view. When the Western Allies inquired about his whereabouts, the Soviets temporized. In April 1946, a Soviet official informed the inter-Allied Kommandatura that Heinrich "had been sent to a labor camp . . . according to Soviet law." In reality, Heinrich had died five months earlier in Soviet captivity.[153]

The case of Karl Heinrich foreshadowed a major political conflict. Berlin had long been an SPD stronghold, and Soviet-communist efforts to exert political control throughout the city inevitably led to clashes within the capital's left-wing political scene. Conversely, as U.S.-Soviet relations soured, American interests began to align with those of the SPD. The new alliance took shape in the winter of

---

150 Rpt, Dana B. Durand, Ch, BOB, to Ch, Foreign Br M, 8 Apr 1948, sub: Transmittal of Report on Berlin Operations Base, in *On the Front Lines of the Cold War: Documents on the Intelligence War in Berlin, 1946 to 1961*, ed. Donald P. Steury (Washington, DC: Center for the Study of Intelligence, 1999), 16.
151 Jochen Staadt, "'Wir packen mit an, Ordnung zu schaffen:' Die Berliner Polizei in der 'Stunde Null'" ["We are helping to create order": The Berlin police at "zero hour"], *Zeitschrift des Forschungsverbundes SED-Staat* 26 (2010), 93.
152 Rpt, OSS, Bibliographical Rpt: Heinrich, Karl, 23 Sep 1944, Folder "Heinrich, Karl XE 208523," INSCOM, IRR, Digitized Name Files, RG 319, NACP.
153 Siegfried Heimann, *Karl Heinrich und die Berliner SPD, die sowjetische Militäradministration und die SED* [Karl Heinrich and the Berlin SPD: The Soviet Military Administration and the SED] (Bonn: Friedrich-Ebert-Stiftung, 2007), 35–36.

1945–1946, when the Soviet Military Administration and the communist party in the Soviet Zone embarked on a campaign to fuse the communists and the social democrats, in effect subordinating the latter to the former.[154] Although the social democrats failed to hold off the merger in Soviet-controlled territory, the campaign met with strong resistance from social democrats in the western sectors of Berlin.

The Americans monitored the campaign closely. Ulrich Biel, the intelligence officer who had interviewed Konrad Adenauer at the end of the war and now served as a public affairs officer in Berlin, had recruited a source inside the SPD. This man, Gustav D. Dahrendorf, told Biel that most social democrats rejected the merger, but that the Soviets coerced opponents through "trickery and outright pressure." Dahrendorf also reported on "acts of political terrorism" and claimed that "right here in the City of Berlin people are being killed and deported." Against the backdrop of the Heinrich case, this statement had the ring of truth.[155]

A Berlin-wide referendum among social democrats, scheduled for 31 March 1946, was to decide the issue. During the ensuing campaign, the U.S. military government discreetly supported the antimerger faction. The American-licensed newspaper, *Der Tagesspiegel*, became a mouthpiece of the opponents, and the Information Control Division distributed much-needed paper for posters, leaflets, and brochures. Biel likely provided the opponents with cigarettes, food, and a venue for confidential meetings at his villa on Milinowskistrasse 27.[156] Only days before the referendum, Clay publicly came out in support of the antimerger faction. Seeing the writing on the wall, Soviet authorities closed the polls in their sector prematurely after only one hour on election day.[157] They were right to be concerned, as 72 percent of party members in the Western sectors voted against the fusion. The result meant that SPD and SED would coexist uneasily in the city for several years.

The story of Ulrich Biel illustrates the intricate relationship between intelligence and politics in the German capital. Born and raised in Berlin, with a partly Jewish background, Biel immigrated to the United States when the Nazis assumed power. During the war, he became a U.S. citizen, was drafted, and trained as a

---

154 For the merger of the two parties in the Soviet Zone, see Chapter 9.
155 Msg, Ulrich E. Biel, to Ch, Public Affairs Br, 18 Feb 1946, sub: Political Intelligence received from Mr. Darendorf [sic], one of the leaders of the Social Democratic Party, Historians Files, CMH.
156 Martin Otto, "Ulrich Biel, ein deutscher Patriot: Der amerikanische Preusse" [Ulrich Biel, a German patriot: The American Prussian] (unpublished manuscript, 2018), 59, Historians Files, CMH.
157 William A. Stivers and Don Carter, *The City Becomes a Symbol: The U.S. Army in the Occupation of Berlin, 1945–1949*, U.S. Army in the Cold War (Washington, DC: U.S. Army Center of Military History, 2017), 156–57.

prisoner-of-war interrogator at Camp Ritchie. In the summer of 1945, the former refugee returned to Berlin as a captain in the U.S. Army.[158] In 1946, he left the Army and joined the military government's Civil Affairs Section, which combined political and intelligence functions. He reported to the section's deputy chief, William Heimlich, formerly chief of the intelligence division in Berlin.[159]

Heimlich, for his part, described the "control" of Biel as a central part of his job. Biel "loved the rough and tumble of precinct politics," Heimlich recalled, and supposedly "would have felt himself a logical candidate for *Oberbürgermeister* [lord mayor]," if it hadn't been for Heimlich's wise guidance.[160] Heimlich's boss, Louis Glaser, was more complimentary: "He [Biel] was a nice man but really tough if you had information that he wanted; he could talk it out of you."[161]

Early on, Biel adopted a hostile stance toward both the KPD and the Soviets. He sided openly and vociferously with the anti-Soviet SPD faction, and his partisanship quickly got him in trouble. In May 1946, a local journalist and CIC source, A. F. Schultes, reported to his case officer, Special Agent Justus J. Shapiro, on a conversation with Curt Swolinzky, a leading SPD social democrat and staunch opponent of the merger. Schultes stated that Swolinzky had made nationalist, anti-Semitic, and anti-Allied remarks, and a CIC investigation confirmed his latent Nazi attitude.[162] Two months later, an "unusually reliable source" told Shapiro that Biel was backing Swolinzky against party opponents "with all possible moral support." According to the source, this support was highly problematic because of Swolinzky's supposedly hardline Marxist views. The source added that Biel "enjoys playing politics behind the scenes, and likes to have nominations, etc., run his way."[163]

Shapiro's source admitted that he did not know Biel personally, and the assertion that the notoriously right-wing Swolinzky, the owner of a small textile business, was a Marxist seems incongruous.[164] That Biel would have supported a

---

158 For Biel's biography, see Otto, "Ulrich Biel."
159 Christoph Weisz, *OMGUS-Handbuch: die amerikanische Militärregierung in Deutschland 1945–1949* [OMGUS Handbook: The American military government in Germany, 1945–1949] (Oldenbourg: De Gruyter, 1995), 705.
160 Interv, Brewster S. Chamberlin with William F. Heimlich, former Ch, G–2, Berlin, 4 Aug 1984, 29, Landesarchiv Berlin.
161 Otto, "Ulrich Biel," 58.
162 Rpt [in German], A. F. Schultes, no addressee, no subject, 25 May 1946, Folder "Swolinsky, Kurt XE 184370," INSCOM, IRR, Digitized Name Files, RG 319, NACP.
163 Memo, Special Agent Justus J. Shapiro, Region VIII, CIC, for Ofcr in Charge, 7 Jul 1946, sub: Biel, Ulrich, Edward, Capt., Folder "Biel, Ulrich Edward Capt. XE 232674," INSCOM, IRR, Digitized Name Files, RG 319, NACP. The "unusually reliable source" may have been Schultes.
164 David E. Barclay, *Schaut auf diese Stadt: Der unbekannte Ernst Reuter* [Look upon this city: The unknown Ernst Reuter] (Berlin: Siedler Verlag, 2000), 208.

staunchly antimerger politician, however, appears probable, and the reference to Swolinzky's supposedly radical leftist views may have been an attempt by one of his internal party rivals to tar Biel as a communist sympathizer. If so, the ploy worked. Shapiro noted that "it seems hardly in accordance" with U.S. policy "to support extreme Marxists," and the CIC opened an investigation "to determine the exact nature of Subject's [i.e., Biel] activities concerning German politics in Berlin."[165] Given that Biel was anything but a supporter of "extreme Marxists," the investigation quickly petered out. The chief of the Civil Affairs Division, Glaser, dismissed the information gleaned by Shapiro's source on Swolinzky as "personal talk" and "innocuous."[166] Biel kept his job, but the Swolinzky episode left a black mark on his record and made some U.S. officials wary of working with him.[167]

With the four principal parties established in Berlin, the city was looking toward the first democratic postwar elections to select representatives for the city council. In June 1946, a U.S. source reviewed each party's prospects based on a Gallup poll. According to this assessment, 35 percent of voters preferred the SPD, 17 percent the communists (SED), 14 percent the CDU, 9 percent the FDP, and 25 percent were mixed or undecided. Military government intelligence believed that the numbers for the CDU were too low, but that the overall estimate of electoral strength was reasonable.[168] Given the massive Soviet support for the SED, and the communists' desire to replace the social democrats as the leading workers' party in the city, this result would have amounted to a devastating defeat for the east.

On election day, 20 October 1946, the Soviets' ambitions in Berlin were soundly dashed. The SPD won a whopping 48.7 percent of the vote, which translated to 63 out of 130 seats—almost but not quite an absolute majority. The CDU came in second at 22.2 percent (29 seats). The SED came in only third, at 19.8 percent (26 seats), followed by the lagging FDP at 9.3 percent (12 seats). When the chief editor of the SED's daily newspaper, *Neues Deutschland*, asked in despair, "what am I supposed to write?," one of his colleagues replied, "Why don't you write: it's all down the drain [*Alles im Eimer*]!"[169]

---

165 Memo, Shapiro for Ofcr in Charge, 7 Jul 1946, sub: Biel, Ulrich, Edward, Capt.
166 Handwritten comments by Glaser in margins of msg, ACofS, G–2, HQ, Berlin District, to Lt. Col. Louis Glaser, 19 Jun 1946, sub: Chairman of SPD – Swolinsky, Folder "Biel, Ulrich Edward Capt. 232674," INSCOM, IRR, Digitized Name Files, RG 319, NACP.
167 Msg, Lt. Col. Eugene Garrison, Intel Div, EUCOM, to Ch, Security Ofc, 28 Nov 1951, re: Biel, Ulrich E., Folder "Biel, Ulrich Edward Capt. XE 232674," INSCOM, IRR, Digitized Name Files, RG 319, NACP.
168 Rpt, Political intelligence rpt no. 35, fortnight ending 15 Jun 1946, Historians Files, CMH.
169 Wolfgang Leonhard, *Die Revolution entlässt ihre Kinder* [The revolution dismisses its children] (Cologne: Kiepenheur and Witsch, 1955), 200.

In view of the SED's defeat at the polls, the Soviets adopted a more authoritarian approach to local politics in their sector while projecting power into the western sectors through the communist-controlled police under Markgraf. The Soviets effectively denied the SPD control in the eastern sector, and their secret services continued to kidnap anticommunist politicians across the city. This hard line aggravated the social democrats and prompted the Americans to push back. As Col. Frank L. Howley, the bellicose American commander of Berlin, put it in his memoirs: "There is only one way to deal with gangsters, Russian-uniformed or otherwise, and that is to treat them like gangsters."[170] The Soviets' aggressive efforts to prop up the SED in Berlin only strengthened the informal alliance between U.S. officials and the anticommunist wing of the social democrats.

The tensions between the two sides manifested in the so-called Ostrowski affair.[171] In December 1946, Berlin's new city parliament elected Otto Ostrowski of the SPD as lord mayor. As the strongest party, the SPD sought to remove communist officials who had been installed by the Red Army in 1945, but they were unable to do so against the wishes of the Soviets. Ostrowski therefore contacted the Soviet city commandant, Maj. Gen. Alexander G. Kotikov, and met with SED leaders to discuss the situation. He had not, however, sufficiently coordinated his initiative with the SPD leadership, including the powerful Swolinzky and the chairman, Franz L. Neumann. When Ostrowski informed them of what he had done after the meeting already had taken place, Swolinzky, Neumann, and others attacked him as disloyal, arrogant, and inefficient. Ugly rumors surfaced about Ostrowski supposedly having divorced his Jewish wife for political reasons under the Nazis. Through informants inside the SPD and the monitoring of Ostrowski's phone, Army Intelligence agencies kept the military government well informed of the unfolding crisis.[172]

Ostrowski was a capable administrator, but he failed to grasp the local implications of the global rivalry between the Soviet Union and the West. "My name is Ostrowski," he told Howley, "but the Russians say it ought to be Westrowski. As far as I'm concerned, I'd like to change it to Centrowski. That's where I stand."[173] This was witty, but Ostrowski's desire to steer a middle course between the two

---

170 F. L. Howley, *Berlin Command* (New York: G. P. Putnam's Sons, 1950), 13.
171 For background, see Gerhard Keiderling, *Um Deutschlands Einheit: Ferdinand Friedensburg und der Kalte Krieg in Berlin, 1945–1952* [On German unity: Ferdinand Friedensburg and the Cold War in Berlin, 1945–1952] (Vienna, Cologne: Böhlau Verlag, 2009), 160–63; Barclay, *Schaut auf diese Stadt*, 215–20; Stivers and Carter, *City Becomes a Symbol*, 190–94.
172 Rpt, Civil Censorship Div, 14 Oct 1946, sub: Ostrowski, (FNU) Dr., Folder "Ostrowski, Otto Dr. D-239054," INSCOM, IRR, Digitized Name Files, RG 319, NACP; Rpt, Herman T. Hunt to Field Ofc Steglitz, Agent's Daily Rpt, 12 Apr 1947, Folder "Ostrowski, Otto Dr. D-239054," INSCOM, IRR, Digitized Name Files, RG 319, NACP.
173 Howley, *Berlin Command*, 144.

sides left him adrift without an anchor. At a meeting of Heimlich and Biel with leading social democrats in February 1947, Biel declared: "Dr. Ostrowski has made a 180° turn toward the Bolsheviks. He must be regarded as a Trojan horse in the SPD. He has to disappear."[174] Less than two months later, the SPD voted him out of office. Years later, Biel confirmed his disdain for Ostrowski by calling him an "idiot" (*Spinner*) for ignoring the realities of the U.S.-Soviet power struggle. Ostrowski, for his part, blamed Biel for his ouster.[175] It is unlikely that Biel, a minor U.S. official, single-handedly engineered the mayor's downfall, but the former Ritchie Boy undoubtedly took sides. His involvement cemented his reputation as the éminence grise of Berlin politics.[176]

Ostrowski's fall opened the door for the man who would dominate Berlin politics over the next several years.[177] A one-time communist, Ernst Reuter had joined the SPD before the war and was a politician of national stature. Under the Nazis, he had spent a year in a concentration camp. Following his release, he fled to Turkey, where he lived in exile from 1935 through the end of the war. His CIC file contained a report from August 1945, when Reuter was still in Turkey, describing him as "intelligent," an "efficient worker," possessing "great knowledge of administrative matters, energetic, entirely absorbed by his work," having "moral and physical courage," being a "good organizer, sober," and as someone who "knows many people." The source of the report was "convinced that Reuter intends to go back to Germany and that he could become a useful adviser in personal matters."[178] It was a prescient assessment.

In 1946, Reuter returned to Berlin, equipped with a global perspective on local affairs matched by few other politicians. A clever tactician and gifted orator, he quickly ascended the political ladder. Within a year, he had cemented his role as the strongman of the SPD in Berlin, and the Americans kept an eye on him. Reuter, noted an intelligence officer, "played his role as a leader during a very difficult period. He was a good actor . . . [and] had extensive experience in urban management as well as the politics of the left, having been a Soviet communist and ending as a strong Socialist who knew the dangers of communism."[179] For the same reasons, the Soviets and the communists distrusted Reuter and sought to block his rise. The SED newspaper *Neues Deutschland* lambasted the popular

---

174 Keiderling, *Um Deutschlands Einheit*, 161.
175 Otto, "Ulrich Biel," 61, 64.
176 Stivers and Carter, *City Becomes a Symbol*, 192–93.
177 For Reuter's biography, see Barclay, *Schaut auf diese Stadt.*
178 Memo, no sender, no addressee, 17 Aug 1945, sub: Reuter, Ernst, Folder "XE 155168 Reuter, Ernst," INSCOM, IRR, Digitized Name Files, RG 319, NACP.
179 Email, Peter M. F. Sichel to Thomas Boghardt, 25 May 2018, Historians Files, CMH.

SPD politician as a "warmonger" (*Kriegshetzer*) with a "fascist heart" who must never become mayor.[180]

For the time being, the Soviets succeeded. When Ostrowski fell from power, the SPD nominated Reuter as the next lord mayor, but the Soviets used their veto right to prevent their archrival from being appointed to this key post. Eventually, the four Allied military governors found a compromise: the SPD would nominate one of Ostrowski's deputies, Louise D. Schröder of the SPD, as acting mayor. Although his failure to succeed Ostrowski disappointed Reuter, the CIC considered Schröder's appointment a safe temporary solution that left Reuter's powerful position intact: "Subject [Schröder] would be able to run the municipality in future with Reuter in the background."[181]

Figure 37: Willy Brandt in uniform as an officer of the Norwegian liaison mission in Berlin, 1946. Archiv der Sozialen Demokratie, Friedrich-Ebert-Stiftung.

Over time, Reuter's ties with the Americans strengthened. His contacts on the U.S. side included Colonel Howley and General Clay, who lauded the social demo-

---

180 "Der Kriegshetzer Ernst Reuter" [The warmonger Ernst Reuter], *Neues Deutschland*, 2 Oct 1948.
181 Memo, no sender, no addressee, 14 Jul 1947, sub: Schroeder, Louise, Folder "Schroeder, Louise Mrs. D 206073," INSCOM, IRR, Digitized Name Files, RG 319, NACP.

crat in his memoirs as "rugged, intelligent, and courageous."[182] Beneath the top military leadership, the CIA struck an informal relationship with Reuter. Henry D. Hecksher and Thomas "Tom" Polgar of the Berlin Operations Base first established contact with Reuter, and he subsequently met regularly with agency officials. According to the CIA deputy station chief Peter Sichel, "we would share intelligence with [Reuter] . . . for his eyes only . . . as [he] shared it with us."[183] Unlike the CIA, the CIC did not establish a covert relationship with Reuter. Given Reuter's overt cooperation with military government, the Corps may have considered it unnecessary to use a clandestine conduit for communicating with him. Instead, the CIC managed to recruit one of Reuter's top lieutenants, a rising star in the Berlin SPD who would play a significant role in West Berlin and West German politics in the decades to come.

Born in 1913, Herbert Ernst Karl Frahm became a social democrat and outspoken left-wing journalist at a young age. To escape Nazi persecution, he immigrated to Norway in 1933, adopting a pseudonym for security purposes. He learned Norwegian and assumed Norwegian citizenship when the Nazis revoked his German citizenship in 1938. In the wake of the German invasion of Norway, he fled to Sweden where he laid low until the end of the war. In late 1946, the Norwegian government sent him, with the rank of major, to Berlin as a press officer attached to the Norwegian military mission. While reporting on conditions in Berlin, he established contact with SPD chairman Kurt Schumacher, who encouraged him to enter German politics and represent him in Berlin. Frahm agreed, reassuming German citizenship and rejoining the SPD. At this point, he chose to adopt his long-time pseudonym as his legal name: Willy Brandt.[184]

In 1947, Brewster H. Morris of the Office of the Political Adviser introduced Brandt, then still serving with the Norwegian military mission, to the CIC in Berlin. Special Agent George D. Swerdlin, who personally vetted Brandt and became his first handler, described him as "an intelligent, energetic man, who may be considered a friend of the Western Powers." Swerdlin also noted that Brandt had "a hatred of communism typical of a true Socialist."[185] In 1948, the CIC and Brandt

---

182 Clay, *Decision in Germany*, 379.
183 Email, Sichel to Boghardt, 25 May 2018. Reuter died prematurely in 1952, at the age of sixty-three.
184 For Brandt's biography, see Peter Merseburger, *Willy Brandt 1913–1992: Visionär und Realist* [Willy Brandt, 1913–1992: Visionary and realist] (Stuttgart, Munich: Deutsche Verlags-Anstalt, 2002).
185 Memo, Special Agent George D. Swerdlin, Region VIII, CIC, for Ofcr in Charge, 25 Jan 1950, folder "D 248037 Brandt, Willy," INSCOM, IRR, Digitized Name Files, RG 319, NACP.

agreed to establish an informal, covert relationship.[186] According to his file, Brandt "was motivated to furnish information to CIC as he believed CIC to be an agency actively engaged in the fight against Communism."[187]

Brandt provided the CIC with intelligence as well as access. He served as a liaison between Schumacher's headquarters in Hanover and the SPD's illegal organization in the Soviet Zone, the so-called Ostbüro (Eastern Bureau). In this position, he forwarded numerous reports from agents in the east to the CIC.[188] In addition, he acted as a conduit to the SPD leadership in the West. When the Army sought to interview top German officials in the course of an investigation of a military government employee, Samuel L. Wahrhaftig, Brandt arranged for a CIC agent to talk to Schumacher.[189] Over time, Brandt grew closer to Reuter, eventually becoming his deputy. As Brandt's significance in Berlin rose, so did his value as an American intelligence source.

Brandt's "loyalty to the SPD"—which, the CIC lamented, "comes before that of any agency of an occupying power"—was the "main drawback" for the Americans who worked with him. Nonetheless, "in specific cases" Brandt aided the Corps "in preference to the SPD." During the early years of his cooperation with the CIC, Brandt never asked for payment. He merely received compensation for his agents, usually in the form of cigarettes and other tradable goods, and reimbursements for expenses. On one occasion, the CIC issued him an airline ticket from Berlin to Frankfurt. Swerdlin noted that Brandt was "very fond of American whiskey, and accepts an occasional present of a bottle given in a sociable manner."[190] Brandt greatly appreciated this gesture. On one occasion, a CIC receipt notes, he received five "A" rations of bottled whisky.[191]

In January 1950, the CIC recruited Brandt formally as an "O-type" or "investigative informant"—that is, a source who provided information from records or agencies to which they had access. He received the designation "O-35-VIII," and on a reliability scale from "A" to "F", the Corps assigned him the second-highest grade: "B" or "usually reliable."[192] Brandt received a monthly retainer of DM

---

186 Rpt, Special Agent George D. Swerdlin, Personality Report, 27 Oct 1948, sub: Brandt, Willy @ Frahm, Willy, Folder "D 248037 Brandt, Willy," INSCOM, IRR, Digitized Name Files, RG 319, NACP.
187 Msg, Maj. Russell B. Remis to Liaison Ofcr, DAD, 23 Jan 1959, sub: Willy Brandt, Mayor of Berlin, Folder "XE 248037 Brandt, Willy," INSCOM, IRR, Digitized Name Files, RG 319, NACP.
188 For more information, see Chapter 9.
189 Memo, Swerdlin for Ofcr in Charge, 25 Jan 1950.
190 Rpt, Swerdlin, Personality Report, 27 Oct 1948, sub: Brandt, Willy @ Frahm, Willy.
191 MFR, "Willy Brandt and SPD East Zone Office," n.d., Folder "D 248037 Brandt, Willy," INSCOM, IRR, Digitized Name Files, RG 319, NACP.
192 Msg, Lt. Col. Richard K. Rudisill, Region VIII, CIC, to HQ, 66th CIC Gp, 27 Jan 1950, sub: Brandt, Willy, Folder "D 248037 Brandt, Willy," INSCOM, IRR, Digitized Name Files, RG 319, NACP.

(deutsche marks) 250 as well as compensation for expenses. In September, Special Agent Gustav Bard replaced Swerdlin as Brandt's handler, and the two met regularly at a safe house on Hagenstrasse in the U.S. sector of Berlin.[193]

The Americans invested heavily in their informant. On 27 July 1950, Brandt— by this time an SPD representative for West Berlin in the Bundestag—and Hans E. Hirschfeld of the West Berlin SPD met secretly with U.S. officials in room 115 of the IG Farben building in Frankfurt.[194] With a warning to treat the following transaction "strictly confidentially," the Americans provided the two men with DM 200,000 in political support. Over the next few years, they funneled another DM 106,000 to Hirschfeld. The former Army Intelligence officer and Information Control Division member Shepard Stone had arranged this deal to strengthen the SPD in Berlin against communist encroachments.[195]

As Brandt continued his political ascent in West Germany, he spent less and less time dealing with matters behind the iron curtain. Consequently, his value as a CIC source of intelligence on East Germany declined, and in September 1952 the Corps dropped him "without prejudice." The two sides parted on friendly terms, and CIC personnel kept in touch with its former informant on an occasional basis.[196] But Brandt was too valuable a resource for the Americans to let go of him altogether. In 1954, he traveled to the United States as part of a goodwill tour for West German officials arranged by the Department of State. The CIA wanted to seize this opportunity to contact Brandt and asked their CIC colleagues if they objected. Trying to shield Brandt from the CIA's advances, the CIC in response demanded that "no efforts whatsoever will be made to approach SUBJECT by members of your organization."[197] According to a former CIA officer, Victor L. Marchetti, the agency ignored this wish.[198]

---

[193] Msg, Lt. Col. Richard K. Rudisill, Region VIII, CIC, to HQ, 66th CIC Gp, 17 Mar 1950, sub: Brandt, Willy, Folder "D 248037 Brandt, Willy," INSCOM, IRR, Digitized Name Files, RG 319, NACP.

[194] With the end of the military government in September 1949, the IG Farben building had become the seat of the recently established U.S. High Commission for Occupied Germany under the leadership of John J. McCloy.

[195] Scott H. Krause, "Neue Westpolitik: The Clandestine Campaign to Westernize the SPD in Cold War Berlin, 1948–1958," Central European History 48, no. 1 (2015), 91–92; "Ein bisschen Druck" [A little pressure], Der Spiegel, 11 Jun 2016.

[196] Msg, Col. Pete N. Derzis, Region VIII, CIC, to CO, 22 Apr 1954, sub: Brandt, Willy, Folder "D 248037 Brandt, Willy," INSCOM, IRR, Digitized Name Files, RG 319, NACP.

[197] Msg, Col. Warren S. Leroy, 66th CIC Gp, to CO, DAD, 9 Mar 1954, Folder "D 248037 Brandt, Willy," INSCOM, IRR, Digitized Name Files, RG 319, NACP.

[198] Victor L. Marchetti and John D. Marks, The CIA and the Cult of Intelligence (New York: Dell, 1974), 64; Viola Herms Drath, Willy Brandt: Prisoner of His Past (Radnor, PA: Chilton Book Company, 1975), 238–39.

Meanwhile, Brandt threw himself into West German politics, serving in both the Bundestag and the West Berlin state parliament. In 1957, he became lord mayor of West Berlin, and in 1969 he was elected chancellor of the Federal Republic of Germany. Given his long-standing ties with American intelligence, it is both ironic and fitting that an espionage affair caused Brandt's eventual downfall. During his chancellorship, West German security identified one of Brandt's closest aides, Günter Guillaume, as an agent of East Germany's Ministry for State Security (Ministerium für Staatssicherheit; commonly known as the Stasi). In April 1974, West German authorities arrested Guillaume. The following month, Brandt resigned as chancellor, ending a decades-long involvement with the world of intelligence.[199]

Conclusion

The democratization of Germany remained a central objective of the U.S. military government, and Army Intelligence assisted materially in the pursuit of this goal. As the U.S. occupation authorities saw it, there was no room, at least in principle, for either former Nazis or communist sympathizers in the new Germany, and all potential candidates for political office had to be evaluated to determine their commitment to democratic ideals. The data collected by the CIC and other agencies put the military government in a position to make informed choices when selecting local administrators. If American officials did not always agree with the decisions made by local politicians, they could be reasonably sure that they had enough information at hand to put local events into a larger context and avoid major surprises. Moreover, Army Intelligence provided accurate threat assessments, as they did in the case of the KPD. Cold War–generated anxiety in the West about international communism easily could have led the military government to ban the KPD. Yet the Army's intelligence sources provided a realistic estimate of the party's weakness, thereby preventing such a politically fraught move.

In addition to safeguarding the budding democracy in the U.S. Zone, the thorough penetration of local politics by Army Intelligence agencies had unanticipated long-term consequences. In the course of vetting and monitoring local officials, U.S. intelligence struck up numerous formal and informal relationships with rising postwar politicians. Virtually every minister-president in the U.S. Zone

---

199 Markus Wolf, *Memoirs of a Spymaster: The Man Who Waged a Secret War against the West* (London: Pimlico, 1997), 151–73. Both Guillaume and his wife Christel were Stasi operatives; posing as refugees from the East, they moved to West Germany in the mid-1950s and infiltrated the Social Democratic Party organization. As head of the Stasi's foreign intelligence division, Wolf handled Guillaume.

and every major leader of a democratic party became involved with one or several U.S. intelligence agencies. Not only did these links generate valuable information for military government, but they also helped bind leading postwar German officials ideologically to the United States. In this way, Army Intelligence agencies helped U.S. officials master the democratization process and laid the foundation for personal alliances that affected American relations with the West German state long after the end of military government.

9 The Soviet Zone

Heinz Raue, a young man from Bitterfeld in central Germany, served as a radio operator with the *Herman Göring Division* of the *Luftwaffe*. In 1945, the U.S. Army captured his unit and turned Raue over to the British, who interned him in Egypt. Upon his release in January 1949, he returned to Bitterfeld, which was now in the Soviet Zone (Map 1). There, he joined the youth organization of the Socialist Unity Party (SED), the Free German Youth (Freie Deutsche Jugend; FDJ). In November 1949, Raue showed up at a Counter Intelligence Corps office in Berlin, bringing along with him internal FDJ documents. Volunteering his services as an informant, he told Special Agent Andrew C. Nelson Jr. that he had joined the communists to spy on them for the Americans. Nelson reviewed the material and concluded: "Source made a good impression . . . and it is believed that he is honest in saying that he joined the FDJ to fight against Communism."[1] Following a background check, the CIC recruited him as "penetration agent" P-15-VIII.[2]

Over the following years, Heinz Raue reported regularly on local FDJ activities and delivered numerous documents from the organization. At his suggestion, the CIC hired his brother Gerhard as a courier to transfer the material safely from the Soviet Zone to Berlin.[3] Code-named P-43-VIII, Gerhard Raue received DM (deutsche marks) 20 to 40 per delivery as well as a one-time Christmas bonus of DM 60.[4] In July 1954, the CIC dropped both agents because of limited funds. The two sides parted on amicable terms. At his last official meeting with the CIC, Gerhard Raue promised that "he would contact his handling agent if he ever comes into possession of valuable information, and he expressed his willingness to be of service to the U.S. Army in case of war in Europe."[5]

The Raue brothers constituted just two of the many American informants in the Soviet Zone, but their case underscores the centrality of the city of Berlin to Army Intelligence in Germany, particularly for collecting information on Soviet

---

[1] Rpt, Special Agent Andrew C. Nelson Jr., Region VIII, CIC, to CO, 9 Nov 1949, sub: Raue, Heinz, Folder "Raue, Heinz D271268," INSCOM, IRR, Digitized Name Files, RG 319, NACP.
[2] Replacement Sheet, Vetting Rpt, 21 Feb 1950, Folder "Raue, Heinz D271268," INSCOM, IRR, Digitized Name Files, RG 319, NACP.
[3] Msg, Lt. Col. Ira K. Ewalt, CO, Region VIII, CIC, to CO, HQ 66th CIC Gp, 19 Jun 1953, sub: Raue, Gerhard, Folder "Raue, Gerhard XE 333153," INSCOM, IRR, Digitized Name Files, RG 319, NACP.
[4] Informant Control Sheet, P-243-VIII, 26 Apr 1954, Folder "Raue, Gerhard XE 333153," INSCOM, IRR, Digitized Name Files, RG 319, NACP; Informant Control Sheet, P-243-VIII, 21 Dec 1953, Folder "Raue, Gerhard XE 333153," INSCOM, IRR, Digitized Name Files, RG 319, NACP.
[5] Msg, Col. Peter M. Derzis, Region VIII, CIC, to CO, 66th CIC Gp, 15 Jul 1954, sub: Raue, Gerhard, Folder "Raue, Gerhard XE 333153," INSCOM, IRR, Digitized Name Files, RG 319, NACP.

Figure 38: A close-up shot of a watchtower in the Soviet internment camp *Spezlager* Sachsenhausen, taken clandestinely by Richard Perla in May or June 1949. The sign reads: "Prohibited zone. No entry. Use of firearms!". Gedenkstätte und Museum Sachsenhausen.

forces. It also reveals that many American informants were not motivated primarily by material compensation but by the heavy hand of Soviet occupation, which inspired fear and hatred in the local population. Espionage was not the only intelligence method that the Americans used to discover what was going on in the Soviet Zone, but to the extent that the Cold War has the reputation of being a proverbial contest of "spy versus spy," its origins lie in postwar Germany, especially in the city of Berlin.

Economic Exploitation

On 22 June 1941, Nazi Germany launched *Operation Barbarossa*, beginning a brutal war of annihilation against their one-time ally, the Soviet Union. According to official Soviet figures, nearly 27 million citizens, including 8.5 million soldiers, perished in the fighting. The Nazis laid waste to 1,710 towns, 70,000 villages, 32,000 factories, 65,000 kilometers of railway tracks, and 100,000 farms, amounting to 30 percent of the Soviet Union's national wealth.[6] A U.S. intelligence assessment of Soviet postwar capabilities estimated that it would take the USSR at least seven years to recover economically from the war.[7] By contrast, the United States had not suffered excessive damage on its soil aside from the Japanese attack on Pearl Harbor in 1941. Soviet sacrifices, Britain's Foreign Secretary Anthony Eden later acknowledged, were "worse than anything we or the Americans were suffering."[8]

Understandably, reparations figured prominently in Moscow's negotiations with the Western Allies. Washington and London generally were sympathetic to Soviet wishes in this area, but the devil was in the details. At the Potsdam Conference, Joseph Stalin demanded $10 billion in reparations, an enormous sum that threatened to cripple Germany and destabilize Europe for years. After the Americans and the British pushed back, the wartime victors reached a compromise of sorts. According to the Potsdam agreement, the Soviets would receive from the Western Zones 10 percent of the industrial capital "as is unnecessary for the German peace economy"—a flexible expression open to interpretation. The agreement also granted Moscow the right to exact reparations from its own occupation zone.[9] The task of monitoring the extent of the Soviet extractions, and their use, fell to American intelligence. By the end of June 1945, the Americans were preparing to take ownership of their sector in Berlin, and Army Intelligence began using the city as a base for operations into the Soviet Zone. Berlin offered the Army a preview of Soviet economic exploitation. In early July, an officer with the Army detachment moving into the designated American sector of Berlin noted that "much machinery and equipment was being shipped out of Berlin to the east."[10] The Strategic Services Unit estimated that during the summer of 1945 the Soviets had dismantled 90 percent of the machinery of Siemens, the largest industrial company in prewar Berlin.[11] The Soviet retaliation against a defeated Germany included the expropriation of property held by German citizens in eastern Europe, as well as the expulsion westward of ethnic Germans living in territories

---

6 Drew Middleton, "Germans' Crimes in Russia Listed," *New York Times*, 9 Feb 1946.
7 Memo, Joint Intel Committee, 18 Jan 1945, sub: Estimate of Soviet Post-War Capabilities, Folder "ABC 336 RUSSIA Sec 1-A," American-British Conversations Corresp Relating to Planning and Combat Opns, 1940–1948, RG 165, NACP.
8 Vladislav M. Zubok, *A Failed Empire: The Soviet Union in the Cold War from Stalin to Gorbachev* (Chapel Hill: University of North Carolina Press, 2009), 2; Michael Neiberg, *Potsdam: The End of World War II and the Remaking of Europe* (New York: Basic Books, 2015), 90–91.
9 Neiberg, *Potsdam*, 198–200.
10 Maj. Gen. John J. Maginnis, *Military Government Journal* (Amherst: University of Massachusetts Press, 1971), entries for 26 June and 2 July 1945.
11 Memo, Strategic Services Unit, Intel Dissemination, 25 Apr 1946, sub: Industry in the Russian and Polish Zone, Strategic Services Unit Intel Rpts, 1945–1946, reel 1, RG 226, NACP.

east of the Oder and Neisse Rivers, now occupied by the Red Army. In October 1945, Brig. Gen. Edwin L. Sibert informed Maj. Gen. Clayton L. Bissell that "reliable observers including an officer from the G 2 Div[ision]" had reported on chaotic conditions in the Soviet Zone caused by the influx of millions of German refugees from the east.[12] Yet even as the situation in Germany stabilized, the Soviets continued to extract economic reparations, often in an arbitrary, haphazard fashion. In 1946, a CIC informant reported on the widespread dismantling of factories and critical infrastructure in the Soviet Zone. Aerial photography not only confirmed agent reports on dismantling activities but also revealed that many of the valuable tools and machine parts were rusting away on railway cars parked on sidings in Germany.[13] In 1947, a staff member of the Reparations and Deliveries Section of the Soviet Military Administration in Karlshorst defected to the American sector and provided Army Intelligence with an insider account of the far-flung dismantling efforts in eastern Germany.[14]

The Soviet Union made no secret of its punitive approach to governance in its designated territories. The intelligence division of Supreme Allied Headquarters noted that the Soviets were "completely indifferent to" German suffering in their efforts to gain the maximum amount of reparations.[15] Over time, this ruthlessness bred discontent even among Moscow's German collaborators. In 1946, a CIC-operated network of informants in the Soviet Zone, code-named HONEYPOT, reported that Soviet policy "has caused members of the communist intelligentsia reat consternation."[16] Disillusionment made some Soviet Zone officials ripe for recruitment by U.S. intelligence. Leo Skrzypczynski, a German industrialist who had spent time in a concentration camp for his underground left-wing activity during the war, was a senior executive for economic affairs in the Soviet Zone and participated regularly in meetings with Soviet officials in Karlshorst. By spring 1946, he had developed serious doubts about Soviet policies and began leaking confidential information to Western press correspondents, including John Scott of *Time-Life* and

---

12 Msg, Brig. Gen. Edwin L. Sibert to Maj. Gen. Clayton L. Bissell, 18 Oct 1945, Folder "From Germany S-20405 thru S-39481," ACoS, G–2 (Intel), "Top Secret" Incoming and Outgoing Cables, 1942–52, RG 319, NACP.
13 Lucius D. Clay, *Decision in Germany* (Garden City, NY: Doubleday, 1950), 124.
14 Rpt, Eugene V. Valic, 7707 EUCOM Intel Center, to CO, 25 Mar 1948, sub: Economic Intelligence Report 27 (Virginia), Folder "Dismantling of Industry in Russian Zone XE 152136," INSCOM, IRR, Impersonal Name Files, RG 319, NACP. The defector's name was Vladimir Ivanovich Zhabinsky, who used the alias Siegfried Rudolf.
15 Rpt, SHAEF, Political Intel Rpt, 21 Jul 1945, Folder "ABC 381 Germany (29 Jan 43) Sec 1-B," American-British Corresp Relating to Planning and Combat Opns, 1940–1948, RG 165, NACP.
16 Rpt, Pinger Rpt no. 95, 6 Dec 1946, sub: Honeypot Report, Folder "Operation Honey Pot (extract) D 129868," INSCOM, IRR, Impersonal Name Files, RG 319, NACP.

Marguerite Higgins and Ned Russell of the *New York Herald Tribune*. In September, the U.S. Constabulary took forty-six documents from Skrzypczynski as he was crossing into Bavaria on an official trip.[17] A few days later, he provided the Strategic Services Unit with a lengthy report on the dismal economic situation in the Soviet Zone.[18] Although Skrzypczynski expressed a desire to move to the United States, he remained in eastern Germany until his death in 1971. Communist officials never discovered his brief collaboration with U.S. intelligence.

Skrzypczynski was not the only official to report to the Americans out of disappointment with the ruthless Soviet economic exploitation effort. In January 1948, an expert on fertilizers, Dr. A. Groh, provided statistics to the intelligence section in Berlin on declining agricultural output in the Soviet Zone.[19] The following year, a penetration agent furnished the CIC with reports from the German Economic Commission, the Soviet Zone's central economic planning agency.[20] And in October 1949, Siegfried Witte, a disgruntled official from the coastal state of Mecklenburg, reported that the Soviets sought to deceive the West about the true amount of resources extracted from eastern Germany. In 1949, Witte noted, the state of Mecklenburg had paid out DM 275 million to the Soviets, but the latter reported that they had received only DM 125 million. The remaining DM 150 million did not appear in Moscow's official accounts.[21]

These reports directly contradicted statements from Soviet officials about the supposedly modest amount of reparations extracted from eastern Germany. During the Moscow conference of foreign ministers in 1947, for example, Stalin told Secretary of State George C. Marshall that the Soviets had removed merely $2 billion of goods from Germany, a number that he felt was "insignificant and much too small."[22] Thanks to U.S. intelligence, Marshall almost certainly would have known

---

[17] Msg, Capt. Mary D. Schurman, Women's Army Corps, HQ, Civil Censorship Div, to HQ, Region IV, CIC, 10 Sep 1946, sub: TCS intercept re Leo Skrzypcczynsky [sic], Folder "11 Dec 06 Leo Skrzypcczynsky [sic] XE 262483," INSCOM, IRR, Personal Name Files, RG 319, NACP.
[18] Rpt no. L-1724, 21 Sep 1946, Folder "L 1675–L 1700," Washington Registry SI [Special Intel] Br Field Files, RG 226, NACP.
[19] Memo, Ofc of the S–2 (Counterintel Section), 16 Jan 1948, sub: Agricultural Conditions in the East Zone, Folder "#2," Rcds Relating to the Soviet Occupation Zone in Germany, 1947–1948, RG 242, NACP.
[20] Memo, Special Agent Kenneth M. Kallstrom, Region VIII, CIC, 13 Jun 1949, sub: DWK Report on the Fulfillment of the 2-year Plan in the Soviet Zone, Folder "RE-279–1950," HQ, EUCOM, Ofc of the Ch of Staff, Intel Div, Administrative Br, Intel Rprts 1948–51, RG 549, NACP.
[21] Rpt, Withold F. Dylewski, Region X, CIC, 2 Oct 1949, sub: Economic Data, Land Mecklenburg, Folder "RE-323-350–1950," HQ, EUCOM, Ofc of the Ch of Staff, Intel Div, Administrative Br, Intel Rprts 1948–51, RG 549, NACP.
[22] Memo of Conversation, 15 Apr 1947, doc. 127, in *Foreign Relations of the United States, 1947, Council of Foreign Ministers; Germany and Austria, Volume II*, ed. William Slany (Washington, DC: Government Printing Office, 1972), 342.

this assertion to be a lie. Over time, the Soviets would remove $14 billion of material from eastern Germany, as well as more than $2 billion worth of goods from the former German territories east of the Oder and Neisse Rivers, which had been annexed by Poland under the August 1945 Potsdam Agreement. In addition, German prisoners of war provided forced labor valued at nearly $10 billion.[23]

U.S. intelligence reports on Soviet reparations practices had a significant impact on American policy. In his memoirs, General Lucius D. Clay explicitly mentioned intelligence reports pointing to large-scale Soviet dismantling activities.[24] In May 1946, Clay decided to cut off reparations deliveries from the U.S. Zone, and subsequent Soviet efforts to put the contentious issue back on the inter-Allied agenda met with Western indifference.[25] Rather than succumb to Soviet demands for a share of the industrial output of the coal-rich Ruhr Valley, the Americans and the British focused on rebuilding their zones independently of Moscow. Two years later, these efforts culminated in the Economic Recovery Program, more commonly known as the Marshall Plan. Named after its architect, Secretary of State Marshall, the plan envisioned over $12 billion of assistance to Western European countries to help rebuild their economies.[26]

As the incoming intelligence provided clarity over the extent of economic exploitation in the Soviet Zone, American officials grew concerned over the use to which Moscow put its bounty. In August 1946, a CIC informant returning from eastern Germany reported that the Soviets had restarted the production lines in the famous Junkers aircraft factories in Bitterfeld and Dessau. According to this source, their output rate approached their top capacity under the Nazis. Junkers had produced the latest jet-fighter planes during the war, a fact highlighted by the American intelligence officer reviewing this report.[27]

In addition to capitalizing on German factories, the Soviets aggressively exploited human capital in their zone. On 22 October 1946, Soviet security and military agencies rounded up several thousand scientists and technicians along with their families and belongings and shipped them to the Soviet Union, where they went to work in the armaments industry. The code name of this operation was

---

23 Ilko-Sascha Kowalczuk and Stefan Wolle, *Roter Stern über Deutschland: Sowjetische Truppen in der DDR* [Red star over Germany: Soviet troops in the GDR] (Berlin: Ch. Links, 2010), 75–76.
24 Clay, *Decision in Germany*, 124.
25 Jean Edward Smith, *Lucius D. Clay: An American Life* (New York: Henry Holt, 1990), 350.
26 For the Marshall Plan, see Benn Steil, *The Marshall Plan: Dawn of the Cold War* (New York: Simon & Schuster, 2018).
27 Memo, Special Agent Stephen W. Mainczyk, Region II, CIC, for Subregional Ch, 6 Aug 1946, sub: Production of War Material in the Russian Zone, Folder "ZF 015104 Germany Russian Zone in Military – Folder 2 of 2," INSCOM, IRR, Impersonal Name Files, RG 319, NACP.

Osoavikhim, echoing the nomenclature of a Soviet civil defense organization. The word choice suggested that, in the minds of Soviet officials, they were recruiting German scientists for the defense of the USSR.

In the ensuing weeks and months, Army Intelligence received numerous reports about this "carefully planned" and smoothly executed operation. The HONEYPOT network estimated the total number of deportees at 10,000.[28] The Pentagon's intelligence division noted, accurately, that Moscow's "acquisition and exploitation of German scientists . . . in the fields of atomic energy (bombs), guided missiles and biological warfare greatly enhances Soviet capabilities."[29] Just as the Americans sought to lay their hands on German scientific and technological experts through operations like Project PAPERCLIP, the Soviets too wanted to acquire as many former enemy scientists as they could find—though their recruitment efforts involved far more coercion than invitation.

Perhaps the single biggest economic prize in the Soviet Zone was a natural resource with critical military potential: uranium. In 1946, the Soviets discovered this key element of the atomic bomb in the *Erzgebirge* (ore mountains), a historic mining area in southern Saxony. The following year, they organized their uranium mining efforts under the umbrella of a Soviet-owned shareholding company known as Wismut AG, which reported directly to Moscow. Eager to extract the maximum allotment of the radioactive element in the minimum amount of time, the Soviets forced more than 100,000 Germans, men and women alike, to work in the uranium mines under appalling conditions. Without protective gear, workers waded ankle-deep in toxic slime, breathing in radioactive dust. Lethal accidents became commonplace. Tens of thousands of workers perished in the mines or in the following years from cancers caused by prolonged radiation exposure.[30]

The Soviets declared the *Erzgebirge* mines off limits for outsiders and sought to shroud the uranium operation in a cloak of secrecy. When Brig. Gen. Walter W. Hess Jr., the commander of the U.S. Military Liaison Mission, asked for permission to visit the mines, General Mikhail S. Malinin, the chief of staff of the Soviet occupation forces, replied that "these mines are not under his jurisdiction and

---

28 Rpt, Pinger Rpt no. 95, 6 Dec 1946, sub: Honeypot Report. This number was probably on the high end.
29 Rpt, Intel Div, to Director of Intel, 5 Aug 1946, sub: Soviet Capabilities to Overrun Europe and Asia, Folder "926079," Rcds of the ACoS, G-2 (Intel), Formerly Top Secret Intel Documents, 1943–59, RG 319, NACP; for a history of Operation Osoaviakhim and its effect on Soviet science, see Norman M. Naimark, *The Russians in Germany: A History of the Soviet Zone of Occupation, 1945–1949* (Cambridge, MA: Belknap Press of Harvard University Press, 1995), 220–28.
30 Naimark, *The Russians in Germany*, 238–48; John Tagliabue, "A Legacy of Ashes: The Uranium Mines of Eastern Germany," *New York Times*, 19 Mar 1991.

Figure 39: Workmen drag reparations equipment from the Daimler-Benz underground engine plant in Obrigheim for shipment to the Soviet Union, July 1946. U.S. Army, NACP.

nothing is known of their existence."[31] Yet the expanse of the project and the awful treatment of the miners, which caused many of them to flee west and tell their tale, made secrecy a virtual impossibility.

The intelligence division in Frankfurt heard rumblings about Soviet mining activities in the *Erzgebirge* as early as the spring 1946. This information originated with the Strategic Services Unit, the Civil Censorship Division, the military attaché in Prague, and various CIC and Third Army units located along the intra-German border. German refugees and the occasional Soviet defector provided the bulk of the information. In late 1948, for example, the Soviet chief of security from a mine at Oberschlema, Ivan N. Polyakov, fled to the U.S. Zone. The U.S. Constabulary picked him up at the border and transferred him to the interrogation center in Oberursel.[32] Drawing on the large volume of reports it received, the division de-

---

31 Naimark, *The Russians in Germany*, 238.
32 Msg, HQ, U.S. Constabulary, G–2 to EUCOM, 3 Jan 1949, Folder "Top Secret IN 1949 to . . . Book I," EUCOM, Ofc of the Ch of Staff, Msg Control Center, Incoming Msgs, Top Secret Sec, 1948–1951, RG 549, NACP; Msg, Lt. Gen. Clarence R. Huebner, EUCOM, to Lt. Col. Paul O. Langguth, Asst Army

scribed the uranium project in detail. Intelligence headquarters in Germany noted the vast scale of the mining effort, the extensive security measures instituted by the Soviets, and the primitive conditions in the mines, which typically had no ventilation systems and generally were "considered unsafe to work." The division also learned that the Soviets did not process the ore in Germany but transported it straight to the USSR for this purpose. According to an interrogation account provided by British intelligence, one of the mines produced an average of 25 to 30 tons of uranium per day.[33]

Uranium from Germany played a crucial part in Moscow's atomic bomb project. According to Central Intelligence Agency estimates, 45 percent of Soviet uranium came from the *Erzgebirge*. In July 1948, the director of central intelligence, R. Adm. Roscoe H. Hillenkoetter, predicted that the Soviets would have a working nuclear weapon by the early 1950s.[34] The Soviets exceeded American expectations, detonating their first atomic bomb in September 1949.[35] The close monitoring of Soviet mining activities in Saxony by Army Intelligence confirmed to the Americans that Moscow had embarked on an accelerated project to develop the bomb, and that the United States would not have an atomic monopoly for much longer.

Political Control

As the war in Europe entered its final days, the Soviets flew a group of ten German Communist Party functionaries from Moscow to Berlin. Their leader, Walter Ulbricht, was a humorless apparatchik who had ensured his survival in Soviet exile through unquestioning obedience to Stalin. His affirmation of loyalty included a willingness to participate in Stalin's purges of fellow communists and to support the imprisonment or execution of those who did not toe the party line. Eventually, Stalin would reward Ulbricht for his fealty by making him the first prime minister of the German Democratic Republic in October 1949. But that prize lay several years in the future. On 30 April 1945, the Ulbricht group arrived

---

Attaché London, 4 Jan 1949, Folder "Top Secret Out Jan 1949 to 30 Jun 1949 Book III," EUCOM, Ofc of the Ch of Staff, Msg Control Center, Incoming Msgs, Top Secret Sec, 1948–1951, RG 549, NACP.

33 Msg, Lt. Col. M. C. Taylor, ODDI, EUCOM, to Director of Intel, War Department Gen Staff, 16 Apr 1947, sub: Status of Uranium Ore Mined in the Erzgebirge Area, Folder "926424," Rcds of the ACoS, G–2 (Intel), Formerly Top Secret Intel Documents, 1943–59, RG 319, NACP.

34 David Holloway, *Stalin and the Bomb: The Soviet Union and Atomic Energy, 1939–1956* (New Haven, CT: Yale University Press, 1994), 177, 220.

35 Michael S. Goodman, *Spying on the Nuclear Bear: Anglo-American Intelligence and the Soviet Bomb* (Stanford, CA: Stanford University Press, 2007), 36–37.

in the bombed-out German capital with the mission of reestablishing the KPD and securing Moscow's interests in the defeated country.[36]

Although the Soviets shrouded the arrival of the group in secrecy, American intelligence quickly discovered its existence. The Office of Strategic Services managed to contact a member of the group and reported on their activities to General Clay.[37] The American deputy military governor was greatly disturbed. In August 1945, he reported to the War Department that Ulbricht's group had reconstituted the KPD and was planning to establish a "bloc of anti-Fascist democratic parties" under communist guidance. Clay had few illusions about the independence of the noncommunist parties in this bloc. "Though little is yet known about individuals in control of these new Social Democrat, Liberal and Christian Democrat Parties," he noted, "it is presumed they were carefully selected on account of their willingness to cooperate in this bloc."[38] Clay's observations were right on the mark. As Ulbricht remarked to his followers: "It has to look democratic, but we have to control everything."[39]

The Americans had not yet licensed any political parties in their zone. By jumping the gun in establishing pseudo-democratic parties under communist tutelage in Berlin, Clay noted, the Soviets were hoping to "set the pattern for all of Germany."[40] The intelligence division at the Pentagon agreed with this assessment and put it into a larger context. "In Eastern Europe, Soviet-occupied countries have had communist dominated governments, which are loyal to Moscow, imposed on them," noted Col. Riley R. Ennis. "In Central Europe where there is joint occupation, the Soviets are striving to eventually set up a unified Germany oriented toward the East. . . . Control of Europe without control of a unified Germany is practically impossible."[41]

---

36 Wolfgang Leonhard, *Die Revolution entlässt ihre Kinder* [The revolution dismisses its children] (Cologne: Kiepenheur and Witsch, 1955), 297–98.
37 Rpt, OSS Mission for Germany, to Gen. Lucius D. Clay, Robert D. Murphy, Brig. Gen. G. Bryan Conrad, Brig. Gen. Edwin L. Sibert, [no first name] Anson, Gen Situation Rpt,1 Sep 1945, Folder "T.S. 103.9a Misc OSS Documents," Ofc of the U.S. Political Advisor for Germany, Berlin, Classified Rcds, 1945, 1947–49, RG 84, NACP.
38 Msg, Gen. Lucius D. Clay, U.S. Gp Control Council, to War Department, 8 Aug 1945, Folder "Germany E, UA, FWD, & CC Series 1945," ACoS, G–2 (Intel), "Top Secret" Incoming and Outgoing Cables, 1942–52, RG 319, NACP.
39 Leonhard, *Die Revolution*, 317.
40 Msg, Clay to War Department, 8 Aug 1945.
41 Memo, Col. R. F. Ennis for Ch, Strategic Plans Section, 27 Jun 1946, sub: Intelligence Estimate of the World Situation and its Military Implications for the United States, Folder "926152," Rcds of the ACoS, G–2 (Intel), Formerly Top Secret Intel Documents, 1943–59, RG 319, NACP. This was, in fact, one of the few instances when Clay acknowledged and concurred with the findings of his

The communists established political control in the Soviet Zone in several stages. Having corralled the newly founded social, Christian, and liberal democratic parties into a communist-dominated "Democratic Bloc" (Demokratischer Block) in April 1946, the KPD bullied the social democrats of the SPD to merge with them into a new party, the SED. Although the SPD had been the larger of the two organizations, communists loyal to Ulbricht pulled all the strings in the newly founded party. All groups had their headquarters in Germany's former capital and maintained that they were representing national interests.[42] For the intelligence division at the Pentagon, the KPD/SPD merger in particular had broader implications. The communists claimed that the merger agreement applied throughout Germany, which would give the new SED a powerful national platform.[43]

The consolidation of communist power in the Soviet Zone involved plenty of coercion. Following the elimination of the SPD, the Christian Democratic Union became the principal target of this heavy-handed approach. In August 1946, the Strategic Services Unit noted that it received numerous reports regarding complaints by CDU members about antagonistic behavior by the SED and its Soviet backers. In one instance, a local Soviet commander removed several politically undesirable members of a CDU delegation. In another, the Soviets threw a CDU member in jail for several hours and questioned him incessantly on his motivation for joining the party.[44] This type of harassment went all the way to the top. In 1947, the director of Moscow's propaganda department in Germany, Col. Sergei I. Tulpanov, berated Soviet Zone CDU chairman Jakob Kaiser in front of other officials about his poor liaison with the Soviets and his contacts with the West. "Speak frankly," Tulpanov told Kaiser, "we will not tell the Americans what you

---

intelligence agencies. More often, he ignored the implications of reports on Soviet oppression in their zone, and during the first two years of the occupation, he sought earnestly to cooperate with Moscow's representatives in creating a united, democratic Germany. Only in response to political directives from Washington did he adopt a more confrontational attitude in the spring of 1947. See Smith, *Clay*, 426.

42 Gerhard Keiderling, "Scheinpluralismus und Blockparteien: Die KPD und die Gründung der Parteien in Berlin 1945" [Sham pluralism and bloc parties: The KPD and the founding of the parties in Berlin, 1945], *Vierteljahrshefte für Zeitgeschichte* 46, no. 2 (Apr 1997): 257–96.

43 Rpt, Intel Div (G–2), 22 Apr 1946, Folder "G–2 Notes for General Council Meeting," Corresp, Rpts, Dirs, and Other Rcds Relating to the Activities and Functions of the Intel Gp, 1943–47, RG 165, NACP. In the event, the SPD, CDU, and liberal parties in the Western zones rejected subordination to the Berlin-based parties.

44 Memo, Strategic Services Unit, Intel Dissemination, 23 Aug 1946, sub: Progress of the CDU in the Russian Zone, reel 4, Strategic Services Unit Intel Rpts, 1945–1946, RG 226, NACP.

have said here." Tulpanov kept his word, but he did not reckon with Army Intelligence. Two weeks later, the CIC had received a transcript of the meeting.[45]

Soviet repression of noncommunist politicians translated into several high-level recruitment opportunities for U.S. intelligence, including two of the CDU's senior leaders. The first chairman of the Christian democrats in the Soviet Zone, Andreas Hermes, clashed repeatedly with the Soviet Military Administration. In late 1945, he moved to the town of Bad Godesberg, near Bonn in the British Zone. His successor, Jakob Kaiser, sought to work with the Soviets but refused to subordinate his party to the communists. In 1947, Colonel Tulpanov forced him to resign; the following year, Kaiser followed Hermes west. Sometime before their departure from the Soviet Zone, the Berlin station of the Strategic Services Unit managed to recruit both of them as informants. According to one intelligence officer, the two "courageous political-penetration agents" provided the U.S. military government with valuable insights into the practice of Soviet-communist rule in the East.[46]

By 1947, political opponents of the communist regime in the Soviet Zone were crossing the intrazonal borders in droves. In the summer, Col. Robert A. Schow of the European intelligence division instructed the European Command Intelligence Center to systematically interrogate "high level sources in the Soviet Zone of Germany concerning SED and KPD activities and intentions."[47] The operation, code-named Sulgrave, quickly yielded results.

In June 1947, the CIC in Berlin learned from a refugee that the minister-president of the Soviet Zone state of Thuringia, Dr. Rudolf Paul, had become deeply disenchanted with his communist overlords. The CIC sent a contact to Paul, inviting him to a secret rendezvous in the American sector of Berlin. Paul accepted and told his CIC interlocutors at their meeting in August that he wanted to defect to the U.S. Zone with his family. The CIC made the necessary arrangements, and in September Paul drove to the American sector in Berlin with his wife and children. The Americans immediately flew them to Frankfurt, where CIA officers interrogated and eventually released him. "I fled for the sake of Ger-

---

45 Memo, Special Agents Kiffin R. Hayes, Albert Holman, and Fred Schwarz, Region VIII, CIC, for CO, 10 Dec 1947, sub: Interview of Col. Tulpanow with Jacob Kaiser (CDU), Folder "XE 182078 Jacob Kaiser folder 2 of 2," INSCOM, IRR, Personal Name Files, RG 319, NACP.
46 Richard W. Cutler, *Counterspy: Memoirs of a Counterintelligence Officer in World War II and the Cold War* (Washington, DC: Brassey's, 2004), 133; David Alvarez and Eduard Mark, *Spying Through a Glass Darkly: American Espionage Against the Soviet Union, 1945–1946* (Lawrence: University Press of Kansas, 2016), 114.
47 Msg, Intel Div, EUCOM, to Intel Div, War Department, 9 Jul 1947, Folder "2. Fr: 'S' Germany 1000–4741 7-1-47–12-31-47," ACoS, G–2 (Intel), "Top Secret" Incoming and Outgoing Cables, 1942–52, RG 319, NACP.

many," he declared while in American custody.[48] Paul provided the Army and the CIA with numerous names and estimates of SED politicians, provided information on the activities of the illegal independent social democratic party in his state, and reported on Soviet efforts to centralize their zone. He also confirmed that even though Moscow had ended its official policy of dismantling German factories, the Soviets continued to do so in secret, much to the dismay of their German auxiliaries. Paul's defection delivered a serious propaganda blow to the Soviets and the SED.[49] When the dust settled, Paul put down roots in Frankfurt, becoming a successful lawyer.

As the fissures between East and West widened, the Soviets officially ended the policy of denazification and initiated an effort to win over Hitler's former adherents. During a visit of an SED delegation to Moscow in 1947, Stalin warned against "pushing all former Nazis to the enemy camp."[50] When one of the visiting German communists, Wilhelm Pieck, asked whether they should establish a party for "nominal Nazis," Stalin agreed and suggested a name for the proposed party: the National-Democratic Party of Germany (National-Demokratische Partei Deutschlands; NDPD). The resemblance of the new party's acronym to that of the dissolved Nazi Party—NSDAP, or Nationalsozialistische Deutsche Arbeiterpartei— was deliberate. Stalin went on to ask the Soviet official taking minutes of the meeting whether they could find a former regional Nazi leader in some prison to head the new party. When the official replied that all leading Nazis likely had been executed, Stalin expressed regret.[51] In March 1948, Colonel Tulpanov formally established the NDPD in the Soviet Zone. Firmly controlled by the SED, the new party sought to attract former Nazis and war veterans, a tactic meant to cut into the electoral support of the semi-independent liberals and Christian democrats.[52]

---

48 MFR, Maj. Joseph M. Stewart, HQ, Region VIII, CIC, 5 Sep 1947, sub: Evacuation of Dr. Rudolf Paul, Folder "Paul, Rudolf XE 186817," Digitized Rcds of the IRR, Intel and Investigative Dossiers, RG 319, NACP; Ltr, Carmel Offie to Robert D. Murphy, 29 Sep 1947, Folder "Top Secret – 1947 – Amb. Murphy's Correspondence," Germany, Ofc of the U.S. Political Adviser for Germany, Berlin, Top Secret Rcds, 1944–1949, RG 84, NACP.
49 Msg, Capt. Henry P. Schardt, HQ, 7707 EUCOM Intel Center, to Director of Intel, CINCEUR, 22 Sep 1947, sub: Interrogation Report of German Political Leader, Folder "Paul, Rudolf XE 186817," Digitized Rcds of the IRR, Intel and Investigative Dossiers, RG 319, NACP.
50 Zubok, *Failed Empire*, 70.
51 Zubok, *Failed Empire*, 71.
52 Gerhard Wettig, ed., *Der Tjul'panov-Bericht: Sowjetische Besatzungspolitik in Deutschland nach dem Zweiten Weltkrieg* [The Tjul'panov report: Soviet occupation policy in Germany after the Second World War] (Göttingen: V&R Unipress, 2012), 97; Leonhard, *Die Revolution*, 427–430. Colonel Tulpanov concurrently licensed another subservient political party, the German Farmers' Party (Deutsche Bauernpartei). Its structure and purpose resembled that of the NDPD.

Although the NDPD leadership remained loyal to the communist regime, many of the party's rank-and-file members were less committed to the Soviet cause. In the early 1950s, Soviet authorities executed several American spies embedded within the NDPD.[53] The Gehlen Organization and private anticommunist groups also recruited NDPD members for espionage operations in the Soviet Zone.[54] The new party may have served its purpose of marginalizing the noncommunist parties in East Germany, but it did not solve the Soviet problem of Western espionage resulting from anticommunist resentment.

The suppression and cooption of noncommunist parties went hand in hand with the establishment of an all-encompassing security apparatus. By 1949, Soviet security agencies employed roughly 10,000 personnel and had recruited more than 3,000 informants to spy on the local population.[55] The Soviet Military Administration set up a draconian justice system enforced by military tribunals and by a complex of internment camps (*Speziallager* or *Spezlager*, "special camps"), usually established on the sites of former concentration camps. The Soviet security forces had strict orders to deal harshly with would-be spies, saboteurs, and traitors: "Operations to accomplish a mission must be conducted with resolve and steadfastness," an instruction manual read. "This includes the use of service arms."[56]

Moscow's security apparatus exacted an enormous human toll. Between 1945 and 1950, the Soviets interned over 120,000 Germans, and the dreadful conditions in the *Spezlager* led to around 43,000 prisoner deaths. Offenders ended up in the camps for a wide range of "anti-Soviet" activities, but "spies, saboteurs, and terrorists" generally faced the stiffest sentences, including long prison terms and execution.[57] Of the 25,300 documented cases processed by Soviet military tribunals

---

53 Arsenij Roginskij, Jörg Rudolph, Frank Drauschke, and Anne Kaminsky. *"Erschossen in Moskau." Die deutschen Opfer des Stalinismus auf dem Moskauer Friedhof Donskoje 1950–1953* ["Shot in Moscow": The German victims of Stalinism in Moscow's Donskoye cemetery, 1950–1953] (Berlin: Metropol, 2005), 164, 257, 307.
54 Edward H. Cookridge, *Gehlen: Spy of the Century* (New York: Random House, 1971), 171; Enrico Heitzer, *Die Kampfgruppe gegen Unmenschlichkeit (KgU): Widerstand und Spionage im Kalten Krieg 1948–1959* [The Fighting Group Against Inhumanity (KgU): Resistance and espionage in the Cold War, 1948–1959] (Cologne: Böhlau Verlag, 2014), 276.
55 Jan Foitzkik and Tatjana W. Zarewskaja-Djakana, eds., *SMAD-Handbuch: Die Sowjetische Militäradministration in Deutschland 1945–1949* [SMAD-Handbook: The Soviet Military Administration in Germany, 1945–1949] (Munich: Oldenbourg, 2009), 71, 83; Jens Gieseke, *Die Stasi, 1945–1990* [The Stasi, 1945–1990] (Munich: DVA, 2011), 40.
56 Foitzik, *SMAD-Handbuch*, 80.
57 Foitzik, *SMAD-Handbuch*, 85.

between 1945 and 1955, 7,704 involved charges of espionage.⁵⁸ The Soviet emphasis on rooting out foreign spies raises the question of whether these efforts affected any Army Intelligence operations. Soviet court-martial records typically referred to a defendant as an agent of "the American secret service," without further specifications.⁵⁹ Often, such claims cannot be verified because no relevant Army Intelligence records have surfaced. In a few cases, however, it is possible to match Soviet documents with U.S. records, shedding some light on the capabilities of Soviet security.

Roger D. Michael served with the *Abwehr* as a military intelligence officer. In 1946, the Strategic Services Unit hired him as a spotter to identify former *Wehrmacht* officers as potential recruits for American intelligence.⁶⁰ In April 1948, Soviet authorities arrested Michael while he was visiting the Soviet sector of Berlin, possibly during an attempt to contact a fellow officer. In the ensuing trial, the Soviets charged him with espionage, although they inaccurately suspected him of having worked for the CIC, rather than the Strategic Services Unit. A military tribunal sentenced him to death, and a firing squad executed him in Moscow on 15 December 1950.⁶¹ Not every case was as straightforward as Michael's. In February 1947, Bavarian police arrested an illegal border crosser named Kurt Lerchner and handed him over to the CIC. Lerchner said Soviet intelligence had coerced him into becoming an informant but he wanted to help the Americans. Yet his confession cut no ice with his interrogator, Special Agent Marco S. Mancuso, who judged Lerchner "as being the type to work only for personal gain." Mancuso recommended that Lerchner be expelled to the Soviet Zone.⁶² As soon as the CIC had carried out Marcuso's recommendation, the Soviets arrested and interrogated Lerchner. Probably under torture, he "confessed" to having been "turned" by the Americans. In December 1947, a Soviet military court sentenced Lerchner to ten years of hard labor for espionage, and deported him as an "especially dangerous

---

58 Andreas Hilger, "Counter-Intelligence Soviet Style: The Activities of Soviet Security Services in East Germany, 1945–1955," *Journal of Intelligence History* 3, no. 1 (Summer 2003), 85–86.
59 See, for example, the case of Richard Bachmann, who was accused of spying for the Americans, sentenced to death, and executed in Moscow on 14 February 1952: Roginskij et al., *"Erschossen in Moskau,"* 106.
60 Msg, Capt. Nathan R. Preston, Third Army, 303d CIC Detachment, to HQ, CIC, USFET, 12 Aug 1946, Folder "Michael, Roger Daniel D048000," INSCOM, IRR, Digitized Name Files, RG 319, NACP.
61 Roginskij et al., *"Erschossen in Moskau,"* 265.
62 Memo, Special Agent Marco S. Mancuso, Region VI, CIC, for Ofcr in Charge, 17 Feb 1947, sub: Project 113/32, re. Lerchner, Kurt, Folder "Lerchner, Kurt XE 160600," INSCOM, IRR, Digitized Name Files, RG 319, NACP.

prisoner" to a prison camp in Siberia. There, he lingered until 1953, when an amnesty in the wake of Stalin's death allowed him to return to Germany.[63]

Lerchner had luck on his side, unlike many others caught by the Soviets. In April 1949, a *Wehrmacht* veteran named Heinz Domaschke offered his services to the CIC while serving time for theft in the Regensburg jail. Domaschke was a KPD member, but he told the CIC that he had joined the communist party solely in order to help the Americans penetrate the apparatus. Maj. William H. Daniels, who handled the case, remained skeptical. Domaschke "appeared very nervous during his interview," Daniels noted. He suspected the prisoner of either trying to enlist the Americans' help to get out of jail or being a Soviet agent seeking to penetrate the CIC. The Corps turned him down and warned other agencies to stay clear of the would-be spy.[64] But Domaschke had not given up on the idea of becoming an American spy. Following his release from prison, he settled in the Soviet Zone and contacted the CIC in Berlin. In 1950, East German security arrested him and found in his possession material that indicated he had gathered information on Soviet forces on behalf of the CIC.[65] The East Germans turned him over to the Soviets, who charged him with espionage and sentenced him to death. A firing squad executed Domaschke in Moscow on 29 May 1951.[66]

Espionage is often a murky business. Even though some official records are available, some cases leave observers with more questions than answers. On 26 August 1948, the official SED newspaper *Neues Deutschland* reported the shooting of a "CIC spy" at the U.S.-Soviet zonal border in Thuringia. Erich Lotz, the paper elaborated, had illegally tried to cross the border into Bavaria. When East German border police attempted to stop him, he fled. Police officers shot him through the stomach, but the "American spy" made it across the border and called for help. Although Bavarian police transferred him to a hospital in Coburg, the wound was fatal, and he died shortly thereafter. Before passing away, however, Lotz told his rescuers that he worked under a cover name, and that his real

---

63 Hilger, "Counter-Intelligence Soviet Style," 92–94. The information on "Kurt L." derives from Soviet documents at the Hannah Arendt Institute for Research on Totalitarianism (Hannah-Arendt-Institut für Totalitarismusforschung; HAIT) in Dresden. Professor Mike Schmeitzner of the HAIT confirmed Lerchner's identity: Email, Mike Schmeitzner to Thomas Boghardt, 30 Jan 2019, Historians Files, CMH.
64 Msg, Maj. William R. Daniels, Region V, CIC, to 7970 CIC Detachment, 30 Aug 1949, sub: Domaschke, Heinz, Folder "Domaschke, Heinz D264570," INSCOM, IRR, Digitized Name Files, RG 319, NACP.
65 Rpt, MfS, Dienststelle Sachsen, Abt. V, Gruppenvorgang 53/50, Sachstandsbericht, Dresden [Saxony Ofc, Dept. V, Gp Process 53/50, Assessment Rpt], 14 Dec 1950, sub: Domaschke, Heinz, MfS BV Dresden AOP 47/52, BStU, Berlin.
66 Roginskij et al., *"Erschossen in Moskau,"* 139.

name was Georg Savieczes. In conclusion, the article noted that Lotz had been on a "top secret" courier mission delivering sensitive intelligence information from the Soviet Zone to the West. He was, the paper asserted, only "one of many" American secret agents engaged in espionage operations against the East.[67]

The reality of the case was more complicated than *Neues Deutschland* suggested to its readers. In response to the allegations of the Soviet Zone press, CIC headquarters in Germany opened an internal investigation, which indicated that Lotz had never worked for the Corps.[68] The investigating special agent, Holmes W. Lemon, commented that a local communist functionary named Wilhelm Hamann had strenuously asserted that Lotz had been "a spy for CIC." According to Hamann, the KPD had informed their comrades in the East about the activities of the alleged secret agent. Lemon concluded that Hamann "is in some way mixed up in the affair" and suggested that further inquiries be made to get to the bottom of the case.[69] Yet these efforts petered out without resolving Lotz's involvement in the world of intelligence.

Even with this small sample size, the cases of Michael, Lerchner, Domaschke, and Lotz suggest that the Soviets caught numerous bona fide American agents while interpreting the term "American spy" very broadly. In the late 1940s and early 1950s, any contact with an American intelligence agency could be a death sentence. Yet if the intent of Moscow's draconian security apparatus was to deter would-be spies, it seems to have failed. Soviet Zone citizens continued to volunteer their services to Army Intelligence agencies through the late 1940s and beyond.

As they consolidated their authority over the territories they administered, the Soviets set up local organizations to support their security and political efforts. Very few of these labors eluded the prying eyes of Army Intelligence. In 1945, the Soviet Military Administration created a central police force, which became known as the Volkspolizei (People's Police). Its units used the World War II–era Enigma machine for encrypted communications. The Allies had broken the Enigma encryption during the war, but the British and the Americans had kept

---

67 "CIC-Spion erschossen" [CIC spy shot], *Neues Deutschland*, 27 Aug 1948.
68 Msg, Special Agent Peter A. Petito, Region III, CIC, to CO, 7970th CIC Grp, 7 Sep 1948, sub: Erich Lotz alias Georg Saviczes, Folder "Lotz, Erich D247027," INSCOM, IRR, Digital Name Files, RG 319, NACP.
69 Msg, Special Agent Holmes W. Lemon, 7970th CIC Gp, to CO, 7 Sep 1948, sub: Erich Lotz alias Georg Saviczes, Folder "Lotz, Erich D247027," INSCOM, IRR, Digital Name Files, RG 319, NACP. The CIC had arrested Hamann in September 1946 for allegedly mistreating fellow inmates at Buchenwald concentration camp under the Nazis. See Lutz Niethammer, ed., *Der 'gesäuberte' Antifaschismus. Die SED und die roten Kapos von Buchenwald* ["Cleansed" antifascism: The SED and the red Kapos of Buchenwald] (Berlin: Akademie-Verlag, 1994), 72.

this success a secret from the Soviets. When the new eastern German police force fell back on the old wartime technology, the Western Allies could monitor police traffic from the Soviet Zone.[70]

In August 1947, the Soviet Military Administration created a secret political police force. Designated as the fifth section of the East German police (K–5), the new organization reported directly to the Soviets. Ostensibly set up to enforce denazification, K–5 focused primarily on the illegal activities of the SPD in the Soviet Zone. Within less than a year, Army Intelligence had procured detailed information about the structure and operations of K–5, obtained mainly from the interrogation of East German officials who had fled to the U.S. Zone.[71] A military government intelligence officer described the organization as "nothing more nor less than the ill-reputed Gestapo of the Nazi period, except that K–5 is under the authority of [the] Soviet Intelligence Service."[72]

Army Intelligence agencies needed even less time to uncover the creation of a paramilitary police force in the Soviet Zone. On 14 May 1948, Colonel Tulpanov instructed leading SED officials to arm and organize 10,000 police officers in barracks for the purpose of fighting "bandits."[73] Less than a month later, the CIC and the CIA picked up the first rumors "plus some substantiated information" about the conscription of German civilians for military service in the Soviet Zone.[74] Reports from deserters allowed the intelligence center in Oberursel in late 1948 to produce an accurate description of the new force, which became known as Barracked People's Police (Kasernierte Volkspolizei; KVP).[75] For the time being, U.S.

---

70 Thomas Boghardt, "Semper Vigilis: The Army Security Agency in Early Cold War Germany," *Army History* 106 (Winter 2018), 21.
71 Msg, Col. Roy M. Thoroughman, 7707 EUCOM Intel Center, to ODI, 7 Oct 1948, sub: Political Police (K–5) and Soviet Control of Justice Officials in the Soviet Zone of Germany, Folder "21c Public Safety (Soviet Zone)," ODI, Excerpts of Miscellaneous Rpts and Publications, Analysis and Research Br, 1947–48, RG 260, NACP.
72 Msg, Lt. Col. William M. Slayden, Ch, Research and Analysis Br, Intel Div, EUCOM, to ODI, 31 Aug 1948, sub: Organization of the Political Police in the Soviet Zone, Folder "21c Public Safety (Soviet Zone)," ODI, Excerpts of Miscellaneous Rpts and Publications, Analysis and Research Br, 1947–48, RG 260, NACP.
73 Torsten Diedrich and Rüdiger Wenzke, *Die getarnte Armee. Geschichte der Kasernierten Volkspolizei der DDR 1952–1956* [The camouflaged army: History of the Barracked People's Police of the GDR] (Berlin: Ch. Links Verlag, 2003), 24.
74 Msg, Lt. Gen. Clarence R. Huebner, EUCOM, to Director of Intel, Pentagon, 21 Jun 1947, Folder "Germany," Rcds of the Chairman, White House Rcds of Fleet Admiral William D. Leahy, 1942–1948, RG 218, NACP.
75 Msg, Col. Roy M. Thoroughman, 7707 ECIC, to ODI, 16 Dec 1948, sub: Recruiting of Members of the Police Force in the Soviet Zone of Germany, Folder "21c Public Safety (Soviet Zone)," Rcds of Functional Ofcs and Div, ODI, Excerpts of Miscellaneous Rpts and Publications, Analysis and Re-

intelligence assessed the KVP's fighting capability as subpar. Disciplinary problems and low morale, the CIA noted in May 1949, suggested that the reliability of the armed police "would be doubtful in the event of a complete Soviet troop withdrawal."[76]

Throughout the late 1940s, Army Intelligence reporting on Soviet policy in Germany suggested that Stalin was pursuing a flexible dual-track strategy. On the one hand, the Soviets created subservient political parties and a powerful security apparatus in their zone, indicating long-term designs on German territory under control of the Red Army. On the other hand, Stalin sought to project Soviet power into the Western zones through German organizations headquartered in Berlin. If he accomplished the latter, the intelligence division at the Pentagon warned, "all of Germany will tend to be increasingly under Soviet-sponsored political influence, to the detriment of Western democratic principles."[77] Although Moscow's strategy appeared muddled and opportunistic at times, and Stalin repeatedly adjusted his diplomacy to circumstances, Army Intelligence accurately captured the essence of Soviet policy in Germany: extending Moscow's influence as far west as possible.[78]

The SPD Ostbüro

As the SPD in the Soviet Zone came under siege, in early 1946 SPD leader Kurt Schumacher established an Ostbüro (Eastern Bureau) in Hanover to assist political refugees seeking to escape from communist oppression. Under the leadership of Siegmund "Siggi" Neumann and Stephan Grzeskowiak (cover name Stephan Thomas), the bureau established contact with disgruntled social democrats across the Soviet Zone to challenge communist rule.[79] In early 1948, the intelligence division in Heidelberg estimated the strength of SPD resistance groups in the Soviet Zone at 10,000.[80] The Ostbüro's access to such a large number of politically moti-

---

search Br, 1947–48, RG 260, NACP. The KVP would become the precursor to the National People's Army (Nationale Volksarmee), the East German military.

76 Rpt, CIA to Director of Intel, 26 May 1949, National Security Archive, https://nsarchive.gwu.edu.
77 Rpt, G–2 Div, 22 Apr 1946, Folder "G–2 Notes for General Council Meeting," Corresp, Rpts, Dirs and Other Rcds Relating to the Activities and Functions of the Intel Gp, 1943–47, RG 165, NACP.
78 Naimark, *Russians in Germany*, 355; see also Wettig, *Tjul'panov Bericht*, 43.
79 Wolfgang Buschfort, *Das Ostbüro der SPD. Von der Gründung der SPD bis zur Berlin-Krise* [The Ostbüro of the SPD: From the founding of the SPD to the Berlin crisis] (Munich: R. Oldenbourg Verlag, 1991), 7, 22.
80 Rpt, ODDI, EUCOM, 25 Mar 1948, sub: Resistance Movement of the Social Democratic Party (SPD) in the Soviet Zone, Folder "925983," Rcds of the ACoS, G–2 (Intel), Formerly Top Secret Intel Documents, 1943–59, RG 319, NACP.

vated individuals opposed to the Soviet-sanctioned political order made the organization an attractive partner for Western intelligence agencies.

Given the Ostbüro's headquarters location in the British Zone and the close relationship between social democrats and local occupation authorities, British intelligence made first contact with this potential wellspring of information.[81] The SPD politician Fritz Heine appears to have been one of the first liaisons between the two sides. Heine, who had plotted against the Nazis during the war, fled to London in 1941. According to a note in Heine's CIC file, British intelligence began collaborating with him during this time.[82] In 1946, he returned to Germany and helped rebuild the SPD. In Hanover, Schumacher put him in charge of managing the western party's relationship with the Ostbüro.

The Americans soon followed the British. The communist takeover of the Soviet Zone SPD in April 1946 resulted in the inclusion of a larger number of disaffected social democrats in the new party. Inadvertently, therefore, the merger opened a window into the new party for U.S. intelligence. In June, a local SED boss and former social democrat reported to the Strategic Services Unit that the new party "has a spy system which reports regularly on the activity and statements of all Social Democrats who still hold any posts at all in the SED."[83] A few months later, "reliable sources both within and outside the SED" reported widespread arrests and harassment of former social democrats across the Soviet Zone.[84]

In 1947, the SPD leadership in Hanover decided to open an Ostbüro branch in Berlin to facilitate contact with social democrats in the Soviet Zone. American intelligence had a strong presence in the city, and this move paved the way for a closer, broader relationship between the two sides. The freshly minted director of Radio in the American Sector and former chief of the Berlin intelligence division, William F. Heimlich, eagerly agreed to help find a suitable headquarters building in the city for Siggi Neumann's group. In May 1948, the Ostbüro moved into a comfortable villa deep in the American sector, on Hammersteinstrasse 14a.[85]

---

81 Buschfort, *Ostbüro*, 57.
82 Index Card, "Name: Heine, Fritz", 12 Oct 1949, Folder "XE 598354 Heine, Fritz," INSCOM, IRR, Digitized Name Files, RG 319, NACP.
83 Memo, Strategic Services Unit, Intel Dissemination, 16 Aug 1946, sub: Political Spying System, reel 3, M1656, Strategic Services Unit Intel Rpts, 1945–1946, RG 226, NACP.
84 Memo, Strategic Services Unit, Intel Dissemination, 28 Aug 1946, sub: Arrests of Social Democrats; Corruption in SED, reel 4, M1656, Strategic Services Unit Intel Rpts, 1945–1946, RG 226, NACP.
85 Buschfort, *Ostbüro*, 35, 67.

Over time, Heimlich developed close ties with several bureau representatives who provided him with information from the Soviet Zone.[86]

Both the CIA and the CIC in Berlin recognized the Ostbüro's intelligence value. Siegfried Höxter, a German-Jewish émigré and former OSS officer, served as the right-hand man of the deputy chief of the CIA's Berlin station, Peter M. F. Sichel, in the recruitment of and liaison with eastern and western SPD circles.[87] Sichel's boss, Dana B. Durand, wrote glowingly about the bureau's intelligence potential.[88] Special Agent Theodor Hans of CIC Region VIII (Berlin) noted that the bureau "was one of the most popular and efficient private and political intelligence and resistance organizations" in the Soviet Zone.[89] The agency and the Corps avidly cultivated Ostbüro members as informants and liaisons.

When Grzeskowiak arrived in Berlin in early 1948 to establish a local Ostbüro branch, he stayed at the house of Willy Brandt, the lieutenant of the city's powerful SPD party boss, Ernst Reuter. Although Siggi Neumann had warned Thomas against involving the gregarious Brandt in the bureau's secretive affairs, the two men hit it off, and Thomas revealed his mission to his host. In due course, Brandt became a key player in the bureau's Berlin business. His house served as a central clearing station for agents and couriers arriving from the Soviet Zone before proceeding to the Ostbüro's office.[90] Because the CIC had recruited Brandt as an informant the previous year, his familiarity with the bureau's sources in the east proved to be a gold mine for American intelligence.[91]

Brandt regularly provided U.S. intelligence with information obtained from Ostbüro sources. Between 7 January 1949 and 3 November 1953, he made contact with his CIC handlers more than two hundred times, relaying roughly the same

---

86 Interv, Brewster Chamberlin with William F. Heimlich, former G–2 Ch, Berlin, 4 and 6 August 1981, 85, Landesarchiv Berlin.
87 Interv, Thomas Boghardt with Peter M. F. Sichel, 7 Mar 2018, Historians Files, CMH; Memo, Robert E. Hallowell, CIC Investigator, Region II, CIC, for Subregional Ch, 8 Aug 1946, sub: Background of 1st Lt. Hoexter, Siegfried, Folder "Hoexter, Siegfried D 219424," INSCOM, IRR, Digitized Name Files.
88 David E. Murphy, Sergei A. Kondrashev, and George Bailey, *Battleground Berlin: CIA vs. KGB in the Cold War* (New Haven, CT: Yale University Press, 1997), 112; Rpt, Dana B. Durand, Ch, BOB, to Ch, Foreign Br M, 8 Apr 1948, sub: Transmittal of Report on Berlin Operations Base, in *On the Front Lines of the Cold War: Documents on the Intelligence War in Berlin, 1946 to 1961*, ed. Donald P. Steury (Washington, DC: Center for the Study of Intelligence, 1999), 25.
89 Testimony, Theodor Hans, *Soviet Terrorism in Germany, Hearing Before the Subcommittee to Investigate the Administration of the Internal Security Act and Other Internal Security Laws of the Committee on the Judiciary, United States Senate*, 86th Cong., 2nd sess., 21 Sep 1960, 18.
90 Buschfort, *Ostbüro*, 67.
91 For more on Brandt and the SPD's work in the Soviet Zone, see Chapter 8.

number of reports. The two sides met at Brandt's house, in his car, or in a CIC safe house. Initially, the Americans paid Brandt in goods, such as cigarettes, coffee, sugar, canned fish, and candy bars. Once the postwar German economy stabilized, the remuneration changed to the new deutsche mark. Typically, Brandt received DM 50 to DM 100 per meeting, but his compensation also included one payment of DM 500 and two of DM 1,000. Brandt used some of the money to cover his expenses, such as gas, office supplies, and photographic equipment.[92] However, he rejected payment for his work as an informant; the extra money probably went to the agents with whom he worked, rather than into his own pocket.[93]

The reports submitted by Brandt covered a wide range of topics. They included the FDJ, the SED, railroads, industrial plants, shipyards, various police units, population statistics, and telephone equipment for the Red Army. He also provided a list of the inmates of the notorious Bautzen prison in Saxony, where the Soviets held political prisoners. On one occasion, Brandt introduced his handler personally to a "possible source on [East German] govt and police."[94] The CIC shared some of the information obtained from Brandt with the 7880th Military Intelligence Detachment and the CIA. Occasionally, other agencies requested and paid for specific intelligence. In October 1951, for instance, the CIA asked for a complete survey of machinery in the German Democratic Republic.[95]

The Ostbüro did not limit its activities to information-gathering operations. In the winter of 1947–1948, a one-time American informant named Hahn fabricated a document, supposedly from communist agitators, calling for a strike among German workers in the coal-rich Ruhr Valley. The ostensible goal of the document, which came to be known as "Protocol M," was to disrupt Marshall Plan aid to Western Europe. Hoping to mobilize the public against communist opposition to the Marshall Plan, Hahn shared his forgery with a man named Kielgast, an SPD Ostbüro associate and British informant. Kielgast, in turn, provided the document to the British as well as to a Berlin newspaper, *Der Kurier*, which published it on 14 January 1948.[96]

---

92 Informant Control Sheets, O-35-VIII, Jan 1949–Nov 1953, Folder "Brandt, Willy XE248037V2," INSCOM, IRR, Digitized Name Files, RG 319, NACP.
93 Rpt, Special Agent George D. Swerdlin, Region VIII, CIC, 27 Oct 1948, sub: Brandt, Willy @ Frahm, Willy, Folder "Brandt, Willy XE248037," INSCOM, IRR, Digitized Name Files, RG 319, NACP.
94 Informant Control Sheet, O-35-VIII, Apr 1950, Folder "Brandt, Willy XE248037V2," INSCOM, IRR, Digitized Name Files, RG 319, NACP.
95 Informant Control Sheet, O-35-VIII, 31 Oct 1951, Folder "Brandt, Willy XE248037V2," INSCOM, IRR, Digitized Name Files, RG 319, NACP.
96 Simon Ollivant, "Protocol 'M,'" in *Deception Operations: Studies in the East-West Conflict*, ed. David A. Charters and Maurice A. J. Tugwell (London: Brassey's, 1990), 276, 284.

At this time, the British eagerly awaited U.S. economic aid, but the Marshall Plan was still undergoing ratification in the U.S. Senate. Highlighting the communist peril, Protocol M promised to galvanize public opinion on this issue and therefore fit neatly into London's political agenda.[97] Eager to get the story out, the Foreign Office quickly endorsed the document rather than seeking to verify its reliability. In short order, major British and American newspapers picked up on the supposed communist conspiracy. On 16 January, the *New York Times* featured the story on page one under the dramatic headline: "Wide Ruhr Strikes Threatened Today in Crisis over Food . . . London Says 'Protocol M', Plot to Sabotage Marshall Plan in Germany, Is Authentic."[98]

Others were not so sure that a communist plot was afoot. Large segments of the German and the British press remained skeptical about the document's authenticity while communist newspapers immediately denounced it as a "lie."[99] The CIC started its own investigation, and in early February it informed the intelligence division in Heidelberg that the document originated with an unnamed anticommunist agent provocateur who sought to turn public opinion against communism.[100] The CIA Berlin station chief noted "its rapid distribution in SPD circles," implicating the "the so-called Ostsekretariat [Eastern Secretariat, i.e., Ostbüro]" as the originator.[101] Although CIC and CIA investigations pointed in the direction of the Ostbüro as the source of Protocol M, military government officials did not act on their reports. The story was already out; they might have felt it would be better to let it run its course.

In London, however, the government faced persistent questions from the press and in Parliament about the document's provenance. In April, the British reluctantly confirmed that Protocol M was a forgery, leading the *New York Times* to comment that British intelligence had been "hoodwinked."[102] The communist press had a field day. "All honest people in Germany should realize," *Neues Deutschland* lectured its readers, "that no means is sufficiently evil not to be used by the enemies of peace and progress in order to push our people anew into self-destruction and therefore into catastrophe."[103] In subsequent articles, the paper cast blame on the

---

97 Steill, *Marshall Plan*, 230.
98 Jack Raymond, "Wide Ruhr Strikes Threatened Today in Crisis over Food," *New York Times*, 16 Jan 1948.
99 "Noch ein 'Angriffsplan'" [Another "plan of attack"], *Neues Deutschland*, 16 Jan 1948.
100 Msg, Intel Div, EUCOM, to Intel Div, Pentagon, 4 Feb 1948, ACoS, G–2 (Intel), "Top Secret" Incoming and Outgoing Cables, 1942–52, RG 319, NACP.
101 Rpt, Durand to Ch, Foreign Br M, 8 Apr 1948, sub: Transmittal of Report on Berlin Operations Base, in Steury, *On the Front Lines of the Cold War*, 25.
102 C. L. Sulzberger, "British Declare 'Protocol M' Fake; Red 'Plot' in Ruhr Ruse by German," *New York Times*, 11 Apr 1948.
103 "Wer hat gelogen?" [Who lied?], *Neues Deutschland*, 13 Apr 1948.

"Wir zehrten damals von den gleichen Versprechen, nur, daß sie es nicht Marshall-Plan nannten."

Figure 40: Soviet propaganda against the Marshall Plan: "Back then, we relied on the same promises, the only difference being that they didn't call it the Marshall Plan!" From the Soviet Zone newspaper *Tägliche Rundschau*, 15 November 1947. *Tägliche Rundschau*.

social democrats and identified the SPD liaison official with the Ostbüro, Fritz Heine, as the mastermind behind Protocol M.[104] Heine's role in this deception operation remains unclear, but the bureau's responsibility was undeniable. Fortunately for the U.S. and British governments, the affair blew over quickly amid the deepening crisis between the Soviets and the West. For Army Intelligence, Protocol M served as a reminder of the risks involved in dealing with a clandestine organization that operated outside the American military government structure.

These risks became even more apparent in the dealings with Ostbüro informants. In late summer 1948, the bureau identified two prospective sources to the CIC, Walter Willfahrt and Alfred Lippschütz. The CIA noted that Willy Brandt had recommended both men, but according to a CIC report, someone else had introduced Willfahrt to the Corps.[105] Lippschütz worked for the Soviet Zone paramilitary po-

---

104 "Das Geheimnis ist gelüftet" [The secret is out], *Neues Deutschland*, 25 Apr 1948.
105 Special Agent George Swerdlin stated that he had been introduced to Willfahrt by one Otto Lange on 27 August 1948: Rpt, Special Agent George D. Swerdlin, Region VIII, CIC, 17 Sep 1948,

lice, and Willfahrt had joined the communications department of the German administration of the interior in East Berlin. Special Agent George D. Swerdlin, who vetted Willfahrt, noted approvingly that "subject appears to be completely honest and frank" and had access to confidential teletype messages of "a major Counter Intelligence target, the German Administration of the Interior."[106] The CIC recruited both as informants.

Only a few months later, in December 1948, Soviet Zone authorities arrested the two men. A Soviet military tribunal sentenced Lippschütz to twenty-five years of hard labor in Siberia. He returned to Berlin following an amnesty in 1956.[107] Presumably, Willfahrt suffered a similar fate. In a postmortem analysis of the case, the CIC identified the problem as "severe indiscretion and total lack of security consciousness on the part of Willfahrt and Lippschütz, plus a very sloppy handling + complex tangle of sub. sources of Region VIII, namely O-35-VIII" and several others. "O-35-VIII" was, of course, Willy Brandt's code name.[108] The communist press subsequently claimed that Brandt had joined the Ostbüro as "an agent of the American secret service."[109] Fortunately for Brandt and the CIC, this outing gained little traction in the West, as the Soviet-controlled press routinely branded anybody opposed to Moscow as an American agent.

The loose handling of agents and couriers, and the failure to keep informants unaware of each other, remained the Ostbüro's Achilles' heel. One Ostbüro member suffered a particularly grim fate because of the organization's lax internal security. Either with the help of a defector or through an inside source, Soviet intelligence found out about Heinz Kühne, who oversaw the bureau's courier network. In February 1949, the Soviets lured him to a house near the Soviet sector under the pretense of an informant wanting to meet with him. Willy Brandt, who was friends with Kühne, lent him his driver and car to get to the rendezvous. As the driver was waiting outside, he suddenly heard screams, then saw several shadowy figures disappear in the dark. The police, who arrived at the scene fifteen minutes later, found several empty vodka bottles, traces of blood, a syringe, and a sock and shoe belonging to Kühne. The Soviets had drugged and kidnapped one of the key members of the Ostbüro.[110]

---

sub: Willfahrt, Walter, Folder "Willfahrt, Walter D247949," INSCOM, IRR, Digitized Name Files, RG 319, NACP.
106 Rpt, Swerdlin, 17 Sep 1948, sub: Willfahrt, Walter. Emphasis in original.
107 "Der Spitzbart muss weg" [The goatee has to go], *Der Tagesspiegel*, 3 Feb 2009.
108 MFR, [T. C.] Hughes, Dec 1949, Folder "Willfahrt, Walter D247949," INSCOM, IRR, Digitized Name Files, RG 319, NACP.
109 "Geheimagent und Kriegshetzer" [Secret agent and warmonger], *Neues Deutschland*, 4 May 1954.
110 Peter Merseburger, *Willy Brandt, 1913–1992: Visionär und Realist* [Willy Brandt, 1913–1992: Visionary and realist] (Stuttgart, Munich: Deutsche Verlags-Anstalt, 2002), 290–92; Buschfort, *Ostbüro*, 40–44.

In East Berlin, his captors tortured Kühne. CIC Special Agent Theodor Hans, who served in Berlin at the time of the kidnapping, testified to Congress that the Soviets preferred

> the so-called water treatment, which consists either of flooding the cell gradually with cold water until the prisoner has to stretch to keep his head above the water level, or dousing the victim alternatingly with ice cold and very hot water for extended periods. The Soviets very often used the rather simple but just as brutal method of forcing the accused to stand for days in knee deep water or submerged up to his hips so that he could not rest or change his position, besides becoming violently ill from exposure, the highly unsanitary conditions—not being permitted to leave the confinement for days—and the further lack of proper nourishment.[111]

Hans noted that the victims of "such torture do not require drugging or stimulation through drugs to induce confessions."[112]

Indeed, Kühne's brutal treatment yielded a rich intelligence harvest. In April 1949, *Neues Deutschland* published an "open letter" from Kühne to the SPD leadership.[113] Presumably, the Soviets had dictated the text to him. In it, the author alleged that he had defected voluntarily, and he disclosed the names of numerous Ostbüro members, including Fritz Heine, Siggi Neumann, and Stephan Grzeskowiak. The letter also named Willy Brandt as a spy for the Norwegian military mission. The Soviets evidently had gained a thorough understanding of the bureau's informant network because the names of Willfahrt, Lippschütz, and several more actual or suspected agents appeared in the text as well. The letter identified another Ostbüro member, Ernst Moewes, as a CIC informant. In fact, the CIC had recruited Moewes in February 1948 and was forced to drop him because of Kühne's confession.[114] The letter further stated that a certain "Oberst [i.e., Colonel] Thomsen" of the CIC was Moewes's handler. "Thomson" or "Thompson" was the alias of CIC Special Agent Severin F. Wallach, who wisely had chosen not to use his real name when working with local informants.

Kühne's fate remains unknown, but his disclosures wreaked havoc with the Ostbüro. According to Special Agent Hans, "the loss of many good sources and contacts through [Kühne], and the drop in prestige were so damaging to the SPD 'Ost-Buero' that for many years the organization did not regain its former signifi-

---

111 Testimony, Hans, *Soviet Terrorism in Germany*, 21 Sep 1960, 24.
112 Testimony, Hans, *Soviet Terrorism in Germany*, 21 Sep 1960, 24.
113 "Die Spionagetätigkeit des 'Ostbüros' der SPD" [The espionage activities of the "Ostbüros" of the SPD], *Neues Deutschland*, 10 Apr 1949.
114 Msg, Maj. Earl S. Browning Jr., 7970 CIC Gp, to CO, Region VIII, CIC, 20 Jul 1949, sub: Moewes, Ernst Carl Julius, Folder "Moewes, Ernst C. J. XE252833," INSCOM, IRR, Digitized Name Files, RG 319, NACP; Msg, Maj. George L. Wilson, 66th CIC Detachment, to CO, 6 Dec 1949, sub: Moewes, Ernst Carl Julius, Folder "Moewes, Ernst C. J. XE252833," INSCOM, IRR, Digitized Name Files, RG 319, NACP.

cance."[115] Kühne's revelations were a severe blow, but for U.S. intelligence, the bureau was too good a source to lose. Both the CIA and CIC expanded their cooperation with the organization in the early 1950s. By this time, the CDU and Free Democratic Party had established Ostbüros of their own, and Army Intelligence reached out to these organizations as well.[116] The operations of political opponents of the SED regime remained vulnerable to penetration and exposure; nevertheless, they continued to provide the Americans with a valuable source of intelligence on conditions behind the Iron Curtain.

The Red Army

The Group of Soviet Occupation Forces in Germany emerged as the principal target of Army Intelligence operations in central Europe. Early collection efforts were not driven principally by Cold War concerns but rather by the fact that the Soviet occupation forces represented the most potent military presence in Europe and the largest concentration of Red Army units outside the Soviet Union. The U.S. Army naturally would want to learn more about this mighty yet obscure entity with which it had to coexist in occupied Germany. As early as September 1945, General Sibert noted in a message to the War Department: "Need for strong Russian Intelligence Section here is obvious."[117]

The intelligence divisions in Europe and Washington began collection efforts separately within a few weeks of the end of the war. Drawing on information provided by Supreme Allied Headquarters, General Bissell's analysts at the Pentagon produced an "intelligence research project" on "developments in Soviet-Occupied Germany and Austria" in June 1945. On the Red Army, the document remained vague. Without giving specific numbers, it noted merely that "redeployment of Soviet forces to the east has begun, but it is not believed to be indicative of large-scale demobilization of the Red Army as a whole."[118]

---

115 Testimony, Hans, *Soviet Terrorism in Germany*, 21 Sep 1960, 18.
116 Wolfgang Buschfort, *Parteien im Kalten Krieg. Die Ostbüros von SPD, CDU and FDP* [Parties in the Cold War: The Ostbüros of the SPD, CDU, and FDP] (Berlin: Ch. Links Verlag, 2000), 42.
117 Msg, Brig. Gen. Edwin L. Sibert to War Department, 19 Sep 1945, Folder "From Germany S-20405 thru S-39481," ACoS, G–2 (Intel), "Top Secret" Incoming and Outgoing Cables, 1942–52, RG 319, NACP.
118 Rpt, Mil Intel Service, Intel Research Project no. 2157-A, 13 Jun 1945, sub: "Developments in Soviet-Occupied Germany and Austria," Rcds of the ACoS, G–2 (Intel), Formerly Top Secret Intel Documents, 1943–59, RG 319, NACP.

As the top intelligence officer in the European Theater, General Sibert stood in a better position than Bissell to collect information on the Red Army. In May 1945, Lt. Col. James O. Boswell, an intelligence officer of the 90th Infantry Division, submitted a report to Sibert's office while on a trip from Czechoslovakia to Austria, ending in Vienna. Boswell described in detail the Soviet units he had encountered along the way and described the dreadful conditions of the civilian population. In Vienna, he wrote, 150,000 cases of rape had been reported. When civilians recognized the small American flag on his vehicle, Boswell wrote, they often asked, "When are the Americans coming?" Others complained that "it was better under the Nazis than it is now." Sibert submitted Boswell's report to Supreme Allied Headquarters and to Bissell's office.[119]

Figure 41: A U.S. Army Signal Corps photograph of a Red Army convoy on the autobahn near Weimar in July 1945. U.S. Army, NACP.

---

[119] Msg, Brig. Gen. Edwin L. Sibert, ACofS, G–2, 12th Army Gp, to SHAEF, ACofS, G–2, 20 Jun 1945, sub: Russian Armed Forces, Annex no. 2, Folder "925229," Rcds of the ACoS, G–2 (Intel), Formerly Top Secret Intel Documents, 1943–59, RG 319, NACP.

A month later, Sibert's office produced an order of battle report on the Soviet forces in central Europe. Based on "bits and pieces regarding Russian dispositions and movements," the report drew primarily on the findings of intelligence officers of the American Third Army and Ninth Army and the British 21st Army Group, who all passed on their observations about Soviet units located opposite their own. The report identified numerous Red Army units in Germany, Austria, and Czechoslovakia, and noted that the Soviets were reorganizing their forces for occupation duty.[120]

Berlin provided the perfect platform for the collection of intelligence on the Red Army. As soon as the Army assumed control of the American sector in July 1945, Soviet defectors began crossing the intersectoral border and surrendered to the Americans. The intelligence division of the Berlin District interrogated them for order of battle information and sent particularly valuable interviewees to the intelligence center in Oberursel.[121] Moreover, given the location of the city deep inside the Soviet Zone, Army Intelligence officers found it easy to conduct reconnaissance trips during the early months of the occupation. In September 1945, for example, General Sibert forwarded order of battle information collected by an officer on a trip near Potsdam. The officer, Sibert informed the War Department, "has this dope [i.e., information] which he rates B–2."[122]

Sibert's early successes did not sit well with Bissell. Driven by a desire for tight control over the Army's intelligence organization and by concerns that aggressive intelligence operations in Europe might upset Moscow, the Army's top military intelligence officer repeatedly curtailed his European counterpart. In July 1945, Bissell denied Sibert's request for the authorization of a high-level espionage mission in the Soviet Zone.[123] In the same month, Bissell arranged for Supreme Allied Headquarters to order Sibert to limit his intelligence efforts "to the measures essential to the security of American Forces in Europe." Instead, he proclaimed, the "War De-

---

120 Msg, Brig. Gen. Edwin L. Sibert, ACofS, G–2, 12th Army Gp, to SHAEF, ACofS, G–2, 20 Jun 1945, sub: Russian Armed Forces, Annex no. 1, Folder "925229," Rcds of the ACoS, G–2 (Intel), Formerly Top Secret Intel Documents, 1943–59, RG 319, NACP.
121 Deposition, Col. John P. Merrill, court-martial of William T. Marchuk, 12 Apr–20 May 1955, WNRC.
122 Msg, Brig. Gen. Edwin L. Sibert to War Department, sub: New Russian Information, 27 Sep 1945, folder "From Germany S-20405 thru S-39481," ACoS, G–2 (Intel), "Top Secret" Incoming and Outgoing Cables, 1942–52, RG 319, NACP.
123 Msg, Maj. Gen. Clayton L. Bissell to Brig. Gen. Edwin L. Sibert, 23 Jul 1945, Folder "#1 to Germany 90804 & 10207 thru 54917," ACoS, G–2 (Intel), "Top Secret" Incoming and Outgoing Cables, 1942–52, RG 319, NACP.

Figure 42: Photograph taken by an Army Intelligence informant of a Soviet artillery unit on the island of Rügen in the Baltic Sea, August 1948. U.S. Army, NACP.

partment will furnish overall . . . intelligence on Russia."[124] When Sibert requested permission to convene a gathering of military attachés in Europe to exchange information on the Soviet armed forces and intelligence activities, Bissell lectured him about "the sound reasons why mass meeting of Military Attachés . . . should not be held."[125]

At the same time, Bissell tried to bypass Sibert by routing intelligence from the European Theater directly to Washington. He arranged with Brig. Gen. George C. McDonald, the chief of Army Air Forces intelligence, to produce a special study

---

124 Msg, Maj. Gen. Clayton L. Bissell to Gen. Dwight D. Eisenhower for Brig. Gen. Edwin L. Sibert, 4 Aug 1945, Folder "#1 to Germany 90804 & 10207 thru 54917," ACoS, G–2 (Intel), "Top Secret" Incoming and Outgoing Cables, 1942–52, RG 319, NACP.
125 Msg, Maj. Gen. Clayton L. Bissell to Brig. Gen. Edwin L. Sibert, 12 Dec 1945, Folder "#2 to Germany 54918 thru 90816," ACoS, G–2 (Intel), "Top Secret" Incoming and Outgoing Cables, 1942–52, RG 319, NACP.

on the Soviet Air Forces based on captured German documents, named Operation CLAMSHELL.[126] He also sent his top expert on the Red Army, Col. Demitri B. Shimkin, to Germany to coordinate the interrogation of Soviet soldiers captured by the *Wehrmacht* who had remained in the West.[127] When the Military Intelligence Service requested information on Soviet units around Berlin from Sibert, the latter responded testily that his office had already initiated such an effort.[128] A month later, he followed up his message with a detailed estimate. According to this document, the total Soviet occupation force in the Berlin area consisted of 39,000 troops, including police, security, and intelligence personnel, as well as 200 to 250 tanks and armored vehicles.[129]

The feud between the two intelligence chiefs came to a head when Bissell transferred the Gehlen group from Oberursel to Washington without informing Sibert.[130] Exasperated at the constant interference, Sibert confronted Bissell during a visit to the Pentagon. Although Bissell made some concessions to Sibert over the use of former German intelligence personnel, he continued to interfere with the European Theater's efforts to collect intelligence on the Soviet armed forces. The simmering conflict between the two generals remained essentially unresolved until Bissell left the post of chief of intelligence in May 1946. His successor, Maj. Gen. Stephen J. Chamberlin, would work more harmoniously with Sibert than did the confrontational Bissell.

Despite their antagonistic relationship, Bissell and Sibert reached an agreement in September 1945 to collaborate on a weekly updated review of the Soviet forces. Compiled by analysts of the intelligence division at the Pentagon, the top secret "Soviet Roundup" drew heavily on information provided by Sibert's office. The intelligence division intended the roundup as a means to inform a tight circle of military and intelligence officials about the latest Soviet order of battle informa-

---

[126] Rpt, Brig. Gen. George C. McDonald, to CG, U.S. Air Forces, 22 Oct 1945, sub: Status of Operation "Clamshell," Folder "926412," Rcds of the ACoS, G–2 (Intel), Formerly Top Secret Intel Documents, 1943–59, RG 319, NACP.
[127] Msg, Mil Intel Service to USFET, 14 Aug 1945, Folder "#1 to Germany 90804 & 10207 thru 54917," ACoS, G–2 (Intel), "Top Secret" Incoming and Outgoing Cables, 1942–52, RG 319, NACP.
[128] Msg, Mil Intel Service to CG, USFET, 8 Aug 1945, Folder "#1 Germany 90804 & 10207 thru 54917," ACoS, G–2 (Intel), "Top Secret" Incoming and Outgoing Cables, 1942–52, RG 319, NACP; Msg, Brig. Gen. Edwin L. Sibert to War Department, 10 Aug 1945, Folder "S91027 thru S 96761 'S' Germany – S 12365 thru S 20404," ACoS, G–2 (Intel), "Top Secret" Incoming and Outgoing Cables, 1942–52, RG 319, NACP.
[129] Msg, Brig. Gen. Edwin L. Sibert to War Department, 6 Sep 1945, sub: Bolero, Folder "From Germany S-20405 thru S-39481," ACoS, G–2 (Intel), "Top Secret" Incoming and Outgoing Cables,1942–52, RG 319, NACP.
[130] For details on the Gehlen Organization, see Chapter 6.

tion, to emphasize specific intelligence targets, and to stimulate discussion about the Red Army among analysts.[131] On 14 September 1945, the director of the Military Intelligence Service, Brig. Gen. Paul E. Peabody, presented the first issue of the new publication.[132] The report assessed Soviet strength in Germany at 6 armies with 60 divisions, totaling 600,000 troops. The analysts may have underestimated the numerical strength of the Red Army in Germany, but they had correctly pinpointed the principal units.[133] In November 1945, the Soviets had seven armies in Germany. The roundup accurately identified the 2d and 3d Shock Armies as well as the 47th Army and the 8th Guards Armies. The roundup also tentatively placed the 5th Shock Army "in the greater Berlin area." In fact, its headquarters were in Potsdam, just outside Berlin. Army Intelligence analysts believed that an additional army might be present in the northern part of the Soviet Zone—and indeed, the 2d Guards Mechanized Army was headquartered in Fürstenberg, roughly 50 miles north of Berlin. Only the 1st Guards Mechanized Army, headquartered in Radebeul in Saxony, escaped the prying eyes of Army Intelligence.[134]

In early 1946, the U.S.-Soviet relationship cooled dramatically. On 9 February, Stalin thundered that the Soviet Union stood in principled opposition to the capitalist and imperialist West. He exhorted his Soviet listeners to increase production and turn the USSR into a superpower within a decade. This, he concluded, was the only condition that would ensure Soviet security "against any eventuality."[135] A little over a week later, on 18 February, the U.S. military attaché to Moscow, Brig. Gen. Frank N. Roberts, warned the intelligence division that the USSR was bent on achieving "dominant world-wide influence," and that "there is no power or combination of powers on the Eurasian continent which is capable of equaling the military strength of the Red Army."[136] Equally alarmed at Stalin's

---

131 Msg, Col. R. F. Ennis, Ch, Intel Gp, to ACofS, G–2, 28 May 1946, sub: Soviet Military Roundup, Folder "H. Collection – Foreign," ODI (G–2), Security-Classified Gen Corresp, 1941–48, RG 165, NACP.
132 Memo, Brig. Gen. Paul E. Peabody, Ch, Mil Intel Service, 14 Sep 1945, sub: Soviet Military Roundup no. 1, Folder "925204," Rcds of the ACoS, G–2 (Intel), Formerly Top Secret Intel Documents, 1943–59, RG 319, NACP.
133 The records of the Soviet forces in postwar Germany remain classified, but Russian and German military historians consider the U.S. estimates for this period to be too low. See Foitzik, *SMAD-Handbuch*, 58; Email, Jan Foitzik to Thomas Boghardt, 2 Jan 2019, Historians Files, CMH.
134 Matthias Uhl, *Krieg um Berlin? Die sowjetische Militär-und Sicherheitspolitik in der zweiten Berlin-Krise 1958–1962* [War over Berlin?: Soviet military and security policy in the second Berlin crisis, 1958–1962] (Munich: Oldenbourg, 2008), 239.
135 Zubok, *Failed Empire*, 52.
136 Rpt, Brig. Gen. F. N. Roberts to Intel Gp, 18 Feb 1946, sub: Estimate of the Situation as of 1 February 1946, Folder "ABC 381 Germany (29 Jan 43) Sec 1-B," American-British Corresp Relating to Planning and Combat Opns, 1940–1948, RG 165, NACP.

bellicosity, the State Department asked the chargé d'affaires at the American embassy in Moscow, George F. Kennan, to produce a thorough analysis of Soviet foreign policy. With the assistance of General Roberts, Kennan did so in a missive known as the "long telegram," which portrayed Moscow's foreign policy as driven by communist ideology rather than pragmatism.[137] The Kremlin, Kennan wrote, viewed a conflict with the capitalist West as inevitable, and "strong resistance" on the part of the United States was the only appropriate answer to Soviet expansionism as well as to the "malignant parasite" of "world communism."[138] Dispatched to Washington on 22 February, Kennan's "long telegram" crystalized American concerns over the Soviet Union and international communism.

On 5 March 1946, Winston Churchill contributed to the war of words with a speech at Westminster College in Fulton, Missouri. "From Stettin in the Baltic to Trieste in the Adriatic," Britain's former prime minister declared, "an iron curtain has descended across the Continent. Behind that line lie all the capitals of the ancient states of Central Europe. Warsaw, Berlin, Prague, Vienna, Budapest, Belgrade, Bucharest and Sofia ... lie in what I must call the Soviet sphere." With President Harry S. Truman seated behind him, Churchill warned his listeners that Moscow wanted "the fruits of war and the indefinite expansion of their power and doctrines." Endorsing Kennan's arguments of the previous month, Churchill advised the American government to push back: "I am convinced that there is nothing they [the Soviets] admire so much as strength, and there is nothing for which they have less respect than for military weakness."[139]

Emboldened by the winds of change from across the Atlantic and freed from Bissell's meddling, Sibert vigorously expanded intelligence operations against the Red Army. Information obtained from German border crossers, Soviet defectors, and British intelligence all contributed to the renewed effort.[140] In the course of the summer of 1946, several Army Intelligence units began recruiting large numbers of sources in the Soviet Zone. Even the CIC, technically a counterespionage

---

137 Memo, Brig. Gen. F. N. Roberts for All Ofcrs, 7 Jun 1946, Folder "Soviet Union," Frank N. Roberts Papers, Truman Library.
138 Telg, George Kennan to George Marshall, 22 Feb 1946, George Elsey Papers, Harry S. Truman Administration File, Truman Library.
139 Martin Walker, *The Cold War: A History* (New York: Owl Books, 1993), 41–42; John Gaddis, *The United States and the Origins of the Cold War, 1941–1947* (New York: Columbia University Press, 1972), 308.
140 Telg, War Department to Brig. Gen. Edwin L. Sibert, 5 Apr 1946, Folder "#1 to Germany 91103 thru 99850 and 80187 thru 89893," ACoS, G–2 (Intel), "Top Secret" Incoming and Outgoing Cables, 1942–52, RG 319, NACP.

agency, joined the game.[141] By September 1946, the Corps reported regularly on the military situation in the Soviet Zone. One informant, code-named CURT, had several subsources across eastern Germany, providing information on Soviet troop concentrations and the strength and activities of individual military units across East Germany.[142]

The sudden escalation of espionage operations in the Soviet Zone threw the Strategic Services Unit for a loop. Pressed by Sibert to improve its order of battle reporting, the unit in March 1946 began recruiting numerous agents, often former *Wehrmacht* officers, who in turn hired multiple subsources. Operation GRAIL, as it was dubbed, eventually involved more than 250 informants. The size of this network was impressive, but security lagged far behind. Many of the agents knew each other or came to know each other's identity in one of the safe houses in the American sector, used for instructions and debriefings but also for "morale boosting" to foster a sense of community.[143] This lack of compartmentalization allowed Soviet counterintelligence to roll up much the GRAIL network, as arrested agents betrayed many others. In retrospect, the head of the CIA's Berlin Operations Base called the operation "disastrous."[144]

Operation RUSTY, the Army-sponsored intelligence effort by a group of former German intelligence officers, was supposed to fill the void left by the Berlin base, but it was ill-prepared to do so. Lt. Col. Hermann Baun, RUSTY's espionage director, sought to reactivate some of his wartime sources.[145] After a number of failed attempts, RUSTY managed to recruit numerous sources in the Soviet Zone, but many of the spy rings proved just as insecure as Operation GRAIL. On one occasion, the CIC learned of a network supposedly involving about 1,200 agents in the Saxon county of Annaberg, adjacent to the Czechoslovak border. Members of the network approached the CIC for help because the Soviets had successfully penetrated it and were in the process of arresting its members. The CIC concluded that the network probably belonged to Operation RUSTY, and recommended that those

---

141 Marc B. Powe and Edward E. Wilson, "The Evolution of American Military Intelligence" (Fort Huachuca, AZ: United States Army Intelligence Center and School, 1973), 86.
142 Rpt, Chisel Rpt no. 73, 10 Sep 1946, sub: Military Situation, Russian Zone, Folder "ZF 015104 Germany Russian Zone in Military – Folder 2 of 2," INSCOM, IRR, Impersonal Name Files, RG 319, NACP.
143 Murphy, Kondrashev, and Bailey, *Battleground Berlin*, 16.
144 Rpt, Durand to Ch, Foreign Br M, 8 Apr 1948, sub: Transmittal of Report on Berlin Operations Base, in Steury, *On the Front Lines of the Cold War*, 10.
145 Magnus Pahl, "Hermann Baun (1897–1951) – Gescheiterter Spionagechef" [Hermann Baun (1897–1951) – Failed espionage chief], in *Spione und Nachrichtenhändler: Geheimdienstkarrieren in Deutschland 1939–1989* [Spies and news traders: Intelligence careers in Germany, 1939–1989], ed. Helmut Müller-Enbergs and Armin Wagner (Berlin: Ch. Links, 2016), 62.

members remaining at liberty be alerted.[146] The Soviets, for their part, claimed that they were arresting over 1,000 American agents per year in the late 1940s.[147]

Despite this turbulence, the analysis of the collected information proceeded apace. The Army's intelligence division expanded the "roundup" into a more detailed publication, the "Notes on Soviet Armed Forces." As the division observed, the demobilization and reorganization of the Red Army in eastern Germany continued, rendering estimates difficult. Consequently, intelligence analyses tended to lag somewhat behind real Soviet troop strength. In November 1946, Army Intelligence estimated the presence of 7 armies and 42 divisions, and 675,000 soldiers in the Soviet Zone.[148] In reality, the Red Army had reduced its presence to 5 armies and 29 divisions by the end of 1946.[149] It took Army Intelligence analysts several months to catch up with the large-scale Soviet force reduction and reorganization. In early 1947, the deputy director of intelligence at the Pentagon, Col. Carter W. Clarke, concluded that the Soviets had withdrawn 175,000 soldiers from Germany, and that the Red Army comprised 500,000 soldiers.[150]

Still, these numbers compared impressively with the American military presence in Germany. The U.S. Army had nearly 2.5 million soldiers in the European Theater at the end of the war but retained only 161,000 men in Germany at the end of 1946.[151] Even this number was deceptive; the only truly operational unit was the U.S. Constabulary, a mobile police force of less than 40,000 men, designed to quell civilian unrest. The only other tactical unit, the 1st Infantry Division, had

---

146 Msg, Special Agent Lee H. Burns, Region VIII, CIC, to CO, 2 Jul 1948, sub: Salzer, Fritz and Lerch, Will, re: Collapse of Intelligence Net in Soviet Zone, Folder "Operation RUSTY Personalities D 169325 (1 of 2)," INSCOM, IRR, Selected Printouts of Digital Intel and Investigative Dossiers, Impersonal Name Files, RG 319, NACP.
147 Armin Wagner and Matthias Uhl, *BND contra Sowjetarmee. Westdeutsche Militärspionage in der DDR* [The BND versus the Soviet Army: West German military espionage in the GDR] (Berlin: Ch. Links, 2007), 38.
148 Memo, Intel Div, War Department Gen Staff, 8 Nov 1946, Notes on Soviet Armed Forces, no. 22, Folder "ABC 336. Russia (22 Aug 43) Sec 2 'Soviet Military Roundup,'" American-British Corresp Relating to Planning and Combat Opns, 1940–1948, RG 165, NACP.
149 Foitzkik and Zarewskaja-Djakana, *SMAD-Handbuch*, 57; Hans-Albert Hoffman and Siegfried Stoof, *Sowjetische Truppen in Deutschland: Ihr Hauptquartier in Wünsdorf 1945–1994. Geschichte, Fakten, Hintergründe* [Soviet troops in Germany: Their headquarters in Wünsdorf 1945–1994. History, facts, background] (No city: Selbstverlag, 2008), 33.
150 Memo, Col. Carter W. Clarke, DDI, for Ch of Staff, sub: Reduction of Soviet Occupation Forces, 17 Feb 1947, folder "091 Russia," Ofc of the Ch of Staff, Top-Secret Gen Corresp, 1941–1947, series 1947, RG 165, NACP.
151 U.S. Department of War, *Strength of the Army* (Washington, DC: Department of War, 1 Jan 1947), 6, 10.

deployed in small detachments across the U.S. Zone, and the European Theater command estimated its combat efficiency at merely 20 percent. Overall, the official history of Army tactical forces during the occupation noted, these troops were "pitifully inadequate" to repulse a foreign aggressor.[152]

Against the backdrop of rising tensions and the imbalance of forces between East and West, Army Intelligence agencies began contemplating the likelihood of an armed clash between the two sides. In June 1946, the intelligence division at the Pentagon drafted a lengthy "Estimate of the World Situation and Its Military Implications for the United States." The weakened state of the Soviet economy, the division inferred, deterred Moscow from initiating a war. Nonetheless, the report described Soviet foreign policy as "generally aggressive" and highlighted Moscow's superiority in conventional forces.[153] Half a year later, the European intelligence division submitted a staff study, war-gaming a conflict between the two sides in Europe. It concluded that the Red Army would easily overrun U.S. and British troops in Germany and seize the English Channel ports within three days.[154]

Army Intelligence estimates of the Soviet forces in Europe informed the first war plan of the Joint Chiefs of Staff against the Soviet Union. Code-named PINCHER, the 1946 plan assumed that an armed conflict would result from a local incident escalating into general war, rather than a deliberate attack. As soon as hostilities had commenced, the PINCHER planners saw no hope for holding continental Europe. American and British forces would withdraw to the British Isles and lend support to Spain, in an effort to defend the westernmost peninsula of Europe against the Red Army. The Middle East, rather than Europe, would become the central battlefield of a drawn-out war, and the Allied air forces would seek to undermine Moscow's war economy by waging a strategic bombing campaign against industrial centers inside the Soviet Union. For the Army, PINCHER stood as a stark reminder of American military inferiority in Europe and Germany.[155]

Meanwhile, U.S. intelligence expanded and adjusted its sources and methods. In 1947, the European Command transferred the 7829th Military Intelligence Pla-

---

[152] Rpt, Historical Div, EUCOM, "Reorganization of Tactical Forces, V-E Day to 1 January 1949" (Karlsruhe: EUCOM, 1950), 3, 9, 16, Historians Files, CMH.
[153] Memo, Intel Div, Pentagon, for Ch, Strategic Plans Section, 27 Jun 1946, sub: Intelligence Estimate of the World Situation and Its Military Implications for the United States, Folder "926152," Rcds of the ACoS, G–2 (Intel), Formerly Top Secret Intel Documents, 1943–59, RG 319, NACP.
[154] G–2, USFET, Intel Staff Study, 26 Dec 1946, sub: Soviet Capabilities in Germany and West Europe, Folder "SD 925908," Rcds of the ACoS, G–2 (Intel), Formerly Top Secret Intel Documents, 1943–59, RG 319, NACP.
[155] Steven T. Ross, *American War Plans 1945–1950* (London: Frank Cass, 1996), 25–52.

toon to Berlin. Within a few years, the unit became the Army's principal espionage arm.[156] Meanwhile, the Strategic Services Unit developed the concept of so-called "tourist missions." By sending individual informants on short-term excursions disguised as business trips or family visits, the CIA compartmented sources from one another, eliminating the possibility of further compromise in case of capture.[157] The CIC, too, honed its espionage techniques. In 1949, the European Command instructed the Corps to launch Operation DEVOTION, a large-scale effort to determine the Soviet order of battle in Thuringia. Individual regions created "positive intelligence teams" that used an approach known as "pyramid practice," involving the dispatch of informants from three different regions to the same target. This technique enabled analysts to check the incoming reports against each other and verify their content.[158]

Although the deployment of large numbers of low-level agents to the Soviet Zone remained a central feature of American intelligence, the various agencies were increasingly effective in placing informants in strategic positions. The CIA managed to recruit a Red Army officer stationed in Dresden, and the CIC had a penetration agent in the Czechoslovak military mission in Berlin.[159] The intelligence section in Berlin successfully recruited several agents working for the Soviet Zone railway administration or living near strategic railway junctions.[160] The reports submitted by these railway spies held particular value to the Army as the Soviets moved most of their forces by train. The intelligence division of the European Command designated a transportation intelligence officer, who analyzed the incoming reports and derived valuable information about Soviet troop movements from them.[161]

The establishment of the United States Military Liaison Mission in the spring of 1947 was a game changer for the Army's military intelligence collection effort. With certain exceptions, officers assigned to the mission had the right to travel freely across the Soviet Zone. From the start, they used their privileged position

---

[156] For more detail on this unit and its operations, see Chapter 3.
[157] Alvarez and Mark, *Spying Through a Glass Darkly*, 79–80.
[158] Maj. Ann Bray et al., eds., *The History of the Counter Intelligence Corps*, vol. 27, *Four Years of Cold War* (Fort Holabird, MD: U.S. Army Intelligence Center, 1959), 101–02.
[159] Peter M. F. Sichel, *The Secrets of My Life: Vintner, Prisoner, Soldier, Spy* (Bloomington, IN: Archway Publishing, 2016), 216; Rpt, Special Agent Hans F. Johnston, Region VIII, CIC, sub: Agent's Daily Report, 8 Oct 1947, Folder "#12 Secret," Rcds Relating Primarily to the Soviet Occupation Zone in Germany, 1947–1948, RG 242, NACP.
[160] Memo, "CHAMPION," Special Intel Memo no. 250, 30 Sep 1947, sub: Military Intelligence from Soviet Zone Germany, Poland, USSR, Folder "#24 Secret," Rcds Relating Primarily to Soviet Occupation Zone in Germany, 1947–1948, RG 242, NACP.
[161] William R. Harris, "March Crisis 1948, Act II," *Studies in Intelligence* 11 (Spring 1967), 15.

to report on Moscow's military forces there. In June, USMLM members visited the town of Wittstock, 40 miles northwest of Berlin. They jotted down the license numbers of Soviet vehicles and noticed that the town housed approximately 3,000 military personnel.[162] Sustained Soviet efforts to contain and penetrate the USMLM illustrate its value to the American intelligence-gathering effort. Within a year of the mission's establishment, its officers reported that the Soviets tightly surveilled their movements and required them to check in with local Soviet commanders. They also stated that the Soviet occupation authorities occasionally arrested USMLM members. Soviet obstruction, the intelligence division in Heidelberg noted, "creates considerable restriction on free travel which repeated protests have failed to correct."[163]

In June 1948, the CIC discovered a Soviet penetration attempt on the liaison mission. A Potsdam resident who went by the unlikely name Giselhal von Szalghapy told the CIC in Berlin that local authorities had ordered him and eight other Germans to appear at the *Arbeitsamt* (employment office). There, they were taken to the Soviet Kommandatura and questioned by a Soviet major, who ordered Szalghapy to penetrate the USMLM by obtaining employment among its staff. Szalghaphy did not show much enthusiasm for the work, and so he did not receive the job. Shortly thereafter, he fled to the American sector in Berlin and told his story to the CIC.[164]

Despite these Soviet containment and penetration efforts, the USMLM's contribution to the American intelligence product would only grow. In the late 1940s, the mission began coordinating its reconnaissance trips with its British and French counterparts, providing continuous coverage of military developments across the Soviet Zone and subsequently, of the German Democratic Republic.[165]

---

162 Rpt, Cpt. Philip Schneider to Ch, U.S. Military Liaison to Soviet Occupied Zone, 18 Jun 1947, sub: Field Report, Folder "TSC # 3901–4000," Top Secret Rpts of Naval Attachés, compiled Feb 1944–Aug 1947, RG 38, NACP. A few years later, the Soviets established one of the largest military training areas in Europe near Wittstock, covering 55 square miles. See Gerd Rosenkranz and Alexander Szandar, "Scharpings Bombodrom" [Scharping's Bombodrome], *Der Spiegel*, 10 Nov 2000.
163 Msg, Lt. Gen. Clarence R. Huebner, HQ, EUCOM, to Maj. Gen. Stephen J. Chamberlin, Intel Div, Department of the Army, 20 Apr 1948, Folder "#1 FR: 'S' Germany 1000–4000 1-1-48–6-9-48," ACoS, G–2 (Intel), "Top Secret" Incoming and Outgoing Cables, 1942–52, RG 319, NACP.
164 Rpt, CIC Region VIII, CI Rpt no. 96, 10 Jun 1948, Folder "CIC Region VIII (Berlin) Periodic Counter Intelligence, Reports," Director of Intel, Analysis, and Research, Misc. Rpts and Publications, 1941–50, RG 260, NACP.
165 Anya Vodopyanov, "A Watchful Eye Behind the Iron Curtain: The U.S. Military Liaison Mission in East Germany, 1953–61" (master's thesis, Stanford University, 2004), 25–26.

Withdrawal of the mission, noted the Department of Defense, "would lose us and our friends much intelligence not obtainable through other means."[166]

The Army's signals intelligence capabilities improved greatly. In the immediate postwar era, the Americans had relied heavily on the British for wireless intercepts from Eastern Europe, but in early 1948 the Army Security Agency's large intercept station at Herzogenaurach, 50 miles south of the interzonal border, became operational. Located on a large plateau approximately 2 miles square and 333 feet above sea level, without mountains in range of vision, Herzo Base provided an ideal location for an electronic listening station.[167] To be sure, Red Army communications proved a tough nut to crack. Many Soviet units used highly secure, lead-encased telephone cables, which defied Western eavesdropping efforts.[168] Nonetheless, Soviet forces generated a large volume of radio communications, and ASA operators produced a steady stream of intercepts. In the summer of 1949, the 114th Signal Service Company handled 420,000 intercepted cipher groups a month at Herzo Base.[169]

By early 1948, the Army's effort to collect intelligence on the Soviet forces in Germany had reached the point of maturity. Drawing on a wide range of sources and methods, intelligence officials composed increasingly nuanced reports. In March 1948, Col. Robert A. Schow's intelligence division in Heidelberg produced a comprehensive "Military Estimate of the Situation," which assessed Soviet strength in Germany at 4 rifle divisions, 10 mechanized divisions, 8 tank divisions, and 6 artillery divisions, numbering 234,000 ground troops. In addition, the Soviets had 89,500 naval, air, security, and military government personnel making a grand total of 332,600. The Soviet Air Forces retained 3,400 aircraft in Germany, including 1,500 fighters, 760 ground attack planes, and 670 bombers.[170] Schow's report slightly underestimated Soviet personnel strength and failed to mention that Moscow had begun to replace its wartime-era propeller-driven aircraft with the MiG-9, the first Soviet jet fighter plane.[171] Overall, however, the report represented a fairly accurate assessment of Soviet strength in Germany.

---

166 Dorothee Mußgnug, *Alliierte Militärmissionen in Deutschland 1946–1990* [Allied military missions in Germany, 1946–1990] (Berlin: Duncker & Humblot, 2001), 35.
167 ASA, "Post War Transition Period: The Army Security Agency 1945–1948" (Washington, DC: ASA, 1952), 72.
168 Kowalczuk and Wolle, *Roter Stern über Deutschland*, 110.
169 Boghardt, "Semper Vigilis," 17.
170 Rpt, ODDI to ACofS, G-2, 1 Mar 1948, sub: Military Estimate of the Situation, Folder "SD 925764," Rcds of the ACoS, G-2 (Intel), Formerly Top Secret Intel Documents, 1943–59, RG 319, NACP.
171 Hoffmann and Stoof, *Sowjetische Truppen in Deutschland*, 34, 42; Email, Jan Foitzik to Thomas Boghardt, 2 Jan 2019, Historians Files, CMH.

Beyond facts and figures, the Army's order of battle analysis looked at the morale and discipline of Soviet soldiers. It found that corruption was rampant and that demobilization caused the Soviet leadership a great deal of trouble. Given the dire economic situation in the Soviet Union, many soldiers resented leaving behind their comparatively comfortable life in Germany, and orders for redeployment to the east often led to desertions. As a result, bands of marauding veterans formed in parts of the Soviet Zone.[172] East of Berlin, Soviet regular troops fought "a hard battle" with bands of deserters, leaving thirty dead. In Frankfurt (Oder), on the German-Polish border, deserters killed the Soviet assistant commandant in broad daylight. Murders, rapes, and robberies committed by deserters against the civilian population continued to undermine the Soviet reputation among Germans.[173]

Nonetheless, the Red Army made for a formidable foe. By early 1948, American troop levels in Germany had declined to slightly over 100,000 soldiers. The combat readiness of the two tactical units, the U.S. Constabulary and the 1st Infantry Division, remained low. The British retained barely 90,000 ground troops in their zone and the French slightly over 50,000. The quality of both had declined significantly since the end of the war, and the French contingent in particular was ill equipped and poorly trained. In the case of an armed conflict with the Soviets, Colonel Schow's intelligence division reckoned, the Red Army units in Germany would be capable of seizing the remaining territory of the country and the northern sea ports. On their own, they would not be able to overrun the whole of Western Europe, but the division noted that Moscow could quickly move reinforcements from Poland and western Russia to accomplish this feat.[174]

Against the backdrop of deteriorating relations with Moscow, from early 1948 the European intelligence division sought to detect signs of an imminent Soviet attack. Throughout the period of military government, they never perceived any such indications.[175] To the contrary, Army Intelligence received numerous reports to the effect that the Soviets had been telling their troops that an American attack

---

172 Msg, Lt. Col. W. R. Rainold, ODDI, to DI, OMGUS, 12 Feb 1948, sub: Report on Soviet Military Espionage Activities, Folder "383.4–1 Espionage," Director of Intel, Analysis and Research Br, Gen Corresp, 1945–49, RG 260, NACP.
173 Rpt, W. F. Heimlich, Dep Br Ch, Civil Administration Br, OMGB, to ODI, OMGUS, 7 Jan 1947, sub: Disorders and Lack of Troop Discipline in Sovzone, Folder "Miscellaneous Reports & Memoranda 1946–48," Director of Intel, Miscellaneous Rpts re. Intel and Document Policies 1944–1948, RG 260, NACP.
174 Rpt, ODDI to ACofS, G–2, 1 Mar 1948, sub: Military Estimate of the Situation.
175 Rpt, Intel Div, EUCOM, 13 Oct 1948, sub: OB Situation During the Period from 15 September to 15 Oct 1948, Folder "927430," Rcds of the ACoS, G–2 (Intel), Formerly Top Secret Intel Documents, 1943–59, RG 319, NACP.

was imminent. The division assumed that that the Soviet command knew about Western military inferiority but did not tell their soldiers because it would make it "a little difficult for them to build up a war psychosis." Instead, Moscow sought to keep their troops from becoming complacent by emphasizing the American monopoly on the atomic bomb and Allied air power. Soviet military training in Germany, the division noted, was based on the precepts that they would defend initially and then launch "a tremendous counter-offensive."[176]

In fact, this assessment reflected official Soviet military doctrine. On 5 November 1946, the Group of Soviet Occupation Forces in Germany issued an operational plan for war with the Western powers. Assuming that Anglo-American forces would conduct their main thrust from Helmstedt in the direction of Berlin, Red Army units would engage them on the territory of the Soviet zone of occupation. Having annihilated the invader, armored divisions would then launch a counteroffensive in the direction of the Rhine River. With variations, this plan remained in place through the 1940s.[177]

The intelligence procured by the Army in Europe shaped strategic assessments of Soviet capabilities and intentions in Washington. Gone were the days when the Pentagon's intelligence division meddled with and sought to short-circuit its European counterpart. Instead, order of battle intelligence from Europe formed a cornerstone of the Army's assessments of Soviet power. In September 1947, for example, the Department of the Army's intelligence division issued a lengthy report on "The Soviets' Occupation Policies in Germany." The order of battle section, identifying four Soviet armies and twenty divisions in Germany, reflected precisely the estimate of the European intelligence division.[178]

The intelligence division in Washington realized that the dismal state of the Soviet economy would not sustain an extended all-out war and therefore mili-

---

[176] Teletype msg, EUCOM, EUCOM teletype msg no. 13, re: DA-1, n.d. [early 1949], EUCOM, Ofc of the Sec of Staff, Sec of the Gen Staff Msg Control Center, Classified Teleconference Msgs, 1945–1951, 1948–1951, RG 549, NACP.

[177] Hoffmann and Stoof, *Sowjetische Truppen in Deutschland*, 42–44. Although the Soviets officially had assumed a defensive posture, the Intelligence Division warned that Moscow "would have no difficulty in provoking an incident and through their propaganda machine interpreting this incident to the troops as an act of aggression by the West." Teletype msg, EUCOM, EUCOM teletype msg no. 13, re: DA-1, n.d. [early 1949].

[178] War Department, Intel Review no. 24, 25 Sep 1947, sub: The Soviets' Occupation Policies in Germany, Folder "14c Policy and General Activity of Occupying Powers (Soviet Zone) Jan '47 to Dec '47 Inc.," ODI, Excerpts of Miscellaneous Rpts and Publications, Analysis and Research Br, 1947–48, RG 260, NACP.

tated against a surprise attack by the Red Army.[179] Nonetheless, military planners had to consider the eventuality of an armed conflict. In January 1947, analysts completed a lengthy research project on the "Possibilities of Trans-Arctic Attack on the United States," listing Canada and Greenland as potential gateways for Moscow's forces.[180] Still, the European Theater remained the Army's top priority, and the estimates of the Pentagon's intelligence division continued to reflect those of its European counterpart. Washington analysts saw "no indication . . . that Soviet troops were planning to take the field in the near future" and noted that the twenty divisions in Germany were "insufficient . . . for aggressive action." Nevertheless, they cautioned, this force was capable of rapid buildup "should Moscow decide to implement its capability of overrunning Western Europe."[181]

The expertise of the intelligence division informed the strategic thinking on the Soviet threat across the War Department and the U.S. government. As early as 1946, the Army's Plans and Operations Division requested a study on "Soviet Capabilities to Overrun Europe and Asia" from their intelligence colleagues. In a detailed war game scenario, the intelligence analysts concluded that the Soviets would be able to field a total of 450 divisions, or about 11 million men, within two months of mobilization. In Europe, the Red Army would execute its main thrust through Germany in a coordinated air and ground attack supported by 40 infantry divisions, 20 armored divisions, and 11,500 aircraft. Within ten days, Soviet forces would reach the Rhine River. Meeting only moderate resistance across Western Europe, they would arrive at the Atlantic in Brittany within 50 days. From there, they would reach the toe of Italy within 90 days, and would capture the Iberian Peninsula within 145 days.[182]

The division's intelligence estimates heavily influenced the deliberations of the Joint Chiefs of Staff. In October 1947, the Joint Intelligence Committee issued a lengthy memorandum "on the probable intentions of the USSR to overrun Western and Northern Europe." Accepting the assessment of the Army in Europe, the committee noted that Moscow did not actively seek war. Nonetheless, Stalin's pol-

---

179 Rpt, Intel Div to Joint Intel Staff, 16 Jan 1946, sub: Intelligence Estimate of the World as of 1 December 1945, Folder "926379," Rcds of the ACoS, G–2 (Intel), Formerly Top Secret Intel Documents, 1943–59, RG 319, NACP.
180 Rpt, War Department, Intel Div, Intel Research Project no. 3506, 13 Jan 1947, sub: Possibilities of Trans-Arctic Attack on the United States, Folder "SD 925922," Rcds of the ACoS, G–2 (Intel), Formerly Top Secret Intel Documents, 1943–59, RG 319, NACP.
181 War Department, Intel Review no. 24, 25 Sep 1947, sub: The Soviets' Occupation Policies in Germany.
182 Memo, Intel Div, for the Director, Plans and Opns Div, 5 Aug 1946, sub: Soviet Capabilities to Overrun Europe and Asia [as of 1 July 1947], Folder "926079," Rcds of the ACoS, G–2 (Intel), Formerly Top Secret Intel Documents, 1943–59, RG 319, NACP.

Figure 43: An Army Intelligence estimate of the advance routes of Soviet forces in case of war in Europe in 1947. U.S. Army, NACP.

icy of exploiting local crises to extend Soviet power raised the possibility that his "courses of action by miscalculation would lead to open warfare." In this case, Western conventional forces could only delay the advance of the Red Army in Europe. Echoing the findings of the analysts from the intelligence division the previous year, the committee concluded the Soviets would quickly overrun Western and Northern Europe.[183]

The evidence of overwhelming Soviet superiority in conventional forces prompted the Joint War Plans Committee to play the atomic card. In July 1947, the committee submitted War Plan BROILER, which assumed a massive Soviet offensive in Europe and the Middle East that would push the Western Allies to the shores of the Atlantic coast and into the Sahara Desert. In an effort to destroy Moscow's war economy and break the Soviet will to fight, the U.S. Air Force would respond by dropping thirty-four atomic bombs on twenty-four cities. By 1949, when the imbalance of conventional forces had further tilted in Moscow's favor, the committee called for atomic attacks on seventy Soviet cities, resulting in the estimated deaths of 2.7 million people, the wounding of 4 million, and the reduction of Soviet industrial capacity by 30 to 40 percent.[184] In 1948, these war plans became integrated into official policy. A directive by the National Security Council (NSC 20/4) identified the Soviet Union as the "gravest threat to the security of the United States within the foreseeable future" and called for the gradual "retraction of undue Russian power and influence." Although the NSC assessment noted that Moscow did not actively plan a surprise attack, it echoed earlier Army Intelligence estimates in that "war might arise through miscalculation, through failure of either side to estimate accurately how far the other can be pushed." If war broke out, the United States would use the atomic bomb to win it. American war aims included the breakup of the Soviet state and the destruction of international communism.[185]

As grandiose as these designs were, they contained a farcical element in that they ignored the limits of American atomic might. In the summer of 1946, the United States possessed merely nine bombs. Two years later, they had fifty, but technical challenges in assembling the devices, a lack of suitable aircraft, and Soviet air defense measures made it highly unlikely that the U.S. Air Force could use them as envisioned.[186] The United States' economic prowess might allow it to win

---

[183] Note, Secs to the Joint Intel Committee on Soviet Military Objectives and Capabilities, 1947–1950, 27 Oct 1947, Folder "ABC 381. U.S.S.R. (2 Mar 46) Sec 1-G," ABC File, RG 186, NACP. Emphasis in original.
[184] Ross, *American War Plans*, 56, 107.
[185] Rpt, NSC, "A Report to the NSC by the Executive Secretary on U.S. Objectives with Respect to the USSR to Counter Soviet Threats to U.S. Security," 2 Nov 1948, Folder "National Security Council – Meetings: 27: November 23, 1948–178-11," President's Secretary's Files, Truman Library; Ross, *American War Plans*, 111–12.
[186] David A. Rosenberg, "U.S. Nuclear Stockpile, 1945 to 1950," *The Bulletin of the Atomic Scientists* (May 1982), 26.

a drawn-out war with the Soviet Union, but the Army had no nuclear-powered magic wand to deal with the Red Army in Europe.

Conclusion

Stalin's plans for postwar Germany continue to be the subject of historical debate. Whether he envisioned an undivided Germany loosely aligned with the Soviet Union or a rump state firmly incorporated into the Soviet sphere of influence in Eastern Europe remains under discussion.[187] The Americans did not have access to the upper echelons of the Soviet leadership—let alone to Stalin personally—and so U.S. intelligence could not offer meaningful insights into the dictator's thinking. Even if the Americans had been able to eavesdrop on Stalin's personal communications or recruit an informant in his inner circle, they may have been unable to predict his policies. Always the opportunist, Stalin himself probably had no clearly defined vision of Germany's future at the end of the war. Rather, he appears to have developed his policies in reaction to events on the ground.[188]

Still, the close monitoring by Army Intelligence of conditions in the Soviet Zone strongly suggested long-term Soviet designs on this territory. The harassment and suppression of noncommunist parties, the large-scale internment of political opponents, and the creation of a Soviet-style security apparatus all pointed to permanent political changes and testified to the gravitational pull of areas under Moscow's control. This type of ground-level monitoring did not require high-level penetrations, but rather needed a mechanism capable of processing and analyzing intelligence obtained through many diverse sources. This was exactly the type of apparatus Army Intelligence possessed.

Ironically, Soviet efforts to suppress political dissent fueled the Army's intelligence operations. Soviet repression exacerbated a sense of outrage among Germans in the Soviet Zone. Despair and anger created thousands of refugees who willingly reported on conditions back home, and many agreed to become American informants. The combination of Army Intelligence capabilities and the punitive Soviet occupation policy produced an intelligence windfall for the Americans. As a result,

---

[187] For two divergent interpretations, see Wilfried Loth, *Stalins ungeliebtes Kind: Warum Moskau die DDR nicht wollte* [Stalin's unloved child: Why Moscow did not want the GDR] (Reinbek: Rohwolt, 1994); and Gerhard Wettig, *Stalin and the Cold War in Europe: The Emergence and Development of East-West Conflict, 1939–1953* (Lanham, MD: Rowman and Littlefield, 2008).
[188] The best English-language history of Soviet policy in Germany remains Naimark, *The Russians in Germany*.

the Army developed an extraordinarily productive intelligence effort directed at the Soviet Zone.[189]

The resulting intelligence at first did not shape American policy. Following his mandate to operate within the Allied framework of Potsdam, General Clay tended to disregard the reporting of his intelligence agencies and sought to work with the Soviets for several years. Over time, however, Army Intelligence estimates from Germany and Europe became a central rationale for the recalibration of American policy toward the Soviet Union. By 1948, the continued, massive presence of the Red Army in central Europe had become a centerpiece of American thinking on Soviet intentions. Starting in the early summer of that year, Stalin's efforts to coerce the incorporation of the Western sectors of Berlin into the Soviet sphere of influence would finally validate the patient warnings of Army Intelligence about Moscow's intentions in Europe.

---

[189] William Stivers, "Was Sovietization Inevitable? U.S. Intelligence Perceptions of Internal Developments in the Soviet Zone of Occupation in Germany," *Journal of Intelligence History* 5, no. 1 (Summer 2005), 70.

10 The Berlin Blockade

On 10 June 1947, the U.S. military attaché to Prague, Col. Egmont F. Koenig, sent a top secret cable to the Intelligence Division at the Pentagon. Under the heading "Political Tension in Czechoslovakia," Koenig warned that the Soviets were cementing their rule in Eastern Europe. In Czechoslovakia, the attaché noted, the powerful Communist Party under Vladimír Clementis was pushing its political rivals to the sidelines: "Although outwardly tranquil," he wrote, "terrific forces are building up inside of the Czechoslovak volcano and an eruption may be expected any time." Koenig went on to describe possible forms of the impending eruption, such as a "forceful seizure of power by the Left" or "Civil war, followed by Russian intervention." He concluded with a call for vigilance: "When the time comes, our Government should know in advance what its answer will be and not caught off balance by the rush of events of which it had no advance notice. HENCE THE ABOVE REPORT."[1]

Like a latter-day Cassandra, the attaché's words fell on deaf ears. The American ambassador to Prague, Laurence A. Steinhardt, dismissed Koenig's warning as "his personal opinion."[2] Nor did the message prompt Washington to take countermeasures. In February 1948, the Czechoslovak communist party launched massive demonstrations; gained control of the state's security apparatus; and hectored the nation's president, Edvard Beneš, into appointing a communist government. On the morning of 10 March, the only remaining noncommunist cabinet member, Foreign Minister Jan G. Masaryk, was found dead in the courtyard below a window of his apartment in the Czech Foreign Ministry. Local authorities ruled his death a suicide, but rumors persisted that he had been murdered. Over the following weeks and months, the communists consolidated their position, abolished democracy, and aligned their country with the Soviet Union.[3] "Things look black," President Harry S. Truman wrote his wife Bess on 3 March. "So that we are faced with exactly the same situation with which Britain and France were faced in 1938/39 with Hitler."[4]

Ominously, Italy appeared to gravitate toward Moscow's orbit as well. Led by the potent Italian Communist Party, a broad popular-front coalition flexed its muscles ahead of the country's first postwar parliamentary elections scheduled

---

[1] Msg, Col. E. F. Koenig, Mil Attaché, Prague, to Intel Div, 10 Jun 1947, sub: Political Tension in Czechoslovakia, Folder "926793," Rcds of the ACoS, G–2 (Intel), Formerly Top Secret Intel Documents, 1943–59, RG 319, NACP.

[2] Msg, Koenig to Intel Div, 10 Jun 1947, sub: Political Tension in Czechoslovakia.

[3] Igor Lukes, *On the Edge of the Cold War: American Diplomats and Spies in Postwar Prague* (New York: Oxford University Press, 2012), 183–202.

[4] Cited in David McCullough, *Truman* (New York: Simon & Schuster, 1992), 603.

for April 1948. This time, the U.S. government took action.⁵ The Central Intelligence Agency and other U.S. organizations intervened heavily in favor of the pro-Western parties; meanwhile, the Army's Intelligence Division began planning for the contingency of a Communist victory at the polls. In March, the Army's intelligence chief, Lt. Gen. Stephen J. Chamberlin, sent his right-hand man, Col. Riley F. Ennis, to a conference of American military attachés in Frankfurt. During the gathering, Ennis handed the attaché to Rome, Col. John M. Willems, a memorandum from the Intelligence Division. The document laid out plans for a coup d'état by the Italian military in the case the Italian Communist Party and its allies won the election.⁶

Back in Rome, Willems discussed the plan with several top embassy officials. The diplomats cautioned that the project carried "with it [the] probability [of] plunging Italy into [a] bloody civil war and seriously hazarding [the] start [of] World War III." But because the scheme represented a "final though desperate action to hold Italy for [the] western bloc," the embassy gave Willems the green light. He contacted leading Italian army and military intelligence officers, but the elections rendered the Army's bold project moot.⁷ With a little help from the United States, the pro-American Christian Democrats won nearly half the votes, besting the communist and socialist parties of the popular front by almost 20 percent. In fending off the spread of Soviet influence in Western Europe, Britain's *Economist* noted approvingly, "America took off the gloves for the first time."⁸

With Czechoslovakia firmly under Moscow's thumb and Italy securely bound to the West, Europe gradually divided into two hostile camps. The hardening of the Iron Curtain across the continent raised serious questions about the future of Germany, the country at the center of Europe and one of the few remaining nations not clearly aligned with either side. The status of the former German capital, Berlin, was especially delicate. Governed jointly by the four Allies yet located deep inside the Soviet zone of occupation, the city held high symbolic value but was acutely vulnerable to outside pressure. Following on the heels of the twin crises in Prague and Rome, Berlin emerged as the principal battleground between

---

5 James E. Miller, "Taking Off the Gloves: The United States and the Italian Elections of 1948," *Diplomatic History* 7, no. 1 (1983): 35–66.
6 Thomas Boghardt, "'By All Feasible Means': New Documents on the American Intervention in Italy's Parliamentary Elections of 1948," Sources and Methods Blog, Cold War International History Project, Wilson Center, 1 May 2017, https://www.wilsoncenter.org/blogs/sources-and-methods.
7 Msg, Col. John M. Willems, Mil Attaché, Rome, to Intel Div, Personal for Chamberlin or Ennis, 30 Mar 1948, Folder "Italy 1948," ACoS, G-2 (Intel), "Top Secret" Incoming and Outgoing Cables, 1942–52, RG 319, NACP.
8 Miller, "Taking Off the Gloves," 53.

the Soviet Union and the West. As the U.S. government's executive agency in the city, the Army and its intelligence organization served as America's vanguard in this contest.

War Scares

By 1947, inter-Allied cooperation on Germany had stalled. In the east, the Soviets were busy consolidating their security apparatus. Meanwhile, Western Europe suffered from high unemployment and a lethargic economy dependent on Germany's recovery for its revival. The continued Allied stalemate over the future of Germany, however, forestalled any efforts to rejuvenate Europe as a whole. Secretary of State George C. Marshall warned publicly: "We cannot ignore the factor of time. The patient is sinking while the doctors deliberate."[9] To invigorate the German economy, the Americans and the British merged their zones in January 1947, creating a unified economic area known as Bizonia. In June, Marshall announced the European Recovery Program, a massive economic aid package to revive the anemic Western European economy. The Marshall Plan, as it came to be known, was to include all countries on the continent that sought assistance, as well as the Western occupation zones of Germany. Even though Western European nations leapt at the opportunity of U.S. aid, the Soviets rejected participation for themselves and for the territories under their control for fear that it would open them up to American influence.[10]

Allied attempts to find a common solution for the future of Germany ended for good during a meeting of the Council of Foreign Ministers in London, beginning 25 November 1947. Germany and Austria were the only items on the agenda. Soviet Foreign Minister Vyacheslav M. Molotov rejected every Western proposal, earning him the nickname "Mr. Nyet" from his colleagues and the press. As Molotov escalated his verbal attacks on the Western negotiators, Marshall terminated the conference with no appointed date for resumption.[11] Shortly thereafter, the Allied Control Council, which coordinated Allied policy in Germany, disintegrated as well. During a stormy meeting in Berlin, the Soviet delegation abruptly stood up, and its chief, Marshal Vasily D. Sokolovsky, avowed: "I see no sense in con-

---

[9] W. R. Smyser, *From Yalta to Berlin: The Cold War Struggle over Germany* (New York: Palgrave Macmillan, 2000), 56.
[10] For the Marshall Plan, see Benn Steil, *The Marshall Plan: Dawn of the Cold War* (New York: Simon & Schuster, 2018).
[11] Smyser, *From Yalta to Berlin*, 59; Jean Edward Smith, *Lucius D. Clay: An American Life* (New York: Henry Holt, 1990), 446.

tinuing this meeting, and I declare it adjourned."[12] The Allied Control Council would never meet again. The Western powers now moved forward with plans for currency reform in their occupation zones and with the creation of a separate West German state. The Soviets dug in their heels and sought to sabotage Western designs.

Joseph Stalin chose Berlin as a pressure point because the postwar zonal borders, which placed the entire city inside the Soviet Zone, gave the Soviets a distinct geopolitical advantage. As a harbinger of things to come, on 6 January 1948 Soviet inspectors boarded a Berlin-bound U.S. military train at Marienborn, the first stop in the Soviet Zone for railway traffic coming from the British Zone. They demanded to check the papers of German passengers, challenging the American understanding—and practice—that Western trains heading toward Berlin would be exempt from Soviet interference or inspection. After a brief standoff, the Soviets retreated, but on 12 January they began demanding Soviet countersignatures on interzonal consignments out of the Western sectors. Three days later, they prohibited German vehicles from entering the Soviet Zone from the Western sectors of Berlin, and later that month they began interfering with British trains running between Berlin and the British Zone. Meanwhile, the Americans noted "ever increasing" efforts to curb Western air travel to and from Berlin.[13] General Lucius D. Clay recalled that Western authorities in Berlin "were convinced that these difficulties were intended as a threat." It was evident, he wrote, "that the 'wraps were off' and that there was 'heavy going' ahead."[14]

The citizens of Berlin acutely felt the rising tensions. Army Intelligence in the city noted the population's growing apprehension over the possibility of an impending Soviet attack. As the Counter Intelligence Corps in Berlin noted, "The feeling that war is imminent has shown a marked increase and is probably based on expected strong Soviet opposition to the unification of the Western Zones."[15] The European Command intelligence division received reports from informants in the Soviet Zone to the effect that "Mongolian troops" were pouring into eastern Germany—a thinly veiled slur suggesting that the new arrivals may have been reinforcements from eastern Russia or the Central Asian Soviet republics. Other informants warned that the Group of Soviet Occupation Forces in Germany had

---

12 Lucius D. Clay, *Decision in Germany* (Garden City, NY: Doubleday, 1950), 356.
13 Daniel F. Harrington, *Berlin on the Brink: The Blockade, the Airlift, and the Early Cold War* (Lexington: University Press of Kentucky, 2012), 43–44.
14 Clay, *Decision in Germany*, 343, 354.
15 Rpt, Region VIII, CIC, 5 Feb 1948, sub: CI Report no. 88, Folder "CIC Region VIII (Berlin) Periodic Counter Intelligence Reports," Director of Intel, Analysis and Research, Misc. Rpts and Publications, 1941–50, RG 260, NACP.

increased its strength from 324,000 to 600,000. The office remained skeptical, however, and rated these reports "F–6," the lowest reliability category. By February, the division had discarded the notion of a major Soviet troop increase in eastern Germany, and estimated the total strength of Soviet forces there as virtually unchanged, at 332,500. The Intelligence Division at the Pentagon, for its part, worried more about Soviet attempts to promote political unrest in Berlin and the Western zones than about an imminent Soviet attack.[16]

Figure 44: Sgt. Marvin E. Sanchez of the 7773d Signal Service Company serving as a radio operator on a train commuting across the Soviet Zone, October 1951. U.S. Army, NACP.

---

16 Msg, Lt. Gen. Clarence R. Huebner to Lt. Gen. Stephen J. Chamberlin, 26 Feb 1948, sub: Russian cable no. 47, Folder "#1 FR: 'S' Germany 1000–4000 1-1-48–6-9-48," ACoS, G–2 (Intel), "Top Secret" Incoming and Outgoing Cables, 1942–52, RG 319, NACP; Msg, Lt. Gen. Stephen J. Chamberlin to CINCEUR, 5 Feb 1948, Folder "14. To: Consolidated Outgoing 43108-95999 (1-1-48–2-14-48," ACoS, G–2 (Intel), "Top Secret" Incoming and Outgoing Cables, 1942–52, RG 319, NACP.

On 1 March, European Command intelligence completed a lengthy estimate of the military situation in Germany and Europe. The report stood by the Army's long-held view that even though the Soviet military had the capability to overrun Germany and parts of Western Europe, Moscow did not intend to go to war—at least not in the short term. The estimate concluded: "The USSR will continue all practices *short of war* to reduce the prestige and efficiency of the Western Bloc and to destroy the effectiveness of the European Recovery Plan."[17] Driving home this point, division chief Col. Robert A. Schow wrote to General Chamberlin three days later that the Soviets fully realized the global implications of a military conflict in Europe: "Such an operation would be the beginning of World War III."[18]

Unfortunately, the two principal recipients of this reassuring assessment failed to consider it. General Clay's top intelligence officer, Maj. Gen. Robert L. Walsh, adopted an alarmist outlook. After the communist coup in Czechoslovakia in February 1948, Walsh repeatedly urged Clay "to warn Washington of impending trouble" with the Soviets. In late March 1948, he told General Clay's deputy, Lt. Gen. George P. Hays, that the Soviets "would do something to make us start a war." Years later, Walsh still believed that the two sides had avoided war in early 1948 only because "Stalin changed his mind."[19]

Clay shared Walsh's concerns. During the London conference in November, which Clay attended, he sensed a distinctly hostile shift in the attitude of the Soviet delegation. On 27 December 1947, he described conditions in Germany as "tense." Though he still discounted the prospect of war, he warned that "we must not be caught as we were at Pearl Harbor." The coup in Czechoslovakia thoroughly startled him, and in early March, Clay questioned Moscow's commitment to peace. In a message to Maj. Gen. Floyd L. Parks, chief of the Army's Public Information Division and formerly in charge of the American occupation in Berlin, Clay qualified his past skepticism of Soviet belligerency with the caveat, "This does not mean that we do not face this danger at some time." He added, "In point of fact, I now doubt if we have as much time as I once thought."[20]

---

[17] Rpt, ODDI, EUCOM, 1 Mar 1948, sub: Military Estimate of the Situation, Folder "SD 925764," Rcds of the ACoS, G–2 (Intel), Formerly Top Secret Intel Documents, 1943–59, RG 319, NACP (emphasis added).
[18] Msg, Col. Robert A. Schow, DDI, to Director of Intel, Washington, 4 Mar 1948, sub: Estimate of Soviet Military Capabilities in Western Europe, Top Secret "ID" Files, RG 319, NACP.
[19] William R. Harris, "March Crisis 1948, Act I," *Studies in Intelligence* 10 (Fall 1966), 6; William R. Harris, "March Crisis 1948, Act II," *Studies in Intelligence* 11 (Spring 1967), 24.
[20] Harris, "March Crisis, Act I," 4–5; Msg, Clay to Parks, 3 Mar 1948, doc. 335, in *The Papers of General Lucius D. Clay, 1945–1949*, ed. Jean Edward Smith (Bloomington: Indiana University Press, 1974), 2:564.

At this delicate moment, Clay's growing concerns over Soviet intentions became mixed up with domestic politics in the United States. As the Berlin crisis unfolded, the Departments of the Army and Defense debated their budgets and the reintroduction of the military draft for the coming fiscal year. Army Secretary Kenneth C. Royall and his staff were pushing for universal military training. In order to sway lawmakers to reinstate the draft, Royall suggested to the chief of the Army's Civil Affairs Division "that a cablegram from [the military governor of Japan, General Douglas] MacArthur in support of selective service would be very helpful now while matter is before the Committees of Congress."[21] For the same, purely domestic reasons, the Department of the Army approached MacArthur's counterpart in Europe, General Clay.

In late February, General Chamberlin visited Germany and met with Clay to discuss the current political and military situation. No official record of their conversation has surfaced. Chamberlin later stated that he had "no recollection" of such a meeting; however, Clay recounted his own memories of the meeting in detail to a Department of Defense historian several years after the crisis. According to the historian's account, Clay expressed to Chamberlin a growing apprehension about Soviet military aggression. Clay said that Chamberlin replied that the Pentagon's Intelligence Division had no evidence of an imminent Soviet attack, but he asked Clay to send a cable "about his fear of possible war" for Chamberlin to "show around the Pentagon."[22] Decades later, Clay told his biographer emphatically that "General Chamberlin came to see me in Berlin in late February. . . . He told me the Army was having trouble getting the draft reinstituted, and they needed a strong message from me that they could use in congressional testimony."[23]

On the morning of 5 March, after Chamberlin had left Germany, Clay sat down with Walsh to discuss his suspicions about the Soviets. The apprehensive Walsh was greatly relieved to hear Clay's concerns: "Lucius," he exhorted his boss, "if you feel there's a good chance of war, we had better get word to Washington." Walsh then grabbed a piece of paper, and Clay dictated to him a message for Chamberlin. Clay's personal aide for intelligence, Capt. Richard R. Hallock, double-encrypted the message in a special cipher and sent it to Washington through Army Security Agency channels.[24] "For many months," the telegram read, "based on logical analysis I have felt and held that war was unlikely for at least ten years. Within the last few weeks, I have felt a subtle change in Soviet attitude which I cannot define but which now gives me a feeling that it may come with dramatic suddenness." Ac-

---

21 Frank Kofsky, *Harry S. Truman and the War Scare of 1948: A Successful Campaign to Deceive the Nation* (New York: St. Martin's Press, 1993), 108.
22 Harris, "March Crisis, Act I," 5–6.
23 Smith, *Clay*, 467; Harrington casts doubt on this version; see *Berlin on the Brink*, 42.
24 Harris, "March Crisis, Act I," 6.

knowledging the lack of corroborating intelligence, Clay went on: "I cannot support this change in my own thinking with any data or outward evidence in relationships other than to describe it as a feeling of a new tenseness in every Soviet individual with whom we have official relations. I am unable to submit any official report in the absence of supporting data but my feeling is real."[25]

Whether Chamberlin had indeed asked Clay for a cable warning about the likelihood of war remains unclear. Given the Army's parallel request to MacArthur, Chamberlin probably had asked for some sort of message to use in the congressional budget committees. If so, Chamberlin would have relayed this request on behalf of Royall or Secretary of Defense James V. Forrestal.[26] Regardless, Clay had expressed concern about Soviet behavior long before Chamberlin's visit. Even if he sent the cable in response to Chamberlin's solicitation and at Walsh's urging, the message expressed his genuine opinion.

Both Clay and Walsh were driven by intuition rather than by hard intelligence assessments. In fact, Clay noted that his war message stemmed from his "feeling" rather than solid evidence. This admission by no means diminished its impact in Washington, where Clay's warning "fell with the force of a blockbuster bomb," according to journalist Walter Millis. General Omar N. Bradley, the Army's chief of staff with the noticeably receding hairline, recalled that the message "lifted me right out of my chair. . . . Had I had enough hair on my head, this cable would probably have stood it on end."[27]

General Chamberlin immediately directed his trusted subordinate, Colonel Ennis of the Intelligence Group, to produce a "crash estimate" on Soviet intentions. Within a day, Ennis wrote up a report countering Clay's claim: "It is unlikely that the Soviets will take military action either to drive us out of Berlin, or Germany, although they have the undoubted capability of initiating offensive operations in Europe and the Middle East without appreciable warning. However, we have no evidence that they intend to do so at the time."[28] A few days later, Ennis consulted with a representative of the European intelligence division, who stated that the Soviets were conducting routine maneuvers, rather than preparing for an attack in Germany.[29]

---

25 Msg, Clay to Chamberlin, 5 Mar 1948, doc. 340, in Smith, *Clay Papers*, 2:568–69.
26 Kofsky, *Truman*, 108.
27 Walter Millis, ed., *The Forrestal Diaries* (New York: Viking Press, 1951), 387; Omar N. Bradley, *A General's Life: An Autobiography by General of the Army Omar N. Bradley* (New York: Simon & Schuster, 1983), 477–78.
28 Harris, "March Crisis, Act I," 9.
29 Memo, Lt. Col. Carl A. Weaver, ODDI, EUCOM, for Col. Riley F. Ennis, 23 Mar 1948, Folder "925974," Rcds of the ACoS, G–2 (Intelligence), Formerly Top Secret Intel Documents, 1943–59, RG 319, NACP.

Ennis's report did not settle matters. Intelligence agencies on both sides of the Atlantic scrambled to verify or refute the military governor's dramatic assertion. On 10 March, General Chamberlin sent an updated set of Elements of Essential Information to military attachés across the globe, asking for specific signs of Soviet initiatives.[30] He also instructed Ennis to travel to Frankfurt to meet with military attachés from Europe and discuss options for increasing intelligence collection on the Soviet Union.[31] In Berlin, the director of the military government's intelligence office, Col. Peter P. Rodes, met with local CIA representatives to discuss Clay's cable.[32] Within less than two weeks of Chamberlin's request, all of these agencies dismissed the notion of an impending attack.

In Washington, the job of collating and analyzing intelligence for the U.S. leadership fell to the CIA. Less than a year old, the agency was still gaining its footing and proved unable to issue an impromptu response to Clay's warning. In frustration, Bradley lamented that "the CIA, recently established for the purpose of answering such questions, was no help whatsoever."[33] Bradley's reaction was a bit harsh, as the CIA immediately assembled an ad hoc interagency intelligence committee, with representatives from Army, Navy, Air Force, and State Department intelligence, to review all available evidence. On 15 March, the agency confirmed Ennis's assessment and informed President Truman that it had found "no reliable evidence that the USSR intends to resort to military action within the next sixty days."[34] Two weeks later, the joint ad hoc committee submitted its final report, concluding even more broadly "that the USSR will not resort to military action during 1948."[35]

But events in Berlin had already overtaken the CIA and its committee's analysis. In late March, Soviet authorities issued weapons to all border personnel and alerted local Germans in border villages to expect the billeting of soldiers in their homes. Shortly thereafter, the Red Army moved several divisions to the borders of Berlin.[36]

---

30 Msg, Lt. Gen. Stephen J. Chamberlin, to All Mil Attachés, HQ, EUCOM, Vienna, Tokyo, 10 Mar 1948, Folder "15. To: Consolidated Outgoing 96000–97999 (2-15-48–3-19-48)," ACoS, G–2 (Intel), "Top Secret" Incoming and Outgoing Cables, 1942–52, RG 319, NACP.

31 Msg, Lt. Gen. Stephen J. Chamberlin to HQ, EUCOM, 13 Mar 1948, Folder "15: Consolidated Outgoing 96000–97999 (2-15-48–3-19-48)," ACoS, G–2 (Intel), "Top Secret" Incoming and Outgoing Cables, 1942–52, RG 319, NACP.

32 Harris, "March Crisis, Act I," 15.

33 Bradley, *A General's Life*, 478.

34 "Notes on the 'March War Scare' of March 1948," May 1953, CIA, CIA Electronic Reading Room, http://www.cia.gov/readingroom.

35 Rpt, CIA, 1 Apr 1948, sub: Possibility of Direct Soviet Military Action During 1948, CIA Electronic Reading Room.

36 Matthias Uhl, *Krieg um Berlin? Die sowjetische Militär-und Sicherheitspolitik in der zweiten Berlin-Krise 1958 bis 1962* [War over Berlin?: Soviet military and security policy in the second Berlin Crisis, 1958–1962] (Munich: Oldenbourg, 2008), 45.

U.S. intelligence quickly picked up on these activities. Placed on around-the-clock border alert, the CIC registered growing numbers of refugees and deserters from the east who brought word about the apparent Soviet mobilization effort.[37] Informants of Operation RUSTY also reported signs of large-scale movements of Soviet combat units. Ominously, intelligence pointed to a strengthening of the Soviet 3d Guards Mechanized Army, whose headquarters was in Luckenwalde about 30 miles south of Berlin.[38]

American officials registered these developments with growing concern. In Berlin, the American commander Col. Frank L. Howley admitted that "Russian military maneuvers just outside the city disturbed me as much as they did the Germans. The Russians might well follow up the blockade by moving into Berlin."[39] Likewise, the alarming reports from Europe created a sense of nervousness in official Washington. Around 4 a.m. on 31 March, Secretary of the Army Royall received an emergency call in his suite in the Mayflower Hotel in Washington, D.C. Standing in his pajamas, he looked out at the streetlights still burning on Connecticut Avenue while the Intelligence Division duty officer apologized for interrupting his sleep and told him that hostilities in central Europe might be imminent. Royall then notified the White House, got dressed, and headed to the Pentagon for a full briefing. To his relief, the meeting dispelled the notion of a new world war.[40]

Army officials fell short of determining the basis for the emergency call to Royall. On 4 April, perhaps prompted by the secretary of war's nocturnal appearance at the Pentagon, General Chamberlin ordered the intelligence division in Heidelberg to send daily situation reports to Washington.[41] The reports included information on the troop movements of the Red Army, the East German border police, war rumors among the local population, and the latest Soviet efforts to interfere with Western access to Berlin. The daily "SITREP" message from the intelligence division in Germany became known in Washington as the Berlin war warning.[42]

---

37 Ofc of the Ch Historian, EUCOM, *The Third Year of the Occupation*, Part 3, *The Third Quarter, 1 January–31 March 1948*, vol. 2, Occupation Forces in Europe Series 1947–48 (Frankfurt: Office of the Chief Historian, EUCOM, 1948), 72–73.
38 Matthew Aid, "SIGINT and the 1948 Berlin Crisis" (unpublished article, n.d.), 5, Historians Files, CMH; Hans-Albert Hoffman and Siegfried Stoof, *Sowjetische Truppen in Deutschland: Ihr Hauptquartier in Wünsdorf 1945–1994. Geschichte, Fakten, Hintergründe* [Soviet troops in Germany: Their headquarters in Wünsdorf 1945–1994. History, facts, background] (No city: Selbstverlag, 2008), 33.
39 F. L. Howley, *Berlin Command* (New York: G. P. Putnam's Sons, 1950), 199.
40 Harris, "March Crisis, Act II," 23, 24.
41 Msg, Lt. Gen. Stephen J. Chamberlin to CINCEUR for Director of Intel, 4 Apr 1948, Folder "350.09 USSR Vol II From 1 July 1948 To 31 Dec 48," Ofc of the Ch of Staff, Sec of the Gen Staff, Classified Gen Corresp, 1948–51, RG 549, NACP.
42 Eduard M. Mark, "A Glooming Peace" (unpublished manuscript, USAF Historical Support Div, n.d.), 280, Historians Files, CMH.

Intelligence officials in Germany yearned to discover what the Soviets really were planning. The European Command in Heidelberg noted that many of the initial estimates on Soviet troop movements had drawn on reports from German informants. Analysts had forwarded the information "without further confirmation in view of the urgency of the situation."[43] Many local spies, however, were untrained in order of battle intelligence and thus susceptible to deception. As Army Intelligence analysts examined the reports, they suspected real Soviet strength was exaggerated.

The United States Military Liaison Mission proved critical in correcting these inflated estimates. Time and again, the European Command dispatched USMLM officers on "field trips" to double-check reports on Soviet troop increases in specific locations.[44] Often, the officers found that the Soviets had not added any forces, or that the increases had been minimal. The European Command informed the Army's Intelligence Division in Washington that "the Mission has maintained that our strength estimate [of the Soviets] is too high, that there are fewer Soviet troops in the Zone since maneuvers than there were before."[45] Other intelligence sources confirmed the mission's skepticism. Electronic intercepts from the ASA did not indicate increased Soviet troop levels or preparations for war.[46] Army Intelligence analysts scouring the reports found that the Soviets had cannibalized some local units to provide their 3d Mechanized Guards Army with a small infusion of men.[47] Moreover, units would have to march from the western Soviet Union through Poland to bolster garrisons in Germany. The U.S. military attaché in Warsaw had a large organization keeping track of such movements, and they did not detect any.[48]

Top Army Intelligence officials in Germany concluded that the Soviets sought to deceive the Americans in order to put pressure on the Allied position in Berlin. In late March, Colonel Schow noted that total Soviet strength in Germany remained unchanged, and Colonel Rodes called the troop movements a "bluff, pure and simple."[49] This assessment became the consensus of Army Intelligence. By

---

43 Msg, Gen Huebner, EUCOM, to Intel Div (Chamberlin), 15 Apr 1948, Folder "#1 FR: 'S' Germany 1000-4000 1-1-48–6-9-48," ACoS, G–2 (Intel), "Top Secret" Incoming and Outgoing Cables, 1942–52, RG 319, NACP.
44 Msg, Huebner to Intel Div (Chamberlin), 15 Apr 1948.
45 Teleconference, 21 Dec 1948, Folder "#1 Topsec Teleconferences 14 Sep 48 (TT 1239) thru 12/31/48 (TT-1752) 10B2," ACoS, G–2 (Intel), "Top Secret" Incoming and Outgoing Cables, 1942–52, RG 319, NACP.
46 Aid, "SIGINT and the 1948 Berlin Crisis," 6.
47 Aid, "SIGINT and the 1948 Berlin Crisis," 6.
48 Harris, "March Crisis, Act II," 15, 25.
49 Harris, "March Crisis, Act II," 20, 24.

June, the intelligence division dismissed earlier reports, suggesting even a moderate troop increase of 30,000, as overly alarmist.[50] The Soviets, noted the division in August, grasped the many risks involved in starting a war and therefore would "not make so great a decision frivolously."[51] By October, the division described the Soviet "show of force" in spring as part of a coordinated deception campaign. In reality, intelligence officials noted, Soviet soldiers in Germany "couldn't care less about what was happening in Berlin or Paris."[52]

The average Russian soldier may not have cared about Berlin, but the Kremlin certainly did. On 28 October 1948, Soviet Defense Minister Nikolai A. Bulganin ordered the transfer of 73,500 soldiers as well as additional tanks, guns, and armored vehicles to Germany. On 25 March 1949, he reported to Stalin on a successful troop transfer. In the same message, he recommended the augmentation of four infantry divisions in Germany from 8,500 to 11,000 men.[53] Within five months, the Red Army had moved nearly as many soldiers to Germany as the U.S. Army had stationed in all of Europe.[54]

Despite the significant numbers, this troop movement largely eluded Army Intelligence. In the summer of 1949, the European Command intelligence division noted "some indication of westward movement of forces into the Zone" but added that this influx was "offset by continued normal flow of troops . . . eastward during the same period." Likewise, the USMLM detected no evidence of war preparations on the part of the Red Army.[55] By the end of the year, the European

---

50 Msg, Huebner to CSGID, 3 Jun 1948, sub: Russian Cable 54 TOPSEC, Folder "#1 FR: 'S' Germany 1000-4000 1-1-48–6-9-48," ACoS, G–2 (Intel), "Top Secret" Incoming and Outgoing Cables, 1942–52, RG 319, NACP.
51 Rpt, Intel Div, EUCOM, 23 Aug 1948, sub: Military Problems of Preventive War as Seen from the Soviet Union, Folder "927743," Rcds of the ACoS, G–2 (Intel), Formerly Top Secret Documents, 1943–59, RG 319, NACP.
52 Teleconference, 19 Oct 1948, Folder "#1 Topsec Teleconferences 14 Sep 48 (TT 1239) thru 12/31/48 (TT-1752) 2 of 2," ACoS, G–2 (Intel), "Top Secret" Incoming and Outgoing Cables. 1942–52, RG 319, NACP.
53 Vestnik Arkhiva Prezidenta Rossiiskoi Federatsii, ed., *Sovetskaia Armiia. Gody reform i ispytanii* [The Soviet Army: Years of reforms and challenges] (Moscow: Istoricheskaia literatura, 2018), vol. 1, 552–70.
54 In January 1949, the Army had 92,028 soldiers stationed in the continental European Theater: U.S. Department of the Army, *Strength of the Army, 1 January 1949* (Washington, DC: Office of the Adjutant General, 1949), 7.
55 Tlg, Gen. Huebner, EUCOM, to Director of Intel, U.S. Army, 28 Aug 1949, Folder "Top Secret Out's 1948 01 Jul to 31 Dec Book IV," EUCOM, Ofc of the Ch of Staff, Sec of the Gen Staff, Msg Control Center, Outgoing Msgs, Top Secret Section, 1948–1951, RG 549, NACP.

Command estimated Soviet troop strength in Germany at 273,000—a figure significantly below the actual number.[56]

The Army may have failed to notice the troop augmentation because the Soviets transferred most of these forces from Austria, rather than from Poland and the western Soviet Union.[57] While the military attaché in Warsaw kept a close eye on east-west train movements between the Soviet Union and Germany, his colleague in Prague struggled to build a similarly efficient organization to monitor north-south movements between Austria and Germany.[58] The Soviets also may have taken special care to disguise their troop augmentation to avoid a Western military response. Whatever the case, Army Intelligence throughout the crisis did not indicate that the Soviets had any desire to go to war over Berlin. Even if the order of battle estimates were faulty during the winter of 1948–1949, they helped avoid setting off additional alarms in Washington and thereby escalating the crisis.

The Blockade

Having failed to impress the Allies with a mock show of force early in 1948, the Soviets ratcheted up the pressure by initiating a blockade of the Western sectors. On 31 March 1948, the Soviet deputy military governor, General Mikhail I. Dratvin, announced a number of restrictions on ground traffic to and from Berlin. Over the next three months, the Soviets imposed a series of ever more stringent limitations on Western access to Berlin by highway, railway, rivers, and canals, but not by air. Colonel Howley described the process as "the slowly tightening moves of a giant boa constrictor—almost imperceptible at the instant of movement but gradually working up to complete constriction."[59] The point of "complete constriction" arrived four days after the currency reform in the Western zones: on 24 June, the Soviets suspended all Western water and land traffic to Berlin.

American intelligence had been conscious to the threat of a blockade. CIA director R. Adm. Roscoe H. Hillenkoetter alerted the president on 22 December 1947 that the breakdown of the foreign ministers' conference in London would prompt the Soviet Union to put pressure on the Western Allies in Berlin. Because the So-

---

56 Teleconference, Lt. Col. Carl A. Weaver and Capt. Laurent D. Pavy, 21 Dec 1948, Folder "#1 Topsec Teleconferences 14 Sep 48 (TT 1239) thru 12/31/48 (TT-1752) 10B2," AcoS, G-2 (Intel), "Top Secret" Incoming and Outgoing Cables, 1942–52, RG 319, NACP.
57 Uhl, *Krieg um Berlin?*, 46–47.
58 Lukes, *On the Edge of the Cold War*, 142–61.
59 Howley, *Berlin Command*, 193.

Figure 45: Berlin-bound trucks being blocked by Soviet forces at the British-Soviet intrazonal border at Helmstedt, June 1948. U.S. Army, NACP.

viets could not expect their Western counterparts to withdraw from Berlin voluntarily, Moscow "will probably use every means short of armed force to compel these powers to leave the city." Hillenkoetter predicted "obstruction to transport and travel," "'failure' of services such as electric supply," "flagrant violations of Kommandatura agreements," and "instigation of unrest among Germans in the US sector."[60] These moves would undermine the American presence in the German capital.

Hillenkoetter's December 1947 memorandum proved prophetic, yet just as with Colonel Koenig's warning about the explosive situation in Czechoslovakia a few months earlier, it was ignored. Only in late March, when the writing was on the wall, did Colonel Howley and his advisers draw up a contingency plan for a blockade. Code-named COUNTERPUNCH, the plan provided for the buildup of food and coal stocks in the Western sectors. Although preparations started late, the Americans in Berlin managed to stockpile supplies for about a month. By radio,

---

60 Memo, Hillenkoetter for Truman, 22 Dec 1947, in *On the Front Lines of the Cold War: Documents on the Intelligence War in Berlin, 1946 to 1961*, ed. Donald P. Steury (Washington, DC: Center for the Study of Intelligence, 1999), 144–45.

Howley broadcast the military government's defiance: "We are not getting out of Berlin. We are going to stay."[61]

Even as the Americans sought to project an image of calm determination in public, a vigorous internal debate about the appropriate course of action roiled the U.S. government. Secretary of the Army Royall saw little value in Berlin, worried about the risks of war, and considered American withdrawal from the city a realistic option.[62] On the other end of the ideological spectrum, Defense Secretary Forrestal and Air Force Chief of Staff General Hoyt S. Vandenberg Jr. suggested to President Truman not to bother with the niceties of diplomacy. Instead, the Americans should implement War Plan BROILER and hit the Soviet Union hard with up to one hundred atomic bombs. Their proposal was as irresponsible as it was unrealistic because the United States had neither enough bombs nor sufficient aircraft to deliver the weapons.[63]

On 1 April, General Clay proposed to the Army's chief of staff, General Bradley, that the Americans enforce their rights by sending an armed convoy from the U.S. Zone through the Soviet Zone to the German capital. Fearing that such an overt provocation would escalate the conflict, Bradley immediately instructed Clay to refrain from doing so because "such an application of military force could lead straight to general war."[64] Nonetheless, Clay reiterated his proposal again eleven days later, this time suggesting a joint Anglo-American-French operation, with each power marching a division from the city of Helmstedt in the British Zone to Berlin, a distance of about 120 miles. Clay predicted the Soviets would "fold up in [the] face of such a move." The British, however, saw "no future in this," as the Soviets could easily stop the Allies with a few tanks, and Bradley politely rejected Clay's proposal for a second time.[65]

Clay refused to take "no" for an answer. On 10 July, after the Soviets had shut down all Western land and sea access routes to Berlin, he once again pitched the idea of an armed convoy to Bradley. "In my own mind," Clay wrote, "I am convinced that [the convoy] would get to Berlin and that the technical difficulties [i.e., the blockade] would cease to exist."[66] The U.S. Constabulary's Brig. Gen. Arthur G. Trudeau, the commander of the 1st Constabulary Brigade which was to lead the breakthrough, recalled that his men were ready and eager to shoot their way into Berlin.[67] Given that the Constabulary was only lightly armed and counted less than

---

61 Howley, *Berlin Command*, 201.
62 Harrington, *Berlin on the Brink*, 84.
63 Russel D. Buhite and William C. Hamel, "War for Peace: The Question of an American Preventive War Against the Soviet Union, 1945–1955," *Diplomatic History* 14, no. 3 (Jun 1990), 375.
64 Bradley, *A General's Life*, 479.
65 Harrington, *Berlin on the Brink*, 59.
66 Msg, Clay to Bradley, 10 Jul 1948, doc. 464, in Smith, *Clay Papers*, 2:734–35.
67 Harrington, *Berlin on the Brink*, 127–28.

16,000 soldiers dispersed across Germany and Austria, Trudeau's statement was mere bravado, bordering on recklessness.[68]

Clay's latest iteration of the convoy proposal prompted a flurry of transatlantic communications and a hastily assembled planning session. A teleconference between the Army's Plans and Operations divisions in Europe and in Washington revealed that Clay's planners had exerted little energy on the project and had too few men and materiel to execute it.[69] A staff study in Washington noted the "prodigious" logistical effort involved in supplying Berlin by convoy: "A system of transportation and traffic control equal to that in effect of the Red Ball Highway of OVERLORD operations . . . during World War II would be necessary." Moreover, the study warned, an armed convoy might trigger "open warfare." In conclusion, the authors counseled against Clay's plan.[70]

Owing to the potentially grave consequences of Clay's proposal, Royall recalled the general to the United States for consultations. During a dinner with Forrestal, Clay argued that, "three weeks ago, he could have put through an armed convoy without difficulty." In the meantime, Clay conceded, the Soviets had become more committed to the blockade, but he still believed, "it could be done without creating a crisis."[71] The next day, Clay made his case for a convoy before President Truman and the National Security Council.[72] It was to no avail. Two weeks later, a report by the Office of the Secretary of Defense to the National Security Council described the chances of piercing the blockade by means of an armed convoy as "remote." The Soviets, the report argued, could easily stop a convoy through "passive interference," such as roadblocks or the demolition of bridges. Based on an assessment of the Joint Chiefs of Staff, the secretary of defense warned that a convoy would carry with it "the distinctly probable consequence of war."[73] By late summer, the Americans had put the idea of an armed convoy to rest.

---

68 Memo, Joint Chs of Staff, 17 Jul 1948, sub: summary of the military situation in Germany, Folder "P&O 381 TS," Plans and Opns Div, Decimal File 1946–1948, RG 319, NACP.
69 Teleconference, Col. R. W. Mayo, Department of the Army, Plans and Opns (Washington), Brig. Gen. V. E. Prichard, EUCOM, Plans and Opns, 13 Jul 1948, doc. 467, in Smith, *Clay Papers*, 2:736–38.
70 Rpt, Lt. Col. Osmanski, Planning and Opns, Strategy Sec, 13 Jul 1948, Folder "P&O 381 US," Plans and Opns Div, Decimal File, 1946–1948, RG 319, NACP.
71 Millis, *Forrestal Diaries*, 459–60.
72 Harrington, *Berlin on the Brink*, 138.
73 Rpt, Sec Def to National Security Council, 28 Jul 1948, sub: The Secretary of Defense on U.S. Military Courses of Action with Respect to the Situation in Berlin, Folder "National Security Council– Meetings: 17: August 5, 1948 178–1," President's Sec Files, The Papers of Harry S. Truman, Truman Library.

Given the serious implications of sending armed forces into Soviet-occupied territory, the absence of intelligence input is striking. Clay apparently formulated his plans without consulting his intelligence officials in Germany. Intelligence officers, in turn, discussed the issue only in passing. On 20 July, the intelligence office of the military government considered an armed convoy briefly in connection with a Soviet propaganda initiative about food supplies for the population of Berlin.[74] Two days later, the CIC in Berlin reported on widespread rumors among the population about an impending Anglo-American attempt to break the blockade by armed trains and a tank force.[75] In Washington, no one asked military intelligence or the CIA for a consequences paper explaining the likely outcomes of any military action. Only a few politicians made informal inquiries on this matter to the ad hoc intelligence committee established during the March crisis. Team members, including General Chamberlin, thought that a convoy would precipitate war, but hesitated to speak out without being officially consulted.[76] Only in August did the CIA submit a report, caveated as "unevaluated information," to the effect that the Soviets would resist by force the intrusion of an armed convoy.[77] In January 1949, the agency submitted a formal memorandum, arguing that a convoy "would involve substantial risk of a general war."[78] By that time, however, the debate about breaking the blockade had already ended.

Clay's inattention to intelligence heightened the risk of an armed escalation. Soviet officers regarded the intra-German demarcation line "as sacred Soviet borders."[79] The Red Army units around Berlin had explicit orders to intercept armed Western convoys.[80] Military leaders in Washington therefore intuitively made the right call to not pursue Clay's proposal, but both they and Clay would have been well advised to request a formal intelligence estimate. Given Army Intelligence's solid grasp on the numbers and distribution of Soviet forces in Germany, such an estimate probably would have revealed the risky nature of Clay's approach.

---

74 Teleconference # 9807, 20 Jul 1948, Folder "#1 Telecons (1-1-48 thru TT-1156, 9-5-48)," ACoS, G–2 (Intel), "Top Secret" Incoming and Outgoing Cables, 1942–52, RG 319, NACP.
75 Rpt, Region VIII, CIC, 22 Jul 1948, Folder "CIC Region VIII (Berlin) Periodic Counter Intelligence Reports," Director of Intel, Analysis and Research, Misc. Rpts and Publications, 1941–50, RG 260, NACP.
76 Harris, "March Crisis, Act II," 30.
77 Rpt, CIA, 6 Aug 1948, sub: Soviet Reaction to Berlin Airlift, CIA Electronic Reading Room.
78 Memo, CIA, Intel Memo no. 118, 11 Jan 1949, sub: Probable Soviet Reaction to a US Attempt to Force the Berlin Blockade, CIA Electronic Reading Room.
79 Victor Gobarev, "Soviet Military Plans and Actions During the First Berlin Crisis, 1948–49," *Journal of Slavic Military Studies* 10, no. 3 (Sep 1997), 16.
80 Uhl, *Krieg um Berlin?*, 45.

With the dismissal of the ill-considered convoy project, the Americans sought another response to the blockade. Eventually, they found it in the airlift (Map 1).[81] Operation VITTLES, as the U.S. Air Force called the effort to supply the beleaguered city by air, began in late June. Initially, the airlift aimed at sustaining only the occupation forces in Berlin, as it appeared inconceivable that the Allies would be able to bring in enough food, fuel, and other essential materials to support the local population. Over time, however, they managed to boost the amount of delivered goods. By September, one cargo plane landed in Berlin every ninety-six seconds. The Anglo-American air forces delivered nearly 7,000 tons of goods in one day alone to the city's Tempelhof and Gatow airfields. This amount narrowly exceeded the daily summertime needs of the city, raising the prospect of breaking the blockade by air.[82]

Given the centrality of the airlift to the survival of West Berlin, U.S. intelligence focused on detecting Soviet attempts to disrupt Allied air traffic. The intelligence service of the recently established U.S. Air Force monitored Soviet aviation while Army Intelligence paid close attention to ground interference with the airlift. Early incidents did not bode well. Already in April, a Soviet Yakovlev Yak–3 fighter jet had collided with a British passenger plane as the latter prepared for landing at Gatow airport in Berlin. The Soviet pilot, as well as all fourteen British crewmembers and passengers, died in the crash. A British investigation found that the Soviet pilot caused the disaster by harassing the slower-moving British plane.[83] In fact, Soviet aircraft were routinely "buzzing" Western planes in the vicinity of Berlin. The crash highlighted the vulnerability of the Anglo-American air bridge.

As the airlift expanded during the summer of 1948, American officials repeatedly dealt with possible Soviet threats. In late June, a report on Soviet barrage balloons in the air corridors prompted top military and intelligence officers in Germany and the United States to discuss countermeasures.[84] In August, the European Command's intelligence division reported that the Soviet Air Forces had increased the number of aircraft in the area of Berlin. And in September and October, the National Security Council repeatedly discussed "possible Soviet interruptions to the airlift."[85]

---

81 Howley, *Berlin Command*, 210; William Stivers, "The Incomplete Blockade: Soviet Zone Supply of West Berlin, 1948–49," *Diplomatic History* 21, no. 4 (Fall 1997), 589.
82 Harrington, *Berlin on the Brink*, 175. In late 1948, the Western Allies added a third airfield, Tegel, in the French sector, to support the airlift.
83 Delbert Clark, "Soviet-British Plane Collision Kills 15; Russian Apologizes," *New York Times*, 6 Apr 1948.
84 Teleconference no. 9703, 30 Jun 1948, Folder "#1 Telecons (1-1-48 thru TT-1156, 9-5-48)," ACoS, G–2 (Intel), "Top Secret" Incoming and Outgoing Cables, 1952–52," RG 319, NACP. The report turned out to be exaggerated.
85 Minutes of the 24th Meeting of the NSC, 14 Oct 1948, Folder "National Security Council–Meetings: 24: October 14, 1948 178–8," President's Secretary's Files, Truman Library.

The Soviets also sought to undermine the airlift through disinformation. On 23 July 1948, the military government's Office of the Director of Intelligence received a report from the commander of naval forces in Germany, containing a warning from one of their sources inside the Soviet Kommandatura in Berlin. This source had informed them that the Soviets planned to close two of the three air corridors within two weeks, and would intermittently close the third. The American intelligence officer evaluating this report commented that the Soviets may have deliberately planted this information to force the Western powers to the negotiating table. In retrospect, this assessment appears accurate, as the Soviets never closed any of the air corridors.[86]

Although the airlift was vulnerable to outside interference, the Soviets never seriously challenged it. Moscow had good reasons for not doing so. The Soviet Military Administration had never formally granted the Western Allies access to Berlin by road, rail, or river; however, they had agreed in November 1945 to allow three air corridors to connect the city's Western sectors with their respective Western zones.[87] Interfering with these clearly defined corridors might trigger war, a risk Stalin wanted to avoid.[88] Moreover, the Kremlin doubted that the West would be capable of sustaining the airlift through the winter. When the airlift failed, Stalin felt, the Allies would be at his mercy. Vladimir S. Semyonov, the political adviser to the Soviet commander in Germany, relished the prospect of "smoking out" the Western powers in Berlin.[89] Or, as Colonel Howley put it, the Soviets "were content to sit back, with cynical satisfaction, and watch the results of their evil work."[90]

For a while, it seemed as if Stalin's gamble would pay off. With winter approaching, the Allies faced a dual challenge. First, the citizens of Berlin required additional delivery of several thousand tons of coal per day for heating purposes. Second, diminishing daylight and deteriorating weather conditions put additional strains on pilots and planes. Intelligence estimates turned decidedly gloomy. The CIA warned in October that, if four-power negotiations over Germany should fail, the "Western position in the city would increasingly deteriorate, and ultimate Western withdrawal would probably become necessary." This move, in turn,

---

[86] Msg, Cdr Naval Forces Germany to ODI, OMGUS, 23 Jul 1948, Folder "91 Soviet Zone," Director of Intel, Analysis and Research Br, Gen Corresp, 1945–49, RG 260, NACP.
[87] Harrington, *Berlin on the Brink*, 22.
[88] Gerhard Wettig, *Stalin and the Cold War in Europe: The Emergence and Development of East-West Conflict 1939–1953* (Lanham, MD: Rowman and Littlefield, 2008), 169.
[89] Jochen Laufer, "Die UdSSR und die Ursprünge der Berlin-Blockade 1944–1948" [The USSR and the origins of the Berlin blockade, 1944–1948], *Deutschland Archiv* 31, no. 4 (1998), 577.
[90] Howley, *Berlin Command*, 194.

"would seriously damage Western, and especially U.S., prestige throughout the world."[91]

An expanded airlift seemed to be the only answer to this bleak scenario. Throughout the summer, Clay implored Washington to send more and larger aircraft to Germany. He insisted that he was "completely confident that given the airplanes we can do the job. . . . We are winning the fight now," he asserted, "and now is the time to maximize our airlift."[92] But in the United States, many senior military figures regarded Berlin as a sideshow and hesitated to fully commit to the city. Doubters included the leadership of the U.S. Air Force, which would have to shoulder most of the additional burden. Committing the bulk of its cargo fleet to the Berlin operation, Air Force officers argued, would severely limit their service's strategic bombing capabilities worldwide. Furthermore, the planes would be sitting ducks for the Soviets if war broke out over Berlin.[93] Fortunately for the people of Berlin, President Truman came down squarely on Clay's side. "We stay in Berlin, period," Truman resolved and ordered a full-scale airlift.[94]

Meanwhile, the U.S. military government retaliated against the Soviets by imposing a counterblockade. The Soviet Zone economy depended heavily on raw materials from the West, and on 24 June General Clay banned the export of roughly twenty critical items, including steel and coal.[95] This measure swiftly yielded results. As CIA director Admiral Hillenkoetter reported to the president, on 28 June Marshal Sokolovsky had convened a meeting in Karlshorst with Soviet officers and the East German industrial committee to discuss the effects of the counterblockade. The East Germans complained that the lack of steel imports and machinery parts threatened to paralyze sugar refineries, canneries, and steel mills, as well as the operations of the Baltic fishing fleet. In turn, Sokolovsky expressed great consternation at their plight; he had been led to believe that East Germany could survive independently. Another Soviet general noted, "We had no idea of this situation. If we had known this, we would not have gone so far." As

---

91 Rpt, CIA to Director of Intel, Department of the Army, 28 Sep 1948, sub: Consequences of a Breakdown in Four-Power Negotiations on Germany, National Security Archive, https://nsarchive.gwu.edu/.
92 Msg, Clay to Bradley, 4 Oct 1948, doc. 557, in Smith, *Clay Papers*, 2:890–91.
93 Harrington, *Berlin on the Brink*, 111.
94 McCullough, *Truman*, 630.
95 Memo, E. O. Brand, Economic Analyst, Intel, OMGUS, to Stearns, ODI, 10 May [or Mar] 1949, sub: Request for Info from Colonel Rodes, Historians Files, CMH; Special Rpt, Innis D. Harris, ODI, 5 Feb 1949, sub: Soviet Zone Industry Under the Counter-Blockade, Historians Files, CMH; William Stivers and Donald A. Carter, *The City Becomes a Symbol: The U.S. Army in the Occupation of the Berlin, 1945–1949*, U.S. Army in the Cold War (Washington, DC: U.S. Army Center of Military History, 2017), 288.

Sokolovsky came to grips with the dire consequences of the counterblockade, he laid out three options to the assembled officials: first, "start a war"; second, "lift travel restrictions on Berlin"; and third, "leave entire Berlin to the West." After the meeting, the director of the Soviet propaganda administration, Col. Sergei I. Tulpanov, observed gloomily "that war was impossible due to bad harvest prospects and that lifting travel restrictions would make the Russians lose face." Hillenkoetter concluded the memo by noting that "the source" of this report "is very reliable and the content is possibly true."[96]

Over the following months, multiple informants confirmed the severity of the counterblockade's impact on the Soviet Zone economy. A document purloined from the East German Economic Commission by an agent of Lt. Col. Harry S. Pretty's intelligence section in Berlin revealed that Soviet Zone imports from the West had dropped sharply in July 1948.[97] In August, a source "close to" Socialist Unity Party boss Walter Ulbricht reported that the East German leader worried about declining East-West trade, because "every ton of steel imported from the Ruhr represented a gain for Communism and a loss for Western Europe."[98] In September and October, informants of the CIC and the intelligence section in Berlin revealed that the counterblockade had successfully upended the Soviet Zone's two-year plan for economic development.[99]

Given the effectiveness of the counterblockade, the U.S. military government gradually expanded the list of banned export materials and tightened the border controls. In January 1949, the three Western military commanders jointly resolved to control the export of raw materials and goods to the Soviet Zone.[100] Four months later, a military government economist reported to Colonel Rodes that it would be an exaggeration to say that Western measures had "busted" the Soviet Zone economy. Nonetheless, he noted, the counterblockade caused shortages for a range of critical items, including heavy engineering equipment, special

---

96 Memo, Roscoe H. Hillenkoetter, DCI, for President Harry S. Truman, 30 Jun 1948, Folder "Memos to and from President 1948–1949," Rcds of the Chairman, White House Rcds of Fleet Admiral William D. Leahy, 1942–1948, RG 218, NACP.
97 Rpt, Lt. Col. Harry S. Pretty, S-2, Berlin, to Intel Div, EUCOM, 8 Mar 1949, sub: Interzonal and Foreign Trade, Historians Files, CMH.
98 Info Rpt, External Survey Detachment 11, 9 Aug 1948, Historians Files, CMH.
99 Rpt, Region VIII, CIC, 14 Sep 1948, sub: Future Political Policies of the SMA for Germany, Historians Files, CMH; Msg, Lt. Col. Harry S. Pretty, to ODI, OMGUS, 12 Oct 1948, sub: Two-Year Plan, Historians Files, CMH.
100 Msg, H. E. Stearns, Intel Br, Berlin, to ODI, OMGUS, 21 Jan 1949, sub: Special Report on Trade between the Western Sectors and the Soviet Area of Control, Historians Files, CMH.

machines, and spare parts.[101] The longer the counterblockade lasted, the more pronounced these deficiencies promised to become.

By early 1949, the Allies had turned around the precarious predicament of their sectors. The airlift ensured the survival of Allied soldiers and local Germans, and the counterblockade put pressure on the Soviets to reconsider their aggressive posture. Meanwhile, intelligence reassured the U.S. leadership in Germany and in the United States that the likelihood of an attack from the East remained remote. With the aid of its intelligence services, the Army had enabled American policymakers to negotiate with Moscow from a position of strength. The military had done its job. It now fell to the diplomats to end the crisis.

The Struggle for Berlin's Hearts and Minds

Inside Berlin, the Allied position remained precarious. Cut off from the Western zones, the United States had only 4,880 military personnel in Berlin in early 1948, and the combined strength of the three Western garrisons amounted to no more than five battalions.[102] This meager force would be hard-pressed to confront large-scale riots, strikes, or other disturbances among the 2.25 million inhabitants of the American, British, and French sectors. The Soviets and their communist German allies understood the Allied weakness and sought to exploit it by sowing dissent between the American occupiers and German civilians.

On 25 April 1948, *Neues Deutschland*, the official SED newspaper in the Soviet Zone, published a lengthy article titled "Serious Acts of Aggression in the U.S. Sector." The authors narrated in considerable detail a dozen instances of American soldiers attacking or mistreating Berliners. "Two uniformed Americans," one example read, "attacked the sixty-year old German Martha Machlanka in [the borough of] Charlottenburg . . . and mistreated her badly. The victim was hospitalized with a severe concussion."[103] When the local CIC investigated these charges, they found that employees of *Neues Deutschland* and other Soviet sector dailies regularly visited Western sector police stations and systematically perused police

---

101 Memo, Anthony Geber, Senior Economic Analyst, for Col. Rodes, n.d. sub: Soviet Zone Economic Developments, Historians Files, CMH.
102 Msg, Gen Lucius D. Clay to Ch of Staff, OMGUS, 2 Apr 1948, Folder "#1 Fr. Germany CC-2765–CC-5919 1-1-48–9-12-48," ACoS, G–2 (Intel), "Top Secret" Incoming and Outgoing Cables, 1942–52, RG 319, NACP; Roger G. Miller, *To Save a City: The Berlin Airlift 1948–1949* (Washington, DC: USAF History Office, 1998), 17.
103 "Schwere Übergriffe im US-Sektor Berlins" [Serious attacks in the U.S. sector of Berlin], *Neues Deutschland*, 25 Apr 1948.

blotters for incidents involving American soldiers. The communist press then "warped and magnified" these stories. "Accusations have even been made," the CIC noted tongue-in-cheek, "that American soldiers have embarked on a grand scale program of biting (or beating—the term is still in debate) Germans without provocation."[104]

Soviet-inspired reports of crimes committed by U.S. soldiers against German civilians in the Soviet-controlled press must have struck many Berliners, and especially women, as ironic. Few had forgotten the physical and sexual violence of Red Army soldiers only a few years earlier. Anecdotal evidence suggests that such press attacks against the Americans had little effect. As a popular contemporary joke in Berlin went: "If there must be a blockade, then it's better to be blockaded by the Soviets and fed by the Americans. Just imagine if it were the other way around!"[105]

The possibility of communist-inspired unrest in the Western sectors posed a more serious threat. On 25 June, Clay's deputy, Lt. Gen. George P. Hays, informed General Chamberlin that Army Intelligence in Berlin had received a report from a "fairly reliable source" with access to communist organizations inside the Soviet sector. The report suggested that members of the SED Central Committee were planning to manufacture a revolutionary "people's movement." According to this information, the Western sectors would "be overrun by strong bands of 'Democratic revolutionaries' on the pretext of demonstrations for the unity of Berlin." Supposedly, the SED assumed that in the ensuing strife, "the Western powers would not take decisive action," and "the anti-Communist forces among the Germans would not receive the necessary material support" from the West.[106]

The prospect of communist-inspired riots rattled American authorities. On the day Hays sent his report to Chamberlin, General Clay opined to Deputy Chief of Staff Lt. Gen. J. Lawton Collins and to Secretary of the Army Royall that the "Principal danger is from Russian-planned German Communist groups out looking for trouble."[107] The report went all the way to the White House. On 30 June, Hillenkoetter submitted a memorandum to President Truman, warning him that

---

104 Rpt, HQ, Region VIII, CIC, 13 May 1948, sub: CI report no. 96, Folder "CIC Region VIII (Berlin) Periodic Counter Intelligence Report," Director of Intel, Analysis and Research, Misc. Rpts and Publications, 1941–50, RG 260, NACP.
105 Cited in Harrington, *Berlin on the Brink*, 230.
106 Msg, Maj. Gen. George P. Hays, ODI, to Chamberlin, 27 Jun 1948, Folder "#1 Fr. Germany CC-2765 – CC-5919 1-1-48–9-12-48," ACoS, G-2 (Intel), "Top Secret" Incoming and Outgoing Cables. 1942–52, RG 319, NACP.
107 Teleconference, Sec Army Kenneth C. Royall, Gen. J. Lawton Collins, Gen. Lucius D. Clay, 25 Jun 1948, doc. 442, in Smith, *Clay Papers*, 2:702.

the "Berlin Communists, under Soviet direction, have been expected to create a 'revolutionary situation' if popular unrest in the city develops sufficiently during the present situation."[108] Hillenkoetter believed that the Soviets were using the threat of creating chaos in Berlin as a scare tactic to pressure the Western powers into making concessions over Germany. The anticipated "revolutionary situation" never materialized. Nonetheless, the incident served as a painful reminder of Western vulnerability to Soviet pressure.

Given the extent to which the Western position in Berlin depended on the attitude of the population in the Western sectors, local Army Intelligence agencies closely monitored Berliners' sentiments toward the blockade. Reports indicated that Berliners' greatest concern revolved around the prospect of American abandonment. On 1 April, the day the Soviets enacted a partial blockade, the CIC in Berlin reported that "rumors of all types" had flooded the city and that the "average Berliner, especially those living in the Western Sectors, fear the possible evacuation [of the Western garrisons] almost to the point of hysteria."[109]

General Clay was keenly attuned to these fears. Although he did not prohibit the evacuation of American dependents from Berlin, he strongly discouraged his personnel from sending their dependents out of the city. As he explained in a teleconference with the Department of the Army: "Withdrawal of dependents from Berlin would create hysteria accompanied by rush of Germans to Communism for safety."[110] Clay and Howley set an example by keeping their own families in Berlin.[111] Outwardly, Clay projected an aura of calm, optimism, and resolve. As he told the German-American journalist Curt Riess at the time: "Nothing has really changed. There have always been crises since I arrived in Berlin. . . . This time it is a case of not succumbing to blackmail." "This statement," Riess recalled, "impressed me more than the record statistics [about the airlift] that were now being published in the newspapers. . . . And the Berliners who read my article were also deeply impressed by what Clay said, just because he had spoken so modestly and unemotionally."[112]

As Berliners came to believe the Americans' assurances about their resolve to remain in the city, their confidence in the Western powers grew. In July 1948, the Soviets announced their intention to feed citizens of the Western sectors provided

---

108 Memo, Hillenkoetter for Truman, 30 Jun 1948.
109 Rpt, Region VIII, CIC, 1 Apr 1948, sub: CI report no. 93, Folder "CIC Region VIII (Berlin) Periodic Counterintelligence Reports," Director of Intel, Analysis and Research, Misc. Rpts and Publications, RG 260, NACP.
110 Clay, *Decision in Germany*, 358.
111 Howley, *Berlin Command*, 221.
112 Curt Riess, *Berlin Berlin 1945–1953* (Berlin: Non-Stop Bücherei, 1953), 106.

they registered in the Soviet sector and purchased the food there. This initiative, which threatened to undermine the rationale of the airlift and the Western presence in Berlin, became the subject of a lengthy teleconference between Army Intelligence personnel in Berlin and Washington. The Office of the Director of Intelligence considered the offer a bluff and doubted the Soviets' ability to feed so many extra mouths. In the event, the discussion proved academic. In what amounted to an impressive demonstration of citizens' belief in the Western commitment to Berlin, less than 100,000 out of over 2 million Berliners living in the western sectors chose to accept the Soviet offer.[113]

According to the Army's intelligence agencies, the airlift itself was the most powerful weapon in the American propaganda arsenal against the Soviets. "'Operation Vittles' is doing more than anything to maintain German morale," reported the CIC in late July 1948. "The people see in this operation the proof that the Western Powers are both willing and able to stand behind the promises they have made."[114] A month later, the Public Safety Branch of the military government in the Berlin Sector wrote in the same vein that "the 'airbridge' is tremendously admired and has confused and frustrated the Soviet threat of 'surrender or starve.'"[115] The timing of these assessments is noteworthy; at this point, the Western air forces had not yet managed to deliver sufficient tonnage on a daily basis to sustain the population of the three Western sectors indefinitely. The airlift therefore made a significant public opinion contribution to Western efforts to defend Berlin against Soviet aggression even before it succeeded logistically.

As Berliners gained confidence in the Americans, they became increasingly hostile to the Soviets and their communist allies. "<u>Politically</u> and <u>morally</u> the Soviets and their SED satellites are completely on the defensive in Berlin," concluded the Public Safety Branch in August 1948.[116] But anticommunism was a double-edged sword. For one, German activists who rallied against Soviet and communist

---

[113] Teleconference 9807, Mr. Watson, Col. Ennis, Lt. Col. S. M. Melnik, Lt. Col. Osmanski, Lt. Col. Emmens, Dr. H. S. Craig, Maj. Gen. Hall, Mr. L. E. DeNeufville, Mr. H. E. Stearns, 20 Jul 1948, sub: Daily cable to Dept. of the Army, Folder "#1 Telecons (1-1-48 thru TT-1156, 9-5-48)," ACoS, G–2 (Intel), "Top Secret" Incoming and Outgoing Cables. 1942–52, RG 319, NACP; Howley, *Berlin Command*, 206.

[114] Rpt, Region VIII, CIC, 22 Jul 1948, Folder "CIC Region VIII (Berlin) Periodic Counter Intelligence Reports," Director of Intel, Analysis and Research, Misc. Rpts and Publications, 1941–50, RG 260, NACP.

[115] Rpt, Ofc of Mil Government, Berlin Sector (OMGBS), 21 Aug 1948, Folder "Pol Reports 11–17," OMGUS, Rcds of the Berlin Sector, Rcds of the Public Safety Br: Intel Rpts, 1946–1950, RG 260, NACP.

[116] Rpt, OMGBS, 7 Aug 1948, Folder "Pol Reports 1–10," OMGUS, Rcds of the Berlin Sector, Rcds of the Public Safety Br: Intel Rpts, 1946–1950, RG 260, NACP. Emphasis in original.

pressure in Berlin became increasingly impatient at continued Western efforts to bring about a negotiated end to the blockade. The Public Safety Branch described them as "disgusted" with the ongoing talks between Western and Soviet representatives in Moscow in late August. Instead, the German activists advocated a firm policy against the Soviets. "If the Western aim is to break the blockade," the branch summarized their arguments, "then the Western Powers must do everything in their power to demonstrate to the Russians that their siege of Berlin is futile and will never bear results."[117] In the fall of 1948, the combination of Soviet pressure from the East and anticommunism in the west threatened to explode the fragile equilibrium in the city.

The regional government, or Magistrat, of Berlin remained responsible for the administration of the entire city. Many of its offices, including the assembly, were located in the Soviet sector, and therefore the Soviets and their communist allies could easily interfere with the administration's proceedings. As the blockade continued, they harassed members of the city government traveling to and from their sector. According to General Vandenberg of the U.S. Air Force, they did so "to gain control of all of Berlin by destroying prestige and power of present city government and by destroying prestige and influence of Western Powers by showing them incapable of supporting city administration and protecting its employees."[118]

Soviet efforts to disrupt the elected Berlin government culminated on 6 September. As members of the city assembly convened for a regular session in the Neues Stadthaus building in the Soviet sector, groups of communist agitators gathered outside. Most worked for Soviet-owned companies and industries. They were under orders to storm the assembly and disrupt its proceedings. The Soviet commandant, Maj. Gen. Alexander G. Kotikov, had refused to provide Soviet sector police to protect the assembly. Therefore, only a handful of policemen and orderlies from the Western sectors were on hand. The demonstrators quickly pushed them aside, hammered down the doors, swarmed through the building, and drove out the lawmakers. The parliamentarians fled and reconvened—without the SED representatives—on the same day at the Taberna Academica, a student-owned venue in the British sector. They would not return to the Neues Stadthaus. Henceforth, Berlin effectively operated under two city governments.[119]

---

117 Rpt, OMGBS, 21 Aug 1948.
118 Msg, Gen. Hoyt S. Vandenberg Jr., Ch of Staff, USAF, to Cdr in Ch of the Atlantic Fleet, 9 Sep 1948, sub: Air Force Intelligence Summary, Folder "Germany," Rcds of the Chairman, White House Rcds of Fleet Adm William D. Leahy, 1942–1948, RG 218, NACP.
119 David E. Barclay, *Schaut auf diese Stadt: Der unbekannte Ernst Reuter* [Look upon this city: The unknown Ernst Reuter] (Berlin: Siedler Verlag, 2000), 192.

Three days later, in the afternoon of 9 September, a crowd of 200,000 to 300,000 demonstrators convened before the old Reichstag building in the British sector to protest against Soviet and SED policy. Several prominent Berlin politicians lambasted the Soviets. Ernst Reuter, the SPD leader whose election as mayor had been blocked by the Soviets, made an emotional appeal to global public opinion: "People of this world. . . . Look upon this city and see that you should not and cannot abandon this city and this people!" As a military government intelligence report noted, at that point "the crowd was well behaved and the speeches drew great applause."[120] After the speeches, however, part of the crowd moved toward the Brandenburg Gate, which marked the border to the Soviet sector. Here, they clashed with Soviet sector police, who began firing into the crowd, wounding several. One youth was shot while attempting to remove the Soviet flag from the gate and died from his wound. Another youth then successfully grabbed the flag and threw it into the crowd, who tore it to pieces and burned the remains.[121] Nearby, German demonstrators smashed the windshield of a jeep carrying a handful of Soviet soldiers. Only the appearance of British military police prevented a further escalation. The British soldiers escorted the Soviet jeep to safety and separated the demonstrators and Soviet sector police.[122] The following day, *Neues Deutschland* denounced the demonstrators as "Nazi goon squads" and vowed to fight until the "unconditional surrender of fascism."[123]

Clay realized the dangers of these unleashed passions. "We are playing with dynamite," he wrote to Under Secretary of the Army William H. Draper Jr. "Mass meetings directed against Soviet military government can easily turn into mass meetings against other occupying powers and can develop into the type of mob government which Hitler played so well to get in power."[124] In this volatile situation, American occupation authorities needed to work with German politicians who could help control public sentiment and support the Western powers. In Ernst Reuter, they found their man. Although Clay and Reuter differed temperamentally and never became close friends, they came to work harmoniously together. In late June 1948, General Clay invited Reuter and his lieutenant, Willy Brandt, to a personal meeting in order to "give them courage" (*Mut zusprechen*)

---

120 Teleconference, 10 Sep 1948, sub: Anti-Communist Demonstration, Folder "#2 Topsec Telecons 9/6/48–12/31-48 (TT-1157)–(TT-1703)," ACoS, G–2 (Intel), "Top Secret" Incoming and Outgoing Cables. 1942–52, RG 319, NACP.
121 Riess, *Berlin Berlin*, 116.
122 Teleconference, 10 Sep 1948, sub: Anti-Communist Demonstration.
123 "Wieder Reichstagsbrandstifter" [Reichstag arsonist again], *Neues Deutschland*, 10 Sep 1948.
124 Msg, Clay to Draper, 11 Sep 1948, Folder "#1 Fr. Germany CC-2765–CC-5919 1-1-48–9-12-48," ACoS, G–2 (Intel), "Top Secret" Incoming and Outgoing Cables, 1942–52, RG 319, NACP.

and get a sense of Berliners' stamina in the face of the blockade. They met at Harnack House, the Army's guesthouse a few blocks from U.S. headquarters in Berlin. There, Reuter told Clay, "we will move forward regardless. Do what you can; we will do what we have committed to."[125] Reuter and Clay also discussed Moscow's objectives and agreed that the Soviets did not seek a war. Impressed with Reuter's resolve, Clay came to regard him as a reliable ally in managing public sentiment. After the clashes between demonstrators and police in a September demonstration, Clay noted he would have "a quiet talk with the responsible Germans"—no doubt a reference to Reuter, who spoke at the demonstration.[126]

The unpopularity of the blockade ruined the appeal of the SED in West Berlin and eliminated the party as a serious political contender. Reuter's sole political challenger in the city remained Ferdinand Friedensburg, the CDU chairman who in the summer of 1948 temporarily stepped in as lord mayor for the gravely ill Louise D. Schröder. Initially, Army Intelligence held Friedensburg in high regard. His entry on the White List noted approvingly that the Nazis had removed him from office in 1933.[127] In 1946, the Soviets dismissed Friedensburg from his job as president of the central administration of the fuel industry in their zone, another point that earned him accolades from Army Intelligence. A top intelligence official described Friedensburg's "absolutely clean" record and praised the mayor as "one of the least diplomatic and most outspoken men among the democratic politicians."[128]

Barred from a political career in the Soviet Zone, Friedensburg focused on Berlin. Despite his earlier dismissal, he was careful not to offend the Soviets, and he emerged as a strong advocate of steering a middle course between the four Allied occupation powers. But Soviet brazenness backed Friedensburg into a corner. In late 1947, Moscow's agents lured the journalist Dieter Friede, who wrote for the U.S.-licensed newspaper *Der Abend*, to the eastern sector of the city where he disappeared. The Berlin police, under its pro-Soviet chief Paul Markgraf, dragged its feet over the investigation. As mayor, Friedensburg was de jure responsible for the police of Greater Berlin. Fearful of tearing the police force apart, he publicly defended the slow official response to Friede's disappearance by suggesting the journalist may have moved from Berlin to one of the western

---

125 Willy Brandt, *Mein Weg nach Berlin* [My path to Berlin] (Munich: Kindler Verlag, 1960), 239; see also Barclay, *Schaut auf diese Stadt*, 242.
126 Msg, Clay to Draper, 11 Sep 1948.
127 Henric L. Würmeling, *Die Weiße Liste und die Stunde Null in Deutschland 1945* [The whitelist and zero hour in Germany, 1945] (Munich: Herbig, 2015), 274.
128 Rpt, Col. T. J. Koenig, Director of Intel, OMGUS, 14 Sep 1946, Folder "OMGUS Intelligence Notes # 21–41, 9.14.46–2.22.47," Historian's Background Files, 1947–1952," RG 549, NACP.

zones. Even CDU leaders disagreed with this improbable explanation. The CIC knew that Soviet intelligence had arrested him.[129] The Soviets sentenced Friede to prison for espionage, sent him to a Siberian labor camp, and eventually released him in 1955.[130] In Berlin, Friedensburg replaced Markgraf with Johannes Stumm, a police veteran and staunchly anticommunist SPD member.[131] This move for all practical purposes split the police into an eastern and a western force.

Friedensburg's stubborn adherence to a policy of collaboration with the Soviets irritated the Americans. In August 1946, an informant of the Strategic Services Unit suspected the CDU politician of secretly working for the Soviets.[132] The following year, Colonel Rodes dismissed Friedensburg as "an able administrator, but certainly not an able politician." If forced to choose between the two sides, Rodes suspected, the mayor "would choose the east."[133] Matters came to a head in July 1948 when Ulrich E. Biel of the Political Affairs Branch paid Friedensburg a visit. Biel told him that Colonel Howley and General Clay did not appreciate his ongoing attempts to reach an agreement with the Soviets. According to Friedensburg, Biel called him a traitor.[134]

Berliners settled the rivalry between Reuter and Friedensburg on 5 December 1948, when the Western sectors elected a new city council. Amid the charged atmosphere of the blockade, more than 86 percent of voters went to the polls. In a resounding victory, the SPD captured 64.5 percent of the vote, its best result in the history of the city. The CDU dropped below 20 percent, while the FDP, who supported Reuter's SPD, gained 16.1 percent. The SED boycotted the elections. The council formally elected Reuter as lord mayor while the Soviets appointed a communist as lord mayor in their sector.[135] Over the following months, Reuter masterfully guided the city through the blockade, closely working with the Americans. As the

---

129 Memo, Special Agent Joseph J. Hotter, Region VIII, CIC, for Ofcr in Charge, 1 Mar 1948, sub: Dieter Friede, Folder "XE 200770 Dieter Friede," INSCOM, IRR, Digitized Name Files, RG 319, NACP.
130 "Berlin Reporter Freed by Soviets: Friede Disappeared in 1947," *New York Times*, 12 Oct 1955.
131 Jochen Staadt, "Wir packen mit an, Ordnung zu schaffen: Die Berliner Polizei in der 'Stunde Null'" [We are helping to create order: The Berlin police at "zero hour"], *Zeitschrift des Forschungsverbundes SED-Staat* 28 (2010), 110, 112, 117.
132 Intel Dissemination, Strategic Services Unit, 23 Aug 1946, sub: Progress of the CDU in the Russian Zone, Strategic Services Unit Intel Rpts, 1945–1946, reel 4, RG 226, NACP.
133 Rpt, Col. Peter P. Rodes, Weekly Intel Report no. 79, 15 Nov 1947, Historians Files, CMH.
134 Martin Otto, "Ulrich Biel, ein deutscher Patriot: Der amerikanische Preusse" [Ulrich Biel, a German patriot: The American Prussian] (unpublished manuscript, 2018), 75, Historians Files, CMH.
135 Stivers and Carter, *City Becomes a Symbol*, 283–84.

CIA's deputy base chief recalled, Reuter "played his role as a leader during a very difficult period."[136]

With a steadfast ally running local politics, the airlift sustaining the civilian population, and the counterblockade putting pressure on Moscow, by early 1949 American authorities in Berlin looked with confidence toward the future.[137] U.S. intelligence suspected that the Soviets, too, realized the tide was turning. In February, the CIA reported that officials from the Soviet Military Administration told SED cochairman Wilhelm Pieck that it would now be "absolutely stupid" for his party to demand withdrawal of the Western powers from Berlin "because it is unrealistic."[138]

Covert Action

The blockade presented challenges as well as opportunities for U.S. intelligence. As the CIA pointed out to the Army's director of intelligence, Soviet measures to restrict traffic to and from the Western sectors slowed the flow of Red Army deserters and diminished U.S. access to informants in the Soviet Zone. Consequently, the CIA lamented, "the general usefulness of Berlin as a center of an intelligence network has been impaired."[139] But to paraphrase an adage, one service's poison is another service's meat. The U.S. Air Force inserted aircraft equipped with cameras into the airlift. The planes produced detailed photographs of military installations and troop movements beneath the air corridors. The value of the resulting photo-intelligence ensured that the observation flights continued throughout the Cold War.[140]

Refugees provided the Allies with another source of information. As the counterblockade weakened the Soviet Zone economy and the SED regime tightened control, East Germans flooded into West Berlin. In 1949, 70,000 refugees crossed the intersectoral border. Led by Marie-Elisabeth Lüders, a former employee of

---

136 Email, Peter M. F. Sichel to Thomas Boghardt, 25 May 2018, Historians Files, CMH.
137 Msg, Hans A. Kallmann to Col. Rodes, 31 Mar 1949, sub: German Reactions in the Soviet Zone, Folder "01 Soviet Zone," Director of Intel, Analysis and Research Br, Gen Corresp, 1945–49, RG 260, NACP.
138 Rpt, CIA, 3 Feb 1949, sub: Meeting of the Landesvorstand Berlin, CIA Electronic Reading Room.
139 Rpt, CIA, to Director of Intel, U.S. Army, 14 Jun 1948, sub: Effect of Soviet Restrictions on U.S. Position in Berlin, National Security Archive.
140 Sven Felix Kellerhoff and Bernd von Kostka, *Hauptstadt der Spione. Geheimdienste in Berlin im Kalten Krieg* [Capital of the spies: Secret services in Berlin during the Cold War] (Berlin: Berlin Story Verlag, 2016), 33.

the Army's intelligence center in Oberammergau, local authorities opened a refugee center to process the newcomers. The CIC and British intelligence sent interrogators to the center to interview the refugees for information on the Soviet Zone. In September, they established the Anglo-American Interrogation Center at Karolingerplatz, which served as both a venue for interviews and a recruiting ground for informants who returned to the Soviet Zone on espionage missions.[141]

In some cases, Soviet policies prompted East Germans to offer their help to the Americans directly. In October 1948, for example, the Office of the Director of Intelligence received a letter from one Max Pelke of the city of Brandenburg in the Soviet Zone. Pelke expressed his wish to join the U.S. Army or the Industrial Police, an Army auxiliary staffed by Germans.[142] He also enclosed information on two friends of his, who wished "to start a resistance movement against Communism" and asked "for advice, financial and material assistance." The military government marked the request, "For action deemed appropriate," but Pelke did not join the Army. Instead, he became involved with local resistance efforts. East German authorities arrested him in 1950 for his connection to the SPD's illegal Ostbüro, and he spent six years in prison.[143]

The blockade emboldened the Americans to broaden their intelligence mission to weaponize the collected information. Propaganda operations formed a crucial aspect of this transformation. In January 1948, Colonel Howley appointed William F. Heimlich, the former Berlin chief of Army Intelligence, as director of Radio in the American Sector, the official U.S. radio station in the city. Howley gave Heimlich a succinct mission for RIAS: purge the radio of "Communistic or extreme Leftist personnel" and shift programming from "neutrality to one of active anti-Communism."[144] Heimlich took to the new mission like a duck to water. Equipped with a background in commercial radio broadcasting and a can-do personality, he rapidly transformed RIAS into a powerful anticommunist propaganda platform. Lambasting the repressive policies in eastern Germany and stoking discontent among citizens behind the Iron Curtain, the radio became a thorn in the side of Soviet Zone authorities.

---

141 Keith R. Allen, *Befragung, Überprüfung, Kontrolle. Die Aufnahme von DDR-Flüchtlingen in West-Berlin bis 1961* [Questioning, verification, control: The admission of GDR refugees in West Berlin through 1961] (Berlin: Ch. Links, 2013), 31–34.
142 Combined Routing Info Filing Form, OMGUS, 5 Oct 1948, sub: Request to start a Resistance Movement, Folder "21c Public Safety (Soviet Zone), ODI, Excerpts or Miscellaneous Rpts and Publications, Analysis and Research Br, 1947–48, RG 260, NACP.
143 Thüringer Landtag Plenarprotokoll, 5. Wahlperiode, 25th session, 18 Jun 2010 (Erfurt, 2010), 2144.
144 Nicholas Schlosser, *Cold War on the Airwaves: The Radio Propaganda War Against East Germany* (Urbana: Illinois University Press, 2015), 31–32.

Heimlich leveraged his intelligence experience in this campaign. Beginning in the summer of 1949, RIAS regularly broadcast "snitch reports" (*Spitzelsendungen*). Having obtained the names and addresses of suspected Soviet informants in the East from intelligence sources, the station exposed them over the airwaves every Thursday night in dramatic fashion. Following an ominous drum beat, a voice would call the citizens of a particular town or city to attention and identify the potential spy in their midst: "Achtung Schwerin, Achtung Schwerin. The name is August Blank, 31 such-and-such Strasse, third floor. He is a spy for the NKVD. He is an informant. We repeat, Achtung Schwerin . . ."[145] The enormously popular "snitch reports" highlighted a particularly unsavory aspect of the Soviet occupation while raising the stakes for communist informants: a hotel owner denounced by RIAS lost all of his guests, and an outed singer was unable to perform without being booed.[146]

The escalation of the propaganda war prompted the Truman administration to authorize more aggressive operations behind the Iron Curtain. In October 1948, the U.S. government's national security policy coordination body, the National Security Council, set up the Office of Policy Coordination as an executive agency for this purpose. Headed by a former OSS officer, Frank G. Wisner, the office was loosely supervised by the CIA.[147] The following month, the council issued Top Secret Directive 20/4, authorizing the CIA and the Office of Policy Coordination to conduct operations to "encourage and promote the gradual retraction of undue Russian power."[148] Wisner's proposed techniques in the pursuit of this goal included "sabotage, countersabotage, and demolition," the support of resistance movements, and the spreading of rumors.[149] The combination of intelligence and political warfare methods came to be known as covert action.

Given Germany's location on the edge of the Soviet bloc and the availability of the Army's logistical machinery, the American occupation zone provided an ideal staging ground for covert action operations in Eastern Europe.[150] Shortly

---

145 Interv, Brewster Chamberlin with William F. Heimlich, former Ch, G–2, Berlin, 4 and 6 August 1981, 85, Landesarchiv Berlin.
146 Kai-Uwe Merz, *Kalter Krieg als antikommunistischer Widerstand. Die Kampfgruppe gegen Unmenschlichkeit 1948–1959* [The Cold War as anticommunist resistance: The Fighting Group Against Inhumanity, 1948–1959] (Munich: Oldenbourg, 1987), 72.
147 David F. Rudgers, "The Origins of Covert Action," *Journal of Contemporary History* 35, no. 2 (Apr 2000), 255.
148 Sarah-Jane Corke, *U.S. Covert Operations and Cold War Strategy: Truman, Secret Warfare and the CIA, 1945–53* (London: Routledge, 2008), 72–73.
149 Memo, Frank G. Wisner for DCI, sub: OPC Projects, 29 Oct 1948, doc. 47, in Michael Warner, ed., *The CIA under Harry Truman* (Washington, DC: CIA, 1994), 241–42.
150 Memo, Frank G. Wisner for Gen Lucius D. Clay, 10 Feb 1949, sub: OPC Activities in Germany, Folder "Top Secret–1949 Amb. Murphy's Correspondence," Ofc of the U.S. Political Adviser for

after the creation of the Office of Policy Coordination, Wisner solicited the support of General Clay and his new director of intelligence, Maj. Gen. William E. Hall.[151] The generals expressed concern about the risks attached to covert action, but they gave the former OSS man their blessing.[152] Wisner wasted no time. In the summer of 1949, he organized the establishment of Radio Free Europe in Munich. Patterned after RIAS, the station broadcast anti-Soviet programs into Eastern Europe.[153] In the early 1950s, the office recruited Polish and Ukrainian émigrés for covert operations behind the Iron Curtain. After training the Eastern Europeans in espionage and subversion techniques in Bavaria and at Fort Bragg in North Carolina, Wisner's outfit parachuted the agents into their homelands to establish resistance movements.[154]

Although Army Intelligence avoided direct involvement in the risky business of covert action, in the course of their day-to-day operations officials inevitably became involved with private organizations engaged in clandestine work. These groups were usually driven by anticommunist zeal, a sentiment that ramped up among Germans in the summer of 1948 owing to the blockade and the release of a large number of political prisoners from the notorious Soviet "special camps" (*Speziallager* or *Spezlager*). German media and RIAS broadcast numerous eyewitness accounts about the appalling conditions in these camps, including graphic descriptions of systematic starvation, torture, and rape. These revelations stoked anger among Berliners and led some of them to channel their rage into action.

The Fighting Group against Inhumanity (Kampfgruppe gegen Unmenschlichkeit; KgU) emerged as the principal anticommunist vehicle in early Cold War Berlin.

Germany, Berlin, Top Secret Rcds, 1944–1949, RG 84, NACP; Nicholas Bethell, *The Great Betrayal: The Untold Story of Kim Philby's Final Act of Treachery* (London: Hodder and Stoughton, 1984), 134.

151 Ltr, Ambassador Robert D. Murphy to Frank G. Wisner, 23 Feb 1949, Folder "Top Secret–1949 Amb. Murphy's Correspondence," Ofc of the U.S. Political Adviser for Germany, Berlin, Top Secret Rcds, 1944–1949, RG 84, NACP.

152 Memo, Frank G. Wisner for Offie, Frank, and Lindsay, 1 Jun 1949, sub: Conversation with Mr. John McCloy, doc. 310, in *Foreign Relations of the United States, Emergence of the Intelligence Establishment, 1945–1950*, ed. C. Thomas Thorne Jr. and David S. Patterson (Washington, DC: Government Printing Office, 1996), 735–36.

153 Corke, *U.S. Covert Operations*, 87.

154 Heinz Höhne, *Der Krieg im Dunkeln: Macht und Einfluss des deutschen und des russischen Geheimdienstes* [The war in the dark: The power and influence of the German and Russian secret services] (Munich: C. Bertelsmann Verlag, 1985), 514. This "totally unrealistic mission," as one intelligence officer called it, failed in the face of draconian countermeasures. Soviet bloc security services arrested, doubled (i.e., turned them into double agents), or executed most of the would-be guerrillas: Harry Rositzke, *The CIA's Secret Operations. Espionage, Counterespionage and Covert Action* (New York: Reader's Digest Press, 1977), 167.

Established in late 1948, the KgU vowed to expose and combat communist power in the Soviet Zone. Its founder, Rainer Hildebrandt, had spent seventeen months as a political prisoner during the Third Reich, and he viewed Soviet-style communism merely as a totalitarian variation of National Socialism. The Soviets, the KgU argued, acted "exactly like Hitler" or even worse.[155] In quasi-religious language, Hildebrandt and his staff lambasted the Soviets as "evil" and "devils," and compared the "infernal" Soviet Zone prison camps to Nazi concentration camps. With the recent experience of the Third Reich in mind, Hildebrandt argued, the failure to resist communism was akin to committing a crime. Therefore, the group chose as its slogan the catchy phrase: "Doing nothing is murder" (*Nichtstun ist Mord*).

The group's noisy anticommunism caught the attention of the CIC. In early January 1949, a female CIC informant and personal friend of Hildebrandt's reported to her handler, Special Agent Richard H. Weber, that she was in contact with the KgU founder. At Hildebrandt's invitation and with CIC approval, she subsequently joined the group and regularly reported on their activities.[156] On 18 January, Special Agents Severin F. Wallach and Theodor Hans (operating under the cover name "Martin") of CIC Region VIII contacted Hildebrandt directly and formally recruited both him and one of his deputies, Heinz Wiechmann, as informants.[157] Wallach became the group's primary handler.

Within a few months, the CIC expanded its support to the KgU. In June 1949, KgU headquarters moved from the British sector to the American sector. The Americans paid the organization's rent and assigned local German auxiliaries of the Industrial Police to provide protection for its members.[158] By the early 1950s, the CIC subsidized the KgU to the tune of DM 3,500—as well as eight cartons of cigarettes—per month.[159] In addition, the Corps shielded the group from penetra-

---

155 Enrico Heitzer, *Die Kampfgruppe gegen Unmenschlichkeit (KgU): Widerstand und Spionage im Kalten Krieg 1948–1959* [The Fighting Group against Inhumanity (KgU): Resistance and espionage in the Cold War, 1948–1959] (Cologne: Böhlau Verlag, 2015), 43–45; Christine Richter, "Der Freiheitskämpfer" [The freedom fighter], *Berliner Zeitung*, 10 Jan 2004.
156 Agent Rpt, Special Agent Richard H. Weber, Projects Section, Region VIII, CIC, 23 Mar 1949, sub: Kampfgruppe gegen die Unmenschlichkeit, Folder "Fighting Group Against Inhumanity XE257711 Part 2 of 2," D-IRR, RG 319, NACP.
157 Agent Rpt, Severin F. Wallach and Theodor Hans, Projects Section, Region VIII, CIC, 17 Mar 1948, sub: Kampfgruppe gegen die Unmenschlichkeit, Folder "Fighting Group Against Inhumanity XE257711 Part 2 of 2," INSCOM, IRR, Digitized Name Files, RG 319, NACP; Heitzer, *Kampfgruppe*, 210.
158 Heitzer, *Kampfgruppe*, 57–58.
159 Msg., Rudolf I. Giessner, Tech Spec Section, to Opns Section, attn.: Major Gallagher, 6 Aug 1953, sub: Kampfgruppe gegen die Unmenschlichkeit, Folder "Fighting Group Against Inhumanity XE 257711 Part 1 of 2," IRR, Digitized Name Files, RG 319, NACP.

tion attempts by agents from the Soviet Zone.[160] In return for this substantial American support, the group delivered tangible results. In early 1949, for example, the CIC translated a KgU pamphlet that claimed that Berlin's Soviet-appointed police chief, Paul Markgraf, had impregnated a female prisoner in the notorious Sachsenhausen prison camp.[161] Whether true or not, the story skillfully linked Berlin's top communist cop to the atrocities associated with the dreaded Soviet political prisons. The KgU also contributed materially to the exposure of Soviet Zone informants. In 1950 alone, the group supposedly identified nearly 20,000 of them. In due course, the KgU became one of the main providers of material for RIAS's popular snitch report broadcasts.[162] Wallach and his team praised the KgU "for the aggressive attitude against Communism and against the inhumanities perpetrated by the Soviet authorities in Berlin."[163]

The KgU's value to the CIC extended beyond propaganda. Through its work with refugees and its efforts to track down missing persons in the Soviets' prison camps, the group gathered a great deal of information about conditions in the Soviet Zone and established contact with individuals hostile to the communist regime.[164] Information from these sources included order of battle intelligence on the Red Army as well as on Soviet intelligence personnel and activities.[165] At their weekly meetings with Hildebrandt, Wallach and Hans received "files and documents" on these subjects.[166] In 1949, the KgU expanded its organization into the West and began producing information on local public figures, politicians, and nationalist groups. Within a year of its initial contact with the KgU, the Corps had reason to be pleased with the results of its collaboration. In an internal report,

---

160 Rpt, Special Agent Kumagai Tanao, Region VIII, CIC, 12 Oct 1949, sub: Kampfgruppe gegen die Unmenschlichkeit, Folder "Fighters Against Inhumanity D 257711," INSCOM, IRR, Digitized Name Files, RG 319, NACP.

161 Text of KgU pamphlet and English translation, "Wir stimmen mit Nein" ["We vote 'No'"], n.d., Folder "Fighting Group Against Inhumanity XE 257711 Part 2 of 2," INSCOM, IRR, Digitized Name Files, RG 319, NACP.

162 Merz, *Kalter Krieg*, 140.

163 Msg, Special Agents Severin F. Wallach and Theodor Hans, to CO, HQ, 7970th CIC Gp, EUCOM, attn.: Mr. Vidal, 14 Mar 1949, sub: Dr. Hildebrandt, Rainer, Folder "Fighting Group Against Inhumanity XE257711 Part 2 of 2," IRR, Digitized Name Files, RG 319, NACP.

164 Heitzer, *Kampfgruppe*, 47–49.

165 Agent Rpt, Special Agent Richard H. Weber, Projects Section, Region VIII, CIC, 23 Mar 1949, sub: Kampfgruppe gegen die Unmenschlichkeit.

166 Msg, Wallach and Hans to CO, HQ, 7970th CIC Gp, EUCOM, attn.: Mr. Vidal, 14 Mar 1949, sub: Dr. Hildebrandt, Rainer.

Special Agent Weber touted the group "as an excellent source of information" and advocated continued support.[167]

The torrent of information provided by the KgU attracted other intelligence services, which circled the group like sharks sensing blood in the water. In the late 1940s, the 7880th Military Intelligence Detachment struck a deal with Hildebrandt. A civilian employee of the detachment, Michael R. Rothkrug, provided the KgU leader with "victuals, air transportation and some money." In exchange, Hildebrandt was to deliver intelligence from the Soviet Zone. When Special Agent Wallach learned of this arrangement, he contacted Rothkrug, and the two American intelligence officials reached an agreement by phone, confirming the CIC as the principal recipient of information from the KgU. In a sign of the growing suspicion and competition for intelligence among the U.S. secret services in Berlin, Wallach never disclosed his real name to Rothkrug, who knew his CIC interlocutor only as "Thompson."[168] Wallach's prudence was well advised, as the Soviets would soon recruit Rothkrug to spy on his own service.[169]

Other services moved even more aggressively to obtain their share of the group's intelligence. In December 1949, the deputy chief of the CIA's Berlin base, Peter M. F. Sichel, informed the commanding officer of the local CIC that the agency was monitoring the phone calls of leading KgU personnel to learn more about their "political ambitions" and about their involvement with "several Allied intelligence services." The CIC complained about this uncoordinated encroachment to the CIA leadership in Germany, which promised to send "a stern letter" to its Berlin base. In an internal note, a CIC officer noted that the Corps would share information with the CIA if the latter "can show a legitimate interest. . . . Otherwise they are out of the picture."[170] Keeping these rival services at bay, however, was easier said than done.

Amply funded and eager to take on the Soviets, the Office of Policy Coordination fought hard to expand its covert action program. Owing to its location deep inside Soviet-controlled territory, Berlin served as a key base for these efforts.

---

167 Rpt, Special Agent Weber, Counterespionage Team, Region VIII, CIC, 1 Dec 1949, sub: Kampfgruppe gegen die Unmenschlichkeit, Folder "Fighters Against Inhumanity D257711," INSCOM, IRR, Digitized Name Files, RG 319, NACP.
168 Statement, Professor Karl Kleist, "Psychiatric Opinion on the Mental Condition of Mr. Michael Rothkrug," 7 Apr 1953, court-martial of Michael R. Rothkrug, Folder "1st [day of trial]," OMGUS/ HICOG Criminal Court Case Files Held in Berlin, 1945–1955, RG 466, NACP.
169 Rpt, MfS, HA II, 10 Jun 1961, "Auskunftsbericht, betr.: Blidin, Leo, geb 1902 in Moskau" [Information report, re: Blidin, Leo, born in Moscow, 1902], 145, MfS-HA II, Nr. 41402, BStU, Berlin.
170 Msg, Peter M. F. Sichel, DAD, to CO, Region VIII, CIC, attn.: Lt. Col. R. E. Rudisell, 2 Dec 1949, sub: Telephone Intercept, Folder "Fighters Against Inhumanity D257711," INSCOM, IRR, Digitized Name Files, RG 319, NACP.

The chief of the office's Berlin station, Michael Josselson, cast a covetous eye on the group with the goal of establishing a "stay-behind" organization that would act as the basis for a guerrilla movement in case of war with the Soviets. In addition, the office sought to use members of the KgU for sabotage operations. Josselson reportedly told his agents, in his less-than-fluent German: "It has to make boom, boom in the [Soviet] Zone!" (*In der Zone muss es bumsen, bumsen!*).[171]

In 1950, the CIA formally integrated the Office of Policy Coordination, creating a powerful intelligence and covert action complex.[172] The following year, Ernst Tillich, a CIA agent (code name "Richard E. Newman") eager to create mayhem in East Germany, replaced the group's cautious and principled leader, Hildebrandt. Some activities under Tillich's aegis were rather harmless. In an early covert action scheme code-named OSTERHASE (Easter Bunny), the group distributed 150,000 flyers announcing a massive price reduction of notoriously scarce goods in the government-controlled stores (Handelsorganisation) in East Germany. The consequent run led to confusion and frustration among East Germans and put a severe strain on the badly managed store chain.[173] Other operations proved more hazardous. The group frequently used caltrops (*Reifentöter*) to deflate the tires of Soviet and East German government vehicles. Reportedly, KgU members also contemplated injecting a lethal poison into meat destined for Soviet troops.[174] In 1952, a court in East Berlin tried several members for planning to blow up a bridge outside southeastern Berlin. The main defendant, Johann Burianek, testified that he had selected the bridge in order to sabotage the "Blue Express" (Blauer Express), a train service between Berlin and Moscow popular with communist functionaries. The Soviet-controlled press had a field day touting Burianek's testimony as evidence of the malfeasance of U.S. intelligence. Eastern propagandists branded the group as mercenaries of the CIC and, using Severin Wallach's cover name, claimed that the special agent had personally sent Burianek on the deadly mission.[175]

The Soviet bloc press campaign prompted an internal CIC investigation of the role of its officials in the attempted bridge bombing and its relationship with the KgU in general. The reporting officer, Maj. Eugene L. Malady, concluded that Wal-

---

171 Richard Helms with William Hood, *A Look Over My Shoulder: A Life in the Central Intelligence Agency* (Novato, CA: Presidio, 2004), 352; Heitzer, *Kampfgruppe*, 74; Höhne, *Der Krieg im Dunkeln*, 516.
172 Corke, *U.S. Covert Operations*, 116.
173 Heitzer, *Kampfgruppe*, 19–21, 295.
174 Heitzer, *Kampfgruppe*, 328–29, 339–43.
175 Heitzer, *Kampfgruppe*, 375; "Vor dem Obersten Gericht began der Prozess gegen die Agenten-bande Burianek" [The trial of the Burianek gang began before the Supreme Court], *Neues Deutschland*, 24 May 1952.

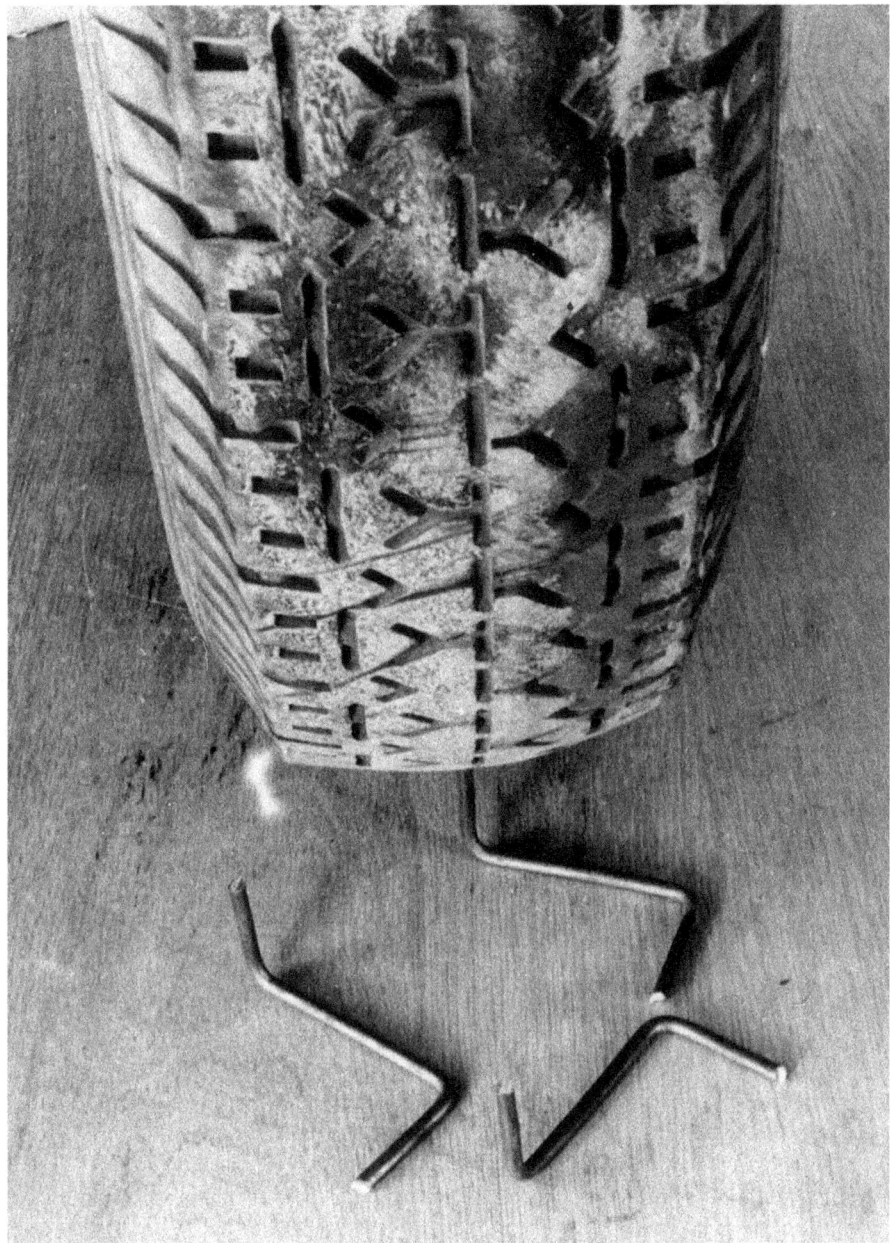

Figure 46: The KgU used caltrops (*Reifentöter*) to incapacitate vehicles of East German or Soviet officials. BStU.

lach probably had not sent Burianek on his sabotage mission, but added the caveat that "we can never be sure whether or not [Wallach] actually is responsible." Malady criticized Wallach for running CIC-KgU liaison operations like a personal fiefdom.[176] A technical specialist, Capt. Rudolf I. Giessner, who looked into funding of the group, found that the CIC provided the monthly subsidy of DM 3,500 without any strings attached. In return, the Corps received almost "nothing in the way of information from the KgU." Giessner recommended that the CIC limit its interactions with the KgU to individual members and cut its generous funding.[177]

Giessner viewed the CIA's growing influence on the KgU as particularly troublesome. He lamented that Wallach and Hans had negotiated a bad intelligence-sharing deal with the agency. The technical specialist considered the agreement "vague and incomplete insofar as who determines who gets what? What amount of money is paid by [CIA] as a subsidy? Do we know who they are? Are we paying the bill for the benefit of other agencies? Are we getting first opportunity at the 'potentials?' It appears to me that we have bought a 'cat-in-the-bag.'"[178] Major Malady concurred. The Corps, he argued, "had been frozen out of access to sources of real interest and was receiving only such dribbles of information as the management of KgU and [CIA] chose to let fall" in the CIC's direction.[179]

Meanwhile, the CIA vigorously affirmed its interest in the group. In a flurry of meetings with top West German government officials and Berlin's lord mayor, Ernst Reuter, the CIA agreed to abstain from recruiting KgU members as informants on the Soviet Zone while retaining its right to work with the group in the fields of propaganda and psychological warfare operations. Following this agreement, representatives of the CIC, the 7880th Military Intelligence Detachment, and the CIA met in Berlin in November 1952 to delineate their respective spheres of interest with regard to the group.[180] The CIC decided to call it quits, winding down its involvement with the KgU. Over the following years, the CIA became the main sponsor of the group as it continued to wage a campaign of violent resistance against the communist regime in East Germany.

---

176 Msg, Maj. Eugene L. Malady, S–3, to Tech Specialist, 8 Aug 1953, sub: Kampfgruppe gegen Unmenschlichkeit, Folder "Fighting Group Against Inhumanity XE 257711 Part 1 of 2," INSCOM, IRR, Digitized Name Files, RG 319, NACP.
177 Msg, Giessner to Opns Section, attn.: Major Gallagher, 6 Aug 1953, sub: Kampfgruppe gegen die Unmenschlichkeit.
178 Msg, Giessner to Opns Section, attn.: Major Gallagher, 6 Aug 1953, sub: Kampfgruppe gegen die Unmenschlichkeit.
179 Msg, Malady to Tech Specialist, 8 Aug 1953, sub: Kampfgruppe gegen Unmenschlichkeit.
180 Msg, Malady to Tech Specialist, 8 Aug 1953, sub: Kampfgruppe gegen Unmenschlichkeit.

The Federal Republic of Germany

On 31 January 1949, Ernst Reuter told *New York Times* correspondent Drew Middleton, "It's over. The Russians know they can't get Berlin by blockade. Soon they will start to find a way out." Indeed, time was working against Moscow. By sustaining Berlin through the winter, the Anglo-American air forces had demonstrated their ability to maintain the airlift indefinitely. Meanwhile, the blockade rallied German public opinion behind the West, and the counterblockade battered on the East German economy. Conceding defeat, Stalin signaled his willingness to end the blockade, and he formally did so in May. In return, the Allies lifted the counterblockade and, in a face-saving gesture to the Kremlin, agreed to another session of the Council of Foreign Ministers to discuss "questions relating to Germany." Predictably, the council accomplished nothing.[181]

By this time, preparations for the establishment of West Germany were in full swing. In June 1948, the Western Allies had launched the currency reform, replacing the Occupation Mark with the deutsche mark, a measure that quickly stabilized the West German economy. In September, representatives of the eleven West German *Länder* formed the parliamentary council in Bonn, with the CDU's Konrad Adenauer as president. In protracted negotiations among themselves and with the Allies, the council hammered out a constitution, or basic law (*Grundgesetz*), for the new state. On 12 May 1949, the same day the Soviets lifted the blockade, General Clay and his British and French colleagues approved the document. This was Clay's last official act as military governor of Germany. Three days later, he returned to the United States.[182] The U.S. government replaced him with John J. McCloy, a diplomat who had long been involved in military, intelligence, and German affairs, to serve as the new U.S. High Commissioner for Germany.[183]

On 23 May 1949, the Federal Republic of Germany formally came into being. Parliamentary elections five months later yielded a narrow plurality of votes for the Christian Democrats. On 15 September, the new parliament (Bundestag) elected Theodor Heuss as president. The freshly minted deputies then proceeded to vote for a chancellor. Konrad Adenauer won with the narrowest possible majority of

---

[181] Smyser, *From Yalta to Berlin*, 85–86.
[182] J. F. J. Gillen, *U.S. Military Government in Germany: American Influence on the Development of Political Institutions* (Karlsruhe: Historical Division, EUCOM, 1950), 215; Clay, *Decision in Germany*, 436.
[183] McCloy initially served as both military governor and high commissioner. On 21 September 1949, when the Office of Military Government dissolved, he continued to serve as U.S. High Commissioner only; see Oliver J. Frederiksen, *The American Military Occupation of Germany, 1945–1953* (Darmstadt: Historical Division, USAREUR, 1953), 149.

one vote—his own. When his victory was announced, the unflappable Rhinelander in his broad Cologne accent said to a fellow parliamentarian that "still things always turned out well" (*et hätt noch immer joot jejange*).[184]

While the Germans were busy preparing for the new state, Army Intelligence quietly laid the groundwork for continuing operations after the end of the military government. The leadership of the American signals intelligence community had recognized the strategic importance of Germany as early as 1946. As the ASA established new intercept stations around the world, Germany became a central part of this global eavesdropping empire, and top intelligence officials expressed the desire to operate sites there "as long as possible."[185] The following year, the Army's director of intelligence, General Chamberlin, requested that General Clay ensure the continuance of "certain communication intelligence facilities," a reference to signals intelligence operations as well as the interception of telephone, telegraph, and postal communications. Clay replied that he had taken appropriate action.[186] In early 1948, ASA chief Col. Harold G. Hayes followed up with a detailed memorandum on signals intelligence requirements for the post–military government period. To carry out its mission in Europe, Hayes argued, the agency needed to retain its intercept facilities at Herzo Base and Scheyern. Both formed "an integral part" of its European signals intelligence organization. In addition, Hayes stated, the ASA required continued access to German communications facilities to monitor German mail, telephones, and telegrams.[187] The CIA, the CIC, and the other European Command intelligence agencies wanted to perpetuate their presence in Germany as well.[188]

Before his departure from Germany, General Clay had assigned the task of representing the Americans in the negotiations over the legal status of U.S. forces in

---

184 Hans-Peter Schwarz, *Konrad Adenauer: A German Politician and Statesman in a Period of War, Revolution and Reconstruction*, vol. 1 (Oxford: Berghahn Books, 1995), 444.
185 ASA, "Post War Transition Period: The Army Security Agency 1945–1948" (Washington, DC: ASA, 1952), 6.
186 Memo, Maj. Gen. Chamberlin for Ch of Staff, 11 Apr 1947, National Security Archive.
187 Msg, Col. Harold G. Hayes, Ch, ASA, to Asst Executive for Planning and Coordination, 4 Feb 1948, sub: State Department Assumption of Responsibility in Occupied Europe, Folder "350.09 (1948) Germany," Rcds of the Army Staff, OASCI, MID, Top Secret Decimal File, 1942–1952, RG 319, NACP.
188 Memo, Campbell, Ofc of the Coordinator and Special Advisor, U.S. Embassy, Bonn, 15 Jun 1956, sub: Sketch of U.S. Formal Intelligence Relationships with West Germany (1945–1955), Folder "GFA 10 – Intelligence (1956)," Ofc of German Affairs, Rcds Relating to the Negotiations of the Status of Forces Agreement (SOFA) with Germany, 1954–1959, RG 59, NACP; Loose leaf, no originator, no sender, n.d., Folder "350.09 (1948) Germany," Rcds of the Army Staff, OASCI, MID, Top Secret Decimal File, 1942–1952, RG 319, NACP.

West Germany to Joseph A. Panuch, his "special adviser for major problems."[189] Panuch took the lead in drafting the Occupation Statute, the document that defined the limited sovereignty the Federal Republic would attain. Panuch took care to define the rights of American intelligence broadly. Under Panuch's plan, the Army and the newly created post of High Commissioner would continue to collect intelligence in Germany with little interference from the new government.[190]

On 21 September, Adenauer drove up to the seat of the High Commission, located atop a mountain at the Hotel Petersberg near Bonn. Here, he was to receive a copy of the Occupation Statute. Standing on a red carpet, the three Allied high commissioners awaited the new chancellor. Diplomatic protocol demanded that Adenauer not step on the carpet, in acknowledgment of the unequal partnership of the new state with the Western Allies. But Adenauer resented his inferior status. As he approached the three commissioners, he boldly stepped on the carpet, thus elevating himself symbolically to the same level as his hosts. Perhaps in an effort not to spoil the ceremony, McCloy and his colleagues overlooked the violation of diplomatic protocol and handed Adenauer the document.[191]

The commissioners could afford to be magnanimous. At the Petersberg meeting, Adenauer may have appeared the Allies' equal, but the reality was different. The Occupation Statute preserved important rights that the Allies had assumed at the end of the war. Only three pages long, it gave the Allies the authority to maintain occupation forces in the federal republic and guaranteed the "protection, prestige, and security of Allied Forces, dependents, employees and representatives."[192] The statute did not specifically mention intelligence, but it did not have to, because the term "Allied Forces" by definition included the covert side of the

---

189 Clay, *Decision in Germany*, 412.
190 Msg, J. Anthony Panuch, Brig. Gen. W. R. Palmer, James L. Sundquist, to Gen. Clay, 12 Apr 1948, sub: Plan Submitted by Commander-in-Chief, EUCOM and Military Governor of Germany (U.S.) to Department of the Army for the Transfer of Military Government Functions to the U.S. High Commissioner for Germany, Folder "Military Gov't of Germany/Cosar Committee Panuch," J. Anthony Panuch Papers, Truman Library.
191 "Adenauers Projekt" [Adenauer's project], *Der Spiegel*, 2 Mar 2009. Years later, McCloy acknowledged Adenauer's resentment but did not mention the red carpet incident: John J. McCloy, "Adenauer und die Hohe Kommission" [Adenauer and the High Commission], in *Konrad Adenauer und seine Zeit. Politik und Persönlichkeit des ersten Bundeskanzlers. Beiträge von Weg-und Zeitgenossen* [Konrad Adenauer and his time: Politics and personality of the first Federal Chancellor. Contributions from fellow travelers and contemporaries], ed. Dieter Blumenwitz et al. (Stuttgart: Deutsche Verlags-Anstalt, 1976), 422.
192 Occupation Statute Defining the Powers to Be Retained by the Occupation Authorities, Signed by the Three Western Foreign Ministers, April 8, 1949 (entered into force on September 21, 1949), in *Documents on Germany 1944–1985*, ed. U.S. Department of State (Washington, DC: State Department, Office of the Historian), 213–15.

Allied military presence in Germany. As Laughlin A. Campbell, a CIC special agent who joined the State Department in 1949, noted: "No specific arrangements concerning intelligence and security were necessary, since these activities had blanket coverage under the wording of the Occupation Statute."[193] West Berlin, which remained under Allied authority, received a separate statute, granting American intelligence similarly extensive rights.[194] The period of military government had come to an end, but Army Intelligence operations in Germany would continue unabated for the foreseeable future.

Conclusion

The Berlin blockade constituted the final stage of the military occupation of Germany. In 1948, the long-festering U.S.-Soviet rivalry broke out into the open and led to the fiercest clash yet between the two camps. It solidified the Iron Curtain and established Germany as the principal battleground of the early Cold War. As such, the blockade sealed the end of the Grand Alliance that had won World War II; in the West, it marked the beginning of a partnership between victors and vanquished.

The story of intelligence in the Berlin blockade was one of opportunities missed and seized. As the Soviets began restricting access to the western sectors of the city, Army Intelligence noted correctly that Red Army strength barely increased, and advised the U.S. leadership in Germany that Moscow was not gearing up for war. The disconnect between General Clay and his intelligence agencies, however, obscured these reassuring reports and contributed to the nervousness of American officials in Germany and in Washington.

As the crisis unfolded, however, the efforts of U.S. intelligence became better integrated into American policy in Germany. Army Intelligence officials kept a close eye on the volatile situation in Berlin and served as mediators between local politicians and U.S. occupation authorities. They contributed greatly to the American propaganda effort, and they skillfully took advantage of rising anticommunist sentiments among the local population to recruit agents and forge strategic partnerships. Reports by Army Intelligence from the Soviet Zone also confirmed the effectiveness of the counterblockade, which played a vital role in Stalin's decision to negotiate an end to the crisis. While the U.S. leadership did not fully exploit the available intelli-

---

193 Memo, L. A. Campbell, Ofc of the Coordinator and Special Adviser, U.S. Embassy, Bonn, 15 Jun 1956, Folder "GFA 10–Intelligence (1956)," Ofc of German Affairs, Rcds Relating to the Negotiations of the Status of Forces Agreement (SOFA) with Germany, 1954–1959, RG 59, NACP.

194 Statement of Principles Governing the Relationship Between The Allied Kommandatura and Greater Berlin, Signed by the Three Western Commandants, Berlin, 14 May 1949, in U.S. Department of State, *Documents on Germany 1944–1985*, 262–64.

Figure 47: Celebrating the end of the blockade, summer 1949. U.S. Army, NACP.

gence, the Army's covert legions nonetheless made a significant contribution to the peaceful resolution of the blockade.

Conclusion

In the five-year-long military occupation of Germany, the U.S. Army accomplished a great deal. The three Western zones, which combined on 23 May 1949 to form the Federal Republic of Germany, were on the road to economic recovery. Moreover, the new state had a democratic system of government, and its duly elected leadership was aligned with the West. The efforts that U.S. military and civilian staff had made to rebuild the war-torn nation, promote democracy, and reestablish civic institutions had given West Germany a path toward a bright future. In other respects, however, the record of the U.S. military government was mixed. Nazi officials were returning to public life, the continued separation of the Soviet Zone had left the German people geographically divided, and inter-Allied cooperation had collapsed. As the relationship between the United States and the Soviet Union grew more antagonistic, the divisions within Europe deepened. In his memoirs, published in 1950, General Lucius D. Clay acknowledged that the Americans had not yet reached the goal of solving "the German problem," but he was cautiously optimistic: "We are well on the way of its solution within a framework acceptable to the free countries of Europe."[1]

American policies shaped postwar Europe, but these decisions did not happen in a void. U.S. leaders in Germany and Washington required firsthand information about conditions on the ground. They also relied on organizations to implement these policies, to protect the military government against threats, and to monitor the ever-shifting landscape of postwar Germany. These missions primarily fell on the shoulders of Army Intelligence. Did America's covert legions deliver?

The answer to this question varies, because the intelligence agencies did not report to a single person or entity. The most important customer of intelligence was—or should have been—the military governor and commander of U.S. Forces in the European Theater. General Clay, however, paid little attention to intelligence. He preferred to gather information from his own sources, and political considerations took precedence in his decision-making. His disregard for intelligence was most obvious in his dealings with the Soviets. He downplayed early intelligence reports on the totalitarian character of Soviet policies in the eastern zone. Yet during the early stages of the Berlin blockade, he also ignored intelligence estimates suggesting that the Soviets were unwilling to go to war. As a result, Clay's alarmist utterances rendered the crisis more volatile than it already was. Overall, if Clay and his top officials had made more of an effort to incorpo-

---

[1] Lucius D. Clay, *Decision in Germany* (Garden City, NY: Doubleday, 1950), ix.

rate Army Intelligence into their assessment of Moscow's policies, the potentially broader perspective could have helped the U.S. military government form a more balanced and steady response to Soviet actions.

This does not mean that the impact of Army Intelligence on the occupation was negligible. Clay and the Joint Chiefs issued orders and directives from Berlin and Washington; on the ground, soldiers and civilians interpreted, implemented, and challenged these instructions.[2] At this level, Army Intelligence personnel exerted enormous influence. The screening of millions of Germans and displaced persons in the context of denazification and emigration could not have been accomplished without the assistance of the Counter Intelligence Corps and other intelligence agencies. The same was true for the exploitation of German science and technology, the identification of capable and untainted administrators, and the monitoring of political parties. Whether one considers any of these policies wise or foolish, they could not have been carried out without the expertise and the resources of Army Intelligence personnel on the ground.

"Intelligence ends with the first shot fired," noted a former Soviet intelligence officer.[3] By this standard, Army Intelligence acquitted itself well. From the summer of 1945 through September 1949, military intelligence assessments from Germany delivered a consistent message to Washington: even though the Red Army was capable of overrunning much of Europe, Moscow did not intend to start a war in the immediate future. At the same time, Army analysts pointed out, war could result from miscalculation or by accident. Through the Department of War, the Department of Defense, and the National Security Council, these assessments fed into American foreign policy. In the field of national security, Army Intelligence played a central role in the transformation of the global order from World War II to the Cold War.

Did Army Intelligence drive the U.S. policy shift from retribution and denazification to reconstruction and anticommunism? Not at first. The tug-of-war between U.S. officials bent on removing and punishing all Nazis and those willing to overlook the unsavory past of individuals with desirable skills began at the onset of the American occupation in late 1944. Tasked to aid in the denazification of Germany, CIC personnel typically fell into the former category—to the extent that two CIC agents described their own role as "tearer-downers" targeting those who had benefited from the Nazi regime, in contrast to the "builder-uppers" of the civil affairs units who needed to find capable Germans to fill critical administra-

---

2 John D. Hess, "Coping with Crisis: Military Government Officials, U.S. Policy, and the Occupation of Bavaria, 1945–1949" (PhD diss., University of Kansas, 2017), 25.
3 Victor Sheymov, *Tower of Secrets: A Real Life Spy Thriller* (New York: HarperCollins, 1993), xi.

tive and government positions.[4] In due course, the shrinking of the military government and the American desire to hand over responsibilities to the Germans fostered a policy of expediency, which meant that many U.S. officials adopted a more forgiving attitude toward former Nazis. The deepening Cold War did not set this trend, but it aided in its acceleration. Within a year of V-E Day, Army Intelligence was shifting the bulk of its personnel and resources from denazification and war crimes investigations to the monitoring and containment of suspected or actual communists. In the world of intelligence, the anticommunist credentials or the Soviet expertise of a German official, even if acquired during the Third Reich, progressively trumped concerns over an individual's Nazi past. U.S. intelligence was not solely responsible for this fundamental shift in American policy in Germany; nevertheless, it helped shape the opinions that underpinned the military government's new priorities.

One of the biggest challenges for Army Intelligence was the decline in qualified personnel after the war as many of the highly talented and educated draftees chose to return to civilian life. Their replacements often had no background in intelligence work, were inadequately trained, and did not speak German. This brain drain gave Army Intelligence and especially its most visible component, the CIC, a bad reputation, to the point where an agent of the Army's own Criminal Investigation Division dismissed the Corps as "a bunch of bums" and "a bunch of hooligans."[5] This verdict was overly simplistic. To be sure, the quality of intelligence personnel in occupied Germany left something to be desired, but U.S. officials sought to respond to these deficiencies and root out those who were truly unfit for the mission. Army authorities repeatedly conducted probes into the corrupt behavior of intelligence personnel. The Air Force even investigated a former intelligence director for black market activities. Although the Army failed to overcome a key challenge—the influx of underqualified personnel—officials made a conscious effort to assign highly qualified and motivated personnel to positions where it mattered most: at the operational level and in leadership positions at the top of the intelligence pyramid.

Despite the demobilization of numerous intelligence veterans in 1945 and 1946, many talented and dedicated operations officers continued to hold key positions. This was true especially in Berlin, which was rapidly evolving into a hot spot of the early Cold War. Men like Severin F. Wallach of the CIC, Peter M. F. Sichel of the

---

4 Interv, Special Agents Harold F. Knapp and James H. Bready, 222d CIC Detachment, 19 May 1945, Folder "Interviews 1945," XXII Corps Engr Section Instructions, Interv Rpts, Sums, and Terrain Studies, compiled 03/1945–09/1945, RG 165, NACP.
5 Ian Sayer and Douglas Botting, *Nazi Gold: The Story of the World's Greatest Robbery – And Its Aftermath* (New York: Granada, 1984), 261.

CIA, and Ulrich E. Biel of the Political Affairs Section served as critical links between the American military government and political activists in the city. It was no coincidence that all three were German émigrés who spoke the language fluently and thoroughly understood local society and politics.

The single most consequential Army Intelligence official in Germany was the chief of the European Theater's intelligence division, Brig. Gen. Edwin L. Sibert. A battle-hardened career soldier, Sibert focused his efforts on the dual totalitarian challenge the Americans were facing: the lingering Nazi ideology and the imminent Soviet-communist threat. He directed intelligence operations in Germany for only two years, but those two years laid a lasting foundation for the American intelligence architecture in Europe. Following Sibert's return to the United States in September 1946, the position of the top U.S. intelligence official in Europe lost some of its relevance. This was partly the result of the personality of Sibert's longest-serving successor, Maj. Gen. Robert L. Walsh, but more so because the Army relocated the office of the chief of intelligence from Frankfurt to Berlin in early 1947. Physically removed from the Army's principal intelligence arm in the U.S. Zone, Walsh was more of a personal adviser to Clay than the head of a major Army organization. Nonetheless, highly competent officers continued to manage the Army's intelligence effort. Sibert's deputy, Col. Robert A. Schow, expertly ran the tactical intelligence organization in Frankfurt and Heidelberg, and Col. Peter P. Rodes built an efficient military government intelligence office in Berlin that stretched across the entire U.S. Zone.

Many of the agencies created under the aegis of General Sibert and his cadre of intelligence specialists in the mid-1940s remained operational long past their creators' departure. Camp King—or "Camp Sibert," as soldiers affectionately called the sprawling Army installation—developed into the nerve center of Army Intelligence in Germany, and it served the Army's needs for nearly half a century. The Berlin Documents Center operated under American ownership until the German government assumed control of it in 1994. Its collections remain a rich archival source on Nazi Germany. The United States Military Liaison Mission monitored the Soviet and East German military through the end of the Cold War. The Army's intelligence training center in Oberammergau eventually became a training and education facility for NATO (North Atlantic Treaty Organization) and it exists to the present day. The covert presence of both the CIA and the Army in Berlin expanded exponentially during the 1950s, turning the city into one of the largest and most significant Western forward bases for covert operations behind the Iron Curtain.

General Sibert's decision to build a German protointelligence organization, Operation RUSTY, yielded a rich harvest. Although RUSTY's contribution to the Army's intelligence product had its limits, the operation allowed the Americans to develop organizational and personal ties to an entity that evolved into West Germany's foreign intelligence service, the Bundesnachrichtendienst (BND). Thanks to the relationships established between the two sides during the years of the occupation, the BND worked closely with the Americans throughout and beyond the Cold War. In his memoirs, Reinhard Gehlen credits General Sibert as "one of the few senior Americans to have seen the coming East-West conflict from the outset. I stand in admiration of Sibert as a general who took this bold step . . . of taking over the intelligence experts of a former enemy for his own country."[6]

The institutional continuity of Army Intelligence in Germany went hand in hand with a lasting legal framework that allowed the Americans to pursue covert operations aggressively in the heart of Europe after 1949. The U.S. government made sure that the special status accorded to their intelligence services in the Occupation Statute were perpetuated under the Status of Forces Agreement, which defined the rights of U.S. military forces in Germany long after the military occupation ended. Army Intelligence continued to monitor mail, telegrams, and phone calls for many years. In the late 1950s, the Western Allies eavesdropped on more than five million phone calls over landlines connecting the Federal Republic of Germany with its eastern and western neighbors. In 1968, the Army's censorship branch tracked nearly eight million letters and packages.[7]

American intelligence agents, too, have long enjoyed a special status in Germany. Apparently, some of these rights survived the end of the Cold War. Sgt. Jeffrey M. Carney is a case in point. Carney was an Air Force intelligence specialist in West Berlin who spied for East German intelligence in the early 1980s. In 1984, he defected to East Berlin, where he received asylum and a new name, "Jens Karney." After the reunification of Germany in 1990, U.S. intelligence located him. In April 1991, the U.S. Air Force Office of Special Investigations, which has operated in Germany since the early Cold War, captured him at his apartment in the former Soviet sector of Berlin and transferred him to the United States. A military court tried Carney for espionage and sentenced him to thirty-eight years in prison, of which he served eleven and a half. Carney's lawyers argued that his capture had been illegal because

---

[6] Reinhard Gehlen, *The Service: The Memoirs of General Reinhard Gehlen*, trans. David Irving (New York: Popular Library, 1972), 121, 123. In the late 1960s, Sibert and Gehlen cooperated on a memoir Sibert wanted to write in his retirement. Sibert's project fell through because his ghostwriter, the journalist Anthony Cave Brown, ran up a large bill at a Munich hotel (while supposedly conducting research) and disappeared without paying. Dispatch, Ch of [CIA] Base, Munich, to Ch, European Div, 10 Dec 1968, sub: Visit to Munich of Anthony Brown, Journalist with Brig. Gen. Edward L. Sibert, CIA Electronic Reading Room, https://www.cia.gov/readingroom/; Email, Ned Sibert to Thomas Boghardt, 27 Apr 2016, Historians Files, CMH.

[7] Josef Foschepoth, *Überwachtes Deutschland: Post-und Telefonüberwachung in der alten Bundesrepublik* [Surveillance Germany: Post and telephone surveillance in the old Federal Republic] (Göttingen: Vandenhoeck and Ruprecht, 2013), 53, 56.

it occurred on the soil of a sovereign foreign state, but the office of Germany's attorney general determined that his case was covered under the Status of Forces Agreement. Notably, a new agreement had been enacted just before Carney's arrest and has remained in force since then. Whatever the legal status of U.S. intelligence in Germany today, its roots go back to the military occupation of the country in the late 1940s.[8]

Modern U.S. intelligence owes a great deal to the Army. The American intelligence community's lead agency, the CIA, profited immensely from its older military brother. The agency recruited heavily among the veterans of the Cold War's first major battlefield. Two CIA directors, Allen W. Dulles and Richard M. Helms, cut their operational teeth in Germany. Highly qualified Army Intelligence veterans, such as General Sibert and Colonel Schow, joined the agency's ranks. In the early 1950s, when the CIA struggled to assert its authority amid the postwar upheavals of the U.S. defense establishment, two Army generals took charge and righted the ship. General Walter B. Smith headed the CIA from 1950 to 1953 and firmly established the agency at the center of American intelligence. Smith, in turn, appointed General Lucian K. Truscott Jr. to sort out the CIA's stations in Germany, where corruption and sloppy tradecraft were undermining the agency's standing.[9]

The Army's legacy is as pronounced in the realm of signals intelligence. In 1949, the Department of Defense sought to combine the cryptographic capabilities of the military services by creating a coordinating agency, the Armed Forces Security Agency (AFSA), but rivalries and competing interests threatened to tear the new umbrella organization apart. In stepped another Army general, Maj. Gen. Ralph J. Canine. A tough and efficient chief of staff of the XII Corps in General Patton's Third Army, Canine was famous for "kicking ass," which was exactly what the dysfunctional American signals intelligence organization needed. In much the same way that General Smith invigorated the CIA, Canine transformed the anemic AFSA into America's premier signals intelligence organization, the National Security Agency (NSA).[10]

As its name indicates, the NSA was partially patterned after the Army Security Agency, and it absorbed numerous components and personnel of its Army predecessor. Thanks to the quasi-extraterritorial rights established by Army Intelligence

---

8 John O. Koehler, *Stasi: The Untold Story of the East German Secret Police* (Boulder, CO: Westview Press, 1999), 236–38; Kristie Macrakis, *Seduced by Secrets: Inside the Stasi's Spy-Tech World* (Cambridge, UK: Cambridge University Press, 2008), 94–102.
9 Evan Thomas, *The Very Best Men: Four Who Dared: The Early Years of the CIA* (New York: Touchstone, 1995), 65–66.
10 Matthew M. Aid, *The Secret Sentry: The Untold History of the National Security Agency* (New York: Bloomsbury Press, 2009), 42.

and advances in technology that allowed for the development of more sophisticated intercept equipment, American signals intelligence facilities proliferated in West Germany and Berlin. According to the East German intelligence service, by 1985 the U.S. military operated five intercept facilities in West Berlin alone. The largest NSA field station was located on the "devil's mountain" (Teufelsberg)—a manmade hill built out of war rubble, which constitutes the highest elevation in the city. From here, U.S. intelligence intercepted signals from deep inside the Warsaw Pact. Targets included the communications of the Soviet and East German air forces; radio traffic of the Soviet, East German, and Polish armies; as well as civilian and military wireless phone conversations.[11]

Beyond their contribution to the making of modern American intelligence, Army Intelligence veterans shaped the culture, politics, and science in Germany and the United States in numerous ways. Some, like Stefan Heym and J. D. Salinger, became famous writers in their countries of birth. Others, like Henry A. Kissinger and Ulrich Biel, pursued careers in politics in Washington and Berlin, respectively. Several became prominent historians. The German-born Hans L. Trefousse, who had participated in the World War II liberation of Paris and Leipzig as an intelligence officer, became a noted scholar of the Civil War and World War II eras.[12] Lt. Col. James L. Collins Jr. was a professional soldier who served with the European Theater intelligence division. He then moved on to various postings in Europe, Korea, and the United States, eventually attaining the rank of brigadier general. Coming full circle, he ended his career as the chief of the Army's historical program, overseeing the publication of an official history of the first two years of the American occupation of Germany.[13]

In the turbulent twentieth century, the Army's discreet intelligence presence in occupied Germany might seem like a moment in time that came and passed quickly. The very term "postwar Germany" implies that the period was merely an appendix to World War II. Likewise, the wording "early Cold War Germany" suggests that the late 1940s were simply a preamble to the "real" Cold War of the decades that followed. In fact, the occupation formed the critical link between World War II and the Cold War, and it constituted a transformative period of historical importance in its own right. The organizations, the operations, and the people of Army Intelligence shaped this process and were shaped by it. Their legacy endures to the present day.

---

11 Maj. Hartmut Heiliger, "Die Feindpotenzen der funkelektronischen Aufklärung des Gegners in Westberlin" [The enemy powers of the radio-electronic reconnaissance of the adversary in West Berlin] (Fachschulabschlussarbeit [i.e., technical college thesis paper], MfS Juristische Hochschule Potsdam, 1985), 19, 20, 22, MfS-HA III, Nr. 14455, BStU, Berlin.
12 Margalit Fox, "Hans L. Trefousse, Historian and Author, 88," *New York Times*, 5 Feb 2010.
13 "James Lawton Collins, Jr.," n.d., General Officers Bios, Historians Files, CMH.

Bibliography

Primary Sources—Archival Collections

National Archives and Records Administration, College Park, Maryland

RG 38: Records of the Office of the Chief of Naval Operations
RG 59: Records of the Department of State
RG 65: Records of the Federal Bureau of Investigation
RG 84: Records of the Foreign Service Posts of the Department of State
RG 107: Records of the Office of the Secretary of War
RG 159: Records of the Office of the Inspector General (Army)
RG 165: Records of the War Department General and Special Staffs
RG 186: Records of the Spanish Governors of Puerto Rico
RG 208: Records of the Office of War Information
RG 218: Records of the Joint Chiefs of Staff
RG 226: Records of the Office of Strategic Services
RG 242: National Archives Collection of Foreign Records Seized
RG 260: Records of the Office of Military Government United States
RG 263: Records of the Central Intelligence Agency
RG 319: Records of the Army Staff
RG 331: Records of Allied Operational and Occupation Headquarters, World War II, 1907–1966
RG 338: Records of U.S. Army Operational, Tactical, and Support Organizations
RG 340: Records of the Office of the Secretary of the Air Force
RG 407: Records of the Adjutant General's Office
RG 457: Records of the National Security Agency
RG 466: Records of the U.S. High Commissioner for Germany
RG 498: Records of Headquarters, European Theater of Operations, United States Army, World War II
RG 549: Records of United States Army, Europe

Dwight D. Eisenhower Presidential Library, Abilene, Kansas

Seventh U.S. Army, Dachau, 1945, 2, online edition
U.S. Army Unit Records, 101st Airborne Division, 1942–1949

Franklin D. Roosevelt Presidential Library, Hyde Park, New York

Henry Morgenthau Jr. Papers

Harry S. Truman Presidential Library, Independence, Missouri

Frank N. Roberts Papers
George Elsey Papers
J. Anthony Panuch Papers
President's Secretary's Files
Rose A. Conway Papers
Stephen J. Spingarn Papers

Lauinger Library, Georgetown University, Washington, D.C.

Anthony Cave Brown Papers

Library of Congress, Washington, D.C.

Foreign Affairs Oral History Collection

Washington National Records Center, National Archives and Records Administration, Suitland, Maryland

Court-martial records of William T. Marchuk

Der Bundesbeauftragte für die Unterlagen des Staatssicherheitsdienstes der ehemaligen Deutschen Demokratischen Republik (BStU, "Stasi Archives"), Berlin

Heiliger, Maj. Hartmut. "Die Feindpotenzen der funkelektronischen Aufklärung des Gegners in Westberlin" [The enemy powers of the radio-electronic reconnaissance of the adversary in West Berlin]. Fachschulabschlussarbeit [i.e., technical college thesis paper], MfS Juristische Hochschule Potsdam, 1985.
MfS HA-II: Records of the 2d Department (Hauptabteilung II, Counter-Espionage) of the Ministry for State Security.
MfS BV Dresden: Records of the Regional Administration (Bezirksverwaltung) Dresden of the Ministry for State Security.

Landesarchiv Berlin

Interv, Dr. Jürgen Wetzel and Dr. Brewster S. Chamberlin with John Backer, Intelligence Officer, 82d Airborne Division, July-August 1945, 14 May 1981.
Interv, Brewster S. Chamberlin with William F. Heimlich, Assistant Chief of Staff, G-2, Berlin Command, 1945-1946, 4 Aug 1981.

Primary Sources—Newspapers

ABC
Berliner Zeitung
Charlotte News
Columbia News
Daily Beast
Federal Information & News Dispatch
Frankfurter Allgemeine Zeitung
Frankfurter Rundschau
Hartford Courant
Life Magazine
Los Angeles Times
Neues Deutschland
New York Times
Der Spiegel
Stars and Stripes
Der Tagesspiegel
Washington Tribune
Washington Post

Primary Sources—Virtual Archives and Document Collections

Central Intelligence Agency (CIA), Langley, Virginia

CIA Electronic Reading Room: http://www.cia.gov/readingroom

National Security Agency, Fort Meade, Maryland

History of the Army Security Agency (ASA): https://www.nsa.gov/news-features/declassified-documents/army-security-agency/
ASA. *Summary Annual Report of the Army Security Agency, Fiscal Year 1946*. Washington, DC: ASA, 1947.
ASA. *Summary Annual Report of the Army Security Agency, Fiscal Year 1947*. Washington, DC: ASA, 1950.

ASA. *Summary Annual Report of the Army Security Agency, Fiscal Year 1948*. Washington, DC: ASA, 1951.
ASA. *Summary Annual Report of the Army Security Agency, Fiscal Year 1949*. Washington, DC: ASA, 1952.
ASA. Post War Transition Period. The Army Security Agency 1945–1948." Washington, DC: ASA, 1952.
ASA. "European Axis Signal Intelligence in World War II as Revealed by 'TICOM' Investigations and by other Prisoner of War Interrogations and Captured Material, Principally German," 9 vols. (ASA, 1 May 1946).

National Security Archive, George Washington University, Washington, D.C.

Digital National Security Archive: https://www.gwu.edu/~nsarchiv/

University of Rochester, Rochester, New York

Living History Project: https://livinghistory.lib.rochester.edu/

U.S. Army Center of Military History, Washington, D.C.

Bray, Maj. Ann, et al., ed. *The History of the Counter Intelligence Corps*. Vol. 2, *Chronology, 1775–1950*. Fort Holabird, MD: U.S. Army Intelligence Center, 1959.
Bray, Maj. Ann, et al., ed. *The History of the Counter Intelligence Corps*. Vol. 16, *To the German Frontier: Part I*. Fort Holabird, MD: U.S. Army Intelligence Center, 1959.
Bray, Maj. Ann, et al., ed. *The History of the Counter Intelligence Corps*. Vol. 18, *The Last German Offensive*. Fort Holabird, MD: U.S. Army Intelligence Center, 1959.
Bray, Maj. Ann, et al., ed. *The History of the Counter Intelligence Corps*. Vol. 19, *The Rhine Breached*. Fort Holabird, MD: U.S. Army Intelligence Center, 1959.
Bray, Maj. Ann, et al., ed. *The History of the Counter Intelligence Corps*. Vol. 20, *Germany Overrun: Part I*. Fort Holabird, MD: U.S. Army Intelligence Center, 1959.
Bray, Maj. Ann, et al., ed. *The History of the Counter Intelligence Corps*. Vol. 21, *Germany Overrun, Part II*. Fort Holabird, MD: U.S. Army Intelligence Center, 1959.
Bray, Maj. Ann, et al., ed. *The History of the Counter Intelligence Corps*. Vol. 25, *Occupation Austria and Italy*. Fort Holabird, MD: U.S. Army Intelligence Center, 1959.
Bray, Maj. Ann, et al., ed. *The History of the Counter Intelligence Corps*. Vol. 26, *German Occupation*. Fort Holabird, MD: U.S. Army Intelligence Center, 1959.
Bray, Maj. Ann, et al., ed. *The History of the Counter Intelligence Corps*. Vol. 27, *Four Years of Cold War*. Fort Holabird, MD: U.S. Army Intelligence Center, 1959.
European Command (EUCOM). *Labor Services and Industrial Police in the European Command, 1945–1950*. Karlsruhe: EUCOM Historical Division, 1952.
Frederiksen, Oliver J. *The American Military Occupation of Germany, 1945– 1953*. Darmstadt: Historical Division, U.S. Army, Europe (USAREUR), 1953.
Geis, Margaret L. *Negro Personnel in the European Command, 1 January 1946–30 June 1950*. Occupation Forces in Europe Series. Karlsruhe: Historical Division, EUCOM, 1952.

Gillen, J. F. J. *U.S. Military Government in Germany: American Influence on the Development of Political Institutions*. Karlsruhe: Historical Division, EUCOM, 1950.

Office of the Chief Historian, EUCOM. *The First Year of the Occupation, 1945-1946*, vol. 2. Occupation Forces in Europe Series, 1945-46. Frankfurt: Office of the Chief Historian, EUCOM, 1947.

Office of the Chief Historian, EUCOM. *The First Year of the Occupation, 1945-1946*. Part 5, *A Survey of Occupation Problems*. Occupation Forces in Europe Series, 1945-46. Frankfurt: Office of the Chief Historian, EUCOM, 1947.

Office of the Chief Historian, EUCOM. *The Second Year of the Occupation*, vol. 2. Occupation Forces in Europe Series 1946-47. Frankfurt: Office of the Chief Historian, EUCOM, 1947.

Office of the Chief Historian, EUCOM. *The Second Year of the Occupation*, vol. 6. Occupation Forces in Europe Series, 1946-1947. Frankfurt: Office of the Chief Historian, EUCOM, 1947.

Office of the Chief Historian, EUCOM. *The Third Year of the Occupation*. Vol. 2, Part 1, *The First Quarter, 1 July-30 September 1947*. Occupation Forces in Europe Series, 1947-48. Frankfurt: Office of the Chief Historian, EUCOM, 1947.

Office of the Chief Historian, EUCOM. *The Third Year of the Occupation*. Vol. 2, Part 2, *The Second Quarter: 1 October-31 December 1947*. Occupation Forces in Europe Series 1947-48. Frankfurt: Office of the Chief Historian, EUCOM, 1948.

Office of the Chief Historian, EUCOM. *The Third Year of the Occupation*. Vol. 2, Part 3, *The Third Quarter, 1 January-31 March 1948*. Occupation Forces in Europe Series, 1947-48. Frankfurt: Office of the Chief Historian, EUCOM, 1947.

Office of the Chief Historian, EUCOM. T*he Third Year of the Occupation*. Vol. 2, Part 4, *The Fourth Quarter, 1 April-30 June 1948*. Occupation Forces in Europe Series, 1947-48. Frankfurt: Office of the Chief Historian, EUCOM, 1947.

Office of the Chief Historian, EUCOM. *The Fourth Year of the Occupation, 1 July-31 December 1948*, vol. 2. Occupation Forces in Europe Series 1948. Karlsruhe: Historical Division, EUCOM, 1949.

Office of the Chief Historian, EUCOM. *A Survey of Soviet Aims, Policies, and Tactics*. Occupation Forces in Europe Series 1947-1948. Frankfurt: Historical Division, EUCOM, 1948.

Office of the Chief Historian, EUCOM. *Censorship*. Occupation Forces in Europe Series, 1945-46. Frankfurt: EUCOM, 1947.

Judge Advocate General School. *Law of Belligerent Occupation*. J.A.G.S. Text 11. Ann Arbor, MI: The Judge Advocate General's School, 1944.

U.S. War Department. *Strength of the Army*. Washington, DC: Department of War, 1 Jan 1947.

U.S. War Department, Adjutant General's Office. *Strength of the Army*. Washington, DC: Government Printing Office, 1 Jul 1948.

U.S. Department of the Army. *Strength of the Army, 1 January 1949*. Washington, DC: Office of the Adjutant General, 1949.

Woodrow Wilson International Center for Scholars, Washington, D.C.

Cold War International History Project — Digital Archive: http://www.wilsoncenter.org/digital-archive

Primary Sources—Published Documents, Document Collections, and Official Publications

Benson, Robert L., and Michael Warner, eds. *Venona: Soviet Espionage and the American Response, 1939-1957*. Washington, DC: CIA, 1996.
Final Report of the Select Committee to Conduct an Investigation and Study of the Facts, Evidence, and Circumstances of the Katyn Forest Massacre, 82d Cong. Washington, DC: U.S. Government Printing Office, 1952.
Gilbert, James L., and John P. Finnegan, eds. *U.S. Army Signals Intelligence in World War II: A Documentary History*. Washington, DC: U.S. Army Center of Military History, 1993.
Ryan, Allan A., Jr., *Klaus Barbie and the United States Government: A Report to the Attorney General of the United States*. Washington, DC: U.S. Department of Justice, 1983.
Slany, William, ed., *Foreign Relations of the United States, 1947, Council of Foreign Ministers; Germany and Austria, Volume II*. Washington, DC: Government Printing Office, 1972.
Soviet Terrorism in Germany, Hearing Before the Subcommittee to Investigate the Administration of the Internal Security Act and Other Internal Security Laws of the Committee on the Judiciary, United States Senate, 86th Cong., 2nd sess., 21 Sep 1960.
Steury, Donald P., ed. *On the Front Lines of the Cold War: Documents on the Intelligence War in Berlin, 1946 to 1961*. Washington, DC: Center for the Study of Intelligence, 1999.
Thorne, C. Thomas, Jr. and David S. Patterson, ed. *Foreign Relations of the United States, Emergence of the Intelligence Establishment, 1945-1950*. Washington, DC: Government Printing Office, 1996.
Thüringer Landtag Plenarprotokoll, 5. Wahlperiode, 25th session, 18 Jun 2010 (Erfurt, 2010).
U.S. Department of State, ed. *Documents on Germany 1944-1985*. Washington, DC: State Department, Office of the Historian, 1985.
Vestnik Arkhiva Prezidenta Rossiiskoi Federatsii, ed. *Sovetskaia Armiia. Gody reform i ispytanii* [The Soviet Army: Years of reforms and challenges], vol. 1. Moscow: Istoricheskaia literatura, 2018.
Warner, Michael, ed. *The CIA under Harry Truman*. Washington, DC: CIA, 1994.

Secondary Literature

5th Armored Division Association. *Paths of Armor: The Fifth Armored Division in World War II*. Nashville, TN: The Battery Press, 1985.
Adenauer, Konrad. *Erinnerungen 1945-1953* [Memoirs, 1945-1953]. Stuttgart: Deutsche Verlags-Anstalt, 1965.
Aid, Matthew M. *The Secret Sentry: The Untold History of the National Security Agency*. London: Bloomsbury Press, 2009.
Aldrich, Richard J. *The Hidden Hand: Britain, America, and Cold War Secret Intelligence*. New York: Overlook Press, 2001.
Allen, Keith R. *Befragung, Überprüfung, Kontrolle: Die Aufnahme von DDR-Flüchtlingen in West-Berlin bis 1961* [Questioning, verification, control: The admission of GDR refugees in West Berlin through 1961]. Berlin: Ch. Links, 2013.
Alvarez, David, and Eduard Mark. *Spying Through a Glass Darkly: American Espionage Against the Soviet Union, 1945-1946*. Lawrence: University Press of Kansas, 2016.

Ambrose, Stephen E. *Citizen Soldiers: The U.S. Army from the Normandy Beaches to the Bulge to the Surrender of Germany, June 7, 1944–May 7, 1945*. New York: Simon & Schuster, 1997.
Ambrose, Stephen E. *Eisenhower and Berlin, 1945: The Decision to Halt at the Elbe*. New York: Norton, 1967.
Andrew, Christopher, and Vasili Mitrokhin. *The Sword and the Shield: The Mitrokhin Archive and the Secret History of the KGB*. New York: Basic Books, 1999.
Anonymous [Marta Hillers]. *A Woman in Berlin: A Diary: Eight Weeks in the Conquered City*. New York: Henry Holt, 2005.
Appelius, Stefan. "Rudolf Harnisch und die Verhaftung der Pinckert-Gruppe" [Rudolf Harnisch and the arrest of the Pinckert-Gruppe]. *Zeitschrift des Forschungsverbundes SED-Staat* 38 (2015): 156–59.
Atkinson, Rick. *The Guns at Last Light: The War in Western Europe, 1944–1945*. London: Picador, 2014.
Bach, Julian. *America's Germany: An Account of the Occupation*. New York: Random House, 1947.
Bamford, James. *Body of Secrets: Anatomy of the Ultra-Secret National Security Agency*. New York: Anchor Books, 2002.
Barclay, David E. *Schaut auf diese Stadt: Der unbekannte Ernst Reuter* [Look upon this city: The unknown Ernst Reuter]. Berlin: Siedler Verlag, 2000.
Bauer, Christian, and Rebekka Göpfert. *Die Ritchie Boys: Deutsche Emigranten im amerikanischen Geheimdienst* [The Ritchie Boys: German emigrants in the American secret service]. Munich: Hoffmann und Campe, 2005.
Bedessem, Edward N. *Central Europe*. U.S. Army Campaigns of World War II. Washington, DC: U.S. Army Center of Military History, 1995.
Beevor, Antony. *The Fall of Berlin 1945*. New York: Viking, 2002.
Bennett, Ralph. *Ultra in the West: The Normandy Campaign 1944–45*. New York: Charles Scribner's Sons, 1979.
Benson, Robert L. *A History of U.S. Communications Intelligence in World War II: Policy and Administration*. Fort Meade, MD: Center for Cryptologic History, National Security Agency, 1997.
Benson, Robert L. *The Venona Story*. Fort Meade, MD: Center for Cryptologic History, National Security Agency, 2001.
Beschloss, Michael R. *The Conquerors: Roosevelt, Truman, and the Destruction of Hitler's Germany, 1941–1945*. New York: Simon & Schuster, 2003.
Bessel, Richard. *Germany 1945: From War to Peace*. New York: Harper, 2009.
Bethell, Nicholas. *The Great Betrayal: The Untold Story of Kim Philby's Final Act of Treachery*. London: Hodder and Stoughton, 1984.
Biddiscombe, Perry. *The Denazification of Germany: A History 1945–1950*. London: Tempus, 2006.
Biddiscombe, Perry. "'The Enemy of Our Enemy': A View of the Edelweiss Piraten from the British and American Archives." *Journal of Contemporary History* 30, no. 1 (1995): 37–63.
Biddiscombe, Perry. *The Last Nazis: SS Werewolf Guerrilla Resistance in Europe, 1944–1947*. Charleston, SC: Tempus, 2000.
Biddiscombe, Perry. "Operation Selection Board: The Growth and Suppression of the Neo-Nazi 'Deutsche Revolution,' 1945–47." *Intelligence and National Security* 11, no. 1 (Jan 1999): 59–77.
Biddiscombe, Perry. "The Problem with Glass Houses: The Soviet Recruitment and Deployment of SS Men as Spies and Saboteurs." *Intelligence and National Security* 15, vol. 3 (2000): 131–45.
Biddiscombe, Perry. *Werwolf!: The History of the National Socialist Guerilla Movement, 1944–1946*. Toronto: Toronto University Press, 1998.
Bidwell, Bruce W. *History of the Military Intelligence Division, Department of the Army General Staff: 1775–1941*. Frederick, MD: University Publications of America, 1986.

Bigelow, Michael E. "A Short History of Army Intelligence." *Military Intelligence Professional Bulletin* 38, no. 3 (Jul-Sep 2012): 1–59.
Bird, Kai. *The Chairman: John J. McCloy and the Making of the American Establishment*. New York: Simon & Schuster, 1992.
Black, Jeremy. *The Politics of James Bond: From Fleming's Novels to the Big Screen*. London: Praeger, 2001.
Boehling, Rebecca. "U.S. Military Occupation, Grass Roots Democracy, and Local German Government." In *American Policy and the Reconstruction of West Germany, 1945–1955*, edited by Jeffrey M. Diefendorf, Axel Frohn, and Hermann-Josef Rupieper, 281–306. Cambridge, UK: Cambridge University Press, 1994.
Boghardt, Thomas. "America's Secret Vanguard: U.S. Army Intelligence Operations in Germany, 1944–1947." *Studies in Intelligence* 57, no. 2 (Jun 2013): 1–18.
Boghardt, Thomas. "The American Candidate: U.S. Intelligence, Theodor Heuss, and the Making of West Germany's First President." *Studies in Intelligence* 64, no. 2 (Jun 2020): 1–12.
Boghardt, Thomas. "Betrayal in Berlin: The Riddle of the 'Walter Affair.'" Sources and Methods, Cold War International History Project, Wilson Center, 17 Aug 2020.
Boghardt, Thomas. "'By All Feasible Means': New Documents on the American Intervention in Italy's Parliamentary Elections of 1948." Sources and Methods, Cold War International History Project, Wilson Center, 1 May 2017.
Boghardt, Thomas. "Dirty Work? The Use of Nazi Informants by U.S. Army Intelligence in Postwar Europe." *Journal of Military History* 79 (Apr 2015): 387–422.
Boghardt, Thomas. "Semper Vigilis: The U.S. Army Security Agency in Early Cold War Germany." *Army History* 106 (Winter 2018): 6–28.
Boyd, Carl. *Hitler's Japanese Confidant: General Ōshima Hiroshi and Magic Intelligence, 1941–1945*. Lawrence: University of Kansas Press, 1993.
Bradley, Omar N. *A General's Life*: *An Autobiography by General of the Army Omar N. Bradley*. New York: Simon and Schuster, 1983.
Bradley, Omar N. *A Soldier's Story*. New York: Holt, 1951.
Bradsher, Greg. "Nazi Gold: The Merkers Mine Treasure." *Prologue Magazine* 31, no. 1 (Spring 1999), online edition.
Brandt, Willy. *Mein Weg nach Berlin* [My path to Berlin]. Munich: Kindler Verlag, 1960.
Breitman, Richard, and Norman J. W. Goda. *Hitler's Shadow: Nazi War Criminals, U.S. Intelligence, and the Cold War*. Washington, DC: National Archives and Records Administration, 2010.
Breitman, Richard, Norman J. W. Goda, Timothy Naftali, and Robert Wolfe, eds. *U.S. Intelligence and the Nazis*. New York: Cambridge University Press, 2005.
Brown, Ralph W., III. "Removing 'Nasty Nazi Habits': The CIC and the Denazification of Heidelberg University, 1945–1946." *The Journal of Intelligence History* 4 (Summer 2004): 25–56.
Budiansky, Stephen. *Battle of Wits: The Complete Story of Codebreaking in World War II*. New York: Free Press, 2000.
Budiansky, Stephen. *Code Warriors: NSA's Codebreakers and the Secret Intelligence War against the Soviet Union*. New York: Penguin Random House, 2016.
Buechner, Howard A. *Dachau: The Hour of the Avenger*. Metairie, LA: Thunderbird Press, 1986.
Buhite, Russel D., and William C. Hamel. "War for Peace: The Question of an American Preventive War Against the Soviet Union, 1945–1955." *Diplomatic History* 14, no. 3 (Jun 1990): 367–384.
Bungert, Heike. "Ein meisterhafter Schachzug: das Nationalkomitee Freies Deutschland in der Beurteilung der Amerikaner, 1943–1945" [A masterful maneuver: The National Committee for a Free Germany in the judgment of the Americans, 1943–1945]. In *Geheimdienstkrieg gegen Deutschland: Subversion, Propaganda und politische Planungen des amerikanischen Geheimdienstes*

im Zweiten Weltkrieg [The intelligence war against Germany: Subversion, propaganda, and political planning by American intelligence in World War II], edited by Jürgen Heideking and Christof Mauch, 90–121. Göttingen: Vandenhoeck & Ruprecht, 1993.

Buscher, Frank M. *The U.S. War Crimes Trial Program in Germany, 1946–1955*. New York: Greenwood Press, 1989.

Buschfort, Wolfgang. *Das Ostbüro der SPD. Von der Gründung der SPD bis zur Berlin-Krise* [The Ostbüro of the SPD: From the founding of the SPD to the Berlin crisis]. Munich: R. Oldenbourg Verlag, 1991.

Buschfort, Wolfgang. *Parteien im Kalten Krieg. Die Ostbüros von SPD, CDU and FDP* [Parties in the Cold War: The Ostbüros of the SPD, CDU, and FDP]. Berlin: Ch. Links Verlag, 2000.

Caddick-Adams, Peter. *Snow & Steel: The Battle of the Bulge, 1944–45*. Oxford: Oxford University Press, 2017.

Casey, William J. *The Secret War Against Hitler*. Washington, DC: Regnery Gateway, 1988.

Chennault, Claire Lee. *Way of a Fighter: The Memoirs of Claire Lee Chennault*. Edited by Robert Hotz. New York: G. P. Putnam's Sons, 1949.

Clare, George. *Before the Wall: Berlin Days, 1946–1948*. New York: Dutton, 1990.

Clay, Lucius D. *Decision in Germany*. Garden City, NY: Doubleday, 1950.

Cole, Hugh M. *The Ardennes: Battle of the Bulge*. United States Army in World War II. Washington, DC: U.S. Army Center of Military History, 1993.

Cookridge, Edward H. *Gehlen: Spy of the Century*. New York: Random House, 1971.

Corke, Sarah-Jane. *U.S. Covert Operations and Cold War Strategy: Truman, Secret Warfare and the CIA, 1945–53*. London: Routledge, 2008.

Crim, Brian E. *Our Germans: Project Paperclip and the National Security State*. Baltimore: Johns Hopkins University Press, 2018.

Critchfield, James H. *Partners at the Creation: The Men Behind Postwar Germany's Defense and Intelligence Establishments*. Annapolis, MD: Naval Institute Press, 2003.

Cutler, Richard. *Counterspy: Memoirs of a Counterintelligence Officer in World War II and the Cold War*. Washington, DC: Brassey's, 2004.

Dabringhaus, Erhard. *Klaus Barbie: The Shocking Story of How the U.S. Used This Nazi War Criminal as an Intelligence Agent*. Washington, DC: Acropolis Books, 1984.

Dallin, David. *Soviet Espionage*. New Haven, CT: Yale University Press, 1955.

Danchev, Alex, and Daniel Todman, eds. *Field Marshal Lord Alanbrooke: War Diaries 1939–1945*. Berkeley: University of California Press, 1957.

Daso, Dik Alan. "Operation LUSTY: The U.S. Army Air Forces' Exploitation of the Luftwaffe's Secret Aeronautical Technology, 1944–45." *Aerospace Power Journal* 16, no. 1 (Spring 2002): 28–40.

Deane, John R. *The Strange Alliance: The Story of Our Efforts at Wartime Co-Operation with Russia*. New York: Viking, 1947.

Diedrich, Tortsen, and Rüdiger Wenzke. *Die getarnte Armee. Geschichte der Kasernierten Volkspolizei der DDR 1952–1956* [The camouflaged army: History of the Barracked People's Police of the GDR]. Berlin: Ch. Links Verlag, 2003.

Domentat, Tamara, and Christina Heimlich. *Heimlich im Kalten Krieg: Die Geschichte von Christina Ohlsen und Bill Heimlich* [Heimlich in the Cold War: The history of Christina Ohlsen and Bill Heimlich]. Berlin: Aufbau-Verlag, 2000.

Dorn, Walter L. *Inspektionsreisen in der US-Zone: Notizen, Denkschriften und Erinnerungen aus dem Nachlass überetzt und herausgegeben von Lutz Niethammer* [Inspection trips in the U.S. Zone: Notes, memoranda and memories from the estate, translated and edited by Lutz Niethammer]. Stuttgart: Deutsche Verlags-Anstalt, 1973.

Douglas, Sarah K. "The Search for Hitler: Hugh Trevor-Roper, Humphrey Searle, and the Last Days of Hitler." *Journal of Military History* 78 (Jan 2014): 159–210.

Drath, Viola Herms. *Willy Brandt: Prisoner of His Past*. Radnor, PA: Chilton Book Company, 1975.

Eckert, Astrid. *The Struggle for the Files: The Western Allies and the Return of German Archives after the Second World War*. Cambridge, UK: Cambridge University Press, 2012.

Eichner, Klaus, and Andreas Dobbert. *Headquarters Germany: Die USA-Geheimdienste in Deutschland* [Headquarters Germany: The U.S. secret services in Germany]. Berlin: edition ost, 2001.

Eisenberg, Carolyn. *Drawing the Line: The American Decision to Divide Germany 1944–1949*. Cambridge, UK: Cambridge University Press, 1996. Eisenhower, Dwight D. *Crusade in Europe: A Personal Account of World War II*. New York: Doubleday, 1948.

Ferguson, Niall. *Kissinger*. Vol. 1, *1923–1968: The Idealist*. New York: Penguin, 2013.

Finnegan, John Patrick, and Romana Danysh. *Military Intelligence*. Army Lineage Series. Washington, DC: U.S. Army Center of Military History, 1998.

Fischer, Benjamin B. "The Katyn Controversy: Stalin's Killing Field." *Studies in Intelligence* (Winter 1999/2000), online edition.

Fishel, Edwin C., and Robert S. Benjamin, eds. *ASA Review* 1, no. 2 (Jul-Aug 1947).

Foitzkik, Jan, and Tatjana W. Zarewskaja-Djakana, eds. *SMAD-Handbuch: Die Sowjetische Militäradministration in Deutschland 1945–1949* [SMAD-Handbook: The Soviet Military Administration in Germany, 1945–1949]. Munich: Oldenbourg, 2009.

Forsyth, Frederick M. *The Odessa File*. New York: Viking Press, 1971.

Foschepoth, Josef. *Überwachtes Deutschland: Post-und Telefonüberwachung in der alten Bundesrepublik* [Surveillance Germany: Post and telephone surveillance in the old Federal Republic]. Göttingen: Vandenhoeck and Ruprecht, 2013.

Friedensburg, Ferdinand. *Es ging um Deutschlands Einheit: Rückschau eines Berliners auf die Jahre nach 1945* [It was about German unity: Reminiscences of a Berliner on the years after 1945]. Berlin: Haude & Spener, 1971.

Fry, Helen. *The London Cage: The Secret History of Britain's World War II Interrogation Centre*. New Haven, CT: Yale University Press, 2017.

Gaddis, John Lewis. *United States and the Origins of the Cold War, 1941–1947*. New York: Columbia University Press, 1972.

Gehlen, Reinhard. *Der Dienst: Erinnerungen, 1942–1971* [The service: Memoirs, 1942–1971]. Mainz-Wiesbaden: Hase & Koehler, 1971.

Gehlen, Reinhard. *The Service: The Memoirs of General Reinhard Gehlen*. Translated by David Irving. New York: Popular Library, 1972.

Gentry, Curt. *J. Edgar Hoover: The Man and the Secrets*. New York: Norton, 2001.

Geraghty, Tony. *Brixmis: The Untold Exploits of Britain's Most Daring Cold War Spy Mission*. London: HarperCollins, 1997.

Gerhardt, Uta. "Die Amerikanischen Militäroffiziere und der Konflikt um die Wiedereröffnung der Universität Heidelberg 1945–1946" [American military officers and the conflict over the reopening of Heidelberg University, 1945–1946]. In *Heidelberg 1945*, edited by Jürgen Heß, Hartmut Lehmann, and Volker Sellin, 28–52. Stuttgart: Franz Steiner Verlag, 1996.

Gieseke, Jens. *Die Stasi, 1945–1990* [The Stasi, 1945–1990]. Munich: DVA, 2011.

Gilbert, James L., John P. Finnegan, and Ann Bray, *In the Shadow of the Sphinx: A History of Army Counterintelligence*. Fort Belvoir, VA: U.S. Army Intelligence and Security Command, 2005.

Gimbel, John. *The American Occupation of Germany*. Stanford, CA: Stanford University Press, 1968.

Gimbel, John. "German Scientists, United States Denazification Policy, and the Paperclip Conspiracy." *International History Review* 12, no. 3 (Aug 1990): 441–65.

Gimbel, John. *Science, Technology, and Reparations: Exploitation and Plunder in Postwar Germany*. Stanford, CA: Stanford University Press, 1990.

Gladwin, Lee A. "Cautious Collaborators: The Struggle for Anglo-American Cryptanalytic Co-operation 1940–43." *Intelligence and National Security* 14, no. 1 (1999): 119–45.
Glantz, Mary E. *FDR and the Soviet Union: The President's Battles over Foreign Policy*. Lawrence: University Press of Kansas, 2017.
Gobarev, Victor. "Soviet Military Plans and Actions During the First Berlin Crisis, 1948–49." *The Journal of Slavic Military* Studies 10, no. 3 (Sep 1997): 1–24.
Goschler, Constantin. "The Attitude towards Jews in Bavaria after the Second World War." *The Leo Baeck Institute Year Book* 36, no. 1 (Jan 1991): 443–58.
Gott, Kendall D. *Mobility, Vigilance and Justice: The U.S. Army Constabulary in Germany 1946–1953*. Fort Leavenworth, KS: Combat Studies Institute Press, 2005.
Goodman, Michael S. *Spying on the Nuclear Bear: Anglo-American Intelligence and the Soviet Bomb*. Stanford, CA: Stanford University Press, 2007.
Grombach, John V. *The Great Liquidator* (Garden City, NY: Doubleday, 1980).
Halbrook, Stephen P. "Operation Sunrise: America's OSS, Swiss Intelligence, and the German Surrender 1945." In *"Operation Sunrise." Atti del convegno internazionale, Locarno, 2 maggio 2005* ["Operation Sunrise": Proceedings of the international conference, Locarno, 2 May 2005]. edited by Marino Viganò and Dominic M. Pedrazzini, 103–30. Lugano: No publisher, 2006.
Harrington, Daniel F. *Berlin on the Brink: The Blockade, the Airlift, and the Early Cold War*. Lexington: University Press of Kentucky, 2012.
Harris, Robert. *Selling Hitler: The Extraordinary Story of the Con Job of the Century*. New York: Pantheon, 1986.
Harris, William R. "March Crisis 1948, Act I." *Studies in Intelligence* 10 (Fall 1966): 1–22.
Harris, William R. "March Crisis 1948, Act II." *Studies in Intelligence* 11 (Spring 1967): 9–36.
Haynes, John Earl, Harvey Klehr, and Alexander Vassiliev. *Spies: The Rise and Fall of the KGB in America*. New Haven, CT: Yale University Press, 2009.
Hechelhammer, Bodo. "Unter amerikanischer Flagge: Die 'Bolero Group' um Reinhard Gehlen" [Under the American flag: The "Bolero Group" around Reinhard Gehlen]. In *Achtung Spione: Geheimdienste in Deutschland 1945–1956* [Attention spies: Secret services in Germany 1945–1956], edited by Magnus Pahl, Gorch Pieken, and Matthias Rogg, 44–55. Dresden: Sandstein Verlag, 2016.
Heimann, Siegfried. *Karl Heinrich und die Berliner SPD, die sowjetische Militäradministration und die SED* [Karl Heinrich and the Berlin SPD: The Soviet Military Administration and the SED]. Bonn: Friedrich-Ebert-Stiftung, 2007.
Heitzer, Enrico. *Affäre Walter: Die vergessene Verhaftungswelle* [The Walter affair: The forgotten wave of arrests]. Berlin: Metropol, 2008.
Heitzer, Enrico. *Die Kampfgruppe gegen Unmenschlichkeit (KgU): Widerstand und Spionage im Kalten Krieg 1948–1959* [The Fighting Group against Inhumanity (KgU): Resistance and espionage in the Cold War, 1948–1959]. Cologne: Böhlau Verlag, 2014.
Helms, Richard, with William Hood. *A Look Over My Shoulder: A Life in the Central Intelligence Agency*. Novato, CA: Presidio, 2004.
Henderson, Bruce. *Sons and Soldiers: The Untold Story of the Jews Who Escaped the Nazis and Returned with the U.S. Army to Fight Hitler*. New York: William Morrow, 2017.
Henke, Klaus-Dietmar. *Die amerikanische Besetzung Deutschlands* [The American occupation of Germany]. Munich: R. Oldenbourg Verlag, 2009.
Henke, Klaus-Dietmar, and Hans Woller. *Lehrjahre der CSU:Eine Nachkriegspartei im Spiegel vertraulicher Berichte an die amerikanische Militärregierung* [Apprenticeship years of the CSU: A

postwar party as reflected in confidential reports to the American military government]. Stuttgart: Deutsche Verlags-Anstalt, 1984.
Hentschel, Volker. *Ludwig Erhard: Ein Politikerleben* [Ludwig Erhard: A political life]. Lech: Olzog, 1996.
Hersh, Burton. *The Old Boys: The American Elite and the Origins of the CIA*. New York: Charles Scribner's Sons, 1992.
Hettler, Friedrich Hermann. *Josef Müller ("Ochsensepp"): Mann des Widerstandes und erster CSU-Vorsitzender* [Josef Müller ("Ochsensepp"): Man of the resistance and first CSU chairman]. Munich: Kommissionsverlag Uni-Druck, 1991.
Hilger, Andreas. "Counter-Intelligence Soviet Style: The Activities of Soviet Security Services in East Germany, 1945–1955." *Journal of Intelligence History* 3, no. 1 (Summer 2003): 83–105.
Hinsley, F. H., E. E. Thomas, C. A. G. Simkins, and C. F. G. Ransom. *British Intelligence in the Second World War*. Vol. 3, Part 2, *Its Influence on Strategy and Operations*. London: Her Majesty's Stationery Office, 1988.
Hoegner, Wilhelm. *Der Schwierige Außenseiter: Erinnerungen eines Abgeordneten, Emigranten und Ministerpräsidenten* [The difficult outsider: Memoirs of an MP, emigrant and prime minister]. Munich: Isar Verlag, 1959.
Hoffman, Hans-Albert, and Siegfried Stoof. *Sowjetische Truppen in Deutschland: Ihr Hauptquartier in Wünsdorf 1945–1994. Geschichte, Fakten, Hintergründe* [Soviet troops in Germany: Their headquarters in Wünsdorf 1945–1994. History, facts, background]. No city: Selbstverlag, 2008.
Hoffmann, Joachim. *Die Geschichte der Wlassow-Armee* [The history of the Vlasov Army]. Freiburg: Rombach, 1986.
Hofmann, George F. *Cold War Casualty: The Court-Martial of Major General Robert W. Grow*. Kent, OH: Kent State University Press, 1993.
Hogan, David W., Jr. "Berlin Revisited—and Revised: Eisenhower's Decision to Halt at the Elbe." In *Victory in Europe 1945: From World War to Cold War*, edited by Arnold A. Offner and Theodore A. Wilson, 77–101. Lawrence: University of Kansas Press, 2000.
Hogan, David W., Jr. *A Command Post at War: First Army Headquarters in Europe, 1943–1945*. Washington, DC: U.S. Army Center of Military History, 2000.
Hogan, Michael J. *A Cross of Iron: Harry S. Truman and the Origins of the National Security State*. Cambridge, UK: Cambridge University Press, 1998.
Höhne, Heinz. *Der Krieg im Dunkeln: Macht und Einfluss des deutschen und des russischen Geheimdienstes* [The war in the dark: The power and influence of the German and Russian secret services]. Munich: C. Bertelsmann Verlag: 1985.
Höhne, Heinz, and Hermann Zolling. *The General Was a Spy: The Truth About General Gehlen and His Spy Ring*. Translated by Richard Barry. New York: Coward, McCann & Geogheghan, 1972.
Holbrook, James R. *Potsdam Mission: Memoir of a U.S. Army Intelligence Officer in Communist East Germany*. Carmel, IN: Cork Hill Press, 2005.
Holloway, David. *Stalin and the Bomb: The Soviet Union and Atomic Energy, 1939–1956*. New Haven, CT: Yale University Press, 1994.
Howe, George F. *American Signal Intelligence in Northwest Africa and Western Europe*. Sources in Cryptologic History, Series iv, Vol. 1. Fort Meade, MD: National Security Agency, 2010.
Howley, Frank L. *Berlin Command*. New York: G. P. Putnam's Sons, 1950.
Hunt, Linda. *Secret Agenda: The U.S. Government, Nazi Scientists and Project Paperclip, 1944–1990*. New York: St. Martin's Press, 1991.
Hunter, Jack. *The Expendable Spy*. New York: E. P. Dutton, 1965.
Hutchinson, Peter. *Stefan Heym: The Perpetual Dissident*. Cambridge, UK: Cambridge University Press, 1992.

Isaacson, Walter. *Kissinger: A Biography*. New York: Simon & Schuster, 1992.
Jacobsen, Annie. *Operation Paperclip: The Secret Intelligence Program That Brought Nazi Scientists to America*. New York: Little, Brown, 2014.
Jardim, Tomaz. *The Mauthausen Trial: American Military Justice in Germany*. Cambridge, MA: Harvard University Press, 2012.
Jeffery, Keith. *The Secret History of MI6, 1909-1949*. New York: Penguin, 2010.
Jessel, Walter. *Class of '31: A German-Jewish Émigré's Journey Across Defeated Germany*. Brookline, MA: Academic Studies Press, 2017.
Jolas, Eugène. *Man from Babel*. Edited by Andreas Kramer and Rainer Rumold. New Haven, CT: Yale University Press, 1998.
Jones, R. V. "Anglo-American Cooperation in the Wizard War." In *In the Name of Intelligence: Essays in Honor of Walter Pforzheimer*, edited by Hayden B. Peake and Samuel Halpern, 299-312. Washington, DC: NIBC Press, 1994.
Jones, Vincent C. *Manhattan: The Army and the Atomic Bomb*, 2d ed. United States Army in World War II. Washington, DC: U.S. Army Center of Military History, 1985.
Kahn, Arthur D. *Experiment in Occupation: Witness to the Turnabout, Anti-Nazi to Cold War, 1944-1946*. University Park: Pennsylvania State University Press, 2004.
Kahn, David. *The Codebreakers: The Comprehensive History of Secret Communication from Ancient Times to the Internet*. New York: Simon & Schuster, 1996.
Kahn, David. *Hitler's Spies: German Military Intelligence in World War II*. New York: Macmillan, 1979.
Kaltenegger, Roland. *Die "Alpenfestung." Der Endkampf um das letzte Bollwerk des Zweiten Weltkrieges* [The "Alpine Fortress": The final battle for the last bulwark of the Second World War]. Würzburg: Flechs, 2015.
Keiderling, Gerhard. "Scheinpluralismus und Blockparteien: Die KPD und die Gründung der Parteien in Berlin 1945" [Sham pluralism and bloc parties: The KPD and the founding of the parties in Berlin, 1945]. *Vierteljahrshefte für Zeitgeschichte* 46, no. 2 (Apr 1997): 257-96.
Keiderling, Gerhard. *Um Deutschlands Einheit: Ferdinand Friedensburg und der Kalte Krieg in Berlin, 1945-1952* [On German unity: Ferdinand Friedensburg and the Cold War in Berlin, 1945-1952]. Vienna, Cologne: Böhlau Verlag, 2009.
Kellerhoff, Sven Felix, and Bernd von Kostka. *Hauptstadt der Spione. Geheimdienste in Berlin im Kalten Krieg* [Capital of the spies: Secret services in Berlin during the Cold War]. Berlin: Berlin Story Verlag, 2016.
Kershaw, Ian. *Hitler, 1936-45: Nemesis*. London: Penguin Press, 2000.
Kirby, Oliver R. "The Origins of the Soviet Problem: A Personal View." *Cryptologic Quarterly* 2, no. 4 (Winter 1992): 51-58.
Koch, Oscar M., with Robert G. Hays. *G-2: Intelligence for Patton*. Atglen, PA: Schiffer Publishing, 1999.
Koch, Scott A. "The Role of U.S. Army Military Attachés Between the World Wars." *Studies in Intelligence* 38, no. 5 (1995): 111-15.
Kock, Peter J. *Bayerns Weg in die Bundesrepublik* [Bavaria's path to the Federal Republic]. Stuttgart: Deutsche Verlags-Anstalt, 1983.
Koehler, John O. *Stasi: The Untold Story of the East German Secret Police*. Boulder, CO: Westview Press, 1999.
Kofsky, Frank. *Harry S. Truman and the War Scare of 1948: A Successful Campaign to Deceive the Nation*. New York: St. Martin's Press, 1993.
Kollander, Patricia, with John O'Sullivan. *"I Must Be a Part of This War": A German American's Fight Against Hitler and Nazism*. New York: Fordham University Press, 2005.

Koop, Volker. *Himmlers letztes Aufgebot: Die NS-Organisation "Werwolf"* [Himmler's last force: The Nazi organization "Werwolf"]. Vienna: Böhlau, 2008.

Kowalczuk, Ilko-Sascha, and Stefan Wolle. *Roter Stern über Deutschland: Sowjetische Truppen in der DDR* [Red star over Germany: Soviet troops in the GDR]. Berlin: Ch. Links, 2010.

Krause, Scott H. "*Neue Westpolitik*: The Clandestine Campaign to Westernize the SPD in Cold War Berlin, 1948–1958." *Central European History* 48, no. 1 (2015): 79–99.

Krieger, Wolfgang. *General Lucius D. Clay und die amerikanische Deutschlandpolitik 1945–1949* [General Lucius D. Clay and the American policy toward Germany, 1945–1949]. Stuttgart: Klett-Cotta, 1987.

Krieger, Wolfgang. "U.S. Patronage of German Postwar Intelligence." In *A Handbook of Intelligence Studies*, edited by Loch Johnson, 28–43. London: Routledge 2007.

Langer, Walter C. *The Mind of Adolf Hitler: The Secret Wartime Report.* New York: Basic Books, 1972.

Lasby, Clarence G. *Project Paperclip: German Scientists and the Cold War.* New York: Athenaeum, 1975.

Laufer, Jochen. "Die UdSSR und die Ursprünge der Berlin-Blockade 1944–1948" [The USSR and the origins of the Berlin blockade, 1944–1948]. *Deutschland Archiv* 31, no. 4 (1998): 564–79.

Laurie, Clayton D. "Goebbels's Iowan: Frederick W. Kaltenbach and Nazi Short-Wave Radio Broadcasts in America, 1939–1945." *The Annals of Iowa* 53, no. 3 (1994): 219–45.

Leonhard, Wolfgang. *Die Revolution entlässt ihre Kinder* [The revolution dismisses its children]. Cologne: Kiepenheur and Witsch, 1955.

Lerner, Daniel. *Sykewar: Psychological Warfare Against Germany, D-Day to VE-Day.* New York: George W. Stewart, 1949.

Löffelsender, Michael. "'A particularly unique role among concentration camps.' Der Dachauer Dora-Prozess 1947." In *Zwangsarbeit im Nationalsozialismus und die Rolle der Justiz. Täterschaft, Nachkriegsprozesse und die Auseinandersetzung um Entschädigungsleistungen* [Forced labor under National Socialism and the role of justice: Culpability, post-war processes and the dispute over compensation payments], edited by Helmut Kramer, Karsten Uhl, and Jens-Christian Wagner, 152–68. Nordhausen: Nordhausen Fachhochschule, 2007.

Longden, Sean. *T-Force: The Race for Nazi War Secrets, 1945.* London: Constable, 2009.

Loth, Wilfried. *Stalins ungeliebtes Kind: Warum Moskau die DDR nicht wollte* [Stalin's unloved child: Why Moscow did not want the GDR]. Reinbek: Rohwolt, 1994.

Lukes, Igor. *On the Edge of the Cold War: American Diplomats and Spies in Postwar Prague.* New York: Oxford University Press, 2012.

MacDonald, Charles B. *The Last Offensive.* United States Army in World War II. Washington, DC: U.S. Army Center of Military History, 1973.

MacDonald, Charles B. *The Siegfried Campaign Line.* United States Army in World War II. Washington, DC: U.S. Army Center of Military History, 2001.

Macdonogh, Giles. "Otto Horcher, Caterer to the Third Reich." *Gastronomica* 7, no. 10 (Winter 2007): 31–38.

Macrakis, Kristie. *Seduced by Secrets: Inside the Stasi's Spy-Tech World.* Cambridge, UK: Cambridge University Press, 2008.

Maddrell, Paul. *Spying on Science: Western Intelligence in Divided Germany, 1945–1961.* Oxford: Oxford University Press, 2006.

Maginnis, John J. *Military Government Journal: Normandy to Berlin.* Amherst: University of Massachusetts Press, 1971.

Major, Patrick. *Death of the KPD: Communism and Anti-Communism in West Germany, 1945–1956.* New York: Oxford University Press, 1998.

Mallett, Derek R. *Hitler's Generals in America: Nazi POWs and Allied Military Intelligence.* Lexington: University Press of Kentucky, 2003.

Marchetti, Victor L., and John D. Marks. *The CIA and the Cult of Intelligence*. New York: Dell, 1974.
Mark, Eduard. "The War Scare of 1946 and Its Consequences," *Diplomatic History* 21, no. 3 (Summer 1997): 383–415.
Matteson, Robert E. "The Last Days of Ernst Kaltenbrunner: Personal Recollections of the Capture and Show Trial of an Intelligence Chief." *Studies in Intelligence* 4, no. 2 (Spring 1960): 9–29.
Matz, Klaus-Jürgen. *Reinhold Maier (1889–1971): Eine politische Biographie* [Reinhold Maier (1889–1971): A political biography]. Düsseldorf: Droste Verlag, 1989.
McCloy, John J. "Adenauer und die Hohe Kommission" [Adenauer and the High Commission]. In *Konrad Adenauer und seine Zeit. Politik und Persönlichkeit des ersten Bundeskanzlers. Beiträge von Weg-und Zeitgenossen* [Konrad Adenauer and his time: Politics and personality of the first Federal Chancellor. Contributions from fellow travelers and contemporaries], edited by Dieter Blumenwitz et al., 421–26. Stuttgart: Deutsche Verlags-Anstalt, 1976.
McCullough, David. *Truman*. New York: Simon & Schuster, 1992.
McKale, Donald M. *Hitler: The Survival Myth*. New York: Stein and Day, 1981.
Meinl, Susanne, andBodo Hechlhammer. *Geheimobjekt Pullach: Von der NS-Mustersiedlung zur Zentrale des BND* [Secret object Pullach: From the Nazi model housing estate to BND headquarters]. Berlin: Ch. Links Verlag, 2014.
Merseburger, Peter. *Der schwierige Deutsche: Kurt Schumacher. Eine Biographie* [The difficult German: Kurt Schumacher. A biography]. Stuttgart: Deutsche Verlags-Anstalt, 1995.
Merseburger, Peter. *Willy Brandt 1913–1992: Visionär und Realist* [Willy Brandt, 1913–1992: Visionary and realist]. Stuttgart, Munich: Deutsche Verlags-Anstalt, 2002.
Merz, Kai-Uwe. *Kalter Krieg als antikommunistischer Widerstand. Die Kampfgruppe gegen Unmenschlichkeit 1948–1959* [The Cold War as anticommunist resistance. The Fighting Group Against Inhumanity, 1948–1959]. Munich: Oldenbourg, 1987.
Milano, James V. and Patrick Brogan. *Soldiers, Spies, and the Rat Line: America's Undeclared War Against the Soviets*. Washington, DC: Brassey's, 1995.
Miller, James E. "Taking Off the Gloves: The United States and the Italian Elections of 1948." *Diplomatic History* 7, no. 1 (1983): 35–66.
Miller, Roger G. *To Save a City: The Berlin Airlift 1948–1949*. Washington, DC: USAF History Office, 1998.
Millis, Walter, ed. *The Forrestal Diaries*. New York: Viking Press, 1951.
Minott, Rodney G. *The Fortress That Never Was: The Myth of Hitler's Bavarian Stronghold*. New York: Holt, Rinehart and Winston, 1964.
Montague, Ludwell L. *General Walter Bedell Smith as Director of Central Intelligence, October 1950–February 1953*. University Park: Pennsylvania State University Press, 1992.
Mosley, Leonard. *Dulles: A Biography of Eleanor, Allen, and John Foster Dulles and Their Family Network*. New York: The Dial Press/James Wade, 1978.
Mowry, David P. "Regierungs-Oberinspektor Fritz Menzer: Cryptographic Inventor Extraordinaire." *Cryptologic Quarterly* 2, nos. 3–4 (Autumn/ Winter 1983–1984): 21–36.
Mühlhausen, Walter. *Demokratischer Neubeginn in Hessen 1945–1949: Lehren aus der Vergangenheit für die Gestaltung der Zukunft* [Democratic new beginning in Hesse, 1945–1949: Lessons from the past for shaping the future]. Wiesbaden: Hessischen Landeszentrale für Politische Bildung, 2005.
Müller, Armin. "Die Technische Nachrichtenbeschaffung der Organisation Gehlen." In *Achtung Spione: Geheimdienste in Deutschland 1945–1956* [Attention spies: Secret services in Germany 1945–1956], edited by Magnus Pahl, Gorch Pieken, and Matthias Rogg, 225–35. Dresden: Sandstein Verlag, 2016.

Müller, Josef. *Bis zur letzten Konsequenz: Ein Leben für Frieden und Freiheit* [To the last consequence: A life for peace and freedom]. Munich: Süddeutscher Verlag, 1975.

Murphy, David E., Sergei A. Kondrashev, and George Bailey. *Battleground Berlin: CIA vs. KGB in the Cold War*. New Haven, CT: Yale University Press, 1997.

Musial, Bogdan. "NS-Kriegsverbrecher vor polnischen Gerichten" [Nazi war criminals before Polish courts]. *Vierteljahrshefte für Zeitgeschichte* 47, no. 1 (Jan 1999): 25–56.

Mußgnug, Dorothee. *Alliierte Militärmissionen in Deutschland 1946–1990* [The Allied military missions in Germany, 1946–1990]. Berlin: Duncker & Humblot, 2001.

Nadich, Judah. *Eisenhower and the Jews*. New York: Twayne Publishers, 1953.

Naimark, Norman M. *The Russians in Germany: A History of the Soviet Zone of Occupation, 1945–1949*. Cambridge, MA: Belknap Press of Harvard University Press, 1995.

Neiberg, Michael. *Potsdam: The End of World War II and the Remaking of Europe*. New York: Basic Books, 2015.

Nelson, Otto L. *National Security and the General Staff*. Washington, DC: Infantry Journal Press, 1946.

"News Notes," *The American Archivist* 10, no. 1 (Jan 1947): 93–112.

Niethammer, Lutz. "Die Amerikanische Besatzungsmacht zwischen Verwaltungstradition und politischen Parteien in Bayern 1945" [The American occupation forces between administrative tradition and political parties in Bavaria, 1945]. *Vierteljahrshefte für Zeitgeschichte* 15, no. 2 (1967): 153–210.

Niethammer, Lutz, ed. *Der 'gesäuberte' Antifaschismus. Die SED und die roten Kapos von Buchenwald* ["Cleansed" antifascism: The SED and the red Kapos of Buchenwald]. Berlin: Akademie-Verlag, 1994.

O'Sullivan, Donal. *Dealing with the Devil: Anglo-Soviet Intelligence Cooperation in the Second World War*. New York: Peter Lang, 2010.

Ollivant, Simon. "Protocol 'M.'" In *Deception Operations: Studies in the East-West Conflict*, edited by David A. Charters and Maurice A. J. Tugwell, 275–96. London: Brassey's, 1990.

Orwell, George. *1984*. New York: Signet, 1950.

Oshinsky, David M. *A Conspiracy So Immense: The World of Joe McCarthy*. Oxford: Oxford University Press, 2005.

Packard, Wyman H. *A Century of U.S. Naval Intelligence*. Washington, DC: Department of the Navy, 1996.

Paddock, Alfred H., Jr., *U.S. Army Special Warfare: Its Origins: Psychological and Unconventional Warfare, 1941–1952*. Washington, DC: National Defense University Press, 1982.

Padover, Saul K. *Experiment in Germany: The Story of an American Intelligence Officer*. New York: Duell, Sloan and Pearce, 1946.

Pahl, Magnus. "Hermann Baun (1897–1951): Der gescheiterte Spionagechef" [Hermann Baun (1897–1951): The failed espionage chief]. In *Spione und Nachrichtenhändler: Geheimdienstkarrieren in Deutschland 1939–1989* [Spies and news traders: Intelligence careers in Germany, 1939–1989], edited by Helmut Müller-Enbergs and Armin Wagner, 38–77. Berlin: Ch. Links Verlag, 2016.

Pardoll, Davis H., and Robert L. Dennis. "Chemotherapy, Pyrotherapy and Penicillin in the Treatment of Gonorrhea." *United States Naval Medical Bulletin* 43, no. 5 (Nov 1944): 988–96.

Parrish, Thomas D. *The American Codebreakers: The U.S. Role in Ultra*. Chelsea, MI: Scarborough House, 1991.

Parrish, Thomas D. *The Ultra Americans: The U.S. Role in Breaking the Nazi Code*. New York: Stein and Day, 1986.

Pash, Boris. *The Alsos Mission*. New York: Charter Books, 1969.

Patton, George S. *War as I Knew It: A Human and Eloquent Story Told by a Great Military Genius*. New York: Houghton Mifflin, 1947.
Petanaude, Bertrand M. "Curse of the Goebbels Diaries." *Hoover Digest* 3 (2012), online edition.
Peterson, Michael L. "BOURBON to Black Friday: The Allied Collaborative COMINT Effort Against the Soviet Union, 1945–1948." Fort Meade, MD: Center for Cryptologic History, National Security Agency, 1995.
Petersen, Neal H., ed. *From Hitler's Doorstep: The Wartime Intelligence Reports of Allen Dulles, 1942–1945*. University Park: Pennsylvania University Press, 1996.
Peterson, Edward N. *The American Occupation of Germany: Retreat to Victory*. Detroit: Wayne State University Press, 1977.
Pirogov, Peter A. *Why I Escaped: The Story of Peter Pirogov*. New York: Duell, Sloan and Pearce, 1950.
Pogue, Forrest C. *The Supreme Command*. United States Army in World War II. Washington, DC: U.S. Army Center of Military History, 1954.
Porch, Douglas. *The French Secret Services: From the Dreyfus Affair to the Gulf War*. New York: Farrar, Straus and Giroux, 2003.
Powe, Marc B., and Edward E. Wilson. "The Evolution of American Military Intelligence." Fort Huachuca, AZ: United States Army Intelligence Center and School, 1973.
Radkau, Joachim. *Theodor Heuss*. Munich: Carl Hanser Verlag, 2013.
Remy, Steven P. *The Malmedy Massacre: The War Crimes Trial Controversy*. Cambridge, MA: Harvard University Press, 2017.
Rezabek, Randy. "TICOM and the Search for OKW/*Chi*." *Cryptologia* 37, no. 2 (Apr 2013): 139–53.
Rezabek, Randy. "TICOM: The Last Great Secret of World War II." *Intelligence and National Security* 27, no. 4 (2012): 513–30.
Riess, Curt. *Berlin Berlin 1945–1953*. Berlin: Non-Stop Bücherei, 1953.
Roginskij, Arsenij, Jörg Rudolph, Frank Drauschke, and Anne Kaminsky. *"Erschossen in Moskau." Die deutschen Opfer des Stalinismus auf dem Moskauer Friedhof Donskoje 1950–1953* ["Shot in Moscow." The German victims of Stalinism in Moscow's Donskoye cemetery, 1950–1953]. Berlin: Metropol, 2005.
Romanus, Charles F., and Riley Sunderland. *Stilwell's Mission to China*. United States Army in World War II. Washington, DC: U.S. Army Center of Military History, 1987.
Rosenberg, David A. "U.S. Nuclear Stockpile, 1945 to 1950." *The Bulletin of the Atomic Scientists* (May 1982): 25–30.
Rosengarten, Adolph D., Jr. "With Ultra from Omaha Beach to Weimar—A Personal View." *Military Affairs* 42, no. 3 (Oct 1978): 127–33.
Rositzke, Harry. *The CIA's Secret Operations: Espionage, Counterespionage, and Covert Action*. New York: Reader's Digest Press, 1977.
Ross, Steven T. *American War Plans 1945–1950*. London: Frank Cass, 1996.
Rudgers, David F. "The Origins of Covert Action." *Journal of Contemporary History* 35, no. 2 (Apr 2000): 249–62.
Ruffner, Kevin C. "The Black Market in Postwar Berlin: Colonel Miller and an Army Scandal." *Prologue Magazine* 34, no. 3 (Fall 2002): 1–20.
Ruffner, Kevin C. "Cold War Allies: The Origins of CIA's Relationship with Ukrainian Nationalists." *Studies in Intelligence* (1998): 19–42.
Ruffner, Kevin C., ed. *Forging an Intelligence Partnership: CIA and the Origins of the BND 1945–49: A Documentary History*, 2 vols. Washington, DC: Center for the Study of Intelligence, 1999.
Sanford, George. *Katyn and the Soviet Massacre of 1940: Truth, Justice and Memory*. London: Routledge, 2005.

Sayer, Ian, and Douglas Botting. *America's Secret Army: The Untold Story of the Counter Intelligence Corps*. London: Fontana, 1990.

Sayer, Ian. *Nazi Gold: The Story of the World's Greatest Robbery – And Its Aftermath*. New York: Granada, 1984.

Schiff, Mel. "President Truman and the Jewish DPs, 1945–46: The Untold Story." *American Jewish History* 99, no. 4 (Oct 2015): 327–52.

Schlosser, Nicholas J. *Cold War on the Airwaves: The Radio Propaganda War Against East Germany*. Champaign: University of Illinois Press, 2015.

Schmidt-Eenboom, Erich. "The Bundesnachrichtendienst, the Bundeswehr and Sigint in the Cold War and After." *Intelligence and National Security* 16, no. 1 (2001): 129–76.

Schwarz, Hans-Peter. *Konrad Adenauer: A German Politician and Statesman in a Period of War, Revolution and Reconstruction*, vol. 1. Oxford: Berghahn Books, 1995.

Schwarzwalder, John. *We Caught Spies: Adventures of an American Counter Intelligence Agent in Europe*. New York: Duell, Sloan and Pearce, 1946.

Selby, Scott Andrew. *The Axmann Conspiracy: The Nazi Plan for a Fourth Reich and How the U.S. Army Defeated It*. New York: Penguin, 2012.

Sereny, Gitta. *The Healing Wound: Experiences and Reflections, Germany 1936–2001*. New York: W. W. Norton, 2001.

Sheymov, Victor. *Tower of Secrets: A Real Life Spy Thriller*. New York: HarperCollins, 1993.

Sichel, Peter M. F. *Secrets of My Life: Vintner, Prisoner, Soldier, Spy*. Bloomington, IN: Archway Publishing, 2006.

Silver, Arnold M. "Questions, Questions, Questions: Memories of Oberursel." *Intelligence and National Security* 8, no. 2 (Apr 1993): 81–90.

Sims, John Cary. "The BRUSA Agreement of May 17, 1943." *Cryptologia* 21, no. 1 (1997): 30–38.

Skorzeny, Otto. *My Commando Operations: The Memoirs of Hitler's Most Daring Commando*. Atglen, PA: Schiffer Publishing, 1995.

Smith, Arthur. *Kidnap City: Cold War Berlin*. Westport, CT: Greenwood, 2002.

Smith, Bradley F. *Sharing Secrets with Stalin: How the Allies Traded Intelligence, 1941–1945*. Lawrence: University Press of Kansas, 1997.

Smith, R. Harris. *OSS: The Secret History of America's First Central Intelligence Agency*. Berkeley: University of California Press, 1972.

Smith, Jean Edward. *Lucius D. Clay: An American Life*. New York: Henry Holt, 1990.

Smith, Jean Edward, ed. *The Papers of General Lucius D. Clay, Germany 1945–1949*, 2 vols., Bloomington: Indiana University Press, 1974.

Smith, W. Thomas Jr. *Encyclopedia of the Central Intelligence Agency*. New York: Facts on File, 2003.

Smyser, W. R. *From Yalta to Berlin: The Cold War Struggle over Germany*. New York: Palgrave Macmillan, 2000.

Srodes, James. *Allen Dulles: Master of Spies*. Washington, DC: Regnery, 1999.

Staadt, Jochen. "'Wir packen mit an, Ordnung zu schaffen:' Die Berliner Polizei in der 'Stunde Null'" ["We are helping to create order": The Berlin police at "zero hour"]. *Zeitschrift des Forschungsverbundes SED-Staat* 26 (2010): 90–117.

Steil, Benn. *The Marshall Plan: Dawn of the Cold War*. New York: Simon & Schuster, 2018.

Steinacher, Gerald. *Nazis on the Run: How Hitler's Henchmen Fled Justice*. Oxford: Oxford University Press, 2011.

Stewart, Richard W., ed. *American Military History*, vol. 2. Washington, DC: U.S. Army Center of Military History, 2005.

Stivers, William. "The Incomplete Blockade: Soviet Zone Supply of West Berlin, 1948–49." *Diplomatic History* 21, no. 4 (Fall 1997): 569–602.
Stivers, William. "Was Sovietization Inevitable? U.S. Intelligence Perceptions of Internal Developments in the Soviet Zone of Occupation in Germany." *Journal of Intelligence History* 5, no. 1 (Summer 2005): 45–70.
Stivers, William, and Donald A. Carter. *The City Becomes a Symbol: The U.S. Army in the Occupation of Berlin, 1945–1949*. U.S. Army in the Cold War. Washington, DC: U.S. Army Center of Military History, 2017.
Strauss, Franz Josef. *Die Erinnerungen* [Memoirs]. Berlin: Siedler Verlag, 1989.
Strong, Kenneth. *Intelligence at the Top: Recollections of an Intelligence Officer*. Garden City, NY: Doubleday, 1969.
Stout, Mark E. "The Pond: Running Agents for State, War, and the CIA." *Studies in Intelligence* 48, no. 3 (2004): online edition.
Sudoplatov, Pavel, and Anatoly Sudoplatov. *Special Tasks: The Memoirs of an Unwanted Witness—A Soviet Spymaster*. Boston: Little, Brown, 1994.
Tagg, Lori. "A Brief History of Training in Army Intelligence." *Military Intelligence Professional Bulletin* 34, no. 3 (Jul-Sep 2012): 82–100.
Taylor, Frederick. *Exorcising Hitler: The Occupation and Denazification of Germany*. London: Bloomsbury, 2012.
Thamm, Gerhardt B. "The Potsdam Archive: Sorting Through 19 Linear Miles of German Records." *Studies in Intelligence* 58, no. 1 (Mar 2014): 1–7.
Thomas, Evan. *The Very Best Men: Four Who Dared: The Early Years of the CIA*. New York: Touchstone, 1995.
Thompson, George R., and Dixie R. Harris. *The Signal Corps: The Outcome*. United States Army in World War II. Washington, DC: U.S. Army Center of Military History, 1991.
Trees, Wolfgang, and Charles Whiting. *Unternehmen Karneval: der Werwolf-Mord an Aachens Oberbürgermeister Oppenhoff* [Operation Carnival: The Werwolf murder of Aachen's Mayor Oppenhoff]. Aachen: Triangel, 1982.
Trevor-Roper, H. R. *The Last Days of Hitler*. London: Cox & Wyman, 1972.
Uhl, Matthias. *Krieg um Berlin? Die sowjetische Militär-und Sicherheitspolitik in der zweiten Berlin-Krise 1958–1962* [War over Berlin?: Soviet military and security policy in the second Berlin crisis, 1958–1962]. Munich: Oldenbourg, 2008.
"United States v. Best." *The American Journal of International Law* 42, no. 3 (Jul 1948): 727–29.
U.S. Air Force (USAF) Intelligence, Surveillance and Reconnaissance Agency. "A Continuing Legacy: From USAFSS to AF ISR Agency, 1948–2012." USAF Intelligence, Surveillance and Reconnaissance Agency History Office, no date.
Vagts, Alfred. *The Military Attaché*. Princeton, NJ: Princeton University Press, 1967.
Von Elbe, Joachim. *Witness to History: A Refugee from the Third Reich Remembers*. Madison: University of Wisconsin Press, 1998.
Wagner, Armin, and Matthias Uhl. *BND contra Sowjetarmee. Westdeutsche Militärspionage in der DDR* [The BND versus the Soviet Army: West German military espionage in the GDR]. Berlin: Ch. Links, 2007.
Walker, Martin. *The Cold War: A History*. New York: Owl Books, 1993.
Walters, Guy. *Hunting Evil: The Nazi War Criminals Who Escaped and the Quest to Bring Them to Justice*. New York: Broadway Books, 2009.
Warner, Michael. "Salvage and Liquidation: The Creation of the Central Intelligence Group." *Studies in Intelligence* 39, no. 5 (1996): 111–30.

Weber, Hermann, and Andreas Herbst, eds. *Deutsche Kommunisten. Biographisches Handbuch 1918 bis 1945* [German communists: Biographical handbook, 1918–1945]. Berlin: Karl Dietz Verlag, 2008).

Wegener, Jens. *Die Organisation Gehlen und die USA. Deutsch-Amerikanische Geheimdienstbeziehungen, 1945–1949* [The Gehlen organization and the United States: German-American intelligence relations, 1945–1949]. Münster: Lit Verlag, 2008.

Weingartner, James J. "Otto Skorzeny and the Laws of War." *Journal of Military History* 55 (Apr 1991): 207–24.

Weingartner, James J. "Unconventional Allies: Colonel Willis Everett and SS-Obersturmbannfuehrer Joachim Peiper." *The Historian* 62, no. 1 (1999): 79–98.

Weisz, Christoph. *OMGUS-Handbuch: Die amerikanische Militärregierung in Deutschland 1945–1949* [OMGUS handbook: The American military government in Germany, 1945–1949]. Oldenbourg: De Gruyter, 1995.

Wengst, Udo. *Thomas Dehler, 1897–1967: Eine politische Biographie* [Thomas Dehler, 1897–1967: A political biography]. Munich: Oldenbourg, 1997.

Wettig, Gerhard, ed. *Der Tjul'panov-Bericht: Sowjetische Besatzungspolitik in Deutschland nach dem Zweiten Weltkrieg* [The Tjul'panov report: Soviet occupation policy in Germany after the Second World War]. Göttingen: V&R Unipress, 2012.

Wettig, Gerhard. *Stalin and the Cold War in Europe: The Emergence and Development of East-West Conflict, 1939–1953*. Lanham, MD: Rowman and Littlefield, 2008.

Williams, Charles. *The Last Great Frenchman: A Life of General de Gaulle*. New York: John Wiley & Sons, 2003.

Winterbotham, F. W. *The Ultra Secret*. New York: Harper & Row, 1974.

Wohlstetter, Roberta. *Pearl Harbor: Decision and Warning*. Stanford, CA: Stanford University Press, 1962.

Wolf, Markus. *Memoirs of a Spymaster: The Man Who Waged a Secret War against the West*. London: Pimlico, 1997.

Wolf, Thomas. *Die Entstehung des BND: Aufbau, Finanzierung, Kontrolle* [The creation of the BND: Development, financing, control]. Berlin: Ch. Links Verlag, 2018.

Wood, James A. "Captive Historians, Captivated Audience: The German Military History Program, 1945–1961." *Journal of Military History* 69, no. 1 (Jan 2005): 123–47.

Würmeling, Henric L. *Die Weiße Liste und die Stunde Null in Deutschland 1945* [The whitelist and zero hour in Germany, 1945]. Munich: Herbig, 2015.

Zarusky, Jürgen. "'That is not the American Way of Fighting': The Shooting of Captured SS-Men During the Liberation of Dachau." In *Dachau and the Nazi Terror 1933–1945*, vol. 2, Studies and Reports, edited by Wolfgang Benz and Barbara Distel, 133–60. Dachau: Verlag Dachauer Hefte, 2002.

Ziemke, Earl F. *The U.S. Army in the Occupation of Germany, 1944–1946*. Army Historical Series. Washington, DC: U.S. Army Center of Military History, 1975.

Zubok, Vladislav M. *A Failed Empire: The Soviet Union in the Cold War from Stalin to Gorbachev*. Chapel Hill: University of North Carolina Press, 2009.

Secondary Sources—Unpublished Works

Aid, Matthew M. "SIGINT and the 1948 Berlin Crisis." Unpublished article, no date.

Fenton, Hayley L. "Notable Ritchie Boys." Unpublished research paper, U.S. Army Center of Military History, 2020.

Hess, John D. "Coping with Crisis: Military Government Officials, U.S. Policy, and the Occupation of Bavaria, 1945–1949." Ph.D. dissertation, University of Kansas, 2017.

Hudson, Walter M. "The U.S. Military Government and Democratic Reform and Denazification in Bavaria, 1945–47." Master's thesis, Command and General Staff College, 2001.

Mark, Eduard M. "A Glooming Peace." Unpublished manuscript, USAF Historical Support Division, no date.

Mullen, Kelsey. "American Intelligence and the Question of Hitler's Death." Undergraduate research thesis, Ohio State University, 2014.

Otto, Martin. "Ulrich Biel, ein deutscher Patriot: Der amerikanische Preusse" [Ulrich Biel, a German patriot: The American Prussian]. Unpublished manuscript, 2018.

Ricks, Molly R. "After Acquittal: Otto Skorzeny's Postwar Life." Unpublished research paper, U.S. Army Center of Military History, 2018.

Ricks, Molly R. "CIC Records on Members of the First West German Parliament." Unpublished research paper, U.S. Army Center of Military History, 2018. Ruffner, Kevin C. "Eagle and Swastika: CIA and Nazi War Criminals and Collaborators." Washington, DC: History Staff, CIA, 2003.

Skowronek, Paul G. "U.S.-Soviet Military Liaison in Germany, Since 1947." Ph.D. dissertation, University of Colorado, 1975.

Spratt, James C. "The History of Camp King." Carlisle, PA: U.S. Army Military History Institute, no date.

Swarc, Alan. "Illegal Immigration to Palestine 1945–1948: The French Connection." Ph.D. dissertation, University College London, 2006.

Vodopyanov, Anya. "A Watchful Eye Behind the Iron Curtain: The U.S. Military Liaison Mission in East Germany, 1953–61." Master's thesis, Stanford University, 2004.

Abbreviations and Glossary of Terms

Text Acronyms and Abbreviations

AFSA	Armed Forces Security Agency
ASA	Army Security Agency
ASAE	Army Security Agency, Europe
BDC	Berlin Documents Center
BND	Bundesnachrichtendienst (West German foreign intelligence service)
CDU	Christian Democratic Union (Christlich Demokratische Union Deutschlands)
CIA	Central Intelligence Agency
CIC	Counter Intelligence Corps
CROWCASS	Central Registry of War Criminals and Security Suspects
CSU	Christian Social Union (Christlich-Soziale Union)
DAD	Department of the Army Detachment (CIA cover name)
DM	deutsche mark
EEI	Essential Elements of Information
E1H2	Cologne military government detachment
F1G2	Aachen military government detachment
FDJ	Free German Youth (Freie Deutsche Jugend); SED youth auxiliary
FDP	Free Democratic Party (Freie Demokratische Partei)
FBI	Federal Bureau of Investigation
FIAT	Field Information Agency, Technical
G–2	Army intelligence
G–5	Army civil affairs
GI	initialism for a U.S. Army soldier
JCS	Joint Chiefs of Staff
K–5	East German political police controlled by the Soviet Military Administration
KGB	Committee for State Security (Komitet Gosudarstvennoy Bezopasnosti)
KgU	Fighting Group against Inhumanity (Kampfgruppe gegen Unmenschlichkeit)
KPD	German Communist Party (Kommunistche Partei Deutschlands)
KVP	Barracked People's Police (Kasernierte Volkspolizei)
LDP	Liberal Democratic Party (Liberal-Demokratische Partei)
MGB	Ministry for State Security (Ministerstvo Gosudarstvennoy Bezopasnosti)
MIS-X	Military Intelligence Service unit involved with escape attempts of downed airmen
MIS-Y	Military Intelligence Service unit involved in interrogation of captured enemy personnel
MITC	Military Intelligence Training Center (Camp Ritchie, Maryland)
NATO	North Atlantic Treaty Organization

NDPD	National-Democratic Party of Germany (National-Demokratische Partei Deutschland)
NKVD	People's Commissariat for Internal Affairs (Naródnyy Komissariát Vnútrennikh Del)
NSA	National Security Agency
NSC	National Security Council
NSDAP	National Socialist German Workers' Party; Nazi Party (Nationalsozialistische Deutsche Arbeiterpartei)
OKW/Chi	Signals Intelligence Agency of the German Army High Command (*Oberkommando der Wehrmacht Chiffrierabteilung*)
OMGUS	Office of Military Government, United States
OSI	Office of Special Investigations (U.S. Air Force intelligence agency)
OSS	Office of Strategic Services
PW	prisoner of war
RIAS	Radio in the American Sector (Rundfunk im amerikanischen Sektor)
S–1	staff administration
S–2	staff intelligence
S–3	staff operations
S–4	staff supply
SA	*Sturmabteilung* (Nazi Party paramilitary forces)
SD	*Sicherheitsdienst* (SS intelligence service)
SED	Socialist Unity Party (Sozialistische Einheitspartei Deutschlands)
SHAEF	Supreme Headquarters Allied Expeditionary Force
SIGINT	signals intelligence
SMERSH	"Death to Spies" (*smert' shpionam*; Soviet counterespionage agency)
SS	*Schutzstaffel* (Nazi Party paramilitary forces)
SPD	Social Democratic Party of Germany (Sozialdemokratische Partei Deutschlands)
Stasi	Ministry for State Security (Ministerium für Staatssicherheit) (East Germany)
T/5	Technician Fifth Grade
TICOM	Target Intelligence Committee
UKUSA agreement	Anglo-American cooperation agreement, March 1946
UNRRA	United Nations Relief and Rehabilitation Administration
USMLM	United States Military Liaison Mission
USSR	Union of Soviet Socialist Republics
V-E Day	Victory in Europe Day
W1	Warrant Officer, Junior Grade
WAV	Economic Reconstruction Union (Wirtschaftliche Aufbau-Vereinigung)

Operations, Projects, and Code Names

A<small>LSOS</small>	Anglo-American mission to investigate Axis Powers' military technology
A<small>SHCAN</small>	detention facility in Mondorf, Luxembourg

BOLERO	European Theater intelligence on the Soviet armed forces
BOLERO GROUP	German veterans selected by United States to analyze postwar Soviet intelligence
BOURBON	decryption of postwar Soviet intelligence
BREAKERS	OSS code name for anti-Hitler German military officials
CHICAGO	CIC informant on Kurt Schumacher
COUNTERPUNCH	U.S. contingency plan for a Soviet blockade of Berlin
CROWN JEWELS	OSS code name for anti-Hitler German civilian officials
CURT	unnamed CIC informant in Soviet Zone
DRAGOON	proposed Allied invasion of southern France
DUSTBIN	detention facility in Paris and later at Kransberg Castle, north of Frankfurt
FISH	high-level German cryptographic machines
HONEYPOT	CIC informant network in Soviet Zone
MAGIC	decrypts of Japanese diplomatic traffic
MARS	CIC code name for Helmuth Kuebler, penetration agent at Zuffenhausen displaced persons camp
ODESSA	organization of former SS members (*Organisation der Ehemaligen SS Angehörigen*)
OSOAVIKHIM	postwar Soviet recruitment of German scientists
OSTERHASE (Easter Bunny)	CIA/KgU covert action against East German government-controlled stores
O-35-VIII	CIC code name for Willy Brandt, SDP politician
P-15-VIII	CIC code name for Heinz Raue, Soviet Zone informant
P-43-VIII	CIC code name for Gerhard Raue, Soviet Zone informant
PURPLE	Japanese cipher machine
ROBOT	Strategic Services Unit code name for Josef Müller, Bavarian politician
SAVOY	OSS code name for Hans A. Kemritz, former *Abwehr* officer
SUNNY	U.S. code name for Sunihild Pfeiffer, double agent
TERMINAL	Allied code name for Potsdam Conference
TURICUM	Munich-based pro-American intelligence network under the leadership of journalist Hans Georg Bentz
ULTRA	Allied efforts to break German ciphers during the war
VICTORIA	Soviet code name for Sunihild Pfeiffer, penetration agent at OMGUS stenographic school
ZIGZAG	OSS code name for Heinz K. H. Krull, former *Abwehr* and *Gestapo* officer
Operation ANYFACE	U.S. operation to shield Ukrainian nationalist Stepan Bandera from Soviet extradition requests
Operation BARBAROSSA	Nazi Germany invasion of Soviet Union, 1941
Operation BASKET/ BASKET CASE	CIC operation against displaced persons posing as "Russian Secret Police"
Operation BEECHNUT	U.S. cryptologic assistance to British intelligence
Operation BINGO	investigation into activities of Soviet liaison officers
Operation BLACKJACK	Third Army intelligence raid on Heilbronn displaced persons camp

Operation CLAMSHELL	U.S. military study on the Soviet Air Forces, based on captured German documents
Operation CHOO CHOO	CIC train security sweep in Bavaria, early 1946
Operation DEVOTION	CIC effort to determine the Soviet order of battle in Thuringia
Operation DOUBLE CHECK	large-scale CIC security sweep, October 1945
Operation FLYPAPER	investigation of Soviet intelligence missions in the U.S. Zone
Operation GISBOMB	Allied plan to bomb German intelligence services
Operation GRAIL	Strategic Services Unit informant network in Soviet Zone
Operation GREIF (Griffin)	German operation to sow confusion behind Allied lines, late 1944
Operation HAGBERRY	CIC investigation of Alexander F. Chikalov
Operation HERBSTNEBEL (Autumn Mist)	German offensive in the Ardennes, late 1944
Operation LIFEBUOY	large-scale denazification screening
Operation Lusty (*Luftwaffe* Secret Technology)	Army Air Forces mission to capture German air force technology and personnel
Operation MARKET-GARDEN	Anglo-American operation to establish Rhine bridgehead, September 1944
Operation MESA	investigation into forcible Soviet repatriation of German scientists
Operation NURSERY	antisubversive CIC campaign against Christian Tessmann & Sons transportation company
Operation RUMMAGE	CIC investigation into recruitment of potential Jewish insurgents in displaced persons camps
Operation RUSTY	German proto-intelligence service
Operation SAND	investigation into Soviet spy ring associated with military government stenographic school
Operation SELECTION BOARD	joint U.S. Army/British Army of the Rhine move to disrupt subversive former SS organizations
Operation SUNRISE [1945]	negotiated surrender of German forces in northern Italy
Operation SUNRISE [1946]	CIC penetration effort of KPD
Operation SYNDICATE	recruitment of intelligence sources in displaced persons camps
Operation TALLY HO	large-scale CIC security sweep, July 1945
Operation VALENTINE	Army sweep to detain *Edelweisspiraten*
Operation VITTLES	U.S. Air Force plan to supply blockaded Berlin by air
Operations Plan ECLIPSE	wartime plan to exploit German cryptologic organizations and personnel in Berlin
Project CASEY JONES	postwar photo intelligence mapping program
Project DICK TRACY	Anglo-American analysis of captured *Luftwaffe* aerial photography of the Soviet Union
Project HAPPINESS	U.S. Zone effort to assess extent of KPD threat
Project HILL	Camp Ritchie historical project involving German veterans
Project OVERCAST	short-term visas for German scientists
Project PAPERCLIP	long-term exploitation of German scientists
Project PATRON	postwar photo intelligence targeting program
Project VENONA	decryption of wartime Soviet intelligence
TRIANGLE Project	collection of information on the Soviet Union from German POWs
Task Force WHITNEY	transfer of Nazi gold and valuables to Frankfurt bank, April 1945

War Plan BROILER	Joint War Plans Committee war plan against the Soviet Union in Europe and the Middle East, 1947
War Plan PINCHER	Joint Chiefs of Staff war plan against the Soviet Union in Europe, 1946

German Terms

Abwehr	German military intelligence
Arbeitsamt	employment office
Belastete	incriminated (denazification classification)
Blauer Express	"Blue Express"; long-distance train between Moscow and Berlin
Bezirk/Bezirke	administrative district of Berlin
Bundestag	West German federal parliament
Edelweisspiraten	Edelweiss pirates (supposed subversive German youth movement)
Einheit Stielau	Stielau unit (German commando force)
Einsatzgruppen	mobile SS death squads
Entlastete	exonerated (denazification classification)
Erzgebirge	ore mountains (mining district in southern Saxony)
Fernamt	telephone exchange
Forschungsamt	Nazi Party cryptologic service
Fragebogen	denazification questionnaire
Fremde Heere Ost	Foreign Armies East
Fremde Heere West	Foreign Armies West
Führerbunker	Adolf Hitler's bunker beneath the Chancellery in Berlin
Gauleiter	leader of a regional branch of the Nazi Party
Gestapo	*Geheime Staatspolizei* (state secret police)
Grundgesetz	basic law (1949 Constitution of the Federal Republic of Germany)
Hauptschuldige	major offenders (denazification classification)
Handelsorganisation	East German government-controlled stores
Heeresgruppe Mitte	Army Group Center
Kampfgruppe Peiper	SS unit believed to bear primary responsibility for the 1944 Malmédy massacre
Kreis	German county
Kriegsakademie	army war college
Kriegsmarine	German navy
Land/Länder	German state
Landrat/Landräte	head of a *Land*; state executive
Luftgau	German air defense
Luftwaffe	German air force
Minderbelastete	less incriminated (denazification classification)
Ministerpräsident	minister-president; governor of a *Land*
Mitläufer	fellow travelers (denazification classification)
Oberbürgermeister	chief mayor
Obergruppenführer	lieutenant general
Oberstgruppenführer	general

Obersturmbannführer	lieutenant colonel
Ostbüro	Eastern Bureau (illegal SPD organization in the Soviet Zone)
Persilscheine	certificates exonerating individual Germans of Naziism
Rassenhygiene	racial hygiene (eugenics)
Reichsbahn	German railway system
Reichsbank	German central bank
Reichsforschungsrat	German Research Council
Reichspost	German postal service
Reichssicherheitshauptamt	Germany security apparatus
Reifentöter	caltrops
Rektor	university president
Schlüsselkasten	cipher box
Schwere Freiheitsberaubung	aggravated deprivation of liberty
Schutzpolizei	uniformed police force (Berlin)
Speziallager (Spezlager)	"special camps"; political prisons run by the Soviet Military Administration in eastern Germany
Spitzelsendungen	"snitch reports"; RIAS broadcasts identifying suspected Soviet informants
Spruchkammer	local German-led denazification tribunal (pl. *Spruchkammern*)
Volkspolizei	People's Police (Soviet Zone central police force)
Wehrmacht	German armed forces
Werwolf	Nazi underground resistance movement

Footnote Abbreviations

ACoS	Assistant Chief of Staff
ASA	Army Security Agency
ASAE	Army Security Agency, Europe
BOB	Berlin Operations Base
BStU	Bundesbeauftragte für die Unterlagen des Staatssicherheitsdienstes der ehemaligen Deutschen Demokratischen Republik (Federal Commissioner for the Records of the State Security Service of the former German Democratic Republic)
CG	Commanding General
CIA	Central Intelligence Agency
CIC	Counter Intelligence Corps
CINCEUR	Commander in Chief, Europe
CMH	U.S. Army Center of Military History
CO	Commanding Officer
DAD	Department of the Army Detachment
DCI	Director of Central Intelligence
DDI	Deputy Director of Intelligence
Dept	Department
DoD	Department of Defense
EUCOM	European Command

FIAT	Field Information Agency, Technical
FRUS	*Foreign Relations of the United States*
G-2	Army intelligence
GCHQ	Government Communications Headquarters (United Kingdom)
HA	Hauptabteilung (Main Department; Stasi)
HAIT	Hannah Arendt Institute for Research on Totalitarianism (Hannah-Arendt-Institut für Totalitarismusforschung)
HICOG	High Commission for Occupied Germany
INSCOM	U.S. Army Intelligence and Security Command
IRR	Records of the Investigative Records Repository
JCS	Joint Chiefs of Staff
JIOA	Joint Intelligence Objectives Agency
MfS	Ministerium für Staatssicherheit (Ministry for State Security; Stasi)
MG	Military Government
MID	Military Intelligence Division
NACP	National Archives and Records Administration, College Park, Maryland
NSA	National Security Agency
OACSI	Office of the Assistant Chief of Staff for Intelligence
ODDI	Office of the Deputy Director of Intelligence
ODI	Office of the Director of Intelligence
OMGB	Office of Military Government, Bavaria
OMGBS	Office of Military Government, Berlin Sector
OMGUS	Office of Military Government, United States
OMGWB	Office of Military Government, Württemberg-Baden
OSS	Office of Strategic Services
RG	Record Group
SHAEF	Supreme Headquarters Allied Expeditionary Force
SMAD	Sowjetische Militäradministration in Deutschland (Soviet Military Administration in Germany)
SOFA	Status of Force Agreement
SRH	Special Research History
TICOM	Target Intelligence Committee
USAF	U.S. Air Force
USAREUR	U.S. Army Europe
USFET	United States Forces in the European Theater
USGCC	U.S. Group Control Council
USMLM	U.S. Military Liaison Mission to the Soviet Occupied Zone
WNRC	Washington National Records Center, Suitland, MD
WWII	World War II

Index

Aachen 39, 42, 54, 281
– denazification in 42–43
– U.S. military government in 39–44, 55–56
Aberdeen Proving Ground 221
Abwehr 66, 125, 138, 241, 244, 249, 323, 364
Adenauer, Auguste 313
Adenauer, Konrad 5, 65, 305–10, 313, 319, 329, 339, 435
Adenauer, Kurt 313
African American U.S. soldiers 26, 279
Aidenbach 180
Air Force, United States 22, 69, 87, 89, 97, 101, 103, 118, 129, 145, 155, 167, 215, 221, 244, 261, 277, 380, 393, 404, 410, 413, 415, 421, 425, 442, 444
Airborne Army, First Allied 233
Airborne Divisions, U.S.
– 17th 256
– 101st 319
Aircraft 25, 33, 39, 62, 118, 178, 232, 248, 277, 355, 388, 391, 393, 410, 413, 415, 425
– B–17 Flying Fortress bomber 54
– Horten Ho 229 single-wing bomber 118
– L–4 Grasshopper airplane 33
– MiG-9 fighter jet 388
– Yakovlev Yak-3 fighter jet 413
Airlift for West Berlin. *See* Berlin airlift
Alaska House. *See* Camp King
Alexanderplatz 212, 272
Allen, Col. Robert S. 70, 279
Allied Control Council 85, 211, 398
Alpine Redoubt. *See* National Redoubt
Alps 59–64, 160, 176, 204
Altman, Klaus. *See* Barbie, Klaus
Altötting 286
Anderson, Gordon M. 69
Anglo-American Interrogation Center 155, 426
Anglo-American War Room 29
Annaberg 383
antibiotics, Army Intelligence use of 259–60, 260n198
anticommunism 8–9, 210–11, 315, 334, 342, 363, 372, 420–21, 424, 426, 428–29, 438, 441–42

anti-Semitism 210, 283–84, 317, 319, 340. *See also* denazification; Holocaust
– of Americans 209, 284
– of Europeans 283, 317, 317n56, 319, 340
Antwerp 39, 44
Appelhülsen 268
Ardennes 44–46, 49–50
Arlington Hall 17, 18, 18n20, 25, 30–31, 31n87, 145–46, 149–50
Armed Forces Security Agency 445
Armies, U.S.
– First 22, 36, 39, 44, 46, 51, 61, 70–71, 206, 229
– Third 22–23, 35–36, 39, 70, 85, 179, 185, 192, 206, 236–37, 241, 246, 249, 282, 357, 378, 445
– Fifth 221
– Seventh 34, 62, 72, 85, 160, 173, 185–87, 203, 207, 246, 282, 289
– Ninth 63, 69, 378
Armored Divisions, U.S.
– 5th 38
– 12th 91
Army Air Division 178
Army Air Forces, United States 22, 69, 87, 90, 97–98, 101, 103, 145, 221, 379
Army, Chief of Staff of the. *See* Marshall, General George C
Army Group, 21st (British Army) 39, 48, 60, 85n11, 234, 378. *See also* British Army of the Rhine
Army Groups, U.S.
– 6th 39, 70
– 12th 3, 17, 21–22, 33, 43, 45, 51, 61–62, 69, 85, 91, 94, 98, 102, 132, 138, 183, 246, 306
Army Intelligence relationships
– with British intelligence 28–31, 29n75, 59, 110, 139, 155, 177–78, 182, 223
– with French intelligence 30, 72, 102, 148, 153–54, 211, 227, 324, 387
– with the Office of Strategic Services 8, 19, 32, 34, 56, 94, 119–28, 174, 273, 308, 359
– with the Strategic Services Unit and the Central Intelligence Agency 127, 273, 386, 425, 428, 432–34, 443–46

Army Language School 146
Army, Secretary of the. *See* Royall, Kenneth C
Army Security Agency (ASA) 2n6, 3, 8, 103, 106, 129, 144–145, 148–50, 238, 240–43, 388, 402, 406, 436
Army Security Agency, Europe (ASAE) 106, 143–50, 240–42
Arnaudow, Dr. Michael 181
Aronovitz, Sidney M. 110
Arouet, Jacques S. 105
Artman, Lt. Col. George 100
ASA. *See* Army Security Agency
ASAE. *See* Army Security Agency, Europe
Aschenauer, Rudolf 210
Aschenbrenner, Lt. Gen. Heinrich 242
Ashcan detention center 151
Asmara 32
Asperg 203
assassinations 49, 52, 54–55, 208, 213n158, 320
atomic weapons. *See* scientific intelligence
Auerbach 196, 199
Augsburg 136, 141, 246
Austria 62, 72, 137, 145, 176, 178, 189, 205, 208, 229, 241, 259, 261–65, 285, 317, 327, 376–78, 398, 408, 411
Austrian Alps. *See* Alps
"Axis Sally." *See* Gillars, Mildred E
Axmann, Artur 195–96

Baer, Ralph H. 26
Backnang 197
Bad Aibling 179, 237, 241
Bad Godesberg 361
Bad Hersfeld 154, 188
Bad Nauheim 108, 134, 294, 319
Bad Tölz 195
Bad Vilbel 145
Bad Wildungen 141
Baker, Capt. Ernest Sidney 69
Baker, Warrant Officer, Junior Grade (W1) Robert 105
Baltimore 136
Bamberg 134, 191, 201
Bandera, Stepan A. 212–13, 213n158
Bankisch, Edith 296
Barbour, Philip L. 110
Barbie, Klaus ["Klaus Altman"] 265–66

Bard, Gustav 347
Barracked People's Police (Kasernierte Volkspolizei; KVP) 367, 367n73
Barsov, Lt. Anatoly 261, 262
Bassubenko, Alexander 260
Battle of the Bulge 42, 44–51, 93, 101, 150, 201, 205, 207–8
Bauer, Karl Heinrich 187
Baun, Lt. Col. Hermann 383
Bautzen prison 371
Bavaria 10, 60, 62, 65, 85, 87, 103, 106, 108–9, 145, 180, 191, 195, 196, 237, 238, 245, 265, 271, 282, 284, 286, 287, 299, 323, 326, 334, 354, 364, 365, 428
– denazification of 185, 186, 230, 317, 320–21
– postwar politics in 311, 312–13, 317–19, 320–22, 323–29
Bavarian Alps. *See* Alps
Bayreuth 141, 314
BDC. *See* Berlin Documents Center
Belgium 38, 46, 54, 98, 157, 206, 281
Belgrade 101, 382
Beneš, Edvard 396
Bentz, Hans Georg 323
Berchtesgaden 237
Berlin 6–7, 9, 10, 19, 28, 32, 60–66, 83, 84, 85–87, 91, 93, 97, 98, 99, 101–7, 111–18, 121–28, 129, 130, 132, 134, 137, 141, 148, 150, 155, 157, 164–67, 168–69, 175, 176, 177–81, 184, 192, 203, 212, 222, 232, 233, 242, 259, 269, 271, 273, 276, 288, 290, 292–93, 296, 297, 299, 301, 303, 308, 314, 326, 337–48, 378, 395, 399, 408, 414, 416, 417. *See also* East Berlin, West Berlin
– American sector 108, 111, 113, 116, 125, 134, 157, 164, 242, 262, 277, 293, 296, 297, 303, 347, 352, 353, 361, 369, 383, 387, 410, 418, 429
– British sector 84, 155, 296, 417, 421, 429
– capture by Red Army 61–66, 175
– French sector 85, 296, 413n82, 417
– intelligence collection in 19, 110–18, 121–28, 129–30, 133, 137–38, 157, 164–66, 168–70, 176–78, 179, 212, 258–60, 293, 299–303, 313, 337, 342–48, 359, 369–71, 385–89, 399, 405, 406, 413, 425–27, 443–46
– safe houses 112, 113, 140, 301, 347, 371, 383

– Soviet sector 177, 181, 262, 296, 301, 339, 341, 364, 374, 378, 417, 420, 421–22, 423, 424, 444
Berlin airlift 6, 98, 413–15, 416, 420, 425, 435. *See also* operations, U.S., Vittles
– morale of Berliners 6–7, 409, 416, 417–21, 422–25
– preparations for 408, 409–11, 413, 414
Berlin blockade 6, 98, 166, 396–439, 440
– allied response. *See* Berlin airlift; operations, U.S., Vittles
– counterblockade 415–17, 425, 435, 438
– political unrest during 409, 41, 421–24
– start of blockade 408–10
Berlin Command 103, 106, 111, 115–18, 126, 168, 313. *See also* Berlin District
Berlin District 103, 106, 111, 112–14, 115, 126, 127, 137, 179, 259, 378. *See also* Berlin Command
Berlin Documents Center (BDC) 103, 106, 164–67, 184, 285, 443
Berlin Documents Center, 6889th. *See* Berlin Documents Center
Berlin Military Post 106, 117
Berlin Operations Base. *See* Central Intelligence Agency
Berne 57–59, 239
Bernkastel-Kues 104
Berzarin, General Nikolai E. 176
Best, Robert Henry 72–73
Betts, Brig. Gen. Thomas J. 28, 102, 223, 247
Bicher, Col. George A. 29, 233, 235
Biel, Capt. Ulrich E. 307, 339–41, 343, 424, 443, 446
Bissell, Maj. Gen. Clayton L. 14, 22, 56, 73, 78, 90, 143, 215, 246–49, 277, 353, 377–80
Bitterfeld 350, 355
Bizonia 398
Black, Lt. Col. Edwin F. 122
Black Forest 222
black market 124–25, 139, 159, 194–95, 268–280, 304, 317, 442
Blakeney, Col. Charles C. 101
Blaubeuren 36
Bletchley Park 17, 30, 71, 233, 235, 238
Blidin, Leo 301–2

blockade by Soviets of West Berlin. *See* Berlin blockade
Blue House. *See* Camp King
BND. *See Bundesnachrichtendienst*
Boker, Capt. John R. 247–48, 250
Bonn 1n1, 361, 435, 437
Bormann, Martin L. 180
Bossard, Samuel B. 253–54, 255, 257
Boswell, Lt. Col. James O. 377
Bowman, Howard C. 26
Boxer, Sgt. John H. 309
"Bracker" [American diplomat] 59
Bradford, Maj. John P. 42
Bradley, General Omar N. 3, 21, 22, 48, 61, 63, 269, 403, 404, 410
Brandenburg 111, 426
Brandenburg Gate 293, 422
Brandt, Willy [Herbert Ernst Karl Frahm; O-35-VIII] vii, 9, 115, 344–48, 370–71, 373, 374, 375, 422
Bratton, Col. Rufus S. 13–14, 111, 175, 177
Braun, Eva 175, 177, 179, 180
Breitingen 56
Bregenz 59
Bremen 10, 85, 87, 103, 106, 108, 110, 121, 129, 134, 141, 157, 159, 310, 316, 330
Bremerhaven 138
British Government Code and Cypher School 30
British intelligence 29–31, 59, 110, 139, 155, 177–78, 182, 223, 233, 369, 372, 382, 426
British Intelligence Objectives Subcommittee 223
British sector of Berlin. *See* Berlin, British sector
British Zone 85, 85n11, 110, 182, 196, 200, 313, 314, 361, 369, 399, 410
British Army of the Rhine 85n11, 103, 178, 196, 199
Brittany 391
Browning, Lt. Col. Earl S. 138, 173, 264
Bruchweiler 56
Bruns, Capt. Curt 46, 205–6
Bucharest 382
Buchenwald concentration camp 284, 332, 366n69
Budapest 382
Buenos Aires 182
Bulgaria 131

Bull, Maj. Gen. Harold R. 294
Bulganin, Nikolai A. 407
Bundesnachrichtendienst (BND) 444
Bundestag 310, 314, 316, 347, 348, 435
Bundy, Maj. William P. 30, 30n84
Burgscheidungen 235
Burianek, Johann 432
Burress, Maj. Gen. Withers A. "Pinky" 97, 99, 253, 274
Busbey, Col. George W. 116–17

Cairo 239
Camp Crowder 25
Camp King 103, 106, 133, 151–55, 236, 240, 242, 244, 246–48, 249, 251, 252, 255, 256, 261, 261n203, 293, 443. *See also* Oberursel
Camp Lindsey 335
Camp Neustadt 214
Camp Nikolaus 256
Camp Overcast 226
Camp Ritchie. *See* Military Intelligence Training Center (MITC); "Ritchie Boys"
Camp Santa Claus. *See* Camp Nikolaus
Camp Sibert. *See* Camp King
Campbell Barracks 88
Campbell, Laughlin A. 105, 438
Campaigne, Lt. Cdr. Howard H. 237
Canada 2, 32, 144, 176, 391
Canaris, Admiral Wilhelm F. 241, 323
Canine, Maj. Gen. Ralph J. 445
Carlebach, Emil 332, 336
Carlisle Barracks 146
Carney, Sgt. Jeffrey M. [Jens Karney] 444
Carnicelli, Pfc. Arthur J. 335
Caserta 146
CDU. *See* Christian Democratic Union
censorship 2, 15, 17, 31, 94, 103, 115, 158, 158n105, 155–60, 190, 199, 202, 306, 322, 330, 333–64, 444. *See also* Civil Censorship Division
Central Intelligence Agency (CIA) 8, 26, 89, 94, 101, 106, 120–21, 126–27, 128, 130, 132, 138, 150, 155, 158, 160, 168, 244, 255, 257, 258, 262, 314, 315, 337, 345, 347, 358, 361–62, 367, 370, 371, 372, 376, 386, 397, 404, 408, 412, 414, 415, 425, 427, 431–34, 436, 443, 445
– Berlin Operations Base 123–26, 127, 128, 345, 383, 431

– relationship with Army Intelligence 121, 126–28, 138, 347, 376
Central Intelligence Group 120, 251, 253, 255, 257
Central Registry of War Criminals and Security Suspects (CROWCASS) 202
Chamberlin, Lt. Gen. Stephen J. 90, 170, 232, 255, 380, 397, 401, 402–4, 405, 412, 418, 436
Chancellor of the Federal Republic of Germany. *See* Adenauer, Konrad; Brandt, Willy; Erhard, Ludwig W
Charité hospital 181
Charlottenburg 417
Chennault, Brig. Gen. Claire L. 22
Cherbourg 88
Chiang Kai-shek, General 22
Chicago (informant) 315
Chikalov, Alexander F. 254
Christian Democratic Union (Christlich Demokratische Union Deutschlands; CDU) 311, 313, 328, 341, 359, 360–61, 362, 376, 397, 423–24, 435
Christian Social Union (Christlich-Soziale Union; CSU) 311, 312, 319, 321–29
Churchill, Winston 61, 62, 63, 65, 66, 71, 83, 239, 288, 382
CIA. *See* Central Intelligence Agency
CIC. *See* Counter Intelligence Corps
cigarettes as currency 126, 140, 249, 271, 273, 293, 323, 339, 346, 371, 429. *See also* black market
Civil Censorship Division 103, 146, 156, 157–58, 159, 190, 202, 203, 210, 289, 322, 357
Civil Censorship Division 7742d, 156, 159
Clair, Marie T. 328
Clark, Dale D. 324
Clarke, Brig. Gen. Carter W. 16, 23, 24, 150, 384
Clay, General Lucius D
– as lieutenant general 87–88
– as military governor of Germany 2, 87–88, 97, 98, 101, 102, 105, 110, 112n89, 128, 151, 166, 185, 189, 200, 209, 225, 227, 255, 257, 273–74, 277–78, 280, 293–94, 311, 316, 319, 321, 327, 332, 337, 339, 344, 355, 359, 359n41, 395, 399–3, 410–12, 415, 418–19, 422–23, 424, 428, 435–36, 438, 440, 441, 443
Clay, Marjorie 277
Clementis, Vladimír 396

code names, groups
- Bolero Group 248-52
- Breakers 59-60, 60n90
- Crown Jewels 57, 119
- Honeypot 353, 356
- Odessa 196, 199, 199n106, 201
- Turicum 323, 323n86, 325, 327
code names, individuals
- Chicago (CIC informant). *See* Chicago (informant)
- Curt (CIC informant). *See* Curt (informant)
- Mars. *See* Kuebler, Helmuth
- O-35-VIII. *See* Brandt, Willy
- P-15-VIII. *See* Raue, Heinz
- P-43-VIII. *See* Raue, Gerhard
- Robot. *See* Müller, Josef
- Savoy. *See* Kemritz, Hans A
- Sunny. *See* Pfeiffer, Sunihild
- Victoria. *See* Pfeiffer, Sunihild
- Zigzag. *See* Krull, Heinz, K. H
code names, intelligence activity. *See also* projects
- Alsos 222-23
- Bolero 248. *See also* code names, groups, Bolero Group
- Bourbon 8, 148, 241
- Eclipse, Operations Plan 233
- Fish (equipment) 30, 236
- Magic 13, 14, 32, 44
- Purple (equipment) 13, 30, 32
- Ultra 8, 30, 30n82, 32, 45, 70-71, 72
code names, military activity
- Counterpunch 409
- Dragoon 34
- Task Force Whitney 269
- War Plan Broiler 393, 410
- War Plan Pincher 385
code names, operations. *See* operations, German; operations, Soviet; operations, U.S.
code names, places
- Ashcan (detention facility) 151
- Dustbin (detention facility) 151, 224, 225, 252
- Terminal. *See* Potsdam Conference
code names, projects. *See* projects
Collins, Lt. Col. James L., Jr. 446
Collins, Lt. Gen. J. Lawton Collins 418
Collins, Col. Richard 91

Cologne 53, 61, 305-7, 313, 436
Combat Commands, U.S.A, 12th Armored Division 91
Combined Intelligence Committee 28
Combined Intelligence Liaison Center 144
Combined Intelligence Objectives Agency 223
Combined Services Detailed Interrogation Center 29
Committee for State Security (Komitet Gosudarstvennoy Bezopasnosti; KGB) 213n158, 288
Composite Group, 7821st. *See* Gehlen Organization; operations, U.S., Rusty
concentration camps 24, 139, 173-74, 187, 197, 202, 205, 280, 284, 311, 314, 323, 332, 334, 343, 353, 363, 366n69, 429
Connor, Lt. Col. William M. 94, 99
Conrad, Brig. Gen. G. Bryan 10
Constabulary Brigade, 1st. *See* U.S. Constabulary
Cook, Col. Earle F. 145
Cooper, Donald H. 105
Corderman, Brig. Gen. W. Preston 16, 144
Corps, U.S.
- V 236
- VI 188
- VII 101
- VIII 46
- XII 217, 445
- XXI 65
- XXII 217
Council of Foreign Ministers 148, 398, 435
- Counter Intelligence Corps (CIC) 3, 17, 18, 35, 36, 40, 41-44, 47, 48, 52, 55, 67, 68-72, 75, 79, 83, 103, 105, 106, 108, 111, 113, 118n119, 120, 126, 133-41, 154, 156, 158, 166, 168, 173, 175, 176, 179-181, 182, 184-85, 186, 187, 190, 191-201, 202-5, 208, 209, 210, 211, 212, 213, 216, 221, 226, 227, 229-30, 231, 242, 254, 261-66, 269, 272-73, 277-79, 282, 284, 285-87, 289, 290-97, 299, 300, 303, 308-9, 310, 313, 316, 320-29, 330, 332, 334-35, 33, 340-41, 343, 344-47, 348, 350, 354, 357, 361, 364-66, 366n69, 367, 369-74, 375, 382, 383, 386-87, 399, 405, 412, 417, 419, 420, 424, 426, 429-34, 436, 438, 441, 442. *See also* individual CounterIntelligence Corps detachments
- criticism of 18, 33, 280, 137

- domestic intelligence activity 18
- informants 3, 9, 140–41, 199, 262, 287, 309, 314, 328, 340, 350, 353, 355, 370, 373–74, 383, 416, 429
- internal problems and investigations 32–33, 117, 136–37, 254, 275, 278–280, 300–3, 374, 432, 434, 442
- regional structure in Germany 33, 40, 113, 115, 132–36, 137–38, 140–41
- special agents 23, 67, 216, 226
- training 23, 136–37, 161

Counter Intelligence Corps detachments
- 29th 68
- 30th 47, 48
- 42d 56
- 89th 69
- 95th 69
- 203d 55
- 218th 268
- 301st 47
- 303d 139
- 307th 72, 187, 208, 286, 290
- 418th 17, 33, 132
- 430th 262, 265
- 970th 94, 100, 133, 134, 141, 264. *See also* Counter Intelligence Group, 7970th

Counter Intelligence Corps regions
- Region I 134, 135, 141, 142
- Region II 134, 135, 141, 142
- Region III 134, 135, 141, 142, 294
- Region IV 134, 135, 141, 142
- Region V 134, 135, 141, 142
- Region VI 134, 135, 141, 142
- Region VII 141, 142
- Region VIII 134, 135, 137, 141, 142, 370, 374, 429
- Region IX 134, 135, 141, 142
- Region X 141, 142
- Region XI 141, 142
- Region XII 141, 142

Counter Intelligence Group, 7970th 141
courts-martial 47, 57, 68, 70, 198, 200, 243, 271, 299, 301, 364, 444
Cox, Joe B. 324
Crandall, Lt. Col. Robert G. 94, 156, 157
Criminal Investigation Division 271, 277, 442
Critchfield, Col. James H. 251n158, 255, 257

CROWCASS. *See* Central Registry of War Criminals and Security Suspects
Crum, Maj. Earl Le Verne 188
cryptologic equipment 25, 30, 145, 234, 239–40
- bombes 30
- Enigma cipher machine 30, 30n82, 70, 239, 241, 366
- Lorenz SZ-42 cipher machine 237
- M-209 portable cipher machine 239
- *Schlüsselkasten* cipher machine 241
- SIGABA cipher machine 70, 238, 239
- T-52 Geheimschreiber teleprinter cipher machine 237
CSU. *See* Christian Social Union
Culp, Col. Clarence M. 134
Cunningham, Robert A. 109
Curt (informant) 383
Czechoslovakia 149, 155, 203, 236, 243, 287, 299, 317, 377, 383, 386, 396, 397, 401, 409

Dabringhaus, Erhard 136
Dachau concentration camp 173–74, 205–8, 210, 264
Dachau trial 205, 231. *See also* war crimes trials
DAD. *See* Department of the Army Detachment
Dahrendorf, Gustav D. 339
Daniels, Maj. William H. 365
Darmstadt 106, 146, 166
de Gaulle, General Charles 30, 71, 85
de Guinzbourg, Victor 72
De Neufville, Lawrence E. 105
Deane, Lt. Col. John R. "Jack" Jr. 249, 251, 252, 253, 256
Deane, Maj. Gen. John R. 73–74, 75
Dearing, Capt. Albin P. 268
defectors 3, 113, 116, 118, 120, 154, 250, 257, 258–63, 266, 272, 287, 291, 301, 332, 353, 353n14, 357, 361–62, 374, 378, 382, 444
Defense, Secretary of. *See* Forrestal, James V
Dehler, Irma 312
Dehler, Thomas 312
demobilization, U.S. military 90, 102, 105, 134, 135, 153, 161, 442
democratization 5, 7, 9, 84, 265, 305–49
- in Bavaria 317–29
- in Berlin 337–48

– political parties and 310–16, 320–22, 324, 327–29, 330–37
denazification 9, 79, 84, 137–38, 166, 170, 173, 182–190, 198, 217, 265, 317, 362, 367
– arrests 183–184, 203, 208n139
– local response to 186–90, 317
– screenings and assessments 185–187, 190, 203, 230
– U.S. policy shift to anticommunism 138, 159–60, 210–11, 217, 264, 441–42
Department of the Army Detachment (DAD) 103, 106, 121, 128. See also Central Intelligence Agency; Office of Strategic Services; Strategic Services Unit.
Department of Defense 89, 388, 402, 441, 445
Department of Justice 232, 266
Department of State 1n1, 26, 88, 119, 148, 152, 163, 214, 215, 231, 232, 239, 251, 347, 382, 404, 438
DeRiemer, Lt. Col. Louis 134
Dessau 355
detention facilities and prison camps 197, 208n139, 284, 310. See also Aschan detention center; Camp King; Camp Nikolaus; Dustbin detention center
– Nazi German 23, 31, 139, 151, 173–73, 186, 201, 204, 205, 231, 280–81, 284, 311, 315, 324, 330, 343, 366, 429n69
– U.S. 34, 151, 154–55, 196, 200, 203, 207, 214, 224, 225
– Soviet 76, 259, 281, 301, 334, 337, 350, 363, 36, 424, 427–28, 430
Detailed Interrogation Center, 6824th 151
deutsche mark (DM) 242, 346–47, 350, 354, 371, 429, 434, 435
Dickson, Col. Benjamin A. "Monk" 20n32, 22, 22n47, 36, 46, 50, 71
Dieburg 192
Dietrich, General Josef "Sepp" 45, 207, 209
displaced persons 67, 139, 154, 193, 202, 268, 280–88, 289, 292, 304, 441. See also United Nations Relief and Rehabilitation Administration
– Jewish 283–85
– violence and 193, 202, 282, 284, 285
Displaced Persons Act of 1948, 285
Domaschke, Heinz 365, 366

Dominik, Dorothea 296
Dönitz, Grand Admiral Karl 57, 234
Dorn, Walter 320
Donovan, William J. "Wild Bill" 19, 20, 34, 324
Draper, William H., Jr. 285, 422
Draganović, Krunoslav S. 263, 265
Dratvin, General Mikhail I. 294, 408
Dreifuss, Walter 325
Dresden 365n63, 386
Dryer, Capt. Cecil. See Struller, Otto R
Duin, Lt. Col. Gerald. H. 251
Dulles, Allen W. 57–59, 60n90, 75, 119, 123, 253, 273, 278, 445
Durand, Dana B. 125, 126, 127, 128, 138, 168, 370
Durant, Col. Jack W. 271
Durchgangslager der Luftwaffe (Dulag Luft) 151
Dundalk 136
Dustbin detention center 151, 224, 225, 225, 252

E1H2 military government detachment 305
Eason, Lt. Col. John D. 105
East Berlin 332, 374, 375, 432, 434, 444. See also Berlin, Soviet sector
East Germany. See German Democratic Republic
East Prussia 84
Eastern Military District 85
economic exploitation 189–190, 351–55, 356, 416. See also reparations
Economic Reconstruction Union (Wirtschaftliche Aufbau-Vereinigung; WAV) 322, 329
Edelweisspiraten (Edelweiss pirates) 194
Eden, Anthony 352
Edmunds, Brig. Gen. James B. 273–74
EEIs. See Essential Elements of Information
Egypt 26, 91, 239, 350
Ehard, Annelore 322
Ehard, Hans 321, 322, 329
Eigruber, August 205
Eilts, Hermann F. 26
Einheit Stielau 47–48
Einsatzgruppen 204
Einstein, Albert 231
Eisenhower, General Dwight D. 2, 21, 28, 31, 42, 48, 60, 62, 63, 64, 65–66, 66n120, 68, 71–72, 83, 87, 97, 102, 169, 185, 226, 233, 247, 248, 269, 283, 284, 317, 320
Eisenhower, Milton 283

Elbe River 61, 63, 64
elections 310, 312, 321, 330, 337, 341, 397, 422, 424, 435. *See also* political parties
Ellis, Col. Burton L. 210
Ennis, Col. Riley R. 90, 359, 397, 403
Epp, Franz Ritter von 319
Erhard, Ludwig W. 328
Erlangen 326
Erskine, Col. David G. 70, 134
Erzgebirge (ore mountains) 356–58
Essential Elements of Information (EEIs) 17, 37, 99, 100, 103, 106, 138, 169
Esslingen 157, 159
European Command 87, 94, 97, 98, 100, 105, 106, 117, 117, 129, 141, 145, 153, 159, 163, 167, 170, 181, 300, 332, 334, 361, 385, 386, 399, 406, 407, 408, 436
European Command Intelligence School, 7712th 161, 163
European Recovery Program. *See* Marshall Plan
European Theater of Operations 3, 17, 28–33, 35, 37, 75, 85, 87, 91, 93–94, 134, 139. *See also* United States Forces in the European Theater
Evans, Lt. Col. Geoffrey H. 235
Everett, Col. Willis M. 209, 209n140
executions 21n37, 24, 209, 281, 333, 363
 – by Americans 47, 48, 57, 200, 201, 208
 – by Germans 173, 201, 205. *See also* Holocaust
 – by Soviets 76, 125, 214, 243, 262, 302, 358, 362–63, 363, 364n59, 428n154
 – Katyn Forest massacres 76, 214–16
 – Malmédy massacre 46
 – of war criminals 205, 207, 362
exploitation of German scientists. *See* scientific exploitation
exploitation of German economic assets. *See* economic exploitation
extradition 211–14, 247, 265

F1G2 military government detachment 39
Faymonville, Col. Philip R. 74
FBI. *See* Federal Bureau of Investigation
FDJ. *See* Free German Youth
FDP. *See* Free Democratic Party
Federal Bureau of Investigation (FBI) 3, 18, 181, 202, 275

Federal Republic of Germany (West Germany) vii, 1n1, 2, 5, 9, 65, 210, 238, 259, 282n55, 307, 311, 313, 316, 317, 329, 337, 345, 347–49, 348n199, 399, 434–38, 440, 443–44, 445–46
Fenn, 2d Lt. Alfred G. 235
Fenner, Wilhelm 240
Fernamt (telephone exchange) 113
FIAT. *See* Field Information Agency, Technical
Field Information Agency, Technical (FIAT) 225, 225n28
Fighting Group against Inhumanity (Kampfgruppe gegen Unmenschlichkeit; KgU) 428–34
Filin (Red Army private) 260–61
Fischhausen 245–46
Fisher, Maj. R. A. 224
Flicke, Wilhelm F. 238
Fleming, Cdr. Ian L. 220n4, 223
Flensburg 234
Ford, Col. Thomas R. 224
Forrestal, James V. 255, 403, 410, 411
Forschungsamt 237
Fox, Thomas D. 335
Fort Bragg 428
Fort Holabird 136
Fort Hunt 15, 35, 244, 250
Fort Monmouth 25
Fragebogen 41, 184
Frahm, Herbert Ernst Karl. *See* Brandt, Willy
France 3, 4, 21, 21n37, 30, 34, 39, 70, 71–72, 98, 124, 148, 150, 151, 157, 161, 175, 176, 197, 211, 226–27, 228, 251, 265–66, 281, 285, 324, 389, 396
Franco, General Francisco 176
Frankfurt (am Main) 34, 85–87, 91, 94, 97, 98, 99–101, 102–5, 107, 108, 109, 111, 113, 115, 116, 117, 119, 120, 133, 134, 141, 144–45, 145, 148, 149, 150, 151, 156–57, 159–60, 167, 170, 203, 224, 228, 230, 242, 250, 260, 263, 269, 270, 272, 285, 289–91, 294, 297, 300, 304, 332, 336, 346, 347, 357, 361, 362, 397, 404, 443, 443
Frankfurt (Oder) 389
fraternization 68, 193
Free Democratic Party (Freie Demokratische Partei; FDP) 310–11, 313, 321, 341, 424

Free German Youth (Freie Deutsche Jugend; FDJ) 350, 371
Freimann 166
Freisler, Roland 87
Fremde Heere Ost (Foreign Armies East). *See* German intelligence
Fremde Heere West (Foreign Armies West). *See* German intelligence
French intelligence 30, 72, 102, 146–48, 153, 179, 211, 265–66, 324, 387
French sector of Berlin. *See* Berlin, French sector
French Zone 85, 139, 211, 296, 389
Friedensburg, Ferdinand 423–24
Fricke, Dr. Walter E. 235
Friede, Dieter 423–24
Fritzlar 146, 285
Führerbunker 175, 178–80
Funk Kaserne 286–87

Gabelia, Capt. George T. 112, 179
Gailey, Brig. Gen. Charles K., Jr. 114, 167
Galloway, Col. Donald H. 128, 253
Garmisch-Partenkirchen 317–18
Garner, Richard. *See* Gehlen, Brig. Gen. Reinhard
Gatow airport 413
Gatzke, Hans W. 27
Gehlen, Brig. Gen. Reinhard [Richard Garner; Dr. Schneider] 244–49, 250–58, 251n158, 380, 444
Gehlen Organization 106, 238, 256–58, 363. *See also* Bundesnachrichtendienst; Operation Rusty
German American Bund 203
German Communist Party (Kommunistische Partei Deutschlands, KPD) 7, 9, 138, 140, 159, 190, 321, 330, 331–37, 338–42, 348, 359, 365–66. *See also* Socialist Unity Party
– activity in U.S. Zone 138, 190, 272, 311, 321, 330–332, 333–34, 335, 336, 348
– activity in Berlin 316, 338–42, 359
– merger with SPD in Berlin 338–40, 360–61
German Democratic Republic (East Germany) 3, 4n9, 112, 129, 129n164, 170, 232, 239, 302, 314, 347, 358, 363, 365, 367, 367n75, 371, 383, 388, 390, 406, 415–16, 426, 432, 434, 445, 446
German émigrés in the U.S. Army 3, 23, 27, 34, 49, 112, 162–63, 188–89, 210, 302, 319, 339, 370, 443
– prevalence of 3, 23–27, 173, 188
– security concerns and 49, 151, 302
German intelligence 35, 67, 69, 79, 125, 247, 249, 380, 383
– *Fremde Heere Ost (Foreign Armies East)* 67, 244, 246–49, 250
– *Fremde Heere West (Foreign Armies West)* 67
German Research Council (Reichsforschungsrat) 224
Gerstenmaier, Eugen 314
Gestapo (Geheime Staatspolizei) 7, 66–67, 69, 119, 138, 166, 183, 250, 178, 313, 336, 336n147, 367
Giesenau 334
Giessen 52, 154
Giessner, Capt. Rudolf I. 434
Gillars, Mildred E. ["Axis Sally"] 203
Glasenbach 241
Glaser, Louis 110, 340, 341
Goebbels, Joseph 55, 80, 175, 183, 276–77
Goebbels, Magda 175
Goudsmit, Dr. Samuel A. 222
Gontard, Maj. Hans 59–60
Göppingen 192
Göring, Hermann W. 263
Görres, Wilhelm 41
Gotha 70
Göttingen 224
Graf, Otto 323
Graubart, Capt. Arthur H. 129
Great Britain 1, 72, 83, 144, 227, 234, 238, 308, 314, 352, 382, 396, 397
Greater Hesse 10, 87, 103, 106, 109, 190, 214, 312, 316, 330
Greece 131
Grevenbroich 54
Groh, Dr. A. 354
Grombach, Col. John V. "Frenchy" 20–21
Grossdeutschland Kaserne. *See* Campbell Barracks
Gross-Gerau 145

Group of Soviet Occupation Forces in Germany. *See* Red Army
Gruhn, Col. Ernest W. 224–25
Grundgesetz (Basic Law, Federal Republic of Germany) 435
Grzeskowiak, Stephan ["Stephan Thomas"] 368, 370, 375
Guderian, General Heinz W. 214, 216
guerrilla movements. *See Werwolf*
Guillaume, Günter 348, 348n199
Güstrow 169
Gutleutkaserne 145
Gutenberger, Karl M. 54–55
Guth, 2d Lt. Paul C. 205

Hahn (informant) 371
Hahn, Otto 222
Haislip, Lt. Gen. Wade H. 85
Halder, General Franz 244
Hale, Lt. Col. Oron J. 179
Hall, Maj. Gen. William E. 97–98, 129, 428
Halle, Capt. Hermann 242
Hallock, Capt. Richard R. 150, 150n46, 402
Hamann, Wilhelm 366, 366n69
Hammitzsch, Martin H. 69, 69n136
Hans, Theodor ["Martin"] 296, 370, 375, 429, 430, 434
Hanover 314, 315, 346, 369–70
Harmon, Maj. Gen. Ernest N. 217
Harnack House 423
Harnisch, Rudolf 254
Harriman, W. Averell 73
Harris, Innis D. 105, 108
Hays, Lt. Gen. George P. 87, 127, 260, 401, 418
Hayes, Col. Harold G. 436
Hearn, Lt. Col. Norman J. 133
Hecksher, Henry D. 26, 345
Heidelberg 87, 100–01, 103, 106, 119, 120, 124, 141, 187, 188, 213, 265, 302, 368, 372, 387, 388, 405, 443
Heidemann, Willi 195–96
Heilbronn 38, 282, 335
Heimlich, William F. 276, 340, 343
– as colonel 111–12, 114, 115n102, 115, 118, 127, 177, 179, 181, 276
– Radio in the American Sector 276, 369, 426
Heine, Fritz 315, 369, 373, 375

Heinrich, Karl 338
Heisenberg, Werner K. 222
Heitzmann, Kurt Heinrich 323–25
Helm, Lt. Col. Hans W. 165–66
Helms, Richard M. 120, 123–24, 445
Helmstedt 390, 410
Hensley, Maj. Robert B. 275
Hentze, Rudolf 241
Hermes, Andreas 361
Herro, Marshall 199
Herz-Krupenko, Lena 286
Herzogenaurach (Herzo Base) 106, 129, 146, 148, 388, 436
Hess, Brig. Gen. Walter W., Jr. 167, 169, 356
Hesse 10, 87, 103, 106, 109, 190, 193, 214, 270–71, 283, 286, 300, 311, 312, 316, 330
Heusinger, Adolf 256
Heuss, Theodor 5, 309, 312, 435
Heuss-Knapp, Elly 309, 309n18
Heym, Stefan 3, 4n9, 5, 134, 446
Higgins, Marguerite 354
Hildebrandt, Rainer 428–29
Hillenkoetter, R. Adm. Roscoe H. 358, 408–09, 415–16, 418
Himmler, Heinrich L. 52, 54, 55, 62, 66
Hirschfeld, Hans E. 347
Hitler, Adolf 6, 42, 44, 51, 59, 60, 62, 69, 72, 87, 93, 123, 174, 176, 178n18, 244n119, 303, 306, 315, 323, 396, 422, 429
– death of 175, 178, 180
– rumors of escape 175–76, 177, 180, 181–82, 198, 264
Hitler, Paula 176
Hitler Youth 53, 54, 57, 183, 191, 194–96, 317
Hodges, General Courtney H. 39, 61, 71
Hoegner, Wilhelm 320–21, 322
Hof 154
Hofer, Franz 59, 60n90
Hoffer, Edward W. 310
Hofgeismar 192–93
Hohenschönhausen (Berlin) 288
Holocaust 158, 188–89, 284. *See also* anti-Semitism; war crimes trials
Holzinger, Sgt. Warner W. 38
Hoover, Herbert C. 276, 280
Hoover, J. Edgar 181
Hopkins, Harry S. 175

Horcher family 263, 263n215
Hotel am Zoo 180
Howley, Edith 6
Howley, Brig. Gen. Frank L. 6–7, 87, 342, 344, 408, 409, 414, 419, 424, 426
Höxter, Siegfried 315, 370
Huebner, Lt. Gen. Clarence R. 88, 167, 168, 170, 260–61, 300, 304
Hülchrath Castle 54
Hummel, Franz 198
Hungary 283
Hunter, 1st Lt. Jack D. [Hans Jäger] 141, 195
Hürtgen Forest 44
Hüttenhain, Dr. Erich 234, 239

IG Farben 85, 223
IG Farben building 85–86, 87, 94, 120, 133, 141, 145, 228, 347, 347n194
IG Farbenindustrie. *See* IG Farben
Illner, Arthur [Richard Stahlmann] 333–34
Infantry Divisions, U.S.
– 1st 384, 389
– 28th 70
– 29th 110
– 30th 48
– 44th 57, 229
– 45th 173
– 69th 63
– 70th 104
– 90th 269, 377
– 99th 46
– 106th 47
Infantry Regiments, U.S.
– 3d 292
– 422d 46
– 423d 46
informants 3, 9, 18, 20–21, 114–15, 116, 120, 125–26, 129, 133, 140–41, 176, 180, 184, 186, 191, 195, 198, 199–200, 206, 217, 244, 253, 254, 262, 263, 264, 266, 272–73, 287, 293, 297–98, 299, 302, 303, 308, 309, 313, 314, 315, 321, 322, 323, 323n85, 325–28, 330, 334, 342, 346–47, 350–51, 353, 355, 361, 363, 364, 370, 371, 373–75, 383, 386, 394, 399–400, 405, 406, 416, 424–26, 427, 429, 430, 434. *See also* individual informants

Information Control Division 108, 132, 186, 322, 323, 339, 346
Ingraham, Col. Gordon D. 152
Inskeep, Col. John L. 94, 100, 134
Intelligence Coordinating Committee 97
Intelligence Division (Washington). *See* Military Intelligence Division (Washington); Military Intelligence Service (Washington)
Intelligence Division (European Theater of Operations). *See* Military Intelligence Service (Washington)
internal investigations 18, 68, 69, 70, 71, 108, 117, 137, 163, 209, 264–65, 270–80, 366, 372, 432–34, 442, 444
International Military Tribunal 148–49, 215
Iran 76, 131
Irwin, Maj. Gen. Stafford LeRoy 90
Ismay, General Hastings I. 66
Italy 4, 14, 19n28, 19, 33, 75, 124, 145, 222, 263, 265, 285, 391, 396–97

Jackson, William H. 253
Jacobs, S. Sgt. Kurt R. 46, 205
Jäger, Hans. *See* Hunter, 1st Lt. Jack D
Japan 13–14, 18n20, 19n28, 19, 30, 32, 44, 73, 111, 134, 226, 226, 234, 352, 402
Jarczyk, Richard 57
Jaspers, Karl 187
JCS. *See* Joint Chiefs of Staff
Jena 235
Jessel, 2d Lt. Walter 230
Jewish emigration to Palestine 30, 139, 283–85
Johnson, Maj. Roy D. 30
Joint Chiefs of Staff (JCS) 17, 19, 28, 84, 86, 182, 189–90, 224, 228, 385, 391, 411, 441
Joint Intelligence Committee (JCS) 17, 28, 56, 78, 79, 224, 228, 229, 391
Joint Intelligence Committee (SHAEF) 28–29, 56
Joint Intelligence Objectives Agency 224–25, 228, 229, 230. *See also* projects, Paperclip
Jones, Maj. Hugh M. 42
Josselson, Michael 432

K-5 (East German political police) 367
Kabus, Siegfried 197–99, 200
Kaisen, Wilhelm 310, 316

Kaiser, Jakob 360
Kallmann, Hans A. 105, 107
Kaltenbach, Dorothea 212
Kaltenbach, Fredrick W. ["Lord Hee-Haw"] 212
Kaltenbrunner, Ernst 204
Karlshorst (Berlin) 288, 301, 326, 353, 415
Karlsruhe 120, 289
Karnau, Hermann 176
Karney, Jens. *See* Carney, Sgt. Jeffrey M
Kassel 103, 106, 121, 241, 272
Katyn Forest massacres 76, 214–16
Keating, Maj. Gen. Frank A. 293
Keck, Lt. Col. John A. 219
Keitel, Field Marshal Wilhelm 122
Kemp, Henry W. 290
Kempka, Erich 179
Kempten 186
Kemritz, Hans A. [Savoy] 126
Kennan, George F. 382
Kettler, Col. Hugo 234, 237, 241
KGB. *See* Committee for State Security
KgU. *See* Fighting Group against Inhumanity
Kibler, Col. Harold R. 18
kidnappings 126, 262, 284, 296, 296, 342, 374
Kielgast (informant) 371
Kimmel-Kaserne 160
Kirchlengern 54
Kissinger, Henry A. 4, 28, 134, 163, 446
Klamm, Gottlieb 198
Kleinschmidt, Clemens 313
Klemperer, Klemens von 27
Kloster Tiefenthal 69
Kluge, John W. 26
Koch, Col. Oscar 23, 36
Koenig, Col. Egmont F. 396, 409
Koenig, Col. Theodore J. 101, 102
Kommandatura 338, 387, 409, 414
Königstein 300
Kotikov, Maj. Gen. Alexander G. 342, 421
Kovalshchuk, General Nikolai K. 288
KPD. *See* German Communist Party
Kraemer, Fritz Gustav Anton 162–63
Krankenhagen 54
Kransberg Castle. *See* Dustbin detention center
Krejci-Graf, Karl 230
Kreuzberg 111
Kriegsmarine 139

Kroner, Brig. Gen. Hayes B. 15, 20
Kronberg 270
Krull, Heinz K. H. [Zigzag] 125
Kubala, Maj. Paul 246
Kuebler, Helmuth [Mars] 290
Kuhn, Fritz J. 203
Kühne, Heinz 374–75
Kulas, Siegfried ["Karl"] 195
Kurochkin, General Pavel A. 293–94
KVP. *See* Barracked People's Police

La Boos, José 264
Lane, Capt. Mary C. 242
Landsberg 284
Landshut 226
Langer, Walter C. 174
language knowledge and training 4, 15, 17, 23, 26, 34, 38, 136, 146, 153, 157, 160–62, 163–64, 204, 214, 301, 302, 443
Lash, Sgt. Joseph P. 18
Lauf 238
LDP. *See* Liberal Democratic Party
Leclerc, General Philippe 71
Lehman, 2d Lt. Charles H. 179
Leipzig 254, 338, 446
Lemon, Holmes W. 366
Lerchner, Kurt 364, 365, 366
Letzelter, Lt. Col. Cyril J. 100
Lewicki, James 219
Lewis, Crosby 120, 252
Liberal Democratic Party (Liberal-Demokratische Partei; LDP) 311, 360
Lichterfelde (Berlin) 125
Liebel, Col. Willard K. 256
Lindau 224
Lippschütz, Alfred 373–74, 375
Lochner, Louis P. 241, 276, 276n29
London 15, 29, 77, 91, 105, 144, 148, 223, 239, 246, 247, 277, 314, 315, 369, 372, 398, 401, 408
London Military Documents Center 33
"Lord Hee-Haw." *See* Kaltenbach, Frederick W
Loritz, Alfred 322
Lorraine 39
Losowsky, Valentin [Walter Vogt] 301
Lotz, Erich [Georg Savieczes] 365–66
Luckenwalde 405

Lüders, Marie-Elisabeth 162, 425–26
Ludwigslust 335
Luftgau 112, 115, 122
Luftwaffe 54, 118, 146, 151, 152, 221, 242, 244, 350
Luxembourg 35, 46, 151, 157
Lyon 265

MacArthur, General Douglas 402, 403
Machlanka, Martha 417
Madrid 263, 263n215
Magdeburg 63
Maginnis, Lt. Col. John J. 111
Magistrat (Berlin) 421
Maier, Gerta 308
Maier, Reinhold 308, 310
Malady, Maj. Eugene L. 432–34
Malinin, General Mikhail S. 167, 168, 170, 356
Malmédy massacre 46, 207–11
Mancuso, Marco S. 364–365
Mann, Klaus 4, 4n9
Mannheim 282
Manteuffel, General Hasso E. von 207
Marburg 235, 334
Marchetti, Victor L. 347
Marchuk, Pfc. William T. 301, 302
Marienborn 399
Markgraf, Paul 338, 342, 423–24, 430
Marr, Lt. Col. Harold E. Jr. 134
Marseilles 285
Marshall, General George C
– Army chief of staff 13–14, 22, 64, 73, 74, 176, 225, 233, 248
– secretary of state 1, 354–55, 398
Marshall Plan 355, 371–72, 373, 398
Masaryk, Jan G. 396
Mason, Frank E. 276, 277
Mathews, Fox 181
Matteson, Robert E. 204
Mauthausen concentration camp 205
Maxwell, Robert W. 290–91
mayors of Berlin. *See* Friedensburg, Ferdinand; Ostrowski, Otto; Schröder, Louise D
mayors of West Berlin. *See* Brandt, Willy; Reuter, Ernst
McCarthy, Joseph R. 210
McCloy, Ellen 313

McCloy, John J. 77, 143, 313, 347n194, 435, 435n183, 437n191
McCormack, Col. Alfred 16, 22, 24
McDonald, Brig. Gen. George C. 379
McNarney, General Joseph T. 87, 97
McNair Barracks 117
Mead, Col. Armistead D. 64
Mead, Senator James M. 274
Mecklenburg 354
Meiningen 170
Menzer, Ostwin Fritz 241–43, 243n112
Merkers salt mine 268–69
Merrill, Col. John P. 116, 116n110, 117, 118, 127, 259–60
Metal, Nicholas 110
Mettig, Lt. Col. Werner 324
Metz 39
MGB. *See* Ministry for State Security (Soviet Union)
Michael, Roger D. 364, 366
Michela, Brig. Gen. Joseph A. "Mike" 8, 74, 78
Middleton, Drew 63, 435
Milano, Col. James V. 263
Miles, Brig. Gen. Sherman 13–14
military attachés 9, 13, 15, 17, 19, 19n28, 19n29, 19n30, 28, 73, 75, 78, 90, 91, 97, 99, 103, 106, 128, 277, 356, 379–80, 381, 396, 398, 403, 409, 408
military districts. *See* Eastern Military District; Western Military District
Military Intelligence Detachment, 7880th 301–02, 302, 431, 434
Military Intelligence Division (Washington) 13, 15–16, 17, 19, 21, 28, 3, 6, 63, 64, 76, 77, 89–91, 98, 103, 105, 106, 111, 139, 143, 145, 163, 165, 221, 231, 244, 246, 255, 256, 257, 334, 355, 359, 361, 367, 379, 380, 384, 116, 391, 397, 399, 402, 404–06
– Eastern Europe Section 77
– Far Eastern Section 13, 111
– German Military Documents Section 15, 151, 152
– Military Intelligence Research Section 15
– Military Intelligence Service. *See* Military Intelligence Service (Washington)
– Signal Security Agency. *See* Signal Security Agency

- U.S. Army Historical Section 244
- XIX Tactical Air Command 69
Military Intelligence Interpreter Teams 111. *See also* Counter Intelligence Corps
Military Intelligence Platoon, 7829th 106, 115, 118, 128, 385
Military Intelligence Service (European Theater of Operations) 17, 31, 31, 217, 230
- Counter Intelligence Corps. *See* Counter Intelligence Corps
- MIS-X 31
- MIS-Y 31
Military Intelligence Service (Washington) 15–16, 17, 20, 21, 22, 31, 35, 74, 90, 91, 143, 217, 219, 250, 280, 280
- Bolero Group. *See* code names, groups, Bolero Group
- Counter Intelligence Corps. *See* Counter Intelligence Corps
- MIS-X 16
- MIS-Y 16
- "The Pond" 20–21
Military Intelligence Service Center 151. *See also* Camp King
Military Intelligence Service Center, 7707th 153. *See also* Camp King
Military Intelligence Training Center (MITC; Camp Ritchie) 2, 17, 25–28, 47, 66, 111, 136, 153, 165, 204, 205, 248, 251, 340. *See also* "Ritchie Boys"
Miller, Col. Francis P. 273–74, 276
Millis, Walter 403
Ministry for State Security (East Germany) (Ministerium für Staatssicherheit, Stasi) 129n164, 348, 348n199
Ministry for State Security (Soviet Union) (Ministerstvo Gosudarstvennoy Bezopasnosti; MGB) 288
missiles 229, 230, 356
- Jupiter-C missile 232
- V-1 flying bomb 35, 229, 231
- V-2 supersonic rocket 35, 169, 229, 230, 231, 232
MITC. *See* Military Intelligence Training Center
Moewes, Ernst 375
Molotov, Vyacheslav M. 326, 398
Mönchengladbach 68, 80

Mondorf 151
Montenegro, Daniel W. 179
Montgomery, Field Marshal Bernard L. 48, 50, 60, 65
Morell, Dr. Theodor G. 178
Morgenthau, Henry J., Jr. 1, 188
Morgenthau Plan 1, 188
Morris, Brewster H. 345
Moscow 8, 19, 19n30, 38, 73, 77, 97, 113, 148, 164, 175, 301, 338, 354, 358, 362, 363, 365, 381, 421, 432
Moscow Declaration 201, 211
Moses, Lt. Col. Merillat 100
Müller, Josef [Robot] 323–28, 329
Müller, Maria 354
Muller, Brig. Gen. Walter J. 347
Munich 121, 134, 141, 157, 159, 166, 173, 193, 195, 200, 212, 213n158, 226, 256, 263, 286, 313, 317, 318, 319, 322–23, 327, 331, 428, 444n6
Murphy, Robert D. 115, 128

Naples 285, 324
Nash, Capt. Kathleen B. 271
National Committee for a Free Germany (Nationalkomitee Freies Deutschland) 77, 290
National Redoubt 57–64
National Security Agency (NSA) 445
National Security Council (NSC) 89, 163, 393, 411, 413, 427, 441
National Socialist German Workers' Party. *See* Nazi Party
National Democratic Party of Germany (National-Demokratische Partei Deutschland; NDPD) 362, 362n52, 363
NATO. *See* North Atlantic Treaty Organization
Nazi Party (National Socialist German Workers' Party; Nationalsozialistische Deutsche Arbeiterpartei; NSDAP) 35, 41, 41, 63, 138, 166, 182, 184, 205, 217, 245n119, 269, 305, 307, 310, 315, 362. *See also* denazification
Nazi Party organizations
- *Forschungsamt* 237
- *Gestapo* (*Geheime Staatspolizei*) 7, 66–67, 69, 119, 138, 166, 183, 250, 256, 279, 313, 336, 336n147, 367
- Hitler Youth 53, 54, 57, 183, 191, 194–96, 317

– *Sturmabteilung* (SA) 36, 183
– *Schutzstaffel* (SS) 6, 35, 44, 46, 47, 52, 54, 59, 62, 66, 138, 153, 173–74, 183, 187, 195, 196, 198–201, 202, 204, 205, 207, 208–10, 230, 253, 263. *See also* Odessa
– *Werwolf* 4, 52–57, 173, 191
NDPD. *See* National Democratic Party of Germany
Neckarsulm 193
Neff, Lt. Col. Paul E. 235
Neisse River 353, 355
Nelson, Andrew C., Jr. 350
Nelson, Col. Olan A. 286
Netherlands 234, 239
Neukölln 111
Neumann, Franz L. 342
Neumann, Siegmund "Siggi" 368, 369, 370, 375
Neuss 69
New Castle Airport 230
Newfoundland 32
Newman, Richard E. *See* Tillich, Ernst
NKVD. *See* People's Commissariat for Internal Affairs
Noce, Lt. Gen. Daniel 277
Noiret, Maj. Gen. Roger 227
nonfraternization policies. *See* fraternization
Nordhausen labor camp 229, 230–72, 232
Normandy 2, 31, 33, 88, 152, 221
North Africa 4, 29, 32, 124
North Atlantic Treaty Organization (NATO) 443
Norway 245
Novak, George J. 36
NSA. *See* National Security Agency
NSC. *See* National Security Council
NSDAP. *See* Nazi Party
Nuremberg 103, 103, 121, 141, 146, 148, 159, 191, 204, 208, 279, 328
Nuremberg trials 204, 208, 215

Oberammergau 103, 106, 160–64, 426, 443
Oberschlema 357
Oberursel 103, 106, 151–55, 200, 203, 208, 236, 242, 249, 251, 252–53, 270, 357, 367, 378, 380. *See also* Camp King
O'Connor, C. J. 105
Occupation Mark 272, 435
Oder River 353, 355

Odessa (Organisation der Ehemaligen SS Angehörigen; Organization of Former SS Members) 197–99, 199n106, 201
Offenbach 157
Office of Alien Property 276
Office of the Deputy Director of Intelligence 98, 101, 104, 105, 215, 258, 300
Office of the Director of Intelligence 99, 101, 102, 103, 104, 107, 165, 168, 225, 309, 336, 414, 420, 426
Office of Military Government, Bavaria 272
Office of Military Government, United States (OMGUS) 84n7, 87, 103, 105, 106, 110, 156, 225, 435n183
Office of Naval Intelligence 28, 155
Office of Special Investigations (U.S. Air Force) 129, 129n164, 44
Office of Strategic Services (OSS) 8, 17, 19–20, 32, 33–34, 56, 59–60, 66, 71, 75, 77, 78n174, 94, 102, 105, 107, 119–23, 124–25, 125–27, 130, 174, 178, 273, 308, 314, 320, 323, 359, 370, 427, 428, *See also* Central Intelligence Agency; Department of the Army Detachment; Strategic Services Unit
– relationship with Army Intelligence 19, 119–21
Offie, Carmel 227
Organization of Former SS Members. *See* Odessa
OKW/Chi. See Signals Intelligence Agency of the German Army High Command
OMGUS. *See* Office of Military Government, United States
operations, German
– Barbarossa 351
– Greif 44, 47, 48, 49, 208
– Herbstnebel 44, 49. *See also* Battle of the Bulge
operations, U.S.
– Anyface 213
– Basket/Basket Case 392
– Beechnut 30–31
– Bingo 287, 292
– Blackjack 282
– Clamshell 380
– Choo Choo 192
– Devotion 386
– Double Check 191

– Flypaper 292
– Gisbomb 69
– Grail 383
– Hagberry 254
– Lifebuoy 185
– Lusty 221
– Market-Garden 39
– Mesa 227
– Nursery 195–96
– Rummage 285
– Rusty 7, 103, 106, 243–58, 383–84, 405, 443. See also Gehlen Organization
– Sand 293–94, 297
– Selection Board 199–200
– Sunrise [1945] 75–76
– Sunrise [1946] 330
– Syndicate 282
– Tally Ho 191
– Valentine 194–95
– Vittles 413, 420. See also Airlift for West Berlin operations, Soviet
– Osoavikhim 355–56
Oppenheim, Sigfrid. See Penham, Daniel F
Oppenhoff, Franz 41–43, 54–55
Ordnance Department 221, 224, 226, 229
– Rocket Branch 229
Orwell, George 132, 219
Osborne, Col. Ralph M. 225
Osenberg, Werner 224, 226
OSI. See Office of Special Investigations (U.S. Air Force intelligence)
Oslo 103, 106, 122
Osmun, Brig. Gen. Russell A. 15, 143
OSS. See Office of Strategic Services
Ostbüro (SPD) 346, 368–76, 426
– informants 370, 370, 371, 373–74
– intelligence activity of 370–72
O'Steen, Lt. Col. James E. 109
Ostrowski, Otto 342–44
Our River 38

Padover, Capt. Saul K. 42–43, 54–55, 189
Palestine 30, 139, 283, 284–85
Pantuhoff, Lt. Col. Oleg J. 169–70, 170n146, 170n149
Panuch, Joseph A. 437
Paris 113, 148, 219, 224, 446

Parks, Maj. Gen. Floyd L. 83, 111, 271, 280, 401
Partridge, Col. Richard C. 101
Pash, Lt. Col. Boris T. 222
Passau 180
Patterson, Lt. Col. John K. 305, 306, 307
Patterson, Robert P. 131, 231
Patton, General George S., Jr. 22, 35, 85, 185, 236, 269, 317
Paul, Rudolf 361–62
Peabody, Brig. Gen. Paul E. 15, 381
Pearl Harbor, attack on 14, 79, 93, 105, 111, 124, 401
Pearson, Drew R. 64, 71, 210, 279
Peenemünde 169
Peiper, Lt. Col. Joachim 46, 207, 209, 211
Pelke, Max 426
Penham, Daniel F. 187
People's Commissariat for Internal Affairs (Naródnyy Komissariát Vnútrennikh Del; NKVD) 74, 212, 288
Pfaffenhofen 106, 146
Pfeiffer, Sunihild [Victoria; Sunny] 292, 294
Philp, Col. William R. "Rusty" 152, 247, 252, 256
Pieck, Wilhelm 362, 425
Pilsen 236
Pirogov, Lt. Peter A. 261–62
Poland 76–77, 131, 211, 214–15, 283, 355, 389, 406, 408
Polgar, Thomas 345
Polish Committee of National Liberation (Polski Komitet Wyzwolenia Narodowego) 77
political parties 9, 75, 78, 80, 93, 311–12, 321, 330, 332, 341, 359–61, 362n52, 363, 368, 394, 396, 441. See also Christian Democratic Union; Christian Social Union; Economic Reconstruction Union; Free Democratic Party; German Communist Party; Liberal Democratic Party; National Democratic Party of Germany; Nazi Party; Social Democratic Party of Germany; Socialist Unity Party
Poll, Albert 294
Polyakov, Ivan N. 357
Poss, Gerhard 300, 302
Potsdam 83, 167, 169, 261, 288, 293, 296, 378, 381, 387

Potsdam Conference 83, 132, 148, 182, 352, 355, 395
Potsdam House. *See* United States Military Liaison Mission
Potter, Col. Frank M., Jr. 109
Prague 4n9, 103, 106, 113, 122, 299, 357, 382, 396, 397, 408
Presecan, Pfc. Joseph 335
Pretty, Lt. Col. Harry S. 117, 118n119, 127, 416
President of the Federal Republic of Germany. *See* Heuss, Theodor
prisoners of war 45, 46–47, 49, 76, 166, 197, 205–07, 208, 214–15, 236–37, 243–58, 305, 319, 326, 355. *See also* Katyn Forest massacres; Malmédy massacre; operations, Rusty
– detention camps for 31, 34, 76, 151, 153, 196
– interrogation of 4, 17, 23, 25, 29, 31, 34–35, 111–12, 139, 151, 152–55, 204, 205, 207, 237–38, 240, 308, 340
– release of German 209–11
projects
– Casey Jones 152
– Dick Tracy 244
– Happiness 331
– Hill 248, 251
– Overcast 226–28
– Paperclip 7, 118, 226, 228–33, 242–43, 356
– Patron 152
– Venona 8, 74–75, 150n66
– Triangle 154
propaganda 15, 19, 25, 42, 52, 55, 56, 57, 60, 66, 77, 175, 180, 182–83, 187, 203, 212, 232, 233, 266, 276, 277, 290, 292, 315, 326, 330, 333, 337, 360, 362, *373*, 390n177, 412, 416, 420, 426–27, 430, 432, 434, 438
prostitution 36, 260
Prützmann, Lt. Gen. Hans A. 52–54, 55, 57
Psychological Warfare Division 42, 57, 108, 189, 308, 309
Pullach 256

Quadripartite Intelligence Committee 102, 180
Quaranta, Francesco S. 166
Quinn, Col. William W. 173

Radio Free Europe 428
Radio in the American Sector (Rundfunk im amerikanischen Sektor; RIAS) 277, 426–27, 429–30
Rainford, Lt. Col. William R. 100
ratlines 263–66
Raue, Gerhard [P-43-VIII] 250
Raue, Heinz [P-15-VIII] 350, 350–51
Raymond, Col. Julian E. 163
reconnaissance 4, 33, 36, 45, 50, 56, 111, 160, 378, 387
Red Army 3, 9, 19, 61, 63, 64, 66, 73, 76–77, 78, 83, 93, 111n84, 131, 175, 177, 234, 235, 243, 251, 258–59, 272, 288, 298, 338, 342, 353, 368, 371, 376–94, 395, 404–05, 407, 412, 418, 425, 430, 438, 441
Red Army units. *See* Units, Soviet
Red Fleet 131
refugees 3, 67, 155, 162, 173, 210, 216, 263, 281, 286, 287, 299, 301, 314, 322, 340, 348n199, 353, 357, 361, 368, 394, 405, 425–26, 430
Regensburg 103, 106, 121, 134, 141, 365
Reich Chancellery 175
Reichsbahn 45
Reichsbank 269, 271
Reichsforschungsrat. *See* German Research Council
Reichspost 157
Reichstag 309, 314, 422
Reimann, Max 159
Reims 175
Reinhardt, Guenther P. 274–76
Reiter Kaserne. *See* Wallace Barracks
Reitsch, Hanna 178–79
Remagen 61, 101
reparations 87, 291, 300, 352–55, 357. *See also* economic exploitation
Reuter, Ernst 115, 343–45, 345n183, 346, 370, 422, 424, 434
Reusch, Gerhard 41
Rhine River 39, 44, 61, 63, 390, 391
Rhineland 68, 93, 104, 307–08, 313
RIAS. *See* Radio in the American Sector
Rickhey, Georg 230, 231, 232
Riess, Curt 419

"Ritchie Boys" 3–4, 4n9, 26–28, 136, 180, 325, 343. *See also* Military Intelligence Training Center
Roberts, Brig. Gen. Frank N. 74, 381
Rodes, John E. 26–27
Rodes, Col. Peter P. 104–05, 105–08, 110, 110, 114, 336, 404, 406, 416, 424, 443
Rome 18, 91, 221, 263, 323, 397
Roosevelt, Eleanor 18
Roosevelt, Franklin D. 1, 18, 61, 62, 64, 68, 71, 73, 77, 169, 239
Rosenfeld, Abraham H. 210
Rosengarten, Lt. Col. Adolph G. 70
Rosenheim 237, 240
Rosenow, Sgt. Kurt 165–66
Rosovsky, Henry 163
Rostock 169
Rothkrug, Michael R. 302, 431
Rothwesten 107, 146
Royall, Kenneth C. 209, 402, 403, 405, 410, 411, 418
Rudolph, Arthur 230, 232–33
Rudolstadt 298
Rudenko, Roman A. 215
Ruhr Valley 63, 355, 371
Rumania 131
Russell, Ned 354
Russian Army of Liberation. *See* Vlasov Army

SA. *See Sturmabteilung*
sabotage 18, 45, 47, 52–53, 56–57, 66–67, 69, 139, 191, 193, 196, 204, 334, 372, 399, 427, 432–34
Sachsenhausen prison camp 351, 430
Salinger, J. D. 4, 4n9, 134, 446
Sands, Col. Thomas J. 290
Saunder, Lt. Jacques 116
Savieczes, Georg. *See* Lotz, Erich
Sawatzki, Albin 229
Saxony 227, 235, 241, 242, 356, 358, 371, 381
Schäffer, Fritz 320, 321
Schardt, Henry P. 26, 154
Schepsis, Capt. Anthony A. 179
Scheyern 145, 436
Schliersee 237, 238, 245
Schneider, Capt. Philip 169
Schneider, Dr. *See* Gehlen, Brig. Gen. Reinhard
Schoenberg (Belgium) 46
Schöneberg (Berlin) 87, 111, 113
Schongau 319
Schoofs, Grete K. 336, 336n147
Schorndorf 282
Schow, Col. Robert A. 98–101, 104–05, 361, 388–89, 401, 406, 443, 445
Schröder, Hans 344
Schröder, Louise D. 344, 423
Schultes, A. F. 340, 340n163
Schumacher, Kurt 314–16, 345–46, 368–69
Schutzpolizei (Berlin) 338
Schutzstaffel (SS) 6, 35–36, 44–47, 52, 54, 59, 62, 66–67, 138, 153, 173–74, 183–84, 187, 195–202, 204–05, 207–08, 210, 230, 253, 263. *See also* Odessa
Schwäbisch Gmünd 191, 282
scientific exploitation, VII 4–5, 9, 118, 221–33. *See also* operations, Soviet, Osoavikhim; projects, Paperclip; Overcast
scientific intelligence, VII 4–5, 221–33, 266
Scott, John 353
SD. *See Sicherheitsdienst*
SED. *See* Socialist Unity Party
segregation in the U.S. armed forces 26. *See also* African American U.S. soldiers
Semler, Johannes 326–9
Semyonov, Vladimir S. 414
Serov, General Ivan A. 288
Sevastopol' 219
Seventh Army Interrogation Center 207, 246
SHAEF. *See* Supreme Headquarters Allied Expeditionary Force
Shapiro, Justus J. 340–41
Shea, Donald T. 109, 109n78
Sheen, Col. Henry G. 18, 18n26, 273
Shimkin, Col. Demitri B. 250, 380
Siberia 22n47, 34, 254, 301, 365, 374
Sibert, Brig. Gen. Edwin L. 3, 5, 9, 22, 34, 45, 50–51, 62–64, 71, 91–94, 97, 99, 102, 111, 115, 121, 127, 130, 138, 139, 152, 160, 177, 180, 195, 227, 246–49, 251–53, 290, 292, 308, 330, 353, 376–80, 382, 383, 443–45
Sichel, Peter M. F. 122, 124–25, 128–29, 150, 257, 314, 315, 345, 370, 431, 442–43
Sicherheitsdienst (SD) 59, 60, 66
Sicily 150

Sidnev, Maj. Gen. Aleksei M. 177
Siegburg 52–53
Signal Corps. *See* U.S. Army Signal Corps
Signal Intelligence Service of the European Theater 29, 103
– Signal Intelligence Division 17, 29, 32, 233, 235
– Signal Security Detachment D 17, 32
Signal Security Agency 16–18, 25, 83–84, 144. *See also* Army Security Agency
– Vint Hill Farms School 25
– Special Branch 16
Signal Service Company, 114th 103, 145, 388
Signal Service Company, 116th 103, 145–46
signals intelligence 8, 13, 16–19, 23–25, 29–30, 32, 33–35, 44, 50, 65, 66, 74, 83–84, 129, 143–50, 157, 160, 233–43, 388, 436, 445–46
Signals Intelligence Agency of the German Army High Command (*Oberkommando der Wehrmacht Chiffrierabteilung;* OKW/Chi) 234
Simpson, Lt. Gen. William H. 63–64
Skorzeny, Lt. Col. Otto 44, 44n21, 45, 47, 48–49, 55, 207, 208–09, 208n139, 263–64, 279
Skrzypczynski, Leo 353–54
Slavin, Maj. Gen. Nikolai V. 73
Slayden, Lt. Col. William M. 100
SMERSH (*smert' shpionam;* "Death to Spies"; Soviet counterespionage agency) 288
Smith, Lt. Col. Baldwin B. 49
Smith, Col. George S. "Budge" 91
Smith, General Walter B. 223, 248, 445
Social Democratic Party of Germany (Sozialdemokratische Partei Deutschlands; SPD) 9, 311, 314–16, 320–21, 334, 338–47, 359–60, 360n43, 367, 368–376, 422, 424
Socialist Unity Party (Sozialistische Einheitspartei Deutschlands; SED) 332, 333, 334, 339, 341–44, 350, 360–62, 365, 367, 369, 371, 376, 416, 417, 418, 420, 422, 423, 424–25
Sofia 382
Sokolovsky, General Vasily D. 260, 262, 398, 415–16
Sonnenfeldt, Helmut 163
Sontra 145
Sophia of Hesse, Princess 270, 270n7
Soviet Air Forces 261, 380, 388, 393, 413
Soviet Army. *See* Red Army
Soviet Military Administration 176, 228, 288, 293–4, 326, 339, 353, 361, 363, 366, 367, 414, 425
Soviet Navy. *See* Red Fleet
Soviet Union (Union of Soviet Socialist Republics; USSR) 1, 2, 8, 19, 19n29, 73, 76, 78, 83, 84, 121n132, 131, 132, 140, 152, 154, 159, 163, 185, 201, 204, 211, 213, 214–15, 226, 228–29, 236, 243–44, 261, 262, 281, 286, 303, 338, 342, 351, 353, 355–56, 376, 381–82, 385, 389, 393, 394–95, 397–98, 404, 406, 408, 410, 440
Soviet sector of Berlin. *See* Berlin, Soviet sector
Soviet Zone 9, 10, 114, 116, 128, 138, 146, 157, 167, 168, 169, 170, 212, 228, 235, 241, 249, 252, 254, 257, 269, 294, 296, 298, 299, 314, 317, 328, 331–34, 336, 339, 346, 350–95, 397–400, 410, 415–17, 423, 425–26, 429, 430, 431–32, 434, 438, 440
Spain 198–99, 208n139, 263, 264, 269, 385
SPD. *See* Social Democratic Party of Germany
Special Committee to Investigate the National Defense Program 274
Speziallager (*Spezlager*) prison camps 351, 363, 428
Spruchkammer(n) denazification tribunals 189–90, 197–98
Squadrons, U.S.
– 2d Army Air Forces, Mobile 103, 145
– 85th Cavalry Reconnaissance, Mechanized, 5th Armored Division 38
SS. *See* Schutzstaffel
Stahlmann, Richard. *See* Illner, Arthur
Stalin, Joseph V. 61, 62, 64, 75, 77, 83, 84, 131, 175, 214, 243, 259, 261, 303, 333, 352, 354, 358, 362, 365, 368, 381, 391, 394, 395, 399, 401, 407, 414, 435, 438
Starr, J. Ward 109
Stasi. *See* Ministry for State Security (East Germany)
Station Complement Unit, 7829th. *See* Military Intelligence Platoon, 7829th
Status of Forces Agreement 444–45
Stauffer, Clarita 264
Staver, Maj. Robert B. 224, 226
Stcherbinine, Michael G. 117, 301, 302
Stearns, Harold E. 107, 109, 110

Stecher, Sidney 199
Steglitz (Berlin) 111, 113
Steinhardt, Laurence A. 396
Stern, Guy 205
Sternberg. Capt. Frederick 112
Stettin 382
Stevens, Lt. Col. Richard D. 94, 134
Stewart, Gordon M. 120, 128
Stewart, Capt. Joseph M. 293
Stielau, 1st Lt. Lothar 47
Stilwell, General Joseph W. 22
Stimson, Henry L. 201, 221
Stock, Christian 316
Stone, Maj. Shepard 309, 347
Storie, Pfc. Gerald E. 238
Stralsund 169
Strategic Services Unit 103, 119–21, 123n142, 127, 252–53, 273, 315, 324, 352, 354, 357, 360, 361, 364, 369, 383, 386, 424. *See also* Central Intelligence Agency; Department of the Army Detachment; Office of Strategic Services
Strauss, Franz Josef 65, 282n55, 319
Strong, Maj. Gen. George V. 14, 20, 51, 77
Strong, Maj. Gen. Kenneth W. D. 28, 45, 51, 69, 247
Struller, Otto R. [Capt. Cecil Dryer] 48
Stumm, Johannes 424
Stuttgart 134, 141, 159, 191, 192, 193, 197–98, 279, 289–92, 295, 309
Sturmabteilung (SA) 36, 183
Sudoplatov, Lt. Gen. Pavel A. 288
Suhling, Lt. Col. William G. 120
Supreme Headquarters Allied Expeditionary Force (Supreme Allied Headquarters; SHAEF) 17, 18n26, 28, 37, 42, 45, 60, 63, 64, 67, 72, 94, 102, 151, 175, 177, 191, 202, 224, 225, 225n28, 233, 240, 246, 247, 284, 308, 376, 377, 378
– Intelligence Division 17, 28, 62–64, 66–67, 91, 94, 99, 100, 165–66, 176, 223, 246–47, 247, 353
– Joint Intelligence Committee 28–29, 56
Suth, Lilli (née Adenauer) 305
Suth, Willi 305
Sweden 146, 345
Swerdlin, George D. 345–47, 374, 373n105
Swiss Alps. *See* Alps
Switzerland 57, 59, 119, 123, 146, 239, 323n86
Swoboda, Maj. Leo A. 40–41

Swolinzky, Curt 340–42
Szalghapy, Giselhal von 387
Szymanski, Lt. Col. Henry I. 76–77

Target Intelligence Committee (TICOM) 233–43
Taylor, Lt. Col. Milton C. 100
Technical Industrial Intelligence Committee 223, 224
Technical Service Unit 9420th, 16, 16n17
telecommunications 2n6, 112–13, 140, 144–45, 148–49, 155–56, 157, 159, 299, 371, 388, 436. *See also* Army Security Agency; Army Security Agency, Europe; signals intelligence; U.S. Army Signal Corps
Tehran Conference 169
Telefunken building. *See* McNair Barracks
Tempelhof airport 83, 124, 413
theater of operations
– European. *See* European Theater of Operations
– Mediterranean 29, 32, 145, 221
– North African 32
Thomas, Stephan. *See* Grzeskowiak, Stephan
Thoroughman, Col. Roy M. 152
Thuringia 170, 227, 268–69, 298, 361, 365, 386
TICOM. *See* Target Intelligence Committee
Tiergarten 272
Tillich, Ernst [Richard E. Newman] 432
Toftoy, Col. Holger N. 229
Torgau 63
Trefousse, Hans L. 34, 446
Trevor-Roper, Maj. Hugh R. 178, 178n18, 180
Treuenbrietzen 297
Trichel, Col. Gervais W. 229
Trier 281
Trieste 382
Trott, 2d Lt. David B. 319
Trudeau, Brig. Gen. Arthur G. 410–11
Truman Doctrine 132
Truman, Elizabeth "Bess" 396
Truman, Harry S. 1–2, 83, 107, 119, 131–32, 209, 231, 283, 285, 285, 382, 396, 404, 410, 411, 415, 418, 427
– as senator 274
Truscott, General Lucian K., Jr. 185, 445

Tulpanov, Col. Sergei I. 326, 328, 360–62, 362n52, 367, 416
Turkey 131, 343
Tyrol 59, 324

Uhlig, Siegfried 242
Ulbricht, Walter 338, 358, 359, 416
Ulm 154, 187, 193
Union of Soviet Socialist Republics. *See* Soviet Union
United Kingdom. *See* Great Britain
United Nations Relief and Rehabilitation Administration (UNRRA) 281, 283, 286
United States Army Air Forces. *See* Army Air Forces, United States
United States Forces in the European Theater 85, 93–94, 103, 133, 225n28, 440
United States Military Liaison Mission (USMLM) 3, 106, 128, 157–70, 261, 356, 387, 387, 406, 407, 443
United States Military Liaison Mission to the Commander-in-Chief of the Soviet Occupied Zone of Germany, 7893d. *See* United States Military Liaison Mission
United States Military Liaison Mission to the Commander-in-Chief of the Soviet Occupied Zone of Germany. *See* United States Military Liaison Mission
units, British 28, 62, 91, 227, 385. *See also* British Army of the Rhine
– Army Group, 21st 39, 48, 60, 85n9, 234, 378
units, French 30, 71–72, 222, 227, 389
– Division Blindée, 2e 71
units, German 24, 38, 44–52, 66, 68, 75, 76
– *Einheit Stielau* 48–9
– *Einsatzgruppen* 204
– *Heeresgruppe Mitte* (*Army Group Center*) 236–37
– *Herman Göring Division* [*Luftwaffe*] 350
– *Kampfgruppe Peiper* 207–08
– *Panzer Army, Fifth* 45
– *Panzer Army, Second* 216
– *Panzer Army, Sixth* 44–4
– *SS Panzer Division "Leibstandarte Adolf Hitler", 1st* 46–47
– *SS Panzer Brigade, 150th* 47

units, Soviet 3, 61, 63, 375, 377–81, 387, 388, 389, 391, 404–06, 412. *See also* Red Army
– Army, 47th 381
– Guards Army, 8th 381
– Guards Infantry Division, 58th 63
– Guards Mechanized Army, 1st 381
– Guards Mechanized Army, 2d 381
– Guards Mechanized Army, 3d 405, 406
– Group of Soviet Occupation Forces in Germany 167, 376, 390, 399
– Shock Army, 2d 381
– Shock Army, 3d 381
– Shock Army, 5th 381
UNRRA. *See* United Nations Relief and Rehabilitation Administration
Unterholzner, Ilse 180
uranium 222–23, 356–58
U.S. Army Signal Corps 16, 84, 113, 144, 150n68, 155–63
U.S. Constabulary 139, 158, 164, 261, 293, 354, 357, 384, 389, 410
– 1st Constabulary Brigade 410
U.S. Combined Intelligence Liaison Center 144
U.S. Forces in Austria 262
U.S. Group Control Council, Germany 87, 101, 122
USMLM. *See* United States Military Liaison Mission
USSR. *See* Soviet Union

Vacca, Peter J. 108–09, 109n78, 321, 322, 324
– as major 109, 321
Vagts, Erich 310
Valic, Capt. Eugene V. 242
Valfer, Ernst S. 284
Van Vliet, Col. John H. 214–15
Vandenberg, General Hoyt S., Jr. 410, 421
– as lieutenant general 253
– as major general 90, 90n24
Vatican 30, 323
Venlo 234
Vichy France 98
Victory Guest House 300
Vienna 72, 129, 137, 377, 382
Vint Hill Farms 25, 32, 146
Vint Hill Farms School. *See* Signal Security Agency

violence against women 83, 114, 114n98, 193–94, 279, 282, 298–99, 418
violence against displaced persons 193, 282, 284, 285–88
Vlasov Army 243–44, 250
Vlasov, Lt. Gen. Andrey A. 243, 254
Vogt, Walter. *See* Losowsky, Valentin
Voice of America 261
Volkspolizei (People's Police, Soviet Zone) 366
von Braun, Magnus 229–30
von Braun, Wernher 229–30, 231, 232–33
Vorarlberg 60
Vosges Mountains 39

Wagner, Dr. Bernhard 186
Wahrhaftig, Samuel L. 346
Waldman, Capt. Eric 250–52, 253, 256
Waldman, Jo-Ann 252
Wallace Barracks 141
Wallach, Severin F. ["Thomsen"; "Thomson"; "Thompson"] 126, 137–38, 179, 181, 293, 296, 375, 429–31, 432, 442
Walker, Lt. Col. Robert T. 145, 299
Walsh, Maj. Gen. Robert L. 97–98, 99, 104–05, 117, 121, 129, 214, 232, 255, 256, 300, 304, 401, 402–03, 443
Wannsee 115
War Department 9, 17, 18–19, 30, 73, 87, 89–90, 103, 119, 144, 151, 164, 226, 228, 231, 246, 248, 251, 255, 271, 359, 376, 378–79, 391
War Department Detachment. *See* Department of the Army Detachment
War, Secretary of. *See* Patterson, Robert P., Stimson, Henry L
war crimes 4, 9, 67, 79, 94, 134, 138, 152, 153, 159, 166, 170, 173, 201–18, 231, 237, 263–66, 296, 319, 442
War Crimes Group in the European Theater 201
war crimes trials 9, 79, 202, 204–11, 213–17, 231, 265. *See also* executions, of war criminals
– accusations of torture 209
– anti-Semitism and 210
Warfield, William C. 26, 26n67
Warsaw 113, 382, 406, 408
Wartenberg, Ralf 204
Washington, D.C. 13, 23, 29, 37, 59–60, 70, 70, 88, 91, 94, 138, 150, 152, 221, 223, 228, 232, 246, 247–48, 250, 251, 255, 258, 262, 277, 337, 376, 379–80, 382, 402–03, 405, 420, 438, 440, 441
"Washington Merry-Go-Round." *See* Pearson, Drew R
Washington Post 48, 210, 279, 327
WAV. *See* Economic Reconstruction Union
Weber, Richard H. 264, 429, 431
Wehrmacht 7, 38, 46, 50, 56, 66, 67, 68, 73, 77, 145, 193, 194, 204, 205, 207, 214n162, 236, 240, 243, 244, 364, 365, 380, 383. *See also* units, German
Weiss, Arnold H. 180, 202
Weizsäcker, Carl Friedrich von 222
Wentworth, Col. Richard D. 94, 100
Werwolf 4, 52–57, 173, 191
Wessel, Lt. Col. Gerhard 249
West Berlin, vii 6, 9, 65, 345, 347, 348, 413, 423, 425, 438, 444, 446. *See also* Berlin airlift; Berlin blockade
West Germany. *See* Federal Republic of Germany
Western Military District 85
Westerstetten 193
Westphalia 54
Wev, Capt. Bouquet N. 224–25
Whidby, Pfc. Claude W. 292
Wiechmann, Heinz 429
Wilder, Billy 187
Wildflecken 283
Wiesbaden 119, 123, 133, 245–47, 247n128, 335
Willems, Col. John M. 397
Willfahrt, Walter 373–75, 373n105
Williams, Brig. Gen. Edgar "Bill" 50
Wilson, Lt. Col. H. E. 134
Wilson, Col. Wilbur 116n110, 117, 127, 292
Wisner, Frank G. 427–28
Wissen 68
Witte, Siegfried 354
Wittenberge 111
Wittstock 387, 387n162
Women's Army Corps 271
Wroblewski, Albert L. 334
Württemberg 56, 308
Württemberg-Baden 10, 87, 103, 106, 109, 198, 309, 309n18, 310, 312
Würzburg 141

Yalta Conference 84, 169, 182, 213, 215, 243, 280
Yeaton, Col. Ivan D. 19n29, 73, 74, 77, 78
Yeo-Thomas, Wg. Cdr. Forest F. E. 208
Yugoslavia 101

Zander, Wilhelm 180
Zapler, T/5 Murray 46–47, 205–06
Zehlendorf 111, 115, 164
Zell 237
Zhukov, Marshal Georgy K. 176
Zinn, Georg A. 316
Zinnecke, Adolf 41
Zschepplin 235
Zschopau 241, 242
Zuffenhausen displaced persons camp 289, 290

www.ingramcontent.com/pod-product-compliance
Lightning Source LLC
Chambersburg PA
CBHW051532230426
43669CB00015B/2578